I FOUGHT A GOOD FIGHT

A HISTORY *of the* LIPAN APACHES

I FOUGHT A GOOD FIGHT

A HISTORY *of the* LIPAN APACHES

SHERRY ROBINSON

University of North Texas Press
Denton, Texas

10 9 8 7 6 5 4 3 2 1

Permissions:
University of North Texas Press
1155 Union Circle #311336
Denton, TX 76203-5017

The paper used in this book meets the minimum requirements of the American National Standard for Permanence of Paper for Printed Library Materials, z39.48.1984. Binding materials have been chosen for durability.

Text design by Rose Design

Library of Congress Cataloging-in-Publication Data

Robinson, Sherry.
  I fought a good fight : a history of the Lipan Apaches / Sherry Robinson.—1st ed.
    p. cm.
  Includes bibliographical references and index.
  ISBN 978-1-57441-506-3 (cloth : alk. paper)—ISBN 978-1-57441-511-7
  1. Lipan Indians—History. I. Title.
  E99.L5R64 2013
  973.04'97—dc23
                    2013003393

The electronic edition of this book was made possible by the support of the Vick Family Foundation.

To: The Lipan Apache People

❖ Contents ❖

❖ List of Illustrations ❖

❖ Maps ❖

❧ Acknowledgments ❧

For those of us who love books and write them, librarians are the stewards of great treasure, as important as bankers. I visited many libraries and archives for this project, and certain institutions stand out for their good will and friendly professionalism: the University of New Mexico's Center for Southwest Research, the New Mexico State Archives, David Schneider and Joe Sabatini at the Albuquerque Public Library's Special Collections Library, The Dolph Briscoe Center for American History at the University of Texas, Provo Special Collections and Manuscripts at Brigham Young University's Harold B. Lee Library, Jim Bradshaw at the Nita Stewart Haley Memorial Library in Midland, Texas, and the Special Collections Library at Texas Tech. I appreciate the information provided by Scott Forsythe at the National Archives.

Books and documents only go so far, however. I was privileged to spend time with Meredith Magoosh Begay and Lucy Evelyn Smith at the Mescalero Apache Reservation. I am forever grateful for Mrs. Begay's willingness to share her knowledge and regret that she didn't live to see the product of our time together. Similarly, I owe a great thanks to Daniel Castro Romero, Jr., for the use of his family history and the Lipan Apache Band's written history, prepared by anthropologist Enrique Maestas. Ellyn Big Rope was also kind in offering her time and insights.

I'm indebted to individuals for allowing me the use of their own documents and for their interest and support: Jackson and the late Gene Harris, historian Marc Simmons, archaeologist Deni Seymour, Bill Cavalliere, and Robert Watt.

For accessible microfilm resources, I thank the cheerful volunteers at the Family History Center of the Church of Jesus Christ of the Latter-day Saints. And I would be remiss to not tip my hat to online resources; particularly valuable have been the Texas State Historical Association's *Handbook of Texas Online and SHQ Online, The Portal to Texas History* of the University of North Texas Libraries' Digital Projects Unit, the University of Texas Perry Castañeda Map Collection, University of New Mexico Libraries' *Celebrating New Mexico Statehood*, the *Atlas of Historic New Mexico Maps* by the New Mexico Humanities Council, and Arizona State University's Documentary Relations of the Southwest master index.

It was my good fortune to find a wonderful translator in Dorothy Mazon, who grew up in northern New Mexico where a great deal of the old Spanish was still spoken. Dorothy enthusiastically waded into stacks of ancient pen scratchings and took an interest in the project. Thanks to Alex Mendoza, who transformed my scribbling into readable maps.

I offer my appreciation to New Mexico's Office of the State Historian for a grant through its Scholars Program that helped pay some of my costs. It's the only program I've found that supports independent researchers.

Writing a book is a solitary process. I'm grateful for the support and encouragement of fellow researchers like Ed Sweeney, Jerry Eagan, Robert Watt, Alicia Delgadillo, Daniel Aranda, Bud Shapard, and Jo Martín. I thank my friend Yvonne Lanelli; house-sitting for her in Alto, New Mexico, allowed me the luxury of uninterrupted writing time within view of the Apaches' sacred peak, Sierra Blanca.

Of course, nobody gets through a project like this without the patience and forbearance of family and friends, and I especially thank my husband for cheering me on.

❧ Introduction ☙

We are Apache, we are Lipan, and I am proud of my heritage.

— *Santos Peralez Castro*[1]

Lipan Apaches often hear from historians that their people are extinct. After one such lecture, a man raised his hand and said, "I'm Lipan. Do I look extinct to you?"

Lipans are some of the least known, least understood of the Southwest's Apache bands. For a small group, they had an outsized impact through three centuries and were often described as the second most powerful tribe in Texas, after the Comanches. Lipans were as clever, fearless, and resourceful as their better publicized cousins to the west and, as a group, far more diverse.

Early Spanish explorers found Lipan ancestors hunting buffalo on the plains. They were members of an Eastern Apache confederacy of about a dozen autonomous groups, each moving frequently over vast distances but staying in contact. They joined for hunting and raiding; if one group suffered losses to war or disease, its survivors found refuge with allied groups until they were strong enough to venture forth again.

Lipan ancestors and their confederates were also links in the chain of traders moving commodities from the buffalo plains to the Pacific coast and Mexico. Their trade relations with the eastern pueblos of New Mexico were so intimate that the Apaches camped outside for extended periods and even joined their Pueblo friends indoors during severe weather. Inevitably, early Lipans and kindred groups became military allies, joined and encouraged their friends in plotting rebellions against the Spanish, and harbored pueblo refugees.

Proximity and alliances gave them early access to horses, and with horses the Lipans expanded their territory southeast across present-day Texas to the Gulf and down the Rio Grande to northern Coahuila. In conquering or absorbing weaker groups, they gained knowledge, territory, trade partners, reinforcements, and, possibly most important to a small group, an expanded pool of marriage partners. Historian Gary Clayton Anderson calls this process "Apacheanization,"[2] but clearly it was a two-way exchange.

Around 1700, ruthless new enemies, the Comanches, swept through the northernmost camps of the confederacy. Many a historian has written that the Eastern Apaches' practice of agriculture pinned them down before a mobile enemy, but the Apaches quickly massed for security and found other ways to acquire guns the Spanish denied them. It took the Comanches fifty years to evict them, and even then, pockets remained. The Lipans returned to fight Comanches at any opportunity.

Lipans did their part to curtail Spanish ambitions in the Southwest long before aggressive northern tribes appeared. During a two-century relationship, Spanish colonies and missions were a source of livestock to raiders, but some Spaniards became trade partners and friends, to the dismay of a succession of governors who railed against the weaponry and ammunition passing into Lipan hands. The Spanish, outnumbered and lacking a consistent Indian policy or even the capacity for efficient decision making, struggled with this enemy whose rules of engagement were alien to them. Viceroys and generals came and went, campaigns were waged, and the Lipans and their allies continued to be a scourge.

During peaceful interludes, some Lipans drew closer than their confederates to the Spanish, Mexicans and Texans. We know these Lipans best; others were visible only through their raids. The friendly Lipans improved trade and enjoyed friendships in the towns; some even attempted mission living while their skeptical relatives watched from a safe distance. In periods of hostility, the once friendly Lipans made good use of their knowledge of roads, ranches and presidios or forts to rain destruction. Exposure to Europeans had a price—greater exposure to the white man's diseases.

When Spain lost its grip on Mexico, Lipans and Comanches aligned themselves with the new government, and yet both tribes later factored into Mexico's desire for colonists in Texas, a development Mexico would regret and Lipans would exploit. Comanches refused peace with the Republic of Texas, but in the early years Lipans liked the scrappy immigrants, who became powerful new allies, and flourished in the new republic, serving as paid scouts and prospering as traders. In a new footnote to Alamo history, Lipans say they were present and lost lives.

◄►

Settlers poured into Texas and brashly invaded Indian territory, sometimes losing their lives in the process, and the Texas Rangers or militias retaliated against the first Indians they came across—often friendly Lipans, camped close to the settlements. Indian agents pushed the tribes beyond imaginary lines until friction and resentment boiled over into clashes.

When Texas became a state, its big landscape couldn't support all its people. Game populations thinned, tribes stole to survive, and the nearly bankrupt republic needed its public lands to settle debts. Anderson calls the removal of tribes and the Texas Indian wars "ethnic cleansing,"[3] a modern label that doesn't fit. Racism was rampant, certainly, but the Texas Indian wars had many causes, not the least of which was tribal aggression. Today, the battles and raids are cited in federal recognition petitions as evidence of a group's determination to hold its lands.

In this backdrop of rising tension, the tragic betrayal and murder of a young Lipan chief ended the Lipans' long alliance with Texas. Again, they struck an arrangement to their advantage as they took refuge in Mexico and became the Texans' sworn enemies. Mexico, embittered at its loss of territory, tolerated Lipan, Mescalero and Kickapoo raids on Texas from sanctuaries in Coahuila, and the three tribes were the subject of many a diplomatic dispatch.

The Civil War emptied forts and siphoned off troops, leaving the frontiers virtually undefended, an invitation to Lipans to return to their old country. At the war's end, as Congress tried to shrink an enlarged military, generals needed new conflicts and found them in the Indian wars. Washington and westerners demanded that the army control Indians on the frontiers and along both borders. The border with Mexico was particularly vexing, wrote historian Robert Wooster. Texans with designs on real estate across the river hoped for another war with Mexico, and the Apaches moving back and forth were sufficient pretext.[4] As the United States increased pressure on Mexico, and a new Mexican regime sought legitimacy, the Lipans and their friends saw their status slip from asset to liability. The Mexican army added its own campaigns to the U.S. army's cross-border raids.

Lipans held out in their old refuges: The endless folds of the Serranía del Burro, the deep limestone canyons of Devils River and the Pecos, the plains vacated by Comanches, the mountainous fingers reaching north from the Rio Grande, and gleaming sand dunes. For years, troops avoided these places; when they entered without trepidation, it was the beginning of the end. Their numbers dwindling, Lipans often joined Mescaleros and both moved to ever more remote hideouts. Despite frightful losses to war and disease, the Lipans never surrendered—they simply melted away, infiltrating reservations in New Mexico and Oklahoma where they had relatives, drifting, family by family, back to places they once lived in Texas, or taking root in Mexican villages.

◄►

This book is neither a chronicle of empire building nor the sad tale of victimization. The Lipans' wealth and territory expanded and contracted. In better times, when trade was good and their enemies in retreat, they might claim all the best country among many watersheds; in drought and famine, stricken by disease, or overwhelmed by their enemies, they retreated to safe havens or the camps of allies.

This pattern has produced a great deal of skewed history. Scholars, relying on the claim of a long-dead captain that the Lipans were subdued once and for all, would declare them impotent. Yet another official, a few years later, would complain that Lipans were a pox on civilization. Historians have often written that the Comanches drove Lipans from their territory and thereafter the Lipans were inconsequential. Subsequent records reveal bitter conflict between Lipans and Comanches; farther along the timeline chroniclers describe an alliance between the two, followed by warfare. And so on. Snapshots in time aren't reliable.

Lacking the numbers and might of the Comanches or the military, Lipans were not only guerilla fighters, they were guerilla traders and guerilla hunters, finding chinks in the Comanche barrier and niches in frontier markets. The Lipans didn't need the Comanches' extensive network; a few traders and middlemen would suffice. Employing various strategies, they supplied themselves from the seemingly forbidden buffalo range, the farmer's pasture, or wild herds of mustangs and cattle.

Boundary surveyor John Russell Bartlett was surprised to learn in 1850 that Lipanería was as large as Comanchería. For nearly their entire written history, the Lipans could be found in the same areas: the lower Pecos River and lower Rio Grande, the Rio San Rodrigo and Serranías del Burro in Coahuila, the Bolsón de Mapími of Coahuila and Chihuahua, the Colorado River and its tributaries in Texas, and the Guadalupe Mountains of New Mexico and Texas. For long periods they also camped on the Concho, Guadalupe, San Sabá, Medina, and the Nueces in Texas; Rio Grande tributaries in Coahuila and Nuevo León, the Gulf Coast of both nations, and the Llano Estacado in New Mexico and Texas.

Migration and forced moves complicate the concept of home for Lipans and many other tribes. They may end up living far from their aboriginal territory and redefine home several times. To paraphrase Augustina Zuazua, the Lipans liked San Antonio and that was their country, but then they went to Zaragosa and made that their country.[5]

Lipans simultaneously inhabited the frontier and both sides of the border. They helped define the frontier as the place beyond the settlements where only Lipans and other "wild tribes" lived. They also raided, traded, fought and lived among Mexicans and Americans. Each nation employed Lipans against the other, leading a few historians to claim that Lipans played one side against the other, which isn't accurate. Lipans habitually chose the side that gave them greatest advantage, and animosity between Mexicans and Americans needed no manipulation. Only after the two nations coordinated their efforts did they finally eliminate their Lipan threat.

◄►

Until recently, Lipans were overlooked by historians. Just two books address Lipan history: *The Lipan Apache in Texas*, by Thomas Schilz, and *The Lipan Apaches: People of Wind and Lightning*, by Thomas Britten, 2009. At seventy pages, the 1987 Schilz book is obviously intended as an overview, but it's riddled with errors. Two examples of many: "The Lipans borrowed a great many of their religious beliefs from the Mescalero Apaches" and "Comanches quickly ousted the Lipans and other Apache bands from the Texas Panhandle and the lands north of the Colorado River."[6]

Schilz's sweeping conclusions often have no basis in fact: "Chiquito and Ramon Castro blamed one another's warriors for breaches in the peace, and the tribal unit of the Lipans began to deteriorate" and "Apaches had little trouble pitting the Americans against" Comanches and Wichitas.[7] At times, Schilz descends into nonsense: "The Apaches loved successful warriors but saw warfare itself as a disturbance in the natural world."

Britten provides a more thorough history, but he writes about the Lipans as if he were inspecting an anthill; a reader gets no sense of the people and places. He has overlooked significant developments—the Eastern Apache confederacy, the French alliance, the Victorio campaign, the reservation period—and pays scant attention to the Lipans' presence in Mexico, Mackenzie's Raid and land claims. We learn nothing of the impact of Chief Picax-ande and Chief Castro. And he seems puzzled by such basics as the use of tipis and wickiups and whether they practiced polygamy.[8]

Both authors are derogatory in tone, not because they're objective but because they accepted judgments of an earlier time without questioning its biases. As a result, they simply pass along and reinforce years of misinformation. Both adopt the view that Lipans were deceitful and manipulative while ignoring evidence of good faith, leading to proclamations like this one: Gifts and any conciliatory gesture "only encouraged the aggression of the Lipans."[9]

Britten's conclusions, like Schilz's, defy logic. He refers to their "decision" to be buffalo-hunting nomads and their "historic unwillingness to place much reliance on agriculture" as risky. (Evidence of their farming is ample.) They had to keep moving because they had so many enemies. (Not so.) And finally, "the Lipans' inability to forge lasting alliances with anyone—either Indian or non-Indian" made them vulnerable. This book will show that Lipans sustained relations with the Llaneros and other bands of the confederacy from prehistoric times until they settled together on the reservation. They were close friends of the Mescalero bands from at least 1730 and probably earlier and with the Tonkawas from 1820 on, and their alliances with other groups extended over decades.[10]

Some of my criticism reflects more than three decades as a practicing journalist. Journalists tell stories. Good journalists get it right. Journalists as historians, says one of the best, Hampton Sides, "delve into their subject and make history come alive for the modern audience," while "academic history is chloroform on paper."[11] He draws lay readers to history and keeps them turning the page, and for that the rest of us should be grateful, but he doesn't use footnotes. I've often thought the methods and goals of historians and journalists are the same; only the vocabulary is different. Journalists have sources, historians have informants; journalists dig, historians research. We all produce a written record, the bones of histories. I'm a creature of both worlds. I tell stories. I bring you as close as I can to the people. I also do painstaking research, fill in historical gaps, and use footnotes.

Journalist Bill Moyers captured the indignation I often felt while working on this book. "Bad history can have consequences as devastating as bad journalism," he said in an address to the Texas State Historical Association. When history goes wrong, "it can denigrate and dehumanize people who have no voice to tell their own stories," but in serving as a witness, "(h)istory, like literature and journalism, finds a moral purpose."

He observed that "some people desperately need to know where they themselves fit into history." I find that particularly true for today's Native people, especially those estranged from their roots. For them, historians recreate a past world where their chiefs, their ancestors, are "players in the unfolding drama of which we are the present cast," as Moyers puts it. The actors change, but the play goes on. Whoever you are, "you have a right to understand your own history, and you have a stake," he said, and everybody "has an obligation to explore who we are and how we got here."[12]

◄►

Old-school historians typically portrayed Lipans as "savages" and blamed them for the failure of missions and every other act of aggression between parties. A "depredation" could mean the murder of a settler or the butchering of a single beef by hungry people. "The history of the Lipan Apaches, and particularly their relationship to the Spaniards, had been so distorted by the ethnocentric bias of some scholars that it was hardly comprehensible," wrote Curtis Tunnell and W. W. Newcomb, Jr.[13]

In the last few decades, historic interpretation has lurched to the other side, with sympathetic portrayals of Native people that incorporate oral history. While the correction is overdue, some new-school historians give us Native people who are blameless victims while villainizing Spaniards, Mexicans and Americans, and a neutral reference to settlers or rangers earns a snub as "hagiography." This isn't interpretation, it's spin, and it doesn't contribute to understanding.

It's now fashionable among revisionists to dismiss the Texas Rangers as frontier bullies and sneer at most of their history as hagiography. Admittedly, they could be brutal, but then so were their adversaries. In fairness, the rangers were often all that stood between settlers and mayhem. There's a larger issue here: We can't just refuse to consider their stories. Legend and lore are as much a part of history as the written record and offer insights, explanations, and even information. Legend is just one attic discovery, one misfiled document away from the legitimacy of the written record.

Is there room for objectivity among the new "Indian-centric" models? Historian John Monnett has called for writing "from both sides of the battle lines" and championed "a new breed of scholars" who "do not begin their studies with pre-conceived theses," leading to bias in the use of supporting documentation. What makes history readable—character development, pacing and storytelling—hasn't changed, he reminds us, and he warns against the "need to overexpose readers to academic jargon [and] fifty dollar words . . ."[14]

In this book I've tried to answer the question, who were the Lipans? I set out with a blank slate, obsessively pursued and sifted information, and shaped a narrative that makes use of stories, which is how Native people tell their own history. I present the good with the bad. Lipans were victims of atrocities; they also committed atrocities.

Presenting a balanced story, when the historical record rarely gives voice to Native people, is always a challenge. Those who write Native histories must depend on accounts written by their enemies, but persistent digging yields the occasional gem—insights from someone who knew the Lipans well or a record keeper who took accurate notes. Oral histories, interviews with Lipans, captivity narratives, and family and tribal histories fill in many blanks and make it possible to reconstruct the Apache view. I've made extensive use of interviews with Lipan people—my own and those of historian Eve Ball, anthropologist Morris Opler, and Daniel Castro Romero, Jr. I have also woven together known facts and values to construct the occasional paragraph from the point of view of the People, the Nde, as they called themselves.

Too many tribal histories stop at the reservation period. Maybe the author thinks there is nothing more to report, or boredom sets in when the shooting stops. Because of the widespread notion that Lipans are extinct, it's important to see them into the present, and much of their past determines their present.

Early in my research, I got a phone call from a Lipan descendent on the Mescalero Apache Reservation in New Mexico. His son wanted to know what it meant to be a Lipan. I explained that I was still learning, but I've kept that boy in my thoughts. What I should have said was, "They never gave up."

❧ Chronology ❧

Before 1000 AD	Athabascan migration south
900 AD	Athabascans possibly at La Junta
1300s or before	Apachean people reach the southern plains
1541	Coronado expedition meets Querechos
1582	Rodriguez-Chamuscado expedition meet Vaqueros
1601	Oñate makes first reference to "Nation called Apache"
1608	Apache raiders begin stealing horses
1640	Taos Pueblo revolt, take refuge at Cuartelejo
1680	Pueblo Revolt
1686	Apaches control the buffalo plains
1692	DeVargas reconquest of New Mexico
1696	Picuris and others rebel, take refuge at Cuartelejo
1700s, early	Lipans obtain peyote ceremony from Carrizos
1706	Ulibarri expedition meets Apaches across mountains and plains; reports of Comanche attacks
1718	Presidio at San Antonio de Béxar constructed
1722	Bourgmont expedition makes peace with Eastern Apaches
1731	Villa of San Fernando de Béxar, Spain's first chartered settlement in Texas
1732	First reference to Lipans as Ypandes, first mention of Natagés as allies

Continued

1739	Cabellos Colorados and eleven other Lipans, first group sent to Mexico City under the Regulation of 1729
1743	Comanches first appear in San Antonio; Ypandes move farther south
1750	Ypandes ally with Bidais
1752	Apaches abandon Cuartelejo, regroup near Pecos Pueblo
1757	San Sabá mission and presidio built
1758	Comanches and Norteños attack San Sabá mission
1758	Lipans relocate in Coahuila
1761	First use of "Lipan"
1762	Mission San Lorenzo de la Santa Cruz and Nuestra Señora de la Candelaria established
1763	France gives Louisiana to Spain
1770s	Lipans divide into Upper Lipans and Lower Lipans
1771	San Lorenzo and Candelaria missions abandoned
1777	Croix and Father Juan Agustin Morfi tour northern Coahuila
1779	Spanish sow conflict between Lipans and Mescaleros
1787–1788	Lipiyan Chief Picax-andé Ins-tinsle and Ugalde make peace
1793	Lipans make peace with Spain
1801	Chief Picax-andé dies in battle with Comanches
1807	Lipans, Comanches and Tawakonis make peace
1810	Comanches break peace with Lipans
1811	Lipans join royalists against Mexican revolutionaries
1813	Recruited by Americans, Lipans join the Republican Army of the North and renew their alliance with Comanches
1815	Lipans and Kiowa Apaches meet again

Continued

1821	Mexico obtains independence, Lipans declare war on Comanches
1822	Lipan Chief Cuelgas de Castro makes peace with Mexico
1835	Texas revolution begins; Lipans serve as scouts and spies
1838	Lipans sign "a treaty of Peace and Perpetual friendship" with Texas
1839	Castro commands his own Lipan ranger company
1840	Young Flacco commands his own ranger company
1842	Castro dies, Young Flacco murdered
1844	Treaties between Texas and Texas tribes
1846	Treaty between United States and Texas tribes; Mexican war begins, Lipans in Mexico migrate north
1850, 1851	Treaties between United States and Texas tribes; Seminoles and Black Seminoles relocate to Texas; Zaragosa provides land for Lipans
1854	Pecos Lipans and John Castro's Lipans move to San Fernando, Coahuila
1856	Chiquito's Lipans move to Coahuila
1857	Seminoles return to United States; Black Seminoles remain in Mexico
1862–1865	Mescaleros at Bosque Redondo
1865	Texas militia attacks peaceful Kickapoos
1866	Lipans take Frank Buckelew captive
1869	Some Lipans living with Kiowa Apaches at Fort Sill
1870	Apaches gravitate to Fort Stanton; first Black Seminole scouts arrive at Fort Duncan
1873	Mescalero Apache Reservation created; arrests cause Apaches to leave reservation; Mackenzie's Raid on May 18 attacks tribes in Remolino; U.S. commissioners try unsuccessfully to remove American tribes from Mexico
1874	Lipan prisoners of Mackenzie's Raid move to Fort Griffin

Continued

1875	Magoosh's last raid
1877	Natzili and Pinole (Llaneros) come in from Staked Plains
1876	Díaz becomes president of Mexico
1878	U.S. Army creates District of the Pecos; Mexican General Trevino begins campaign against Lipans and Mescaleros; Lincoln County War gunplay
1879	Victorio goes on war path, joined by Mescaleros and Lipans
1880	Lipan scouts used in Victorio campaign and border conflicts; reservation Apaches disarmed and dismounted; Victorio ambushed in Mexico
1881	Last Indian raid in Texas; Alsate and Colorado shot; Mescaleros and Lipans return to reservation; Fort Griffin closed
1884	Tonkawas and Lipans removed to Indian Territory
1885-1886	Geronimo outbreak, Lipans and Mescalero scout against him
1896	Fort Stanton closed
1898	Natzili's death
1904	Venego's band arrives from Mexico
1915	Magoosh's death
1948	The Apache Nation (Lipans and Mescaleros) files claim with Indian Claims Commission
1976	Commission awards five million dollars to the Lipans and equal amount to the Mescaleros
1998	The Lipan Apache Band of Texas incorporated
2007	The Lipan Apache Tribe of Texas Inc. separated from the Lipan Apache Band of Texas

Creation Story

Now this story shows how some people were in the old days.

— Percy Big Mouth

Lipans were Apache at heart, but as a result of their long history of befriending or absorbing other groups, their cultural table was a smorgasbord of adopted habits and traditions. Unlike other Apaches, they farmed, ate fish and bear, counted coup, and used sign language. They spoke good Spanish. They lived in artfully painted tipis on the plains, wickiups in the mountains, and jacales in Mexico.

Lipans were typically described as handsome people dressed in skillfully made buckskin clothing. Many an observer found the Lipans more fastidious and their skins better cured. A Spanish officer in 1896 observed "a certain neatness and martial bearing that differentiates them markedly from the other nations, in which dirt and filth are so common."[1]

Unlike other Apaches, they were tall; Lipan men, at nearly six feet, would have towered over other Apaches. Friends and adversaries alike marveled at their intelligence; they were quick studies, especially in the use of a new tool or weapon. They could count up to a thousand, and their counting system had a root of ten. They could not only determine the time but reduce it to fractions, and they could predict eclipses and other astronomical events.[2]

Families were matrilineal. When a man married, he joined his wife's extended family. Lipans were the only Apaches who didn't avoid their in-laws. Leaders were always men, but first-hand accounts reveal that certain women commanded great respect and often served as messengers, an important task. Lipan women didn't ride into battle as their Mescalero sisters did, but when the camp was attacked, they fought fiercely. In conflicts women also loaded guns and guarded the horses.

Lipan children were trained early to use a slingshot and bow and arrow—more than one visitor marveled at the accuracy of small, naked boys shooting their arrows—and to build a fire with a fire drill. They chased birds and butterflies to strengthen legs and lungs and were made to plunge into cold water to develop stamina. From Coyote Tales told at night, children learned it was important to be brave, generous, and honest, and to help others and treat guests well. The stories also taught lessons about vanity, lechery, gluttony and deception. Sometimes Coyote sounded all-too-human: "I'm a fine looking fellow, yet the girls don't pay any attention to me."

Topography figured into offense and defense. Like other Apaches, Lipans typically fought from ambush or struck in fleet, targeted raids and vanished, but they were also capable of staged, coordinated fighting in the open. They camped with mountains or canyons at their backs and discouraged pursuers by racing over the most miserable, steep or thorny route, scaling imposing mountains and doubling back on trails. If their losses grew intolerable, they scattered in all directions and regrouped later.

A man distinguished himself by showing courage in battle. The hero of a folk tale is described this way: "This man was a real Lipan. He'd fight with anything—the wild animals or the enemy. He was not afraid of anything at all."[3] As a man's reputation for bravery and wisdom grew, he could be recognized as a head man, captain or chief, but he was only a leader as long as his people were willing to follow him. They could leave when they wanted, and he exercised no authority over them. Similarly, leadership wasn't hereditary, although a son might become chief.[4]

The warrior's arsenal included his gun, bow, lance, club, knife and shield. By the mid-1800s, they occasionally used the tomahawk. Lipans valued the latest firearms but never abandoned the bow and arrow. A warrior could fire a dozen arrows while the enemy fumbled with his muzzle loader. Like other plains warriors, they counted coup. "It was a great thing among the Lipan to be the first to touch a fallen enemy," said Antonio Apache. "They would race out, even though it was dangerous, to be first to touch the fallen foe."

If a raid had gone well, they celebrated with a dance. "When the Lipan were defeated in a big fight and lost some of their men, they didn't come right into camp," said Antonio Apache. "They would stop where the people could see them. They would get off their horses. Then the people in camp knew what had happened. They waited till sundown and then came into the camps. There would be no dancing or greeting. Nothing would be said to them (to shame them)."[5]

Although their written history tends to focus on conflict, Apaches weren't always at war, and Lipan folk tales describe happier times: "Those people down there danced every night. They had good times every day."[6] They loved games—hoop and pole for the men, the stave game for the women—and they played cards and raced horses.

Lipans, like other Apaches, believed in one deity. They possessed sacred objects and employed masked individuals to represent supernaturals. The Lipan medicine man was both religious authority and healer. There were ceremonies to cure the sick, bless dwellings, improve the hunt or raid, deliver misfortune to the enemy, change the weather, and find lost objects. They observed an elaborate girls' puberty ceremony.

The Lipan afterlife rewarded the good and punished the bad. Their oral accounts often describe a place, possibly in the underworld, divided by a hill. On the south side was a beautiful, green place with cottonwoods growing along a good stream, where men played hoop and pole. On the north side, which was shrouded in smoke and mist, witches and evil people were tormented by fire and had only snakes and lizards to eat.[7] Lipans observed the Apache custom of destroying the belongings of the deceased, killing the person's horse, and moving camp. Mourners cut their hair and wore old clothing, and the individual's name was not spoken again.

Lipans learned the peyote ceremony in Mexico from its originators, the Julimes (later called Carrizos), and practiced it for more than a century before teaching it to Mescaleros, Naishans (formerly called Kiowa Apaches), Kickapoos, and Comanches.

◄►

"Among us Lipans, our story goes like this. I'm trying to write about how the things start on this wide lands. In the beginning; the people were down in the lower world." This is the way Percy Big Mouth began the Lipan Creation Story for his young friend, Gene Neyland, in the 1940s. Self-conscious about his third-grade education, he wrote, "Well Gene please don't mind my mistakes and the poor English as I'm trying my best, and on the Indian story, correct the right words in its place. Iron them out good." Here is his Creation Story, ironed out a bit:[8]

There were all sorts of peoples. They use one language. Then someone suggest they have a council.

"Let's find another place to move," someone said.

"To where we move?"

"You see there a light above. Suppose we send someone up there to find out about the upper world."

"How about the wind?"

So they asked him, and the wind agreed to go up and see how it look. It's the whirlwind. He came to the new world above. Nothing but the water covered the earth. Then the wind start to get busy, rolled the water up like curtain. [Land appeared. The water was at one side.] The upper world is ready for the people below.

Then they sent the raven [crow][9] up to look over the dry land. There are lot of dead fish and some other things that live in the water.

The raven never thought of going back down, as he having a feast all by himself.

So they held a council again to send someone else and decided to send Beaver. When he came up, there was dry land and the clear river flowing. He is so happy in the new world, he never thought of going back to tell the others. He started to get busy building dams.

The people below wonder what happen to the Beaver. This time they send the gray Badger out. He go this way and that way, all around. Most of the places are dried up, beautiful streams running. He came back. He's faithful to his fellows. They all happy, when the Badger got back and told them about the upper world.

They sent four others—Mirage, Wind, Lightning, and Water. They fixed the earth so the animal, the fowl and all the different trees and all the plant started to grow. The little spring ran out from the hills. Oh, it's sure beautiful on the new world above.

Now all these were the peoples: Trees, little bushes, weeds of different kinds, animals of all sorts, fowls of all different kinds, insects. They all happy, they all talk one language, even the rocks. They all understand each other. They are the first peoples. They moved around the edge of the earth clockwise.

Then the real humans came out after them . . . [When they started from the place of emergence, the western tribe are first to stop, Western Apaches.][10] As they went along clockwise, different peoples dropped off. As they stopped they became different tribes and had different languages. "You shall be such and such a people and speak this language," they were told. That is how all these different tribes and languages were made. [They used the dog for a horse at this time as they moved north. At the very end of the journey the Tonkawa dropped off with the Lipan. The Lipan were the very last to stop the journey and find a home. Now the people were all fixed.][11]

These two are the leader: the Sun, and the Moon. The sun is a man, and the moon is a woman. They were with these people. Their rays shine down on them. In the day time the sun show them their way to go; at night, the moon. These two said, "We separate, but we will meet each other." That is when it eclipses.

Then at last they start out on their journey over the wide world. The grey willow said, "I stop here and live, where nice little brook flowing." Then little later the alligator-bark juniper stopped. He was wearing turquoise beads around his neck, which became his berries. [Traveling on, more junipers stopped. Their turquoise or reddish beads became berries] Next oak stopped. He was wearing black stones on his head. These are his acorns now. [As they went along, three more oaks stopped, and a chokecherry, mulberry and other trees.]

There was a river running southward. As they were moving along, they never stop to set up (camp) but just kept moving. Then someone said, "Sleep." So they stop at this place. They wanted to move on, but someone put a white walking cane over them. They went to sleep. One day and night passed. Someone said, "Morning."

The Sun and Moon left them and said, "Go ahead. There is nothing will disturb you people. Everything on ahead is good for you people. They told the people they should keep moving, no matter what happen on this earth. So the Sun is the War Hero;[12] the moon is Changing Woman.

There are several large Giants living in different places who were eating people who come near their home. Of these Giant people are Big Owl, Antelope, Buffalo, Peccary, Flicker, Giant with four others.

Now Changing Woman was living on a high mountain at a place they call Rock Nose just on the border of New Mexico [in the Guadalupe Mountains]. There was a cave on the southeast side where Changing Woman was living when the earth is very young.

Every time she have a child, Big Owl come and eat the child. As the story goes among the Apaches Tribes, the giant was visiting all the time. The woman having a hard time, trying to raise a child, so she went to a little spring and lay down. It rained and the rain entered her body. Then a child began to develop within her. This child was going to be a great person. In four days he came.]

She had a boy she call Child of the Water. Then Giant came. He thought he smell a baby. The woman said, no. The giant looked all around but can't find the child and left. She was hiding the boy. When the giant came again, the little boy was already walking around, and he ran to his hiding place in a hole the woman dug under her fireplace. The giant looked around.

"I'm sure there must be a child somewhere, 'cause I saw his foot track." He hunted around, but never found the child. The woman kept a large flat rock over the hole and built a fire on the flat rock.

The little boy came out. He's big enough to shoot bow and arrow now, so the woman made bow and four arrows and teach the boy how to handle the bow and arrow. When the giant came again, this time the little boy didn't run back in his hiding place. Big Owl saw the boy and said, "I want that little boy." He tried to think of some trick so that he could get that little child.

But the mother said, "I got that child from the Water, so it's a Thunder Child. I'm going to rear that boy for Thunder. You mustn't try to bother that child." The Giant Owl went off but came back again but couldn't persuade her to give him up.

The boy grew to be a young man. He could take care of himself anywhere. He had his bow and arrow, and could fight anything. Then Big Owl came again but didn't bother him because he was afraid.

The young man, Killer-of-Enemies, said he would go down to the flats and get after the buffalo. He saw a buffalo under a mesquite tree. It was open country all around and no one could approach him. Killer-of-Enemies was great, but he asked for a little help. He prayed. That was to show that no matter how strong we are, we must ask for a little help. With help from gopher, who dug four trenches, he killed the buffalo, who was killing the people. Then he told buffalo, "You must be useful to the people." The buffalo said he would, "but they must not throw my flesh around carelessly. So today the hunter has to be careful about this.[13]

Next Killer-of-Enemies killed the Antelope, who was killing the people. He made four arrows of the sotol stalk. The black arrow he shot to the east, and black smoke rose. The antelope ran over there and returned. He shot a blue arrow to the south, and blue smoke rose. The antelope ran to the south and came back. Killer-of-Enemies shot the yellow arrow to the west, where yellow smoke appeared. Finally he shot the white arrow to the north, and white smoke rose. He was so tired when he returned, Killer-of-Enemies killed him with a war club. He told the antelope the people would use his skin and his flesh. Antelope said he would agree, but the people must not leave any fur on the meat and never swallow it that way.

After this, Killer-of Enemies killed the Eagle and his wife and told one of their children that he would grow no larger. He too must help the people, and they would respect him highly and use his feathers in ceremonies and prayers. He plucked feathers from the dead father and blew them upward, creating all sorts of birds.

The final challenge for Killer-of-Enemies was a monster bird that lived among the prairie dogs and killed with its eyes. The prairie dogs always warned him when anyone was coming. With help from the grey lizard, who showed how to approach without being seen, Killer-of-Enemies first blinded the monster bird and his family by throwing hot buffalo fat in their eyes and then killed them with his war club. Killer-of-Enemies told him, from now on you have no power with your eyes. You're just a plain burrowing owl.[14]

Killer-of-Enemies had killed all the enemies of the people. He also created both the deer and the horse and gave them to the people. He and Changing Woman still live in the Guadalupe Mountains.[15]

◄►

Culture heroes who slay monsters are familiar icons of Apachean mythology, but just four groups—Lipans, Navajos, Western Apaches and Jicarilla Apaches—tell origin stories of emerging from an underworld and name their culture hero Killer-of-Enemies. These and other similarities are evidence of an early link, according to anthropologist Morris Opler. Lipan and Jicarilla stories were nearly identical.[16] The story incorporates such important cultural elements as the four directions and their associated colors and their beliefs about animals like the buffalo, antelope, eagle and horse.

The Lipan creation story, told in abridged form here, also incorporates some history—use of the dog travois, association with the Tonkawas, and origins in the north. "I have heard that at the time of the emergence some people went to the north, so far to the north that they came to a land where it was dark all the time," said Antonio Apache, who was Opler's informant along with Percy Big Mouth and his aunt Stella La Paz in 1935.[17]

Percy was proud of his people's history and culture and often shared his knowledge. Born in 1889 to a Mescalero father, Big Mouth, and a Lipan mother, Zotsaha, Percy was Lipan in the Apache way.[18] In the 1940s, as a ranger on Sierra Blanca for the Mescalero Apache Tribe, the outgoing Percy enjoyed chatting with tourists and, for his friends, wrote down stories in longhand on Big Chief tablets.

One of those friends was Martha Gene Neyland. Another was Sue Edwards, whom met Percy in 1941, when her father brought a group of Boy Scouts from Stamford, Texas. The first evening, "without a sound, Percy appeared at the edge of our camp circle," Sue wrote. The visitors neglected to bring extra plates and cutlery, "but my father was the first to offer his plate." The gesture was the beginning of a long friendship.

Every night, Percy joined their camp, ate dinner and told Apache stories. He also taught them dances, drum making, and tracking. The Boy Scouts—and Sue—gave him their full attention, which must have been gratifying. Apache young people didn't care to hear about the old ways, and sharing with these white youngsters was Percy's way of keeping the culture alive.

"Draw a mental picture, if you can, of all of us sitting on the edge of our seats around the dancing flames of a campfire, eyes as wide and unblinking as hoot-owls, mouths ajar, minds drinking every word and imaginations in full exercise . . . We were experiencing something most children can only dream about," Sue wrote.

Percy Big Mouth, 1940s. *Courtesy of Gene and Jackson Harris.* Percy and his family always believed that his twisted spine was the result of a childhood fall from a horse, but Jackson Harris, a physician, believes Percy suffered from Potts Disease—tuberculosis of the spine.

Percy gave up his ranger job in 1949 to care for Old Dad, and Percy began sending Apache stories. Over the next few years, he wrote hundreds of pages of myths and legends: "Now Sue, the Indian story I wrote for you is a great one. When an Indian want to hear a real old story like that, they roll a cigarette for the person who know an old story. When he accepted the cigarette, then he tell his story. They even give a horse in the old time days."[19]

Percy Big Mouth died of a heart attack in December 1958, five weeks after his father's death at the age of 108.[20] Eve Ball wrote of Percy, "It is not an exaggeration to say that he was one of the best known and most beloved individuals on the reservation."[21]

CHAPTER

Early Encounters

They are men who move here and there, to wherever it seems best
to them . . .

— *Captain Juan Jaramillo*[1]

I n the endless, undulating spring grasses of the plains, the People
could see the approach of friends and enemies. These strangers
were even more obvious, sitting astride great beasts, the sun reflecting off armor and weapons. The People had heard about these men
who made themselves ugly with facial hair. Any self-respecting warrior would use flints to tweeze all the hair from his face, including
eyebrows and eyelashes. They knew of the beasts as well—snorting,
heavy-footed animals that could bear much heavier loads than the
medium-sized, shaggy dogs the People harnessed to carry their possessions when they moved camp. These creatures had terrified the Pueblo
people on first sight.

The People were neither frightened nor alarmed at the strangers'
approach. Their camp and its two hundred tipis housed at least a thousand people, and even though some of the men were away hunting buffalo, they were well defended. Their group and allied bands numbered
in the thousands. Their enemies feared them, and the newcomers were
few. These plains dwellers were called Kiraush by the Pueblos. The
Spanish would call them Querechos, Vaqueros and finally Apaches.
They called themselves Ndé, the People.[2]

"Although these [people] saw the expedition, they did not move nor did they make any commotion. Instead, they came out of their tents to look openly," wrote Pedro de Castañeda, an expedition member. Using their hands, the people asked what the expedition was and expressed themselves so well "that it seemed as if they were talking."[3]

Francisco Vasquez Coronado, the expedition leader, wrote to the king: "They do not cultivate the land, but eat raw meat and drink the blood of the cattle [bison] they kill." Their well-constructed tents, as well as their clothing, also came from the bison. Dogs carried tents, poles, and belongings. "These people have the best physique of any I have seen in the Indies,"[4] Coronado said, and Casteñeda agreed: "They have better figures, are better warriors and are more feared."[5]

Furrows left by dragging tipi poles led the explorers to the Querechos in May 1541. They were near the Canadian River on the present-day New Mexico-Texas border.[6] The Spaniards, unnerved and disoriented by a landscape level as a tablet from horizon to horizon, were startled to find Indian buffalo hunters[7] and marveled at their use of the bison. "They dry the flesh in the sun, cutting it thin like a leaf, and when dry they grind it like meal to keep it and make a sort of sea soup of it to eat by throwing a handful into a pot and seasoning it with fat," Castañeda wrote.

For liquids they "empty a large gut and fill it with blood and carry this around the neck to drink when they are thirsty." They also opened the bison's stomach, squeezed out the chewed grass and drank the juice. Their tanning skills were superior. For skinning, they used a small flint, edged with their teeth and attached to a stick, as easily as an iron tool.[8] The Querechos departed, but the Spaniards were still seeing their camps two days later.[9]

The Lipan Apache Band of Texas considers these people its ancestors, and substantial historic evidence supports that claim.[10] Others refer to the Querechos as Plains Apaches, a grouping that included the ancestors of the Lipans, Mescaleros and Kiowa Apaches, or the Eastern Apaches, made up of these groups plus Jicarillas.[11]

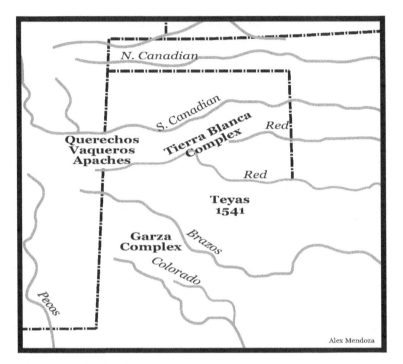

Map 1 Eastern Apaches, 1500s

Continuing east for five days, Coronado and his party met the Teyas, a Caddoan group sometimes mistaken for Apaches. Coronado himself referred to the Teyas as "another sort of people" and "enemies of those that I had seen in the last settlement."[12]

Archaeologists call these settlements the Tierra Blanca and Garza complexes of the Texas Panhandle-Plains. Querechos lived in the Tierra Blanca complex on the Llano Estacado (Staked Plains) north of the Red River. Teyas inhabited the Garza Complex along the upper forks of the Brazos River near present Lubbock. The two groups didn't mix.[13]

From stories about Teyas or Querechos attacking pueblos sixteen years earlier, the Spaniards assumed, as did archaeologists until recently, that those events heralded the arrival of the Apaches on the plains,[14] but they actually appeared much earlier. Apache ancestors separated from Canadian Athabascans in the first millennium and followed game animals south to the northern Rocky Mountain region, where they adapted to Plains bison hunting, apparently introducing the bow and arrow. Before A.D. 1000 they migrated south in small groups, reaching the southern Rocky Mountains and plains of present Colorado by the fourteenth to fifteenth century.

For years, scholars have debated routes taken by the Athabascans: mountains, plains, or both? The consensus favors multiple groups following different routes, which explains the different tribes and bands.[15] As for the eastern groups, archeologists Kevin Gilmore and Sean Larmore suggest they migrated along Colorado's front range and the western edge of the plains, reaching the area well before 1400.[16]

Bison increased on the middle Pecos, southern Llano Estacado and Panhandle Plains around A.D. 1300 and so did humans, who either adopted or brought new technology—more efficient arrow points, scrapers, drills and knives. The first Apaches were hunting bison on the Texas High Plains by this time. They may have dislodged Caddoans, who moved to the northeast.[17]

"Apaches have been here quite a bit longer than archeologists think," wrote archaeologist Deni Seymour, who has studied sites in southeastern New Mexico and West Texas. Athabascans and non-Athabascans entered the southern Southwest by at least the fourteenth century, probably by the thirteenth century or earlier, and in smaller numbers. She believes new sites will continue pushing the arrival time earlier.[18]

Apaches joined the trade network that brought obsidian from the Jemez Mountains, turquoise from the Cerillos mines, marine shells from the Pacific Coast and Gulf of California, and pottery from the pueblos of the upper Rio Grande.[19] In this commerce, the Apaches provided bison meat, robes and tallow, along with Alibates chert, finished tools, and freshwater shell ornaments that probably came from the headwaters of the Colorado and Concho rivers in Texas. They made pottery and traded for it. In the course of business, the plains Apaches drew closer to eastern pueblos, making friends and exchanging gifts.[20] They began to favor Pecos Pueblo until they virtually monopolized trade there, edging out rival Caddoan traders.[21]

◄►

The Canadian River, more than a thousand miles long, spills from the eastern flanks of the Sangre de Cristo range near the present New Mexico-Colorado border and flows slowly east to the Raton area and then south, its waters red with clay. Steep, rugged canyons cut into Dakota sandstone form the Canadian Breaks, along with a scattering of buttes and flat-topped mesas rising from the sandy floor. This was Apache country. Where the river entered the elevated, grassy expanse known as the Staked Plains, or Llano Estacado, this too was Apache country. After slinking across Texas, it emptied in Oklahoma at the Arkansas River.[22] The Apaches were here too.

After Coronado, the People didn't see Spaniards again for forty years. In that time they learned that the bearded ones stole people from the tribes and kept them to labor in the mines and fields. They also knew of Spaniards who carried no weapons but prayed to a cross they wore. When the small expedition led by Father Agustín Rodriguez and Captain Francisco Sánchez Chamuscado approached in 1582, Indian people fled, believing them to be slavers.[23] At a pueblo in New Mexico's Galisteo Basin, the Spaniards heard about people who lived on game and bison meat during the winter and in summers searched for prickly pears and dates. They lived in huts of cattle (buffalo) hides and moved from place to place. They were enemies but also came to trade buckskins, buffalo hides and meat for corn and blankets. "They said that the Indians who followed these herds were very brave, fine hunters with bow and arrow who would kill us," wrote an expedition member.[24]

In October the Spaniards found people they called Vaqueros on the Pecos River,[25] two days from their homes on the Canadian River. "Here we were met by over four hundred warlike men armed with bows and arrows," wrote a soldier, Hernán Gallegos. "They asked us by means of signs what we wanted. We told them we were coming to visit them and that they were our friends. Nevertheless they were intent on shooting arrows at us."

The explorers withdrew, and, from a distance, made the sign of the cross with their hands; the Vaqueros reciprocated, welcoming the Spaniards cheerfully. By way of salutation, a Spaniard fired his harquebus, which so startled the Vaqueros, they dropped to the ground in terror and let the Spanish know they shouldn't do it again. The party learned that the Vaqueros "roamed over the greater part of the plains and along the rivers, lakes, and salt water holes. When it was cold or snowed they sought shelter in the extensions and slopes of the sierra," wrote the historian Baltasar de Obregón.

The party wandered without finding bison, returned to the Vaqueros' camp, and seized a man to guide them, avoiding a fight only because of their guns. After three days, they reached the Canadian, where they found buffalo by the thousands. They shot forty, to the delight of the guide who had never seen guns used for hunting. The expedition then turned back, sending the guide ahead laden with meat as a reward for his services. Back in camp, he told his people about the hunt. They were then glad to welcome the Spaniards, who shared meat with the leaders.[26]

◄ ►

Eleven years later Jusephe Gutierrez, an Indian from Mexico, survived a disastrous expedition with the Spaniards, when expedition members became lost and separated on the buffalo plains. Gutierrez was rescued and cared for (or captured, depending on the account) by Vaquero Indians and lived with them for a year before making his way home. He described wetlands along the Canadian River, great herds of bison, and plum trees. Hearing the report, Juan Perez de Oñate sent his sargento mayor to investigate.[27]

In 1598, Vincente de Zaldívar Mendoza, with Gutierrez as a guide, led a fall expedition, which found Vaqueros in the same location. After presenting gifts and food, a man shouted to others who were hiding, and they all approached the Spaniards. "They are strong people, fine bowmen," he said. They gladly supplied a guide who led them to bison, but farther on, three other Indians were "greatly upset at seeing us marching through those lands." Zaldívar rode to their camp accompanied by a single soldier and an interpreter and told the three he wanted only to see them and be their friend. Not far from camp, "a great many people came out to meet him, by fours and by sixes," seeking his friendship by raising their right palms toward the sun and turning it toward their guest.

The next day, the people brought toasted corn meal. Zaldívar reciprocated with gifts and told them Governor Oñate would help those who were loyal and punish those who were not. They asked for help against the Jumanos. On the return, they found a camp of "fifty round tents of tanned hides, all bright red and white, with buttons and straps to close their openings as artfully made as they are in Italy, and the tents so large that the simplest among them easily held four separate beds and mattresses [of cedar or pine boughs covered with leaves or straw and topped with soft skins], and so skillfully tanned that even in a pouring rain the water cannot penetrate them . . ." Zaldívar traded for one of the tents and found that it weighed no more than fifty pounds.

He was fascinated with the dog travois: "(T)hese move in a long string, harnessed at the chest and haunches; and even carrying at least a hundred pounds they lope along as fast as their masters, and it is quite a sight, and a very amusing one, to see them trotting on their way, one after the other, the tips of the poles dragging behind them, and almost all of them with sores on their shoulders."[28]

◀▶

If the Spaniards found the Apaches' dog travois amusing, imagine what the Apaches thought about Oñate's convoy of more than seven hundred horses and mules, six mule carts, two ox carts, four pieces of artillery, and servants enough to tend it all, just to support seventy men. The colonizer of New Mexico thought the Vaqueros and Apaches were different groups, but by 1601 he referred to them as "the nation called Apache," the first known reference, probably from Awátche, the Ute word for Apaches. By the 1630s the name was in common use.[29]

Near the Canadian River, its verdant banks covered with vines and fruit, they encountered Apaches. The river here was "one of the best rivers which we had seen in all the Indies." When some Apaches appeared in his camp, Oñate and his men gave them so many presents that they soon returned with men, women and children, who raised their hands in friendship and brought the Spaniards some tasty black and yellow fruits the size of small tomatoes, which grew in abundance on the Canadian. The party found good springs and groves of trees as the land leveled out, and they met more Apaches. The Spaniards enjoyed a movable feast with abundant fish, plums "as mellow and good as those which grow in the choicest orchards of our land," and grapevines with "sweet and delicious grapes." The masses of gentle bison were fat and easy to kill.[30]

Five expeditions over sixty years found Apaches—numerous and comfortable—on or near the Canadian River, and they considered it their country.[31] Despite their brief encounters, the Spanish learned that the People moved from place to place and lived from the buffalo, skillfully tanning and making clothing, tipis. They traded surplus meat, robes, fat and tallow with Pecos, Picuris and Taos pueblos, as well as other tribes to the east and southeast; the exchange was so well established, they even wintered with nearby pueblos. The Querechos were courageous, intelligent and adept at making themselves understood. Feared as warriors, they were enemies of two other tribes. Castañeda's observation that they were "faithful friends" confirms amicable relations, at least initially, but the Spaniards' early willingness to take what they wanted would soon sour these relations.[32]

CHAPTER

Friends and Enemies

It is a nation so bellicose, all of it, that it has been the crucible for the courage of the Spaniards . . .

— Father Alonso de Benavides, 1630[1]

A cho Apache warriors spent weeks making arrows, choosing the hardest wood, straightening the shaft with their teeth, attaching sharp points of stone or bone. When it was time, they left their camp on the eastern flank of the Sangre de Cristo Mountains and, carrying bows nearly as tall as themselves, along with clubs and lances, passed silently along slopes and canyons to join their Taos Pueblo brothers. In the early morning of August 10, 1680, the combined groups attacked settlers and missionaries in the Taos area and killed all but two. Acho Apaches, members of a band later called Lipan,[2] were also involved in fighting at Picurís Pueblo and La Cañada.[3]

Devastation exploded across northern New Mexico, as the Pueblos and their allies made good on years of threats. In coordinated attacks, they killed twenty-one priests, settlers and soldiers and destroyed about sixty missions and many haciendas. Utes and Navajos also joined, but the Apaches were a pronounced presence. During the siege of Santa Fe, a Pueblo leader demanded the return of Indian captives "and likewise that all the Apache men and women whom the Spaniards had captured in war be turned over to them, inasmuch as some Apaches who were among them were asking for them." Pueblo captives said they and the Apaches had devastated the country from Taos to Isleta. Governor Antonio de Otermín didn't believe the rebels had Apaches among them, certain the two tribes were enemies, and refused the demand.[4]

Contrary to Otermín's (and some historians') perceptions, Apaches were not the Huns of the Southwest. Historian Ramón Gutiérrez describes Apaches and Pueblos as competitors for resources, speculates that Pueblo farming was a byproduct of Apache invasion, and concludes Pueblos traded under threat.[5] The reality was that each Apache unit was autonomous; a group might have close ties with one pueblo, hostile relations with another. Apaches from the plains considered the people of Pecos, Taos and Picuris pueblos their good friends and trusted trading partners. Pecos, perched atop a mesa with a commanding view of a broad valley that opened to the plains, became a trade center.

The Apaches' arrival was an event. After days of travel, an entire band would spill into the valley, its hundreds of dogs loaded with dried buffalo meat, fat, tallow and tanned hides. Parfleches bulged with goods from tribes farther east. The cacophony of barking dogs, shouted orders, greetings called out and running children enveloped the pueblo as the Apaches set up camp. Soon they made their way to houses, where they bartered for decorated cotton blankets, pottery and maize.[6] Of course, they had gifts for their friends, and it was a time for feasts.

The Spanish also became trading partners. Because the crown allowed commerce only with Mexico, whose merchants extracted a high price, colonists valued exchange with the Eastern Apaches, but the Spanish unbalanced the system. Tribute they demanded from the Pueblos eliminated surplus maize previously bartered for the Apaches' bison products; this supplemental food source evaporated just as large game was becoming scarce. Apaches were well aware of the onerous tribute system and could see that Pueblo people were virtual slaves to the Spaniards.[7]

Pueblo herders began to escape on horseback and took refuge with Apaches on the plains, no doubt teaching them how to ride. Raiders on foot began appropriating horses from Spanish herds as early as 1608. Lipans say they were among the first Indians, after the Pueblos, to have horses.[8] Apache raiders became so efficient the Spanish could scarcely defend themselves. Leaving their families in a secluded place defended by a few men, they set out in small parties on foot and traveled by night without making fires. Small parties met at an appointed time and place near the country they intended to invade. From an overlook they identified distant settlements, haciendas, and herds and then reconnoitered on foot after painting their bodies with mud and otherwise camouflaging themselves. Moving soundlessly, they could observe sleeping soldiers or livestock and communicate with each other by mimicking birds or coyotes. Once they acquired horses, they covered the hooves with hides to avoid leaving tracks and led them over hard or rocky ground until the day of the raid. At a safe distance, they divided their booty and escaped in different directions to frustrate pursuers.[9] "(T)hey travel unbelievable distances in one night and make their retreat like swift eagles, rendering it very difficult to overtake them," wrote the Catholic historian Juan Domingo Arricivita.[10]

As early as 1630, the Spanish understood certain Apache basics—that even though they moved around in search of game, they planted crops on their own land. They were well dressed in buckskin, "and the women gallantly and honestly clad," wrote Father Alonso de Benavides. "They are wont to have the wives as they can support; and upon her whom they take in adultery they . . . cut off her ears and nose; and they repudiate her. They are very obedient to their elders and hold them in great respect. They teach and chastise their children . . . They pride themselves much on speaking the truth, and hold for dishonored him whom they catch in a lie . . ."[11] Father Alonso de Posada in 1686 observed that Apaches weren't "governed by chiefs or hereditary princes, but rather by those who give proof in war of being the bravest." He observed that they held their wives "in special esteem" and took care to wear clean clothing.[12]

◀ ▶

Conspiracies to drive off the parasitic conquerors corresponded with the early raids, and Apaches also attacked pueblos they considered too close to the Spanish. "Picurís, Taos, Pecos, Apaches and Vaqueros . . . have formed a league among themselves and with other barbarous nations to exterminate our friends," wrote Father Francisco de Velasco in April 1609. "All the hostile tribes surrounding the nations among whom the Spaniards are now settled think that the Spaniards are scoundrels and people who are concerned only with their own interests. Many times these hostile natives have selfishly persuaded the peaceful Indians that the latter should throw off the heavy Spanish yoke . . ."

The viceroy instructed Oñate's successor to congregate Indian pueblos in new locations away from "the Apaches, who are usually a refuge and shelter for our enemies, [where they] hatch their plots against the whole land . . ."[13] Schemes festered through the 1600s. In 1640 a group from Taos Pueblo revolted, killed the priest and other Spaniards, destroyed the church and fled to the Apache village called El Cuartelejo on the plains. These refugees had a profound impact. Anthropologists believe the Cuartelejo Apaches learned farming and pottery-making from their Pueblo guests, and the practices spread to other Apache groups. The Taos people remained until Juan de Archuleta and twenty soldiers and Indian auxiliaries retrieved them in 1664, but some escaped and remained at El Cuartelejo and others may have joined them.[14] As unrest grew, the Spanish repeatedly punished Pueblo people severely "as traitors and confederates of the Apaches."[15]

During these years, a drought baked pastures into straw and withered crops in the field. Desperate Apaches brought in slaves and even their own children to trade to the priests for a little meat or flour. Pueblo people starved to death in their homes, and yet Governor Diego de Peñalosa in 1664 barred enemy Indians from trading in the pueblos, which exacerbated hostilities and intensified food shortages. Hundreds of Indians died of starvation. Apaches burned and pillaged Pueblo villages, carried away captives, stole livestock and even absconded with images, ornaments and jewels from the missions. "(T)he whole land is at war with the widespread heathen nation of the Apache Indians," wrote Father Juan Bernal.[16]

◄►

Apache unrest had simmered for years. The governors of New Mexico found no gold, but slaves were a valuable commodity. Spanish law forbade slavery but permitted capture of unconverted Indians during punitive expeditions, which was all the excuse Spaniards needed. They attacked Apache trading expeditions and even seized Apaches who came to ask for food during famines. Nearly every Spanish home had some of these servants (called *genizaros*), but the biggest profiteers were the governors, who sold hundreds of slaves to the southern mines.[17]

Around 1627 or 1628 Governor Phelipe Sotelo Ossorio sent a slaving expedition to the plains that struck peaceful Apaches and killed their chief, a Christian convert who held out the rosary he was wearing as he pleaded for his life. Priests were incensed, as were Apaches and settlers.[18] In 1638 a party sent by Governor Luís de Rosas attacked friendly Apaches who customarily traded at Pecos, killing some and taking others captive. Rosas kept a few as laborers in his Santa Fe weaving shop and sold the rest.[19]

The worst of the lot was Governor Bernardo López de Mendizábal, whose greed for slaves was such that during harvest time in 1659 he sent a slaving expedition of eight hundred Pueblo men and forty Spaniards to supply El Parral and its mines. He had already exported more than seventy Indian men and women on the pretext of punishing them and was accused of "forcing the citizens to sell their Apaches to him or seizing them outright, to increase the number he could offer for sale." Apaches "conceived a mortal hatred for our holy faith and enmity for the Spanish nation," wrote a captain.[20]

A few Spaniards cultivated friendly relations in their years of trading. Captain Diego Romero, in the summer of 1660, led a trading expedition for Governor Mendizábal that included a delegation from Pecos

Pueblo. He probably reached the Red River near the present Texas-Oklahoma border and found a village with dozens of colorful tipis. Late in the evening about thirty Apache men came to Romero's camp, formed a circle around him and announced they had come to make him chief captain, an honorary title. They placed Romero and the Pecos leader on a new buffalo robe and carried them to their camp, singing and playing reed whistles and flutes. From a place of honor on a pile of hides they were the subjects of an elaborate ceremony of speech, chanting, mock battles, and a tobacco pipe shared around a circle. Romero apparently married a woman, Apache way, and slept with her. Proudly wearing a gift feather in his hat and his close ties with the Apaches drew the unkind attention of the Inquisition.[21]

◀ ▶

Governor Otermín promised peace to nine Apache leaders who came to Pecos but sent them as prisoners to El Parral and sold their wives and children. Two of these men escaped and returned to tell their stories, further inflaming hatred against the Spaniards. Apaches from the plains continued trading in New Mexico but stopped bringing their wives and children and generally confined their visits to border pueblos like Pecos.[22]

Otermín ignored the ominous reports of his subordinates and the warnings of clerics. Now surrounded by angry hordes, the rebellion out of his control, he fought his way out of Santa Fe and fled south, where he learned that the rebels planned to destroy Isleta Pueblo for failing to support the revolt and give the Isleta women and children to Apaches to compensate them for their losses to Spaniards. Apaches harried the refugees far down the Rio Grande valley. Months later, from the safety of El Paso, he decided against a return to New Mexico because he lacked arms and provisions and heard the rebels and Apaches had fortified themselves in pueblos and estancias. By 1681 the alliance had dissolved, but rebel leaders and others were still bitter about the Spaniards' treatment of Apaches.[23]

How deeply were Apaches embroiled in the Pueblo Revolt? Anthropologist Albert Schroeder argued that Apaches played an insignificant role, but they not only fought alongside their Pueblo allies, they gave them a strategic and psychological edge. Otermín blamed the Apaches for unrest, as many an official would from then on; the alternative was to admit his own failings. The Apaches' raids and ambushes, he said, were intended to destroy New Mexico and "bring the Christian Indians into confederation with them, which they attempted and accomplished so many times."[24]

Otermín and his predecessors railed against the alliances without gauging the depth of resentment; they twisted or flouted Spanish law and shrugged off criticism from priests and settlers—for decades. We can assume the Apaches made revenge raids but stopped short of all-out war, probably because they lacked universal support for war; not all bands participated in the Pueblo Revolt. Writing eighty years later, Father Juan Sanz Lejaún lamented the wasted potential because the governors "attend only to filling their own pockets." Describing the tribute, forced labor, required participation in Spanish military campaigns, and other abuses, he observed, "When all this work is known to the heathen, who are always coming in and going out of the pueblos and hearing the complaints of the reduced Indians, what new reductions can be expected?"[25]

CHAPTER

The Confederacy

*They were coming to give me many manifestations of gratitude . . .
[from] all the tribes that were living along the banks of all the streams I
had seen and others that I had failed to cross, and others that I will meet
further on.*

— Juan de Ulibarri, 1706[1]

After the Pueblo people could see only the backs of the fleeing Spanish, after they mourned their dead, after they celebrated their victories, they had the Spanish flocks and herds at their disposal: thousands of animals. They exchanged horses with Plains tribes for buffalo robes and dried meat.[2] Passed through trade networks, mostly to the east, horses would transform plains society. Apaches now had ready access to horses, and used them to expand their territory. They could move quickly, carry heavier loads, and range farther in search of game and seasonal plants. Lipan ancestors moved southeast to the Colorado River in Texas and followed it into the rugged Lomería Grande (Hill Country). Some migrated all the way to the Texas coast. Their early trade in fresh-water shell ornaments hints that they were already familiar with the area, and now they stayed. Resident groups presented little challenge.

Just three years after the Pueblo Revolt, Chief Juan Sebeata, whose Jumanos were displaced from the upper Colorado, asked Governor Otermín for help against the Apaches. In December 1683 Otermín dispatched Juan Dominguez de Mendoza.[3] Other groups also approached Mendoza asking "that for the love of God I should make war on the hostile Apaches, who were enemies of theirs and of the Spaniards," and Mendoza agreed. The Spaniards then spent weeks chasing spurious reports of Apache raids until Mendoza concluded that Juan Sebeata was lying and sent the chief and his spies on their way.[4]

In May 1684 Apaches attacked the expedition three times from the north. Historians have speculated that the Apaches may not have been living there, but if they swept the previous occupants from their lands, they were fairly well established. Their new territory began at the headwaters of the upper Colorado, where the Staked Plains meet the Edwards Plateau, and extended along such tributaries as the Concho, San Sabá, Llano, and Pedernales rivers and their tributaries. It was country as pleasant and agreeable as the Canadian. The Concho yielded shells and pearls, a valuable trade commodity. Soaring live oaks shaded generous pasture, where wild hens set up a commotion at dawn. The bottom lands of the Colorado were rich in nut-bearing trees, grapes, mulberries, and groves of plum trees. Here lived bear, deer, antelope, and endless herds of buffalo. The broken, tree- and brush-covered Hill Country offered protected havens for rancherías; in the valleys was tall grass for horses.[5]

Lipan ancestors were also living on the coast, below the Nueces River, and had been there for some time. Even though the neighboring Karankawas were hostile, the Lipans adopted some of their habits, including bare feet, and learned to eat fish and shellfish. From the Tamaulipecan tribes they learned to use pottery and probably learned to make it.[6]

By 1686 Apaches controlled the buffalo plains. To the east, they invaded lands of the Quivira (southern Kansa) and Teja tribes. When they traded Quivira captives for horses at Pecos Pueblo, they said they had killed many important captains and other Indians of those nations. To the southeast, the Apaches drove the Ahijados, Cuytoas and Escanjaques from the Nueces River to the Rio Grande. The Jumanos retreated to the junction of the Rio Grande and Conchos River in Coahuila.[7]

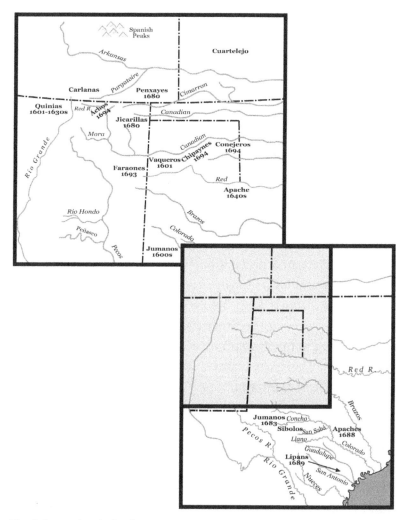

Map 2 Eastern Apache Bands, 1600s

"They have struck fear to all other tribes and have overrun, ruined and cast most of them out of their own lands," wrote Father Alonso de Posada in 1686. "This tribe occupies, defends and considers itself owner of four hundred leagues of land east and west and two hundred leagues north and south. In some places along their borders they claim even more territory. Its center is the plains of Sibola."[8]

Their enemies turned the tables briefly in 1688 when the Ervipi-ames (Coahuiltecans),[9] Jumanos (Taovayas),[10] and Tejas, aided by Frenchmen, destroyed an Apache ranchería near the Colorado. The following year, Apaches living in the hills northwest of present San Antonio, killed Frenchmen who frequented the Tejas camps, and the Tejas guided four Frenchmen across the Colorado farther east to keep the densely wooded Monte Grande between them and the Apaches. The Tejas (also called Texas, the namesake of the state) asked the Spanish for help in 1692, and that August they joined for a campaign. Apaches attacked them as they slept, and only Spanish firearms saved them from destruction; the new allies later struck a devastating blow, killing 136 Apaches.[11]

The often repeated declaration that Comanches pushed Lipans into Texas is groundless.[12] Lipan ancestors were entrenched in Texas and northern Coahuila long before Comanches appeared. Eastern Apaches roamed over vast territory even before they had horses; after-ward, they added to their territory, easily conquering and/or absorbing the inhabitants. Their new country was not only rich in resources, it was the path of least resistance.

◄►

Diego de Vargas in 1692 prepared to retake New Mexico. In Santa Fe, he found the Pueblo people still incensed at the Spaniards' brutal betrayal of the Apaches. "(W)hen the Spaniards formerly lived in this kingdom, they offered peace to the Apaches and then hunted them down and killed them," Vargas wrote. The people of Pecos Pueblo said they didn't want to be friends and would live with the Taos people or the Apaches rather than surrender.[13]

When Vargas launched his reconquest in 1693, he found a few friendly and a few ambivalent pueblos. He met stiff resistance at Taos, Picurís, Cochiti and Jemez. The rebels were allied with Canadian River Apaches (kin to the Acho Apaches involved in the 1680 revolt) and the aggressive Faraon Apaches, so named because they reminded the

Spaniards of Egyptian pharaohs, who lived between the Pecos and the Rio Grande south of Santa Fe. By April the Tewas, Tanos, Jemez, Apaches Colorados (Canadian River Apaches), and Navajos had allied to destroy the Keres, who were cooperating with the Spaniards.[14]

Not all Apaches wanted a fight. Certain eastern groups "have and have always had particular care in maintaining peace with the Spaniards," wrote Father Posada, "in order that they might have commerce with them, having an outlet for their dressed skins and hides."[15] In March 1694 the governor of Pecos brought in three Apaches who had been friendly to the Spaniards before the revolt and wished to resume trading at Pecos. Vargas assured them they would be welcome and sent a party of soldiers and settlers with them to Pecos. The Apaches were generous with their buffalo meat and tanned skins and said the rest of their ranchería would be at Pecos in October, and the Spaniards could come for the trade fairs as they once did.

The Pecos governor returned to Santa Fe in May, this time with the leader of the Apache rancherías on the buffalo plains, who said his people were friends of the Spaniards before and wanted to re-establish trade relations. They would come when the maize was ripe and bring buffalo, elk and buckskins to trade with the Spaniards. He gave Vargas three handsomely decorated buffalo hides and an elk-hide camp tent. As they ate, Vargas learned that the chief's villages were fourteen days away. Asked why he wasn't a Christian, the Apache leader said he could be baptized on the spot, and if the Spaniards would kill the rebels, he and his people would live in pueblos and become Christians.

Vargas showed him a silver plate, hoping the chief had seen this metal in his country. A day's ride from Santa Fe, he responded, on the edge of a small mountain, were cliffs of ore the Indians called "white iron" because it was too hard and heavy to move. Vargas gave him an iron ax and told him to bring a sample on his next visit. Vargas inquired about Quivira, the mythical village of gold sought by the first Spanish explorers. We often go there to fight and capture young people to trade for horses, he said. Then he departed to begin his planting.

In July Vargas found Acho Apaches living in the Sangre de Cristo mountains along the edge of the Canadian. The Achos and Utes were then at odds.[16] Meanwhile, some Chipaines Apaches from the east, who were trading at Picurís in May, reported that light-haired white men (Frenchmen) defeated a large group of Conejeros Apaches who lived farther east. The same Chipaines returned in September after moving west to avoid the many Frenchmen on the plains. These groups have been called Jicarillas or Faraons,[17] but the Apaches living along the Canadian—the Chipaines, Conejeros, Rio Colorados, and Achos—were Lipan ancestors, members of the same band Coronado found near the river in 1541.[18]

Vargas managed to subdue Taos and Picurís pueblos, but trouble was in the air like electricity before a thunderstorm. Priests, weathering disrespect and threats, feared for their lives. In March 1696 Faraons camped at Pecos Pueblo and on the Pecos River. A month later messengers sprinted to various pueblos and to the Apaches. Allies waited with horses and supplies in remote locations, and several Spaniards had already fallen to rebels.[19]

In mid-October Picurís, Tewa and Tano people fled east, accompanied by Apaches. Vargas pursued, leading fifty Spaniards and more than sixty Pecos and Tesuque allies. They came upon an abandoned camp of thirty-one Apache lodges and hurried east in rain and snow, following a trail littered with tipi poles, metates and cooking utensils. On October 26, he caught up with them as they scrambled up the slope of a ravine. Some escaped, others died trying, and the majority, eighty-four people, surrendered. The captive Apaches were divided among the soldiers and settlers in the campaign and became slaves.

Picurís Chief Don Lorenzo and others escaped with the remaining Apaches, traveling down the Mora River to the Canadian, which they followed into the Texas Panhandle. There they camped for some time in the country of the Chipaines before they sought refuge at El Cuartelejo, as the Taos people had a half century before.[20] About ten years later, Don Lorenzo sent a messenger asking the Spanish for forgiveness and aid. In 1706 Sergeant-Major Juan de Ulibarri, who presumed they were captives, rode east to set them free.[21]

Ulibarri's company of soldiers, settlers and Indian auxiliaries left on July 20, crossed the mountains east of Taos, and descended to the plains near a branch of Moras Creek, where they could see faint Apache trails. East of present Cimarron on Rayado Creek they met friendly Conejero, Acho and Río Colorado Apaches returning from a visit to Taos Pueblo. They said they "were very happy that we Spaniards were coming into their lands and among their rancherías without doing them any injury."

The three groups had drawn closer for defense, the Achos moving south to put some distance between themselves and hostile Utes, and the Conejeros moving southwest from their home farther east on the Canadian River.[22] They warned the Spaniards to guard against the Penxayes, Flechas de Palo, Lemitas and Trementinas, who "had always been very bad thieves and had even injured them."[23]

In histories of this period, it's often difficult to tell one group from another. The Spanish named various Apache groups for a leader, landmark, or physical characteristic. Occasionally they employed the Spanish pronunciation of an Apache word. The names could change, and the groups themselves were as fluid as a school of fish, joining to hunt or raid and separating later. The four supposedly hostile groups were also Apaches. The Flechas de Palo and Penxayes, who lived from the mid-Purgatoire River to Raton Ridge, were affiliated with Carlana Apaches whose country lay between the Purgatoire and Arkansas near the present New Mexico-Colorado border. The other two groups, Trementinas and Lemitas, were Faraons, known to have unfriendly relations with the pueblos.[24]

Ulibarri gave the Achos, Rio Colorados and Conejeros gifts of tobacco, knives, pinole (toasted, ground corn with brown sugar, anise or cinnamon used to make mush), corn and biscuits. Four days later in the north, they encountered Jicarilla, Flechas de Palo and Carlana Apaches, who came out of the mountains to visit, led by several chiefs. The head chief, Ysdalnisdael, was lame.

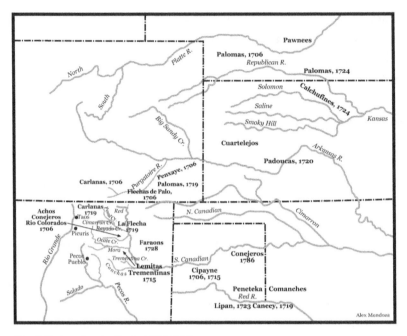

Map 3 Eastern Apache Bands, 1706–1726

These friendly people thanked Ulibarri for themselves and head Chief Ucate[25] for entering their country without harming them and said that on the Spaniards' return they would be with the Jicarillas. They promised him raisins, a delicacy, and assured him that all the groups he had encountered and others he had yet to meet were good people, "who hadn't stolen anything from anyone" because they were busy with their own fields of corn, beans and pumpkins. The Apaches' remarks indicate they expected punishment for past raids or thought they might be blamed for the raids of others, like the Faraons.[26]

Ulibarri entrusted his worn-out horses to their care, gave them tobacco, knives and biscuits, and rode on. As they approached the cone-shaped volcano, Capulin Mountain, there were prunes, a cherry-like fruit and grapes. On the Purgatoire in present southeastern Colorado some Penxayes approached the expedition warily, but the Spaniards' pledge of friendship "pleased them highly."[27] Days later

Ulibarri encountered more Penxayes hurrying to join their people before an impending attack by Comanches and Utes.

The expedition lost its way repeatedly in the short-grass plains,[28] despite "hummocks of grass placed a short distance apart on the trail by the Apaches, who lose even themselves there." At an Apache ranchería his men found a chief and several others willing to lead them to their villages on the plains. The next day the chief rode with Ulibarri through broad, pleasant river valleys toward the first ranchería, called Tachichichi, near present Leoti, Kansas. The Apaches, delighted to see them, offered food. A Picuris man reported that "everyone was very happy, both the Picuris who were with him as well as the Apaches." They spent the day discussing peace, and the Apaches talked about the hostilities between themselves and the Pawnees and northern Jumanos (Taovayas).

At a second ranchería called Persiuncula, many chiefs welcomed them. The Apaches had gathered crops of Indian corn, watermelons, pumpkins, and kidney beans, and their wheat was maturing. "They came without arms, very happy and kindly disposed. They brought us much buffalo meat, roasting ears of Indian corn, tamales, plums and other things to eat," Ulibarri wrote.

On the last hill before El Cuartelejo, Spaniards and Christian Indians worshipped at a cross built by the Apaches and then took the cross and made a procession to the nearby village, where Don Lorenzo and other Picuris people lived.[29] Ulibarri was surprised to see so many Apaches wearing Catholic medals, crosses, and rosaries. In their years of trading, they explained, they understood the Spaniards wearing crosses and rosaries were valiant, and "when the Apaches fight with their enemies, the Pawnees and the Jumanos, and become tired, they remember the great Captain of the Spaniards who is in the heavens and then their weariness leaves them and they feel refreshed." He said the Apaches worshipped nightly.

Ulibarri received all the people in his camp, gave them gifts, and assured them of his good intentions. He told them he would take home the Picuris, whom they had enslaved, and if they objected, they "would

experience the severity of our arms." The Apaches said they were willing to give up the Picuris, but if they were to believe his friendship was
sincere, he should accompany them on a seven-day journey to attack
the Pawnees. Ulibarri's response: Another time, maybe. His horses
were worn out, and he was anxious to return home.

They showed him a French gun. Pawnees, aided by the French, had
attacked them as they hunted buffalo to prepare this feast. After their
enemies retreated, the Apache chief sent some warriors to follow their
route. A Frenchman and his wife had fallen behind, and the Apaches
killed them. The Apaches had other firearms, including three carbines,
which they had taken from the Pawnees. They said the Pawnees sold
captive Apache women and children to the French just as they themselves sold captive Pawnees to the Spanish.

Ulibarri dispatched men to retrieve Picuris people in other
rancherías—Nanahe, Adidasde and Sanasesli. The latter was a large
village forty leagues away. While he awaited their arrival, crowds of
Apaches streamed into the main camp. In long conversations, he
learned that the Apaches were familiar with five major rivers: the
Napestle (from "napesti," or flint arrow), or Arkansas; Nisquisandi
(Osage); Sitascahe (Platte, where the Pawnees lived); Daenasgaes
(Missouri); and Nasatha (Mississippi). All the tribes, they said, traded
with white men to the east (French or English) who provided hatch-
ets, sword blades, harquebuses and copper items. To the north were
Apaches called the "Pelones," who lived on the other side of sand
dunes—actually, Palomas who lived in the Nebraska Sand Hills. The
Spanish would later learn of the Escalchufines (or Calchufines), who
lived farther east from the Cuartelejos and Palomas.[30]

On the return trip, the expedition met the same friendly Apaches,
who said the rumored attack on the Penxayes had occurred. Utes
and Comanches also attacked a ranchería of the Carlanas and the
Sierra Blancas, who lived on the south slope of the Spanish Peaks
and Raton Ridge.[31]

◄►

Vargas made contact, friendly and otherwise, with Apaches who belonged to a confederacy that stretched from the mountains to the distant plains. Each group cultivated its own relationship with both Spaniards and pueblos; to Vargas, some of these groups were hostile, while others sought friendship and trade. In the early 1700s, Spanish expeditions found them friendly, which signaled more than an attitude adjustment—they were facing new enemies.

Ulibarri was apparently the first Spaniard to visit the Cuartelejo villages. The Spanish until then had known them only as buffalo hunters from the east, and even adventurous traders like Diego Romero conducted business in temporary camps. Ulibarri, bearing gifts, was prepared for diplomacy, and it paid off. He peacefully accomplished his mission while learning about these Apaches: Their country was blessed with fruit and game, and they were skilled farmers. They provided well for themselves but lacked manufactured goods and horses. Their travels had taken them as far as the Mississippi River. They'd clashed with the Pawnees, Taovayas, and Tejas, and a new nation, the Comanches.

◄►

Villages of Cuartelejos, Palomas and Escalchufines on the plains of Kansas and Nebraska are known to archaeologists as the Dismal River Complex. Apaches had lived here for at least a century when Ulibarri visited; Oñate in 1598 heard of Vaqueros living in large pueblos on the buffalo plains.[32]

Their unique, semi-permanent dwellings featured five vertical center posts nine feet tall arranged in a pentagon around a fireplace and connected by beams across the top. Small poles pushed into the ground and leaning against the connecting beams, like the ribs of an umbrella, extended the space. About twenty-five feet in diameter, they were probably covered with grass or brush. Neither hogan nor Plains earth lodge, they were the Apaches' own creation and the inspiration for the name, El Cuartelejo.[33]

There were two related groups: hunter-gatherers on the High Plains and southern Rocky Mountains of Colorado and Wyoming, and, in southern Colorado and northern New Mexico, people who combined hunting with some agriculture.[34]

Game was plentiful—bison, antelope, mule deer, prairie dogs, coyotes and prairie chickens. They hunted bison, deer, and beaver and also ate turtles and mussels but not fish or fowl. One animal not in evidence was the horse. They grew corn and squash using bison scapula digging tools; El Cuartelejo even had irrigation ditches. Wild foods included plums, chokecherries, hackberries and black walnuts. To cook green corn and probably other foods in large quantities, they used baking pits—not typical Plains cooking but typically Apache.

They made pottery Plains style without coiling and adorned themselves with tubular bone beads, small turquoise trade beads, copper, and iron conical jingles. The Dismal River artists used spongy bone paint brushes and pigments of red hematite, yellow limonite, white caliche and black charcoal. There was little European trade material.[35]

After years of debate over the identities of Dismal River inhabitants, anthropologist Karl Schlesier in 1972 combined the historical and archaeological records to offer a new interpretation that demonstrated ties among the Dismal River people and other far-flung Apache groups. Schlesier saw the complex as five clusters, each having several bands or groups.

The northernmost group lived in the Sand Hills of northwestern Nebraska near the upper Calamus and Loup River forks and the Dismal River. They hunted as far west as Wyoming and north into South Dakota. Schlesier speculated that they were Naishan (Kiowa Apaches). This would explain the consistent beliefs, culture and language among the Jicarillas, Lipans and Naishan. The second cluster stretched from the Arkansas River in western Kansas to the Republican River in Nebraska and included the headwaters of the Smoky Hill, Saline, Solomon and Republican Rivers. Schlesier thought these were the villages of Cuartelejos, Palomas and Escalchufines,[36] but Palomas were also farther east in present Oklahoma. On the Rocky Mountain front range was the Colorado cluster, composed of Carlanas, Sierra Blancas,[37] Penxayes, Flechas de Palos and Jicarillas, and their country extended from the headwaters of the Arkansas River south to the upper Canadian in New Mexico. The Panhandle cluster (those once called Querechos and Vaqueros) lived along the Canadian River from eastern New Mexico into Texas and on the upper branches of the Red River in New Mexico. They were the Chipaines, Rio Colorados, Achos, and Conejeros—ancestors of the Lipans.[38] The Pecos cluster consisted of the Faraons, who lived on the northern Pecos River, and the Siete Rios (Seven Rivers), who lived on the middle Pecos.[39]

Apache scholar Albert Schroeder generally agreed with Schlesier's interpretation. "It is a real interesting piece of historical reconstruction, and I like it," he wrote to Schlesier.[40] Viewed through a historical lens, the theory still holds up. The Achos and Conejeros could have joined other nearby groups but instead moved closer to the Rio Colorados, an indication of kinship. Similarly, the Carlanas and Flechas de Palo said they would seek out the Jicarillas, and later the Carlanas[41] and Sierra Blancas are described as living close together. This was probably an old pattern; they had come together and parted many times to trade, raid, hunt and make war. Many of these names would disappear, but the Eastern Apaches would regroup and relocate while sustaining their strong alliance.

◄►

In 1712 Governor Juan Ignacio Florez Mogollón, attempting to snuff the influence of pagan Indians, forbade Spaniards and Pueblos from attending the trade fairs.[42] Faraon raiding increased, and by 1715 the warm relations between the eastern pueblos and eastern Apaches was in tatters. In July Mogollón debated how to campaign against the "Apaches, Chipaynes, and Faraones or Limitas."[43] Like his countrymen, Mogollón had trouble sorting out the various groups, and so did Don Geronimo, lieutenant governor of Taos Pueblo.

Don Geronimo said the Chipaines, who lived in a village of thirty houses of wood covered with clay on the Canadian River, mingled with other Plains Indians during the annual trading held in Pecos, but on their way home they stole animals from Pecos and even from the Jicarilla Apaches. The Chipaines "and the Faraon nation are one and the same." His comment was a figure of speech indicating the closeness of the two groups, but historians have taken him literally. The Chipaines (an early Lipan group) and Limitas (a Faraon[44] group) sometimes camped together but were distinct groups. Pecos people understood the difference; they called the Faraons "thieving Indian pirates."[45]

The Taos Pueblo people wanted arms to pursue these Apaches and offered to guide the Spaniards. The Jicarillas also volunteered to join a campaign. The best time for an attack, said Don Geronimo, was in mid-August, when they harvested their corn, buried it, and left to hunt buffalo. Later, a more credible source, the venerable Don Lorenzo, identified arrows left behind as those of the Trementinas or Limitas Apaches (Faraons). The same day Apaches took the Picurís horse herd, which the pueblo's young men retrieved. A council agreed they must make war on the Apaches and chose September.[46]

On August 30 General Juan Páez Hurtado set out with 37 soldiers, 18 settlers and 146 Indians from Taos, Picuris, Tiguex and Pecos. Mogollón ordered Hurtado to avoid mistreating other Apaches on the route and to bring him the Chipaines or Limitas women and children. After crossing the mountains, the group followed the Canadian River downstream below present Tucumcari, New Mexico, but didn't find any Apaches. Hurtado suspected their quarry had been warned.[47]

CHAPTER

5

Carlana

[The French and Pawnees] can without impediment penetrate into that realm if our allies, the Carlana Apaches, do not block their passage . . . Inform [the Texas governor] how affectionate are the Apaches of La Jicarilla, in El Cuartelejo and in the Sierra Blanca towards our people . . .

— *Juan de Olivan Revolledo, 1720.*[1]

Chief Carlana heard from other Apaches that the Spanish governor was in their land, but he didn't believe it. No governor had ever come to their country. He rode to the top of a tall hill and looked out. In the distance he made out a halo of dust. Carlana hurried to find the Spaniards so he might ride with them against the invaders. Already the Comanches had displaced Carlana's people and attacked the Jicarillas so many times they feared for their survival. The small, isolated camps were easy pickings for the Comanches, who had many warriors.

In late September 1719, Carlana found Governor Antonio de Valverde on a river the Apaches called La Flecha (the Cimarron, just north of the confluence with Ponil Creek). Apaches, probably Flechas de Palo, lived there in nine houses; one adobe house was topped by a cross.[2] Valverde was eating as Carlana approached and greeted the governor.

"Ave Maria," said Carlana in a clear voice.

"Sin pecado concevida," the governor replied.

Valverde gave the chief his own plate of boiled meat and vegetables. Carlana ate the mutton but not the chicken. (Apaches didn't eat poultry.) He told Valverde that because of Ute and Comanche attacks, he fled his country with half of his people to get help from the Jicarillas; the rest went to live with Apaches farther inland, led by Chief Flaco. The Carlanas lived in the northern Sangre de Cristo Mountains, a southern spur of the Rocky Mountains, and in the Sierra Blanca range near present Raton, where the mountains melt into a mesa reaching east into rolling prairie, green or gold with the change of seasons, and buttes stand square-shouldered on the horizon.

The allied Comanches and Utes had rained devastation on the Eastern Apaches and Spanish settlements for nearly twenty years, and Valverde intended to punish them, which cheered Carlana. He and his people would guide them to the land of the enemy and show them all the best places and springs. Near Rayado Creek,[3] the expedition entered several villages where unnamed Apaches and Jicarillas complained bitterly that Utes and Comanches had attacked their villages many times and killed and captured so many of their people, that they hardly knew where to live. They'd even burned their piles of maize. These enemies might return and finish them off. An old Apache woman on horseback arrived to say her people would place themselves at Valverde's service.

Chief Carlana and his people had abandoned their home in the Spanish Peaks and erected their twenty-seven tipis at a Jicarilla village of seven terraced houses on Ponil Creek, where proficient farmers with irrigation ditches were harvesting corn. Carlana and the Jicarillas repeated their offers to accompany the Spaniards. At the Canadian, twenty (Flechas de Palo) Apaches appeared. They too had been attacked by Comanches and joined the expedition. On September 27 Chief Carlana reappeared with sixty-nine Apaches. "They circled the camp on their horses, jubilantly singing and shouting. In the evening these same messengers danced according to their custom, some covered with red and others with white paint . . . After they had danced for a good part of the night, [Valverde] ordered them entertained and feasted," wrote the expedition chronicler.

The next day Carlana sent out seven young scouts armed with arrows, machetes and oval leather shields. About two-by-three feet, their tough convex shields were made from wet hide tightly stretched and molded in a shallow depression in the ground; arrows and even bullets were known to glance off these convex shields unless they hit dead center. Other Apaches hunted game and one day drove deer into camp with "great glee and shouting." They were in a favorite hunting ground near present Walsenburg, Colorado, which they had avoided out of fear for the Utes.

When the expedition caught up with Carlana's spies, they had sobering news. Five enemies had gone to Carlana's former home and, not finding any Apaches, turned around. Other Apache spies found three trails of fresh tracks and approached as close as they dared, while hiding in thickets. Pushing north, Valverde ordered his soldiers to march at night, on the Apaches' advice, while the remainder of the party followed. Apache spies stole forward, finding trails and a succession of abandoned enemy camps, each larger than the one before.

Valverde noticed that Carlana wasn't eating and assumed he was frustrated at not finding enemies; he tried to console the chief with meat, tobacco and pinole. Carlana was probably frustrated by Valverde's leisurely pace. The expedition ambled a few leagues each day, stopping often for the governor to hunt or entertain. With its fine wines and silver goblets, the expedition was more a gentleman's excursion. Apache warriors, in contrast, carried little besides their weapons and ate infrequently or not at all.

To the east they found another empty camp, this one large enough for a thousand people. Hundreds of horses dragging tent poles scratched out a veritable highway, now heading northeast. Carlana knew this route had too few springs to support Valverde's large party and its many horses. The governor called a council of soldiers and settlers, who'd had ample time to ponder an engagement with these enemies, and decided to turn back. It must have been a sharp disappointment to Carlana.

That evening ten Apaches arrived from Cuartelejo to say their chiefs were on the Río Napestle (Arkansas) with all their people, on their way to meet Valverde. The expedition moved toward them and reached the pleasant waters of the Arkansas, where distant bison herds carpeted the plains. On the twenty-fifth, nearly a thousand people— Cuartelejos, Palomas and others—camped on the other side of the river. The Apaches were a match for their nearby enemies in numbers but not in weaponry or mounts; the more remote groups were still using the dog travois.

One Apache was recovering from a gunshot wound in the abdomen. As the Palomas planted corn, the French, Pawnees and Jumanos (Taovayas) ambushed them. "[T]hey gave him a bullet, as he expressed it," Velarde wrote. Only the cover of nightfall allowed them to escape. The Pawnees and their allies now held the Palomas' land. The French, living with the Pawnees and Taovayas in two large, fortified settlements on the Arkansas River in present northern Oklahoma, provided their new friends long guns and taught them to shoot. They also carried small guns in their belts. Each day their enemies came closer. Female captives who escaped said the French had three other settlements on the other side of the Mississippi, which provided arms and supplies. Astonished by this information, Valverde promised the Apaches help against their enemies so they could live in their own land and vowed to expel the French, but he was out of supplies.[4] Watching the Spanish lumber back toward the horizon, Carlana must have considered his options and found them wanting.

With Spain and France at war, the viceroy ordered a reconnaissance to locate the French, and Valverde delegated the job to his lieutenant-general, Pedro de Villasur. The expedition left Santa Fe with forty-two soldiers, three settlers or traders, a priest and sixty Indian auxiliaries and proceeded north, probably along the same route Valverde had taken. At Carlana's camp, they presented tobacco, maize, hats, short swords and knives to the Carlanas, Jicarillas and Cuartelejos who would serve as guides. The Apaches apparently conveyed them across their own territory and turned around. The expedition, a fraction of the size they accompanied the year before and led by an inexperienced commander, must have seemed to the Apaches like the rabbit taunting the mountain lion. This time there were no offers to fight alongside the Spanish.

The expedition plodded on fifty to seventy leagues farther to the South Platte without finding any Pawnees. In a council they opted to continue looking "or to learn whether the Apaches had deceived us . . ." They weren't deceived. On August 12, 1720, Pawnees and Frenchmen attacked Villasur's party, killing forty-five members, including Villasur. Twelve Spaniards and forty-eight Indian auxiliaries fled.[5]

The badly wounded survivors dragged themselves to the Cuartelejos, "who came out to meet them with great tenderness" and "kept them in their company with much kindness for two days, supporting and succoring them with their poor provisions." The party returned to Santa Fe in September, a month after the war ended between Spain and France. Charles L. Kenner wrote that the Cuarteljos, "[c]linging pathetically to the only possible source of aid . . . begged the Spaniards to return" and join them in a campaign.[6] There was nothing pathetic about the invitation. The Apaches understandably sought allies against their enemies, and, in fact, the Cuartelejos were holding out remarkably well against a much larger enemy.

◄►

The Comanches penetrated the region in greater numbers. The Apaches fought valiantly, but simply couldn't defend themselves against such forces. Many young men died, and the Comanches captured numbers of women and children. On November 8, 1723, Carlana and two other captains came to Santa Fe seeking help, this time from Governor Juan Domingo de Bustamante. They offered to obey the king, settle in pueblos, accept baptism and instruction by missionaries, and answer to an alcalde. A council of war in Santa Fe voted to accept the offer, hoping this would inspire other Eastern Apaches to do the same.

Bustamante rode within a fortnight. At La Jicarilla the Apaches received him warmly. Carlana, six other captains and fifty warriors, one carrying a cross, joined him. In the next camp Captain Churlique greeted Bustamante carrying an engraving of the Virgin Mary wrapped in buckskin. In the third camp, Captain Cojo, who previously had resisted baptism, was now amenable. At each camp, the Apaches promised to be baptized and obey the king, and Bustamante promised to protect them.

Then negotiations reached a sticking point. Before he would defend them, Bustamante wanted the Apaches to divide up the lands and live in assigned places; before the Apaches would give up their freedom, they wanted the governor to campaign against the Comanches. And they wanted to confer with other captains before they made a decision, which they would do by spring, said Cojo.[7]

◀▶

Three months before Valverde's tour, in summer 1719, Jean Baptiste Bénard de La Harpe rode northwest to explore the region and open trade. The French were beginning to understand that the plains Apaches they called Cancy (probably from the Caddo name Kántsi) and Padouca were key to trade on the southern plains.[8] The Cancy, probably Palomas, occupied a large village on the Red River, surrounded by beautiful prairies and groves of trees; deer and buffalo were plentiful. The Spanish were mining there, and when the Apaches' enemies approached, the Spanish turned large guns on them. The Apaches had swords and lances but not guns. "The advantage that the Cancy have over their enemies is that they have good horses, whereas the other nations have very few," he wrote.[9]

The party detoured twice to avoid large parties of Cancy warriors. In 1714 and 1717, Apaches attacked French parties at the same place on the Colorado River.[10] In the second incident, "when they saw that we would not run and that we would not hand over our goods, after they had shot many arrows at us," the Apaches stole twenty-three mules and a Spanish mulatto woman who was the mule driver, wrote Francois Dion Deprez Derbanne, who concluded that the Apaches were the only tribe that couldn't be pacified.[11]

La Harpe thought otherwise. After a Tawakoni chief told him they had eaten seventeen Cancys during a public feast, La Harpe regretted not arriving "in time to save the lives of these poor unfortunates," whom he could have returned to their people to make friends. The Frenchman was also interested in the Padoucas, a name the French used for a large tribe farther north known to be unaffiliated with the Spanish and enemies of the Pawnees, probably Kiowa Apaches.[12]

The French, who knew the Apaches only as enemies, grew more determined to break the Spanish trade barrier. To do that, they needed peace with the Eastern Apaches. They would learn that these intimidating people responded warmly to sincere overtures of friendship. In 1722 French authorities ordered Etienne Vénard de Bourgmont to make peace with the Apaches in Kansas and broker a peace between them and the tribes who were French allies. Bourgmont reached Apache territory but turned back, too sick to continue. He sent Francois Gaillard as his emissary with two freed Apache captives, a young woman and teenage boy, along with two Kansa Indians.

In late August, they approached some hunters, and the freed captives caught their attention by throwing their robes in the air three times. As the hunters approached, Gaillard and the Kansa Indians were apprehensive, but the captives explained their presence, and the hunters escorted Gaillard's party to their chief in the Cuartelejo village. The two captives praised the French, told of valuable gifts the French were bringing, and said the French chief would arrive when he was well.

The chief and head men received the Frenchman warmly, took him to their dwellings, and exchanged gifts. Gaillard's gun drew their intense interest. He obliged by showing them how to load and fire and then presented the firearm to the head chief, who gave Gaillard a horse and bison robe. Bourgmont's stand-in made a good impression.

Next Gaillard and the two Kansas took twenty Apaches to the Kansa summer hunting grounds. After a few tense moments, the Kansa people treated their former enemies to a three-day feast. The Apaches brought a group of Kansa men and three women to their camp for feasting, entertainment and gifts—horses and robes "trimmed with smaller skins and decorated with porcupine quills." His orders executed, Gaillard sent five Apaches to meet Bourgmont at the Kansa village and bring him back.

In late September Gaillard and some six hundred warriors and their families, from eight Apache villages, journeyed 200 miles east to meet Bourgmont. The head chief gave them seven days to reach the Kansa village and no more than four days' stay before reporting back. On October 2 Bourgmont received them formally, and his soldiers fired their fusils, startling the Apaches, who still weren't accustomed to guns. He then took them into his tent to receive gifts.

In the next few days, chiefs of other tribes arrived, summoned by Bourgmont, and the Frenchman began to craft his peace. He told the assembled group of French allies—Kansas, Otoes, Iowas, Missouris and Panimahas (Skiri Pawnees)—that he was authorized to make peace among them. They stood and shouted their approval. The Apache chief invited his former adversaries to visit. Later the Apaches performed a dance, and they smoked pipes together.

On October 8, Bourgmont and representatives from each tribe set out for Apache country. After ten days' travel, the party announced its approach with smoke signals, answered by smoke from the west. Eighty Apaches appeared with their head chief and Gaillard, and the Apaches provided horses to take everyone to a sprawling camp of one hundred-forty dwellings near the Smoky Hills of present eastern Kansas. The French counted eight hundred Apache warriors, fifteen hundred women and two thousand children.[13] Apache men wore trousers of dressed skin, gathered at the bottom to fit into high-topped moccasins. Women wore blouses and skirts of dressed skins, fringed at the bottom.

Over the next few days, they dined on buffalo meat stewed in a pot, various sun-dried meats and prunes ground with their pits and cooked. A Frenchman wrote that the Apaches offered their daughters to guests, but he misunderstood; the Apaches most likely wanted

French sons-in-law. It wasn't unusual for the Eastern Apaches to seal a new alliance through marriage.

Bourgmont himself received royal treatment. A large group of warriors spread a buffalo robe on the ground. On it they placed Bourgmont, his young son and two Frenchmen and carried them to the lodge of the head chief for a feast and celebration. Apaches loved children and were obviously delighted that Bourgmont brought his son. They took turns entertaining the boy every day and returned him to his father at night. The son of the head chief gave young Bourgmont a string of turquoise—the diamonds of the desert, traded from Pueblo people in New Mexico, and probably the young Apache's most valued possession.

On the second day Bourgmont unpacked his goods, and, like any good salesman, arranged appealing displays: stacks of muskets, sabers, pickaxes, gunpowder, balls, gunflints, red and blue Limbourg blankets, mirrors, Flemish knives, other knives, shirts, scissors, combs, awls, needles, kettles, hawkbells, vermillion, beads, rings and brass wire. He asked the Apache chiefs, elders and influential people to make peace with the tribes who were French allies and allow French traders to pass freely. He gave a flag to the head chief, who accepted it with his own speech, a portion of which follows:

"For a long time we have desired to make peace with the French and from now on we will go and see the French; we will bring horses there to trade with them and we will readily make peace with all the nations you just mentioned. We are very pleased about this treaty and now, as they are witness, I am very pleased that they hear it and that they see it. Therefore, they can come to see us; we will go to them with the peace pipe and this will be very good. We will hunt, each one of us, in peace; it is already a long time that we have desired this, and therefore, my Father, we all promise you, in the name of our entire people, that we have heard your word, and that it is good."

Apaches accepted the gifts, astounded that the French gave them so freely. The Spanish brought horses and a few knives, awls and axes of poor quality, "but they are not like you, who gives us here a quantity of merchandise, such as we have never seen before." The head chief sent seven horses to the Frenchman.

One Frenchman recorded a buffalo hunt. In groups of fifty to one hundred families, "[t]hey start to torment them and run them hard until their tongues stick out a foot. Then they choose the fattest ones and shoot arrows into them which penetrate a foot into the animals' bellies. Choosing the fattest ones in sight, they kill like that all they want. Many of the horses are killed also. They never have colts, for their mares always abort on the hunt."

The head chief told Bourgmont that twelve villages obeyed his will. The warriors he saw were "only a fourth of the number who are under my command . . . [I]f you should ever need two thousand warriors, you have only to ask." He would have more horses to give Frenchmen, he said, because in three or four months, many warriors would journey to Spanish country, where a horse was worth three bison robes.

The Cuartelejos alone didn't have that many warriors; the chief described the Eastern Apache Confederacy. Its known groups then numbered about a dozen, and the numbers would remain consistent over a long period. The two thousand warriors indicated a population of ten thousand people. In his remarks, the head chief also revealed a chain of command: "I am heeded and obeyed in all the villages of our tribe . . . they go neither to war nor to the Spaniards without my permission."

The French described a "very large" tribe whose country extended over 200 leagues (500 to 600 miles). After four decades of pressure from their enemies, the Cuartelejos held their country. The northernmost bands had moved south to occupy and hold desirable country along the Red and Colorado Rivers. And yet, some of the remote groups were still using stone-age tools, and all the Eastern Apaches needed guns and European goods. They were so eager to trade with the French that they asked Bourgmont to leave some of his men with them. Bourgmont departed on October 22, with a large supply of food for his journey. The head chief scooped up a handful of dirt and shouted, "Now I regard the Spaniards as I do this dirt. And you," he said to Bourgmont, "I regard you as the sun."[14]

◄ ►

The unsuspecting Spanish began to notice a shift in the balance of power on the plains. Apaches showed up to trade carrying French muskets and said they took them from the Pawnees in battle. By 1724 only the Jicarillas still wanted Spanish protection.[15] In 1726 Comanche prisoners said white men accompanied the Escalchufines and Palomas Apaches who captured them, and there were reports of Frenchmen living at El Cuartelejo who joined a large force of Palomas, Cuartelejos and Carlanas to try and force the Comanches from the region.

An uneasy Bustamante concluded that the "French have conquered and won over to their side most of the heathen Indians who inhabit the plains . . ." French access to the plains, he fumed, "is by means of the alliance and trade which they have with the said Apaches, who conduct them to these places." Bustamante proposed a campaign, but the viceroy believed the French wanted only to trade.

In this time, the Palomas, Escalchufines and Lipans had removed to the Colorado River in Texas and as far east as present Oklahoma to the Red River. They had horses, when their enemies didn't, and they gathered in larger camps to better withstand attacks by superior numbers. The Comanches found it harder to dislodge the combined Apache forces in Kansas, Texas and Oklahoma, as well as the feisty Faraons on the Pecos. By 1728 the French couldn't afford to support all their new friends, and the alliances fell apart, but even then the Carlanas, Cuartelejos and their confederates held out on the plains.[16] As these names evaporated from Spanish records, historians assumed they were absorbed by the Jicarillas, Lipans or Mescaleros.[17] In fact, they maintained their identity, autonomy and their independence but would be known by different names.

CHAPTER

Early Texas

(L)ittle by little the Apaches are showing their claws.

— *Father Francisco Hidalgo, 1723*

The People must have been incensed as they spied Spaniards clearing land to build a fort and mission in the middle of country they'd held for forty years. In 1718 the presidio at San Antonio de Béxar rose on the San Antonio River, and the Franciscans founded the Mission San Antonio de Valero for the Coahuiltecan tribes. They would add four more missions by 1731.[1] The presidio's last stone was barely in place when the Apaches began raiding.

The Marqués of San Miguel de Aguayo, governor of Texas and Coahuila, tried to make peace with the Apaches in 1720. Their eloquent response: red cloth dangling from arrows stuck in the ground. In April 1721, the Apaches attacked a pack train, killed the driver and wounded a soldier. Aguayo sent detachments to patrol the area and take any Apaches alive, but they avoided contact and continued raiding.[2]

Texas colonists were still unfamiliar with Apaches. In one early incident, two settlers looking for some missing horses encountered Indians they didn't recognize and assumed they were friendly local Indians. The Apaches killed one man; the other raced away on a fast horse. Captain Nicolas Flores sent out fifteen men who found the victim's mutilated body but not his horse.[3] Subsequently, Flores took an aggressive approach, recovering fifty stolen horses, along with the heads of four offending Apaches. He was so vigilant that no horses were taken from Béxar for over a year.

In August 1723, five Apache captains, as the Spanish called leaders of smaller groups, met near the Rio Colorado in Texas,[4] and each sent twelve men to raid the presidial herd. Despite locked corral gates and guards, they made off with eighty horses, returned to the rendezvous point where they separated the horses, and each captain rode home to his own ranchería (encampment). Flores led thirty soldiers and thirty Tonkawa Indians in a dogged pursuit, carrying just two pack-loads of flour and relying for meat on buffalo and deer. At the Apaches' meeting place they could see tracks angling like spokes in five directions. Choosing one set, they followed it northwest for thirty-six days to a camp of two hundred Apaches (possibly on the Concho near present Brownwood).

The warriors came out to meet him, Flores claimed. In a punishing six-hour battle, thirty-four Apaches and a chief died, and twenty women and children were captured. The Spanish recovered 120 horses and mules, along with such plunder as saddles, bridles, and knives. Flores and three others were wounded. Father José Gonzalez, of the San Antonio mission, told a different story: "They fell upon it with such violence that the Apaches, caught unawares, even though they were fifty men, instead of defending their women and children, became panicky and all together took to flight along a mountainous stream, in which some of them died." Four soldiers corroborated the priest's statement.[5]

The Apaches had many horses, as well as good saddles with iron stirrups. They protected themselves and their horses with armor of buffalo hide, painted blue, red, green or white. Apaches had taken a lesson from Spanish soldiers, who had abandoned their metal armor for a knee-length sleeveless coat made of seven layers of buckskin, which could withstand arrows. They didn't have firearms, but in their arrows and lances, they had entered the Iron Age.[6]

Among the prisoners was an attractive, charismatic woman the priest believed could be an emissary to her people, and he badgered Flores into giving him responsibility for her. Through another captive who could speak Spanish, Father Gonzalez told her the Spanish wanted peace and would send missionaries to instruct them in the Catholic faith. This woman had probably gained the priest's attention because she was a person of importance, treated by her people with respect and deference. In this and many other encounters, Apache women would represent their people to the Spanish, carry important messages from the chiefs and demonstrate influence among their people.[7]

Flores questioned the woman. Why were the Apaches hostile and stealing horses? It was because of her people's trade in horses and slaves, she answered, with "other Spaniards" up north—the French. She assured him the Apache chiefs wanted to be friends. Asked where they obtained their corn, beans, sugar and salt, she said they had houses and fields near the Spanish, and there lived their great chief, "who governs all these five captains; that no one can go anywhere without his permission."[8]

The Spanish in Texas learned, at about the same time Bustamante was hearing it in New Mexico, that the Eastern Apaches weren't just scattered bands but an organized alliance that obeyed one great chief, and these groups weren't living nearby but instead raiding from their traditional homes. The priest and captain gave her gifts and a horse. Flores told her that he would release the other captives if their chiefs would come in and make peace. She promised to return in twenty days and alert them with a smoke signal. Back at her rancheria, more than five hundred people gathered to attack the mission and presidio. The woman presented the Spaniards' peace proposal so persuasively that they decided to delay their attack. They debated for five days. Her chief called four other chiefs in for a council, and the principal chief deliberated alone. He didn't trust the Spanish enough to come in person, so he sent his brother, his brother's wife and three others to see if the offer was genuine.

About three weeks later, the female emissary returned with the five people. The chief's brother presented a gold-tipped cane to Flores, probably the staff of command Ulibarri had given to Yndatiyuhe in 1706 at Cuartelejo, along with a buffalo skin adorned with a painted sun. Flores and Father Gonzalez entertained them for three days. Promising to communicate everything to their chief and return with an answer, they left on November 1. However, a Coahuila Indian who had just escaped from the Apaches said they were still angry about Flores's campaign and had joined to attack Béxar. When the woman returned, they decided to delay their revenge on the chance they could recover the captives. A Spanish captive confirmed the story; the Apaches were always ready to make war on the Spanish, she said, and many tribes had gathered to attack Béxar.

About thirty Apaches returned in late December. Father Gonzalez pressed Flores to release the captives, but he refused until all the chiefs agreed to make peace. Apache warriors offered themselves in place of the captive children, but Flores again refused. Angrily, they said, "Take girl!" and left a twelve-year-old girl, apparently believing the Spaniards were only interested in slaves. They said that when winter ended, four chiefs would return to make peace; the fifth chief didn't want to be a friend of the Spanish.[9]

The captain seemed more interested in worldly gain than in peace, reported Father Francisco Hidalgo. Father Gonzalez succeeded temporarily in having Flores removed for jeopardizing the peace. Apache attacks abated for a time, but the chiefs never returned and hostilities resumed. Lying in wait, they picked off the viceroy's courier, stole horses, and attacked mission Indians. Father Hidalgo was willing to travel to the Apaches, accompanied by a single lay brother, and try to convert them. Fernando Pérez de Almazán, governor of Texas, was less optimistic. The chiefs had not returned, and the Apaches, he said, were getting worse every day.[10]

◄►

Supposedly in 1723 the Lipans fought an epic, nine-day battle with Comanches. "Indians of the Lipana Nation and Apaches" living three hundred leagues from San Antonio in numerous camps on the banks of the Rio del Fierro (possibly the Red River) suffered "a continuous war with the numerous and fierce nation of the Comanches." This decisive battle forced the Lipans and their allies to give up their homeland and seek refuge between the Colorado and Brazos, "where they would not be persecuted by their enemies." They still didn't feel safe and moved farther south to the Béxar area. Their hatred of the Comanches was such that "if after death they were to meet, their bones would fight one another."[11]

The hatred was real but probably not the battle. The teller of this tale, decades after it allegedly occurred, was the Apache-hating Texas Governor Domingo Cabello. Lipan anthropologist Enrique Maestas dismisses the story as folklore or one of many battles between Apaches and Comanches. Anthropologist Morris Opler wrote that "authenticated nine-day battles between tribes are not too common in American Indian annals. Yet this bit of recorded hearsay—far removed in time and space from the putative event—has been cited with all earnestness again and again."[12] The Lipans were still in their same haunts along the Canadian in 1723 and had frequented the Béxar area long before they were allegedly driven there by Comanches.

◄►

Apache raids tapered off after 1725, and by July 4, 1726, Almazán could report that San Antonio was quiet. Spaniards were mystified, but the Apaches, with new allies and generous trading partners in the French, were otherwise occupied. During this unusual calm Pedro de Rivera investigated conditions in the northern provinces and stunned northern settlements by recommending a reduction in forces. The garrison at Béxar "has no other enemies in its neighborhood than the Apache Indians, who inhabit the Lomeria Grande, which nation is not so large as to cause anxiety to that presidio," he reported after a visit in 1727; the presidio's location was well situated to restrain them.[13]

The viceroy reduced garrisons and revamped policy with the Regulation of 1729, which prohibited attacks on friendly, neutral and even hostile tribes until every attempt to pacify them had failed; forbade Spanish authorities from siding with one tribe against another unless a tribe asked for help; and prohibited soldiers from creating unrest in Indian villages, exploiting them or dividing captive families. If enemy tribes asked for peace, the authorities must accept as long as there was a written and signed agreement.[14]

In 1731 the villa of San Fernando de Béxar became Spain's first chartered settlement in Texas, which was still a thinly settled, remote expanse between the prosperous states to the south and hostile Indians and French opportunists to the north.[15] That year the Apaches stepped up their attacks, and this time it wasn't in small parties or by stealth at night. In January fifty Apaches attacked two priests and a small party escorted by four soldiers who were traveling from San Antonio to the Rio Grande, taking their mules, horses and goods. They killed and wounded settlers and soldiers, captured children, and spirited away entire herds of burros and horses. Hardly a day passed without some injury. Almazán wanted to punish them, but realized that military campaigns seemed to inflame their hatred.

In August the Apaches began gathering to mount a combined attack on the settlement, and on September 18 they stole sixty horses from the presidio. Captain Juan Antonio Pérez set out immediately and sent ahead a sergeant with five soldiers. When Pérez overtook his advance party about a league from the presidio, they were holding off forty warriors and would have died without his timely arrival. Relief was short-lived: Hundreds of Apaches, mounted and armed, emerged from hiding.

"They attacked us with the greatest audacity, emboldened by their vastly superior numbers. There must have been five hundred of them, all mounted and well armed, while we had only twenty-five men altogether. Realizing our weakness, the Indians attacked so furiously that we had no room in which to defend ourselves. They advanced in a crescent, pressing our center as vigorously as they did both wings, but because my men were so few we could not defend all sides at once . . ."

After two hours of intense fighting, the Spanish had two dead and thirteen wounded, and their horses were mostly disabled. The soldiers decided to make their stand on foot beneath a tree, and take as many Apaches with them as they could. Suddenly, "the enemy, for no apparent reason, took off at top speed and disappeared . . ."[16] If not for divine providence the entire settlement might have been wiped out, Almazán said, because San Antonio would have been nearly unprotected. The abrupt retreat was less divine intervention than typical Apache warfare. Apaches couldn't afford to lose men and rarely risked them needlessly; destroying Pérez and a few soldiers would have cost many warriors. They chose to depart with their stolen horses.

After this battle, the Spanish in Texas for the first time identified three groups—Apaches, Pelones, and Jumanes—who "have annihilated and terrorized all the nations living in these parts and admit no others to their friendship," wrote Almazán.[17] Two years earlier, Captain Joseph Antonio de Eca y Múzquiz, serving in Coahuila, reached the same conclusions after puzzling over which groups were troubling his area. Raiders lived in the area of San Rodrigo Spring, the canyons on both sides of the lower Pecos and lands from the Rio San Diego to the Burro and Santa Rosa Mountains,[18] all Lipan haunts.

Within a few years of driving the Jumanos south, Eastern Apaches made the Jumanos their allies. They grew so close, they even shared the same chief, and Spaniards at times called them "los Apaches Jumanes."[19] As historian Gary Clayton Anderson wrote, "the Apaches were not simply the brutal, cruel people of Spanish folklore. Rather they had worked to gain access to Jumano towns and used marriage and exchange as a means of expanding alliances."[20]

The people described only as "Apaches" may have been Faraons or Natagés, who lived from the Pecos to the Conchos in Mexico,[21] or they could have been bands still unknown to the Spanish. "Pelones," or "bald ones," were probably Natagés, who cut their hair short like priests. The Spanish also called some northern Apaches "Pelones" who were actually Palomas and confederates of the Cuartelejos.[22] Almazán perceived a quality in this adversaries that would infuriate a long succession of commanders—their gift for transforming enemies into allies. He wanted a substantial campaign to punish them all.[23]

◄ ►

Breathlessly, an Indian spy reported the biggest ranchería he had ever seen—four hundred tents with eight hundred Apache warriors from four tribes. Governor Juan Antonio de Bustillo y Zevallos moved his troops deeper into the wooded hill country north of Béxar to within five leagues of the encampment on the San Sabá River. During the night they inched closer. With a hundred chosen men, he attacked by morning's light.

The Apaches must have been expecting them. There was no panicked scramble for weapons and horses in the dawn chill. Warriors fought from horseback, protected by leather breastplates. They waited for the Spaniards to fire and then, as soldiers reloaded their muskets, shot their arrows and plunged forward to fight hand to hand. For five hours, they repeated this sequence. If a warrior fell, the others dragged his body away. At one point in the battle, they grieved audibly as they carried away a prominent chief who bore a silver-headed cane of authority awarded by Spaniards. Finally, unable to prevail against Spanish fire power, the Apaches withdrew.

Bustillo claimed to kill two hundred Apaches. He captured thirty women and children, seven hundred horses and one hundred muleloads of booty. His loss was seven wounded, one mortally, but Apaches harried the expedition and stole horses all the way back to San Antonio. After that October 1732 battle, Bustillo's most experienced soldiers "expressed amazement at what they saw, for they had been in many engagements with various Indian nations, but never in their lives had they seen anything to equal the valor and daring of these warriors," wrote Almazán.[24] Long accustomed to the Apaches' strike-and-vanish raids and ambushes, they marveled that Apaches could execute a coordinated, mounted attack.

The enemies in this battle were "Apaches, Ypandis, Ysandis and Chentis." This is the first reference to Lipans as Ypandis (also Ypandes or Ipandes). The others were probably Natagés. This was a small ranchería, said a captive woman. To the north a larger camp, entirely Ypande, stretched across four leagues, and nearby were Jumanos and others—all joined to make war on the Spaniards.[25] Between San Antonio and New Mexico were thirty-seven different Apache groups, Bustillo learned. This new intelligence revealed the combined strength of the Ypandes and their allies and hints for the first time that they were now allied with the Natagés, an aggressive band from southern New Mexico. The ever-shifting faces of the enemy made them hard to identify, and, if Bustillo had understood band autonomy, would have explained the alternating friendship and hostility that confounded Béxar residents.

While Bustillo's men were away, Apaches raided the village's stock. Citizens asked him to not distribute captives but instead use them to make peace; one or two captive women might serve as messengers. The presidial garrison too asked the governor to negotiate peace with the Apaches or face "total destruction by this host of enemies." Father Gabriel de Vergara seconded these opinions and asked the viceroy again to establish missions for the Apaches, who were well supplied with arms and horses. "I need not mention their bravery, audacity, and horsemanship, for you have witnessed these things with your own eyes," he said. The Apaches, he insisted, would support missions.

On January 4, 1733, the governor sent two women, one Apache and one Pelón (probably Natagé), with messages for their chiefs. A month later one messenger returned with the chief's representative, who said they were gathering their people to make peace, and four chiefs would arrive with many people to talk. Bustillo entertained them for three days, and they promised to return in two moons.

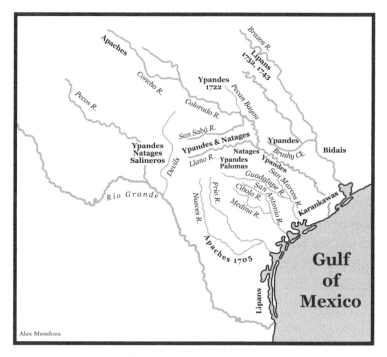

Map 4 Ypandes and their Allies, 1700–1745

Apaches began coming and going from Béxar and seemed to get along with the residents. On March 27 three men and a woman visited to trade. As they departed, accompanied as usual by a few soldiers, a band of about two dozen Apaches approached. The soldiers awaited their arrival, but as the Indians approached they formed two wings. The soldiers realized their intentions too late. They were found mutilated, their bones stripped of flesh. With this act, hostilities and raids resumed. Priests kept terrified mission Indians in place with difficulty, and soldiers asked to remove their families to safety. Historians have cited this act as an example of "Apache perfidy" or betrayal, but it was an expression of their fury over unreturned captives.[26]

That summer Joseph de Urrutia became San Antonio's presidial captain, elevated because of his forty years' experience with Indians. Apaches resumed trading there the following year. Their loads of buffalo meat and hides were eagerly received at the presidio, which was too thinly manned to send hunting parties. One party even offered to compensate the settlers for the deaths of the two soldiers, and they generously fed a patrol visiting an Apache camp on the Guadalupe River.[27]

To the south, Coahuila was not enjoying peace. Raiding eroded populations and their herds until some settlements were hollow as a dried gourd. On May 3, 1735, more than a hundred Apaches in four groups simultaneously struck a ranch, a mission and a citizen, spiriting away fifty horses. When hostilities spread north in 1736, the Apaches abandoned their trade with Béxar. Over the next year, attacks became oppressively routine—murders, captured children and stolen horses. Heightened fears called forth a bureaucratic solution: No citizen could fire a gun unless he saw an Indian entering; any shot fired would signal an Indian attack. For any other shooting, they must have a license.[28]

CHAPTER

The Trials of Cabellos Colorados

[T]he Indians have spread terror over this entire region; but it will be nothing as compared with what we may fear from now on, for never have they been so aggressive as in the present year.

— *Fernando Pérez de Almazán, 1731*[1]

One name began to surface. From the Mission of San Francisco de la Espada, raiders took forty horses and left behind a tired horse—the one Alferez Juan Galvan had given the Ypande (Lipan) Chief Cabellos Colorados. The latter was said to have an agreement with the great chief of all the Apaches to steal the horses of presidios at Béxar, Rio Grande, Coahuila, and Sacramento so that his confederates could slaughter the inhabitants. Cabellos Colorados was known in San Antonio, where he and his people traded. His wife—Urrutia referred to her as "Capitana"—led a party of three women and a man to sell or trade buffalo meat. He treated them well and was confident of their friendship, but the chief later seized two San Antonio citizens, who became slaves employed in dressing skins and died trying to escape.

On December 11, 1737, the chief's luck ran out. Soldiers counting the herd at dawn caught an Apache and learned that ten leagues away was a small party led by Cabellos Colorados. They captured the entire group, including the chief, his wife and baby daughter. "The Indian Woman Captain is now a prisoner by order of the Governor," a subordinate reported. Cabellos Colorados asked that a messenger inform the tribe of their capture so they might return the stolen horses. The woman chosen promised to return within twenty days; forty days later, she said her people had sixteen horses to exchange for the prisoners. When a great many horses appeared, Urrutia sent a spy, who reported more than a thousand armed Indians. The Apaches stayed five days, but Urrutia didn't ride out to meet them.

The female messenger insisted the great chief was bringing horses soon, and she and others visited sporadically to deliver buffalo meat for the prisoners. In August the Tejas attacked their ranchería, killed twelve people, captured five boys and stole all the horses they intended to return to the Spaniards, along with many of their own horses. The great chief still wanted to gain the release of Cabellos Colorados and the others, said an old man. Urrutia replied that he wanted to witness the good behavior of the Apaches for a while longer. He assured them the prisoners were well treated and living comfortably. Cabellos Colorados himself was in prison, however, because the Spanish considered him dangerous.

The old man begged the governor to release an old woman he held among the captives and offered a horse and mule. Urrutia joked that he would release the woman if the two one-eyed Indians with the old man took her place. They all laughed, and the exchange was made. The woman must have been important for two warriors to give themselves up.

The Apaches demonstrated their good faith by committing no depredations at Béxar, but the Spanish interpreted the quiet as evidence of the captured chief's guilt. In October, their patience exhausted, the Apaches renewed their raids.[2] In early 1739 Cabellos Colorados, his wife and small daughter, five men, and four women were convicted of violating a peace treaty and became the first group sent to Mexico City under the Regulation of 1729. They would soon wish the Spaniards had just killed them.

On foot, they left San Antonio on February 18, 1739, and reached Mexico City at the end of May. Spanish law was still decades from mandating adequate food and humane treatment of captives. Two prisoners died on the way and the rest were jailed in the hellish Real Carcel de la Corte. In the next five months amidst disease and squalor, Cabellos Colorados and three others breathed their last. The captive Manuela Josefa contracted leprosy and was moved to a hospital. By October three skeletal men were barely alive—Joseph and Joaquin, about twenty-five, and Timoteo, about sixty. The surviving women, all in their forties, were Antonia, Juana Teresa and Maria, wife of the chief, along with her child. They too were "very thin," according to a report to the viceroy.

Mexican officials took an interest and suggested home care before any more of them died. By November 4, the oldest woman, Antonia, was dying and would be buried in the cathedral cemetery. The other women were so sick they had to be carried down the stairs of the house. An official took Maria to a private home to recuperate.

On November 19 the auditor, Pedro Malo, visited the prison and learned that two more men had perished; the last man remaining would die the next day. Malo ordered that Maria be reunited with her daughter, Maria Guadalupe, and returned to her nation. Another functionary retrieved the child but found that the last two survivors were too sick to eat. He ordered them taken to the hospital and baptized.[3] The records don't say if the Capitana and her daughter ever made it home.[4]

The trials of Cabellos Colorados and his group, the first people sent away under the Reglamento of 1729, illustrate the policy's contradictions and weaknesses. Spaniards could no longer pardon captured hostiles, nor could they distribute captives of any age or sex, which precluded the more humane solution of placing the women and child as servants. Although the regulation called for the viceroy to decide their disposition, there is no such record, and officials in Mexico City jailed them until a few bureaucrats took pity on the last few survivors. No other Apache captives met the same sentence for at least three decades.[5]

◄►

Because Cabellos Colorados was an important chief and his wife was highly esteemed, the Apaches' revenge raids left San Antonio in a constant state of terror. Some families moved away, and those remaining were afraid to tend their stock. Mission Indians were deserting. Apaches slipped into the presidio at night, crept soundlessly to the plaza, and took horses tied to the doors of houses.

Urrutia asked the viceroy's permission for a campaign of two hundred men plus Indian allies. He would underwrite the cost of the campaign by selling captives, and all participants would share in the plunder. That, said Father Benito Fernandez de Santa Ana, was the real reason for the campaign, which got underway in the winter of 1739. The campaigns gained nothing "either for God or the king" and only amplified the Indians' hatred.[6]

◄ ►

Apaches penetrated Comanche country three hundred leagues to the northeast and met the Comanches, a group so large and so fierce they put the Apaches' steely courage to the test. The Comanches followed the Apaches back to their own country and met in battle. The outnumbered Comanches fought bravely to the last man. The Apaches told that man to return to his people and warn them what awaited if they came into Apachería again.[7] This tactic usually worked for the Apaches, but this time, the survivor led more Comanches back to Apache country.[8] Father Santa Ana told this story in 1743 after Comanches made their first appearance near San Antonio. Unlike Domingo Cabello's yarn about a nine-day battle in 1723, the priest's story is credible. It also indicates that the Apaches traveled an immense distance to meet the Comanches, and it was Apache aggression that brought the Comanches south. Before about 1740 the Lipans and Palomas were more concerned with other enemies.

The Palomas in December 1739 asked Urrutia for permission to live on the Guadalupe River about twenty-five leagues northeast of San Antonio, where they were joined by the Lipan chief, Cuero de Coyote. Both groups said Tejas with guns had killed many of their people. French explorers in 1740 saw only two male and three female "Padokas" near the Canadian; at the sight of the Frenchmen's horses and goods traded from Comanches, the Apaches threw down their meat and fled.[9]

After that the Ypandes, in six or seven small groups with five hundred warriors, edged closer to San Antonio; the Pelones, who were the first Apaches driven from their lands to the Red River, counted eight hundred warriors, said Father Santa Ana. (Either the "Pelones" were the Palomas, or Spaniards in Texas and New Mexico called them by different names.) "The Ipandes, who comprise the largest number, have been earnestly asking for a mission in their land," he wrote 1743. "As their petition was not answered, they thought that the pledge made to them was not being fulfilled, and so they renewed their incursions, which they had suspended for many months."[10]

The Ypandes were "intimate friends and relatives" of the Natagés, who also moved south and ranged from the Pecos to the Conchos in Coahuila. The two groups shared a Natagé chief in 1745. They joined on the Pecos in June and July, and in autumn they migrated together to the San Sabá, Llano, Almagre (Honey Creek) and Pedernales Rivers. Emboldened by their larger numbers, they hunted buffalo on the Colorado. San Antonio was now the "nucleus of the Apache," said Governor Tomás Felipe de Winthuisen.[11]

Because the Apaches had a healthy fear of Comanches, the time was ripe for a mission, Father Santa Ana told the viceroy. He suggested a presidio in the hills north of San Antonio near the Pedernales, Llano and San Sabá Rivers, where the Apaches felt safe, and he reminded the viceroy of the gold, silver and iron that surely glittered in Apache country.

◄►

Toribio de Urrutia succeeded his father as captain at Béxar in 1740; the old Indian fighter would die a year later. Cut from the same cloth, young Urrutia agitated for a campaign. That would only make the Apaches worse, argued the priest. The viceroy waffled, but after losing a hundred troops and most of their horses in Coahuila, followed by an attack the following year on Santa Rosa, he allowed Urrutia his campaign. In April 1745 he fell upon an Ypande rancheria ten leagues north of the Colorado where most of the inhabitants were away, so it wasn't difficult to take captives. The young daughter of the big Ypande chief, her cousin, and a related woman with two small children were among the captives.

Two months later some 350 Ypandes and Natagés, including women and children, attacked the presidio at night, an unusual occurrence because Apaches rarely fought at night and normally left their women and children in a safe place. The Apaches planned to burn the presidio while its occupants slept. Some waited in ambush just outside while others gathered at the fort. When a boy caught sight of them and began shouting, citizens rushed from their houses and held the Apaches back. The raiders divided and attacked the presidio by another street and would have overwhelmed its defenders if not for the timely arrival of a hundred mission Indians, who furiously drove off the Apaches and chased them all the way to the Medina.

An Apache captive took advantage of the melee to rejoin his people. To questions from the Ypande chief, the escapee responded that the Spanish treated the captives kindly and would return them if the Ypandes would submit to royal authority and live in a town. "This moved the chieftain to shed tears, to give up the campaign, and to order all his men to fall back, although his allies, the Natagés, were very much displeased," said Father Santa Ana.

An Apache who came to the presidio looking for his brother found only his clothing and realized he was dead. Tearfully, he said his people retreated to their country; their captains were deceived into thinking fewer people lived at San Antonio. The Ypandes declared peace, resumed visiting, and renewed their campaign for a mission. They had asked many times before and bureaucratic indecision led them to believe the Spanish didn't want peace. The Natagés, of course, were still opposed.

Father Santa Ana made excuses. He told the Ypandes he didn't have a presidio. They replied he could start a mission without a presidio. He said he didn't know how to build houses and cut down trees. They responded that they knew how to build houses and cut down trees. He told them they didn't know how to plow and sow, and they said three of their people could plow, and they would teach the others.[12]

Meanwhile, a priest built a new mission in 1746 for enemy Tonkawas who made just one request and waited only a year. Adding injury to insult, the unauthorized mission rose at the confluence of the San Xavier River and Brushy Creek—gateway to the Lomería de los Apaches and a pass they used to reach the buffalo plains. Apache camps lined the heavily wooded Brushy Creek, a place so familiar to Lipans that nearby Lipan Creek would be named for them. Despite predictable Apache assaults Spanish authorities approved three missions and a presidio.[13]

◄►

The People could hardly remember a time of such hardship. They had lost many warriors, women and children to diseases their medicine men were powerless to cure, and now they were besieged by a sickness the Spanish called *viruelas*. Still they fought the soldiers and lost more warriors, wives and children. Their enemies in the north were as numerous as cactus spines and growing every day. And they'd seen no rain for such a long time that cattle were bony, and hunters returned ashamed, with their heads down. Then the woman came back, the relative of a chief, who said their family members taken by the Spanish were unharmed and would be returned if only they would stop fighting and settle at missions. The chiefs were willing to hear more.

The priests finally persuaded Urrutia that he would never subdue the Apaches by warfare alone, and he began to see the logic of combining military might with promises of food and protection at missions. When he undertook another campaign in 1748, the priests asked him to conduct a different kind of war: Apaches wouldn't be killed except in self-defense, and captives would be treated well.[14]

Urrutia left San Antonio on February 2, 1749, with about two hundred men, most of them Indian allies. At a small rancheria, which put up little resistance, he captured three old women and five children and took them back to San Antonio, where the priest was kind. "All of this was done to the great wonder of the Apaches, for they had never seen such humanity among the Spaniards," Father Santa Ana wrote.

While Urrutia was away, Apaches angrily attacked Mission Concepción, killing sheep and stealing a large number of cattle. He set off again in March with about three hundred men. Not far away, near the Guadalupe River, they found a buffalo hunting camp with few men present; the Spanish easily captured thirty men, ninety women and forty-seven children. The men were jailed and the women and children entrusted to missionaries and citizens with instructions to be good to them but permit none to escape. Soldiers and residents clamored for the captives to be distributed, but Father Santa Ana refused.

The captain and the cleric had their opportunity. A female captive who was related to the primary chief relayed their message. The assembled chiefs decided they would parley and sent three women—the wife of the principal chief, accompanied by another woman, and the original messenger. The leading woman delivered her message to the priest and the captain. Eight more people came later that day, confirming the message. Even if the principal chief and the Natagés didn't accept peace, the Ypandes would. From May 20 until early August many Ypandes visited from the north, including their leader.

The Spanish had broken such peace-for-prisoners promises before, but circumstances softened the Ypandes' reluctance. They could see the mission Indians harvesting maize, beans, cotton, and Castilian corn for sugar. They had cattle, sheep and goats and operated a weaving workshop. The Indian villages had houses with beds, chests, pots and other good things. When the priest suggested to some young Apache women, including the attractive niece of the principal chief, Boca Comida, that they marry the missions' Indian men, they accepted. Ten Apaches married mission Indians and stayed in the mission.[15]

On August 16 four chiefs—two Ypandes and two others—arrived with four hundred people intent on making peace and recovering their captured relatives. With great joy, Captain Urrutia, his troops, the missionaries, and citizens of San Antonio met the Apaches two leagues out and returned to a great reception hall newly built for the occasion where they feasted on beef, corn, squash and fruit. The next day they attended Mass, commenced talks, and ratified a peace that ended thirty years of hostilities. At a celebration, soldiers, priests and citizens lined one side of the plaza and on the other stood chiefs and tribal members, including the newly released captives.

A story repeated endlessly is that they sealed the agreement by burying a live horse, a hatchet, a lance and six arrows in the plaza. This is another tale from Domingo Cabello, source of the legendary 1723 Apache-Comanche battle. Historian William Edward Dunn noted that priests, who documented every other development in the period, reported no such event.[16]

The documented peace was less dramatic. When the treaty was final on November 28 and 29, the Lipans received their captives, including two taken by the governor over the priest's objections. Boca Comida, the principal chief and two other Ypande chiefs were ready to come in. The peace was well timed, Urrutia thought. Two months earlier the Apaches allied with the Caudachos, beneficiaries of French largesse. Missions might control the Apaches and break this alliance. If not, this new source of firearms would allow them to inflict more damage.[17]

As people streamed in, an alarmed Father Dolores wondered how he would feed them all, when all of Texas was beset by a drought. How would the Apaches influence mission Indians? He knew of their dances "and beverages [peyote] that they use in their great fiestas." He instructed the new arrivals to camp on the Guadalupe River, fifteen leagues from San Antonio.

Just as relieved settlers were starting to work their farms, Ypandes sent by Captain Coquín warned Urrutia that the Natagés and Julimes were planning to go on the warpath. The Spanish dismissed the warning and even thought the Apaches made it up to receive gifts. Coquín sent a second warning, which got Urrutia's attention. His message to the presidio of the Rio Grande arrived after the Natagés killed Father Silva and his companions near the fort. Ypandes visiting San Antonio feared they would be blamed, but Urrutia reassured them and returned the favor, warning them the Tejas planned an attack.

The Ypandes continued to show their good faith—feeding a lost soldier, bringing an orphan to the priest, rescuing an Indian who fled an epidemic raging at the mission—and yet the Spaniards were still uneasy because Boca Comida had not come in. Unknown to them, the great chief's camp was ravaged by smallpox, and he himself died. His successor visited the mission with his relatives, saying he wished to continue the peace. When he pledged to bring all his people there and await a mission, Father Dolores wavered and sent them back to their country.

Still more leaders expressed their desire to settle at the mission. Father Santa Ana had prayed for this change of heart but fretted that pastures were thin, and the mission's cattle near the Guadalupe River might be too much temptation for the Apaches. Father Dolores appealed to the captain for support. Urrutia had orders to wait for all the Apaches to arrive, assess their attitude and then assign them land that was safe and sheltered but didn't afford an easy escape.

Father Santa Ana journeyed to Mexico City to plead personally for Apache missions.[18] He described the Lipans' repeated requests for a mission. If not for slaving expeditions to satisfy the Spanish "avarice for prisoners," the Apaches would already be living at missions, he said. He wanted only the number of people they could support and clothe—no more than a hundred—but expected more than three hundred and saw no way to maintain such a large number. He also wanted a presidio to compel the Apaches to sow and cultivate their fields. Otherwise they would divide into small bands and go out to hunt bison, deer and bear (unlike their western cousins, Lipans ate bear meat) and gather "fruits of the land."[19]

In May 1750 Ypandes and Natagés relocated to the Medina River and its canopy of pecans and cypress, putting San Antonio between them and the Comanches, which was disconcerting to Urrutia and the settlers. Soon after, they made peace at the presidio and mission La Bahia del Espiritu Santo (near present Goliad) and approached their former enemies, the Akokisas, Mayeyes, Cocos and Bidais, creating a fruitful alliance that would last many years. That summer rumors predicted a war on the Apaches by interior tribes, and in August Caddo groups tried to recruit mission Indians at San Xavier as they awaited other allies. The war never materialized,[20] but it was apparent the Texas Apaches faced a daunting array of enemies.

Trail of the Dead

(W)e must be on our guard against them because of their number, audacity, inconstancy, and secrecy.

— *Captain Joseph de Berroterán, 1748*[1]

C hief Pascual heard from Indian people at La Junta that a Spanish captain wanted to speak to him, that the Spanish would give him his own pueblo and mission, but he didn't know this captain, and he had other things on his mind. He was still angry about what happened at the water hole, Acatita la Grande. Tobosos killed four of his warriors, and he couldn't find a way to avenge their deaths, probably because there were so few Tobosos left.

Apaches and Tobosos[2] had long shared the Bolsón de Mapimí, an arid expanse of dry basins and isolated mountain ranges that stretched endlessly, it seemed to Spanish soldiers, toward a brown horizon. From the eastern flanks of the Sierra Madre, several streams drained into the Mapimí basin, providing just enough water to sustain those who knew how to find it.[3] From here, raiders could descend on settlements in Coahuila to the east and Nueva Vizcaya to the west.

The Spanish solved one problem by eliminating the Tobosos,[4] only to create another: Apaches expanded to take their place. Captain Joseph de Berroterán, captain for life at the presidio of San Francisco de Conchos, befriended Chief Pascual and his people, who had previously lived in Nueva Vizcaya, the Tarahumara region, and southwestern

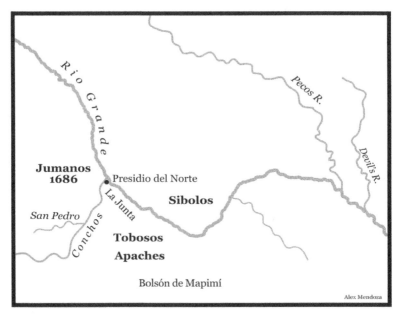

Map 5 La Junta, 1600s

Chihuahua. Pascual in 1730 led four hundred people to the Mapimí presidio to seek peace; in the 1740s, living in the Bolsón de Mapimí on the edge of Spanish settlements, they were guilty only of minor depredations. They had even helped Berroterán flush out rebel Conchos Indians who were raiding in Coahuila.

Still, the captain considered the brief periods of peace in 1742 "convalescence from a bad illness and preparation for another more serious one threatened by the Apaches, who have penetrated the frontiers, and the many others who can follow them northward." The Bolsón de Mapimí could accommodate thousands of hostile Indians. "All the mountains and rough country are impassable to our [forces] but accessible to the enemy."

Defense now featured "flying companies" to engage and pursue Apaches, but Berroterán knew from his long service on the frontier that campaigns into the Bolsón failed. Spaniards suffered from the harsh desert and scarce water, and the uncluttered landscape gave the enemy full view of troop movements. As soldiers wore themselves out in the arid waste, Apaches were safe in their refuges and could easily descend again. The more practical approach, he concluded, was peace through gifts and diplomacy, backed by military force. Berroterán's approach was still working in 1748. The Apaches "apparently have not begun to rob and murder yet, due to the peace that their chief, Pascual, has made with me and the friendly relationship that we have entered into . . ."[5]

◄►

Pascual, who led a plains group closely tied to the Lipans and Natagés, was one of two friendly Apache chiefs that Captain Joseph de Ydoiaga heard about when he began exploring Coahuila in 1747. The Indians at La Junta were on good terms with Pascual, whose people lived about forty miles south between the Conchos and the Bolsón de Mapimí, and with El Ligero, who was a Lipan whose range included La Junta.

As the expedition drew closer, Pascual moved his people into the mountains. Ydoiaga was sorry Pascual had left, he told the people at La Junta, because he wanted to talk; the chief could come in with his people without fear. When the baptized Faraon Apache, Alonzo, told Pascual a second time that the Spanish captain wished to see him, he decided to see what the captain wanted.

Ydoiaga camped at La Junta on January 1, 1748, and two days later Pascual came to visit. As they ate, the captain asked Pascual why he had gone to the mountains and was now here alone. Pascual said he wasn't sure of the captain's intentions, but when the other Indians assured him he would be treated well, he came at once. He didn't bring his family because he lacked horses and the weather was cold. (More than likely, he still wasn't sure of the captain's intentions.) He hoped to bring his people and Chief Ligero to talk about settling.

Ydoiaga wondered why Pascual no longer took hides to trade at the Conchos presidio. Hunting was poor, he replied, and he didn't have enough to trade. Pascual inquired about his friend Berroterán and was told the captain was traveling. The news pleased Pascual because he'd heard Berroterán was in prison.[6] Ydoiaga gave the chief meat, pinole and tobacco for his return trip. A month later, at the pueblo of San Juan at La Junta, the captain met El Ligero, an old man who led 150 families. El Ligero asked for a letter allowing him to trade his tanned skins safely with both Indians and Spaniards.[7]

◄ ►

Ydoiaga's expedition was one of three sent in 1747 to identify the best site for a new presidio at a place the Spanish called La Junta de los Rios del Norte y Conchos. There the Conchos River, flowing north from the Sierra Madre Occidental, created a verdant oasis surrounded by mountains at its junction with the smaller Rio Grande. (The towns of Presidio and Ojinaga would later take root there.)

Indian people had inhabited the area for centuries. Some with habits remarkably similar to early Athabascans were present as early as 900 A.D. and introduced the bow and arrow, the snub-nosed scraper and finely worked knives of stone. From 1400 to 1700, plains hunters—either Jumanos or Apaches—brought change to La Junta's housing, pottery and probably its culture.

Ypandes lived there part of the year with their friends, the Jumanos and Sibolos, who also joined them in the north to gather fruit and pick pecans along the brisk waters of the San Sabá, Llano, Almagre (Honey Creek) and Pedernales Rivers and then hunt buffalo on the Colorado. The Sibolos, like the Jumanos, were driven from their homes by Apaches, who were now their allies.[8] Natagés and Faraons also frequented the area. Pedro de Rábago y Terán, governor of Coahuila, heard many variations in spoken Apache around La Junta and could distinguish the Ypande dialect from the others. Ypandes were so familiar with the area and had so many allies, he suspected southern roots rather than northern.[9]

The church tried to establish missions, but La Junta's Indian pueblos were such a mother lode to Spanish slavers selling mine labor that the

Indians periodically rebelled and deserted. The authorities, of course, blamed the unrest on Apaches. In 1715, when two missionaries came to re-establish missions, the Julimes Indians mentioned an Apache friend, already baptized, who planned to bring his people in to be baptized when teaching missionaries arrived. This band of about sixty families lived above and below La Junta. Because of smallpox in his rancheria, he arrived too late to see the fathers but told the Indians at La Junta he would come back when he returned from the Colorado River.[10]

From the Julimes, later called Carrizos, the Lipans and Tonkawas learned the peyote ceremony—the first tribes north of the Rio Grande to adopt the practice. In the region of Coahuila where the Carrizos lived, the small, rounded cactus was common; their mission, founded in 1673, was called Santo Nombre de Jesus de Peyotes. Later, they moved north to La Junta.

Like other Lipan alliances, this one probably had unfriendly beginnings; the Lipan word for Carrizos is "Enemy Camped About Water." Threatened by Lipan and Comanche raids, Carrizos entered missions in northern Coahuila, took refuge in Laredo, or joined the Lipans.[11] When the Spanish built the Mission of Peyotes south of present Eagle Pass in 1770, they encouraged the Lipans to live nearby, but the priest railed against the Apache and Carrizo "use of these drinks in their sorcery." Lipans would later bring the ceremony to the Mescaleros, Kiowa Apaches and Comanches.[12]

◄►

In November 1747 Governor Rábago y Terán departed Sacramento to reconnoiter the banks of the Rio Grande. Traveling west along an old trail, the expedition passed through a succession of abandoned rancherías, where they found carved stakes for spreading tents to dry, pumpkin vines, and a baking pit used for horse meat. They struck a much-used trail toward buffalo grounds in the northeast.

At one dusty Indian settlement, San Cristobal Poblado, were herds of horses and mules with Spanish brands, some belonging to his own men or their relatives, but Rábago, "fearing the audacity of these Indians," kept his men from seizing the animals by promising to trade for expedition horses. Rábago also ransomed two captive mission Indian women from Coahuila "sold to these Indians by Apaches when they come to trade at this pueblo." On their return, they found a place on the Conchos where "the Apaches come to trade when they are afraid to enter the pueblos" and saw a multitude of hoof prints and footprints that crossed over their own about a week earlier.

On January 13 they returned to Monclova. In their absence a large party of Apaches had surprised four soldiers from the presidio of San Antonio de Béxar and cut their bodies to pieces. Some of the attackers wore rosaries.[13] Rábago recommended a presidio on either bank of the Rio Grande at its junction with the Conchos, but the Presidio del Norte didn't materialize until 1760.

The governor decided to take the fight from Coahuila to Apache country. Marching north in August 1748, he gathered soldiers, residents and mission Indians as he followed the Apaches' trail past San Antonio to the Colorado. Two spirals of smoke drew them farther northwest to a month-old camp pocked by many hoof prints and footprints. Following more smoke twisting slowly from two fires, scouts stole forward and saw Apaches gathering their horses.

On October 5 Rábago's men rose before dawn. He moved forward with four squads of soldiers and residents (twenty-five men and their commanders). Attacking at first light, they killed nine men and captured fourteen women and children. The rest escaped through thick woods and a deep stream. The Spanish rounded up seventy-three horses and mules with various brands, along with some unbranded colts.

Refreshed by this victory Rábago pressed on, but he quickly discovered that another enemy had struck first. Moving through deserted camps, he saw so many lifeless victims of measles that he called the place El Real de los Muertos (Trail of the Dead). Under normal circumstances, Apaches would have buried their dead with ceremony, dressing the deceased in his or her best clothing and sending weapons, food and water with them to the afterlife. That these unfortunates were abandoned meant the survivors were overwhelmed by the number of dead and feared the disease themselves. Rábago considered it "divine punishment."

The weakened Apaches made a stand where they could, exchanging fire with soldiers, setting brush fires, and stalking the expedition to recover captives or animals. Rábago's men passed a camp near the headwaters of the Medina, where they took captives and rounded up horses and continued finding rancherías with corpses. Now discovered, Rábago changed course and headed southwest, adding to their growing population of captives, who succumbed to illness daily. Back on the Colorado, hoof prints and signs of dragged poles led southeast to still more abandoned camps and decaying bodies. Changing course again, they rode northwest, where scouts said they would find the Natagés. Passing more abandoned camps and paintings on large rocks, they began following the Nogales River.

The next morning, an Apache sprinted into a large ranchería to warn his people. He would have come sooner, he told them, but he shadowed the Spaniards hoping to steal a horse. The Apaches quickly rounded up more than a thousand horses and mules. Within moments of seeing the dust of Rábago's squads, they collected everything they could carry, packed horses and mules, suspended infants in cradle-boards, and melted into the hills, leaving sentinels behind.

Rábago's squads found only empty tents and scraps of food. One sentinel gave his life to slow the soldiers' march, and they retrieved sixty-eight horses and mules bearing brands from Coahuila, Santa Rosa and the Rio Grande. The captive Marcos Martinez Morada strode out to greet them. He and another man had been taken four months earlier in Chihuahua. "His companion had been crucified, inhumanely burned with red hot coal and torches and eaten alive little by little. This young man was defended by an Indian who became his master."[14] Lipans were known for their cruelty and torture of captives; this story is consistent with other accounts of the period.[15]

Three hundred warriors gathered here to plan an attack on some presidios, Morada said. "They had not carried out their plan because the Indians expected from the Mission San Juan de la Junta had not arrived." It seems the people Ydoiaga visited at La Junta were more than just trading partners of the Apaches.

As the party moved down the Nogales River toward San Antonio, a scout approached two Indians hunting deer, thinking they were his fellow auxiliaries. They shot him in the head with an arrow and fled with a horse loaded with meat. Incredibly, the scout survived. Rábago continued to surprise Apache camps, but many escaped into craggy cliffs. When they reached San Antonio on October 10, they attempted to treat the sick Indian women, but just thirty survived of more than one hundred captives; Rábago distributed them to residents in San Antonio, San Juan Bautista and Monclova and to officers of the campaign.[16]

◄ ►

Governor Tomás Vélez Cachupín arrived in New Mexico in 1749. The Carlanas, Cuartelejos, Lipans and other Apaches were living in Texas "with little communication with the province and with not a few indications of enmity," he wrote, and so he worked hard to restore good relations. Instead of punitive expeditions, which rarely accomplished anything, he tried to make peace on terms that offered something to both sides. Vélez was nothing if not a realist. "There is not a nation among the numerous ones which live around this government in which a kind word does not have more effect than the execution of the sword," he said.

By winter in 1752, they had abandoned El Cuartelejo and regrouped near Pecos Pueblo.[17] Three hundred men and their families were "living so sociably and neighborly as to indicate their general love for this province." They left their women and children in the pueblo while they hunted buffalo. "I keep them in this limited area with whatever guile I can," he said, in case of Comanche attacks and used them as auxiliaries and spies. "They are so active and astute" and knew the country so well that they could effectively reconnoiter for one hundred leagues.

The Comanches, he said, could be the ruin of the province, and for that reason also, "the greatest consideration becomes keeping the Carlanas and the rest of the Plains Indians at peace, always sympathetic and linked to our interests." He concluded in September that "the Apaches, Carlanas, Palomas, and Cuartelejos will continue trustworthy."

Two years later the departing governor recommended trade protocols to his successor: Keep the Utes and Apaches from injuring the Comanches, mediate among the groups, and monitor the trade of horses and ransoming of captives. The fairs were a source of goods, but they were also the source of insults, real and imagined, and the settlers cheated the Indians so often that Vélez attended the fairs in person to settle disputes and prevent the settlers from stealing the Indians' herds and goods. The governor's candid instructions revealed sharp practices that were probably common over the years; settlers weren't just the long-suffering targets of Indian depredations.

Vélez also urged his successor to preserve the Apaches' friendship but prevent the Natagés and Carlanas from forming an alliance. The Natagés were then trading stolen horses and mules for the Carlanas' buffalo meat and hides. He considered the Natagés a bad influence, a sentiment shared by his Texas peers. By 1758 the Carlanas were living south of Pecos Pueblo on the Pecos River. Together with the Cuartelejos and affiliated groups, they continued moving south and were gone when Vélez returned in 1762.[18] They would reappear on the Southern Plains, living between the Lipans and the Natagés, and remain closely tied to both.

CHAPTER

The Saga of San Sabá

The Apaches were evidently unimpressed by the strength of the new Presidio, for they quite refused to settle at the Mission. Indeed the whole establishment stood like bait at the very edge of the Comanche territory.

— *Colonel Diego Ortiz Parrilla, 1758*[1]

When the viceroy finally agreed to a mission for the Apaches, in August 1756, it was fifteen years after their first request, thirteen years after Father Santa Ana's first request, eleven years after the Ypande chief's request, and seven years after the peace agreement at San Antonio. The Apaches had kept their peace in San Antonio and traded with the citizens,[2] adjusted their territories, made new allies, fought their enemies, and, in general, managed nicely without Spanish help. So their lack of enthusiasm as the long-promised mission rose on the banks of the San Sabá might be forgiven.

The Spanish bureaucratic machinery had jammed with internal conflict, politics and indecision. Jacinto de Barrios Jáuregui, governor of Texas, was the final obstacle, rudely rebuffing priests and Ypandes who sought his support.[3] After the viceroy overruled Barrios, it took another two years and two exploratory expeditions to find a site.

In summer 1753 Lieutenant Juan Galván and Father Miguel de Aranda of Mission Concepción found two promising locations on the San Sabá near present Menard. The Apaches were overjoyed to see them. "They began coming to my camp at once, firing salvos, surrendering their arms and kissing the hand of the father," said Galván, indicating that the Apaches had firearms and ammunition enough to waste it on salvos.[4]

Authorities next sent Pedro de Rábago y Terán, scourge of diseased Apaches, whose investigation in late 1754 and early 1755 confirmed abundant supplies of wood and pasture, as well as possible silver deposits. After crossing the Pedernales, he reached the camps of Chief Chiquito (also called Tacú), who had 467 people with him, and Chief Pintas, who had a hundred. Both were delighted to learn that the Spaniards planned a mission for them. On the Concho River, they said, were ten more chiefs whose people roamed as far as Comanche country. They too wanted a mission.[5]

An expedition sent in November 1755 to look for mineral deposits in the Llano and upper Colorado region found Apaches on the Guadalupe. A chief told Lieutenant Governor Bernardo de Miranda of rich silver deposits six days' journey above the Llano in Comanche country. Pointing to the silver buckles on Miranda's shoes, he told the wide-eyed explorers there was an entire mountain of pure silver.[6] The Apaches must have laughed heartily as the gullible Spaniards rode away.

◄ ►

While the viceroy deliberated, Apaches sought alternatives. Some tried to join the San Xavier missions.[7] Ypandes approached Father Alonso Giraldo de Terreros at San Juan Bautista, who was planning a mission for Natagés, Sibolos and Tucubantes. (The latter may well have been Ypandes, the people of Tacú.) In June 1754, more than nine hundred Apaches led by three chiefs camped along both banks of the Rio Grande near San Fernando de Austria in Coahuila. Some were Apaches who had lived there before, but others were the people who had been at San Antonio.

On the Rio Escondido two leagues from the villa and west of the Presidio del Rio Grande, the new San Lorenzo mission opened on December 21, 1754. By the end of March it had eighty-three resident Apaches, including three chiefs—El Gordo, El de Godo and Bigotes—who said they were there because Father Dolores refused to give them missions in Texas. After Father Terreros left, his replacements failed to gain the Apaches' trust or stem mounting discontent, and on October 4, 1755, they revolted, sacked the mission, set fire to the buildings and left.[8] Three Apache chiefs then led nearly a thousand people to the San Xavier mission, which Rábago had relocated to the San Marcos River, halfway between the former site and San Antonio. There an epidemic swept the missions, taking Rábago's life before authorities transferred the mission and presidio again, this time to serve Apaches on the San Sabá.[9]

The viceroy in 1756 designated two leaders: Father Terreros and Colonel Diego Ortiz Parrilla, former governor of Sinaloa and Sonora.[10] That fall Parrilla began making arrangements and recruiting soldiers, as the priest bought large inventories of supplies. Father Terreros arrived in San Antonio with four other priests and nine Tlaxcaltecan[11] families from Saltillo who would teach the neophytes at San Sabá and proudly showed visiting Apaches his stock of gifts and supplies. Two visiting chiefs repeated their desire to gather in missions and apologized for the absence of friends who were far away—the Natagés, Mescaleros, Pelones, Come Nopales and Come Caballos (prickly pear eaters and horse eaters).

After long preparation, Parrilla's soldiers and their families, missionaries and Tlaxcaltecans set out for the San Sabá and arrived on April 18, 1757. Parrilla explored the San Sabá to its source without finding a single Apache. Choking down their disappointment, they established the Santa Cruz de San Sabá Mission on the south bank of the river in open, gently rolling country with lush pastures threaded by creeks and streams and shaded by pecans, oaks and cottonwoods. It had everything to offer but protection—no canyon walls, mountain flanks or rocky hillsides for defense. It was not a place the Apaches would have chosen.

Missionaries and Tlaxcaltecans built living quarters and a temporary church protected by a log palisade with a large gate secured by bars. They cleared fields, planted crops and started digging an irrigation ditch. Two miles above, Parrilla began building the Presidio de

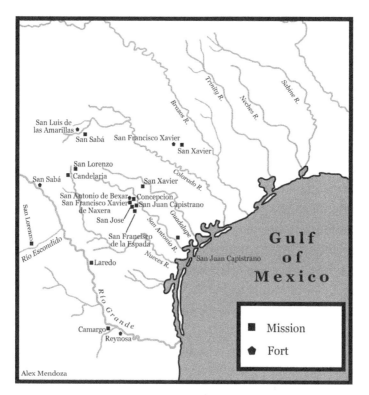

Map 6 Spanish Forts and Missions, 1700s

San Luis de las Amarillas, a cluster of adobe buildings surrounded by a log stockade, with several gun platforms.[12]

Missionaries anxiously watched for Apaches to crest distant hills, unaware they were living farther south. When Tacú visited San Antonio, Father Dolores scolded him for not keeping his promise to live at the San Sabá mission, and he departed immediately with three hundred people. Apaches began arriving from the south until, by mid-June, some three thousand Apaches camped near the mission with substantial herds of horses and mules. Warriors numbered about seven hundred, some armed with French guns, the rest with bows and arrows. Tacú had to leave because his brother and sister were seriously ill, which suggests his band had been at the San Xavier mission.

Historians have described the Apaches as haughty and indifferent, as if they were supposed to be grateful and attentive after fifteen years of excuses. Chiefs and captains told Parrilla they had been far away and scattered, primarily hunting buffalo. Father Dolores gave them maize, but they needed powder and balls to kill game, they said. They were all hungry.

They were also angry that Tejas attacked Ypandes on the San Xavier road, killing Pierna Gorda, Chief Casa Blanca's brother, along with his wife and two children.[13] Casa Blanca said that if his people could not agree to settle and be obedient, it was because they were accustomed to keep moving, but they did want peace and friendship with the Spanish. He himself had never promised to settle and intended to hunt buffalo and fight the Comanches. He vowed to avenge his brother's death.

Casa Blanca's scouts had found tracks of Comanches on their way to meet with the Tejas. He knew they planned to make all-out war on the Apaches. If he settled in the open country of San Sabá, his people would be easy targets. The Apaches' seven hundred warriors had to protect 2,000 people plus 2,700 head of stock. The presidio's hundred soldiers would hardly make a difference. Casa Blanca couldn't very well sit and wait for an onslaught by a bigger enemy. He left the next day.

Tacú said he was still committed to the mission but was honor bound to join Casa Blanca, whose people pleaded tearfully with him to not abandon them in their fight with the Comanches. He couldn't deny them, he said sadly, and he needed buffalo meat. He would return and live at the mission, he assured the priests. The Spaniards (and historians) denounced this setback as a broken promise and Apache perfidy, but return he did in early July with a large quantity of meat. They seemed edgy. Having met their enemies in battle, they needed to put some distance behind them. Discouraged priests began leaving until only three remained. Small Apache groups passed through sporadically and, expecting the silhouettes of their enemies to darken the horizon, hurried on. They were also beset by another epidemic and scattered to minimize its impacts.[14]

As Apaches grew scarce, their enemies weren't far behind. In San Antonio northern tribes boasted that they would wipe out the Apaches, and if the Spanish defended them, they would fight the Spanish too.[15] On March 2, 1758, raiders stole sixty-two horses at San Sabá. Soldiers pursued half-heartedly and returned with alarming stories: the countryside was alive with hostile Indians. Parrilla pleaded with the missionaries to come to the presidio for protection, but Father Terreros refused.[16]

◄ ►

At dawn on March 16, the mission guard Juan Leal, cutting stakes on the river bank, looked up to see an unending host of Indians crossing the river. Frozen in horror, he watched their numbers multiply until they filled the country as far as he could see. The shouting invaders quickly surrounded the mission. Father Miguel de Molina "saw nothing but Indians on every hand, armed with guns and arrayed in the most horrible attire. Besides the paint on their faces, red and black, they were adorned with the pelts and tails of wild beasts, wrapped around them or hanging down from their heads, as well as deer horns."

Most carried firearms, ammunition in large powder horns and pouches, swords, lances and cutlasses. They wore battle dress of helmets, leather jerkins or breastplates traded from the French. Leal had never before "seen so many barbarians together, armed with guns and handling them so skillfully." Soldiers estimated their numbers at fifteen hundred to two thousand. They recognized Tejas, Tonkawas, Bidais and other northerners; few recognized the Comanches, who were the majority.

Invaders told the guards that they had no quarrel with the Spanish and wished only to kill Apaches. Some said they were looking for Apaches who had killed their people near the Concho. Without waiting for guards to unlock the gates, the Norteños wrenched off the crossbars with their hands, poured inside the stockade and began looting. By the end of the day Father Terreros, Father Santiestevan, four soldiers and two residents would be dead, another five soldiers seriously wounded and the mission burned to the ground. Parrilla's men attempted a rescue but, wildly outnumbered, fell back. After midnight Father Molina and a handful of surviving Spaniards and Apaches escaped.[17]

One Apache brought seven people to safety on a hidden path; another hid two Spanish children and then took them to the presidio, carrying the smallest on his back. A third Apache led his horse carrying a woman whose husband had died on the way. Large numbers of Apaches took refuge at the mission of San Antonio, expressing their grief for the murders as they watched anxiously for signs of their enemies. They offered to scout or accompany any punitive expedition.[18]

◄ ►

The saga of San Sabá is one of the most familiar chapters in early Texas history. Apaches are usually blamed in the retelling, but that ignores the Apaches' changing circumstances and absolves the Spanish and northern Indians for their roles in the massacre. The Spanish themselves reached some disturbing conclusions: First, the mission represented to attackers a new alliance between the Spanish and the Norteños' enemies. Second, the French supplied weapons and fomented hostilities; many of the horses and mules taken from San Sabá later turned up at Natchitoches. Third, the mission's own stores were a great temptation.[19]

Distant officialdom blamed the Apaches, but those closest to the massacre thought otherwise. Parrilla wrote that the Apaches "are now beyond the dangerous territories, which they deserted with good cause." Father Molina concurred. "It is well known that the home of the Apaches is far away, closer to our settlements along the rivers."[20]

The Spanish left behind pages of testimony. The Ypandes left behind their own testimony. At Paint Rock, a limestone cliff overlooking the Concho where artists of different tribes painted some 1,500 images, two in particular are probably the work of Lipans: a red devil with a pitchfork and pointed tail, and a mission with a long row of windows and two towers, each topped by a cross with black clouds that depict its burning. According to Lipan oral history, the grandfather of Cuelgas de Castro, who would become a great chief, left a mark on a stone near San Sabá: A broken arrow pointing down.[21]

◄ ►

Tacú was astonished. The captain and the brown robe—the same religious who denied them a mission before—said it was time the People settled at the San Sabá mission. It was hardly six moons since the Spanish proved that even they weren't safe there, and those of the People foolish enough to stay barely escaped with their lives. The Apaches always intended to settle at a mission, Tacú told the Spaniards, but first they wanted to punish their enemies. The Comanches troubled them wherever they decided to live, and they were forced to move from place to place, enduring hardships and always keeping watch. If they settled into towns, they would be helpless to defend themselves, but by striking back, they would gain some relief and reduce their risk, Tacú said.[22]

Parrilla had already proposed moving the now useless presidio and establishing new Apache missions on the San Marcos or Guadalupe rivers, closer to the Ypande camps, but a junta concluded that moving the San Sabá presidio would be a sign of weakness. The church sent new missionaries, housed at the presidio. As before, Apaches visited in small groups but didn't linger.[23]

Ypandes massed on the Medina, and Father Dolores wondered if they too would be Norteño targets. They visited in large parties, and when they offered to protect the San Antonio missions, the priest sent them to scout the area and prove their fidelity.[24] The greater body poured south from Texas into Coahuila and hunkered down on the Rio Grande and most of its tributaries—the Moras, Piedra Pinta, San Diego, San Rodrigo, San Antonio and Escondido Rivers, all familiar, safe places. The Escondido, like the San Rodrigo, headed in the Burro mountains; the pecan, cypress, oak, and mulberry trees along its banks drew nesting eagles, later inspiring the name of nearby Eagle Pass. By April 1759 there were 2,500 Apaches between the Rio Grande and the Santa Rosa mountains.

Ypandes joined this exodus. Gran Cabezón, Boruca, Bordado and other captains camped along both sides of the Rio Grande. Some didn't feel safe until they reached the Gulf Coast. Chief Pastellan (who had received a mission at San Juan Bautista in 1750 and deserted the first night) camped with his people at El Escondido and asked for peace at the Sacramento presidio.

Governor Angel de Martos y Navarette instructed the commander to treat Pastellan well and accept his peace offer but find out "what is the real motive of the said Apache Indians in advancing upon our frontiers." Navarette assumed the Apaches had been living at San Sabá and could have warned Parrilla of the impending attack. He maligned them for not resisting the Comanches and not seeking Spanish military support. "Everywhere they foment disorder and continual brawling, but they claim that others are the aggressors and not they themselves," said Navarette.[25]

Mescaleros, Natagés, Atascosas (an Ypande group living on the river of that name), Jumanos and Ypandes united to make war on the Comanches and Norteños, and attacks and counter-attacks consumed the rest of that year. In December musket-toting raiders from eleven tribes surprised Tacú's buffalo camp perched on a hill by the Concho River. Surrounded and overwhelmed, all he could do was run. By different routes, Tacú and others reached San Sabá.

◄ ►

Parrilla was itching to punish the northern tribes and imagined they were no more challenging than the Moors he had fought in North Africa. A junta in January 1759 prescribed a campaign against the Tawakonis, Tonkawas, Wichitas, Taovayas and Iscanis—the probable attackers—but not the Comanches, who were both numerous and far distant. Parrilla would be given six hundred men, to include soldiers, militia, Tlaxcaltecan Indians and mission Indians. Ypandés were their only friends among all the Apaches, but the junta was reluctant to involve them in a campaign; they might think the Spanish needed them or join in such numbers that provisions and discipline would be a problem. They decided to hire about twenty-five Apaches as guides and scouts.[26]

When Parrilla marched north in August 1759, his forces included just thirty soldiers and his small San Sabá garrison. The rest was a patchwork of 50 mission Indians, a large contingent of Ypandes, and 450 poorly armed, ill prepared and resentful militiamen from distant settlements. The mission Indians and Apaches carried mostly bows and arrows.[27] At the Guadalupe River, more than seven hundred Apaches—men, women and children—joined for protection while they hunted buffalo.

Within days, an Apache chief became guide. Apaches knew the country well. On the eighteenth day they found horses and mules taken from the San Sabá presidio. Two days later, near the present Eastland-Stephens county line, a number of Apaches turned back to rejoin their families. The 134 remaining Apaches, including some women, "were determined to make a campaign against the enemy."

Beyond the muddy Brazos, scouts returned, shouting they had seen the enemy. Apaches, mission Indians and soldiers set out and found only two horses and some abandoned huts; their occupants fled through the woods, setting fires to warn their people. Past Rock Creek, across plains, scouts tracked many people traveling eastward to a Tonkawa ranchería with fires. With this news, the expedition traveled all night and attacked at dawn on October 2, killing 55 and taking 149 captives. Others escaped through the woods. Prisoners described a village nearby, protected by a stockade and surrounded by a moat, where three Frenchmen lived.[28]

On October 9 sixty to seventy warriors attacked Parrilla's army. One charge sent them running, and the Spaniards chased them through the forest until they plunged onto the river bank opposite the fortified village whose inhabitants opened fire, laughing and challenging them to enter. Parrilla arranged his troops with the main body in the center, the mission Indians and Tlaxcaltecans on the right wing and the Apaches and some Spaniards on the left wing. From noon until darkness they

fought—charging and falling back. Blasts of the Spanish cannons produced more laughter from the enemy. Some Ypandes searched up and
down the river for another way into the Taovaya camp but found just
two entrances, heavily guarded.

Quavering militiamen began scurrying back to camp or hiding
in the woods. In the waning light, enemy Indians tried to cut off the
line of retreat and weakened the left wing. Some soldiers broke and
ran and then all the Spaniards raced into the woods, leaving behind
their cannons. Troops refused to obey orders; the few who tried to
save the artillery were gunned down. Parrilla repulsed several charges
with difficulty.

After the enemy withdrew, Parrilla deliberated. They could see the
Taovayas' high, oval-shaped huts, along with the Comanches' tipis,
partially surrounded by a palisade. Over the center of the village bil-
lowed a French flag. All the tribes of the northern alliance, thousands
of people, appeared to be gathered there, and Apache scouts said more
were streaming in. The confident Norteños didn't bother posting a
guard as they celebrated that night.

Parrilla remained three days before deciding his men had "a lack
of spirit for fighting the kind of Indians which have been seen." Eleven
Spaniards, one Tlaxcaltecan and one Apache were dead; fourteen Spaniards and one Apache were wounded; and thirteen Spaniards deserted,
but they had killed more than a hundred and still had their captives.

The disgruntled Ypandes departed. It wasn't their way to throw
their lives away in a mismatched fight alongside unworthy allies, nor
would they dally indecisively before an enemy, and they were satisfied with the losses they inflicted. Parrilla complained that some of the
Ypandes retreated "impetuously," and "took their horses and many of
ours," and yet they served "loyally and affectionately" in the campaign.
They quickly rejoined the families they left with the Natagés. Parrilla
was confident that "once they observed one of our campaigns against
their enemies," they would return to San Sabá, but this campaign hardly
inspired confidence.[29]

CHAPTER

Missions Impossible

Those we call the Lipanes have come in large numbers.

— *Father Jiménez, 1763*

Apaches admired a forceful speaker, and this captain spoke boldly to them: The Comanches have taken your lands and your buffalo. Five times I have provided escorts for your hunting parties. You would be better off to live in a village at the mission. The friendly captain entertained them well and, from his own pocket, bought gifts of tobacco, corn, piloncillos (bricks of brown sugar), bridles, spurs, iron parts for saddles, and clothing.

In October 1760 Captain Felipe de Rábago y Terán (who will be referred to here as Terán to distinguish him from his uncle, Pedro) replaced Parrilla. Some Apaches probably remembered him from San Xavier, where he was yanked from command and chastised for incompetence, debauchery and suspected crimes. Young Terán seemed to embrace his post at San Sabá as a chance at redemption. Energetically, he recruited new soldiers, replenished the horse herd and replaced the wooden stockade with stone. That summer and fall, several Lipan chiefs camped nearby, encouraged by the formidable wall rising around the fort. Just the sight of it had already discouraged two raiding parties.[1]

Terán was the first to call the Ypandes "Lipan" in July 1761, when he mentioned "los Yndios Apaches y Lipanes" in a letter."[2] The origin

San Sabá Presidio ruins (*Sherry Robinson photo*)

of the name is uncertain. Picuris Pueblo people called them Nipan-nano, according to John Bourke. "The Apaches have told me that the Lipans were their people and that the word Lipunin meant Buckskin, or the people who dressed in that material or had much of it." Albert Schroeder wrote that Lipans took their name from a chief named Pan (Pan-n'de, or people of Pan), which became Ypan'de.[3]

Late that year Gran Cabezón, a Lipan who had just become principal chief of ten Apache bands, said he was willing to settle at a mission but not San Sabá. His people liked that place, he said. It had good land and plenty of water, but it wasn't safe. If they stayed, their enemies would attack them again. He himself had visited the mission but never promised to live there. The chiefs had chosen another place known to the Apaches but not to their enemies. Father Diego Jiménez, president of the Rio Grande missions, considered the proposed site practical, but questioned their commitment: "[T]hese Indians, if I am not mistaken, agree to be congregated half willingly and half unwillingly, as if constrained."

The chiefs set three conditions: More soldiers to accompany them on a buffalo hunt, the return of a Natagé captain's daughter held in

Nuevo León, and soldiers to join them in raids against the Comanches during prickly pear season. Terán agreed to the first two but wisely talked the Lipans out of a campaign, saying it would only bring the northern tribes south to retaliate. In late December they returned from their fall hunt ready to settle, even though their brothers to the northwest thought they were fools for enslaving themselves in a mission. Gran Cabezón couldn't order all the bands to join a mission—the principal chief didn't have that kind of authority—but he could lead by example and bring in his own people. He was also the first Lipan to become the confederacy's ambassador and spokesman.

◄►

Steep, rugged hills on both sides of the Upper Nueces valley sheltered El Cañon (present Camp Wood) from weather and offered defensible positions in an attack. The river ran clear and glassy southward through the canyon from its source about thirty miles north in the limestone flanks of the Edwards Plateau. Elms, cottonwoods, oaks, pecan trees and evergreens would provide timber and firewood, and rich land could be cultivated. When Lipans and soldiers reached the spot in early January 1762, Cabezón declared that his people would live here.[4]

On January 23 everyone gathered, and José Antonio, a Lipan interpreter who spoke good Castilian Spanish, explained the privileges and responsibilities of mission life to three hundred members of Gran Cabezón's band as hundreds more watched from a distance. Following blessings and a procession, Gran Cabezón said his people were happy and wanted the Catholic king to protect, defend and govern them. The chief uprooted some grass, drew water, and sprinkled some stones he had picked up, the Lipans' way of taking possession. Father Jiménez named the mission San Lorenzo de la Santa Cruz.

The priest still had his doubts. Compared to the docile Coahuiltecans, the Lipans were proud, savvy, courageous and haughty. They ate well on bison and game, owned herds of horses, and used saddles and bridles. They raised corn, melons, squash and tobacco. With Europeans, they traded for brass utensils, clothing and some firearms. The Lipans' medicine men mistrusted him. Father Jiménez wanted Terán to remain with enough soldiers to defend against Comanches and mold the Lipans to the routine and discipline of mission life, but Terán, anxious to return to San Sabá, assigned a lieutenant and twenty men as guards.[5]

As the mission got under way, groups of curious Apaches began visiting. El Turnio demanded his own mission. Using kernels of corn, the chief communicated that he had 114 armed warriors; his band probably numbered four hundred to five hundred people. Terán refused at first, but El Turnio was stubborn, and Terán didn't want to lose his allegiance. On February 6, 1762, he established a second mission, Nuestra Señora de la Candelaria, about ten miles south of San Lorenzo (near present Montell) and thinned his ranks to provide thirty soldiers. El Turnio said he would live there and support his family, but "they would leave the mission whenever fruits and *cogollitos* were in season."

By fruits, El Turnio likely meant prickly pear *tunas*, a Lipan staple consumed raw after brushing off the stickers. Cogollitos were probably the hearts of sotol, maguey, palmilla or agave, which Lipans baked for two days in a large pit lined with heated rocks and covered with grass and earth. The cooled hearts could be eaten, but Lipans preferred to pound them into thin sheets, which could be dried and ground into flour.[6]

The optimistic commander and hopeful priest had now established two missions within a month, and neither had official sanction. They began to petition their superiors. Within a week each mission counted four hundred residents. Instructed by Coahuiltecans, the Lipans made adobe bricks, built a church and carefully tended their corn, but their crops quickly disappeared. "[W]e have had so many Indians come in that, like locusts, they have cleaned out the field," a priest complained.

That summer the Spaniards recorded twelve band chiefs but named just eight: Gran Cabezón, El Turnio, Teja, Boruca, Panocha, Bordado, El Lumen and El Cojo. The core groups, probably Lipans, were those of Gran Cabezón, El Turnio, Teja, and Boruca. Other bands passed through or camped nearby. Terán hoped they would see the light; even the Mescaleros and Natagés might follow because "these nations are closely tied to the Lipans."

Still, the missions were short on food, and without the viceroy's blessing and financial support, their survival was tenuous. In June the Lipan men departed for a buffalo hunt, and the priests couldn't object. The troublemaker El Lumen had a dream that the missionaries and soldiers left the missions, taking the Lipan women, children and horses with them. The hunters hurried back to find their families living peacefully. When El Lumen next suspected that the Lipan women were living with the priests, soldiers and Coahuiltecans and that the missionaries intended to kill them, his fellow captains dismissed his wild accusations and told him to leave if he didn't trust the Spaniards. He did.

In September Gran Cabezón, Teja, Boruca, and Bordado were off gathering prickly pear tunas and then hunting buffalo, each time with permission, but the continuing shortage of food and insufficient guard compromised the priests' control. Cojo left without permission; his group would soon desert.

All year, Comanches raided Lipans camped nearby. Mission guards were unable or unwilling to pursue them, which didn't reassure the mission Lipans. By fall, rumors of attacks rippled the mission's thin fabric of order. Father Jiménez tried to reassure the Lipans that Comanches promised to leave mission Lipans alone, but the Lipans didn't believe it, and Father Jiménez didn't either. The Texas governor compounded their fears by making peace with the Comanches. The Lipans "suspect treachery on our part," Father Jiménez wrote.

Come December and January every able-bodied man, boy and some women left to hunt buffalo. No longer cowed by the Comanches, they sent spies to Comanche territory to locate enemy camps before the hunt. Afterward, warriors sent the women and old men back to the missions with the products of their hunt and rode on to fight their enemies. For four satisfying years, they could retreat to the safety of the missions. The Comanches might follow, but they hadn't yet breached El Cañón.

◄ ►

Father Jiménez grew jittery about the northern tribes. Captive Lipans who escaped from their enemies said the Comanches knew about the new missions and were spying on them. He and Terán asked again for support and supplies, but the viceroy still had not warmed to these missions. The two men were too isolated to know that this remote outpost was immaterial. When it appeared England would prevail in the Seven Years' War, France in 1763 gave Louisiana to Spain, its ally. France was too generous. Spain was barely managing its own far-flung, thinly populated empire.

In late 1764 smallpox infested the mission, and fleeing Lipans left their sick behind, despite the missionaries' pleas to remain. In this dark period, the Lipans began seeing an old man who could appear and disappear. "The old man advises them to have a continuous war with the neighboring nations and with the Spaniards," Father Jiménez reported. The old man warned them against baptism and promised that they would be reunited. He would die in battle only to reappear and encourage his people to fight, promising that they too would return to life. Sometimes he appeared as a woman, who was always the same age.

Anthropologists consider such movements a sign of cultural upheaval and social disorganization. The Lipans were suspended between new and old ways. They settled into mission life and listened to the priests, but they were trapped like rabbits as their enemies drew closer, and they still had to provide their own food. By the end of 1764 each mission still had four hundred people, but come December and January every able-bodied man, boy and some women would leave to hunt buffalo cows. In May and June they hunted bulls. The night before they gathered for ceremonials to pray for a good hunt or hold a war dance, knowing they could encounter Comanches. The missionaries were sure the prince of darkness was at work. Lipans resumed raiding in Chihuahua, despite the priests' disapproval, and showed off their newly acquired loot.

◄►

On the morning of January 21, 1766, in the mission's fifth year, four hundred Norteños attacked the Mission San Lorenzo and the Lipan village. They killed six people, took twenty-five captives and all the stock, and challenged the Apaches to come out and fight. The attackers slept that night in an Apache camp.[7] Terán sent forty-one soldiers to block the raiders' escape. From a hilltop, they used their cannon so effectively that the blood of two hundred enemies flowed downhill and pooled at the base. The stricken Wichitas, Comanches, Caddos and Tonkawas could be heard wailing as they left.[8]

Now angrier, Norteños throttled the presidio, the missions and any Lipans they managed to catch. El Turnio abandoned the Candelaria mission. In October 1766 three hundred attackers stormed the walls of San Lorenzo. Soldiers, aided by swivel guns, repulsed them, but they returned a month later. Soldiers again took up their positions, augmented by women in soldiers' coats and hats who stood along the walls with guns. It was an effective bit of theater. At the sight of numerous armed soldiers, the attackers fired one volley and retreated to an oak grove nearby and exchanged gunfire until nightfall.

The following winter, the presidio at San Sabá was under virtual siege and running out of food. The faithful Lipan interpreter José Antonio died outside the presidio. "The flesh from both thighs was torn and the right hand was cut off," Terán wrote. Late in 1767, Lipans who had retreated to the Rio Grande thought it might be safe to hunt buffalo and return to the mission, but a league from San Lorenzo, the enemy caught them, killing or capturing more than thirty people and taking all their meat and more than a thousand horses. After that, no Lipans remained in San Lorenzo or even Central Texas.[9] On December 10, 1767, the Norteños drove off the presidio's entire cattle herd as half-starved soldiers cowered behind the stockade. Four attacks later, the Spanish learned from a captive that the French were saying the presidio held many supplies and that a large number of Apaches lived there with the Spaniards.[10]

◄►

Spanish bureaucrats and church historians again blamed the missions' failure on the "ungrateful, treacherous" Lipans, and yet for five years, Gran Cabezón, El Turnio, and their people made a good-faith effort to live in missions. Other mission Indians traded their freedom for food and protection; the Lipans received neither. The remaining chiefs had been forthright about their opposition. The Lipans' goal was an alliance with the Spanish, and missions were a condition of that alliance. We can only imagine the regret and recrimination in councils as allies chided the Lipans for trusting the Spaniards again, with the same disappointing result.

Spaniards rarely saw their own hand in outcomes. Realistically, without the viceroy's approval and material support, the missions were doomed. Two Texas governors resented Terán's attempt to establish a new jurisdiction, and their opposition swayed the viceroy. The missions' failure was not a failure of people but of bureaucracy. San Lorenzo, abandoned by the Spanish in 1771, was the last attempt to settle any tribe at a mission. Historians have observed that such mobile, independent spirits "were hardly worth the candle," as historian Herbert Bolton put it,[11] and yet some Lipans did embrace the church.

Valentina Sambrano Castro, a descendent of Lipan chiefs, recalled traveling through Menard as a child in the early 1900s. Men using mules and flat sleds dragged blocks of granite from the presidio ruins. "My mother was mad. She kept saying, 'They are robbing our history.'" Four days before her death in December 2001 at 87, she said, "I also want to tell you that we, our people, never stopped loving our mission and that almost all of the family still practices the Catholic way of life."[12]

◄ ►

Lipan camps dotted both sides of the Rio Grande and its tributaries all the way to the coast. The river they called "Big Water Flows"[13] was one of the longest in North America. Rising high in the San Juan Mountains of present Colorado, it cleaved New Mexico in half on its way south, and sliced the soaring canyons of the Big Bend through the Chisos

Mountains and Sierra del Carmen as it angled toward the Gulf of Mexico. New mission refugees joined those who had left San Sabá ten years earlier, who in turn had joined Lipans long resident in the area.

Gran Cabezón, Boruca, Zapato Bordado, Casaca Colorada, and Canos clustered on the San Rodrigo and at San Vicente, a well-used ford near Big Bend on the Apaches' north-south highway (later called the Comanche Trail). Lipans overran the area from San Fernando (Zaragoza) south to the Sabinas River. Cut off from the buffalo grounds and having no particular reason to remain friends of the Spanish, the Lipans were raiding widely, alone or with allies—the Natagés, Mescaleros, Carlanas, and Salineros, who lived along the Pecos in New Mexico. The Bidais kept them amply supplied with rifles, powder and bullets traded from the French,[14] and Lipans also traded directly with the French at Opelousas and Natchitoches in Louisiana.

Lipans near the Santa Rosa Mountains typically joined the Natagés for forays into Nueva Vizcaya and Coahuila. Some suspected that the friendly Lipans near La Junta guided other Apaches to Spanish settlements; the Spaniards called them *entregadores* (deliverers). Apaches living in the Sierra Colorado, former refuge of Tobosos, struck at will from Chihuahua to Coahuila; Lipans in the Big Bend ranged to the Conchos River, northern Durango and western Coahuila.

In discussing Lipans, the Spaniards could hardly summon enough adjectives. The "infidel Lipans" were a "depraved nation" sheltered at the presidios from "pursuit of their innumerable enemies," said the Marqués de Rubí, who heard many a story about the Apaches as he traveled along the northern frontier. Rubí, said Antonio Bonilla, "describes with inimitable accuracy the perfidious, brutal character of the horribly vile Lipan Apache nation."

Sent by the king to inspect presidios and make recommendations, Rubí crossed 7,600 miles in twenty-three months.[15] On July 11, 1767, he reached the Rio Grande, where he found Lipans peacefully tending their fields on the south side of the river. The party crossed using a Lipan boat, probably a raft of logs and hides pulled by swimmers.[16] Examining the

Lipan missions, they scoffed at the forlorn Candelaria and San Lorenzo and declared the San Sabá garrison the worst in the kingdom.[17]

Nicolás de Lafora, captain of the Spanish Royal Engineers and Rubí's assistant, blamed the Spaniards' humiliating defeats on conditions at the presidios, the poor preparation of soldiers, and their captains' ill-conceived strategies. They found irregularities in soldiers' pay, guns of various calibers, poor quality swords, few lances, and inadequate powder. Inexperienced captains waged war against fleet, agile enemies as if they were European battalions. Soldiers encumbered with supplies and weapons "never can run as fast nor for so long a time as an Indian, whose arms and equipment increase his weight very little . . ." And when the enemy abandoned his horse and darted up an arroyo or an escarpment, the soldier was ill prepared to pursue and fight on foot. And yet, the enemies abandoned precaution "the moment they think they are safe within their own territory," so the only way to subdue them was "continuous offensive war in their own territory."[18] A century later, the United States Army would reach the same conclusion.

Rubí saw no advantage in befriending the Apaches: They should be driven from every Spanish mission, presidio and settlement on the frontier and exterminated or forced to enter missions in the interior. "We should consider as our frontier neighbors and transborder counterparts . . . only the perfidious Lipan Apaches," he said. Their presence, he warned, would only draw their enemies.[19]

Rubí proposed choking off Apache raiding trails with an outer line of fifteen presidios from the Gulf of California to the Bahia del Espiritu Santo in Texas. A campaign could trap the Lipans between Spanish forces and the northern tribes. It was a marked shift in policy. While some opposed the loss of their presidios, bureaucrats in Texas began to extol the Comanches as potential allies and disparage the Lipans as a waste of the king's resources. Anybody who had befriended or defended the Apaches, like Terán (who already had plenty of enemies), would be tarred with the same brush. Settlers, however, feared the northerners more.[20]

CHAPTER

Coahuila

[A]mong all the nations [the Apaches] are the most fearsome not only because of the firearms that they now have acquired . . . but also for their valor and intrepidity and because they are not accustomed to flee, preferring to win the engagement or die . . .

— Hugo Oconór, 1777[1]

C oahuila, the Lipans' new refuge, sprawled from the Medina River to the Big Bend of the Rio Grande to the Bolsón de Mapimí. Settlements were isolated, and the presidios undermanned. In spring 1770, three thousand Apaches camped across the Rio Grande from the presidio of San Juan Bautista, and Governor Jacobo Ugarte y Loyola had just 115 soldiers at the presidios of Monclova, San Juan Bautista del Río Grande and Santa Rosa del Sacramento. Settlers began to slip away. In July 1771 Apaches brazenly attacked the presidio of Santa Rosa at noon with the governor present and stole six hundred horses. Soldiers pursued, but their horses wore out after 180 miles.[2]

That October, Bernardo de Gálvez led a campaign beyond the Pecos and attacked an Apache camp at dawn, killing twenty-eight Apaches and seizing thirty-six prisoners and the horse herd. Gálvez would conduct three campaigns against Apaches identified as Lipan, Natagé, "Culcogendi," and "Tisyeendis." This is one of the earliest references to the Cuelcahen Ndé, or People of the Tall Grass, and the Tú sís Ndé, Big Water People.[3] The People of the Tall Grass would later be called Llaneros. The Big Water People were a Lipan band.

On May 18, 1772, more than three hundred Lipan warriors swept the haciendas of Sardinas, Posuelos, and San Miguel, the ranchos of

Los Menchacas and Santa Gertrudis, and the towns of Nadadores and San Buenaventura. Within two hours, they killed 23 people and took 22 captives and 954 horses and mules. Losses would have been worse, Ugarte said, if his troops hadn't arrived when they did.

It was another argument against moving the presidios, as far as Ugarte was concerned. Towns and haciendas would go undefended, and enemies in rugged mountains were in no danger of pursuit.[4] The trouble was "the multitude of Lipans" pretending to be friends who stole, murdered and took innocent children as captives. The Mescaleros and Natagés were doing their share of killing and robbing, and the Julimeños kept Lipans apprised of Spanish movements. The only remedy, Ugarte told the viceroy, was to move them all to presidios or send them overseas. Viceroy Antonio María Bucareli waved off his concerns but had to admit "the Lipans hold many horses, mules, and captives which they bring daily to trade in the presidios of Monclova and Aguaverde."

The Lipans and their allies, now concentrated in Coahuila and little dissipated by war and disease, were flexing their muscles. Because they knew of Spanish overtures to their enemies, they began to reach out to other tribes. The evolving alliances and attendant uncertainties were fertile ground for intrigue in which individuals could upend the well-laid plans of leaders.[5]

In Texas, Governor Juan María Vicencio, Barón de Ripperdá, wanted to "cut off the pernicious friendship" between the Apaches and the Bidais, who were then attempting to broker a peace between the Apaches and the Tejas. In July the Tejas visited some fifteen hundred Lipan warriors gathered on the Nueces, Frio and Rio Grande. The following month a French agent in Ripperdá's employ, Athanasio de Mézierés, pressured the Bidais to end their friendship with the Apaches and successfully nipped the budding Teja-Apache alliance.[6]

Ripperdá was trying to draw the Nations of the North into an alliance, but a single Apache neophyte hindered his plans. José Miguel grew up at the San Antonio mission but disappeared periodically to go live with his people. When he left seven months earlier, he took his wife, her father and mother, and ten mission Indians. During a visit by the Northern Nations, he returned to San Antonio, killed three Comanches, and carried off three women and a girl. He also killed the Taovaya chief who came to ratify a treaty with Ripperdá and took from the dead chief a Spanish flag and Ripperdá's gifts.

Ripperdá jailed José Miguel in July. From behind bars, the irrepressible Apache tried to entice visiting Wichitas to join him with promises of horses. José Miguel later claimed that he would rejoin the mission and bring in the rest of the apostates if they let him go with the priest who was seeking his release. Ripperdá would have sent José Miguel to labor in the mines, but the priest wouldn't hear of it.[7]

◄ ►

Hugo O'Conor, an Irish expatriate, called Oconór by the Spanish, became the new commandant inspector of the northern frontier. In early December 1772 he set out with three flying companies and Indian auxiliaries to select sites for the relocated presidios prescribed by the Regulation of 1772. If possible, they would deliver a blow to Lipans and other Apaches. Oconór ordered a presidio at La Junta. To the east, along the Big Bend of the Rio Grande, he chose the Arroyo of San Carlos for the relocated Cerro Gordo presidio. Following fresh tracks, they struck a camp on December 25, killing three and recovering two hundred stolen horses. At the San Vicente ford the concentration of tracks pitting the sand spoke of high traffic—perfect for the relocated presidio of San Sabá.

Unnerved by Oconór's presence, Lipan chiefs Bigotes and Juan Tuerto came to San Fernando in early January 1773 to seek peace with the Red Captain, as Indian people named him for the color of his hair. Bigotes "marveled to see so many Spaniards," said Oconór.[8] The Spanish knew Bigotes as one of the chiefs who sought a mission in Texas, lived at the Escondido mission in Coahuila where the Apaches rebelled, and camped near the Mission San Lorenzo without joining it.[9] A few days later, chiefs Casaca Colorada, Panocha and Zapato Bordado joined them; the latter two had lived at San Lorenzo. The three were among a veritable city of Lipans with more than a thousand warriors at the confluence of the Pecos and Rio Grande, a stronghold of deep canyons. They negotiated with the Red Captain for several weeks, as large numbers of miserable, hungry Lipans streamed in to San Fernando.

The Irishman demanded that they turn over all their Spanish prisoners, livestock and goods and agree to live in pueblos and missions. This time, nobody offered himself for lessons in Spanish civics and religion. They denied having Spanish prisoners, livestock or goods and adamantly refused to enter missions, but they would join the Red Captain in a war against the Comanches. Oconór agreed to the alliance. He had no intention of honoring it, and neither did they.

In April 1773 Lipans rode along with Oconór and his troops as they reconnoitered more sites. Upstream from the confluence of the San Rodrigo and the Rio Grande were many Lipan camps, all the more reason to build on that spot the new presidio of Santiago de Monclova. Twelve days later, he sited the Santa Rosa presidio at the Arroyo of Aguaverde.[10]

While troops were absent, Lipans attacked a priest and three armed civilians on the road from Monclova to the Rio Grande missions, wounding three and taking their baggage and mules. The priest recognized the son of Bigotes and others from his ranchería. Not long after, Indians drove off a herd of cows from Santa Rosa. Citizens were terrified, and Ugarte feared the miners would quit working.[11] Two recovered captive Spanish girls said Mescaleros planned to join the Lipans in destroying Coahuila's two new presidios, as well as Santa Rosa and San Fernando. Already concerned about the vulnerability of his embryonic presidios, Oconór determined to make a preemptive attack on the Apaches above Big Bend.

In numbing cold after a late November storm, they clashed in a rugged canyon of the Sierra del Mogano. Hundreds of warriors raced toward their attackers but fell back before the Spanish charge and scattered, their blood staining snow-covered rocks. More than forty Apaches died, and although many of the wounded escaped into the mountains, the Spanish would find thirty-six of their bodies months later in a large cave. The attack so alarmed the Lipans that they abandoned their camps along the Pecos and scattered.[12]

Lipans had suffered another setback not long before. A presidial commander of Monclova heard such a thunderous tramp of horses' hooves, he couldn't imagine where they could be coming from. It was the sound of fleeing Lipans. An exhausted man staggered into a camp near Aguaverde to warn that Comanches and Lipans were fighting on the Rio San Diego, near Santa Rosa. Despite their shock at finding more than three hundred Comanches upon them, the Lipans fought valiantly from morning to night and lost just seven killed and three taken captive, but Captains Malla, Panocha, and Rivera lost their horses, "of which there were many," said Adjutant Inspector Roque de Medina.

Comanches had now breached the Lipans' safe havens in Coahuila. Where would they be safe? They took Medina to their rancherías at Sacramento and on the San Diego so he could see what the Comanches had done. The Lipan captains wanted Medina to accompany them in pursuit of their enemies, but he demurred, saying he didn't have enough horses. Because you are afraid, they said angrily, you should give us your powder and shot, and we will go alone.

Medina retorted that he would do neither. He castigated them for not defending the Spaniards against their Mescalero friends and disparaged their peace as insincere. Our enemies have robbed us, and now you want to rob us too, Panocha said heatedly. Medina departed in a huff. Lipans pulled up their camps and moved closer to the Santa Rosa and Monclova presidios and the Rio San Diego headwaters.[13]

Ugarte was sure the Lipans would recoup their losses from Coahuila's herds and demanded that Oconór go to Aguaverde. In late March 1774, Oconór found the presidios at San Carlos and San Vicente quiet, but to placate Ugarte, he surprised a Lipan camp on the Rio Grande and took forty prisoners. That fall Oconór made peace with Cabello Largo, principal chief of the Lipans, and Viceroy Bucareli conferred on him the title "General of the Lipan Apaches."[14]

◄ ►

The clatter of guns and swords, the staccato of voices, and rumble of horses plodding across the northern provinces announced the beginning of one of the biggest campaigns ever attempted against the Apaches. In September 1775 more than two thousand troops from four provinces would form themselves into the pincers of Oconór's multi-pronged attack. Ugarte, with 325 soldiers, armed settlers and Indian allies, would march north to the old San Sabá presidio and turn west toward the Pecos. They would join Captain Raphael Martínez Pacheco's ninety men and continue up the Pecos, driving the Apaches west into the Big Bend mountains, where Captain Manuel Muñoz's 120 men would be waiting. Oconór, with 294 soldiers, would proceed north from Nueva Vizcaya.[15]

Ugarte hadn't counted on two obstacles: the unpalatable taste, steep banks and swift current of the lower Pecos, later called "the most formidable natural obstacle in Texas," and the Lipans. At Nogalera the newly anointed Lipan general, Cabello Largo, asked if his people were the targets of this campaign. Ugarte assured him they weren't. Cabello Largo spent the night in their camp and then announced a buffalo hunt. The next day more Lipan captains arrived: Poca Ropa, Boca Tuerta, El Cielo, El Flaco, Panocha, Rivera, Javielillo, Pajarito, and Manteca Mucha.

From the San Rodrigo presidio, Ugarte's troops headed for the Llano. Two days out, they passed Lipan rancherías that were curiously devoid of women and children, probably because they were hiding in the high country. The following day, eight more Lipans appeared to retrieve horses they left at the start of the buffalo hunt. Cabello Largo ordered two of them to serve as guides to San Sabá. Troops scouting that river found no sign of Apaches, including the Lipans hunting buffalo. In mid-October Ugarte's spies wandered along the steep, barren canyons of the Rio San Pedro (Devils River) without detecting any sign of Apaches other than tracks leaving the San Pedro that joined and traveled north. Those tracks were about twenty days old—the amount of time the expedition had been underway.

Along the Pecos and San Pedro, in the Guadalupe Mountains, parties of soldiers and spies peered into canyons, studied likely camping places and water holes, and followed old trails, but the Apaches had vanished, leaving abandoned rancherías as evidence of their passing. On the Pecos was a well-established but vacant camp with corn fields.

"The signs show there were many of them," wrote Captain Vicente Rodriguez. "After they harvested the fields, the people scattered, some to the north and some to the south. There were many watermelons and other kinds of melons they plant. The grazing was good in this place." Back on the San Pedro in early December soldiers found that about one hundred animals, coming from the headwaters of the Concho, crossed their own tracks as they traveled upriver.

Not until December 22 did they find some Apaches to engage. Six leagues from the San Pedro headwaters, they saw four Indians leaving a bend in the river, and many more descending a mountain. The auxiliaries sent to cut them off were attacked. Only the timely arrival of Lieutenant Juan Bautista de Elguezabal and his fifty men saved them. Troops managed to kill three and wound three of the sixty Apaches sprinting over rough terrain.[16]

Oconór had little luck catching Gileño Apaches in southwestern New Mexico, so he joined troops from San Elizario and El Paso to attack a large band of Mescaleros in the Sacramento Mountains of New Mexico. They killed forty Apaches and took eight prisoners and three hundred horses. In the same camp were Gileños, Natagés, the Lipan bands of El Ligero and Bigotes,[17] and a band not previously known.

Spies captured an Indian man and woman on the Pecos who said they were looking for the Lipans. They had escaped from the battle in the Sacramentos where they said the leather jackets killed or captured all the Lipiyanes, members of the confederacy who would soon take their place on the historical stage. Overall, Oconór was disappointed. Ugarte had only six casualties to report. Raiding resumed soon after the campaign ended.[18]

◄►

Poca Ropa, possibly anticipating more hostilities, came on September 4, 1776, to assure Ugarte of his friendship. The new principal chief blamed

Mescaleros for recent raids and offered to lead troops to their camps. Poca Ropa later delivered five Mescaleros, but Ugarte wasn't persuaded.[19]

Ten days later a new campaign was under way. Oconór would lead one detachment toward the Mimbres Mountains of southern New Mexico and then turn toward El Paso. Muñoz would lead a second prong from his presidio of La Junta to the northern Big Bend area and continue towards El Paso. If the Apaches escaped their trap, the two columns would move north, and a third prong from New Mexico, commanded by Lieutenant Diego de Borica, would press south along the Rio Grande.

Striking five times between September 14 and the end of October, they killed twenty-seven and captured eighteen. In El Paso Oconór collapsed, his strength spent. Lieutenant Colonel Francisco Bellido pushed on to the Pecos and by December 10 his men had killed forty Apaches and captured forty-six, plus 119 animals. Oconór rallied for a march into the Sacramento and Sierra Blanca mountains and blocked any escape westward; the New Mexicans prevented an escape north. Apaches hurried northeast toward their reliable havens on the Pecos and, assuming they were out of danger, either stopped to hunt buffalo or joined hunters. A Comanche war party descended on their camp and slaughtered three hundred families. Only two people escaped. The Spanish were shocked at what they saw: tipis splattered with blood, bodies everywhere, so much buffalo meat, the Comanches left it to rot along with the bodies. Oconór estimated the Apaches remaining in the region at no more than twenty families.

The Irishman, and a few historians, believed he had broken the Apache grip on the northern provinces,[20] but he had broken only his own health. The Spanish always underestimated Apache numbers and resourcefulness. Their population was so large and dispersed that for every Apache counted in one camp, there were many more in remote locations. After losses, they replenished their numbers with captives. Their trade network was so resilient that even as Spanish commanders plotted against them, their countrymen were trading gunpowder for horses. Eastern Apaches would bedevil the region for another century.

CHAPTER

Labors and Designs

[T]he astute Lipanes now engage in the manufacture of powder, having learned the ingredients of which it is composed, perhaps, from some of our own people . . .

— Croix, 1778[1]

In their villages along the Rio Grande, the People grew corn and gathered seeds and grains. It was difficult to hunt buffalo, but they had all the wild cattle and horses they could take. The Spanish captains prodded them to move across the river, but it wasn't safe. The Comanches, as numerous as thistles, still threatened, and the treacherous governor, Ripperdá, favored their enemies. More relatives joined their camps, and the larger camps kept their enemies away. Their allies, the Lipiyans, lived nearby and would ride with them. So would the Natagés. They still had many friends among the Spanish people. They would stay here, with plenty of rough country at their backs, where they had everything they needed.[2]

◀ ▶

On a bright, moonlit night in June 1776, Indians attacked eight men and a woman who left the Rio Grande Presidio. Two men, Juan Trabieso and Francisco Casanoba, were lanced, and the Indians made off with horses, mules and merchandise. When raiders took the reins from her hand, María Josepha de Flores recognized them as Lipans and Apaches, even though their faces were smeared with mud. She threw herself to the ground and crawled away on all fours through the horses as the others fled. She arrived back at the presidio a week later.[3]

Familiar with the settlements, the Lipans and their allies could readily raid, replenish their herds, and increase their numbers with captive children, who "are worse in war action, as they serve as guides and act with greater cruelty than the savages," said officials.[4]

Juan Domingo Ochoa, a teenager captured while herding goats near Saltillo in 1776, saw them kill a herder who put up a fight. At Rancho de la Popa they killed two women and took three infants and some horses. Two of the infants died of hunger on the journey. Spaniards caught up with them at Popa Peak, and the Apaches defended themselves with guns, bows, arrows and lances.

At their ranchería, they beat Juan Domingo, cut off his left ear, and ordered him to care for the horses of his new master. Many families lived in the camp; one group had just joined after fleeing from Comanches. He saw other Spanish captives—boys and women from Coahuila and Nueva Vizcaya. A mulatto man with an Apache wife and a former inmate of the Durango jail lived in this group and tried to persuade the boy to remain by extolling the free life of the Indians. When the men were out raiding, Juan Domingo escaped.[5]

◄ ►

In 1776 Frenchman Teodoro de Croix took command of the newly created Provincias Internas, which included Nueva Vizcaya, Coahuila, Texas, New Mexico, Sinaloa, Sonora and the Californias. Relocating the presidios was a failure, he said. Apache raids, more frequent and more damaging than before, had all but ruined both Coahuila and Nueva Vizcaya. Presidial horse herds were worn out from chasing Lipans and Mescaleros.[6]

Lipans, with their herds of mostly stolen stock, hovered near the same presidial line intended to keep them in check. Some were friendly to the Spanish, "but mixed in with them in disguise are those who commit hostilities against the said line," said Ripperdá. Croix ordered the presidio of Monclova to be returned to its namesake and Aguaverde and San Sabá to be moved to Santa Rosa and San Fernando.[7]

Croix had no faith in peace with Apaches, a tribe of individualists scattered broadly across the landscape. Because they seemed to fear only the Comanches, an alliance with the Comanches seemed the most promising strategy. Provincial authorities were inclined to agree, but had reservations. Northern tribes had honored their treaties but not the Comanches, and yet if the Spanish allied with Lipans, they would still be troubled by Lipan depredations while inviting greater harm from the Comanches.

The Comanches had five thousand warriors. Apaches had the same number only if Navajos and Gileños were counted, which meant the Eastern Apaches were outnumbered. The scale tipped farther with the combined 1,500 warriors of the Tejas, Taovayas, Tawakonis, Yscanis, Quitseis, and Tonkawas. And they were amply supplied with English and French guns.[8]

◄ ►

In his report to Croix, Oconór described Eastern Apachería using their Spanish and Apache names: Faraones (Selcaisendé), Ranchería of Pasqual (Culcahende), Ranchería of El Ligero (Chahugindé), Ranchería of Alonso (Yncagende), Ranchería of Capitan Bigotes (Sigilande), Mescaleros (Zetosendé), and Natagés (Zetocendé). (The *jen-ne* or *ende* means "people.")[9] Most of these groups were the extant members of the northern confederacy; their southern allies were the Mescaleros and Natagés.

By at least 1771 the Lipans were divided into two groups. Upper Lipans, who called themselves Tuedinendé or Tuetinnini (No Water People), lived to the north in Coahuila, along the Pecos, and in western Texas and were often with Natagés and Mescaleros. Lower Lipans, who called themselves Tusisndé (Big Water People), lived on the Gulf Coast and the lower Rio Grande in southeastern Texas, Nuevo León and Tamaulipas.[10]

Pasqual's Culcahende, also called Cuelcahendé and Llaneros, could only be the reconstituted Cuartelejos; they lived between the Lipans and Natagés and were closely allied with both. The Lipiyanes, known by then but not included in Oconór's report, were most likely the Carlanas who once lived in northern New Mexico.

Twenty years later, Antonio Cordero, who could speak Apache, would describe the same groups and territories but state that the Llaneros, called Cuelcajen-ne, had three subdivisions—Natagés, Lipiyanes and Llaneros—and occupied the plains and sands between the Pecos and the Colorado. However, repeated references in Spanish reports list them separately with different leaders and territories. Mescaleros, or Sejen-ne, lived west of the Llaneros in the mountains near the Pecos and appeared more often in the Bolsón de Mapimí as Lipans collected in the east. Mescaleros and Natagés had virtually the same Apache name, leading some scholars to believe they were the same group, but they too were closely related, separate groups. A Spanish governor described the Lipans, Lipiyans and Natagés as friends who were separate from the Mescaleros. The Faraons, or Yntajen-ne, lived in the Sierra Blanca and Sacramento Mountains of southeastern New Mexico and often joined the Mescaleros and Natagés in raids.[11]

◄ ►

Oconór informed Croix that the Lipans were at peace, for the most part, and it didn't seem proper to punish all for the excesses of a few. The Lipans should be accorded, under a provision of the Regulation of 1772 requiring good relations with peaceful tribes, "the best treatment and friendship, tolerating in them some mistakes or slight excesses."[12] Croix was unmoved. In his own melodramatic view, the Lipans "came into the presidios, overbearing and proud, and with hands bloody from victims, vassals of the king, whom they had sacrificed to their fury . . ."

Touring the provinces in 1777, he and Father Juan Agustin Morfi solemnly witnessed one abandoned ranch after another in northern Coahuila—silent, windblown testimony to Apache attacks. Croix believed his arrival with troops calmed the Lipans' unrest: "They immediately gave guarantees, which remorse for their crimes and fear of their punishment extracted." Lipans offered to deliver two rancherías of Mescaleros camped close to the presidio of Aguaverde as a gesture of good faith; after a half-hearted raid, they moved their families far away. Croix considered it "a happy beginning of my labors and designs."

At the Presidio del Rio Grande, near present Guerrero, they met more Lipans. "On getting up from siesta we found the fort full of Lipan Apaches," Morfi wrote. "It was the band of Josecillo el Manso, who under the guise of peace had come to find out what was going on." Josecillo, born at the Mission of Peyotes, was captured by the Lipans at age six or seven and raised as a Lipan. "Through industry and shame-lessness he came to be a chief. He is very bold and has done great dam-age in the province . . ." Lipans circulated in the streets and on the plaza, visiting friends.[13]

The Lipans, said Father Morfi, "are tall, straight, well formed, robust, free and easy, of regular features," and they were astute and bold. He allowed that some Lipans "have more honor than they are credited with." They were clean and decent in their dress but "of las-civious customs," probably a reference to polygamy, but while the captains might have several wives, most Lipans had just one. "They are zealous of the honor of their wives and daughters," he wrote. Morfi remarked on prostitutes "who accompany them on their mili-tary routes and on hunting parties, the wives remaining in charge of the family and household at the rancheria." These were probably female captives.

Men became captains after performing deeds of valor; the greater the valor, the more respect given. Lipans ate buffalo, venison, bear and cattle but differed from other Apaches in not eating horse meat. Even though Morfi had seen the Lipans' cornfields, he said "their laziness and wandering spirit make them enemies of cultivation."

Morfí mistakenly believed that Lipans worshipped the sun "and other ridiculous figures made by their hands." Religious acts involved smoking tobacco or other herbs and blowing the smoke to "the object of their barbarous adoration." Apaches recognized a supreme being, but it wasn't the whites' God of wrath or reward. Medicine men carried figures made of stuffed skins resembling a human with a painted face. They weren't idols but objects they considered sacred. The medicine men—Morfi considered them charlatans—were akin to priests who also practiced the healing arts and blessed any new tipi or wickiup during a ceremony.[14]

◄ ►

Croix convened regional councils as he traveled, from December 1777 to April 1778. His plan was to unite the tribes of the north with hunters from Louisiana, commanded by Bernardo de Gálvez, in a joint campaign against the Eastern Apaches. The seasoned officers on the councils approved his plan but wanted at least three thousand men.[15] Until then they should suspend hostilities against the Lipans. "It is considered very urgent to increase the forces to keep the Lipans, who are the right arm of the Apache (nation) from bringing about the ruin of these provinces quickly," Croix wrote.

The Frenchman rode toward Chihuahua, dogged by Lipans who probably helped five hundred Mescaleros attack the party.[16] When Croix reached Chihuahua in April, the Gileños had asked for peace, and so had Apaches living in the Sacramento, Petaca and Organ ranges of New Mexico, probably Mescaleros, Natagés, and Faraons. Croix ordered presidial commanders to accept nothing short of total surrender and an agreement to settle in designated pueblos. The Mescaleros refused those terms but promised to stop raiding.[17]

Croix's goal in September became the defeat of the Lipans and other eastern Apaches, but forcing them from their lands meant the Comanches and other northern tribes could move closer and cause new trouble. Athanase de Méziéres, Spain's agent to the northern tribes, was stitching together an alliance of Comanches and Norteños,[18] when international conflict doomed the grand plans.

In February 1779 the king informed Croix that he opposed a war on the Apaches. Spain was about to enter the American colonists' war against Great Britain (Spain declared war on June 21). He was unwilling to send more men and resources to the northern provinces, and he objected to exterminating any Indians, preferring persuasion and peace. Croix's stipulations were overly rigid, he said; the Apaches should be allowed to live in their usual way. Generous gifts would lead them to appreciate Spanish life. He even recommended providing firearms for their hunting and defense. The Lipans, Croix sniffed, "are not worthy of the sovereign piety."[19]

Croix was left with the puny tools of diplomacy and intrigue, but in this regard, circumstances shaped up nicely. Domingo Cabello y Robles became governor of Texas in 1778. As governor of Nicaragua, Cabello increased Indian tribute payments and campaigned against Indians committing depredations. Now he railed at the weakness of Texas, which was at the mercy of its tribes and without the soldiers to subjugate them.[20] Treachery, however, proved as useful as soldiers.

When the Lipans returned to Texas, they were on good terms with the new governor, or so they thought. Cabello gave a gun to Josecillo's son, Xaviercillo, with Croix's blessings, and he reciprocated with live bison and buffalo skins to honor the king. On March 6, 1779, eighty Lipans and Natagés camped outside the San Antonio presidio. Chiefs El Joyoso, Jiró, Agur, Roque, Xaviercillo, and the sons of Manteca Mucha and Casaca had urgent business with Cabello. He allowed them in without weapons.[21]

Joyoso, the spokesman, shook Cabello's hand. Tonkawas and others had killed or captured more than three hundred people and stolen many horses, he said. Certain the Tonkawas then hunting between the Guadalupe and Colorado rivers had participated, they were bent on revenge and wanted the governor's help. Cabello declined. The Tonkawas were his friends, he said, and he wouldn't fight them unless they gave him cause. He gave the Apaches each two piloncillos and a box of cigars, and they left.

Eleven days later they returned proudly with four Tonkawa scalps, four captives and booty. Joyoso gave a girl captive to "his very good friend Don Luis Menchaca." Cabello offered eight horses for a woman and two boys, thinking the boys could be converted and that restoring the woman would warm his friendship with the Tonkawas. The Lipans refused,[22] but to demonstrate their good will, they promised to stop raiding, broke up many of their camps, and delivered more than thirty horses stolen from San Fernando.

Captain Francisco Martinez sensed an opportunity. Preying on the Lipans' fears of seeing the Norteños among their rancherías using Spanish weapons, he provoked a Lipan raid on the Mescaleros, who struck back. Gloating over "the excellent beginnings of their disunion," Croix anticipated the "forced reduction of one or the other."[23]

It was a peculiar development. Apache bands operated independently and played their hands as they saw fit. The more aggressive groups might steal horses from fellow Apaches, but affiliated groups didn't fight one another. This eruption reflected long simmering differences. Mescaleros had such contempt for Lipans because of their friendship with the Spanish that they stopped intermarrying; Lipans, who were sometimes blamed for Mescalero raids, disparaged the Mescaleros as troublemakers.

In late April rumors burned through San Antonio that in Coahuila Governor Juan de Ugalde and his presidial captains were discussing peace with the Mescaleros to gain their alliance in a war on the Lipans. San Antonio citizens were "very anxious about the harm which will befall their friends the Apache-Lipans" and had such affection for the Lipans that Cabello feared they would inform them.[24] That summer the Lipans and Mescaleros clashed. Many Lipans died, and the Mescaleros took six hundred horses plus plunder. Ugalde calmed the Lipans before they could avenge their losses. Croix was elated.[25]

In early August Joyoso came to Menchaca, alone and on foot. Relating his troubles with the Natagés and Mescaleros, he asked his friend if the Spaniards of San Antonio were also against him. Menchaca responded truthfully that there were no movements against the Lipans there.[26] Weeks later Cabello was settling into a long visit with five Tejas, when he learned that five Lipan chiefs and a great number of their people were on their way. The governor's face betrayed his apprehensions, arousing his visitors, but, regaining his composure, he informed the Tejas about the approaching Lipans and inflated the story to say the Lipans were looking for a fight, and the Tejas should leave and spread the word.

The next afternoon, five Lipan chiefs dismounted at Cabello's house—Josef Grande, Josef Chiquito, Joyoso, El Manco Roque, and Manteca Mucha. Outside the gate were six hundred of their people, with sixteen stolen mules to return. It's unfortunate the Tejas aren't here because we wish to make friends and return captives, they said. We will befriend other tribes as well but not the Comanches. That was the last thing Cabello wanted: "[I]t behooves us to cultivate their old enmity."[27]

Croix debated anew which group was more deserving of his favor. The Lipans' "old although unfaithful friendship" plus their renewed fears of the northern tribes "would make them more faithful in our alliance." On the other hand, Spain would then have to defend the Lipans against all their enemies and incur the wrath of the Norteños. The Mescaleros were "more perfidious, cruel, and barbarous than the Lipan [and] not worthy of our honorable alliance," and yet in September Croix formalized peace with the Mescaleros, reasoning that peace with both would provoke the insecurity of both.[28]

◄►

Cabello and Méziéres in September 1779 entertained the Tonkawa Chief Mocho and seventy-five of his people, who enjoyed Spanish hospitality until early October. During a dance the alcalde spotted a Lipan in the crowd. Back from a buffalo hunt and camped in the hills of Puerto Viejo, eight leagues away, they wanted to know when the Tonkawas were leaving. That night Joyoso and Josef Chiquito called young Francisco Menchaca by name as he returned to his house and told the boy not to be afraid. They outnumbered the Tonkawas, they said, and if not for the governor, would have trounced them. They asked again when the Tonkawas would leave; they were eager to see Cabello. Awakened abruptly, Cabello snapped that he didn't know when the Tonkawas would leave and ordered the Lipans to let the Tonkawas pass without a fight. The following day he made Mocho a captain and encouraged the Tonkawas to be on their way.[29]

On October 26 Roque, Joyoso, Josef Chiquito and Manteca Mucha got their audience. "Utterly inflamed" in their feelings toward the Natagés, Mescaleros and Gileños, they vowed revenge and asked Cabello's help. He would only help if they spoke with Croix in Chihuahua and chose one leader to negotiate because their profusion of chiefs "was annoying me greatly." Traveling to Chihuahua was inconceivable—they had too many enemies there. The chiefs left abruptly after learning the Comanches had just stolen four hundred of their horses.[30]

Reminders of their common enemies brought reconciliation. Lipans in particular faced greater hardships. Unable to hunt buffalo, they were reduced to stealing cattle and traveled all the way to the coast to hunt deer. Their enemies no longer found them on the banks of the Rio Grande because they hovered near presidios. The Mescaleros resumed raiding.

Croix's divide-and-conquer scheme misfired, along with his Comanche strategy. Comanches had overrun the province and stolen so many horses and mules from the Béxar presidio that Cabello couldn't retaliate. In January 1780 Lipans provided horses and mules to soldiers for a campaign against the Comanches. The Spanish killed nine or ten Comanches and lost a soldier, whom the Lipans mourned. When Chief Casaca and some of his people asked to trade for Comanche spoils, the abrasive Cabello insulted their courage and told them to get their own by fighting the Comanches as the Spaniards did. Croix's attitude toward the Lipans softened. Like Oconór, he advised his successor in April to overlook their defects.[31]

That fall, Comanches attacked Laredo, ran off more than three hundred horses, and retreated through an Apache camp, an old tactic. On October 8, citizens surprised Lipans camped at the Nueces, killing two men and a woman and taking more than five hundred horses and mules. "The Lipan-Apaches are so inflamed about the episode that they are planning the most terrible revenge against the people of Laredo and the other populated areas along the Rio Grande," Cabello wrote.[32] The Lipans poured hostilities on Camargo, Mier, Reynosa, Revilla and Laredo until farmers couldn't irrigate, sow crops or tend cattle. Residents wouldn't venture more than five leagues from their villages, and merchants refused to travel the roads.[33]

On January 14, 1781, Lipans arrived in Béxar on foot "and in utter defeat." They were hunting buffalo near the Pedernales River when Comanches attacked. They fought hard but without guns saved themselves only by hiding in the woods. One man was killed, and they lost all their horses. Cabello was convinced that half were Comanches, while the rest were the Tawakonis and Taovayas he had just entertained and given ammunition.[34]

◄►

Disease, an enemy with unlimited weaponry, waged its own war. In 1778 a smallpox epidemic swept into Texas from Louisiana, descending upon Indians and Spaniards alike. After ravaging Béxar, Bucareli and Natchitoches, it spread to smaller tribes, nearly wiping out the Adaes and reducing the Bidais to a remnant. During the summer it spread to the Tawakonis, Taovayas, Tonkawas and Kadohadachos. It was also devastating to the Comanches.

The Apaches, scattered over a distance, may have been spared, but in fall 1780 a double epidemic of smallpox and diphtheria struck down many Lipans before it waned a few months later.[35] Cabello hoped "that not a single Lipan-Apache lives through it." When smallpox entered Béxar, it taught the governor some humility: "One does not hear or see anything day or night except the tolling of bells and the sight of burials."

Lipans, "decimated to a degree inexpressible," flocked into the missions, "which have been inundated with such people," Cabello wrote. "But their coming to the missions is not saving these people from nevertheless dying in great numbers." Lipans abandoned victims in the place they died, leaving their possessions and horses. Cabello feared that some new disease might arise "from the infestation of so many cadavers that are being left to the elements . . ."

Just three years earlier, Father Morfi observed that disease had limited, but not necessarily reduced, the Lipan population. "[I]f it were not for their having suffered from smallpox and continual warfare, in which they live," he wrote, they would populate the region, "such being the fecundity with which they propagate their specie." This double epidemic, beyond the ministrations of priests and skills of medicine men, devastated the Lipans and began the long decline of their population. The most deadly was smallpox, which stalked the population every sixteen years and lingered for a year at a time, reported a French scientist in 1827. Tribes responded by "seeking the emptiest, most deserted places they can find, abandoning the sick along the way and changing their camp each time one of them dies."[36]

CHAPTER

New Allies

The Lipan Indians . . . can easily make an alliance with other Indians
in the interior, which they regularly do . . .

— *Revilla Gigedo, 1783*[1]

After losing all their chiefs in the epidemic, Tonkawas embraced
El Mocho, a Lipan captive they raised from childhood. On
November 24, 1780, Mocho slipped into Cabello's house at 6 a.m.
and explained that he would have attacked the Lipans and stolen their
horses, but Comanches and others hindered his movements, and he
heard that smallpox was everywhere. Cabello snapped that the Lipans
were so reduced by disease that the Tonkawas could easily have taken
their horses. The next day several Lipans showed up. Come to our
camp, and we will give you horses, they told Mocho. Cabello snarled
that the Lipans would just kill him and dance with his scalp, and Mocho
declined. After more Lipans arrived with the same offer, Cabello gave
Mocho and his companion horses so they could leave in the night.[2]
In 1782 their paths merged. Mocho proposed a trade fair in November and December. Cabello ordered the Tonkawas to stay away from
Lipans and threatened to kill Mocho if he persisted. The Tonkawas
ignored him. Cabello asked for soldiers to punish anyone trading with
the Lipans, but Croix couldn't spare a man.

◄►

In November 1782 four thousand people of many nations gathered beneath the dense, cypress canopy along the spring-fed Guadalupe. Women prepared their best foods for feasts, and people drew their fanciest buckskins from parfleches for dances. Amid the laughter and embraces were tears, as people learned of family and friends lost to disease and war. The People lost their share, but the epidemics bypassed distant, isolated groups, who now reinforced their decimated brothers and sisters. The People were still strong and had so many weapons that they no longer clung to the skirts of the presidios. Boldly, they reclaimed their old country. They hunted buffalo again.

Their chiefs had always extended their hands to make friends of other nations, but now they desired even more allies, even among those who were enemies. Here were Tejas and Tonkawas, who suffered more from the sickness than themselves. The People drove before them many, many horses—a few taken from presidios, the rest Spanish horses that stampeded during storms and mixed with mustang herds. Usually, the Spanish paid them for such horses, but they hoped to trade for guns.[3]

Their carefully tended friendships and alliances had allowed the Lipans to resist thirty years of Spanish meddling. They still traded horses and mules for rifles and powder from the Cocos, Mayeyes, Bidais, Atakapas, and the Akokisas.[4] Big Water Lipans living near the coast and Bahía del Espíritu Santo transformed their off-and-on relationship with the Karankawas into an alliance, thanks to Chief Josecillo. When the Karankawas killed hapless sailors who landed on the coast, they sold the firearms to Lipans.[5] Through the Mayeyes, a Tonkawan group, they could reach the rest of the Tonkawas (Tonkawas proper, the Yojuanes, and the Yerbipiames.) All of these groups were so diminished by disease that new alliances presented not just strategic advantage but lifelines in a shifting political landscape.

When the trade fair got underway, the interpreter Andrés Courbiére, wearing Indian attire, circulated among two thousand Apaches (Lipans, Mescaleros and Natagés), about six hundred Tonkawas, and three hundred Tejas, Akokisas, Bidais, Cocos and Mayeyes. During the fair, Tonkawas joined the Lipans to fight a big war party of Tawakonis, Taovayas, Wichitas and Iscanis on the Colorado River. The Apaches brought more than three thousand horses to trade but by the fair's end on December 25 had acquired a disappointing 270 guns because Spain's war with Great Britain had siphoned away weapons.

Mocho circulated through the gathering, trying to unite tribes under his leadership. He boasted that he would defeat the Spaniards and their friends and staged a reunion with his Lipan relatives, to little effect; Apache leaders didn't trust him. Croix ordered Mocho's assassination, but Felipe de Neve, who replaced Croix in 1783, recommended that "death is dealt to him at the hand of his own."[6] The Spaniards dispatched the troublesome chief the following summer.[7]

◄ ►

Cabello chastised the Tejas for their new alliance with the Lipans, when they visited in September 1783. To win back their chief, Baltazar Bigotes, he ostentatiously presented him with a uniform, baton, flag and patent, and one of his own horses. The Teja then rode away in the company of Lipans and bestowed rifles, horses and mules, including those Cabello had given him, on Lipans who appeared along the road.[8] Through 1783, the Lipans withstood their enemies, and Cabello used them as guides and trackers, and yet their doubts about the governor thickened like dust. Lipan Chiefs Aga and Zapato Sas produced a Comanche captive who admitted his people were gathering many warriors to steal the presidio's horse herd, but Cabello seemed unmoved.[9]

The Lipans' enemies stepped up hostilities. Comanches surprised two hundred Lipans on a buffalo hunt in March 1784, and survivors limped into San Antonio afoot and unarmed; trackers found Comanches burning the Lipans' weapons and buffalo meat. In May Lipans, alerted by Béxar residents, attacked a war party of Taovayas; a captive said Cabello invited the northern chiefs to come and make war on the Lipans. With proof of Cabello's treachery, Chief Casaca and other Lipan leaders angrily confronted the governor on June 16. He attempted to placate them, but they broke with Cabello soon after.[10]

◄ ►

Talk of another trade fair circulated in spring 1785. The ever useful Courbiére promised Bidais, Cocos, Mayeyes, Akokisas and Tonkawas that a trader would supply their every need if they broke with the Lipans, and they agreed. "But I doubt that they will comply, for it is impossible for any Indian to do a good thing," Cabello grumbled. His plots to isolate the Lipans only drove the forbidden exchange underground; their allies needed horses, and the Lipans had them in abundance. The Lipans, as planned, met their trading partners, Tejas included, at the mouth of the San Antonio River.[11]

Next they added the Kadohadachos, who were supplied by Louisiana traders, to their trading circle. Sergeant Manuel de Urrutia visited a Lipan camp of some two thousand people with three thousand horses. Nearby, another two thousand hunted buffalo. Alarmed that hunting on such a scale might destroy the buffalo herd, Urrutia took them to task, but they refused to stop; hunting en masse was necessary for self-protection. The sergeant spied Kadohadachos in the camp with a sizable store of firearms, powder and shot. The Lipans were so well supplied that "rare is the Indian among them who does not have two fusils with sufficient powder and bullets."

Cabello redoubled his efforts. He ordered the commander at La Bahía to detain any Indians carrying arms and ammunition to the Lipans and directed Lieutenant Governor Antonio Gil Ybarbo, at Nacogdoches, to crack down on traders. Ybarbo removed a renegade trader but found nine more Frenchmen trading with the Taovayas and Wichitas, who were stealing horses and mules from the Bexar presidio. In February 1786 Cabello sent a messenger to the Tonkawas: Miguel Peres, a Tonkawa taken captive as a child by Lipans campaigning with Parrilla in 1759. Lipans sold the boy to a Spaniard, who raised him as his own. Happily for Cabello, Peres's brother succeeded El Mocho as chief. Miguel Peres conveyed Cabello's displeasure over his people's friendship with the Lipans and reminded his brother of Mocho's fate.[12]

The governor meanwhile negotiated an agreement with three western Comanche chiefs to declare all Apaches enemies. Lipans sent 158 warriors to intercept the Comanches. They didn't attack but told the Spanish escort that, considering all the trouble Comanches had caused, Cabello was sick in the head for making peace with them. In April fifty Comanches led by the great Chief Cabeza Rapada went looking for Apaches and found the hunting camp of three hundred "Apaches, Mescaleros and Lipiyanes" on the rolling plains between the Pecos, the San Sabá and the Concho. The Apaches attacked furiously, surrounding the Comanches and killing twenty, including Cabeza Rapada. The Apaches lost nine, including one of their own chiefs. Cabeza Rapada's distraught people quickly formed a revenge raid led by the other great chief, Camisa de Hiero.[13]

On May 22, 1786, the Lipans of Chief Cuernitos and his son, Chief Panocha, were camped on the Rio Colorado with 160 armed warriors, when Norteños attacked a small hunting party and killed two men and took a woman captive. A survivor rushed into camp at daybreak shouting that more than three hundred Indians were on their way, and the Tonkawas were with them. The Lipans sent their women, elders and children to hide while the warriors prepared to meet the enemy.

It was an epic battle, from the first gray light of morning until the scarlet sky yielded to dusk, a battle the Lipans would sing of for a long time. Outnumbered, the two chiefs and thirty of their best warriors held off the Comanches and fought to the death, allowing the rest of their people to escape. Among the dead were two women who chose to remain behind to load guns, tend the wounded and possibly to take up the positions of the fallen men.

Word of their valor and sacrifice spread quickly. The survivors and other Lipan camps regrouped on the Nueces to mourn their dead, particularly Cuernitos, "for they looked on him with much respect and attention, and they obeyed all he ordered them [to do]," Cabello wrote.

Added to their grief was the sting of the Tonkawas' betrayal. Two Spaniards who visited the new camp to recover stolen horses found the
Lipans so despondent they hardly knew them.[14]

Survivors mourned as a group. Men wept, women wailed and everyone cut their hair and wore old clothing. Because Apaches believed that
a ghost could harm the living unless it quickly traveled to the afterworld
and remained there, it was their custom to destroy the possessions of
the deceased. They wreathed themselves in the smoke of burning sage,
juniper or another ghost medicine and sprinkled ashes on themselves
and around the camp to discourage any lingering or returning ghosts.
They ceased speaking the names of the departed chiefs and warriors
and referred to them in other ways.[15]

◄►

Zapato Sas, respected leader of the Big Water Lipans, succeeded
Chief Cuernitos. On June 24, 1786, he presented himself to Cabello
to be recognized as principal chief. Like many of his predecessors, he
preferred diplomacy and persuasion over conflict. The Lipans' long
association with the Spanish was a fact of life, and he wanted to maintain good relations, even if his confederates disapproved. Zapato Sas
was well aware of Cabello's deceit, but humbled by recent losses, he
offered to locate anywhere Cabello wanted, as long as the governor
sent traders.

"Zapato Sas is quite valiant," Cabello observed, and that made him
potentially dangerous. The governor suggested he move to the Frio
headwaters, a location the northern nations considered "quite convenient for making a great strike against them." The governor eagerly
awaited the Lipans' destruction.[16] In early September the Taovayas,
Wichitas, and Tawakonis set out to attack the Lipans they thought
were on the Colorado and Guadalupe Rivers but learned the Lipans
were instead on the Frio. They didn't want to travel that far, but they
didn't return empty handed. On their way home some raided the
Béxar herd.[17]

Zapato Sas returned alive and well on September 19 to hear Cabello's answer. The governor complained of stolen horses and slaughtered cattle but would permit a buffalo hunt near the abandoned San Sabá mission. To show his "great affection," he gave Zapato Sas a loincloth and two good knives for skinning and dressing. In December 1787 the Taovayas, Wichitas and Tawakonis caught Zapato Sas traveling toward his main village with enough people for six tipis. They fought furiously all day long until the northerners made off with all the chief's horses, which they used to attack the Lipans' main village just as Zapato Sas was arriving. The next day an evenly matched battle pitted Lipans, with about four hundred eighty warriors bearing four hundred rifles, against four hundred enemy warriors armed with rifles. Losses were unknown, but the northerners took six hundred horses and mules.[18]

Two months later, Cabello's reign of intrigue ended. History would remember his peace with the Comanches, but in reality his machinations stoked conflict. Texas was no more secure. Cabello's new allies needed horses to fight the Apaches, and the Apaches needed horses to trade for guns. The Lipans he tried so hard to suppress had more allies and more guns than ever. Only the traders prospered.

◄►

The new interim governor of Texas on December 3, 1786, was Raphael Martínez Pacheco. He quickly sought the Lipans, who "were perpetrating more destruction and extortions than did the enemy at war. And all of this was happening because that nation felt my predecessor's contempt for them." He began negotiating with them on December 26, concerned less about provoking the northern tribes than becoming obligated to any one tribe.

Pacheco was a veteran of Ocónor's Apache campaigns and other Indian wars but, as commander of La Bahía presidio in 1772, had also been friends with the Lipan Chief Pobea, who had married Chief Boruca's two daughters. In January 1787 Pacheco welcomed seven Lipan chiefs. The most prominent was Chief Soxaís, who told Pacheco that his old friend Pobea "did not allow any of his people to come to fight, nor did his son."[19] By February the Lipans were at peace. Pacheco rewarded them with gifts intended for the Comanches and Nations of the North and had their rifles repaired and their clothing mended. In return, he expected them to settle at a mission and live by their own industry.[20]

Again, the clergy balked. Father José Raphael Oliva scarcely had enough meat and corn for the Indians already living there. Burdened with the Lipans, he said, they would be ruined, and "the Lipans would end up with everything." Pacheco ignored Father Oliva[21] and sent Lieutenant Jose Antonio Curvelo with a priest and soldiers to the large camp of Zapato Sas and other chiefs, two days southwest of San Antonio at El Atascoso, a shady retreat among ancient live oaks where the Atascosa River crossed El Camino Real.

On February 25 five chiefs greeted them warmly and more people joined in great rejoicing, Curvelo wrote. That evening, after prayers, the Lipans held a dance in their honor that lasted until dawn.[22] Chief Chiquito, son of Casaca, arrived later with all his people, "showing great joy at seeing us."[23] Their joy had much to do with the provisions Curvelo brought. The Lipans were starving. For two years a drought had seared the region. Cattle were bony and buffalo scarce. Measles wracked the camps. Need was so great, the chiefs asked Curvelo for his remaining supplies to feed their women and children.[24]

As Curvelo was departing, Chief Casaca arrived from the presidio and began shouting that Pacheco was on his way with troops to take them captive and kill any who resisted. Weeping women and children began to run. Curvelo's interpreter told the lieutenant that Casaca "had told them a thousand and one lies." He sent two Lipans to overtake their people.[25]

Casaca may have been mistaken, but he wasn't lying. Juan de Ugalde, commanding general of the Eastern Provinces, had waged brutal war on the Mescaleros since January 19, 1787. He employed fourteen scouts, including eight Lipans, who wore Mescalero moccasins to avoid betraying their presence. In the Chisos Mountains, Ugalde assaulted Mescaleros who had just signed a peace treaty at the Presidio del Norte. Informed of the treaty, Ugalde dismissed it furiously and resolved anew to continue attacking Apaches. A third attack failed to surprise the Mescaleros. It seems the Lipan scouts were not wearing Mescalero moccasins.[26]

That spring Chief Canoso's Lipans began living at the Mission of San Antonio Valero, where Pacheco provided for them generously. They helped retrieve a citizen's mules and horses, served as scouts, found new routes, and captured guardhouse escapees.[27] Pacheco's superiors berated him for potentially upsetting the peace with Comanches and Nations of the North by befriending Lipans. If the Lipans wanted to live in towns, said Ugarte, commanding general of the western provinces, they could settle in Coahuila, where the northern tribes didn't go. Ugalde deplored Pacheco's lavish gift giving, and yet he admitted that for the previous nine years, the Lipans weren't guilty of "the crimes which are attributed to them." Like Oconór and Croix, he believed the entire nation shouldn't be blamed for the actions of a few.

Pacheco argued that in his long experience, the Lipans were more likely to keep their promises. Every measure exercised in the last thirty years, including the military buildup, had failed to stem the provinces' misfortunes, he said. He was so certain of his plan, he spent six thousand pesos of his own money. In all his actions, he said, he was abiding by the Gálvez doctrine.[28]

◄►

Viceroy Bernardo de Gálvez revamped frontier policies on August 26, 1786, with his "Instructions for Governing the Interior Provinces of New Spain." Observing that a bad peace was preferable to a successful war, he called for peace with the tribes who asked. Both sides should observe the terms of the peace, but "certain trifling defects" in the Indians should be overlooked. Past treaties failed, he said, because they provided no advantages to Indians, and they couldn't sustain themselves on hunting and warfare. "And so, if they do not rob, they perish of hunger and misery." Satisfying their needs for horses and mules, he knew from experience, would cost less than additional troops.

"I am very much in favor of the special ruination of the Apaches," he wrote, but he wanted to quickly establish trade for livestock with the Lipans, which would reduce their raiding. The Lipans would readily depend on the Spaniards for guns and ammunition, "and it is an error to believe that firearms used by the Indians do us greater harm than the bow and arrow."

His instructions regarding another commodity are chilling: The Apaches were not yet acquainted with liquor, but with a little effort "they will acquire a taste for these drinks," which would become valuable in trade and "allow the greatest profit to our merchants."[29]

CHAPTER

Picax-andé

Picax-andé's strength is manifested more each day by the great numbers of important Apache chiefs who submit to him, a natural prince, through whose mouth they believe the gods speak.

— Ugalde, 1788

The Lipiyans, a fierce Apache group, were still holding out on the plains near the Colorado River, despite the Comanche menace. Their leader was Picax-andé Ins-tinsle, which meant "Strong Arm." The Spanish called him Brazo de Fierro. The Lipiyans were well equipped with guns, arrows, bows, lances, shields and leather armor, Ugalde wrote. "They are brave warriors, as they have shown in the many battles fought against the warlike Comanche nation," and had given no thought of abandoning their lands despite their proximity to Comanches, "nor do they ask peace at our presidios."

Ugalde learned of the holdouts from captives during his Mescalero campaign and headed north with his troops, accompanied by five Lipans and four Mescaleros. Picax-andé, likewise, heard about Ugalde from Apaches fleeing Spanish attacks. On July 10, 1787, near the lower Pecos, the Lipiyan chief and the Spanish chief met. "Without pausing, he crossed the river to present himself," wrote Ugalde. His men respectfully held the chief's stirrup and bridle, and he dismounted. Picax-andé was "about fifty years of age, with the face and bearing of a soldier."

Ugalde conducted him to a hastily arranged court, seating the chief on his right, with the officers and chaplain sitting in a circle and the

Lipiyans, Lipans and Mescaleros behind Ugalde. Amused at holding court "out in the sun, surrounded by humanity in ragged skins, caked with sweat and dust, among rocks and cactus," he offered meat, pinole, biscuits and cigarettes.

Picax-andé spoke: "There are only three chieftains: the Great One above, you, and I. The first is looking down upon us and listening to what we say so that we shall see who is lacking in truth." In his simple but eloquent declaration, Picax-andé made it clear he considered himself Ugalde's equal. He also expressed a core Apache value—telling the truth.

Each man made a long speech about his respective strengths. Picax-andé described his victories over the Comanches and said his people had never attacked Spaniards. He was at peace with the pueblos of Pecos and Galisteo in New Mexico. Ugalde warned the chief that he had no hope for success against the Spaniards. The two men made a preliminary agreement to ally and spent the next day conferring. The following morning, Picax-andé departed quickly to prepare for a raid on the Comanches, and Ugalde continued downstream.[1]

Picax-andé and Ugalde had great expectations of one another. The Lipiyans were an Apache island in a sea of their enemies, and they too were suffering from the drought. Picax-andé wanted to resettle his people in a new location, and he needed allies against the Comanches. Ugalde hoped the great Picax-andé would be the key to peace with all the Apaches.

◄►

Picax-andé had lived his entire life during a turbulent time for his people. Expelled from their homeland in northern New Mexico, the Lipiyans (formerly, Carlanas) re-established themselves in new country from the Pecos to the Colorado and the rolling plains and sand dunes in between. The chief was born here in a place called the Arenales (the Sands), most likely present Monahans Sandhills.[2]

For 40,000 years, the slender tributaries of the Pecos abraded rock from the New Mexico mountains and ferried it southeast, where it

The Sands, Monahans Sandhills (*Sherry Robinson photo*)

collected on bars and flood plains. Northwest winds scooped up the fine particles, flung them east, and then shaped the growing white mounds into dunes, domes and ridges rising thirty feet above the surface. Thousands of acres of sandhills formed a barrier to enemies and a refuge and home for people from the Anasazi to the Apaches who knew how to find water. American soldiers were later astonished to find springs here.[3]

The Lipiyans' adopted homeland provided so well they had little need to trouble the Spanish. They had wild mustangs to spare. Watersheds yielded plums, pears, and grapes. Rabbits, antelope and buffalo were plentiful. Picax-andé's country, Ugalde said, was "a veritable Promised Land, for it has all that is necessary for human life."[4]

At a tender age, Picax-andé's father and male relatives would have taught him to run, fight, hunt and use weapons. Like other Apache boys, he learned to stalk small game silently and shoot arrows with great accuracy.[5] Boys ran long distances to build strength and stamina and engaged in staged fights with other boys. As an adolescent, he joined the men for raids to gain horses and booty or exact revenge; after proving his worth, he became a warrior.

The Lipiyans joined allied groups to hunt, raid and hold ceremonies, their combined numbers insuring not only a good hunt but a safe return. In one of these encampments, Picax-andé first saw the Mescalero woman who would become his wife. They may have chosen each other, but the fact that her brother, Alegre, married Picax-andé's sister indicates an arranged marriage, intended to bind the Lipiyans and Mescaleros.

His relatives would have made the first overture by presenting gifts—usually horses, buffalo robes or guns—to the woman's parents. After their families reached an understanding, they married.[6] Custom required a husband to join his wife's family to support and protect them, but Picax-andé remained among his own people, joined by his wife. If he had more than one wife, it was never reported by Spanish visitors to his camp.

He probably earned his name in a single battle, raising a Strong Arm against the enemy. During one clash, the Comanches shot him, but he fought his way out, the Comanches said, because he was very brave.[7] Many such episodes made him a legend among his people. Apaches followed only "the most intrepid, wisest, and most distinguished" man among them, and "never does flattery, intrigue or bribery figure in it" nor does hereditary position or fortune, wrote Gálvez, with grudging admiration.

Good outcomes and evidence of his wisdom and spiritual power earned the fidelity of his own people and allied groups. Picax-andé and the captains who joined him understood that only together were they a match for the Comanches, but even then, it took a strong man to hold together an Apache alliance. Picax-andé led out of charisma, diplomacy, strategy, politics, and fear. Such qualities made him all the more attractive to Ugalde. In October, at Ugalde's request, the viceroy agreed to recognize Picax-andé Ins-tinsle with a formal commission as head chief of the Lipiyans, Lipans, Mescaleros, Sendés (Natagés), Nit-ajendes (Faraons) and Cachu-endes (probably Llaneros).[8]

◄►

The timing of this alliance was as fortuitous for Picax-andé as it was for Ugalde. The Lipiyan chief's overtures in New Mexico had come to naught. In November 1786 two Lipiyan chiefs asked Governor Juan Bautista de Anza, who mistook them for Lipans, to re-establish the trade they enjoyed at Pecos Pueblo four decades earlier; citizens too wanted trade with the Lipiyans. They moved to Coahuila to get away from the Comanches, they explained, and would observe the same friendship and good conduct in New Mexico that they did in Coahuila. Anza wanted written proof from the governor of Coahuila and told them not to disturb his peace with the Comanches. They agreed to both conditions "since they are quite eager to move back here next year."

To Ugarte, peace with the Comanches was "too important to expose to some risk just to please the Lipans who are in no way deserving of favors which might prove dangerous." He suspected the request was really a ruse to spy. The Comanches vehemently opposed peace with Apaches because "they would be transformed into women if we cut off and deprived them of opportunities to employ their warlike energies . . ."

The Spaniards in New Mexico confused Lipiyans with Lipans, which doomed the Lipiyans' efforts to return to familiar country and freely associate with their old friends, the Jicarillas.[9] Ugarte urged Anza to persuade the "Lipans" to return to Coahuila and "make them understand their trade and communication with [New Mexico] is not desired..." Eight times between November 1786 and June 16, 1787, Apaches asked for peace in New Mexico but afterward did some minor pilfering. Picax-andé visited Anza's successor, Governor Fernando de la Concha in November 1787, bearing a passport from Ugalde. This time he asked for nothing other than permission to visit the Jicarillas. He departed to hunt buffalo, accompanied by Utes.

In January 1788 (before his peace with Texas Lipans) Ugarte ordered Concha to make war on all Apaches except the Lipans and to deny the Lipans trade and protection in New Mexico. Concha began supplying horses, guns and ammunition to the Comanches and paying salaries to their chiefs; he offered a horse and bridle plus two large knives for each Apache they brought to Santa Fe.[10]

◄►

Rebuffed in New Mexico, Picax-andé focused on Ugalde. When Captain Domingo Diaz, of the Presidio del Norte, sent the chief two horses and asked him to visit, Picax-andé returned the horses and said he "only desired to bind himself in friendship to the Great Captain of Coahuila." Diaz wrote that "this chieftain is the idol of all of them, and the one whom they all obey and many accept him as their chief."

In late February 1788, Picax-andé and his large contingent crossed the Rio Grande on their way to Santa Rosa. Upper Lipan leaders "presented themselves before him" and rode on to the headwaters of the Rio de San Rodrigo. Picax-andé camped on the San Rodrigo on February 27 and seized three Lipan chiefs who "had not done their duty in the battle which he had had with the Taovaya nation." At the headwaters he asked the Spanish to lend him forty horses to replace his exhausted animals. He got his horses the next day, but Apaches stopped the surprised Spaniards at the edge of their camp because they were in the midst of a ceremony.

Lieutenant José Menchaca removed to a hill and watched in fascination as the Apaches gathered in deep silence before a large tipi, which they entered four by four. Each group remained a short time and left to make room for others. Nobody ate or drank until the ceremony ended. Later, Menchaca delivered gifts of cattle, cornbread, cornmeal and cigarettes, which Picax-andé ordered to be distributed fairly among his people. Ceremonies continued another three days.

Menchaca was impressed by "the sustained manner of treatment accorded a chieftain in whose presence the head men of the greatest and richest rancherías of the Lipans, Lipiyans, Mescaleros, Sendes, Nit-ajendes, and Cachuendes did not dare to lift their eyes, into whose tent no one entered unless he were summoned, and whose person was respected above all with a reverence for which there could be found no equal among the gentile nations of the frontiers . . ."[11] From Menchaca's observations, it's clear that Picax-andé was also a powerful medicine man.

Picax-andé reached San Fernando on March 2, accompanied by six captains and fourteen important leaders of allied groups, including Upper and Lower Lipans.[12] At Ugalde's home in Santa Rosa, the two leaders embraced as three cannons boomed a salutation. Ugalde took Picax-andé to a reception room, where they exchanged speeches. Ugalde described his wish to strengthen the peace between their people. Picax-andé said that as chief of many chiefs, he wielded great power, but he had never used that power against the Spaniards. He never thought a treaty was necessary, he said, because they are easily broken and often a cause of unnecessary war.

At noon Ugalde conducted Picax-andé to a table in the great hall. To accommodate four guards who refused to leave the chief's side, Ugalde placed another table adjoining his own. There they talked for the rest of that afternoon, evening and the next two days. Picax-andé proposed an alliance against the Comanches, which historian Al Nelson saw as "the last throw of a bankrupt gambler," but the Apaches had made the proposal so many times, it seems more of a standard request. Ugalde responded that he would not make war against people observing peace with Spain, and yet, he himself was not a friend of the Comanches.

The only discordant note was word that a Spanish captive escaped from Picax-andé's camp and said others were still held. Ugalde didn't want to challenge his guest but broached the subject indirectly. The next morning Picax-andé told Ugalde he wanted to go with him to church. "[H]e entered and remained throughout the service, as thoughtful and attentive as the most scrupulously observant Catholic of our Sacred Religion," Ugalde wrote. Afterward, he said it was "a very good function and that he had enjoyed it very much." The chief avoided every question about his own religious beliefs.

The most important Spanish and Apache leaders convened in the reception hall to see Picax-andé commissioned as principal chief. At the chief's request, Ugalde changed Picax-andé's name to Manuel (for the viceroy) Picax-andé Yns-tinsle de Ugalde and presented a cane and a document decorated with a royal coat-of-arms and figures representing Ugalde and Picax-andé clasping hands. The chief embraced Ugalde and every other Spaniard in the room but not the Apaches. Only his guards were allowed to touch him, although he did permit certain important chiefs to approach him with grave respect. The day ended with celebrations in the plaza. Ugalde believed peace was at hand in Coahuila, Texas and Nuevo Leon as long as the Spaniards were firm in war and observant in peace. "We can profit from the abilities of the Captain Manuel Picax-andé," he wrote.[13]

Word reached Picax-andé of an epidemic among his people, and he moved camp to the forks of the Rio de San Antonio, two days from Santa Rosa. When Ugalde visited, he was treated to an Apache reception: Riders formed two wings and moved in perfect order to intercept the line of march. The armed Apaches increased the speed of their horses to a full gallop and, to a drum and flute, acted out an attack with timed firing of volleys. In their midst, surrounded by unmounted men, was Manuel Picax-andé Ynstinsle de Ugalde, elaborately painted, dressed in a scarlet Spanish uniform ornamented with silver, and holding his cane of office.

That afternoon Picax-andé turned over three Spanish captives. He understood Ugalde's remarks, he said. His people didn't take the captives but bought them fairly from the Mescaleros, Sendés and Gileños, and this was his first opportunity to restore them. The next morning, Picax-andé raised a final issue: The Comanches received weapons, ammunition and supplies in Santa Fe and San Antonio. The Apaches were now at peace and asked that he stop supplying their enemies. Ugalde said the trade would cease in his jurisdiction, a promise he kept.[14]

It might have been a bright beginning, but "Ugalde's choice had been made for him, the future of the Apaches had been fixed and their death warrant signed" during Croix's meetings during the winter of 1777–1778, wrote Nelson, when officials, including Ugalde, chose to ally with the Comanches. "Picax-ande, a frontier statesman of highest caliber," saw the Comanches as "the disturbing force on the frontier." By eliminating this pressure, the Apaches could spread out, and greater security and better hunting would relieve their need to raid. Official policy would doom the Apaches while the Comanches would "become a greater scourge to their erstwhile allies than the hard-pressed Apaches had ever been."[15]

◄►

In spring 1788 Ugarte, on a mission to make peace with Texas tribes, encountered Lipans, who filed by to shake his hand. They knew of his campaigns against Mescaleros and Navajos and the peace he maintained for eleven years. The Lipans' interpreter assumed he was there to bring them into missions, but Ugarte knew missions had failed. At their Atascoso camp more Lipans boomed a noisy musket salute. An "eloquent Indian," a kind of town crier called a *tatole*,[16] assembled five hundred people, who sat in a great circle around Ugarte. They talked for the next three hours. That day, April 13, 1788, they approved a treaty and then celebrated with food and dances lasting all night.

At San Antonio Ugarte found the Tú sís ndé (Big Water People), whose "most noted Captain Zapato Sas" promised to abide by the treaty but objected strongly to the Spanish peace with Comanches. "The Lipanes have been friends of the Spanish for a long time," he said. "There is no one present who hasn't been born, lived, or died under the eyes of the Spanish. This will never be so with the Comanches and other northern nations." Arming them facilitated forays against Lipans, but the Spanish had never given arms to the Lipans. Ugarte found the complaint reasonable. In September Ugarte believed hostilities were ended. "One or the other Indian might steal a horse, a mule or a cow to eat, but the same thing can happen among us."[17]

Meanwhile, Chief Aga's diplomatic visit to Ugalde at Santa Rosa in November 1787 proved fruitful. "His demeanor, formality, and appearance have pleased me greatly," Ugalde wrote. He asked Pacheco to "attend him with particular favor" and give him a gun from the supply set aside for the Comanches.[18] In May 1788 Ugalde informed Santa Fe and San Elizario that "the Lipanes will not be pursued because of their arms . . ." He directed Upper and Lower Lipans to camp in one place, and in September their ranchería stretched from El Atascoso to the Nueces, but such a concentration proved taxing on the region's resources. Settlers described an expanse littered with so many skinned buffalo carcasses that not even the vultures could consume it all.[19]

Spy vs. Spy

I had treated him with the greatest sincerity and generosity of which I
was capable . . . To this he responds by becoming the worst enemy
of the Provinces and seducing the Lipanes to declare themselves a
scourge as well.

— Ugalde, 1789[1]

T he Mescaleros, who had lived at peace near Santa Rosa and the
Presidio del Norte, abruptly broke their peace on April 8, 1788.
Picax-andé distanced himself, literally. He and the Lipans were hungry
and had gone buffalo hunting, he said in a message to Ugalde, "but not
without praying to God for your health." He knew of the destruction
caused by the Mescaleros and, as Ugalde's friend, was prepared to punish them, he said. Ugalde declared unforgiving war on the Mescaleros
but rejected help from the Comanches and Taovayas out of respect
for the Lipiyans and looked to Picax-andé for help. He demurred; his
people were sick, his horses were in poor condition, and they lacked
necessities, or so he said.[2]

When he met with Ugalde in December, Picax-andé attempted to
mediate differences and began by relaying Mescalero grievances: They
were incensed that their relatives, even captains, were still captives
despite the peace, and they were blamed unjustly for raids by the Gileños. Ugalde wouldn't hear it. Exaggerations, he sputtered. He would
make war on the Mescaleros again, and he expected Picax-andé to join
him. "He should have wanted to join us in the attack on the Mescaleros
to assist his people," Ugalde said, but Picax-andé was cool to the idea.

"He said he only came in obedience to my call and had to return to his rancheria immediately and to those of the Lipanes."

Suspicious, Ugalde ordered Alferez Casimiro Valdés to escort Picax-andé back to his ranchería, ostensibly as protection but in reality to spy. Picax-andé accepted reluctantly.[3] On January 3, 1789, they rode out. Picax-andé's camp of 273 tipis and 157 wickiups was at the confluence of the Rio San Rodrigo, San Antonio, and Rio Grande, a good place to fatten horses, hunt deer, and gather berries, prickly pear tunas and nuts. As they approached, he ordered a smoke signal to let his people know he was arriving, and they all came out to meet him.

Picax-andé dismounted and smoked the pipe three times, the custom before speaking to his people. He described the fine reception he was given by his friend Ugalde and exhorted the people to recognize him as their captain. When he said Valdés was a supporter, the people cheered and embraced Valdés. If it sounded like a political speech, it was. It took a great deal of persuasion to keep Apaches united.

The sprawling camp glowed with evening fires. Valdés retired to a comfortable tent decorated with skins that had been prepared for him. The next morning, the chief invited Valdés to stay awhile. Just the night before, he said, two Mescalero captains happened to arrive for a visit. One was the brother of his wife and the other was a new captain he liked. They were north on the Pecos during the recent troubles. Picax-andé hoped Valdés would let them enter in peace.

If Valdés understood Apache ways, he would have recognized in that instant why Picax-andé would never attack the Mescaleros: His wife was Mescalero, and he was obligated to her people, which meant he was balanced precariously between his relatives and the Spanish. That morning Picax-andé told his people the commanding general was very angry with the Mescaleros who had violated the peace and would punish them harshly.

Picax-andé's guests were his brother-in-law Alegre and a greatly esteemed young man the Spaniards called Zanagate. The interpreter, who had been a captive of the Mescaleros, told Valdés that other

Mescaleros were slipping into the more distant tents and rancherías. There were eighteen tents of Mescaleros and a third captain who had broken the peace in Santa Rosa. They were present to do their own spying; they wanted to gauge the Spanish friendship for the chief. In mid-afternoon Alegre and Zanagate told Valdés that on Picax-andé's orders they would join the other Mescaleros who were keeping peace in Santa Rosa. They promised to do no harm and not separate from Picax-andé.[4]

Valdés left the next day and returned on January 17. The two men talked into the night. The Spaniard tried in vain to learn the intentions of both the chief and the Mescaleros. Three more Mescalero captains happened to arrive for a visit, along with the Lipan captain Dabeq-silsete. The Lipan and Valdés had been raised together as children and shared the same name, Casimiro. That evening they ate together privately. Valdés told Dabeq-silsete, as Ugalde had instructed, that if he was faithful he would be the greatest captain of his nation and began questioning the Lipan about Picax-andé. I consider you a brother, Dabeq-silsete responded, but if I tell you these things, the Lipiyans will learn of it and Picax-andé will kill me or take away my ranchería and ruin me.

Valdés promised to tell only his commander. Dabeq-silsete said Picax-andé himself would not rob or harm the Spanish, but he supported others who did—the Mescaleros, Natagés, Faraons, and Cachuendes (Llaneros). He had seen them return from raids and give Picax-andé some of the booty. If Valdés looked at the horses on the sly, he would see many branded animals, stolen after celebrating peace. Picax-andé wouldn't oppose his relatives and would always aid them, said Dabeq-silsete. He himself thought sheltering the Mescaleros was foolish.

At sunrise, Picax-andé addressed his people. Ugalde was gathering a great force for a campaign against the Mescaleros and could descend on the Lipiyans as well. The Mescaleros deserved to be annihilated and forgotten forever, he said. He assured Valdés that he preferred to be friends, but if one among them did wrong, that one should be held accountable, not the entire group. Then the chief's wife addressed the crowd. Speaking forcefully, she said they should realize how well they were treated by the Spanish. They didn't want to be seen as wrongdoers, especially by the commanding general.

That afternoon, with Valdés present, Picax-andé told all his captains of the dream he had. The Great Captain above told him not to fail in what he promised the Spaniards or he could die. His Capitan Grande above wouldn't help in battle unless Picax-andé obeyed; wherever he might be, the Capitan Grande above would find him and fill him with fear. The Great Captain had revealed this to him in a voice of iron that reached from the earth to the sky.

In the evening the Apaches held a Spanish-style dance for Valdés. With drums, flutes, and other musical instruments, they went singing to the tents of Valdés and Picax-andé and formed a circle for the dance. To the Spaniard's surprise, the people wore expensive, Spanish clothing. Valdés tried to buy some of the clothing to show his commander, but they wouldn't sell. Picax-andé said such music brought out the best in a truthful man like himself. The Lipiyans left the next day for a buffalo hunt, allowing Valdés to confirm that among the horse herd were a dozen stolen animals.[5]

Picax-andé had exerted his best efforts to keep the Mescaleros on the right trail, but the intelligence was lost on Ugalde, who lost the little patience he possessed. He now understood Picax-andé would never fight Mescaleros. Peace with the Lipiyans was a mistake, he concluded. Picax-andé was a threat. "I judge nothing is more important now than to remove the powerful head of the Eastern branches for his long leadership, for his recognized bravery, (in which the Indians feel there is no equal) and above all for his superstitious dominion over them which causes them to obey without question."

When a Mescalero emissary inquired about renewing the peace, Ugalde offered to meet with their leaders. Five captains came in with their people and on March 24, 1789, Ugalde clapped them all in jail.

He declared war on all the Apaches except the Lipans and marched in August, attacking Lipiyán and Mescalero camps at the Piedras Negras crossing of the Rio Grande.[6] The Lipans were so closely tied to both groups that they were caught in the turmoil.

◄►

Two Lipans rushed into the San Antonio Valero mission on August 25 and excitedly told their people that Ugalde had slaughtered many Mescaleros and the Lipans living with them west of the Rio Grande. Their chiefs sent them to warn the mission Lipans to leave or the Spaniards would do the same to them. Gripped by fear, men, women and children ran away on foot. Their rescue party gathered more than a hundred horses from eight ranches and a mission to speed the getaway, and they headed for the hills of San Sabá.

Unfortunately, fifteen of the stolen horses belonged to Lieutenant Curvelo. San Antonio citizens were accustomed to visit Lipan camps to claim strayed or stolen animals, so Curvelo, who knew the Lipans well, thought nothing of setting out alone and unarmed to recover his horses.[7] When he failed to return, Pacheco dispatched the Lipan tracker José Antonio and nine of Curvelo's relatives. Two days later, they found his body and assumed the Lipans killed him.

Near Los Almagres the fleeing Apaches killed five miners. Although Pacheco suspected that Mescaleros had roused the Lipans, he was furious. He had risked his reputation and couldn't help but feel betrayed by the rebellion of the mission Lipans he had treated so well. "Because the Lipanes themselves have created the excuse, the time is right to accomplish their extermination, since they have squandered such a good opportunity to settle in towns or missions in order to preserve their lives," he said. Comanches and Tonkawas vowed to join with other nations to annihilate the Lipans, but Pacheco wanted the Spaniards to strike first, to avenge the murders and "take all their horses before the other nations fall upon them."[8] In early December three Lipans climbed over the wall in San Antonio to tell Pacheco that

Mescaleros, not Lipans, killed Curvelo and the miners. The Lipans were then on their way to the hills along the Frio and Medina. One Lipan, a Christian named José Joaquín, stayed behind.

Ugalde planned to "give a crushing blow to the hostile Apache nations," the Lipiyans, Lipans and Mescaleros united under Picax-andé. They were well armed and well mounted and had erected a palisade fortification around their camp at the junction of the San Sabá and Colorado rivers. Ugalde seemed more perturbed at the Lipans because he had made the greatest effort "to maintain the most scrupulous good faith and to prevent their being exterminated, as has been proposed several times by the authorities of these Interior Provinces."

Ugalde's force, with about two hundred Comanche warriors and eight chiefs, camped at the abandoned San Sabá presidio in mid-December and sent word to Pacheco to gather and equip eighty-five men to join him.[9] On December 24, forty-four soldiers and fifty-two citizens rode out under the command of Alférez Manuel de Urrutia, who took his friend, the Lipan José Joaquín. On the march, José Joaquín tried to kill Urrutia with a blow from his pike, but Urrutia dodged, and the Lipan died instead.

Four days later, six Lipan warriors "in a very agitated state" entered Pacheco's room, where he lay in bed with chills and fever. They greeted him in sign language, and he responded in kind. He ordered something for them to smoke while he dressed. They told him their people were gathered in canyons along the Medina, and they were starving. Pacheco ordered meat from the kitchen and surreptitiously directed twelve soldiers armed with small weapons to move quietly around the back of the house and remain in the passage to the kitchen. When the Lipans made to leave, Pacheco kept them with a promise that meat was cooking. He signaled his troops to enter and tie up the Lipans. The six warriors quickly drew knives and arrows for a fight.

"Their leader [Santa Rosa], the strongest one, advanced directly at my gun barrel," Pacheco wrote. He held the barrel against Santa Rosa's chest. "I dared not fire it at him lest I kill one of our own men. I was able to grab the sword which I had put on and with it I ran him through. Of the six, five were killed, because only in that way could they be subdued." The survivor was taken to the guardhouse. Pacheco's room was "covered in blood as though five bulls had been slaughtered. The bed, the walls, chairs and tables were bloody."

When the six men failed to return, two more came in to find out what happened and were jailed.

On January 9, 1790, Ugalde and the Comanches met the united groups of Apaches at the Arroyo de la Soledad (Sabinal River Canyon) on the Rio Frio west of San Antonio. Already weakened by a battle with the Norteños weeks earlier, the Apaches were overwhelmed. The Spanish and their allies killed two chiefs, twenty-eight women and one child and captured thirty women and children, eight hundred horses and a great deal of loot. "He left them destroyed and despoiled of all the goods they possessed," said Pacheco. The Spanish lost only three soldiers killed and four wounded. In Pacheco's thirty-five years of experience with Apaches in Texas, it was the first such attack on "such a considerable group as the Lipan, not counting the others who united with them." For this campaign, Ugalde would be memorialized by attaching his name (incorrectly, as "Uvalde") to the battlefield, a town and a county.[10]

◄►

Swept unjustly into Ugalde's campaign, the People were attacked in Coahuila and Texas. Aga and the other chiefs were as puzzled as they were indignant. They had done nothing but live in good faith, even eating and drinking together with the Spanish. They served Ugalde as scouts. And yet Ugalde, with soldiers and citizens they knew, attacked peaceful camps, killed their men and took their women and children captive.[11] The long drought caused great suffering as well, and they were compelled to raid the missions and their cattle herds in competition with their enemies, the Comanches, who were also hungry.[12] The People moved their camps and declared war.

◄►

A vaquero dashed into Laredo on April 7, 1790, to say a great number of hostile Lipans were approaching. The alcalde and priest pleaded with a sergeant to move the powder magazine from a warehouse on the outskirts of town to a secure structure. The sergeant was confident his men could repel an attack, but to placate the officials, he sent a scouting party that met the Lipans and, outnumbered, retreated to the barracks. The Lipans opened fire on the sergeant's poorly prepared troops, who found themselves absurdly short of ammunition and withdrew. The Lipans now had control of the magazine. That called for a victory dance. They threatened to lay siege to the town but satisfied themselves with several skirmishes before moving down the river to a ranch, where they helped themselves to horses and cattle. They returned nightly for several more raids.[13] From March through July in the towns of Revilla, Laredo and Mier, twenty-nine people died, seven were taken captive, and many mules and horses were missing. In September Lipans raided the Presidio del Rio Grande, taking 1,490 animals. Only fifty were recovered, and a sergeant, a cabo and twenty soldiers died.[14]

◄►

As Ugalde blasted his way through the Texas hills, a bureaucratic sea change was underway. Viceroy Manuel Antonio Flores, who applauded Ugalde's every move, departed in October 1789. The Conde de Revilla Gigedo, the new viceroy, was appalled by Ugalde's blatant bad faith with the Mescaleros, his conflicting reports about the Lipiyans, and his attacks on peaceful Lipans. In April 1790 he ordered Ugalde to return from his campaign and surrender his command, but Ugalde remained out of reach. As the viceroy was ordering him to desist, he attacked three Lipan camps in the Guadalupe Mountains.[15]

Ugarte became the improbable agent of peace as new commander of the eight internal provinces. When Mescaleros came to El Paso to seek peace, Ugarte readily accepted. He removed Pacheco for his murder of the Lipans in his room and replaced him with the seasoned Manuel Muñoz. Though unsympathetic to Apaches, Muñoz was capable of objectivity. His first act was to release the two Lipans whose only crime was to inquire after their missing men.

The new commandante directed Captain Domingo Diaz, at the Presidio del Norte, to conciliate and calm the Indians and persuade the principal chiefs to come in and talk, even as Ugalde was still prosecuting his war. The Mescalero captains Alegre and José and the Llanero captain Volante were a league away on the banks of the Rio Conchos. El Natagé and Cuerno Verde were in the Sierra del Carmen, which straddled Coahuila and West Texas, and Picax-andé, called El Calvo [Bald One] in the west, was in the Sierra Oscura, a small range near present Carrizozo, New Mexico.[16]

Nobody seemed to know the Lipans' whereabouts. Chief Moreno was far to the north, making peace at San Ildefonso Pueblo in the company of plains Jicarillas. It was rumored the Lipans waged war in the guise of Faraons and Llaneros.[17] Ugarte ordered the governors of Coahuila and Nuevo Leon to grant peace to the Lipans if they sought it and asked the Mescalero captains to remind the Lipans of their old friendship with the Spanish.[18]

In August 1790 six Lipan captains—Canoso, Zapato Sas, Roque Torres, Chiquito, Tomey and Casachiquita—sent the trusted Chief Aga to San Antonio with six warriors and two women. Aga complained sadly about the injustice of Ugalde's attacks. The Upper Lipans agreed to stop fighting, but the Lower Lipans, a larger group, were still at war. On October 26 Upper Lipans living between the Sacramento Mountains and Sierra Blanca in New Mexico asked Volante if they might enter the peace. The Natagés were also willing to negotiate, so long as the Spaniards recognized Picax-andé as the principal chief.[19] As Ugarte turned over his command to Pedro de Nava, it appeared all Nava needed to do was finalize the peace.

CHAPTER

Betrayal

The reason for the Lipans' hostility, which caused them to leave their lands, was because their rancherías were attacked by Ugalde. Since that time they have scattered because they mistrust us.

— Manuel Muñoz, 1791[1]

Nava made peace with the Upper Lipans on February 8, 1791, in San Fernando and recognized Chief José Antonio as their principal leader. Nava's conditions were that José Antonio would punish wrongdoers and force them to make restitution or turn them over to the Spanish; the Lipans would restore captives; and when they rounded up mustangs, they would return animals with known brands. They could enter frontier towns to trade as long as they did no damage. And they must break with El Calvo (Picax-andé) and ally with the Spanish. José Antonio agreed to Nava's terms but said they had no captives. He promised to whip robbers, kill murderers, and return animals taken from corrals, but they expected to be paid for catching stock running free. Breaking with Picax-andé would take time, he said.[2]

Turning his attention to the Lower Lipans, led by Canoso, Zapato Sas, and José Lombrana, Nava sent Chiquito's brother with a message: Accept peace willingly or by force. By March the Lower Lipans were visiting San Antonio and La Bahia, and Zapato Sas and other captains were pleased to camp in their old country near the Nueces, which is where Muñoz wanted them. A campaign now seemed unnecessary, Muñoz said. On April 13, Zapato Sas, Aga and his brother Rivera promised to observe the same treaty.[3]

Peace was nearly in hand, when the new comandante-general of the eastern provinces arrived. Ramón de Castro was cut from the same cloth as Ugalde. He ordered Muñoz to ready a two-month expedition using Comanches as auxiliaries.[4] Unaware of this change, Chief José Lombrana arrived to discuss peace at Santa Rosa on May 1, 1791. With him were three warriors, three women, and one captive. They turned in their weapons but kept some knives and guns concealed in their clothing. Castro, offended that all the captains hadn't come in, ordered them to appear within twenty days. Until then, Lombrana and the others were to remain in a small house as hostages. Lombrana and two warriors escaped in the night. When Castro came with soldiers to contain the others, a warrior came forward, embraced Castro and stabbed him twice in the back. Castro shot him, and troops then killed the women. A sergeant and a soldier also died and seven were wounded. Castro survived.[5]

Less than two weeks later, Chiquito, an Upper Lipan who participated in Lieutenant Colonel Manuel Echeagaray's campaign in Chihuahua, asked for peace. Echeagaray told Chiquito the Chiricahuas intended to kill him and assigned a "guard," who escorted the chief and his family to Arispe. Held in a two-room house, Chiquito complained that he came in peace and good faith and now he and his people were being treated like prisoners. Around 11:30 p.m. on May 12, as the sentry lit a candle, a Lipan stepped outside to smoke a cigarette and then returned, leaving the door open. The sentry was placing the candle in the lamp when the Lipans tried to lance him. He yelled for the guard to take arms and thrust aside three lances thrown at him. Chiquito and nine warriors snatched up five muskets and a bow and arrows and escaped on foot with two women and three children. Four soldiers were injured. On the same night, Chiquito's son and his ranchería disappeared. Echeagaray caught up with Chiquito, but he eluded capture because the scouts fired prematurely. They killed a young boy and captured a boy, a baby girl and a warrior.[6]

"Captain Chiquito, who came in peace of his own free will with his family and ranchería . . . should remain at liberty, as there is no cause for capturing him," said an officer. "On the contrary, there was no treaty and good faith was promised. All Apacheria could mistrust us and we would lose a chance to make alliance with them and friendship."[7]

◄►

The People saw suspiciously large numbers of Taovayas in Bahía. Word of José Lombrana's betrayal traveled from camp to camp. The priests wouldn't allow them to visit their relatives at the missions. When they entered San Antonio to trade, they slept outside the walls, and some never got off their horses. Distant camps combined in one large village on the Atascoso. There, Chief Canoso traded for weapons with the Bidais and other faithful allies.[8]

Muñoz, still protesting that the Lipans had caused no trouble, followed orders to invite Comanches to join an expedition and sent spies to reconnoiter the Atascoso. In New Mexico, Concha outfitted a Comanche expedition. By July 1791 a thousand men were ready to attack, but the Norteños, avoiding remote Apache country, confined their campaign to the banks of the Pecos, Arkansas, and Colorado Rivers, where they found no Apaches. Many Lipans were camped near Presidio del Norte "waiting for the peace which they have sought," Nava wrote.[9] However, Lieutenant Vicente Troncoso and one hundred-fifty men penetrated the Sacramento Mountains in New Mexico and attacked Apaches, who escaped and took refuge around El Paso.[10]

Despite the Spaniards' manifest bad faith, Lipans still wondered if peace had a chance. On September 5, 1791, an aged Lipan came to the Mission of San José, sent by Zapato Sas, Canoso, Chiquito, José Lombrano and Pinto, to learn whether the Spanish wanted peace or wanted to fight. The Lipans didn't want to fight, he said, and weren't angry. Castro made the old man a prisoner.[11]

The Spaniards began to have second thoughts. Concha told his superiors that they wouldn't have so much trouble with these Apaches if they had, as he suggested, prevented the Comanches from "throwing the Lipans, Lipiyanes and Llaneros from their lands . . ."[12] He pointed out "the sad effects we experienced . . . for having looked with indifference on the destruction of the Apache lands" of the three groups. Now the Spanish were vulnerable to such new enemies as the Pawnees and Aricaras, and it was important to maintain the Comanches as barriers. Nava questioned the Comanches' mettle as allies. The Comanches found it difficult to pursue Apaches in their own country, even with tracks. The resourceful Apaches dug for water with sticks and used gourds to scoop it out for their horses. The Comanches refused to enter those places because they would lose horses with little certainty of gain. Muñoz told the viceroy it was clear the Lipans wanted to make peace, but Castro was determined to make war. Recounting the injustices suffered by the Lipans since he had been in Texas, he said, "Good treatment, kind words, truth, and evidence of benefits is what is needed."[13]

◄►

The People were attacked in Texas and Coahuila, enemies possessed most of their stock, and the treacherous chief named Castro hated them. They could see the Mescaleros, Llaneros and Faraons enjoying peace and Spanish provisions at El Norte. It was risky, but they would send emissaries again, beginning with the friendly captain at El Norte.

José Antonio sent eight Upper Lipans to the Presidio del Norte on January 3, 1792, to seek Díaz's help. Viceroy Revilla Gigedo ordered Nava to treat them well and rebuild the old friendship, while he attempted to tame Castro.[14] A month later, José Antonio, Moreno, Bidatja, and Tunayilten sent three representatives to Nava. The unjust treatment of José Lombrana and the others sorely tried their trust, said the emissary Bilcusatliche, but after Cax, son of Volante, described the Llaneros' good treatment in Nueva Vizcaya, the Lipans decided to ask Nava for peace. The Upper Lipans were then united in 291 tents on the Pecos, eighty leagues away. (This suggests an Upper Lipan population of about 1,455.) Twice as many Lower Lipans could be found on the Nogalera, the San Sabá, and the Nueces.[15] They were all poor, the emissary said. Picax-andé was not with them, but they desired good relations between that chief and the Spanish.

"This Indian, after tearfully expressing the high cost to all of his nation of the peace broken by Ugalde, in which the Alferez Casimiro Valdes played a role, explained that bad treatment and lack of good faith they had experienced forced them to continue the war against their will," Nava wrote.[16]

Three days later, a soldier intercepted a Lipan named Pacheco trying to enter San Fernando at night. Pacheco, who wasn't trying to hide and readily turned over his weapons, said he came from a united camp of Lipans at the headwaters of the San Sabá whose captains desired peace. They also asked about their earlier representative, who was imprisoned.[17] Castro didn't believe a word of it. He doubted that the independent Lipans appointed emissaries to represent them and claimed they only asked for peace after being threatened with war. It was impossible to tell Lipans from Lipiyans by language, character, costume or physiognomy and equally impossible to part them from each other or from El Calvo (Picax-andé), he said. The time was ripe "to put the Apaches between two fires and destroy them."[18]

The Lipans grew more desperate. In March 1792, after waiting eighteen months for peace, Zapato Sas and a party of twenty-nine weak and starving warriors entered Nuevo Santander to raid. The group divided, some going to Reynosa, others to Camargo. Well-armed troops from Laredo caught them on March 16. They killed Zapato Sas and fifteen young warriors and recovered a captive and spoils. Citizens overtook eight Lipans, killing one, capturing another, and recovering five hundred animals.[19]

◄ ►

Picax-andé reappeared that spring. He sought nothing from the Spanish, including their blessings. "Brazo de Hierro (Arm of Iron), known in the country of the east by the name Picax-andé and here as Calvo, was in the Presidio del Norte with Captain Natagé in April, both making propositions that they should live with their people in the sands without hostility," said Díaz. The Spanish wanted them closer, but they stubbornly insisted on living in the Arenales (sands) where they were born and raised and where they were safe from the Comanches. We can live on buffalo, native plants and wild game—familiar foods we have been without for a long time, they said. We will stay in the sands until the end of our days. We have never done any harm in Coahuila and always wanted peace with the Spanish.

With them were two Utes whose nation had a longstanding friendship with the Lipiyans and the Lipans. For the buffalo hunt that year, they planned a formidable gathering of two thousand Lipans, Llaneros, Natagés and Utes on the banks of the Pecos. Together they would avenge a Comanche attack on the Lipans during the previous year's buffalo hunt. The Comanche Nation isn't as big or brave as you think, they told Díaz. The Utes are more numerous, and even though the Utes and Comanches pretend to be at peace in New Mexico, they are enemies in the field. "The Utes come in great parties to visit El Calvo and Natagé, as well as the Lipans," Díaz said.[20]

The two chiefs wanted only to be left alone in their own country, but their independence discomfited Nava, as did the Upper Lipans' dependence on "El Calvo and Natagé of the sands." He failed to see that the Upper Lipans fared better than Zapato Sas and his people because their strong alliance afforded them secure access to the buffalo range. Revilla Gigedo worried that an alliance between Utes and Lipans could upset the peace in New Mexico. On July 8 Picax-andé visited Díaz, who, as ordered, tried to persuade the chief to settle nearby, where he could receive provisions and live in tranquility, as opposed to the Arenales, where his enemies were so close. I can't abandon my homeland, where we have everything we need, Picax-andé said. I have no enemies except the Comanches, and I am willing to die fighting them.[21]

On May 7, 1792, the Comanche Chief Ecueracapa, outfitted by Concha, led more than five hundred men in a campaign against the Lipans, Lipiyans and Llaneros. They divided into two groups. Ecueracapa entered the Sierra Blanca in southern New Mexico, where they found three small Apache camps, killing the captain and four warriors and taking four women captive. The second group, led by Quenarucaro, made for the plains. After fourteen days they saw a sizable ranchería of Apaches, but because they were visible in the flat expanse, they had to attack from a distance on the run. The Apaches had a head start, and the Comanches killed just six warriors and captured four women and nine children, plus some horses.[22] The Spanish used gallons of ink describing the Apaches as perfidious but didn't seem to regard themselves as perfidious for arming the Lipans' enemies, even as the Lipans sought peace.

In early June parties of Lipans visited El Norte and Bahía Espiritu Santo to learn the viceroy's decision, but Nava could tell them nothing.[23] Cabello Colorado and his people, who were living on the coast, in July joined the Upper and Lower Lipans still assembled on the banks of the Pecos. Castro sent Pedro Menchaca, who had a rapport with the Lipans, to visit them on the pretext of buying hides and learn their strength. Castro then informed the Comanches and Nations of the North of their whereabouts.[24]

◀ ▶

On August 22, 1792, Revilla Gigedo ordered that all the Lipans who asked for peace should have it, which detonated a showdown with Castro. Their war of words, one of the most unusual exchanges recorded between Spanish authorities, is a study in conflicting policy toward Lipans. Tossing aside protocol and caring little whom he offended, Castro composed a scorching 127-point tirade. Revilla Gigedo fired back, point by point.

Castro insisted on attacking the Lipans; Revilla Gigedo insisted on compassion: "Their misery and lack of resources are more worthy of pity than of hate." Castro criticized Nava for accepting peace with the Lipans and added that a discussion of the matter requires "a better pen than mine," to which Revilla Gigedo responded, "Poorly cut pens should remain in the inkwell." The viceroy chastised Castro for mistreating Lipan emissaries. "If the barbarous Indians had done such things to us, we would not tire of declaring them perfidious and treacherous," he wrote. He also scolded Castro for misinterpreting his orders, belaboring his difficulties, and undermining solutions.

Castro considered the peace ill timed and unwise—the same as "sowing the ground with spines and thistles." Revilla Gigedo said he had already ordered the peace. If Spain could negotiate with the despised Mohammedans to maintain peace, he said, they could treat with the Lipans. God made the Lipans and the Spanish. The Apaches would only be punished for cause and not when they asked for peace. "Peace must be finalized, and Commanding General Don Ramon de Castro will not take part because I have appointed another to arrange the truce and celebration of peace with the Lipans," he wrote.[25] On November 23, 1792, a royal decree united the two commands under Nava.

◀▶

The People began to have doubts. They knew the Comanches had used Spanish guns against them the previous spring. The governors said one thing and did another. The Upper Lipan Captain Antearas said he would never agree to peace. He had many Spanish captives in his service and didn't want to give them up. And the Spanish might punish him. His words drew a rumble of agreement. Peace meant they would have to stop raiding. They had many mules but very few horses. Picaxandé was among them again after a journey north. The Utes would ride with them on the buffalo hunt. This strong ally strengthened their desire to remain independent.

Adjutant Inspector Diego Borica, learning about this change of attitude from a Mescalero spy, stewed over the alliance of Apaches and Utes. The combined Apaches formed quite a large group, all under the "pernicious influence" of El Calvo. On October 9, 1792, he called in the Mescalero captains Alegre (Picax-andé's brother-in-law) and José and the Llanero captain Volante and told them their people and the Spanish would all suffer if the Lipans were admitted to peace at El Norte. The frequent visits of Picax-andé and his allies would undermine any peace, he complained. They listened in silence, then departed, saying they would "fix it" if Borica would not act against them.

The following day, in public view, several members of José's group killed two Lipans and their families, relatives of Pino Blanco, who came to ask for peace. When Borica reprimanded the three captains, they said they were only trying to please him, and the people were witches who could do harm for any simple reason. They said El Calvo would meet the same fate when he arrived for the peace talks. When word of the killings reached the Lipans, they stayed away from Presidio del Norte,[26] and the peace stalled.

Nava in December 1792 ordered Concha to disrupt the Lipans' friendship with the Utes, capture Picax-andé, and mount a campaign. He had soldiers, citizens and Indians ready to descend on the Apaches' big Pecos camp, but heavy snow held them back. Before they could act, Utes and Navajos destroyed a Comanche buffalo hunting party, taking women and children captive and making off with the horse herd. The Comanches retaliated against the Utes, and Concha was suddenly facing a new Indian war.[27] After that, mentions of Apaches grew scarce in reports from New Mexico; Concha was preoccupied with the unraveling alliance.

◄►

Three priests, escorted by soldiers, went to see Canoso in early December 1792. He was living near San Antonio. Canoso embraced Father Velasco, and they spent the day together. The priest returned with the Lipans Bautista, Jacinto and Curbelo, who spent the night. Jacinto had nothing good to say about Aguagrande: "San Antonio, amigo mucho. Aguagrande, amigo nada." (By Aguagrande, they meant the presidio at Laredo.) The next day, Canoso and a large number of warriors and boys, all armed, came to the Spaniards' camp, where a priest gave them food and tobacco. A priest's horse caught the attention of one man. Raising the saddle skirt on the animal, he saw puncture wounds and began speaking excitedly, drawing more than three hundred warriors. The horse must have received its wounds when Zapato Sas was killed, the man alleged, a hint that this was the chief's mount. A soldier said the Comanches killed him. That's a lie, said the Lipan, the soldiers of Aguagrande killed Zapato Sas, and we will have revenge. Expecting trouble, Chief José Antonio told the priests they should go, and they departed hastily, leaving the horse behind at the chief's request.[28]

CHAPTER

War and Peace

The Apache is proud of nothing, except of being brave, and this attitude reaching such a degree, that he despises the man of whom no bold deed is known . . .

— *Antonio Cordero, 1796*[1]

José Antonio asked for peace for his entire nation in January 1793, but the mantle of principal chief had passed to Canoso, Chiquito and Moreno, who were hunting buffalo. They would come in and negotiate when they returned. Nava was beginning to understand the diversity of Lipanería and found it to be a far more varied group than the other Apaches in his territories. For that reason, he suggested flexible terms. Nava's proposed articles of peace included the usual demands to cease hostilities, return captives and turn over branded animals, along with the usual promises of rations and trade. The Spanish also offered to designate territory where Lipans could hunt and gather unhindered. If Picax-andé asked for peace, "let him enter and treat him in all good faith," Nava said. If he was willing to go to Santa Fe, he could be considered friendly. "If he goes to his rancheria, tell him we have learned of the bad advice given to the Mescaleros and Lipans to separate them from our friendship and alliance: in the future he needs to be more loyal."[2]

By May some two thousand Apaches—Chiricahuas, Gileños, Mimbrenos, Mescaleros and a few Faraons—were settled in eight groups, seven of them at presidios. The Lipans were in their familiar country; the Lipiyans and Natagés remained in the Arenales.[3] In July

Lipans celebrated their hard won peace in San Antonio and San Fernando. They promised to stop pilfering livestock if the Spanish allowed them to trade buffalo robes in the settlements. In a major concession, the Lipans said they would sacrifice their valuable trade with the Bidais and kindred tribes, and the Spanish said they would press the Norteños to keep peace with the Lipans.[4]

Lipans settled back into their former territories and happily took up old habits—hunting buffalo in spring and fall and trading in San Antonio. For the next decade, they visited San Antonio monthly, as did the Comanches, to receive supplies and gifts. "At the present time they are acting in good faith, and have separated themselves from our enemies, not so much by reason of affection as out of respect for our weapons," wrote Lieutenant Colonel Antonio Cordero in 1796.[5]

Cordero, who could speak Apache, wrote a report that year relied on by both his contemporaries and historians. Apaches were, in general, so robust that they were "almost insensible to the rigors of the seasons" and so agile and nimble that they could outperform a horse in rugged territory. They ate with gusto when they had an abundance of food, but "in times of calamity and scarcity he bears hunger and thirst to an incredible degree, without losing his fortitude." The health of the camp was utmost; they wouldn't hesitate to abandon the sick if they might infect others. Apaches routinely used the lance, bow and arrows. The eastern bands had some firearms, but because they couldn't repair them they often converted them to new uses in lances, knives and arrowheads.[6]

◄►

The peace, which lasted for years, was one that Gálvez might have blessed—not perfect, pocked by periodic thievery and misunderstandings, but altogether better than a good war. Lipans and Comanches still fought, but the crippling battles of the previous decades seemed to end with the Spanish peace. After Comanches made off with most of Canoso's horses, his band crossed the Rio Grande and settled south of Laredo. Moreno and Chiquito soon joined him.

Chiquito became principal chief in January 1799 and negotiated a treaty with the governor of Nuevo Santander that allowed them to live below Laredo, between the Rio Grande and the Rio Salado. Some Lipans stayed on at the San Antonio de Valero, San Francisco de Espada, and San José de Aguayo missions in and around San Antonio and at La Bahía del Espíritu Santo and Nuestra Señora del Refugio missions near the Gulf of Mexico.[7]

With peace, the Lipans' numbers grew, and by 1804 they were "probably the most populous of all the Apache tribes," according to a civilian bureaucrat. The Spanish continued to fan their hatred of the Comanches and Nations of the North to keep them from allying, "as they have already attempted to do."[8]

After the United States received Louisiana from France in 1804, its Indian agent, Dr. John Sibley, attempted to influence the region's tribes. "Lapans . . . are a shrewd and comparatively an enlightened people and remarkably honest," he wrote. Cordero, hoping to shape an alliance among tribes to protect the Texas borders from this potential new aggressor, in summer 1806 suggested the unthinkable—peace among the Comanches, Lipans and Tonkawas. They weren't opposed; chiefs of these tribes admitted that the long years of warfare had damaged them all. With Cordero presiding, the Lipans, Comanches and Tawakonis reached a historic accord in spring 1807. Lipans, represented by Canoso and Moreno, and Comanches agreed to hunting territories divided by the Lomería de San Sabá (hills dividing the upper Colorado and Nueces river systems). Although Sibley believed the Lipans were "warmly attached to the Americans, and extremely anxious to come under their protection," Lipans remained faithful to the crown. The peace lasted until 1810, when Comanches resumed raids on Lipan and Spanish horse herds to support their trade with the Americans.[9]

◄►

The olive branch remained out of reach to Picax-andé (El Calvo). Hoping the New Mexicans would be more approachable than they were ten years earlier, he asked for peace on September 24, 1797, in the new town of San Miguel del Vado, about twenty-five miles from Pecos Pueblo in New Mexico. The Mescaleros and Faraons, again at war with the Spanish, were in his camps in the Arenales and in their own country. Troops had not managed to strike a meaningful blow against them.

Governor Fernando Chacón turned him down and, on Nava's orders, tried to set the Comanches on them. He expected the Comanches to accept his challenge gladly, but they had just sent most of their young men against the Apaches and didn't welcome another campaign. Nava was adamant; the Comanches should ride, regardless of the difficulties, and campaign with vigor. He corrected Chacón, who referred to "Lipans." Operations should target the Mescaleros, Faraons, and "Lipiyans or Llaneros,"[10] he said. "You are mistaken in regard to the [other] group. The Lipans live at peace on the frontier of Coahuila and Texas." El Calvo, Nava explained, "is the principal chief of the Lipiyan or Llanero Apaches, although you think he is Lipan. He has nearly always been at war with us and the Comanches. In a word, they are different nations . . . the Lipiyan and the Lipan. They are both Apaches, but the second group does not merit our attacks."[11]

In spring 1798, troops from Coahuila and Texas struck the Lipiyans and Mescaleros, killing eleven warriors and taking fifty-four captives, plus more than two hundred horses. Picax-andé "strongly insisted that they be admitted in peace." Nava told him he could live on the frontier of Coahuila, knowing it was an unpalatable option, and predicted the chief's renewed efforts to make peace in New Mexico, possibly by trying to pass as another tribe or even blending in with peaceful Indians.[12]

In November four warriors Chacón believed to be Llaneros, accompanied by two Jicarillas, introduced themselves as Jicarillas who wanted to reunite with their people. Chacón doubted their story and had them escorted far from the province, warning that if they returned, they would be punished. He alerted all the outposts but knew they could easily mingle with the Jicarillas, who traded in secret with Lipiyans and

Faraons on the plains.[13] In December 1800 troops making a reconnaissance through New Mexico found that a large group of Apaches with an estimated 207 men had been living in the Capitan Mountains but departed for the plains, pursued by seventy Comanches in four parties who intended to attack them and steal their horses.[14]

Given no quarter by the Spanish and increasingly pressed by his enemies, Chief Picax-andé died in battle with the Comanches in 1801, very likely of a Spanish bullet. He would have been in his mid-sixties. After filling their reports with the chief during his life, the bureaucrats devoted a single line to his death. Picax-andé should take his place alongside Cochise, Geronimo and Victorio as one of the greatest Apache leaders in history—possibly the greatest. The others united disparate Apache groups to outmaneuver American and Mexican armies, but their alliances were short-lived. Picax-andé brought together far-flung groups from at least seven autonomous Apache bands and the Utes to hold his homeland against Comanches, Northern Nations and the Spanish. His alliance held at least fourteen years and was ultimately too threatening to the Spanish.

"[A]n impartial judge could soon see that every charge we might make against them would be offset by as many crimes committed by our side," wrote Lieutenant José María Cortés in 1799.

◄ ►

Delgadito and Picado became the principal Lipiyan captains. Too few to return to their own country and fearing another Comanche attack, the Lipiyans spent the winter with Natagés, Mescaleros, Faraons, Llaneros, and Upper Lipans in the Sacramento Mountains of New Mexico.[15] After raiding in Nueva Vizcaya, they had plenty of meat and horses and were probably well armed, as well.

In late April 1801, after another Spanish sweep of the Capitan and Sierra Blanca areas of New Mexico, the Lipiyan Captain Capote arrived at El Vado and said sixteen rancherías wanted to make peace and do some trading. Thinking Capote was Jicarilla, the Spanish commissioner sent four genízaros (Indian captives raised as Spaniards) to guide the Apaches to safety while a Spanish patrol passed through, and the Apaches warned others. They returned in early May, along with four rancherías of plains Jicarillas, who showed the Lipiyans where they could find water and pasture. They planned to steal horses and exchange them for mustangs or horses with unknown brands.

Chacón ordered them back to their own country, but after learning the Lipiyans came to join their relatives and friends, the Jicarillas, as well as Utes and Navajos to take revenge on the Comanches, the governor had a change of heart. The Jicarillas' long friendship with the Lipiyanes and Llaneros showed bad faith, Chacón fumed, and the possibility of an alliance among Jicarillas, Llaneros, Lipiyans and Navajos was unthinkable. Chacon's fears may have been heightened by a report the year before of a new group among the Nations of the North who spoke the same language as the Navajos and Apaches. Known later as Kiowa Apaches and in modern times as Naishan, they told the Spaniards they were separated from their people when the Comanches overran their country and wanted to be friends of the Jicarillas and Navajos. The last thing Chacón wanted was a larger Apache Nation.[16]

His troops attacked the Apaches twice in the mountains and took all their horses—thirty-one bony, sore-hooved animals—along with tents and supplies. The Lipiyans and Jicarillas fled to the plains in two groups, joining four days later. Next, a small party of Apaches (Delgadito, Picado and eight others) entered Taos Pueblo hoping to disappear among the Jicarillas and Utes. The Pueblo people shouted a war cry and rushed them before they could reach their weapons, but they resisted fiercely. The alférez refused to let a Ute captain speak to the captives. Comanches captured seven more, including Captain Capote, "whose capture has been of the greatest importance because he has sometimes pretended to be Jicarilla and at others, Llanero. He has committed continual robberies and murders," Nava said. Chacón sent them south; if they survived they probably spent their lives in Spanish workhouses.[17]

In less than a year, the Lipiyans lost not only Picax-andé but three of their most important captains. They returned to the plains with the Llaneros and Jicarillas. They still had firearms, but lacking ammunition or access to a gunsmith, they converted their broken guns to lances, knives, arrowheads, and tools.[18] At that point Picax-andé's people might have allowed themselves to be absorbed by an ally, but against all odds they held out. In 1812, the Apaches surrounding New Mexico, wrote Pedro Bautista Pino, were the Gileños, Llaneros, Mescaleros, Carlanes, and the Lipanes.[19] Pino called them by their old name, "Carlanes," but the persecuted Lipiyanes survived.

◀▶

Father Miguel Hidalgo's torch of revolution began to inflame Mexico in 1810, and Spain withdrew troops to contain the insurgency. Apaches kept "the frontiers of three provinces in a continual state of alarm," reported explorer Zebulon Pike.[20] The Lipans maintained their peace, and Texas Governor Manuel María de Salcedo recruited Lipan warriors to the royalists' cause. Ignacio Elizondo had three hundred Lipans with him when he ambushed Father Hidalgo and his fellow revolutionaries at Acatita de Baján, southeast of Monclova, on March 21, 1811. Royalists encouraged Lipans and other tribes to plunder Texas, Coahuila and Nuevo Santander, all Republican strongholds.[21]

Two of Hidalgo's sympathizers, José Bernardo Maximiliano Gutiérrez de Lara and José Menchaca, son of the Lipans' old friend Luis Menchaca, rode to Texas. Gutiérrez's promise to free the tribes from Spain if they would join him nearly cost his life. Spain was no longer a threat to them.[22] In early 1812 Gutiérrez and Augustus William Magee plotted to raise an army, wrench Texas from the Spaniards, and establish an independent republic. When their Republican Army of the North captured Nacogdoches and La Bahía, the Lower Lipans, who were closest to the action, must have reassessed their loyalties. They began supplying rebel troops with dressed deer skins and moccasins "in exchange for a few loads of ammunition—manifesting great joy in the vicinity of such neighbors, tendering their services if they were desired," said a participant.[23]

Colonel Samuel Kemper and Major Reuben Ross dispatched John McFarland to recruit Lipans and Tonkawas in February 1813, and he returned with three hundred men, mostly Lipans, who joined the rebels en route to San Antonio. This large force of Lipans would have been nearly every fighting man among the Lower Lipans. The Republican Army then numbered about 800 Americans, 180 Mexicans, and 325 Lipans, Tonkawas and Coushattas.[24]

On a prairie near the junction of the Rosillo and Salado Creeks, nine miles southeast of San Antonio, republicans met 2,500 royalists. Insurgents planned to begin their attack with a drum tap, but the Indians, positioned on the extreme right under Ross, didn't understand the order and charged prematurely. As a result "they suffered greatly, losing some of their principal men in a hand-to-hand fight; but they fought with the most desperate courage, killing large numbers of the Mexicans," wrote Colonel W. D. C. Hall. When the Americans attacked, they quickly routed the enemy and on March 29 took San Antonio. The warriors murdered many who surrendered, probably in revenge for their losses.[25]

In June Elizondo's army of green troops and presidial soldiers reached the Alazán, a small stream about five miles from Béxar. Rebel troops silently formed a battle line close to the enemy's picket guard. Major Henry Perry directed the Indian auxiliaries to stay behind until the battle began and then move between the Spanish encampment and its herd, stampede the animals, and run them far from camp. As the Spaniards celebrated mass, rebels opened fire and charged. After a bloody exchange, Elizondo's troops were forced to retreat.

Warriors stampeded the stock, as ordered, and some remained with the animals while about two hundred returned to the battle and waited to see which side would prevail. "[I]f the fight went against us they would escape with all the mules and horses; if the scale would turn in our favor, at the right moment they would swoop down on the fleeing

Spaniards," wrote Captain Carlos Beltran. The rout began quickly, and Mexican allies joined the Indians "dealing out death and destruction to Elizondo's forces, not sparing age, sex or even the wounded."[26]

General Joaquín de Arredondo entered Texas in July with a massive army. José Alvarez de Toledo, now commanding the renamed Republican Army of North Mexico, reorganized it in two divisions—Mexicans and Indians under Miguel Menchaca (cousin of José) and Americans under Perry. Menchaca, a Mexican, didn't trust Toledo, a Spaniard, and Menchaca's men shared his sentiments.[27] Twenty miles south of San Antonio, in the midst of an oak and hickory forest along the Medina, the two armies met. The Battle of the Medina, on August 18, 1813, was the bloodiest ever fought on Texas soil. The Republican Army, numbering about 1,400, engaged an advance led by Elizondo that scuffled and fell back several times, drawing insurgents to Arredondo's main body of men, who numbered more than 1,800. After a brutal, four-hour battle, the victory was Arredondo's.[28]

In this battle, only about one hundred Indians, mostly Lipans, participated. The Lipans fought bravely, but as Arredondo's reserves cut them to pieces, their ranks broke.[29] From the Lipans' perspective, they'd already taken the worst during the Salado battle and couldn't afford to lose more men. Apaches attack intrepidly, Cordero said, but "if they do not obtain the upper hand immediately and see that luck is against them, they do not hesitate to flee . . ." Elizondo and two hundred cavalrymen captured an unknown number of fleeing Indians. "The pursuit was violent and barbarous . . ." wrote Vicente Filisola. Few Indians and Americans escaped "from that terrible fight, and the wounded and their prisoners taken by the infantry were ordered shot the same day."[30]

Surviving Lipans retreated with the Americans to the Sabine. Some battle refugees joined American traders at Nacogdoches and began a lucrative but forbidden trade with Lipans and Comanches. The relationship became so close that the traders sometimes accompanied their Indian customers on raids. In October Arredondo sent troops to Nacogdoches, where they descended on a Lipan village of three hundred lodges, scattering the residents and taking nearly everything they owned.[31] Lipans returned to their country and left the rebels and royalists to their war, but now they had fine double-barrel guns and ammunition supplied by American traders. Around 1813, Lipans and Comanches renewed their alliance and together harried Mexico when peace had filled pastures with cattle.[32]

It was the Spaniards' dreaded nightmare. Familiar with roads, villages and farms, the Lipans guided the Comanches to better spoils, attacking settlements, killing men on the spot and carrying off women and small children. Fields and herds that once blanketed the region disappeared—Camargo was hardest hit—and only forlorn crosses told the story. With no fear of enemy ambush, Lipans lived in unaccustomed tranquility, hunting buffalo, picking pecans, and tending their fields. They enjoyed trade fairs like the one held in 1815 in the home country of the Caddos and Wichitas on the headwaters of the Brazos. Lipans, Comanches, Tawakonis, Delawares, and Kiowas peacefully ate buffalo, gambled and danced into the night.[33]

In this period, Chariticas (Arapahoes) and Naishans (Kiowa Apaches) descended from the north to the headwaters of the Brazos, where they encountered a party of Comanches and Lipans. The Naishans were astonished to hear their language spoken by Lipans. They held a great council and passed the pipe.[34] After making contact with Jicarillas and Navajos in 1800, they had lived in Comanche territory. This was their first meeting with Lipans.[35]

◀▶

Antonio Martínez, the last Spanish governor of Texas, presided over a province on the brink of ruin. His troops were hungry, unclothed and without horses, and the garrison itself was too small for either a punitive expedition or protection. Local government in Béxar demanded what little grain the farmers put aside, and Indian raiders were so brazen they assaulted Spaniards almost at their doorsteps.

The "infamous Lipans . . . constantly trouble us," Martínez wrote. Lipans seemed to own the roads to La Bahía and the Rio Grande. He estimated Lipan warriors living between the Rio Grande and the Guadalupe at an astronomical 25,000 warriors—it must have seemed that way to the beleaguered governor—and the Comanches at 18,000 warriors. Their attacks "have almost destroyed this province," he wrote.[36]

During 1818 various combinations of Lipans, Comanches and Wichitas descended on settlers and soldiers alike,[37] but after Indians attacked settlers west of Hedionda, at the headwaters of the Sabine, on September 3, Antonio Músquiz led seven soldiers and twelve citizens who knew the country. All had firearms and horses despite the scarcity of both. In the Cañón del Cedral (near the Brazos in present Bosque County), they found seventeen Lipans and opened fire, driving them back as the Lipans returned fire. With fierce fighting on both sides, about fifty warriors arrived to reinforce the others.

Músquiz believed they had a stronghold in the mountains. He formed his small party in a square and during a blazing, three-hour battle, the outnumbered Spaniards inched their way up to the high ground where the Lipans were entrenched with their families, forcing them to flee. The Lipans lost four and had many wounded. The Spaniards lost one soldier and two citizens, plus two wounded, including Músquiz himself.[38] Late that year Martínez mustered six hundred soldiers and trounced Lipans on the Guadalupe. One of the Lipans' American friends was killed and another lost two fingers.[39]

Although the tribes harried both sides in the war for independence, it appeared to Texans that Lipans and Comanches favored the insurgents. "[T]he Camanches and Lee Panes, the most powerful tribes of Indians in this country and who are at war with the royalists, are waiting impatiently expecting the approach of the army of the republic, and promise an effective co-operation in the reduction of St. Antonio and La Bahia," a newspaper reported in 1819. As the sun set over Spanish Texas, troops and horses were dying of hunger, most of the weapons were broken and useless, and the defenseless citizens were dying every day at the hands of Indians, Martinez wrote. Lipans, on the other hand, were faring nicely. In 1820 the Lipans possessed "a considerable knowledge of the art of war," resisted settling, practiced their traditional religious beliefs, and spoke and understood Spanish well, according to one report.[40]

During more than two centuries, the Spanish increased their knowledge of Lipans but not their understanding, while the Lipans knew and understood the Spanish. Despite the occasional glimmer of insight from a Gálvez or a Cordero, Spaniards remained inflexible in their terms, insisting that independent, nomadic people live in villages and become Catholic citizens. They ignored advice from seasoned leaders like Croix to overlook the Lipans' occasional thefts, they held the Lipans accountable for every incident, and then they betrayed them to win peace with the Comanches and northern tribes, for whom they willingly overlooked the occasional theft. Their calculated choice didn't pay off in the end.

CHAPTER

Castro

The Lipans have a chief who is quite civilized. Castro, as he is called,
speaks good Spanish and has a feeling for justice and equity.

— Jean Louis Berlandier, 1828[1]

Comanches claimed to be friends, but still they attacked the People's relatives—the Sejende, the Cuelcajende, the Natagés and the Túédinendé—to the west. The Comanches declared war impulsively, without first summoning a council to deliberate. They didn't observe the laws of hospitality. As allies, the Comanches were unworthy. When the two Spaniards came to tell the People that Mexico was free of the Spanish king and encourage them to break with the Comanches, the People obliged. They didn't need the Comanches. They would go to Mexico City and negotiate their own peace.[2]

When Spain finally released her grip on Mexico, Commandant-General Gaspar López on November 3, 1821, sent a proclamation to all the chiefs or captains of Indian tribes announcing the change of government. He directed Francisco Ruiz and Vicente Tarín, known to have influence with the Comanches and Lipans, to visit both tribes. The Lipans were living near Laredo and in Coahuila at Santa Rosa and Aguaverde; in Texas on the San Sabá, Guadalupe, San Marcos, and Colorado rivers; and on the Gulf Coast between present Houston and Galveston and at the mouth of the Rio Grande. "In my opinion, the Lipans are the best horsemen," Ruiz reported. They were "very adept" with their weapons and known to steal Spanish livestock and alter the brand with gunpowder or a branding iron but "do seem to have a disposition toward cultivating the soil." Citizens, however, were still bitter about depredations.[3]

A three-man commission in late December recommended renewed friendship with the Caddo tribes but not the troublesome Lipans and Comanches, who had terrorized the country since 1810. Commissioners proposed a humane war, but the dwindling treasury precluded any campaigns.[4] After Ruiz's visit, Lipans decided to broker their own peace with Mexico, and in spring 1822 the Lipan chiefs Cuelga de Castro, El Cojo, and Poca Ropa rode to Mexico City to negotiate with the new government.

Castro and El Cojo were dawn and dusk in temperament. Castro, "who enjoyed a good reputation among his own people and the military commandants, [was] a man remarkable for his urbanity and his propensity towards civilized life," while El Cojo was "a ferocious man, treacherous and celebrated for his thefts and brigandage," an observer would later write. Castro would become the Lipans' most prominent chief, and under his leadership the Lipans' relations with both Mexico and Texas evolved beyond trade and military alliances to cultural adaptation.

Castro, then about thirty, had been a chief for two years. He was born around 1792 to Chief Josef Chiquito and Maria, according to the Castro family oral history, in a place near present San Sabá called Lipans' Field (*Labor de los Lipanes*). There they grew corn and watermelons and traded stolen mules and horses to the Americans for weapons and farm tools. Arredondo once sent two hundred cavalrymen against this camp, but the Lipans escaped except for a blind man.

Spanish missionaries gave Castro his name. "Cuelga de" is the Hispanicized version of Cúelcahén Ndé (Tall Grass People), or Llaneros. Castro may have been a Llanero married to a Lipan; Apache way, it made him Lipan. The origin of "Castro" in the chief's name is lost to history, but it's not hard to imagine that the missionaries wanted to honor the new comandante-general of the eastern provinces by naming the child for Ramón de Castro.[5]

Chief Castro possessed a handsome face, if little animated, and spoke good Spanish. He had a pet buffalo cow trained to follow his saddle mule. Military commanders considered him the most approachable of Apaches when they wanted to complain about crimes or make sure criminals were punished. As the new government and the Eastern Apaches sorted out their relationship, they looked to Castro, whose natural statesmanship set him apart. El Cojo, by comparison, was an older man and more inclined to hostility. In 1814, he made peace in San Antonio and Coahuila, broke it the following year, and later joined Comanches and Wichitas in raids. He was still at war in 1820. Poca Ropa, also an older man, had more in common with Castro; as principal chief in 1776, he tried to negotiate with Ugarte.

In the Mexican capital, the three chiefs were housed in the Colegio Apostolico de San Fernando, a monastery where the Mexican leadership hoped they would observe the fathers' good example. They remained for several months and witnessed the coronation of Agustín de Iturbide, who presided briefly as emperor.[6] On September 18, 1822, only Castro and Poca Ropa signed the peace treaty. They vowed to forgive the offenses and damages inflicted on them earlier and to respect the new government. The Mexicans promised them some unclaimed land and water where they could grow crops, pasture their horses, and receive government protection. The Lipans could round up wild horses and unbranded livestock and return branded animals to their owners for a reward. They would join in fighting common enemies and could trade for weapons used in self-defense.[7]

On their return, the Lipans stole all the horses from a Comanche camp, and Comanches pursued them along the jade waters of the Medina to the Lipan ranchería, where the Lipans met them with heavy gunfire. The Lipans cut the throats of Comanche men married to Lipan women. Lipans no longer feared Comanches, and they had been at war with the Norteños since 1820, when Tawakonis attacked Lipans on the Colorado. Eighty-five warriors went out to meet the enemy and fought to the death, allowing their people to escape. Lipans made friends again with the Karankawas and Tonkawas, this time for good. Lipans could travel at will in Karankawa and Tonkawa territories and even sat in their councils as advisors.[8]

The Mexicans were delighted with these developments but still had to factor Lipans and Comanches into Texas colonization. Pioneer Noah Smithwick wrote that because Mexico couldn't hold the territory against the two tribes, it opened Texas to the Anglo Americans. Economic considerations played a larger role in colonization, but Smithwick's assertion can't be denied. In 1823 the Mexican government approved Stephen Austin's colony in east central Texas and subsequently passed laws to bring immigrants to "vacant lands," which were actually portions of Lipan, Karankawa and Tonkawa country.[9] The Mexicans opened a spigot they could never close.

◄►

In February 1828, messengers informed General Anastasio Bustamante that Lipans led by Castro and El Cojo would soon arrive in Laredo. An officer and troops received them and presented bread and a bottle of mescal, a customary greeting. About one hundred fifty families, their faces painted with vermillion, rode in. "Everything about those indigenes had an aspect at once barbarous and nomadic. [N]one had those triple chins induced by the artistry of our cooking. Yet not one showed any signs of actual privation, nor could any be considered as thin or emaciated," reported Jean Louis Berlandier, a French botanist and zoologist with General Manuel de Mier y Terán, who was charged with reporting on the natural resources of Texas and its Indian and American inhabitants.[10] Berlandier's reports, much quoted by historians and anthropologists, are valuable for their objectivity and detail.

Lipans were tall. The men stood 5 feet 10 inches to 6 feet 1 inches; the women were about 5 feet 4 inches, the height of the average man at that time. They were "erect, lithe, well proportioned, graceful in their movements, and by comparison with any I have seen, by far the most agile natives in the country," Berlandier wrote. They pulled out all their facial hair, "being particularly careful to remove the eyebrows" and dressed in clean clothing of "extremely well-worked" deerskin and the finest and best painted buffalo robes.[11]

"The Lipan wears a belt from which he hangs a bit of cloth in front and behind to hide his nakedness. Often a dagger hangs at his belt. A buffalo hide, tanned and decorated with painting, often hieroglyphic, serves him as a cloak. When it is cold the fur side of the mantle is turned inside, while in milder weather it is worn outside." A man might also wear *mitazas* (a trouser slit up the outer leg and fastened with buttons) and sandals rather than moccasins.

"Their hair is worn either loose or fastened at the nape, sometimes braided and decorated with buckles or plaques of silver, but they never cut it." A man's hair wasn't necessarily his own. "To the hair which nature gave them they add that of others, sometimes their wives', sometimes even horsehair, in order to make a braid that reaches to their knees."

Lipan women in their dress "are the most decent of the natives. A sort of jacket of deerskin, covered with intricate decorations of glass beads, hides the upper part of their bodies. A deerskin skirt falls to the knee. Very

"Lipanes" by Lino Sanchez y Tapia, 1828, *from the collection of Gilcrease Museum, Tulsa, Oklahoma*

long stockings of softly tanned deerskin serve for slippers as well. . . . The young women wear their long hair loose upon their shoulders . . ."

Weapons were the lance, gun and bow. "Their lance is usually tipped with the straight blade of a Spanish saber, 2 ½ feet or so in length, with a shaft 8 or 9 feet long. They adorn it with feathers and various gaudy ornaments." The Frenchman assumed warriors would be clumsy with such a weapon, but Apaches could charge with a lance grasped in both hands as they guided their horses with their knees. The lance was "truly a formidable weapon, which they handle and throw with surprising and fatal dexterity, when in pursuit of a flying enemy," wrote Francis Latham, an American observer.[12] Berlandier said the Lipans used guns only in special circumstances and still relied on bows for hunting and warfare. "In their hands the bow is undoubtedly the most fearfully deadly of weapons."

As horsemen, Lipans were second to none. "Although little protected against thorns, they penetrate forests at full gallop where a civilized and well-dressed man would enter only with care," Berlandier wrote. They could "lie along the side of their mounts, holding on by a leg and the mane in a manner so perfect that one believes he is looking only at a herd of wild horses . . . [T]hey could fall quickly on their unsuspecting enemies with an extraordinary velocity."

Berlandier admired their mental quickness. A Lipan examining a compass, probably for the first time, explained it in Spanish: "That point shows the north, and with that, one cannot get lost when the sun does not appear." And the Frenchman recorded Gálvez's revenge: Lipans were fond of liquor and given to drunken fighting among themselves. "I myself have seen them stab their comrades and then flee," he said.

The night before they left, "the Lipans roamed through the streets after sundown, singing their songs of peace." They approached the main square for a dance and lined up single file, "standing very close to one another, and walking so slowly that at first they did not appear to be moving at all." Singers gathered around a buffalo hide, which they held taut and struck like a drum.

Weeks later at Béxar, Berlandier witnessed Comanches hurrying away at word of approaching Lipans, who chased them more than thirty leagues to the banks of the Colorado and relieved them of more than two hundred horses.[13] It may have been repayment for an attack a year earlier by a large group of Comanches and Wacos on Castro's Lipans and some Tonkawas on the San Marcos. In that fight, the Lipans took a beating and lost five or six hundred horses. They retreated down the river to De León's Colony.[14] In their near constant conflicts, the Lipans, "although more courageous and more warlike than the Comanches, are forced to yield to numbers," Berlandier wrote. Lipans rarely attacked Comanches directly, but with ruse and surprise, "their audacity sometimes procures them a notable advantage."

The Lipans still observed the truce and had "begun to learn the ways of society," Berlandier wrote. "I have no doubt that, once established on lands of their own, with protection against their enemies, this people would in very short order begin to be useful to their fellow citizens, particularly if they were given agricultural implements." Having seen *Labor de los Lipanes*, he said, "They can farm successfully and lead a nomadic life." Berlandier may have been the first to see the diminished nomadic tribes—some had already disappeared—but the "adventurers who live on the frontiers of the Republic" furnishing arms and munitions in exchange for stolen goods encouraged their audacity.[15]

General Mier disliked the Lipans and considered them more formidable than Comanches. He recommended two thousand troops for a six-month war against Lipans, Comanches and Norteños. After that Mexico could "do with them what the North Americans have done with their savages: subjugate them and send them beyond their borders." This wouldn't be easy, he admitted. The Mexican government established garrisons on the Brazos, Galveston Bay and the Nueces and gave them Aztec names, reflecting Mier's desire to Mexicanize Texas. Lipantitlán, on the Nueces just below San Patricio at a favorite Lipan campsite, was intended "to wipe out the tribes of the Lipans." Instead, Lipans congregated at the outpost.[16]

◄►

The bustling hide trade at Nacogdoches in 1828 consumed 40,000 deer skins, 1,500 bear skins, 1,200 otter pelts and 600 beaver pelts in less than a year brought in by Lipans and other tribes. These people of nature, it seems, were not above the kinds of excesses later blamed on white men. At the same time, buffalo hunters, Indian and non-Indian, were "contributing greatly to the destruction of an animal which is so useful for its flesh, and whose hide serves as a garment for all indigenes and for diverse uses among civilized peoples," Berlandier said.[17]

This wasn't the first caution about environmental change. Nava in 1792 ordered Lipans to stop wantonly destroying wild animals during their hunts because it could eliminate a species, to the injury of both Lipans and Spaniards, "who had a right to conserve it within their territories."[18] Grasslands too were deteriorating as European stock spread mesquite pods from the arroyos; the plain around San Antonio grew thick with mesquite and juniper. In 1777 Father Morfi observed that as mustangs and cattle proliferated, the populations of buffalo, elk and antelope declined.[19]

On the other hand, the *mesteños* (wild mustangs) were themselves a resource. Descended from the Spanish barb, they were particularly at home on the range in Texas. Small but powerful with a long, thick mane and tail, they grazed by the thousands, but capturing and taming them was so taxing, Governor Martínez once said that "only six or eight out of a hundred, and sometimes none, can be kept from escaping." For at least half a century, the Lipans, who lived on the "mustang prairie" of South Texas, energetically captured, broke and traded mustangs to Spaniards and Americans. "The Lipans are a fine group of men, skilled at warfare, excellent horsemen, and with great talent for breaking and training wild horses," Berlandier wrote.[20]

Unlike their western relatives, who readily ate horsemeat, Lipans only ate horse meat when they had no other game. They dried the horse hide and used it to protect their possessions when they were on the move. The mane and tail could be transformed into rope, cinches and bridle rings. The horse rib was employed as a hide scraper. "There were many wild horses. The Lipan nearly every day went out there to get the fine horses, the best they could get," said Antonio Apache.[21]

◄►

The human landscape was also changing. As the Yanquis multiplied, jaws tightened across Texas and northern Mexico. Mexicans began to fear the United States would use Anglo-American colonies to seize Texas. Texans began to question President Antonio Lopez de Santa Anna's growing dictatorial powers and Mexico's attempts to control colonization. The population of Anglo Americans began to rise along the coast and in east Texas, but Lipans and Comanches still had the upper hand in central Texas.[22]

Stephen Austin considered a formal alliance with the Lipans against other tribes but believed "such an alliance would establish in their minds the right to live on the country permanently." He recognized their value as friends, however. In January 1825, he issued a passport describing Juan Novale as "a principal chief of the Lipan Nation of Indians who are the friends and brothers of the American settlers in this province." He asked Americans who encountered the chief "to receive him in friendship and treat him with kindness and attention."[23]

Lipans and Mexicans were comfortable in their longstanding protocols, but Lipans and American colonists struggled with cultural differences. Americans took offense at the Lipans' expectation of gifts and hospitality. "Parties of Tankaways, Lepans, and other tribes . . . were beggarly and insolent," complained Austin's cousin. The first Irish colonists at Refugio in 1831 refused to give gifts, and the insulted Lipan chief became threatening. Settlers assembled their militia and fired their small cannon. The Lipans fled, only to return and ask the immigrants to fire the cannon again. The Irish refused. The Lipans wanted to camp there for the night, but the colony's leader told them to find another camp site. They departed and didn't return.[24]

Americans flogged Tonkawas for thievery and then began shooting them. Stealing persisted. Finally, colonists surrounded the Tonkawas in an open field at Columbus and, rifles in hand, were about to finish them off, when Chief Castro rode in with 450 warriors. A written agreement between Castro and Austin allowed the Lipans to take responsibility for the Tonkawas and keep them out of white settlements. Castro settled his new wards between the Nueces and the Rio Grande, where they remained for about two years.[25]

Meanwhile, Mexico protected its peace with the Lipans, even as relations with other tribes crumbled, and Lipans reciprocated. Lipan warriors regularly joined Mexican campaigns against Comanches, and Lipans led by Tres Manos threatened to annihilate a party led by James Bowie seeking the legendary Los Almagres mine near the former San Sabá mission. In return for his help, the Mexican government gave Castro a lieutenant colonel's commission and a salary. Mexicans also supplied Lipans with arms and ammunition. When Castro's father-in-law was murdered while traveling to Laredo with a fine mule in 1832, the matter was so important that Mier, then commanding the Eastern Interior Provinces, ordered an investigation.[26]

Lipans became so familiar with Mexican institutions, they appeared before the Laredo town council for various reasons—to protest the appointment of a European of low rank as commander, to object to the town's hospitality toward Comanches—and used the courts to try and recover horses stolen from them. Castro in January 1835 asked for and received Mexican permission to settle one hundred families on land belonging to Fernando Garcia at Carricitos in Tamaulipas so that they could farm and raise cattle.[27]

The Lipans thrived during this peace with Mexico and traded with Mexicans and Americans. In time, Castro, Chief Flacco, and the Lower Lipans gravitated towards the Americans, while the Upper Lipans drew closer to the Mexicans. In 1835 Santa Anna (Lipans called him Little Bull) dissolved the Texas government, appointed a military governor, and sent troops to Texas. Both sides were hounded by wild tribes on the frontier, but both counted the Lipans as allies.[28]

CHAPTER

Friendship for the Texians

Familiar with his fame as a Statesman and a Warrior, and confiding in his attachment to the American people, the Government of Texas is proud to receive General De Castro on terms of amity and friendship.

— *Mirabeau B. Lamar, 1838*[1]

When the first shot of the Texas Revolution detonated years of friction and resentment in October 1835, some Lipans were already serving as spies and scouts. The mayor of Reynosa reported in November that "some groups of Lipans acting like rebels are going about causing damage to the ranches near the salt source."[2] Many Lipans remained in Coahuila to sit out the conflict; some moved back and forth across the Rio Grande to avoid battles; others took advantage of the chaos to raid. Incursions by all tribes were unintentionally most helpful to the Texans. Santa Anna, making his way north, expected the tribes to side with Mexico, but below the Rio Grande, they pilfered supplies and attacked troops.[3]

In January 1836 Hugh Love proposed enlisting Indian tribes for six months or more at the same pay as regular troops, providing ammunition, and giving them horses and half of all other plunder taken from the enemy. He also suggested that commissioners treat with the frontier tribes and "grant the lands promised them." The overtures failed, and settlers were "entirely unprotected by any military force, or plan of general defence," reported an advisory committee, which asked the acting governor to sweep "from the country, & from the earth, if possible, these restless & bloody savages . . ." In February the committee called for a "Ranging corps."[4]

◄ ►

Lipans were there when the Alamo, a makeshift fort patched together from the old San Antonio de Valero Mission, earned its place in history on March 6, 1836. Marcelo de Castro, a brother of Cuelga de Castro, said his people approached to help the Alamo defenders. Apprehended by Mexican soldiers, they had to watch the battle from a distance. "We were hunting. We were far. We return quickly. We witnessed smoke coming from the Alamo," said Calixto Gonzalez Castro. "We were forced by soldiers from entering the Alamo. We witnessed how the Mexican soldiers tossed and burned the bodies of the dead Texans into large fires. We lost family at the Alamo. We buried our dead."[5]

Chief Magoosh, an Upper Lipan, was born near San Antonio in 1821 just weeks after the Mexican flag replaced the Spanish flag. "My grandfather saw the fall of the Alamo when he was a boy. The Apaches were sympathetic with the Americans. They hated the Mexicans," said Richard Magoosh, the chief's grandson.[6]

"My great grandfather escaped [from the Mexicans] and walked this way and rejoined the People," said Meredith Magoosh Begay, a great-granddaughter. "He had worn out his moccasins and walked barefoot through thorns. He killed a deer and used a deerskin to wrap his feet. He sat on top of a hill. He saw kids and yelled. Two girls ran back to their mother and father, saying, 'A ghost is calling us.' Men got on horses to find him. They gave him a horse." The two girls who saw him were Augustina Zuazua and Rose Tahnito, who came to the Mescalero Apache Reservation from Mexico in 1905.[7]

Because this was Lipan country, it's reasonable to assume they were present. Historians are still debating the number of Alamo defenders, and Calixto Castro's recollection indicates that the Lipans weren't necessarily inside the Alamo but were captured and died trying to reach the Alamo. The revolution ended officially on April 21, 1836, but not the hostilities and intrigues, and both sides wanted Indian allies. In August Thomas Rusk, trailing defeated Mexican troops to make sure they crossed the Rio Grande, was cheered to learn that "the Comanches & Lipatlans can be enlisted . . ."[8]

If the tribes had known what was in store, they might have chosen differently. In 1836 Mexican Secretary of War José María Tornel wrote prophetically that as the United States' population increased, its government began to see the inconvenience of Indian treaties. The attitude of white people toward nonwhites "was sufficient for the expulsion of the men of bronze, the redmen, and for the despoliation of their property . . . What was there to restrain Anglo-American greed? Nothing! Might was on their side, the miserable Indians had nothing but their weakness."[9]

◄ ►

With a brutal, expensive war for independence concluded, the new Republic of Texas badly needed to curtail its Indian war. In his inaugural address, President Sam Houston urged Texans to "abstain from aggression, establish commerce with the different tribes, supply their useful and necessary wants, [and] maintain even-handed Justice with them." Houston invited Lipans and other tribes to meetings where they could air grievances and establish trust that could lead to treaties. Castro and the Lipans liked Houston and visited the new president often. The republic's Congress supported Houston's Indian policy and gave him Indian agents and trading posts but ordered a regiment of 280 mounted riflemen to the frontier to enforce trade laws, remove white trespassers from Indian lands and apprehend Indian raiders.[10]

The population then included about 20,000 Indian people (900 Lipans), 30,000 Anglo-Americans, and 3,500 people of Mexican or Spanish descent. The republic's Standing Committee on Indian Affairs pronounced the Lipans, Karankawas and Tonkawas "part of the Mexican nation and no longer to be considered as a different People from that nation." This was the first instance of sustained confusion about whether Lipans were American or Mexican.

Mexicans, still seething at their loss, promised the tribes they could possess Texas. In the lingering animosity, the Lower Lipans carefully maintained their neutrality,[11] which occasioned doubts on both sides. Castro had permission to live near Laredo, but Mexican authorities didn't want him to learn how thinly guarded the town was and "want to carry out the plans he has with the colonists." They monitored Lipans living at Santa Rosa in Coahuila, fearing Castro's influence. In March 1837 a Texan spy came across Castro and forty warriors at Pintas Creek and concluded that "they are hostile to our cause . . ."[12] The Mexicans had more reason to worry. Lipans, Mescaleros, Comanches, and Kiowas were then raiding on the Lower Rio Grande, but the Mexican government couldn't provide relief because of its losses during the disastrous Texas campaigns.[13]

Houston's policy was as pragmatic as it was altruistic. The Indians of the prairies would not be conquered by any number of troops, he wrote in 1838, but they could become friends through trade. "The executive has never yet known a treaty made with an Indian tribe first infracted or violated by them. Everything will be gained by peace, but nothing will be gained by war."[14]

On January 8, 1838, at Live Oak Point on the Gulf Coast near present Corpus Christi, Chief Castro signed "a treaty of Peace and Perpetual friendship." Texas promised to protect the Lipans as long as they remained at peace and didn't disturb Texans or their property. The Texans were to appoint traders, establish trading posts in Lipan territory, and provide $250 in gifts for Castro to distribute. Lipans pledged to deliver livestock or other property, for which they would be paid. If any Lipan committed a violent act or stole property, Castro would deliver him to authorities; if a Texan harmed a Lipan or stole property, the offender would be punished under Texas law. Both Texans and Lipans were guaranteed safe passage when traveling peacefully. James Power, who lived nearby, signed for Texas. "After they signed the treaty, we drank, ate and received many gifts . . ." said Modesto González Castro. Gifts included cloaks, knives, scissors, fur hats, powder flasks and bolts of calico.[15]

Two months later, Castro, one of his sons and a handful of warriors arrived in Houston during Independence Day celebrations. Castro professed his desire to be a friend to the new government. Mexicans had murdered Lipans in the past, he said, and he was confident the Texans would prevail. He was greatly disappointed to learn Houston was in Nacogdoches, but Vice President Mirabeau B. Lamar said he "received them with great kindness and assured them that our government would offer them its protection and aid."

Lamar made sure the Lipans received good rifles, blankets, and American clothes and even took them to a ball, where they made quite an impression. "They are a fine looking and an intelegent tribe and very warlike," wrote a guest. Castro complimented the ladies and honored Erastus "Deaf" Smith, saying, "Castro with two men would go any place; Deaf Smith would go alone." (The intrepid Smith was a spy, scout, soldier and captain in the Texas Revolution; Houston called him "my stay in darkest hour.")

After twelve days, Castro departed for the west after promising to help Texans maintain their new republic and soon moved his camp below Austin. "He is a sagacious, shrewd, and intelligent Indian and is familiar with Mexican politics," wrote Secretary of State Robert Irion to Houston. "He vows eternal hatred to the Mexicans and friendship for the Texians. He is at war with the Comanche and will not make peace with them, until they shall have concluded a permanent treaty with us."[16]

Castro and his people now frequented the Texas settlements, and their close encounters were good for many an anecdote that illustrate their relations. Nicholas Fagan, traveling alone to La Bahía, once spotted a group of Indians approaching. Expecting Comanches or Wacos, he dismounted and stood with his gun cocked. Castro recognized Fagan and ordered his men to halt. Approaching the wary settler alone, Castro told Fagan he was a brave man to leave his horse and stand ready to fight single-handed with a whole group of Indians. It was a high compliment from an Apache. Fagan's daughter recalled that the Lipans were a "comely set of people," who dressed somewhat like white people.[17]

On one occasion, twenty-five Lipans visited Victoria to trade. With them was a Dr. Hanam, who had been a physician in Matagorda but abandoned his wife for a Lipan beauty. The two bought a jar of preserves from John Linn's store and sat on the step to eat it. Asked why he would turn his back on civilization to live with Indians, the doctor claimed he was studying medicinal roots and herbs. After this visit, Lipans and Comanches fought, and the doctor abruptly ended his "studies" and moved to Alabama.[18]

Travelers also admired Lipan women. Francis Latham described them as "elegant specimens of aboriginal or native American female beauty." He called one particularly striking girl "a native queen of the prairie" for her Grecian forehead and nose, graceful movement, erect posture, long braids falling to her waist, and well-crafted clothing. William Bollaert claimed that because the "Lipan women are known for their prettiness and good figures," the Comanches raided Lipans to steal their women. In truth, the tribes routinely took women captives, but on one occasion Bollaert's statement was true.[19]

Chief Magoosh and his No Water Lipans were living on the Rio Grande below El Paso. While the warriors were away hunting buffalo, Comanches raided the village and carried off all the Lipan girls and young women. On their return the Lipan men overtook the Comanches and defeated them. In a hand-to-hand fight, a big Comanche killed Magoosh's brother and, badly wounded, came at Magoosh with a broken arrow. Magoosh, who was about twenty, dispatched him with a knife. It was the first time he'd killed a man.[20]

◄►

Despite treaties and Houston's good intentions, land-hungry white settlers plunged into Indian country, antagonizing tribes and becoming "victims to their own indiscretion and temerity," Houston wrote. Repeated pleas and warnings to land surveyors fell on deaf ears. Houston's Indian commissioner was himself a surveyor.[21] Would-be president Mirabeau Lamar manipulated the waning popularity of

Houston's Indian policy to his advantage, although even Lamar was accused of giving "the Lipan Indians fine cloaths at the expense of the government."

In December 1838 Lamar became president. Earlier that year, he told Castro that his government's policy would be "to maintain amicable and pacific relations with all nations and tribes."[22] Now he said bluntly that native people should be pursued and their sanctuaries destroyed. He subscribed to the United States' policy of pushing them west. Backed by the Texas Congress, Lamar built forts, recruited hundreds of mounted volunteers, and waged new Indian wars. By August his policies were bankrupting the republic. Anson Jones, the republic's minister to the United States, wrote that Texas had enough army and navy officers to defend Russia but couldn't support them much longer. The republic's Indian policy was wrong, he said. "We should be at peace with them, for we can make nothing by war."[23]

Through it all, Castro deftly nurtured a friendship with the belligerent president. The Lipans kept their peace and found new opportunities as scouts and guides with both volunteers and the reorganized, energized rangers. Castro, with the rank of captain, commanded his own Lipan ranger company,[24] which included his son Juan (also called John), who was a colonel, and forty-one privates.[25] While it might appear that the Lipans were trying to stay in the Texans' good graces by serving as auxiliaries—that they might even have been pawns of the Texas Rangers—the Lipans were simply upholding what they saw as an excellent alliance, which allowed them to fight Comanches. In the many times they tried to enlist the Spanish in a campaign against the Comanches, this is the type of alliance they had in mind.

"This tribe seems to have had a flair for diplomacy. It sized up the political situation around it and . . . leagued itself with the strongest, serving with a fair degree of loyalty," wrote historian Hobart Huson. "Thus they successively served with the Spanish, Mexican, and Texian armies, principally as scouts and spies and occasionally as line soldiers."[26]

CHAPTER

Flacco

> At the head of the Lipan tribe was old Chief Flacco, whose son, young Flacco, was the idol of the tribe. Brave and unswerving in his fidelity to the whites, his many services had likewise won him the friendship of all who knew him.
>
> — *Noah Smithwick*[1]

Flacco was a favorite among rangers. Son of the Lipan Chief Flacco and husband of Castro's daughter María, young Flacco proved himself a reliable and fearless scout and spy during the Texas Revolution. As early as 1835, he reported from Zacatecas on Santa Anna's troop strength in battles with his enemies within Mexico. Not yet twenty-five, he had taken the scalps of eight enemies.[2]

"He is the pride and the flower of his tribe, and is as fierce and as brave, as a lion," wrote a newspaper correspondent. "He is tall, straight and active, and a most splendid and graceful rider; and when beheld, as I have seen him, at full speed on his noble war-horse, painted for battle, and armed with bow, shield, tomahawk and lance, he cuts a most martial and dashing figure. Young Flacco is altogether a noble looking fellow, with a generous expression of countenance, a dark and steadfast eye, and a proudly curled lip, which never deigns to tolerate a laugh, and but seldom indulges in the relaxation of a smile."[3]

Flacco wore a string of beads and numerous silver arm and wrist bands. A wide belt across his chest supported the quiver on his back, and a second belt held his hunting knife. Buckskin leggings, decorated with figures in red and black, came to his knees and were attached by thongs to his belt. His moccasins were beaded and fringed.⁴

The rangers were a critical force in Lamar's goal of driving hostile Indians out of eastern Texas and beyond the settlements, and Lipans eagerly joined the ruthless campaigns against Comanches. Subjected to more than a century of Comanche hostility, Lipans would not have faulted ranger tactics, but in time they too would be ranger targets. Early on, however, Castro, Flacco and the Lipans were pivotal figures in some often-repeated ranger stories that shed light on the Lipans' services to the republic.

In January 1839 Lipan hunters discovered a Comanche camp on the San Gabriel, about fifty miles from Austin, and raced back to warn the settlements. Volunteers quickly organized under Captain John Henry Moore. He had fifty-five white rangers and Castro's ranger company, plus the Tonkawa Captain Placído and his twelve men. With scanty rations, the rangers marched up the Colorado in freezing temperatures, following a spy detachment of two Texans and two Lipans. At the headwaters of the San Gabriel, a storm forced them to take shelter, and some of the horses froze to death. "The Indians, loth to see so much good meat go to waste, ate the flesh," wrote Captain Noah Smithwick.

The storm abated on February 13. Scouting ahead, Smithwick and a Lipan spotted a pillar of smoke rising from the San Sabá. They needn't go any farther, the Lipan said, because he knew exactly where the enemy camped. They turned back and rode late into the night. From behind, the howl of a wolf halted the Lipan in his tracks. Minutes later, an answering howl. Wolves or Comanches? Smithwick felt cold chills crawl over his skin. The Lipan, motionless as a statue, kept listening. After a third howl, the Lipan said, with some relief, "Umph, lobo." Continuing on, Smithwick shot a turkey, but they didn't stop until the Lipan found a suitable place—a dry ravine where no trees would reflect the firelight. While Smithwick slept, the Lipan stood guard and roasted the turkey. The next day they rejoined Moore and camped at

Spring Creek, a few miles from the Comanches. Two volunteers and two Lipans crept forward after dark and found the Comanche camp enlarged by other groups setting up their winter quarters. "Disconcerted by the unexpected intelligence, Colonel Moore rather demurred to attacking, but we had come out to hunt a fight and were willing to take the responsibility," Smithwick wrote.

Stealing through timber, the rangers edged closer. A mile out they dismounted and tied their horses. Moore directed Juan Castro and seven Lipans to stampede the Comanches' horses. Captain William Eastland was to form the right wing of the attack, the Bastrop company under Smithwick, the center, and the Lipans under Castro, the left. They planned to keep the timber at their backs and run the Comanches onto the plains, where they would be vulnerable. But they were spotted, and in the cold, pre-dawn light, rangers—Texan and Lipan—vaulted into the village, throwing open tipi flaps and shooting Comanches where they lay.

"Taken completely by surprise the savages bounded from their lodges and scattered like partridges," Smithwick wrote. "Our men rushed right in among the lodges. The women and children screaming, dogs barking, men yelling and shooting, in a moment transformed the peaceful scene on which the day had just dawned into pandemonium."

The rangers, unsettled by the number of Comanches, fired all their weapons at the same time, a tactical error that required pausing together to reload. Moore ordered a retreat—to reload and regroup, he would later say—but the order "threw our men into confusion," said Smithwick. "Quick to grasp and take advantage of the situation the Indians rallied and drove us back to cover of a ravine . . ."

"Old Castro was so disgusted when Colonel Moore ordered a retreat that he withdrew his command and left . . . Old Castro told Colonel Moore at the time that such a thing as ordering a retreat when the enemy was routed and flying had never before been heard of." Castro obviously thought Moore a coward and a fool, but two Lipans remained—Flacco and Juan Sais, a war chief. Juan Castro, meanwhile, ran off part of the Comanches' horses, but Comanches seized the rangers' unguarded horses.

As the Texans pulled back, the Comanches formed a line and advanced. One warrior strode ahead of the others, challenging the Texans, and a ranger shot him. The downed Comanche lay on his back and shot arrows in a high arch that found the Texans "till young Flacco ran out in the midst of a perfect rain of arrows and dispatched him with his lance." Flacco took the man's shield but the Comanches' furious charge kept him from claiming the scalp. They had barely reloaded, when the Comanches charged in front and on both flanks repeatedly. After a time, they withdrew, and the Texans removed to a cedar brake about a mile away.

A Lipan woman who lived among the Comanches approached with a white flag, and Juan Sais interpreted. "She said we had killed some of their bravest men, and asked how many of our men were killed. The wily old chief assured her that we hadn't received a scratch," Smithwick wrote. The woman also said the Comanches had five white captives and offered to exchange them for Comanche captives. The Lipans had already "killed or otherwise disposed of [their captives] without advice from me," Moore wrote; two rangers hoping to recover their relatives were painfully disappointed.

Because the Comanches had their horses, "we were left afoot more than one hundred miles from home, with two disabled men to carry," Smithwick wrote. "So ended our disastrous expedition." Moore figured Comanche casualties were steep. He lost one soldier killed and six wounded. The Lipans under Juan Castro made off with ninety-three horses and mules and later turned in forty-six of them.[5]

In December, Castro and the Tonkawa Chief Plácido with their two hundred men joined Colonel Edward Burleson and his three hundred troops to eject Comanches from the San Sabá country. They found instead a party of Cherokees and attacked them at Pecan Bayou on December 25. The Lipans and Tonkawas, Burleson wrote, "performed their duty with fidelity as scouts, and with bravery in the field."[6]

The rangers in May 1840 awarded Flacco his own command. "He now considers himself a Texas Captain and is highly proud of his new office," reported the Austin newspaper. "Me no fight like Indian any longer and steal horses," he reportedly said. "Me Texian officer and fight like Texians. Me kill Mexicans and no steal." (Quotations like these should be taken with a grain of salt. Flacco may not have spoken parlor English, but writers of the day habitually made Indians sound ignorant.)[7]

In 1840 Castro gave Moore another chance. The chief and sixteen other Lipans, with Flacco as his lieutenant, joined Moore's force of ninety white rangers in another hunt for Comanches. En route, they rediscovered the old San Sabá presidio in good condition, with most of its walls standing. Crossing the Concho, they turned toward the Colorado, and the Lipans found a trail, which they followed up the Red Fork of the Colorado. On October 23 Lipan scouts came upon pecan trees the Comanches were cutting to harvest nuts. Moore sent his two most astute Lipan spies on the best horses to locate the Comanches; his men waited, huddled against a sharp north wind. As evening approached, Castro climbed a tall hill nearby to look for his men and spotted them several miles away. With their shields, they signaled that they had found Comanches.

The party rode up the Colorado and camped, and Moore sent the Lipan scouts out again that night. Texans shivered in their wet clothing while the Lipans slept comfortably in tipis and buffalo robes. The scouts returned around 3 a.m. to report the Comanche camp in a horseshoe bend of the river. They estimated sixty families and one hundred twenty-five warriors. Opposite the camp was a high, somewhat steep bluff. Moore's men advanced within a mile or two of the Comanches. He stationed men on the bluff across the river.

At daybreak they inched within three hundred yards of the sleeping camp, but a Comanche guard yelled a warning. The Texans charged, but before they could do their worst, every warrior and many women prepared to fight. Brawling mostly hand-to-hand, the rangers overwhelmed the Comanches. Those who escaped the first attack became targets for the sharpshooters on the bluff.[8] In the thirty-minute engagement one hundred twenty-eight Comanches died. The Texans had two wounded and took five hundred horses. This time, Castro and Moore had a higher opinion of one another. "Great credit is due the Lipan chief Castro and his men, several of whom served ably as spies," Moore wrote.[9]

On the way back, the party met a small group of "Seratic" Indians near the old San Sabá mission, and Castro spoke with them. Their eight hundred people lived on the Rio Grande and wanted to be friends with the Texans and fight Comanches. These Seratics (from the Shoshonean *charitica*, pronounced saritika) were most likely Llaneros. They later sent two of their captains to treat with Texas at Castro's invitation. David Burnet perceived an "affinity" between the Lipans, Mescaleros and Seratics and believed that together they outnumbered the Comanches.[10]

In late December, after a skirmish between Lipans and Comanches on Elm Creek, Lipans and Tonkawas awaited volunteers for an incursion on hostiles living on the Brazos. Settlements were rapidly expanding, and it was important to dislodge the Indians from "those fertile lands," said a newspaper.[11] The Lipans would soon find themselves among the undesirables.

◄ ►

Flacco's favorite ranger was the brave, unpretentious Jack Hays. Members of his company traveled fast and light, not taking anything they couldn't carry on a horse, and lived on wild game or, if their luck was bad, horse meat.[12] Even so, they were less Spartan than Apaches. Once, when Hays was searching for Mexican bandits, his men stopped at midday to eat, and a recruit offered Flacco some food. Leaning against a tree with his arms folded, Flacco declined. "No, warriors never eat much on warpath . . . Too much eat, too much eat. Captain Hays great chief, but American eat too much on warpath."[13]

From Flacco, Hays learned the fine art of trailing, and the two discussed differences in fighting tactics of the different tribes. If Hays wanted information without attracting attention, he traveled alone and on foot. Comanches visiting San Antonio once asked Flacco about this dangerous habit. Flacco replied, "Me and Blue Wing no afraid to go to hell together. Captain Jack, great brave, no afraid to go to hell by himself."[14]

One of the best known exploits of the two men was the Llano fight. On July 19, 1841, Hays marched to the Frio, leading forty-three rangers, including seven Lipans[15] under Flacco. Several weeks earlier Hays had overwhelmed a Comanche party here and believed they were still nearby. Passing through the rugged country at the head of the Frio's western branch, they found the abandoned camp of about two hundred people. The Comanches had burned the prairie, driving out game and leaving nothing for horses or men to eat. The Lipan scouts began following a small trail and flushed a party of Comanche hunters. Hays and twenty-five men with the strongest horses pursued, but the hunters warned their camp. By the time Hays arrived, women and children were escaping, and about fifty warriors engaged them in a running fight over six miles of rough terrain. The Comanches' tactic was to retreat, stop and form a line, prepare their weapons and fire when the Texans were in range. After two hours of these maneuvers, the rangers' horses were too tired to close in for a good shot.

Hays and some men with the best horses formed an advance. Flacco's horse seemed fresh. One man's horse was so spirited he was afraid to give the animal its head, so Hays proposed a temporary trade. Dashing up to the enemy, Hays fired and then tried to return to his men, but the horse bolted straight toward the middle of the Comanche line. Flacco surged forward to join Hays. As the captain's crazed mount broke through the line, he fired a shot to either side, which found their marks and spooked the horse into running even faster. Flacco was close behind. The Comanches began to surround them, but Hays spurred the horse in a large circle back to the Rangers, shooting a warrior who

attempted to block him, with Flacco still on his heels. Flacco later said
he wouldn't be left behind by anyone but observed that Captain Jack
was "bravo too much."[16]

◄►

The People's tipis, cloud white against the fading light of a clear day,
were scattered over several acres on a grassy bank of the Colorado
below Austin at Hornsby Prairie. Inside, the lodges were carpeted with
a variety of well dressed robes and skins. The camp bustled with preparations for the evening—cooking food, securing nearly a thousand
mules and horses. Small naked boys shot arrows with great accuracy.

"A number of boys, with whips and shouts, were forcing the
immense drove of horses into the limited circuit of the village; still farther, out upon the prairie, some thirty or forty young blades, painted
as striped as the pole of a barber, and all superbly mounted, were dashing about, apparently deeply interested in a race between several fleet
and spirited nags, which was just then about to be run. In one place,
a crowd of old warriors could be seen collected around Onsise [Juan
Sais], their military Chief; in another place, Flacco, in earnest consulta-
tion with some of the powerful Captains of the tribe. Decrepit old men
sat smoking around the doors of the lodges; children and dogs went
running and tumbling upon the grass, and the elderly squaws were
tying their horses with long hair ropes, to stakes that were driven into
the ground, or busily engaged in cooking; while the young warriors
and unmarried damsels were gathered here and there, in small squads
or walked from lodge to lodge, with an air of proud disinterestedness,
among the busy scenes." In the gathering darkness, hundreds of campfires threw a golden light on lodges, people and horses. The next day,
the village disappeared.

"The lodges were all packed upon the backs of mules, and the poles
that supported them dragging upon the ground, and the whole tribe
were in the act of again returning to the wilderness . . . There were
no idlers: all were busy about something, preparatory to their exit."

One person caught a mule, another packed an unruly mustang. A horse kicked, a second one reared, a third plunged and rolled violently. One packed horse, its poles dangling, spooked, which triggered a stampede of the entire herd. Great feats of speed, horsemanship and skill with the lasso were required before horses galloping across the plain were again contained. By that time, many families had started out, winding their way as far as the eye could see.[17]

The People prospered in the Republic of Texas. Their young men were proud to ride with the rangers. Raids on Mexicans and Comanches provided wealth in horses and goods, and they sold horses, buffalo robes, and beautifully tanned and decorated hides. Many even had money; their buffalo robes fetched two dollars each in Houston. There was no hunger, want, or fear. Their chief was respected by Texans and feared by Mexicans.

CHAPTER

Pathetic Incident

The whites were greatly alarmed over the consequences of the das-
tardly outrage, knowing that, if the Lipans learned of it they would take
indiscriminate revenge on the settlers.

— Noah Smithwick[1]

Castro, said the *Texas Sentinel*, "is a man of great courage, wonderful sagacity, and uncommon physical powers; and is also distinguished for his fidelity to the Texian." The Lipans and Tonkawas had so
often proven their friendship in campaigns against hostile Indians "that
a squad of their spies are considered an indispensable acquisition on all
such expeditions." Newspapers routinely reported Castro's good deeds,
and he basked in the affections and esteem of Texans. However, he was
increasingly challenged to maintain a balance between the desires of
his own people and the expectations of the whites. Newcomers, who
didn't know one Indian from another, arrived in ever larger numbers. If
a horse was stolen, they shot any Indian they saw. Lipans took to shouting "Lipan! Lipan!" when they met a Texan to avoid a similar fate. And
after losing several men to poisoned liquor, they didn't drink whiskey
until they first saw white men drink it.[2]

Castro tried to maintain order, but young men are young men, and
his warriors wanted to raid. Incursions into Chihuahua became such
a problem that a two-hundred-man junta organized to repulse tribes
raiding from Texas. A further complication was the arrival of Upper
Lipans from the west. They joined Castro's people near Bexar,[3] but

their seventy warriors weren't necessarily under Castro's control. The Lipans and their confederates in Coahuila and along the Pecos were also outside Castro's influence, and Texans didn't understand that.

Lipan raids in the Refugio area prompted Captain John Scott to gather some volunteers to punish them, and he foolishly took his ten-year-old son, Henry. They followed a trail across the Nueces to the Rio Grande. Near present Brownsville, they were ambushed. Many volunteers died, including Scott, and the raiders took Henry and escaped into Mexico. After a few weeks the boy escaped in the night on a pony picketed nearby.[4] Because Lipans always secured their captives, we can assume they probably considered Henry a liability and staged his escape.[5]

The Texas Congress proposed setting aside a tract on the Colorado for the Lipans and another on the Brazos for the Tonkawas. Proponents claimed these reservations "would form a barrier to the incursions of the northern savages," but recognized that the two tribes would be exposed to attack and probably wouldn't stay.[6] The measure failed.

During 1841 Lipans became the subject of complaints in both Mexico and Texas. Manuel Lafuente in Laredo reported that fifty Lipans in Béxar were preparing to raid in his area and warned Castro that if the thefts and destruction continued, he would call out the militia. Castro promised to obey, but he'd made such promises before, the mayor said. He asked Lamar to "set aside a remote place for them where they cannot harm anyone."[7] More than once the Lipans, all too visible, were unfairly accused of murders and thievery committed by other tribes or Mexican scoundrels. In October 1841 a sheriff ordered the arrest of Castro and Flacco, then camped on the Colorado near Austin, for a murder in Travis County but then changed his mind, probably reminded by wiser heads of the Lipans' faithful service.[8]

The Lipans lost horses to white thieves. Noah Smithwick, a justice of the peace at Webber's Prairie, described one incident: "[T]hree worthless scamps made a raid on the Lipan Indians and stole a number of their best horses. The Indians missed them almost immediately, and getting track of them, came to me to assist them in their recovery."

Smithwick sent two white men with Castro and a party of Lipans, and they overtook the thieves near La Grange. "The ringleaders decamped, leaving a half-witted fellow to bear the consequences. The captive was brought back to me. In a quandary as to what to do with him, I turned to old Castro.

"'What shall I do with him?' I asked.

"The old chief looked contemptuously at the poor trembling wretch, who, frightened out of what little wit he possessed, was literally crying.

"'Oh,' said he, 'turn him loose.'" Castro gave the two white men a pony for their trouble. Smithwick often reflected that if an Indian stole a white man's horse, "hanging was the penalty if he could be caught."[9]

◄ ►

In September 1841, Texans re-elected Sam Houston. As president of a nearly insolvent republic, he again made a priority of peace with the Texas tribes through treaties and posts manned by licensed traders. Fair treatment and trade would be powerful incentives for tribes to preserve the peace, he reasoned, and reputable trading houses "will not cost the government one dollar to the hundred which have been expended to keep up a mockery of war."

He asked merchant G. W. Adams to establish a trading house on the Brazos. "Do request the people not to make the Lipans and the Toncahuas our enemies," he said. Houston preferred to keep them as friends and didn't want any new enemies. "Do these tribes justice—keep liquor from them, and we will have no trouble."[10]

Houston disbanded most of the regular army and mustered in four new ranger companies, but he encouraged restraint among the rangers and ordered them to protect Indian lands from white squatters and illegal traders. Concerned that "some persons on the frontier . . . have a disposition to molest the Tancahua and Lipan Indians," Houston ordered Major Thomas Smith, commander of the rangers, to restore any property stolen from Indians and preserve their friendship.[11]

Houston looked to Indian agents like Colonel L. B. Franks, appointed for the Lipans and Tonkawas on February 1, 1842, to secure peace, but the government's bare coffers compromised his plans. Joseph Taylor, sub-agent to the Lipans and Tonkawas, resigned after a ranger seized his horses for service. Houston couldn't object: "There is not one dollar in the Treasury, which has not been cancelled." In August Houston instructed a new agent to protect them "in the enjoyment of their just rights."[12]

◄ ►

Santa Anna, still fuming over the loss of Texas and further galled at Lamar's brash claim to half of New Mexico, sent troops north in early 1842. They briefly occupied Béxar, Goliad and Refugio. On March 6 Captain Miguel Aznar attacked a party of Lipans who arrived in Refugio the night before from the Rio Grande, killing Castro's nephew and son-in-law. The Mexicans took forty horses and mules, stolen on the Rio Grande, and distributed them among soldiers without horses.

Two days later, a revenge party of three hundred Lipans, Tonkawas and Mescaleros attacked Captain Ramón Valera's camp at Santa Gertrudis and set fire to the prairie grass, which choked Mexican troops as the Indians charged repeatedly. The Mexicans threw back their attackers, Valera reported, but the horse herd stampeded and scattered "so that only the famous skill of the enemy could manage to round them up at a distance . . ." Unable to recover their dead, "the defeated remnant suddenly took to flight raising, as is their custom, a long howl with their wailing." Valera assumed Texans had armed the Indian party.[13]

At that time, Texans were mobilizing. Secretary of War George Washington Hockley organized spy companies to leave March 6 and sent with them Flacco and a small group of Lipans. Flacco and John Castro, commanding fifty-two Lipans, operated at times with Hays and at times under direct orders from Hockley. Castro remained in Austin, which was quickly becoming a ghost town. The Lipans' active involvement spurred rumors in Mexico that Texans, with a thousand Lipans,

were advancing toward the Rio Grande to steal cattle and deprive the
Mexican army of needed supplies.

On Flacco's return, Hockley reported the young warrior's excellent work and noted again the Lipans' value to the spy service. Houston
promoted him to colonel for his courage, loyalty and service to Texas
and presented him with a full colonel's uniform, including a sword and
plumed hat. Flacco kept these prized possessions in a rawhide box and
wore them only on ceremonial occasions. A clerk taught him to write
his name, which he penned Spanish style—"Flacco Colonel."[14]

In June Castro, Flacco, John Castro and a few warriors journeyed
to Houston to seek payment for their services. Hockley asked that the
long-standing claim be paid, but the republic was broke, and unpaid
troops devastated large areas in the state. The Lipans returned to service. Castro accepted new orders and carried a letter from Houston
asking Texas citizens to give the Lipans "evidences of friendship" and
necessary supplies of beef. Besides their valuable service in the past,
"they may, in the future, be very successfully employed in the prosecu-
tion of the war against Mexico."[15]

On June 22 Castro left Houston to gather his men and the Tonkawas, proceed to Corpus Christi, and accompany the Army of the Southwest to the Rio Grande. Without a doubt, they were more disciplined
than the scruffy assemblage they joined. The Texans marched south
and occupied a hillock near Lipantitlan. Lipans and Tonkawas probably
formed the backbone of spy companies sent by Adjutant General James
Davis. After Lipans reported that General Antonio Canales reached the
Nueces, Texans and Mexicans faced one another on July 7 at the Battle
of Lipantitlan. Both sides declared victory and returned home.

On July 20, 1842, a newspaper reported that "Castro, the Lipan
Chief, died lately of a fever, near Austin."[16] He was about fifty. According to family oral history, the venerable Chief Cuelga de Castro died of
cirrhosis of the liver while hunting near Sam Houston's home on the
Brazos River and was buried with full military honors in the Old Missionary Cemetery at San Antonio.[17] The long peace he enabled was

nearly at an end. His sons would try to carry on his diplomatic legacy, but the Texas he embraced would never be seen again.

In November the Lipans divided. John (also called Juan) Castro led his people, with seventy warriors, south to join Lipans living in Mexico; Ramón Castro and his group remained in the north.[18] John Castro would return by 1844. "John Castro, son of the late distinguished General Castro, of the Lipan tribe, has given renewed assurances of a friendly disposition entertained for the Texians by a people so long advised by his father," Houston wrote. He asked citizens to be kind and generous. "They are valuable to us as friends—they are good watches upon our frontier. Were they our enemies, it would do us much injury."[19]

◄ ►

Texans demanded a strike against Santa Anna, and Houston reluctantly sanctioned a campaign under Alexander Somervell. His poorly organized expedition plodded out of San Antonio on November 25, 1842. Hays commanded a battalion of 125 scouts, which included Flacco and Luis, an Apache from New Mexico. "Taking a deaf mute Lipan, whose sense of sight was peculiarly acute, young Flacco led the van, bearing an honorable part in all the engagements along the Rio Grande," for which they received spoils—mostly guns, ammunition, horses and blankets, wrote Smithwick.

Riding ahead, Hays, Flacco and others flushed two Mexican spies between the Nueces and Laredo. In a spirited chase, Flacco led slightly in a field of some twenty-five horses, followed closely by Hays, who injured his horse in the race. They caught one spy, but the other escaped and would likely warn Laredo. Behind them, Somervell ordered a detour to the Laredo road; horses and livestock muddled through bog and chaparral for two days. On December 6, Flacco reported that Hays and his party reached Laredo and found no significant Mexican force. Laredo surrendered to the Texans, and the alcalde and several Mexicans came out to shake hands, but as one approached Flacco he leveled his lance. Because of hearsay that Mexicans killed John Castro and nearly all his people on their way to the Rio Grande, Flacco swore his lasting hatred of Mexicans. He refused to speak to a single Mexican.

On December 11 Somervell admitted the expedition was a failure and told his men they could leave without dishonor. Somervell and two hundred men returned home, and five hundred crossed into Mexico. Luis wanted to rejoin his tribe, and Hays suggested to Flacco that he leave with Somervell, a suggestion Flacco would likely have taken as an order. Somervell offered Flacco a reward to return to the Nueces and bring in some horses they left. Accompanied by Luis, two Mexicans and several Texans, Flacco began driving the horses back to Texas. Luis became ill, and he and Flacco stopped on the Medina while the Texans reportedly went on. The next morning the two white men, Tom Thernon and James B. Reavis (or Ravis), were reported missing and days later were seen in Seguin with Flacco's horses. Reavis shot Flacco while he was sleeping and made off with his horses, wrote Lamar.

James O. Rice found the bodies of Flacco and Luis near the road about twenty miles west of Bexar. Fearing repercussions, the Texans made it appear that Mexicans murdered the two men and also spread rumors that six dead Cherokees were found nearby, but when Old Flacco and the Lipans investigated, they concluded the murderers were some of Somervell's men.

"They seem confident that he has been murdered by white men," reported a newspaper, which predicted they would "avenge the supposed injury." The account questioned the Lipans' friendship and hinted they were responsible for depredations in the previous six months. "Of the integrity and honesty of Flacco, no one has had a doubt, and had it not been for his efforts to keep the others within bounds, it is thought by many they would heretofore have been more open in their hostility."[20]

Old Flacco visited Smithwick to learn what happened. He and his wife had been frequent visitors, often arriving with gifts of game and small beaded moccasins for Smithwick's little boy. "I dared not tell him the truth," Smithwick wrote.

To Houston, the chief wrote on March 24, 1843: "I am in bad health & fild with sorrow on account of the death of my son I wish you would giv me all the information you can I sent you a mustang stallon to the care of Col. Burleson which he will return to you Sence the death of my Sone I wish my name altered & call Senior Yawney I dislike to hear the name of Flacco."[21] At the chief's request, Smithwick wrote to Houston and General Burleson; both responded that Mexican bandits murdered young Flacco and his companion, and a letter from the Lipans' friend José Antonio Navarro corroborated the story. Houston's letter of sympathy, written on March 28, has appeared in nearly every collection of Texas materials, usually in prose, but the original was a prose poem:

"My heart is sad!
A dark cloud rests upon your nation.
Grief has sounded in your camp;
The voice of Flacco is silent.
His words are not heard in Council;
The Chief is no more.
His life has fled to the Great Spirit;
His eyes are closed;
His heart no longer leaps
At the sight of the buffalo.
The voices of your camp
Are no longer heard to cry
"Flacco has returned from the chase."
Your chiefs look down on the earth
And groan in trouble.
Your warriors weep.
The loud voice of grief is heard
From your women and children.
The song of birds is silent.

The ears of your people
Hear no pleasant sound.
Sorrow whispers in the winds,
The noise of the tempest passes.
It is not heard.
Your hearts are heavy.
The name of Flacco brought
Joy to all hearts.
Joy was on every face,
Your people were happy.
Flacco is no longer seen in the fight.
His voice is no longer heard in battle.
The enemy no longer
Makes a path for his glory.
His valor is no longer
A guard for his people.
The might of your nation is broken.
Flacco was a friend to his white brothers.
They will not forget him;
They will remember the red warrior.
His father will not be forgotten.
We will be Kind to the Lipans.
Grass will not grow
On the path between us.
Let your wise men give the counsel of peace.
Let your young men walk in the white path.
The grey headed men of your nation
Will teach wisdom.
Thy brother, Sam Houston"[22]

The famous letter was one part sentiment, one part political persuasion: "I hope it will be interpreted to him with care," he wrote Indian agent Benjamin Bryant. "I send him four plugs of tobacco. To his wife I send eleven shawls, the mother of young Flacco that was slain. Of his murder I know nothing, only it is said that Mexicans from the Rio Grande killed him . . . If the Lipans and the Toncahua will go out to take satisfaction for his death, tell them by no means to harm women and children."[23]

Smithwick rode thirty miles to the Lipan camp with the letters. "It was a delicate mission, for I knew that old Flacco idolized his son, who was indeed a noble young chief. I interpreted such portions of the letters as I deemed expedient, being very careful to leave no room for doubt as to the Mexican robber story."

Accustomed to Indian stoicism in the face of tragedy, Smithwick was unprepared for Old Flacco's grief. "Tears rained down the old man's face while sobs fairly shook his frame. I felt how useless words were in such a crisis. I could only express my sympathy by the tears that welled up to my own eyes."

When Flacco grew calm, he thanked Smithwick and the others who offered their sympathies. Then he said, "It has always been our custom to destroy everything belonging to the dead, but my son was the white man's friend and I want to do with his things as white men do." Smithwick suggested to Flacco that he keep his son's things. "Oh no, no," he said. "I don't want them where I can see them. It makes me sorry. I want to forget."

A few days later, Old Flacco sent four of his son's horses—a saddle horse for Smithwick, a mare and colt for General Burleson and a young mustang that young Flacco had caught and trained for Houston. He entrusted Houston's horse to a mail carrier, but it didn't arrive. Days later Old Flacco and his wife visited Smithwick again. They obviously hadn't been eating. Smithwick's wife prepared dinner, and Smithwick persuaded them to eat. "It was the last time I ever saw them, as the tribe shortly after left the country . . ." Believing Texans had murdered their beloved Flacco, his group moved across the Rio Grande and turned their wrath on their former allies. In a handwritten account, Smithwick called the murder "one of the most pathetic incidents in the history of Texas."

John and Ramón Castro were angry about Flacco's death and grieved along with his widow, their sister María, according to Lipan oral history. Ramón didn't trust Texans to protect them, and he argued with John. Ramón's group remained in the Bastrop area, camped on Cedar Creek with the Tonkawas until that summer, when they were struck by an epidemic that was particularly deadly among men; the two groups lost a fifth of their warriors. Settlers, convinced they were stealing horses, wanted them to leave. They moved that fall to the Guadalupe, where the cypress bowers and cool, blue-green waters had always been inviting.[24]

Flacco's people took their revenge. Settlers hauling a load of corn a few miles from Austin were attacked by fifty Indians they believed were Lipans. A heavy rain had impaired their guns, leaving them all but defenseless; two settlers died and three escaped into the timber. Earlier, Lipans were suspected of killing travelers on the western roads and attacking settlers near Austin and Corpus Christi.[25] It was the end of an era. Lipans and Americans would still ride together, but Flacco's death broke the trust, and there was no Castro to mend it.

Reavis was never brought to justice. The murderers calculated that when the army disbanded, men would be eager to get home and not want to pursue the murderers, wrote Judge Dudley Wooten. "They were seen with Flacco's horse and saddle and could easily have been arrested; but military authority had ceased, and mob authority did not assert itself in the hour of need. The Lipans cannot be blamed for making war on the white people. The nation which, having reasonable means of finding out the culprits, fails to punish such a crime, is guilty of the crime itself as 'accessory after the fact.' "[26]

Promises, Promises

The Lipan are a tribe of considerable importance, and may be ranked next to the Comanche among the Indians of Texas.

— David Burnet, 1847[1]

As Houston nervously stonewalled Old Flacco, General G. W. Terrell pledged during the first council at Tehuacana Creek in March 1843 that white people would do justice to Indian people and that "none shall intrude upon them." Terrell also promised them "a country to live in, in Texas," and "a great abundance of buffalo and other wild game to feed the red men who come to live in Texas."[2]

On February 3, 1844, following a series of councils, Houston signed a new treaty with all the Texas tribes except the Comanches and Kiowas. It embodied all the principles of his peace policy but didn't draw a line between settlers and tribes. Ramón Castro and his brother Seuge represented the Lipans. They were already at peace with the Comanches, and for months five Caddos had camped with Lipans on Boregas Creek, south of San Antonio. Lipans were also on tributaries of the Guadalupe northwest of Gonzales and ranged between the headwaters of the Llano and Frio. In June Comanches defeated by Mexicans near Matamoros fell in with a party of Lipans who brought them to their well-stocked camp on the Frio and gave them supplies and horses.[3]

On October 7 at Tawakoni Creek, Houston gathered the tribes for another council. "I want the Lipan and all the other Indians to become friendly, as brothers, and to bury the tomahawk," Houston said. "The Comanche and Lipan have made peace, and I want them to keep it fast."[4] Representing the Lipans were principal chiefs Chiquito, Juan Castro, and Roan. With them were Seuge Castro, Flacco Chico (Little Flacco, probably Young Flacco's son), and Castillo. This list squares more or less with an agent's tally of primary leaders: Lemas Castro, principal chief; Ramón Castro and Juan (John) Castro, war chiefs; Captain Roan, war chief; Captain Chiquito, civil chief; and Captain Chico, civil chief.[5]

Two days later the republic forged another treaty. The tribes promised not to treat with any nation (namely, Mexico) at war with Texas, nor would they steal. They would trade only with Texans, and Texas would establish trading posts for them, operated by men of good character. No whiskey would be sold to Indians. The Texans promised to keep bad men from the Indians' hunting grounds, to supply weapons for hunting, and to send blacksmiths and teachers. Should the Indians go to war, they would confine their aggression to warriors and not kill, capture, or injure women and children. They agreed to give up their captives. The tribes refused to designate a permanent dividing line but agreed that the line of trading houses could serve as a boundary between Indians and whites.

Signing for the Lipans were Ramón Castro and Captain Chico. President Anson Jones signed on February 5, 1845.[6] Jones continued Houston's peace policy, convinced it was cheaper and more humane to buy friendship with the tribes than to fight them. The total cost of Indian affairs in Houston's second term was $139,092; Anson Jones would spend $45,000 in 1845. (Ramón Castro received gifts during his November visit; he surprised Jones by asking for an umbrella.) Lamar's persecution of tribes had cost $2,552,319.[7]

◄►

On September 19, 1845, Indian commissioners convened the tribes at Tehuacana Creek. Ramón Castro, Chiquito and Captain Chico, along

the settlements because they were often with Lipans who visited, authorities removed the Lipans from the San Antonio River to the San Gabriel, above Austin.[13]

Neighbors bristled at false and inflammatory reports in the press. In October 1845, he rode into Austin with Lipans and Tonkawas to assail the *Texas National Register* for a report that John Castro was hostile. Another story had Captain Hays killing two Comanches found in John Castro's camp with American horses, but Hays hadn't been in the Lipan camp for months. The truth: On October 27, Castro rode sixty miles in one day to find Neighbors and report that Comanches came to his camp with two American horses and other plunder. The agent, with an army detail, arrested the Comanches in the Lipan camp. A third claimed John Castro was in frequent communication with the Seratics, and was "well known" to be hostile.

"The Indians in my charge have for the last six months shown every disposition to be true friends to Texas," he wrote. "They have rendered services to the government as spies, against both the hostile Indians and Mexicans; in fact, are exceedingly anxious to be so employed." Printed yarns kept white settlers stirred up, while rumors about attacks by frontiersmen circulated among the tribes, keeping them agitated as well.[14]

◄►

With Texas statehood around the corner, not to mention war with Mexico, the Commissioner of Indian Affairs in fall 1845 ordered Pierce M. Butler and Colonel L. G. Lewis to negotiate a treaty between the United States and the wild tribes. In mid-February 1846, Lipans accompanied Butler and Lewis to Comanche Peak for a council, where participants in beaded finery also enjoyed feasts, dances and games. A Lipan woman married a Kichai man. She was "dressed in fringed buckskin jacket, and also fringed bootees ornamented with slaybells [small tin bells], and her ladyship thickly painted, dress and all," wrote Elijah Hicks, a Cherokee judge and former editor. The couple, covered with one blanket, walked among the lodges with a drum beating. Hicks was taken with the Lipans: "My tent door and fire side has been constantly thronged with Lipan naked boys, with calico clouts dragging to the ground, old grannies, children and misses dressed in buck Skin Capes & petticoats & bootees, all elegantly fringed and would be a rich dress any where."[15]

Commissioners told the assembled tribes that they wanted to make a permanent peace and end horse stealing. The chiefs wanted their war captains and as many of their people as possible to hear the white men. They had made treaties before, and when the white men failed to keep their word, the people held their chiefs responsible.[16] After the chiefs returned with 19,000 of their people—Comanches, Lipans, Tonkawas, Caddoes, and Wichitas—they finalized the treaty. They still didn't have a boundary line, but the United States pledged to pay tribes an annuity and provide a blacksmith. Licensed traders would live among them, but if chiefs complained of unfair dealings, the license would be revoked. Tribes and Texans would give up captives. Felons of either race would be tried by law, and both had to stop stealing horses. Anyone selling liquor to Indians would be punished. The terms were standard, but the treaty marked a turning point: Tribes acknowledged for the first time the Americans' dominant position, wrote historian F. Todd Smith.[17] Forty-one chiefs, including Lipans, would travel to Washington and meet President James Polk, who signed the treaty March 8, 1847.

The council was still in session when Neighbors arrived with news that Texans accused Lipans camped on the Colorado (Ramón Castro's people) of stealing stock and killed many people, including women and children. The news "caused the most heart-rending national mourning by the Lipan women encamped here, loud with their shrieks which lost their sound in the distant heaven," wrote Hicks. Even then, Ramón Castro tried to observe the treaty in good faith. Late in 1846 he delivered three horses.[18]

New treaties raised anxieties across the border. Convinced that Texans were arming the tribes to make war on the Mexican frontier, Mexico ended its peace with the "barbarian tribes" in February 1845. A month later Colonel Calisto Bravo, in Laredo, got wind of a new threat. At the headwaters of the Colorado, supposedly, were fifteen hundred Lipans planning to invade Mexico. Rumors continued to fester about various combinations of Indians and Texans massing at different locations for an invasion, but Mexico still hoped to pacify the Lipans. In September Bravo sent spies to Béxar to watch the Texans' movements and instructed them to bring back a Lipan to learn if peace was possible. Lipans were afraid to visit Laredo, but three Lipans, two men and a woman, would go if their friends Esteban Rodrigues and Francisco Jaures came to get them.[19] It was evidently a successful visit.

◄ ►

One unfortunate turn in council deliberations occurred when Butler and Lewis learned that two young Lipan warriors killed two Germans gathering timber at the head of the Medina. Because the Germans couldn't speak English, Spanish or any Indian languages and wore wooden shoes, the Lipans concluded they must be intruders. The warriors must have been newcomers; resident Lipans were well acquainted with Germans. After Butler ordered the Lipan chief to produce the two men to stand trial for murder, the group fled to Mexico. Commissioners had a poor understanding of Texas Indians, said ranger Buck Barry. "The tribe of Lipans, that had befriended Texas in all her struggles, this tribe had no sins to attone for. If Texas was annexed, the Lipans would be annexed also."[20]

Lipans were on good terms with the German immigrants who populated the new towns of Castroville, New Braunfels and Fredericksburg after 1844. Frontier novices, the Germans needed venison, and their wagonloads of supplies offered new trade opportunities. John Castro was well known; at New Braunfels, he took wine and cake as a guest of Prince Carl of Solms-Braunfels.[21]

Visiting Lipans often wore religious medals and cherished the small prints of saints the priest at Castrovillle gave them. One Sunday the Lipans arrived during Mass and positioned themselves before the chapel. "They seemed delighted with the sacred music, and made movements corresponding with the congregation during the celebration of divine service," wrote Father Emmanuel Domenech. Most likely, they had spent time in missions.

"One of the Lipan chiefs, named Castro, was far from being a person of savage character. He had a daughter of singular beauty, who died soon after completing her eighteenth year," Father Domenech recalled. During her illness she stayed at the home of the colony's founder, where she heard her first piano music. Bewildered at first, she touched the wood, examined the instrument on all sides, and "then gave way to alternate fits of laughter and tears . . . every note seemed to electrify her . . ."[22]

Along with wine, cake and music, the Germans brought artists who left behind some spectacular visual records of Texas tribes. They documented daily life and humanized the people rather than demonizing them, as Frederick Remington did, even though the artists were well aware of raids and atrocities attributed to their subjects. Theodore Gentilz first encountered Indian people as a surveyor in 1844 for colonizer Henri Castro, and enjoyed portraying their tranquil, daily life. "Camp of the Lipans," done in 1845, is one of the best representations of Lipans. His idyllic scene captures Lipans at ease and a warrior "fishing" with bow and arrow.[23]

Portrait painter Richard Petri made friends with natives by handing out sketches. One of his most memorable portraits is a rendering of a young Lipan man wearing a gorget of three crescents, possibly made by Petri's brother-in-law, artist Hermann Lungkwitz; Indians brought silver to his shop to be fashioned into ornaments. A small painting of a girl eating watermelon is probably Lipan. When Petri initially asked to paint the child, the mother asked him to wait until she could make new clothing.[24]

In fall of 1845, after General Zachary Taylor sent troops to Corpus Christi, Juan Castro guided Colonel William G. Cooke, responsible for raising troops for Taylor, to Corpus Christi. Local people accused Castro of leading Lipans in a raid on Refugio a year earlier and threatened his life, and so the army housed Castro in the soldiers' quarters for

"Plains Indian with Hair-Pipe Breastplate," 1852, by Friedrich Richard Petri, di_04093, *Dolph Briscoe Center for American History, The University of Texas at Austin*

protection. Neighbors had blasted a newspaper for the Refugio report and said John Castro had been with him at the time. Riding back to his camp, Castro was shot and wounded by parties hiding in a thicket, treated by the army, and escorted to his camp by Cooke. He was probably scouting or spying on Mexican movements for the Americans. In 1846 the state Senate formally received John Castro.[25]

Disagreement over the boundary became the lit fuse that exploded as the Mexican War in 1846. Whether the border was the Rio Grande or the Nueces, it was another of the white men's invisible lines; Lipan country lay on both sides of the river. It must have been a surprise to the 2,500 Lipan families who migrated north to what they considered Indian country to learn they couldn't stay. When Mexico forced their sons into the army, they fled with sizable herds from twenty-six villages and joined other Lipans scattered from the Colorado, eighty miles above Austin, to the mouth of the Pecos. They were planting corn on the San Sabá when they learned of the commissioners' peace talks, and three of their chiefs attended to assure the Americans of their friendship. Texans were mystified by the new arrivals.

"They resemble the Lipans in their language and customs; their warriors are large and well formed men and so closely resemble those of the Lipans that it is difficult to distinguish them," reported a newspaper. They too made peace with the Comanches but had no confidence in them after seeing the Comanches with horses stolen from them in Mexico. Believing they were forced to choose between two great evils, they wanted to be under the protection of the United States and have a home assigned to them.[26]

Butler and Lewis described the new arrivals as "Es ree que tees" (*esikwita*, also *essequeta*, the Comanche word for Lipans),[27] who numbered about 3,500, plus five hundred Mescaleros.[28] Combine this number with the

"Plains Indian Girl with a Melon," by Friedrich Richard Petri, di_04092. *Dolph Briscoe Center for American History, The University of Texas at Austin*

900 Lipans previously estimated to be in Texas, and the population of 4,400 is about the same as it was in 1792, which indicates the Lipans had recovered their losses from war and disease but hadn't grown.

When Governor James Pinckney Henderson learned of Essequetas' presence "with the intention of remaining," he instructed Neighbors to assure them of friendship but make no promises they could stay. In fact, he should avoid discussing their settlement and inform the Lipans "that the State of Texas has the Exclusive right to the land they occupy . . ." Several chiefs visited the governor and were told they could stay temporarily if they planted corn.[29]

Governor George Tyler Wood, the state's second governor, wanted the government to run all the Indians out of Texas, but Captain James H. Ralston, at San Antonio, argued that most Indian aggression stemmed from "improper encroachments by white men on Indian rights," so it was the government's duty to defend Indian rights.[30] Secretary of State David Burnet believed subjugation or removal of tribes was inevitable and necessary for "the progress of civilization," and yet he seemed unwilling to remove the Lipans. "They have never made war upon our frontier; and their present equivocal condition is to be regretted. They are more enterprising and warlike than the Comanche, who regard them with a respect, in which fear is a chief ingredient."[31] Financial pressures prevailed. Rather than settling tribes on their own lands, Texas chose to use land to retire debts of the republic and handed the United States responsibility for 124,000 Indian people.[32] This fact argues against "ethnic cleansing." The desire for land was paramount, and tribes represented an obstacle. Prevailing attitudes and prejudices were just another argument for removal.

Lipans had flourished during a long period of peace, but their well being and their presence hinged on their usefulness to Texans, as they themselves recognized in their repeated offers to serve as scouts. For a time, powerful friends spoke for them, but their foothold was slipping.

CHAPTER

Chiquito

Unless some measures are adopted to check the disposition of the rangers to attack parties of friendly Indians whom they meet, it must ere long, involve us in a war with them.

— *Robert S. Neighbors, 1848*[1]

Three hundred Comanches raided Goliad one night in early 1847 and drove off the horses. Lipans, camped nearby, gave chase along with some settlers. A shortcut brought them ahead of the raiders, and they hid in the tall grass. Lipans fired on the Comanches, who were riding in their direction, then slipped away, took up a new position, and fired again. Like wraiths, they appeared and disappeared with each volley. The Comanches abandoned their prizes.[2] This event was one of the last gestures of friendship. After this, relations with Texans began to deteriorate.

May 1847 marks a turning point. Sixty or seventy Lipans stole several hundred horses and mules from a hacienda near Parras, Coahuila, and killed several men. The owner sought help from occupying American troops, and they hid in a corral at El Pozo, which had the only well in fifty miles. When the Lipans rode in, soldiers rushed out, and the Lipans "received them with contempt," according to physician A. Wislizenus. The American riflemen did little damage in the first charge, but after they dismounted, their aim improved. The Lipans fought with determination. Bravest of all was their medicine man, wearing a headdress of feathers and thorns.

As their losses mounted, the Lipans retreated, leaving fifteen dead, along with thirteen captives and all their booty. The fallen Indians were well proportioned and very muscular, the physician wrote. Mexicans stripped the bodies, and Wislizenus himself took the slain medicine man's skull, which he sent to a craniologist in Philadelphia. Mexicans said the Lipans lived in the mountains of the Bolsón and raided far to the south. They often passed through El Pozo and were so arrogant, they notified the Mexicans in advance to fill basins for their arrival. The Mexicans were afraid to disobey. One irony of the war was that Mexicans feared tribes more than they did Americans. Decades of attacks by Comanches, Kiowas and Apaches had so depopulated and weakened the northern Mexican states that they could muster little resistance during the Mexican War, wrote historian Brian DeLay.[3]

A month after the fight at El Pozo, Lipans on a revenge raid attacked a courier on the Laredo road bearing dispatches from Jack Hays to General Taylor. Hays sent rangers to recover the materials, and they fired on Lipans, wounding one or two, but the Lipans escaped. Neighbors was helpless. The Lipans were living on the Rio Grande and the Nueces, beyond his control. He sent for their chiefs,[4] but before they could communicate, rangers led by Captain Bezaleel W. Armstrong attacked a Lipan camp, killing more than thirty Lipans in their sleep. They fled to the Pecos, joining other Apaches far from the reach of the rangers or Neighbors.[5]

Just four years earlier, in the emotional wake of Flacco's murder, the rangers had promised to protect his people. Armstrong's attack introduced a long period of conflict between Lipans and rangers—all protested furiously by Neighbors and other agents. The rangers were also gaining notoriety for their excesses along the border and their mistreatment of Hispanic people. "These blood-thirsty men, who have neither faith nor moral feeling, massacred a whole division of the Lipan tribe, who were quietly encamped near Castroville: they slew all, neither woman nor child was spared," wrote Father Domenech. "They rifled the dead bodies of their clothing, in which half the assassins clothed themselves, and then amused themselves by a sham battle." The priest considered rangers "the very dregs of society, and the most degraded of human creatures."[6]

In January 1848 the ranger company of Captain J. B. Gillett, who used an Apache scalp as a holster cover, lost some horses, so he and his men attacked a small Lipan camp, killing seven people. A passing Comanche raiding party had taken the horses. After two more unwarranted attacks, Neighbors protested that rangers, instead of recovering a stolen horse through an agent, attacked and massacred the first Indians they found. Any more attacks "must involve us in difficulties with the wild Indians that it would be impossible to adjust without much blood."[7]

◄►

The white people multiplied like mosquitos after a rain. The People were being pushed this way and that by rangers and soldiers and sometimes settlers. They hardly got their corn planted in one place before they were ordered to leave. The People were accustomed to moving, but now they felt like wild animals, wandering here, running there. A man couldn't sit before his lodge, smoke and watch his children in peace, and the women never knew when they would have to drop everything, snatch up their children and run for their lives.

Chiquito, a civil chief, and Chipota, a war chief, led their group northwest to a spring at the headwaters of the Frio, where the mountains were cloaked with dense thickets of blackberries, grape vines, and plum trees, as well as cedars and silver birches. Both men were in their sixties and not inclined to impetuous actions, but they knew the treaties were scratches in the sand. They began raiding. During one sweep, they stole a mule and horse belonging to Bigfoot Wallace, a hero of the revolution and legend among rangers. Chief Chipota's daughter,[8] recognized the animals and warned her people that the big ranger would come after them.

Wallace let a month pass before he organized a pursuit, reasoning that the Lipans wouldn't expect a reprisal so late. He raised about thirty men and rode through Bandera Pass to the Guadalupe valley. The trail was obliterated, but Wallace knew if he could get within a dozen miles of their camp, he'd pick up the tracks of hunting parties. At the head of the Guadalupe they found ample signs. Wallace and one other man continued on foot toward the head of the Frio. Spotting smoke, Wallace reached for his spyglass and saw two women smoking bees out of a tree to collect honey.

The next day, smoke drew them to the Frio's east fork headwaters, and Wallace led his men down a draw between timbered ridges. On the southern ridge two Lipan boys drove two hundred horses and mules to water, which masked the sound of the approaching rangers. They charged into the camp, surprising the Lipans, who were feasting on buffalo meat, their shields and bows on the ground or hung in trees. Shouting and gunfire stampeded the Lipan herd, adding to the confusion. The chief's daughter sprinted through the stampeding horses toward Wallace, screaming, "El Capitan! El Capitan! Wallaky! Wallaky!" Wallace told her to grab the tail of his buckskin hunting shirt, and she stayed close to Wallace, parroting his movements for the remainder of the fight.

Ten Lipans died and the rest scattered. Wallace's men collected 190 horses and mules—but not Wallace's horse and mule—along with shields, bows and moccasins. One shield was decorated with two rattlesnake tails, each with thirty-two rattles. He told the wailing girl not to "take on" and left her with an old woman to await the return of their people.[9] Wallace had compassion enough to spare the girl but otherwise felt no remorse. In a fictional account, an acquaintance of Wallace's thought some regrets were in order, so he invented them: "I sincerely wished on her account that I had permitted her tribe to go unpunished . . ."[10]

◄ ►

Chiquito, his people secure again in the rugged canyons of the Guadalupe headwaters, stepped back on the peace path. In April 1848 he found Neighbors about one hundred miles north of Austin. Asked why they stayed away from the previous year's council, Chiquito said that after Armstrong attacked them and they moved to the Pecos, they were afraid to approach the white settlements until they learned of Neighbors' promise of friendship. The agent said they were "much disposed for peace."[11]

Lipans objected to military enforcement of an imaginary line ten miles above Torrey's Trading Post, which "deprives them by force of what they consider to be their rights when there is no treaty defining their boundary," Neighbors wrote. The agent was still troubled by the rangers' rash attacks and indignant that traders were "supplying as much whiskey as they can sell." Despite treaty obligations, neither agents nor the federal government had authority to keep unruly white people out of Indian country or prevent the sale of liquor.[12]

Chiquito's Lipans tried to show their good faith. In August, Chipota, himself a former ranger, rode hard and without sleep to inform the rangers that a party of Comanches visited his camp, announced their intention to steal horses from Captain Highsmith's company, and threatened punishment if the Lipans didn't join them. They rode in the direction of San Antonio after snatching up a Lipan woman and a horse. Chipota considered Highsmith a friend and warned him that the Comanches and other tribes planned to attack white people.[13] The Comanches made good on their threat in October. Can-See-Nothing, a Comanche chief, brought seven horses stolen from rangers to the Lipan camp. "The Americans will follow the trail to my camp and will fight me and my people for what you have done," Chiquito said.

"I don't care," said Can-See-Nothing. "You and your men have [guided] the Americans to the Comanche camps."

Soldiers led by Lieutenant H. M. C. Brown trailed the stolen horses to Chiquito's camp, killed thirty Lipans and took two hundred of their horses. Had they asked, Chiquito said, he would have helped them catch the Comanches. The army promised to recover the Lipans' horses, but not one was returned. Chiquito's people fled and began taking revenge.

In a month's time, about twenty Texans were dead or missing and forty horses and mules were stolen between San Antonio and the Guadalupe River. Can-See-Nothing later admitted to Neighbors that he stole the horses but refused to give them up.

Captain John York organized volunteers from De Witt County to drive Chiquito from the area. In a scrape west of the San Antonio River, the Lipans prevailed. Chiquito later told Neighbors that the last man he killed was probably York. Neighbors added, "That was not the last. You killed a man near where I live, and cut him all to pieces."

"No, my people did not kill him. Two of them saw two Tonkawas; each one had a man's thigh tied to his saddle. The Lipans do not eat their enemies."[14]

◄ ►

Lipans became scarce in Texas. Some were living to the northwest, some were on the Pecos, many were back in Mexico, and all were at war, doing a great deal of damage around San Antonio, Corpus Christi and along the Rio Grande. An army quartermaster considered them well armed and "perhaps, the bravest and most daring" of tribes.

In early 1849 Neighbors estimated five hundred Lipans with one hundred warriors (probably the most visible Lower Lipans), fifteen hundred Mescaleros with three hundred warriors, and fifteen hundred "Euquatops" (probably the Upper Lipans and their allies) with three hundred warriors. He hadn't spoken with the Lipans for months and thought it would be impossible to make amends without money or presents. They were often beyond the Texas frontier settlements among the "wild tribes with whom they kept up a constant traffic and have always been suspected of doing much mischief, both in stealing and killing," sharing their knowledge of the settlements with their aggressive cousins.[15]

Who were the wild tribes? The known Eastern Apache bands then included Jicarillas, Mescaleros, "Sacramentos," Agua Nuevas, Lipans, "Carrijalanians," (Carlanas, or Lipiyans) and "Yanéros" (Llaneros).[16]

The Agua Nuevas were a Mescalero band ranging from Presidio del Norte to San Elizario on both sides of the border. The Sacramentos, probably the former Natagés or Faraons, lived in the Organ, Sacramento and Sierra Blanca Mountains of southern New Mexico. Llaneros were still on the plains between the Pecos and Rio Grande.[17]

Reports of Lipan forays peppered authorities in 1849: They carried away children, took hundreds of horses and cattle from Texas ranches, and killed a wagon driver near La Mesa. At times they were joined by Comanches.[18] Neighbors was then on his way out. After the Whig victory in the 1848 election, the government replaced Neighbors with Judge John H. Rollins, an asthmatic. "[M]en incompetent, both physically and mentally, were placed in charge of the Indians," wrote Houston. "The consequence was that the Indians had not a friend to travel with them [nor] one who had been associated with them in their hunts."[19]

In March 1850 four dragoons escorting a wagon near Fort Inge stopped to rest at a water hole and perished after being surrounded by hostile Lipans. Captain William J. Hardee followed the attackers' trail to the Rio Grande. Indian spies watched travelers between the fort and Eagle Pass. "If the party is large and shows indication of pursuit, they fly into the mountains, scatter and elude detection; if on the other hand the party be small, they unite and attack it," he said. In July Hardee directed an expedition against the Lipans. Soldiers moved down the left bank of the Frio, Bigfoot Wallace with his rangers moved down the right bank of the Nueces, and Hardee himself scoured the country in between. They attacked two parties, killing nine and wounding nine. Hardee kept up his sweeps all summer, starting one patrol as soon as another finished.[20]

Henry found them in September. "The Lipans are decidedly for peace. They have always been friends of the Texans and they desire to be so still," Henry wrote. They told him they wanted an area designated for their home where they could raise corn. They had apparently broken with the Comanches and repeated their desire to join the Americans and fight their old enemies. When Kiowas approached menacingly, Lipans told the Kiowas they would have to fight Lipans too. Chiquito conducted Major Henry to Lipan Creek and the trail to San Sabá.[6]

In November Lipans, Buffalo Hump's Comanches, Caddos, Quapas, Tawakonis and Wacos met on Spring Creek, near the San Sabá. Their treaty, signed on December 10, contained the usual language about trade, captives, crimes, and liquor. Signing for the Lipans were Chiquito, Chipota, Yekehtasna and Kehrauch. General George M. Brooke directed his officers "to carry out the spirit of this Treaty so far as can consistently be done" and hoped Texas citizens would be accommodating, but the unauthorized, unapproved treaty wasn't binding.[7]

Lipans visited Fredericksburg and Fort Martin Scott regularly during 1851 and notified troops of fresh trails leading to the Rio Grande, but if they expected the government to feed them, they were disappointed. There was no such provision. "[I]t would be folly to advise them to make fields where they would be dispossessed in less than a year and they must and will steal," Rollins wrote.[8] In October, a month after Comanches struck Chiquito's camp on the Concho, Lipans, Mescaleros and Southern Comanches met agent John Rogers at the San Sabá treaty grounds. Rogers grandly declared that the president would provide "such portions of the Country as you desire" and "comfortable homes," but exhorted them to "go to work" because the buffalo, deer, bear and mustang were gone. Lipans gave up fourteen Mexican captives.

Chiquito told Rogers: "[I] request and desire that our great chief the president of the United States would procure a home for me and my people and protect us from further persecution, homes that [we] may call our own and not be driven from them as we have been," said Chiquito. "[We] wish to raise corn and know how to do it. [We] feel like Americans and are willing to abide and be governed by their laws . . . We are poor and denied the privilege of catching mustangs to sell and to eat."

Chief Quaco said he was grateful to the president and the agent for food and clothing. "I have been and will continue to be the friend of the white man and people of the United States. They have been good to me." He had many children. He was tired of moving around and wanted a home where he could bring together his family, his horses and his livestock. He was poor but willing to work if the United States would help and protect him.

Colonel Lamos (Lemas Castro), an old Lipan chief, said he now had hope of being settled where he could have his children around him and not roam about like wild animals. He could see before him the beef, corn, corn meal, blankets and other things they needed. "This gives me confidence in the great chief and I believe him our friend and we will stand by him." Manuel Hernandes, a head man standing in for Chief Shanaca, said he too was willing to live by the nation's laws. He was "tired of being driven about from place to place."[9]

The treaty, signed on October 28, 1851, reaffirmed the Treaty of 1846 and contained the usual assurances but not a word about land for the tribes. Lipans who signed were Chiquito, Coyote, Quaco, Chipota, Manuel, Colonel Lamos, John Castro, John Flacco and Manuel Hernandes.[10] Ramón Castro was notably absent.

Rollins left his position soon after but vented his frustrations about the "repeated promises and repeated failures" of government in a fifteen-page letter to his successor. Hostilities, he was certain, were inevitable. "[A] desire to fight and exterminate the Indians strongly pervades the minds of the people of Texas," and they missed few opportunities to "magnify Indian cruelties and provoke open hostilities." The rangers' "assistance is to be feared rather than desired . . . [N]early if not all differences with the Indians that have agitated and excited the country for the past three years have grown out of the employment of volunteers and their badly advised conduct."

Security was not possible without killing every Indian in Texas, Rollins concluded. It was more practical to remove them to unoccupied territory, but he didn't endorse this idea either. Even if land was available, "these Indians are too wild to understand, too independent to submit to it, and such is their aversion to removal that they would defend to the last a country which they believe, with some justice, to belong exclusively to themselves."[11]

◄ ►

When Major George Thomas Howard, a former ranger, replaced Rollins in January 1852, the press assumed Howard would be "[a]fflicted with no sentimental tenderness for the Indian." Howard reported unsentimentally that the Lipans and Comanches were starving and that both had concluded it was better to die fighting. Said Chiquito: "The country here where, until within a short time, the white man has never seen, is now dotted over with the tents of soldiers. They prevent us from going into the country and stop our usual incursions into Mexico, where we have always been accustomed to go and get our supplies."[12]

The Lipans planted corn and pumpkins that spring but relied on the beef and corn Howard gave them at Fort Martin Scott, and because passing gold seekers left behind new epidemics, they also asked to be vaccinated. That summer the Lipans near Fredericksburg were stealing food to survive. "They have nothing to subsist upon, and hunger compels them to commit these outrages," citizens wrote in a petition. The Lipans asked repeatedly to hunt wild horses, but Howard refused because of citizen and military objections.[13]

As reports of thefts mounted, agent Horace Capron's solution that summer was to relocate Chiquito, Chipota, Castro (probably Rámon Castro) and their people, along with the Mescalero chief José Maria Flores, near Fort Mason. They left behind a few young men to harvest their corn. Days later Chiquito, the other chiefs, and a group of warriors rode in, anxious for Howard to know that the young men they left got drunk and stole horses. They intended to pursue the rascals and return the horses. Chiquito, despite his age, vowed to bring them in himself. The Lipan chiefs couldn't control their young men "when the Whites let them have liquor," Howard told citizens, and as agent he had no authority to prohibit this trade. He silenced complainers by reminding them of the Lipans' long service to Texas.[14]

Their new location, between the Llano and San Sabá, was in their traditional range, but they were cut off from portions of their country, and the post commander, Philip St. George Cooke, required passes for them to visit the settlements. Unable to trade, they were reduced to begging at the fort and stealing from settlers. In desperation, some traveled without passes, becoming fugitives "to be hunted to death," Capron lamented. The government sent impractical gifts, which the Lipans quickly traded for food at lopsided exchange rates. The press echoed agents' pleas for food and not "trifles and tinsels." "There is no exaggerating the starving condition of these Indians, and with every disposition on their part to be friendly, they are forced into predatory excursions to sustain life," Capron wrote in September. Washington turned a deaf ear.[15]

"What have we got left? The game, our main dependence, is killed and driven off, and we are forced into the most sterile and barren portions of [country] to starve," Lipans said late that year. Capron couldn't bear the sight of their suffering and hurried away.[16]

◄ ►

West Texas in mid-century was largely unmapped and unknown. In the six-hundred mile expanse between San Antonio and El Paso, the only water, other than the odd water hole, flowed in the Rio Grande and the Pecos. It was the ideal sanctuary for Apaches, but Americans searching for new routes in 1850 began to penetrate country previously unknown to them. In spring of 1850 Lieutenant William Whiting led an expedition to identify a commercial and military route, the future San Antonio-El Paso road, and came upon the Pecos almost by surprise. The discolored, treeless river, "a pocket edition of the lower Rio Grande," wasn't visible "until the traveler is right upon the bank," he said.

On March 9 Chief Capote and two wives cautiously approached Whiting's camp and asked the Americans to come out and talk. His people were up the river, he said, and his chief wanted to speak with them. Capote asked them to wait while he brought him back. Whiting suspected that the chief really wanted to get his families and horse herd to safety, but he waited. They didn't return. "These Lipan are a brave and well-armed tribe of Indians; but their numbers have been much reduced of late years, the Rangers having severely beaten them in several fights. Their whole number of warriors probably does not pass one hundred," he wrote. The next day Whiting's party continued up the river where they found the Lipans' hastily abandoned camp.[17]

From the Pecos, the expedition traveled northwest. At a prominent peak, hostile Mescaleros led by Chief Gómez surrounded them. Whiting convinced Gómez they were only trying to get through to Presidio del Norte or El Paso, and the Apaches guided them over the mountain to a camp site. About 10 p.m. the Mescalero Guero Carranza urged them to leave. Some Apaches had returned from a raid in Mexico, where they lost men in a fight. They were angry, he told them, and might attack you if you remain. Whiting's men built up their fire and slipped into the night.[18] On the return trip Whiting encountered Capote and his people in about the same place. Thirty Lipans approached to talk, but after his close call with the Mescaleros, he and his men were in no mood for conversation.

There was cause for Gómez's animosity and Capote's caution. Gómez had been friendly until the state of Chihuahua offered a bounty for Indian scalps. That year American scalp hunters killed and scalped members of Gómez's band, which inflamed Apaches across the frontier against white men. Former ranger Jack Hays accepted a position as sub-agent to the Gila Apaches in New Mexico in early 1850 but found them so hostile, he resigned his post before serving a day.[19]

As Whiting explored west Texas, Captain Henry B. Judd led an expedition two hundred miles down the Pecos from Las Vegas, New Mexico, and found that "the true position of the Rio Pecos is very far to the eastward of that indicated on any of our maps." After five days, they descended steep and rugged sand hills to the fertile bottom lands of the Pecos at the Bosque Redondo, a twenty-mile long cottonwood grove. The area was a neutral ground where several tribes met traders and grazed their herds on the valley's rich grass. "From the middle of May until the early part of August, these plains are covered with their lodges and their feeding herds," Judd wrote. Sixty miles farther was a second cottonwood forest, Bosque Grande. Judd wrote prophetically that both places should be considered important military positions.[20]

At the Bosque Redondo that summer, two Comanche chiefs joined "Apaches," Jicarillas and Mescaleros in making a treaty with the United States. Signers of the treaty were El Pluma, Barranquito and Santa Ana for the Mescaleros, Lobo and José Largo for the plains Jicarillas,[21] and Cuentas Azules for the Llaneros and their confederates.[22] This suggests that the reference to "Apaches" often found in army correspondence about Eastern Apaches indicates Llaneros, although it could also mean the officers didn't know the band affiliation.

Lipans tell a story about a big camp on the Pecos with Mescaleros, Chiricahuas (called Blue Mountain People by Lipans and Mescaleros) and Northern Lipans. Comanches had been raiding in Mexico and came upon the small Lipan camp outside the bigger camp. The two Comanche chiefs debated whether to socialize with the Lipans or fight them. One argued that they could kill all the men and take their women, children and horses. The other countered that they would only lose men: "I have heard that they are good fighters and often have killed many of our men."

The aggressive chief won out. They took the Lipans' horses. The Lipans got ready to fight. Among them was a Jicarilla Apache, who came out singing his war song and shaking a gourd rattle. The other Apaches joined them. Both sides lined up and charged. It was a hard fight, back and forth. The Lipans lost two of their leaders. An Apache killed the chief who wanted to fight and scalped him. He waved the scalp. Then they killed another Comanche chief and wounded the chief who hadn't wanted to fight. The Comanches, weakened by the loss of their chiefs, began to pull back. A Lipan charged into the Comanche line with his lance and killed those who were behind. The Comanches stepped up their retreat, but the Apaches followed and killed more. They drove the Comanches right into their camps. An Apache whose son was one of the first to die said, "Let them go. Let them tell their people back home what happened and how the fight started."[23]

◄ ►

In October 1850 John Russell Bartlett, a U.S. boundary commissioner, had a close encounter with Lipans. Near the Concho, Chief Chipota approached the party with his hand extended and produced papers from various American officials verifying his identity and the fact that he recently signed a peace treaty. The documents asked Americans to treat him kindly. "The chief was about sixty years of age, rather corpulent, owing to the life of ease which he gave us to understand he had been leading, and was mounted on a mule so disproportionately small, as to present a most ludicrous appearance," Bartlett wrote. Chipota "had a pleasant benevolent countenance" and was well dressed in buckskin. Slung across his back was a quiver of bobcat skin and at his side was a pouch of the same material.

Chipota had been following them for two days, he said in Spanish. His people were camped a few miles away. "Chipota knew enough of civilization to be aware that when distinguished gentlemen meet, it was customary to take a drink; and finding no proffer of such civilities on my part, he gave me to understand that he would not object to a glass of whiskey." Bartlett informed the chief that he didn't drink whiskey but offered him a meal at their next stop and invited Chipota to join him in his carriage.

The chief was delighted. He tried to maintain his dignity but couldn't stifle his curiosity about Bartlett's Sharp's rifle and other firearms. Picking up a telescope, Chipota asked how it was fired. Bartlett adjusted the glass, pointed it at a distant tree and invited Chipota to take a look. "His credulity had been overtasked, and it was hard to convince him that it was the same far-off tree. I told him that we used that to see the Indians at a distance and could always tell when they were about, or had stolen any mules." He was miffed at the theft of his party's mules and suspected that the thieves were Indians.

Bartlett said he'd like to meet Chipota's people. At day's end, Chipota departed and returned with Chiquito, who also produced his papers. The Lipans said they lived from Zacatecas in Mexico to the Colorado River of Texas and from the coast to the borders of New Mexico; during the winter, they stayed in the Bolsón de Mapimí. In this statement, they revealed that Lipans still occupied most of the same territory since the late 1600s, and Lipanería was as broad as Comanchería. Bartlett bought a mule from Chipota and offered ten dollars each in cash or goods for the return of mules they'd lost, but the Lipans insisted they hadn't seen them. They stayed for dinner and spent the night.

Among the Lipans was a strikingly handsome, athletic young man who wore only a breech cloth and necklace of bone. At first he was unwilling to speak to the Americans but then conversed with a few who knew Spanish. He asked one young American if he was married, and the American produced a miniature of a beautiful woman. The small image charmed the young Lipan so much that he asked repeatedly to see it. The next morning he tried to barter for it, even offering his horse. "Failing to acquire it, the young man begged one more sight of the enchanting image, which he was permitted to enjoy; he gave it one long and affectionate look, leaped upon his horse, and rode off."

The next day, teamsters chased a loose mule for more than an hour and gave up. Bartlett offered the young Lipan a red shirt if he could catch the animal. To Lipans accustomed to capturing mustangs, this was sport. The youth leaped on his horse, which had no saddle, and, taking a long lasso in hand, dashed off at full gallop after the frightened mule. Following an exciting chase, the young warrior got within forty feet and threw his lasso over the mule's head, bringing it to a stop. The Lipans, enriched with shirts and other gifts, departed, "apparently delighted with their visit."[24]

CHAPTER

Refuge

I believe that the white man's God is a very rich God, and he gives the white man everything he wants; but the Indian's God is a very poor God and he has nothing to give us, and the Indians have got nothing. That is the difference between the white man and the Indian.

— Lipan chief to Sam Houston, 1853[1]

The Americans decided, as the Spanish had before them, that they needed a line of forts. By late 1849 the army had 1,205 soldiers at thirteen posts to watch over 2,000 miles of frontier. Most were new recruits with no knowledge of Texas, and three-fourths were foot soldiers who were useless against mounted Indian parties. It wasn't difficult for tribes to monitor their comings and goings. As citizens clamored for greater protection, the War Department responded with more troops and more forts. By 1852 Texas accounted for 3,016 out of 10,000 of the army's soldiers. The millions spent were mostly wasted, groused Houston. He was certain he could keep peace for $100,000 a year, but peace, however inexpensive, was unpopular. "The Indians must be pursued, hunted, run down, and killed, driven beyond the limits of the State," thundered the *Texas State Gazette.*[2]

With "the tide of western migration still flowing" and the war over, wrote anthropologist Morris Opler, the army's next mission was to "precede and protect the western line of settlement and to drive out any Indian occupants of lands claimed or coveted by the white man." During the 1850s the Lipans often found themselves on the defensive, and yet they could still draw on allies for strength and refuge. Their numbers were smaller, but they weren't necessarily weak. Population estimates, which typically tallied one group and failed to account for distant groups, are unreliable. As one observer predicted their demise, another, like W. B. Parker, who accompanied the Marcy expedition during the summer of 1854, said: "The Apaches and Lipans are very numerous, fierce and warlike. They are more generally supplied with firearms than other tribes and are in a state of constant hostility to the whites."[3]

◄►

In December 1852 "Indians" attacked a ranch forty miles south on the San Antonio River. They announced defiantly that they were Lipans and challenged their victims to a fight before wounding several men and making off with twenty-five horses. One man said he recognized Chief Manuel. Capron and Howard were suspicious; it just wasn't the way Lipans fought, and they knew Manuel was at Fort Mason. The commander and others could vouch for him. The agents informed General William S. Harney the intruders were more likely Mexicans and Americans dressed as Indians.

Regardless, Harney gave the order to kill all the men and take the women and children captive. Deploying troops from Fort McKavett, Fort Chadbourne and Fort Terrett to block their retreat to the north, west and south, Major Philip St. George Cooke forced the fleeing Lipans southeast. On January 12, 1853, at the Guadalupe River, Manuel and his people appeared willing to surrender but then slipped past troops, who overtook them. Most escaped, but Cooke took eighteen prisoners and more than a hundred horses and burned their lodges. Soldiers killed several men and captured a few women and children. The rest scattered, "stripped of their horses and mules, their clothing and wampum; their camp burned, and even the presents lately distributed among them by the Indian Agents, and their blankets, have been taken from them as trophies of war," Capron wrote. He called the attack "shocking to every feeling of humanity." The survivors, driven from their winter camp, were now loose on the border "destitute and fired with revenge," Capron said.[4] The following month, he persuaded a few Lipans to meet Howard at Fort Martin Scott, where Major James Longstreet returned captured horses and supplies.[5]

◄ ►

Neighbors returned in August 1853 as supervising agent for Texas and assigned Howard to the Lipans, Mescaleros and Tonkawas. Large groups of Lipans and Mescaleros were then on the upper Nueces. They wanted to plant corn but hesitated. "In every attempt we have ever made to raise a crop, we have been driven from them before they could mature by the encroachment of the white man," they told Howard.[6]

For a time in 1854 Ramón Castro's group lived on Cibolo Creek, near Selma, where the hunting was good and the Lipans got on well with the settlers. Their camp lay across the creek from the Friesenhahn homestead and two miles from pioneer William Davenport, and their children played together. Settlers were impressed with the clay ovens Lipans used to bake sotol and other foods. William Davenport described sitting on the porch and listening to the coyotes howl. "Mr. Castro sometimes comes over with his wife and we all sit and talk and listen to the night together," Davenport wrote in 1854. "Just yesterday I went with Mr. Castro and some other Apache gentlemen to hunt. I was so surprised to see the land I was taken to. The cliffs here are white, with caves in them. I watched in surprise as the Apache men ran the buffalo over the side of the cliff to fall on the rocks below. I went with them, and they gave me and Nancy a half bull to smoke for the winter. Nancy learned how to cure the hide from watching the Apache ladies." After one hunt, the Lipans asked to borrow a horse to transport a deer they killed. "I had no problem. I knew Chief Castro, and he always brought everything back," Davenport wrote."[7]

◄ ►

In early March 1854 Lipans attacked loaded Mexican carts near Laredo and swept away herds of cattle and horses. Citizens had so few horses left, they couldn't even pursue thieves, and the nine companies of infantry stationed nearby had no more than twenty horses. They blamed Chiquito's group, but Howard insisted that his interpreter was constantly in camp with them. When soldiers confronted Chipota at Fort Inge, he denied his band's role in any depredations but admitted it could be other Lipans. Laredoans threatened to "use force to take them, even should it involve the destruction of the whole tribe." A ranger company could punish "these tame pets of the United States." General Persifor F. Smith ordered five detachments of Mounted Rifles to hunt down the raiders.[8]

That spring Mounted Rifles from Fort Merrill found a party of Lipans at Lake Trinidad, about forty miles southwest of the fort. "Had the Rifles reflected for a moment, they would have acted on the maxim 'a good retreat is better than a bad battle,' as they were without any other arms than their revolvers, half of which were not loaded, and of those that were, some were injured by damp," recalled veterans John and William Wright. They charged the Lipans. "The Indians, raising their war-whoop, boldly stood the shock, and began to gallop around them in rings, firing their arrows and rifles among their victims, who soon became aware of their critical situation." The soldiers, with little ammunition and only two sabers, had no choice but to fight their way through the circling warriors and run for their lives. A teen-aged warrior fired an arrow through the commander's arm and killed another man.

Troops escaped mostly by bluffing—threatening to fire revolvers—but half the soldiers were wounded, most of them severely. Two other men, separated during the retreat, were killed. A soldier who summoned reinforcements and returned with the hospital steward blundered into the Lipans' camp and plunged through; Lipans jumped to their feet to fire at them and chased them as they raced for Lake Trinidad. Two days later, twenty men rode to Baluarta where they found the same Lipans, led by Castillo, camped at a pond and charged them. The Lipans were ready. They had streaked their faces with red and yellow paint from the buckskin bags they carried. On their left arms, protecting one side of their bodies, were large round or oval shields, also painted yellow and red, usually in circles. Made of buffalo skin taken from the neck, the toughest part of the animal, and doubled two or three times, the shields could withstand a pistol shot. The Lipans always carried their shields, but the Comanches only used them in time of war.

The warriors were already on their horses and "received them with a smart fire of rifles and arrows." A rifle ball dropped the commanding officer's horse, and he pitched to the ground. A warrior seized the moment to kill him, but the commander got up, fired at the warrior, unhorsed him and took his horse. In a brutal fight for the next thirty minutes, "the Indians perform[ed] the most extraordinary evolutions as they sent their tomahawks bright glancing through the air, or shot their arrows with winged speed, and a movement wonderfully rapid and graceful, resembling that of some expert violinist performing a quick and difficult piece of music." At length, the battle favored the Rifles, and they chased the Lipans into the chaparral. The Lipans lost four men, "but many more must have been mortally wounded, as a red man, like a deer, will continue to run while any life is in his body." They also lost their plunder, possessions, animals and some weapons.[9]

◄►

In spring 1854 John Castro's group planted corn on Blanco Creek, a Frio tributary. Three hundred Tonkawas, led by Chief Placído, camped on the Frio a few miles from Fort Inge; nearby, in the Sabinal Valley, Chiquito's band was planting corn and melons in fenced fields. Complaints reached Governor Elisha M. Pease about depredations on the Leona, Sabinal and Rio Seco, and settlers near Fort Inge considered the Lipans and Tonkawas an "unmitigated nuisance." Howard ordered the Lipans to abandon their fields and move to the Nueces. They refused. After conferring with Chiquito, John Castro set out with three family members and some of his men to speak to Howard.[10]

Outside Castroville, they fell in with Frederick Law Olmsted and his traveling companion. Castro wore an elaborately beaded buckskin

Lipan Warrior. Drawing by Arthur Scott, ca. 1854–1857, Report on the United States and Mexican Boundary Survey, 1856. According to Daniel Castro Romero, Jr., this is Chief John Castro; his striped shirt stayed in the family for years.

shirt and a wreath of fresh oak leaves on his head. Heavy brass rings dangled from his ears, and vermillion streaked his hairless face, "including the edge of the eyelids, whose motion had a horrid effect . . . His face was not without some natural dignity and force, but the predominant expression was wily and brutal," Olmsted wrote. Castro's daughter "was a girl of delicate features and slight proportions, showing signs of fatigue and hardship. She rode astride, like the rest, dressed in a tolerably neat and pretty buckskin cape, with fringed leggings. The horses of the party, though probably the best belonging to the tribe, were small, worn, and inferior. The mule on which the chief rode was alone in tolerable working condition."

Earlier, Olmsted had visited Castro's camp at the head of the Leona, three miles north of Fort Inge, and counted about one hundred people, including some Tonkawas and Mescaleros. Travelers always found the Lipans handsome and their villages picturesque. The man who would become America's pioneer landscape architect saw only "miserable squalor, foul obscenity, and disgusting brutishness," but then he had similar opinions of Texans and Mexicans. A more perceptive visitor might have discerned great need in the Lipans' begging for a dime or in the handful of bony Mexican horses staked outside the camp. Reading Wood Black's house, he wrote, was "overrun with a swarm of these vagabonds." Black, a Quaker who settled in the area in 1852, was on good terms with Indian people. He helped negotiate treaties and traded extensively with peaceful tribes like the Lipans and Tonkawas.[11]

In conversation Castro learned Olmsted was traveling to San Antonio from San Fernando. Castro asked if there were Indians in San Fernando, and Olmsted responded there were many—Lipans, Mescaleros, Kickapoos, Comanches, Tonkawas and Seminoles. "All drunks. All fools," Olmsted said, provoking laughter from the chief, who repeated the comment for the amusement of his men. Castro began to converse "on the various merits of whiskey, corn, horses, and Germans." They separated at Castroville. When Olmsted caught up with Castro and his men near San Antonio, they were drunk.

The day before Castro's arrival, unknown Indians killed a set-tler named Forester and three of his children. Castro offered to track the killers for a party of citizens and troops and left his daughter and two relatives with Howard as a guarantee. For two days he guided the group but deserted in the night on one of Howard's horses. The party assumed Castro's furtive departure was evidence of Lipan guilt, but one of the men had threatened him. Castro later returned the horse. Castro's men escaped before the Texans could arrest them, but How-ard ordered the chief's family held. When troops found Castro's camp deserted, they arrested Chiquito and some of his people and brought them to Fort Inge. Neighbors later freed Chiquito, who, despite his poor treatment, offered to help find the murderer.[12] The Foresters' kill-ers, it turned out, were Northern Comanches and Wichitas. Chiquito's Lipans abandoned their fields and camped near Fort Inge, where they served as guides, trailers and spies and helped cattlemen round up lost cattle. For John Castro, it was the last straw. He and his people crossed the Rio Grande and reached San Fernando by April 27, 1854, where he found old friends and new allies.[13]

◄►

Chief Wild Cat, an enterprising Seminole, envisioned a confederacy of tribes from both Indian Territory and the Texas plains. During 1846 he met with Kickapoos, Lipans and Tonkawas but got nowhere. Unde-terred, he explored trade ties with them during the Butler and Lewis treaty talks.[14] His plans finally took root in Mexico. In 1850 Wild Cat's Seminoles, along with mixed-race black Seminoles and former slaves protected by the Seminoles, were welcomed in Mexico as military col-onists and received citizenship and camp sites near Zaragoza, Piedras Negras, and Santa Rosa. In return, they helped citizens and troops repel and pursue Comanches, Lipans and Mescaleros and fend off Texas fili-busters, getting paid in booty and sometimes wages.[15]

In a few years, Wild Cat's refugee colonies harbored Kickapoos, Tonkawas, Comanches, Mescaleros, and Lipans. In January 1854, before John Castro's arrival, Lipans came from the Pecos at the invitation of Mexican authorities, who offered them land and security. One group of Lipans camped across the river from Laredo and Fort Duncan. The governor of Coahuila believed they were too few to be a threat and appointed an agent to watch them. "There is nothing to fear from this tribe," he said. Neighbors tried to keep them in Texas but could offer them nothing, including protection.[16]

◄►

The only solution, Neighbors believed, was reservations. During summer 1854 he and Captain Randolph B. Marcy marked off eight leagues on the Brazos River near Fort Belknap for the Caddos, Wichitas, Anadarkos, Wacos, Tawakonies, Tonkawas, Kichais and Delawares. The Southern Comanches would live on their old winter grounds forty-five miles west on the Clear Fork of the Brazos. For the Lipans and Mescaleros, they surveyed a four-league parcel adjoining the Caddo reservation, but Neighbors wasn't optimistic. He hadn't spoken to either group, "but as many of the Lipan are now hostile it seems doubtful if they will come into the measure at all."[17]

Despite official indifference, the agent pushed relentlessly. The Southern Comanches, Lipans, Caddos, Ionies, Wacos, Tawakonis, Tonkawas and Mescaleros, which he estimated at 3,500, were hemmed in on the south by white settlements and on the north by Northern Comanches and Kiowas, vulnerable to attacks by both, "and compelled to carry on something like an armed neutrality with both," he said. Months passed with no word from Washington, as the Texas Legislature passed resolution after resolution beseeching the United States to collect and settle these tribes. Finally, the exasperated agent took his argument to Washington and extracted approval. By the end of 1855, he had the two reservations settled. Some Lipans came in to the Brazos reserve, but the majority remained out of reach.[18]

In late September a group of immigrants herding cattle to California said Mescaleros and Lipans stole their livestock. Captain John G. Walker and forty-two Mounted Rifles set out. A day and a half and seventy miles later, they found an Apache camp of sixty to seventy lodges at the base of the Sierra Diablo. Half of Walker's divided command stumbled into the middle of the ranchería, and Apaches attacked. When the remaining troops arrived, they pushed back the Apaches. After a short, brutal fight, the "sides of the mountains were literally covered with mounted and dismounted warriors" and escaping women and children. As soldiers began destroying lodges and food supplies, the Apaches regrouped in the surrounding heights and fired down volleys of arrows. Walker, his shirt shredded by arrows, withdrew, but he discovered a place within sight of the road to Presidio del Norte near the Pecos and Rio Grande, where wood and water could be found, which was "the center of the region infested by the Apache and Mescalero Indians."[19]

◄►

By 1855, most Lipans were south of the border, but it took a year before that fact was widely known. In March, certain that Chiquito's people supplied information to hostile Mescaleros about traffic on the El Paso Road, General Smith wanted to strike, over Neighbors' objections.[20] After unknown Indians stole horses above Goliad and citizens tracked them to the Rio Grande, they learned that three hundred Lipans were living in Mexico near the trail they were following and had about fifteen hundred horses, which they admitted stealing. Ranger Peter Tumlinson and cattleman Levi English later found ten Lipans on the headwaters of the Medina and killed five, recovering twenty-eight horses and saddles taken from the Goliad area.

Citizens papered Governor Pease with inventories of thefts and reports of attacks and demanded that he call out the rangers. They thought the marauders were Lipans, Comanches and possibly some of Wild Cat's Seminoles. "The Indians generally come in on foot & their presence is not known until they have perpetrated their outrages and are on the retreat," wrote a resident.[21] A good governor, Pease knew that if he called out the rangers, they might undermine efforts to settle tribes on reservations and provoke a general war. In September Pease asked Smith for soldiers, but Smith couldn't oblige.[22]

With no other option, Pease asked ranger James Callahan to form a volunteer company for three months to protect settlers on the Guadalupe and its tributaries. The state couldn't pay for provisions, horses, weapons or wages, and yet Callahan easily raised and outfitted a company. Ostensibly he was chasing Lipans, but "men of means, influence and character" had publicly pledged aid to anyone willing to capture runaway slaves in Mexico.[23] The expedition departed on September 18, 1855, on a scout after the Lipans "wherever we may find them" and fought some of Wild Cat's Seminoles and fugitive slaves about thirty miles from Bandera. On the Leona they found fresh trails of a large force and asked for help. Sixty men joined from Seguin and San Antonio. From the Nueces fresh tracks led through arid terrain where mesquite, scrub oak and prickly pear raised spiny barriers all the way to the Rio Grande. Scouts said an Indian camp with many stolen horses was about nine miles away. Major Sidney Burbank told them they had no business in Mexico and refused to let them cross near Fort Duncan, so they crossed downstream and assured citizens of Piedras Negras that they only wanted to punish Indians.

On October 3 Callahan started down the road to San Fernando. That afternoon, dust rose from a stand of timber near the road, where men and horses awaited, sunlight reflecting off their weapons. Three well-dressed Indians rode from the woods. The rangers formed a line facing the woods and dismounted. An Indian force of about one hundred-fifty to two hundred emerged from the trees and formed its own line facing the Texans. One of the chiefs tried unsuccessfully to draw the rangers from their position or provoke them into shooting. Riding closer, he shot an arrow over them. Two rangers fired and hit the chief's horse, but he managed to reach the woods.

Then about two hundred men on foot, mostly Mexicans, came from the trees and formed their line at a right angle to the Indians and the rangers. Callahan decided to charge the Indian line. The rangers held their fire until they were close and then blasted, killing many. Callahan moved his men to a stream bed, and the Indians set fire to the tall grass, trying to burn the Texans out. Several crept close and opened fire. Sporadic shooting continued until sunset, when Mexicans and Indians retreated to San Fernando, ending the battle. Callahan retreated toward the Rio Grande. Both sides claimed victory and disputed their losses. From Piedras Negras, Callahan wrote of his betrayal by Mexicans and asserted that the "Seminoles, muscaleroes and Lipans are all determined to scourge Texas with blood and outrage so long as they remain unchastised." He believed all three tribes participated in the fight. After a two-day stay, the rangers torched shacks and fences on the outskirts of town, lost control of their blaze, and burned most of Piedras Negras to the ground.[24]

Across the river at Eagle Pass, the thinly manned Fort Duncan provided little protection, said Jane Cazneau, an Eagle Pass resident. The tribes "pour down from their distant fastnesses, far beyond Eagle Pass, in parties of from a dozen up to some hundred warriors, mounted on the fleetest of their desert steeds, and free from every incumbrance but their light trappings . . ." As the settlements pressed deeper into the frontier, their herds and flocks "became a perpetual fountain of supply to these roving Indians."

Wild Cat could have been a powerful protector if the United States had given his band a home and rations, Cazneau maintained. It would be both humane and economical "to create a kind of border militia of the friendly tribes . . . We owe something very different to the Indians on our borders from the mockery of gifts and treaties, which we have dealt them—gifts of rum to destroy, treaties that covered their sure destruction with specious promises of peace and protection. Yet we call ourselves Christians and thank God we are not wicked, like other nations."[25]

CHAPTER

The Last Extremity

The Lipans tho' contemptible in number cannot be put down without the simultaneous action of the troops on both sides of the border.

— Albert S. Johnston, 1856[1]

Fed up with their treatment at Fort Inge, Chiquito's people, along with the Tonkawas, moved to a favorite camping site among the live oak, pecans and white oak lining Las Moras and Pinto Creeks. The sparkling water from Las Moras spring had great power: It was said that whoever bathed there could not deceive. Hunting was good. Buffalo, deer, antelope, and mustangs grazed on the prairies, and patches of chaparral harbored rabbits and peccaries. Their young men were valued as scouts at Fort Clark.[2]

General Zenas R. Bliss recalled that an army patrol, riding east from Fort Clark in single file with the Lipans in front, surprised three Comanches. The scouts "threw off their blankets and, with a yell, darted after the Comanches." The commotion caused the army mules to throw their riders, and only the two officers and a drummer boy remaining mounted. Two Comanches on horses got away. A scout overtook the third, who was riding a mule. "He ran up to the Comanche and ran his lance through his back and he fell forward on his mule's neck and hung on to the mane. The Lipan then ran past him and as he went by, he threw the butt of his lance to the left and made a 'right point' cutting the Indian's throat as cleanly as if he had been standing beside him on the ground."

When the Tonkawas were taken to their reservation, the Lipans, who "were at that time a quite powerful tribe," refused to go; they and some Tonkawas joined the Lipans in Mexico, Bliss wrote.[3] Chiquito's Lipans were in Mexico by late January 1856. He and Comanchito told a visiting Texan that they wanted peace but were now at war. When we lived in Texas, they said, we were always blamed for horse stealing. Now we will give the Americans real cause to blame us. They had swept the ranches on the river, taking nearly fifty horses and killing a man. "It is now really dangerous to travel three miles from Galveston unless in the company of an armed party," wrote the *Galveston Weekly News*.[4]

The Texas Legislature passed bills to regulate trade, prohibit liquor sales to Indians, and create a reservation of five square leagues west of the Pecos for the Lipans and Mescaleros.[5] Neighbors was encouraged but still hadn't seen the estimated two thousand "Lipans and Muskaleros and the Apaches at the Guadaloupe Mountains." Mexican authorities refused to let him speak to Lipans near Piedras Negras, saying they had agents and were under Mexican protection. Meanwhile, the American government declared hostile any Indians outside reservation boundaries.[6]

◀ ▶

Callahan's raid in 1855 stoked debate in Mexico. The Texans invaded because of these Indians, said Father Ignacio Galindo; he predicted the Texans would be back, and so the government should "remove any motive for difficulties with our neighbors." Santiago Vidaurri, governor and military commander of Nuevo León and Coahuila, was furious about the filibuster, but he shared the priest's fear. He warned Lipans, who were then raiding in Nuevo León, that any complaints would be cause for their extermination. When Texans made new allegations, he sent troops in March 1856. One detachment captured a party of six-ty-three near Gigedo and attempted to take them to the Río Sabinas, but the Lipans tried to escape. When the women began killing their infants rather than see them taken captive, it so enraged the soldiers, they killed forty-one people. A second force attacked and captured seventy-four Lipans. After killing most of the warriors, they believed the insignificant number of survivors "cannot inspire any fears for the future." Mexicans were certain "the history of the Lipans is brought to an end."[7] More than one hundred people escaped and, joined by eighty Tonkawas, fled to Texas, where Captain Gordon Granger, of the Mounted Rifles, pursued, killing some and wounding others. The survivors joined Apaches on the Pecos. Within months, Lipans mounted coordinated actions near the Nueces and San Antonio in tandem with Comanches. "All the troops at my disposition," wrote Colonel Albert Sidney Johnston, "have been kept actively and vigorously employed."[8]

◄ ►

The army began sending small parties of mounted soldiers on frequent scouts. A young Philip H. Sheridan, stationed at Fort Duncan, found that "almost constant scouting became a daily occupation." After Lipans skirted the garrison there, they killed a herder but paid dearly— the herder killed two and seriously wounded a third. Chased by the Mounted Rifles, raiders stood across the Rio Grande challenging the soldiers to come after them. That night Sheridan and another officer attended a party in Piedras Negras where two Lipans were their fellow guests. "As soon as they saw us they strung their bows for a fight, and we drew our six-shooters, but the Mexicans quickly closed in around the Indians and forced them out of the house . . . and they escaped."[9]

Under Fort Mason's aggressive strategy of "patrol, pursue and punish," troops followed every Indian trail. The Rifles, stationed at Fort Inge, did little else but scout for Lipans. Officers tried sending female captives to persuade their people, believed to still be "in a very destitute condition in the country about the heart of the Nueces," to go live on reservations. In July 1856 cavalry detachments clashed with Lipans on the Nueces and Llano and believed the Lipans were living on the headwaters of Devils River and entering the settlements through passes in the Sabinal and Bandera areas. Colonel George P. Buell ordered troops to pursue them "to the last extremity." Nobody knew where the last extremity might be; the Apache haunts were "scarcely known at all," Buell admitted; neither did they know their numbers, their bands, or their allies. Six months later exploration of the Pecos and Devils Rivers hadn't even identified a good ford.[10]

In September Captain James Oakes and sixty-three men invaded the Lipans' long-time stronghold, a nearly impenetrable fortress of rocky canyons and rugged heights at the junction of the Pecos and Rio Grande. They surprised three parties of Lipans, killing four, wounding four and capturing their animals. The rest escaped across the Rio Grande. Johnston was certain they had rendered hideaways unsafe for what he assumed was "the remnant of the Lipan tribe united to a fragment of the Tonkaways."[11]

Six months later, troops would find those remnants larger than they assumed. Lieutenant John Bell Hood, bored with routine camp duties at Fort Mason, set out in July 1857 with twenty-four Second Cavalry troops, "all eager for a chase as well as a fray" with "the red men of the forests." Near the Concho they found the trail of an Indian party riding for Mexico by way of the Devils River headwaters. Several days later, another party joined the original group, for a total of about fifty warriors. They followed the trail to Devils River. "As no troops had ever been that far out before, all the country west of Fort Clark had been almost given to the Indians and a scout had never been made west of Devils River," wrote Bliss. "As may be supposed, it was a pretty wild and dangerous place and entirely unknown, except within a mile or two of the road."[12]

Devils River, washing over sand and gravel for ninety-four miles on its way to the Pecos, had plenty of hiding places in its limestone canyons. The Spanish called it the Rio San Pedro, but ranger Jack Hays, peering into its forbidding depths, said it looked more like the devil's river than Saint Peter's. To the Lipans, the glassy water with deep, green pools, the plunging canyons, the banks carpeted with abundant grass and shaded by oaks and junipers were welcome shelter. Ramon Castro and his people joined other Apaches and some Comanches here.[13] On

July 20, in the range bordering the river, a large white flag rose from a ridge where horses grazed. Hood knew that Tonkawas were expected at the reservation who would signal their presence with a white flag. Not knowing if these were Tonkawas or hostile Indians, the soldiers formed a line and moved forward cautiously. Within twenty paces, the few Indians they could see threw the flag to the ground and fired. A large pile of brush burst into flames in front of the soldiers. Warriors, yelling furiously, rose from hiding places around them, and others charged down the slope, seizing some of the army horses by their bridle reins. A mounted party attacked the left of the army line with lances. Stripped to the waist for battle, their attackers wore horns or wreaths of feathers on their heads; they carried rifles, bows and arrows. Smoke and crackling of the blaze melded with shouting and gunfire to create an infernal clamor. Soldiers discharged their rifles and then drew their revolvers. The warriors fired their rifles and handed them to women, who ran to the rear, reloaded and returned them. Fighting was so close and frenzied that Indians beat the army horses' heads with their shields. When Hood's men ran out of ammunition, they fell back to reload.

"Soon afterward arose from beyond the burning heap one continuous mourning howl, such as can alone come forth from the heart of the red man in deep distress. These sounds of sorrow revealed to me that we were in little danger of a renewal of the assault." By nightfall, the Indians had gathered their dead and wounded and departed toward the Rio Grande. Hood's adversaries were Lipans and Comanches. If they had taken better aim or successfully flustered the army horses, Hood reflected in his memoir, he and his men might have met "a similar fate to that of the gallant Custer and his noble band." He estimated ten warriors killed and twelve wounded, while he suffered six dead or wounded.[14]

◄►

Lipans and Comanches had urgent reasons to renew their friendship. War and disease had reduced both their tribes, and the Seminoles, prodded by their Mexican sponsors, attacked the Lipans repeatedly.

After Wild Cat died in a smallpox outbreak, his alliances dissolved. Lipans and Comanches continued their incursions in November 1857 by raiding Laredo. Soldiers from Fort McIntosh pursued but couldn't catch them. Laredoans were again irate, but Neighbors insisted the culprits numbered no more than twenty, operating on the fringes of the frontier. They were impossible to capture, he said, because they "penetrate the settlements on foot, keep concealed until they have provided themselves with the best horses in the country, and when pursued, travel from seventy to one hundred miles per day . . ." Neighbors hadn't seen the Apaches. He was preoccupied with keeping order on the reservations, as "designing men" used forays by Northern Comanches and Kiowas to prejudice the public against reserve Indians.[15]

Ranger John S. "Rip" Ford protested that Texans were still unprotected from Indian rampages. The government could quote troop numbers all it wanted, but they were still largely infantry, operating "against the best horsemen in the world." But for his rangers, he claimed, the Comanches, Lipans, Kickapoos, Kiowas and others could depredate as they pleased. "American traders have engaged in this nefarious and unholy traffic, and have actually bartered arms, ammunition, provisions &c to the Indians for horses plundered from the people of Texas," he wrote. Texas will never know peace "as long as we have a horse left, or as long as there is an Indian left to steal him." Ford's remedy was to call up the rangers for an all-out war that would wipe out Indians and punish traders. But settlers, wrote one petitioner, feared that Indians would "seek revenge for the chastisement that Capt Ford gave them and come down amongst us and kill our citizens and Steal our property."[16]

◄►

Generals David E. Twiggs and Winfield Scott decided in January 1859 to launch offensives into Lipan and Comanche territories. Secretary of War J. B. Floyd also took the bold step of giving Twiggs permission to pursue Indian raiders across the border but advised caution in dealing with peaceful groups. Ramon Castro's sizable group was camped on a grassy flat at Dolan Falls, where the creek of that name sprayed over limestone and joined Devils River. In May, eight miles north of the river's mouth, they ambushed cavalry and dragoons from Fort Clark and pinned them against canyon walls. Only after an intense, day-long battle were troops able to fight their way out. In September, after Lipans stole 130 horses from the Frio area and carried away two boys, Lieutenant William B. Hazen with ten men followed in a heavy rain and caught up with them at the head of the Nueces. In a running fight, they killed one warrior and wounded another. The rest escaped by running down a steep ravine and into a dense cedar brake, but they left behind their horses and the captives.[17]

◄►

The two reservations became lightning rods for white antagonism, provoked by the raids of non-reservation Indians and a thinly veiled desire for land. In February 1859 Neighbors and other agents concluded glumly that the reservations couldn't be sustained in Texas and began moving the tribes to Indian Territory. Neighbors completed the last relocation in August, escorting the Southern Comanches "out of the land of the philistines," as he put it. Some Lipans sought refuge at the new reservation on the Washita. On his return he stopped at Fort Belknap. There, on September 14, 1859, Ed Cornett, a stranger to Neighbors, shot the agent in the back. Twenty minutes later, he was dead. Lieutenant William E. Burnet, of the First Infantry, predicted, "The Indians will be very apt to lead those people a lively dance this winter, and I think, they have justly earned it: they made war on the Troop[s] (in the papers) drove off the friendly Indians who were a great protection against the Comanches and murdered the Government officer in charge of the Indians, simply for doing his duty faithfully and fearlessly." In a final ironic turn, rangers—always a headache to Neighbors—brought Cornett to justice without the inconvenience of judge or jury. The federal Office of Indian Affairs concluded that because Texas had officially shed its tribes, it no longer needed agents. The Lipans lost the man who knew them best, and he wouldn't be replaced.[18]

That fall Houston was re-elected governor, and among the sizable crowd in Austin for his inauguration were Lipans and Mescaleros, who still regarded the aging general as a friend.[19] Any possibility that Texas would revive Houston's Indian policies expired when Houston refused to take an oath of loyalty to the Confederate States of America and was removed from office. After that, the Lipans were known only by their raids. The army kept troops posted at the headwaters of the Nueces, the mouth of Pendencia Creek, and on the Frio below its junction with the Leona—all traditional Lipan country. Texas wasn't completely protected from marauding Indians, admitted Secretary of War Robert E. Lee,[20] but the army had other priorities.

◄ ►

The Union ruptured in 1861. General Twiggs surrendered Texas military posts to the Confederacy in February, and the federal government removed its troops from the frontier. The Confederate government placated distraught settlers by sending the First Regiment of Texas Mounted Riflemen and an artillery battery, but they focused largely on Comanches and Kiowas in the northwest. All too aware of the war between the whites, tribes raided freely.[21]

Texas Confederates divided the frontier into three districts, but even with constant scouts, the thinly manned posts were easily penetrated. The Confederate and Texas governments were soon at odds over financial responsibility and priorities; every man mustered into the frontier regiment was a man who wasn't fighting for the South. In the Third Frontier District, Lipan country, frontier defenders busied themselves with German opposition to conscription, gangs of armed deserters, and outlaws. "The Indians seemed to be the least talked of, the least thought of, and the least dreaded of all the evils that threatened and afflicted the Frontier," wrote a Third District commander.[22]

One of few skirmishes with Lipans was in October 1861, when Sergeant W. Barrett and seventeen men from Fort Inge chased Lipan raiders. In a steady rain, the Lipans crossed and recrossed Barrocito Creek, south of Laredo, to lose their pursuers. Army horses got stuck in the boggy crossings and had to be pulled out, and rifles and ammunition were soaked. As the sun melted into grey gloom, Lipans jumped from the scrub in a small clearing and ambushed the soldiers, who reached for their guns only to find them unusable. They drew their sabers. Three men who dismounted and engaged the Lipans hand to hand managed to kill several warriors before they too were killed. In a half-hour fight, ten Lipans died, but in the waning light Lipans were gaining the upper hand, and the soldiers retreated.[23]

In 1863, citizens complained that "the country seems to be literally swarming with Indians," but Texas could no longer afford the Frontier Regiment. Late that year the state replaced it with a loosely organized militia, which was less expensive but incapable of taking campaigns into distant Indian strongholds. Attacks escalated. The militia's legacy was bitter. Its last major operation in January 1865 was an attack on peaceful Kickapoos passing through on their way to Mexico. Kickapoos crushed the volunteers and retained a hatred for Texans. It wasn't long before Lipans and Kickapoos were raiding together. "Of all these tribes these Kickapoos and Lipans are specially distinguished for a bitter animosity to the inhabitants of Texas," a settler testified.[24]

Confederates bungled their opportunity to enlist Mexico in combined campaigns against the Apaches and Comanches. In early 1861 Lipans and Mescaleros from the Pecos attacked Resurección in northern Coahuila, killing several residents and carrying off five children. Captain H. A. Hamner, Confederate commander of Fort Clark, and Jack County volunteers made an unauthorized entry into Mexico and, accompanied by Mexican citizens, pursued the Apaches without catching them. Back in Resurección, Hamner attempted to claim a black man as his slave, but indignant Mexicans objected. At Fort Duncan, Colonel John R. Baylor, an Indian hater who had led a vigilante attack on the

Brazos agency (one of Neighbors' "designing men"), complained about Lipan raids from Mexico. Through Hamner, he proposed that the Confederate States and Mexico join in fighting Lipans and Comanches. The Mexicans declined and demanded that the Americans stop raids by Lipans and Mescaleros from Texas.[25]

Apaches entered at least two treaties with the Confederates—one with Kiowas, Comanches, Kiowa Apaches and one group of Lipans in 1865[26] and one with Mescaleros. Within months Mescaleros destroyed much of Fort Davis and also fought Union forces in New Mexico led by General James H. Carleton. Colonel Kit Carson's campaign in 1863 prompted many to flee into the Guadalupe Mountains and continue south, but about four hundred Mescaleros were sent to the Bosque Redondo on the Pecos.[27] Lipan Chief Magoosh, who met Kit Carson when Union troops reoccupied Fort Stanton, said he helped gather Lipans and Mescaleros for internment. "There were Lipans at Bosque Redondo. They had relatives here, and they visited and stayed," said Meredith Magoosh Begay. "They got caught in the roundup and sent to the Bosque Redondo."[28]

Carleton's experiment foundered in 1864, when he brought nine thousand Navajos, the Mescaleros' enemies, to the small reserve. With more people to feed, the army reduced the size of rations, and hunger and disease ravaged the camps. On the night of November 3, 1865, the Mescaleros fled. They reappeared on the Pecos, in the Davis and Guadalupe Mountains, and with Comanches on the plains. They also headed "clear down to the border and to the Lipan country," said Percy Big Mouth.[29]

In March 1866, John and James Edgar led two loaded wagon trains, several days apart, from San Antonio to El Paso. Each had twenty wagons and two hundred mules. After an Apache attack, one train turned back to Fort Stockton; the other lost more than a hundred mules in a fierce storm. Combining the two trains, they reached El Paso with half their original cargo. On the return trip, sixty or seventy Lipans and Mescaleros opened fire on the advance party, which scurried back to the wagons. The following day Navajos from the Bosque Redondo joined the siege. After several days, they parleyed. The attackers said they were starving. They would leave if the traders gave them some corn. The traders knew a good deal when they heard one.[30]

◄ ►

When the Civil War ended, Lipans seemed to be everywhere, afraid of nothing. They were often reinforced by angry Mescalero refugees from the Bosque Redondo, Gila Apaches from southwestern New Mexico, and Kickapoos from Mexico. The northernmost Lipans joined Kiowas, Comanches and their Naishan (Kiowa Apache) cousins and sometimes drew dissatisfied reservation Indians to their ranks. A stream of reports detailed killings, stolen goods and livestock, ransacked wagon trains, and abducted children. At year end, citizens estimated the Lipans and Kickapoos had taken about a thousand head of cattle. "The Rebellion had the effect to move the settlements of the frontier back," wrote Bliss. "Owing to the absence of troops the Indians had become as bad between the Frio and Rio Grande as they were before the war."[31] Settlers expected troops to return to the frontier, but federal officers weren't anxious to defend their former enemies. Sheridan, military commander of Texas and Louisiana, asserted, "Texas has not yet suffered from the war and will require some intimidation."[32]

◄ ►

Soldiers at Fort Lancaster were taking horses to water the afternoon of December 26, 1867, when upwards of nine hundred Lipans, Kickapoos, Mexicans, and white renegades descended on the post from three directions. One well-mounted party of about two hundred from the north stampeded the herd; about sixty of them rode through and around the camp toward the south. Soldiers seized their guns to fend them off and hurriedly drove the herd to the corral's entrance, but raiders approaching from the south raised the bar. Captain William Frohock, of the Ninth Cavalry, dispersed his troops to defend the north,

west and south sides of the camp, but "so close upon us were the savages" that they couldn't control the panicked horses long enough to get
the corral open. They repulsed the advance from the north, but hostiles from the west closed around the frightened horses and charged
southward, bursting through the army's line and then passing through
their own line.

Warriors formed battle lines that extended over a mile to cover their
exit. As Frohock and part of one company advanced on the lines, they
broke and reformed to the rear, "keeping the horses behind them and
themselves beyond the reach of our shots." The original force from the
north attempted a second charge, which forced Frohock to recall pursuers to repel the attack. The warriors simply reformed a line beyond
reach of their bullets and remained there. "Large parties had now
appeared upon the surrounding hills and coming up the cañons. Two-
thirds of them were dismounted." Soldiers reported seeing English-
speaking white men among them who wore Confederate uniforms; the
Indians were all painted. Frohock himself saw a white man and Mexicans with the Indians. They carried away their dead and wounded and
rode off to the southeast, leaving the ground strewn with bows, arrows,
an occasional pistol, coats and blankets.[33]

Officers assumed white men orchestrated this event, but Lipans
had shown themselves capable of executing bold, complex strikes.
As they had in the past, they would maximize old and new alliances
to such an extent that their diminishing numbers wouldn't be apparent for years. The Kickapoos, however, would quickly prove to be a
mixed blessing.

The Captives

The [Lipan] when traveling never followed a road or even a path if it were near a settlement, and never crossed either unless forced to do so. If it was necessary for him to do this, he removed every sign of his trail before pressing on.

— *Frank Buckelew*[1]

George Schwander, a newcomer at Camp Wood in 1864, herded sheep past the ruins of the Mission of San Lorenzo, which had sheltered Lipans a century earlier. One fall morning he left home with a flock of sheep. His wife and six-year-old son, Albert, stayed behind with the ewes and lambs. That day five Lipans approached, and Mrs. Schwander told Albert to run and hide. They killed her with arrows, ransacked the house, and took the boy.

"When the Indians had plundered all they wanted to, we started out afoot and walked all day through brush and over rocky ground," Albert recalled in the first narrative by a Lipan captive. The Lipans reached their camp that night and were joined by a large band. "[T]hey stretched me out on the ground. My feet were bruised and swollen and I was tired and almost dead with fear." The Lipans held a big dance, led by their chief, wearing "a crown of bright colored feathers" that stretched down his back. They danced through the night, the men leaping up and down and striking the ground with their lances.

"The next day they tore the top of my garments off, and I suffered from cold, but at their command had to keep going. The band we met had horses, and they whipped me with a rawhide rope because I couldn't catch the horses for them, as I was so small.

"I rode behind one of the warriors, and I remember we had only boiled meat (cattle or buffalo) without any salt or seasoning. The bread was made from prickly pear apples, mashed up and put on a rock to dry. I was very sick from eating the Indian diet."

When George Schwander returned that night to find his family missing, he hurried on foot to Uvalde, forty miles away. A posse followed the trail across the Pecos and camped in the rain. Over Schwander's protests, they built a fire. At midnight, someone threw dry wood on the fire, causing it to blaze up, and "a shower of arrows and bullets fell about the little group." One arrow lodged in a posse member's hip. They threw a buffalo robe over the flames. The Lipans cursed them in Spanish, saying they killed the woman and had the boy. They told the Texans to wait and they would give them a fight in the morning. That night Albert slept on the ground between two warriors, who kept him in place with their arms. Instead of fighting, the Lipans slipped away, rode along the Rio Grande to Paso del Norte, and crossed into Mexico. At Cuatro Cienegas in Coahuila, the Lipans traded Albert to a Mexican for liquor and a horse. The man was kind to the boy and would have kept him, but a miller named John Crawford notified Schwander, who then ransomed his son.[2]

Lipans commonly had Mexican captives but rarely white Americans. They may have felt, as their western cousins did, that white children were more trouble than they were worth, or their long association with white people may have made them reluctant, but war and disease had taken such a toll that they needed new tribal members, particularly boys. Bravado aside, their encounter with the posse probably gave them pause. More whites would come looking for the boy, and they couldn't afford to lose men.

◄ ►

Frank Buckelew became an involuntary guest of the Lipans on March 11, 1866.[3] Thanks to his recollections, we have one of the few intimate accounts of their life in this period. Thirteen-year-old Buckelew was on the head of Sabinal Creek with another boy when he saw cattle dart from a thicket and spotted a warrior, who rose to one knee, placed an arrow in his bow, and spoke. Buckelew knew he would die if he attempted to run, so he turned to face the man, who was having a good laugh at the sight of the other boy running hysterically. He tapped Buckelew sharply on the head and said, "Vamos."

In the thicket, three Indian men took his clothes, put them on and strutted about. One plucked a long, thorny, catclaw switch, struck Buckelew with it and told him to move. Buckelew trotted after the two, driven by repeated whacks from the switch. They quickly crossed the canyon bottom and climbed the side "with the alertness and agility of squirrels while I found it extremely difficult and tedious," he said. At the top, another man rested on the edge of a projecting rock. He extended his hand to the boy and said, "Howdy! How old you be? You be Englishman or you be Dutchman? You be Englishman me killie you; you be Dutchman me no killie you."

Buckelew had heard that Indians didn't keep captives over the age of ten, so he told the man he was ten and that he was English. The latter information probably saved his life because the Lipans were then angry that Germans from Stringtown, beset by a series of murders, had attacked a peaceful Lipan camp on the Medina. Several people died before the Lipans forced them to retreat. The man studied Buckelew and responded, "Heap big ten-year-old boy." (The dialogue used in this second-hand account, written in the 1920s, is probably an approximation of how the writer thought Indians spoke.) Buckelew had just met Costilietos (also, Costilitos), a war chief of the Lipans. Relieved to find an English-speaking Indian, Buckelew pleaded for his freedom, but the chief said he intended to take him home, make him an Indian, and give him a bow and arrows and a pony. Costilietos no doubt considered that an appealing offer.

They continued up the bluff. "Perfect ease of movement and silence characterized every step. Not a word was spoken, and not an unusual

noise made as they walked straining eye and ear to catch the least indication of the presence of an enemy." When they reached a point opposite Buckelew's house, they stopped and ordered the boy to call out
to his people, which he did. His sister saw him and screamed, which
informed the Lipans there were no men at home. Buckelew sat down
to remove thorns from his feet, and one man helped him, less out of
compassion than a need for him to move quickly. They gave him a pair
of moccasins. The Lipans thoroughly covered their trail and proceeded
on. "When I became the least bit careless in my walk, which I was several times, and made an unnecessary noise, I was at once reminded of
my awkwardness by a tap on the shoulder or head by one of the Indians." In silence, they followed the river high on the bluff and descended
at dusk for a drink.

Pausing on the bank, the Lipans took arrows from their quivers one
at a time and passed them deliberately between their teeth to straighten
them. They refilled their water bags, made from a portion of cow stomach and closed by a drawstring of deer sinew. The dripping bag hung
from the right hip. They gave Buckelew his own water bag and continued
for several more hours through a light rain, stopping for the night in a
cedar thicket near a small creek. They retired without eating. Buckelew
slept that night in the clutch of a warrior to prevent him from escaping.

The next morning, the men threw their blankets over their shoulders and arranged weapons and tools to allow the greatest freedom
of movement. Seeing cattle, one man left the party and shot a fat red
heifer using an old flintlock rifle. The Lipans customarily cut out the
liver and ate it raw. When Buckelew hesitated, the chief told him, "You
eat. It be good for you." They removed the skin and cut the meat into
small pieces, which they roasted slowly over a fire and ate half-cooked.
The large bones were placed on the fire, cooked briefly and then broken to yield the marrow, a delicacy to the Lipans. It was the first food
they'd eaten since his capture.

The Lipans slowed without relaxing their guard. At day's end they
stopped in a brushy ravine during a wild thunderstorm. Sheets of water

driven by a cold norther pelted the sleeping party. The Lipans moved a bit of soggy blanket over their faces and otherwise exhibited no sign of discomfort. In the morning, the boy watched in fascination as they started a fire without matches. Their usual method was to rub together flint and steel, but in wet weather it was more reliable to employ a sotol stalk about the size of a broom handle with a hole bored in the center and a notch cut on one side. Holding the sotol on the ground, an Indian could place a smaller stick in the hole and turn it rapidly until a fine wood dust emerged from the hole, became heated, began to smoke, and fell on cedar bark or another flammable material placed at the lower end of the notch. This could be fanned into a flame. Buckelew would become adept at starting fires using both methods.

On the third day they turned west, passing around the headwaters of the Sabinal. Near the headwaters of the Frio, one man shot a steer. The chief and two men departed, and the remaining warrior and Buckelew prepared the beef. Then the man removed Buckelew's eyebrows with a tweezer—a cruel act, to the boy, but basic grooming to the Lipans. He later noticed the men using a bit of looking glass and tweezers to remove all hair from their faces. They detested beards, he learned. The three Lipans returned with seven young calf hides of the same size. They cooked and ate part of the meat and carried the remainder to the top of a nearby mountain. Here they cut sticks several feet long, tied them at the top like a tipi, and built a small fire near the center. They draped the thinly sliced meat carefully over this frame, cooked the meat all the next day, and then placed their jerky on the small calf hides. With deer sinew they fashioned the hides into parfleches, which they wore like a backpack. Jerky "was the staple food of the Indian's daily diet and each Indian carried his own."

Costilietos departed, saying: "Now I leave you. Two my men take you to my wigwam; me tell my men be good to you; me go back with other men, get more horses; me like heap horses; me come to you soon; then you be my boy again. Good-bye." They continued west, passing along a divide near the head of the Frio. The man with the rifle shot a deer but didn't bother to take any meat—he was simply improving his marksmanship. Later, he was excited to shoot a sizable buffalo. The Lipans sat down to enjoy a cigarette made from the shuck of a sotol while they waited for the beast to die and then ate the liver. They skinned the buffalo and cut the hide in three strips, removed the tenderloin and sliced it in strips, and rolled the meat up in the hides. Each man carried a roll on his shoulders. The rest they left for wolves. That night they allowed Buckelew to sleep alone because any escape would have been futile. He had been a captive one week.

The next day they stopped on the Nueces headwaters, and Buckelew could hear the ruckus of white men getting drunk at a nearby store. That night they hogtied the boy while they stole two horses and a mule. Now mounted, they took a more northerly course into open valleys and low, grassy hills and picked up their pace. After riding all night, they stopped at a rich bee cave and had venison and honey for breakfast. The men collected more honey in a hide. The party rode several times around the base of a steep hill, probably to confuse searchers, and resumed their previous journey west. From a cave they retrieved cached saddles and lances. The saddles were a pair of wooden, X-shaped pieces connected with more wood and covered by rawhide—crude but more comfortable than riding bareback.

Crossing Devils River midway between Beaver Lake and the headwaters, they continued to a small lake on top of a narrow divide. The next morning they reached the government road to forts Clark, Mason and McKavett, but before crossing, they examined it at length, and one man climbed a tree for a better view. Then they crossed and erased all signs of their presence. Across a steep canyon in the Pecos, they could see the Lipan village and forded five miles upriver. His companions threw off their burdens and jumped in the water for a swim, motioning for the boy to join them, and he was surprised to see these somber men play in the water like children.

If Buckelew thought he was safe, he was mistaken. An old woman approached and began whipping him with a quirt, drawing blood. He then had to run a gauntlet of boys, girls and old women who struck him with quirts or clubs as he passed through. The force of the blows increased as he passed from small children to the larger boys and girls and old women. Buckelew needed all his resolve to remain standing. Then began a loud howling. The first old woman motioned him to come and put his head in her lap, which marked the end of his apparent initiation rite. He would now learn to be a Lipan. He found their cuisine monotonous and in time used his new skills with the bow and arrow to kill a duck. Back in the village, he began to prepare it for cooking, when a man knocked it from his hand with disgust. Buckelew learned to eat birds on the sly.

Generally each warrior provided for his own family. When they took many deer, antelope, bear or buffalo, they held a common feast, with everyone sharing equally. Nearly every warrior had a separate herd of horses and a herder. That became Buckelew's job. They moved often in search of fresh pasture. One day they prepared for a hunt. Men and boys riding fast ponies formed a circle in a grassy valley. Another group moved to the center of the valley where they could see hundreds of antelope. As the animals attempted to escape, the men closed in, firing arrows and bullets from one side of the circle, which drove them to the other side of the circle where more were killed. Many escaped. The Lipans were so excited and intent on the hunt "that they seemed utterly reckless of their lives."

One day the Lipans were relaxing in camp when a cloud of dust from the north heralded the unexpected approach of a party. They hustled women, children and livestock to safety, and the warriors prepared to fight. Chief Costilietos took command. "The need for and the power of this great old war chief now became evident," Buckalew said. The Lipans watched from their side of the creek. Kickapoos galloped into view and began to circle closer to the stream bank. Costilietos prepared his warriors to dash across the stream and engage them. Recognizing the Lipans' strength and their willingness to fight, the Kickapoos reassessed. Their chief and two warriors rode forward, asking through signs to talk. Costilietos did likewise. They met midway and after a lengthy discussion the parties returned. The two chiefs announced their decisions, whooped and rode together as friends. The Kickapoos camped opposite the Lipans, and the Lipans brought back their women, children and herds.

Now they would feast. They built a large, circular structure of brush and wood, thirty to forty feet in diameter with an opening at the top for the smoke to escape and a large arched door. Warriors dressed as animals with horns on their heads danced to music made by striking smooth, dry sticks together, rattling strings of disc-shaped bones and beating drums of deer hide stretched over a piece of hollowed log. There was gambling, horse racing, and target shooting with bows and arrows. The Kickapoos stayed for about a month before returning to their own hunting grounds. They were still in sight when the Lipans discovered they were missing more than a hundred ponies and made hasty preparations to go in pursuit but thought better of the idea and let the Kickapoos keep their horses.

Buckelew witnessed many a ceremony—weddings, mourning and probably the girls' puberty rites—but seemed most impressed with the ceremonies performed with every solar or lunar eclipse. He was astounded that these "savages" had advanced knowledge of the eclipse. Long into the night of the event, they played their percussion instruments and chanted.

One day a Lipan party returned from a raid into the Bandera area, and when they distributed clothing, Buckelew recognized boys' garments belonging to the Kincheloe family and his aunt's mare. The Lipans had killed two women, pillaged the house but not burned it, and not harmed the children. Pursued by settlers, they lost one man, and another broke a leg. The dead man's widow cut her hair, dressed in mourning garb and spent several days in a secluded place weeping for her husband.

The Mexicans were then enemies, and the Lipans stayed on the north side of the border between the Rio Grande and the Pecos. One day an old Mexican man brought news of a peace treaty. The Mexicans now welcomed Lipans to hunt and trade if they would release Mexican captives. When six captive boys learned of their impending release, three wanted to return, and three chose to stay with the Lipans. They left immediately. They were then about a hundred miles up the river from San Vicente. Along the way, the Lipans killed enough small Mexican hogs (probably peccaries) to provide food for the remaining journey. After a large rattlesnake bit a horse, several old women left the camp and returned with roots and herbs, which they beat, kneaded and mixed into a poultice that was placed it over the bite. Before long, the horse was healed.

The group reached San Vicente in January 1867 and camped about two miles away. The Big Bend village offered meager food supplies, and the Lipans quickly exhausted their inventory of cattle and were reduced to eating parched corn. Buckelew supplemented his diet by trading the bows and arrows he made for tortillas. Both Mexicans and Lipans enjoyed gambling and drinking mescal, but he didn't see any heavy drinking by either. Only once did he see Lipans squabble while inebriated, and the drunks' friends tied them hand and foot until they sobered up.

Mexican people began visiting the camp, and an old man asked Buckelew if he'd like to escape. He wanted to leave but knew he would have to be as cunning as a Lipan to succeed. With the help of a young Mexican employee of W. B. Hudson across the river, he stole two of the strongest horses and ran away in the night. Hudson was probably startled to see young Buckelew on his doorstep dressed in a blanket with paint on his face, hair to his shoulders, and no eyebrows. Hudson returned Buckelew to his sister.[4]

◄►

Brothers Clinton and Jefferson Smith, aged eleven and nine, were herding sheep for their father near Boerne, Texas, on February 26, 1871, when a group of ten Lipans and fifteen Comanches captured them.

They crossed the Guadalupe and stopped briefly on the Pedernales. Bound with buckskin, the exhausted boys slept on a wet saddle blanket. The next day they traveled northwest. Mid-morning, their captors killed a cow and, not wishing to make a fire, devoured it raw. Clinton and Jefferson refused to eat, but after two more days, gladly ate a raw cow's liver tossed to them. Later that day, the raiders roped a wild horse, tied the boys on it, and drove the horse with them.

For several days their captors would split up, reunite and divide again, often setting fire to the dry grass or using skunk musk to confuse the rangers' dogs and communicating with smoke signals. They kept an eye on rangers through field glasses. The group traveled until late at night and took up the trail again before dawn. Nearing Fort Concho, the warriors surmised correctly that troops were in the field looking for them, so they stole past the sleeping fort, doubled back on their trail, crossed the river at Fort Concho, and camped at a pond. The rangers found Jeff's bloody shoe at this pond, but after a chase of nearly two hundred miles, they were out of supplies and turned back.

Continuing northwest, they recovered cached supplies from a cave. At an Indian trail they left small stones to tell the phase of the moon and the direction taken. (Lipans set out a row of stones in places they knew their people would be, such as a spring, said Antonio Apache. "The stones go in the direction they moved. If they moved a long way, the row of rocks is long. They didn't mark trees. They used only rocks and smoke signals" until they obtained mirrors.) Several months after reaching the main group, Jeff was sold to Geronimo, so the two boys saw each other only when the Comanches and Geronimo's Apaches camped together. In the next year or so Clinton and the Comanches met Lipans, "a fierce tribe," near Fort Sill in Oklahoma and sometimes camped with them. Jeff Smith recalled that his captors met a large party of Lipans in New Mexico. "The Lipans had a trading point somewhere with the Mexicans, and would exchange horses and mules for sugar, coffee, whiskey, tobacco, guns, pistols, beads, red calico and other articles." Geronimo suspected the Mexicans were trying to get Lipans to capture him for a reward, "so we did not tarry long with this tribe."[5]

In April 1873 a Mexican trader informed the U.S. commercial agent at Piedras Negras that a white boy was in a camp of Lipans, Mescaleros, Kickapoos and Comanches in San Rodrigo Canyon, about sixty miles from the Texas border. He ransomed Jeff from his Lipan captor for $150 in gold.[6] On May 1 Jeff was turned over to Thomas G. Williams, a government representative, who promptly cut his hair and insisted that he wear the white man's uncomfortable clothing. The boy had forgotten English and slept on the floor, which he found more comfortable than a bed.[7]

CHAPTER

Mescalero

In these parts the Kickapoo and Lipan Tribes commit most all the stealing and murdering . . . [A] whole regiment of mounted troops stationed along our borders will not prevent these savages from making
successful raids to this part of Texas.

— *Judge H. I. Richards, 1867*

Lipans and Kickapoos became such a menace that Texans began to
suspect Mexican civil authorities were informing them of troop
movements and opportunities to steal. Their camps in Mexico were
the size of villages, and they continually replenished their large herds of
horses and cattle from Texas, selling livestock to Mexicans and American fugitives living in Mexico.[1] Demands for extradition of certain Indians alarmed tribes and Mexicans, who feared another Callahan-style
invasion, so the tribes broke up their camps, divided into smaller, more
mobile groups, and dispersed. This "relieved [Mexicans] of the presence & embarrassments of so great a body of consumers at one local-
ity," wrote Stephen Brown, who was to meet with Indian leaders and
negotiate their removal on behalf of Major General Joseph Reynolds.
He only met once with a few chiefs, but they were ready to return to
their former homes. When they first came to Mexico, they were rich
and comfortable but were now poor and dependent on raiding and on
the Mexicans. Some were serving as scouts in the Mexican army; others were servants or laborers. They didn't dare express their unhappi-
ness. To the Mexicans, the tribes were a boon to trade and a source of
protection against other tribes, but Brown believed they would be "the

scapegoats for the unlawful deeds & depredations of all the bad characters that gather along both frontiers."[2]

◄ ►

Lipans tell a story about a Southern Lipan and Northern Lipan who were looking for horses when they found a Kickapoo camp. They watched it for a day, and saw a Kickapoo drive the horses to good grass and return to his camp. They were good horses. By moonlight, they rounded up the horses and started off, riding all night and the next day and that night until midnight. Finally, they stopped to sleep. They continued for two more days until they reached home. A big group of Kickapoos set out to recover their horses and picked up the trail. Near the Lipan camp, a hunter spotted them. The chief ordered the women to gather their things and begin moving out. He chose seven brave men to join him in holding off the Kickapoos. One was a Big Water Lipan from Coahuila, another was a Mexican captive raised with that band, and the rest were Lipans from New Mexico. One had taken the horses and was riding one of the Kickapoos' horses.

From the top of a hill a man saw the Kickapoos approaching slowly, leading their horses so they would appear to be a group of wild horses. When they saw the Lipan, they mounted up and chased him. He signaled to the other men to ride in the opposite direction from the camp. He himself headed for the plains, and the Kickapoos chased him a long way. When the Mexican captive's horse gave out, the chief's brother suggested they leave him. The chief said, "No, in my fighting against the enemy I have never given my men away and let them fall into the hands of the enemy." He took the man on his horse. Even though the chief's horse was strong and the Kickapoos' horses were tired, they began to catch up. The chief stopped, made his ceremony over his shield, said his prayer and lifted his shield four times to the sun. His men heard the growl of a bear come from his shield.

He told four men to get off their horses and face the enemy. He and another man remained mounted. When the Kickapoos began to shoot, the Lipans charged, but the Kickapoos' arrows hit the chief's shield and flew over. A Kickapoo with a muzzle loader wounded the chief in the hip. The Lipans killed a Kickapoo, let the Kickapoos fire their guns again, and then pressed them, killing three more Kickapoos, one by gunshot and two by lance. The Kickapoos withdrew to reload, and a Lipan lanced a man. More Kickapoos came. The man with the lance hit a Kickapoo wearing a headdress and tore off the man's quiver. The chief and the other Lipan on horseback were also driving back the Kickapoos. When the chief saw there were so many Kickapoos coming that they wouldn't have a chance, he signaled to his men on foot to go back. They caught horses and began to move away slowly with the Kickapoos behind them.

The chief was starting to feel his wound and told the Southern Lipan, as he handed him his shield, "It's your turn to start the fight now." That man was on one of the stolen horses, and it was fresh and spirited. The approaching Kickapoos talked it over and let the Lipans go. They gathered their dead and began to cry. When the Lipans were out of sight, they stopped too. The chief was in pain and wanted to stop riding. His wound was more serious than he thought. He sent a man to the Lipan camp with a message for their people that he fought a good fight: "You saw with your eyes what I did . . . I didn't keep my distance. I was right there with them; that's how I got wounded, for they are good fighters, too. Go back and tell what I did. I am the chief. I say it myself. Tell those people not to feel badly about what happens to me. If I go down it is all right. I am just one man." Years later, when the Lipans and Kickapoos were friends, they talked about that fight. "Yes, we lost our very highest chief in that fight," the Kickapoos said. "And the Northern Lipans lost their highest chief too," they said.

Later on, the Kickapoos set out to avenge their chief. The Lipans were camped at Natagé Point on the north side of the San Diego River in Coahuila. At sunset they were playing hoop and pole under some pecan trees when forty Kickapoos crept up through a thicket. A Lipan sitting against a tree watching the game saw movement from the corner of his eye. Turning his head slowly, he saw a Kickapoo's feathers. The enemy was waiting for the pole to be thrown before attacking because the men always gathered closely to look at the position of the pole.

The man sitting against the tree called out a warning, threw his blanket aside, and reached for his weapons. Before most of the Lipans could pick up their weapons the Kickapoos were running amongst them. Just two Lipans were armed, one with a rifle and one with bow and arrows. The rifle was only a single shot, and the man knew if he fired, they would get past him. He pointed it at the Kickapoos and held them off for a time, but a Kickapoo stabbed him from behind with a lance. He was still moving, so another Kickapoo hit him on the head and a third took his scalp. Still alive, he crawled away, pulled the lance from his body and used it as a cane. He made his way back to his people and later recovered. The other Lipan fought valiantly with bows and arrows but was overwhelmed and killed. The Kickapoos killed men, women and children. Later, when Lipans and Kickapoos were friends, a man in the original fight chided them: "What I did was what men do, but the way you people did not long ago, sneaking up on our camps and killing children who could do no harm—that is not the way men fight."

◄►

This incident took place on May 27, 1868. The Kickapoos killed five men and six women and children, wounded seven men and took away two boys, twenty-five horses and three tents, along with two carbines, five tomahawks, three six-shooters and bows and arrows. A resident of Musquis, where the Kickapoos were on good terms, took up a collection for the Kickapoos' "great and important service to the state." Zaragosa (formerly San Fernando), a town on the Escondido the Lipans called Many Houses, had befriended the Lipans. A resident asked the government to make the Kickapoos return the horses and boys. The Lipan chiefs Gicare, Soli and Costilitos (Costilietos) brought their families in to receive a response.[3]

Lipans had been in Zaragosa since 1850, when the Mexicans gave them a place to live near the old church and presidio, hoping the

Lipans' presence would deter Comanche attacks, and they encouraged the Lipans and Mescaleros to bring in their stolen stock to sell. Lipans also settled at Hacienda Patiño, between Morelos and Zaragosa; at Remolino on the San Rodrigo, northwest of Zaragosa; and in the mountains southwest of Zaragosa, near the village of Norte. By 1868 the groups at Hacienda Patiño and Remolino numbered between eighty and one hundred people. Smaller family groups were at Monclova Viejo and San Juan Bautista. In addition, Lipans and Mescaleros lived near San Carlos in the Big Bend, and "wild" Lipans were still living in the mountains. Diplomatic efforts to draw the Kickapoos and Lipans back to the United States came to naught. After another fight with Kickapoos, the Lipans and Mescaleros retreated to Monclova Viejo, about twenty-five miles above Piedras Negras.[4]

The man who died fighting with bows and arrows was one of four children of Big Water Lipan parents. His siblings were Chivato, born in 1852; Dinero, born in 1860; and Pe-chá, born between 1863 and 1869.

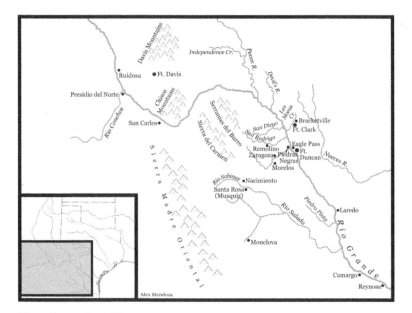

Map 8 Lipans after 1850

The family had been in Mexico at least three generations. Their great-grandfather introduced peyote to the Lipans.[5]

The Lipan story continues: The dead man's father was angry. He went out with his sons Chivato and Dinero, along with Miguel Zuazua, Cardinal Rodriguez and Santavi. They took some horses from the Kickapoos and rode slowly for several days. The horses' owner chose eleven men who could stand a hard fight, and they left right away. The dead Lipan's father stopped to rest. Cardinal Rodriguez argued that they should keep going, that this was a poor place to stop. He climbed a hill and saw two Kickapoos coming with more behind them. He shouted to the others. Two Kickapoos got off their horses. The avenging father waited with his two sons. A Kickapoo came forward, fired his gun and took out his knife. The Lipan father fired his .44 and killed the Kickapoo. The other Kickapoo continued fighting. Rodriguez came running down the hill, dropped into an arroyo and fired but missed. A Kickapoo returned fire.

As more Kickapoos arrived, they wounded three Lipans, and the Lipans ran. The father and his sons mounted up and rode away. The father picked up a man who had his testicle shot off and took him to shelter in some bushes. He gave the man some herbs, performed a ceremony and told him, "Walk now and don't give up." The Lipans scattered. Dinero ran off by himself. When he fired at Kickapoos chasing the other Lipans, they turned and chased him. The other Lipans ran up a hill, and Dinero reached the foot of another hill with the Kickpoos on his heels. He curled up behind his big shield. Two Kickapoos took aim but missed him. He ran on with the Kickapoos still close behind. A shot brought down Dinero. His pistol was fastened to his hand, so he didn't lose it. He reloaded and fired at the Kickapoo leader, who dodged and was only grazed.

When the Lipans realized Dinero wasn't with them, Chivato ran down a hill toward the sounds of gunfire and started shooting at the Kickapoos, but a Kickapoo shot him in the chest. When the Kickapoo prepared to finish him off, Chivato raised his gun and killed the man. He fired again at the Kickapoos and started back up the hill. He hid behind some brush and started for a big rock, when a bullet hit him in the leg and another struck above the groin. He struggled behind the rock and continued over the hill. Dinero managed to follow his brother over the hill. Dinero gave Chivato some medicine he had, a root, and Chivato's mind began to clear.

The two made their way to another hiding place. The Kickapoos trailed them by their blood. Some young men wanted to run ahead, but an older man cautioned: "He is waiting for us there. Another of us will be killed." While the Kickapoos argued, the brothers moved to another hill. Chivato said, "You'd better go on. Let them finish me. I can't go any further. Fix my gun." The brothers prepared their weapons and waited. The Kickapoos didn't come for them but turned around, picked up their men who were mortally wounded and started for home. Chivato and Dinero recovered, and Cardinal Rodriguez, Miguel Zuazua and Santavi survived.

Mexican people blamed the Lipans for problems, so authorities ordered troops to subdue them. Chivato's mother had a premonition and began sending Chivato, Dinero and their baby sister away every day. She told them to take the goats and go a few miles away into the hills to the west. If Chivato heard shooting, he was to stay away until nightfall. One day, the troops did come to Zaragosa and nearly annihilated the Lipans. Chivato left his brother and sister in a safe place and returned to the village. Everyone was dead, it seemed. Later he would learn only thirteen people survived. He saw the bodies of people and animals strewn everywhere, unburied. His father was dead. With her dying words, his mother urged him to get some supplies and take his brother and sister to Texas.

They headed north. Stopping at a water hole one day, they looked up and found Mescaleros watching them. They told the Mescalero leader what happened in Zaragosa, and he invited the boys to come along. The Mescaleros gave them food and fresh horses. They rode to what is now Roswell, New Mexico, up the Hondo Valley and into the mountains that would become the Mescalero Apache Reservation.

They told the Mescaleros they hated Mexican soldiers, and the Mescaleros promised them a chance at revenge. After a while, they accompanied raiding parties into Mexico to steal horses from Mexican troops and later rode with Mexican bandits.[6]

Apaches clustered in the Sierra Diablo, nineteen miles of rough, jutting, saddle-emptying mountains. On October 18, 1867, Captain Frank Wilson and more than a hundred men from Fort Union and Fort Stanton in New Mexico caught up with the thirty or forty warriors they trailed south from the Sacramento and Guadalupe Mountains. Troops killed six and found the Apaches' winter camps tucked into jagged canyons where access was so difficult and water so scarce, only forty-three of Wilson's men could even reach them.

"The Indians showing fight, an engagement ensued, which lasted some three hours," he wrote. When several hundred more warriors materialized in the surrounding heights, Wilson "deemed it best to retire." He guessed at twenty-five to thirty killed or wounded, "but as they were

Sierra Diablo in northwestern Texas (*Sherry Robinson, photographer*)

carried off the field as fast as they fell, their number could not be ascertained; one of their rancherías was burned to avoid its falling into our hands." Six troops were killed or wounded—two by musket balls, the rest by arrows. "It will take a considerable force to dislodge them."[7]

Mescaleros, joined at times by Lipans and Comanches, were living in the Guadalupe Mountains and sixty miles south in Sierra Diablos in 1869, when they began drifting back to Fort Stanton in New Mexico. They wanted to live at peace, said Lieutenant A. G. Hennisee, but he was hard pressed to provide for them. He recommended a reservation.[8] New Mexico citizens in March 1870 sent a man to ask the Mescaleros if they would live on a reservation. He found Chief Francisco Llanero with fifty men and women and some Comanches at Bull Spring, at the base of the Guadalupes. Yes, they would live on a reservation if it was in their own country, and they would pass the news. Francisco Llanero said he wasn't the head chief, but he would try to persuade the others.[9] The name indicates the Llanero Apaches maintained their autonomy but were closely associated with the Mescaleros; the Americans saw them as one tribe.

Apaches from across the region began collecting at Fort Stanton; by early 1871 they numbered five or six hundred. Chief José La Paz announced in February 1871 that the entire tribe wanted peace, and would come in as soon as grass on the Staked Plains was long enough for them to graze their animals. Agent A. J. Curtis continued sending messengers to the plains and by year end counted about 830, including 440 Aguas Nuevas (Mescaleros who lived at a town by that name on the Rio Grande below Fort Quitman), 350 Lipans (Magoosh and his people), and 310 Warm Springs Apaches (Gileños).[10]

Meanwhile, groups of Apaches and Comanches were still on the Staked Plains. An old Apache woman on a good mule told a patrol in July that two tribes of Apaches (probably Mescaleros and Llaneros) and one of Lipans had just made peace with the Comanches after a council on the Pecos where they also traded with comancheros. The Apaches returned to Fort Stanton to make peace.[11] In August 1872, unidentified Indians took a herd of cattle near the falls of the Pecos, about forty miles above Horsehead Crossing. Captain J. P. Dodge, leading troops of the Ninth Cavalry from Fort Stockton, struck east across the Pecos and came upon a well-provisioned camp of ten lodges in an arroyo next to some holes of rain water; its occupants departed so hastily that food was still cooking. Following the trail of forty horses at a trot, they topped a rise and looked out over a landscape empty of humanity. The Apaches had evaporated like steam.[12]

That month, the number of Apaches at Fort Stanton rose to 1,805 people, all well behaved, "considering that very few of them have ever lived on a reservation, and that they came from the 'war path,'" Curtis wrote. The government ignored his proposals for a reservation, as it had Hennisee's. The Apaches kept their part of the bargain, Curtis told President Grant, but the government had not. Rations were insufficient, and wild game was disappearing. They were inadequately clothed and "deplorably destitute."[13] Curtis resigned in frustration.

◀▶

The blue pyramids of the Sacramento Mountains, which beckoned dusty travelers from the plains, sheltered Apache movement from the northernmost hill of the Guadalupes forty miles north of the Texas line and north for ninety miles, embracing the 12,003-foot Sierra Blanca, the Apaches' sacred peak. On May 29, 1873, the government created the Mescalero Apache Reservation. Apaches, agents and military officers believed it would solve a lot of problems, but it only created new ones.

Set in the traditional country of the Natagés and Faraons, who were absorbed by the Mescaleros, the reservation was well familiar to Upper Lipans and Llaneros. It answered the Apaches' requests for land of their own where they might settle, and it promised to end roaming and raiding, which would simplify military operations. However, the Apaches would need food and supplies, and that simple function opened the door to corruption and inefficiency that compromised the reservation's mission for years, and by concentrating Apaches and their herds, the reservation was a magnet to vengeful settlers and rustlers.

The post trader, L. G. Murphy & Co., was "a den of infamy and its toleration a disgrace to the public service," railed Captain James Randlett.[14] The army was just beginning to recognize the rampant lawlessness and corruption that would boil over a few years later in the Lincoln County War. Major Lawrence Murphy served at the Bosque Redondo, where he got to know the Mescaleros. In 1866, when his regiment disbanded, Murphy and another former officer became traders at Fort Stanton, nearby Lincoln and the Mescalero Agency. Before long, he was falsifying vouchers, inflating counts of Apaches, misrepresenting beef weights and dealing in stolen cattle.[15]

Food, issued irregularly, was barely fit to eat; blankets failed to arrive. The Office of Indian Affairs, unsure if its agents were under Murphy's influence, hired and fired, exacerbating instability on the reservation. The chiefs strived to keep their people on the reservation, but if restless—or hungry—young men chose to raid, it was out of their control. After L. Edwin Dudley, New Mexico's Superintendent of Indian Affairs, had two chiefs arrested and threatened to hold them until stolen stock was returned, alarmed Apaches left the reservation for the plains, the mountains and Mexico.[16] Dudley's actions were "the worst that could possibly have been adopted. Infallibility is their prerogative. There is no appeal," wrote Lawrence Murphy. Dudley and the agent "surrendered their judgment . . . to a military officer who knew as little of the Indian character or disposition as did anyone within my experience." Murphy may have been a scoundrel, but his assessment of the situation is correct.[17]

Randlett tracked one large group through the Guadalupes to the Pecos and out on the Staked Plains. They chose a well fortified site at the base of a mesa, cut their tipi poles and began to settle in. Discovering they were followed, the group splintered, some heading for Sulphur Springs on the Staked Plains, many running for Mexico. The occasional child's moccasin left in the trail hinted at their haste. "They evidently intend to live off the settlers on the Pecos, and seem to direct all their venom against Mr. Chisum," Randlett observed. Cattleman John Chisum established his operation along the Pecos in 1865, squarely in the middle of traditional Apache country. He blamed the Mescaleros for his losses, but Chisum's cattle fed many a settler and enriched untold numbers of rustlers.[18]

Some destitute Apaches made their way back to Fort Stanton in March 1874, and more were on the plains. Over the summer more Apaches reappeared, well armed and with many horses.[19] In early 1875 Chisum's cowboys and Pecos Valley settlers attacked reservation Apaches in their camps, killing several people and stealing their horses; some Apaches retaliated and fled. On the night of January 15, rumors of the cowboys' return flew from camp to camp, and nearly all the Apaches ran away from the reserve.[20] Agent W. D. Crothers waited until spring before sending an employee, Andrew Sharpe, to find them. Searching over mountains and plains, he found a camp in the Smoke Mountains.[21] This was most likely the Eagle Mountains, a grass-covered range broken by sandstone that rises sharply from the West Texas desert floor. Eagle Springs in the northeastern foothills delivered plenty of good water even in dry weather. From the Eagle Mountains, the Apaches could make their way north, sheltered by the Sierra Diablos and the Guadalupes or move south to Mexico by way of the Sierra Vieja.[22]

"They were well armed with breech loading guns and had a large number of horses in their possession," Crothers wrote. Sharpe persuaded them to leave only after providing cattle at his own expense. In mid-October, about two hundred-fifty people returned. Another two bands were still on the plains.[23] As soon as the returning Apaches made camp, settlers began attacking. On the afternoon of June 18, 1876, all the Apaches left, taking their own stock and some from nearby ranches. For three weeks they had fed their grain rations to their livestock to build stamina. Troops pursued for about ten miles before darkness eclipsed the trail. About a week later, half returned; another 150 reached Mexico in August.[24]

CHAPTER

Day of the Screams

The worst of them were the Lipan, a small body, and the Kickapoos
numbering several hundred.

— Zenas R. Bliss[1]

When army regulars finally reoccupied frontier posts, they were
often Buffalo Soldiers, black men with white officers of the
Ninth and Tenth Cavalry and the Twenty-fourth and Twenty-fifth
Infantry, who would prove to be unshakable combatants.[2] Apaches
understood they faced a new adversary, but they regained the upper
hand temporarily when General J. J. Reynolds withdrew troops to
contend with the growing threat of the Ku Klux Klan, which was robbing and killing "union men and Negroes," as well as army officers and
soldiers. Combined parties of Indians and Mexicans blazed a trail of
destruction between the Nueces and the Rio Grande. They couldn't be
stopped as long as they had no assigned lands, Reynolds said.[3]

In May 1869 about one hundred-fifty raiders attacked a wagon
train and made off with all the mules, escaping toward the Rio Grande.
In June Ninth Cavalry troops from Fort Clark fought on the Pecos with
Lipans and recovered mules stolen from a government pack train, along
with animals taken from Fort Clark three years earlier.[4] Hardly a week
passed without a raid by Lipans, Mescaleros or Kickapoos, separately
or together and often joined by Mexicans. They typically forded the
Rio Grande at San Diego and cut a broad loop from San Antonio to

Laredo, killing shepherds and travelers, attacking ranches, driving off herds and leaving a trail of broken-down animals, victims, and pillaged haciendas. Texans were sure Mexican traders had spies in the field to advise the tribes of opportunities and keep them supplied with arms, ammunition and liquor.[5]

◄ ►

The army needed scouts against these raiders, and Major Zenas R. Bliss, then with the Twenty-fifth Infantry at Fort Duncan, believed Black Seminoles were the solution. They had stayed in Coahuila after the Seminole Tribe returned to the United States following Wild Cat's death in 1857, and were joined by others of Black-Indian ancestry, freed slaves and runaways. To protect them from filibusters and slavers, the Mexican government relocated them from the border to Laguna de Parras in southwestern Coahuila, where they became targets of Comanche and Apache raids. They proved to be a match.

After raiders took the young son of Dick Grayson, John Horse gathered thirty or forty men and left others to guard their families. The heavily armed group followed the raiders for several days, until John Horse halted. The trail was too obvious, he said. He sent scouts ahead, and his men formed a semicircle, with the convex side outward. Those with well-trained horses and rifles stayed in the saddle; others with cumbersome weapons or skittish horses dismounted and fixed staves. Inexperienced men held the horses in the middle of the semicircle.

They waited. Suddenly, shots tore the silence, and their scouts exploded from a distant thicket, riding hard on lathered horses. They had found a big camp of Comanches, Lipans and Mescaleros, who were close behind. John Horse ordered his men to stand their ground as the sizable Indian party approached. He took aim at a Comanche riding ahead of the others, and his bullet found its target. The others fired, with equally deadly results. Warriors surrounded the black men, believing they could still overwhelm them. John Horse and some of his men bluffed, pointing empty guns at the approaching warriors while others reloaded. The circling warriors tightened their ring, shooting and firing arrows as they suspended themselves from their horses' far side. When they charged, the Black Seminoles jumped on their horses to meet the attack and used their guns as clubs. They also wielded machetes, severing lance points. Forming a circle to reload, they surprised their attackers with a new burst of fire and more losses. The warriors turned and retreated. The Black men pursued, killing a few more. At the Indian camp, they rescued the captive boy and burned the lodges.[6]

Groups led by John Horse, Gopher John (known to Lipans as Laughing Dog), and John Kibbetts were willing to work as scouts for the United States and began arriving at Fort Duncan in July 1870; more Black Seminoles were recruited for service at Fort Clark. Most of these men were African in appearance but dressed like Seminoles, and a few wore buffalo-horn war bonnets. They spoke English and Spanish, knew the terrain and were no strangers to frontier combat. They were acquainted with the Lipans and Comanches and even traded with them but were never friends. The Seminole Negro Indian Scouts became some of the most effective scouts ever to serve the army—uncanny trailers who could stay out for months and live on half-rations, game or even rattlesnakes, if necessary. Bliss called them "splendid fighters."[7] Recruiting the Black Seminoles was the military's most effective single move against the hostile tribes in Mexico.

◀ ▶

When the army brass converged on Fort Clark in April 1873, they had one urgent topic: What were they going to do about the Lipans and Kickapoos? Livestock numbers on the upper Rio Grande were a tenth of what they had been in 1865; losses soared to an estimated $48 million.[8] General Philip Sheridan, Secretary of War William Belknap and Colonel Wesley Meritt fixed on Colonel Ranald B. Mackenzie as the man for their mission. Called "the most promising young officer in the Army" by Ulysses S. Grant, Mackenzie had received seven brevets for gallantry in the Civil War, but his severe wounds would torment him all his life. Fellow officers acknowledged his courage but also knew he could be irritable, demanding, impetuous and explosive.

To Mackenzie's mind, the only way to stop the raids was to invade Indian strongholds and destroy them, a tactic he'd demonstrated in campaigns against Comanches on the Staked Plains, although a white captive said his soldiers massacred women, babies and old men. However, Mexico refused to sanction the American army's movement inside its borders,[9] and an invasion of Mexico could provoke war, Mackenzie told his superiors. He asked for written orders. Sheridan pounded the table and shouted, "Damn the orders! Damn the authority! You are to go ahead on your own plan of action, and your authority and backing shall be General Grant and myself." Sheridan wanted "a campaign of annihilation, obliteration and destruction."

Mackenzie set out in the night with nearly four hundred men. With them were thirty-four Black Seminole scouts who had lived near the Kickapoos in Coahuila. Their relatives at Nacimiento provided useful intelligence on the Kickapoo, Lipan and Mescalero villages north of them and west of Remolino at the San Rodrigo headwaters. They crossed the Rio Grande at sunset on May 17 and rode hard for sixty-three miles. The next day dawned bright and cloudless. The villages stretched before them along the turquoise waters of the San Rodrigo, which slowly wound its way east to the Rio Grande. It was a place Lipans had inhabited for a hundred years. Each village numbered between fifty and sixty lodges. John Castro's Lipan village lay a quarter mile beyond the Kickapoos. Cooled by breezes rolling off the hills, the soldiers moved quickly up the stream bed, around the base of a hill and down a long slope until they reached the sleeping Kickapoo village.

Mackenzie made two decisions that Custer failed to make three years later at the Little Big Horn. First, Mackenzie's men carried their reserve ammunition in their shirt pockets and not on pack mules or their horses, where the enemy might gain access. Second, he resisted the suggestion of his Black Seminole scouts that they split up and attack all three villages or at least send troops around the Lipan village toward the mountains to cut off their escape. The scouts wanted to attack the Lipans and Mescaleros first; they had been friendly with the Kickapoos but never liked the Apaches and bitterly remembered their raids.

Troops charged over rocky, open ground covered by mesquite, prickly pear and Spanish dagger. Surprising and overwhelming the Kickapoos, they destroyed the village within minutes and quickly made for the Lipan village and then the Mescalero village. The Lipans, male and female, fought fiercely. Most escaped to the mountains, as did the Mescaleros in the more distant camp.[10] During the fight, scout Tony Wilson had a Lipan in his sights. Just as he fired, his target raised an arm, revealing too late that she was female. Shooting a woman troubled Wilson for the rest of his life. Apparently when a woman wanted to surrender, she raised her hand and soldiers would stop shooting at her. Apache men never used the gesture, preferring death to the humiliation of capture.[11]

◄►

Stories of that day passed through generations of Castros. "My grandfather said that during the morning hours . . . soldiers, Mexicans and Americans, surprised the [Kickapoo] rancheria and Lipan Apache [rancheria] while the people were still asleep. Many woke up to the screams of women, men, children being shot at and bayoneted to death," said Valentina Castro Sambrano, granddaughter of Calixtro Gonzalez Castro. He told her it was a day she was not to forget.

Soldiers fired into tents and small huts. They even killed Mexicans who happened to be staying there. Lipans customarily dug holes large enough to shelter a person, who could then hide by pulling up a large weed attached to a rope. John Castro's daughter, Juanita, jumped in a hole with her baby brother, Miguel Gonzalez Castro. She held Miguel to her chest and put her hand over his mouth, trying to keep him from crying, but a soldier heard the baby and thrust his bayonet into the tumbleweed brush repeatedly, stabbing the baby in the heart and killing him. The terrified girl continued to grip the rope, holding the dead, bleeding infant. Castro's sons Calixtro, who was fifteen, and Manuel dived into another hole and covered themselves. [12] Many Lipans managed to escape by hiding in the ravine. The soldiers didn't look for them because they were preoccupied with killing the others.

Afterward, the survivors walked for days to reach relatives in Texas or Mexico. John Castro was badly wounded; his brother Ramon was dead, and so was John's wife Francisca (a Lipan-Kickapoo). With Manuel he walked for weeks to reach McAllen, Texas, where they found Calixtro and Juanita, the only other family members to survive. He vowed never to allow such a tragedy to happen to his people again. Castro told his people to change their surnames and not reveal they were Lipans or speak the Lipan language out of fear they would be hunted down and killed. He changed his name to Porfirio Gonzales, "when the soldiers would come looking for the Indians—us," his grandson recalled. Many of Castro's Lipans never regrouped. Instead, they melted into the populations of various Mexican towns.

Thereafter, the Castro family began family gatherings with an offering called the "grandfather plate," in which food and drink are placed in the fire pit. "We did this to remember the family we lost at Mackenzie Raid and for the lost souls in other tragedies," said Frank Vasquez Castro. The gesture also welcomes the spirits of ancestors to share their wisdom. "It is believed that the only place one can talk or mention a lost family member's name in public is at family reunions in the company of the family's root or soul," wrote Daniel Castro Romero, Jr. [13]

◄►

To historians, May 18, 1873, was Mackenzie's Raid. To Lipans, it was *Dia de los Gritos*, Day of the Screams. Mackenzie reported just nineteen warriors killed, but many more, including women and children, died outside the villages when soldiers discovered their hiding places. "The exact number will never be known," wrote soldier Robert G. Carter. The wounded were also uncounted. The army took forty women and children captive and destroyed all three villages, burning lodges and food supplies. The Lipans' losses would have been worse if their camp had been attacked first or simultaneously by a split command, and if Mackenzie's mules hadn't been exhausted. It helped, too, that many Lipans left early that morning to go hunting.

One of the captives was Chief Costilietos. Scout Renty Grayson lassoed the old man as he was fleeing; other scouts captured his daughter, Teresita. Costilietos admitted to leading a raid by Kickapoos, Lipans and Mescaleros not long before in the Nueces Valley. In a fight near Howard's Wells on April 20, an officer of the Ninth Cavalry died.

A Black Seminole Scout brought in one Lipan warrior without disarming him. "The moment I saw the look of rage at what he had witnessed come over his face, I feared trouble," Carter wrote. "As soon as he had recovered from his amazement and apparent stupor and fairly realized, by the blazing villages, prisoners, women and children standing under guard, etc., what had happened and how he had been duped, with a defiant whoop, he brought his rifle down like a flash upon [Captain Clarence] Mauck." Carter raised his own carbine, cocked and fired without aiming. "He gave a loud, piercing yell, threw up his gun, which went off in the air, and toppled off his pony, dead before he touched the ground."[14]

Mexicans later disputed reports of Indian thievery, saying they were simply an excuse for invading Mexico. The Lipans, Kickapoos and Mescaleros maintained themselves on the fruits of their labors, evidenced by their abandoned fields. Costilietos, then in his eighties, supported himself with a little trading. The Indians defended themselves valiantly, and sold their lives dearly, Mexicans said. When there were no more men to kill, the Americans took out their wrath on women, killing fifteen.[15]

Captives were taken to San Antonio. "They should be kept in a corral and allowed to cook their own food so as to change their mode of living as little as possible, in order to prevent injury to their health," Mackenzie wrote. He sent them on to Fort Gibson and then Fort Sill but recommended that Costilietos be allowed to stay, probably because

This undated photograph taken in San Antonio is identified only as "Indian chief and daughters," but a note on the back says "Lipan Apaches." Chief Costilietos, known to be elderly, was the only chief captured in 1873. *H. A. Doerr, photographer. DeGrolyer Library, Southern Methodist University, Dallas, Texas. Ag2008.0005*

the government's commercial agent suggested sending the old man as a messenger to his tribe "to bring them to terms." Mackenzie told Costilietos he would arrange for Chief Castile, of the Tonkawas, and the Lipan scout Johnson to see him.[16] On June 27, Costilietos vanished; his body was found a week later by the side of the road. Teresita stayed and later married Black Seminole scout James Perryman, who had enlisted just before Mackenzie's raid; their commanding officer, Lieutenant John L. Bullis, performed the ceremony.[17]

Lipans and Mescaleros with about seventy-five warriors regrouped on Sulphur Creek, six miles from Remolino, and on a flat hill called El Burro about thirty miles northwest of Remolino. Mexican authorities at Zaragosa issued them ammunition for hunts in response to their request to draw beef, but they visited warily in parties of fifteen to twenty-five men to trade buckskins for ammunition.[18] On the morning of October 6, 1873, about forty Lipans appeared among sheep ranches on the San Antonio road. Firing arrows and guns, they wounded three herders, one mortally, and then divided, taking eighteen brood mares and killing others that wouldn't be driven easily. Lipans took revenge for Mackenzie's raid across all the frontier towns.

"The victims sacrificed have been innumerable, especially on the three occasions when the American troops have chastised Indians who were living in peace in Mexico," said a Mexican report.[19] In January 1874 Ignacio Mariscal, Mexico's minister to the United States, protested Mackenzie's raid. Mexico, he said, would help stop border depredations but would not suffer armed invasions by foreigners.[20]

◄ ►

The Secretary of the Interior appointed commissioners to remove Kickapoos, Potawatomies, Lipans and Mescaleros from Mexico. Governor Victoriano Cepeda, of Coahuila, was cooperating, but Mackenzie's raid was poorly timed, commissioners grumbled. The feeling was mutual. Mackenzie wanted them to finish up so he could attack again. "The Indians can easily move their Camps so far back into the Mountains and so far away from the river that they can only be reached by operating for a considerable time on the other side of the Rio Grande. I believe that if the Mescaleras or Lepans could be hit pretty hard that the Kickpoos would conclude to come out," he wrote. The press, which lionized Mackenzie, agreed, but Mackenzie's superiors were having second thoughts. Sherman advised him to use "caution if not restraint" in sending spies into Mexico "to hunt up camps with a view to a future attack," which could stir up complications with Mexico. Sheridan directed General Christopher C. Augur "to tighten up a little on Col Mackenzie," and Augur enjoined Mackenzie from crossing the border again "without further provocation."[21]

On July 11, 1873, Commissioner Henry M. Atkinson met with Kickapoos, Potawatomies, Lipans and Mescaleros. All said they would return to the United States. Commissioner Thomas G. Williams on July

28 was optimistic about a speedy removal of the Kickapoos and Pota-watomies, but the Lipans and Mescaleros would only be persuaded if commissioners visited them with escorts of both Mexican and American troops. Earlier, returning captive Jeff Smith told Williams that the Lipans bought ammunition at San Antonio. The raiders, he said, were primarily Lipans with a few Mexicans.[22]

The commissioners asked for $45,000 to collect, maintain and transport some three hundred Kickapoos and $70,000 to do the same for 1,500 Lipans and Mescaleros, an indication of their numbers in Mexico. When the Mescaleros decided against leaving, a frustrated Atkinson wrote to Mackenzie that he intended to bring in the Kicka-poos as quickly as possible "and will leave the Lepans and Mescelleros to your tender Mercies."[23] About half the Kickapoos and all the Pota-watomies started back to the United States with the two commission-ers on August 28. The rest of the Kickapoos promised to leave Mexico if they heard favorable reports from their kin. They never left.[24] Lipans and Mescaleros refused to "entertain any proposition to limit their place of residence," wrote Augur, who was increasing troop strength at Fort Clark.[25]

◄►

The Lipan prisoners Mackenzie sent to Fort Sill asked to join the Tonkawas at Fort Griffin and become scouts, an arrangement Costili-etos had requested. Mackenzie said he would ask if the Tonkawa chief and the Lipan scout Johnson could visit him. Tonkawas had taken ref-uge at several forts after a massacre of their people by Comanches and other tribes early in the Civil War. They moved to Fort Griffin in 1868 and made their homes on the Clear Fork of the Brazos. There Lieuten-ant Richard Pratt, who would later found an Indian school, shaped the demoralized Tonkawas into an effective trailing and fighting force.

In December 1869 Lipans wrote a pictorial letter to the Tonkawas asking to join them at Fort Griffin. "[T]he Lapans are anxious to come to this point to settle down with the Tonkawas and to be at peace with the military," wrote Captain J. W. Clous. "To accomplish all this, they claim the good office of Castile and his Tribe who are the friends of the whites and who by their friendship are in good circumstances while the Lapans are poor." When they arrived in 1874, they erected seven tipis in a pecan grove on Collins Creek, west of the fort.[26]

Lipan scouts joined the army's 1874 campaign against Kiowas and Comanches. After learning on September 20 that a large group had moved north into the Palo Duro Canyon area, Mackenzie sent Johnson to locate the camp. Two days later he returned, saying the enemy was at hand. When Mackenzie's men descended the canyon walls, scouts led the charge. Some of the Tonkawa women, taking revenge for the slaughter of their people by Comanches, fought alongside their husbands. After routing the Comanches, troops burned the camp. Mackenzie gave Johnson his choice of forty horses to reward his discovery and then let the other scouts make selections. Troops shot the remaining 1,450 horses to keep the enemy on foot.[27]

Johnson was the scout sergeant. His mother was Lipan and his father Mexican or Tonkawa; Apache way, that made him Lipan.[28] Three years earlier, Johnson had served with Mackenzie, tracking Kicking Bird and the Kiowas after they broke from the Fort Sill reservation. Most of the Lipan scouts were about five-foot-seven or eight inches. Two Lipans, known as Bill Turner and Jack, at five-foot-ten-inches, and Johnson, at five-foot-eleven-inches, could have stood shoulder to shoulder with the tallest Black Seminole scouts, who were also known for their height. The Lipan scouts accepted American names when they enlisted but still painted themselves red and yellow.[29] Johnson's responsibility among his own people was to train the boys as warriors. Carrying a whip, he made them jump in the river, even if they had to cut a hole in the ice.[30]

Johnson was friendly with the Creaton family in the town of Fort Griffin, and during frequent visits at their home got to know Ida Creaton. A story told in 1928 was that one Sunday, dressed in a store-bought suit, Johnson paid a call and offered John Creaton twenty ponies for his sister. Creaton refused. A few weeks later Johnson showed up at

Top: In the first picture, the Lipans are saying they recognize the strength of the army.

Bottom left: In the second picture, Lipans say they want to meet soldiers and the Tonkawas near Fort Griffin.

Bottom right: In the third picture, Lipans show they want to be friends with the soldiers and the Tonkawas.

Ida Creaton and Johnson, probably 1874. *Henry S. Shuster, photographer. DeGrolyer Library, Southern Methodist University, Dallas, Texas. Ag2008.0005*

the Creaton house drunk and lunged at John, who struck Johnson on the chin and carried the scout sergeant to the fort, where he spent some time cooling off in the guardhouse.[31] This yarn could be dismissed except for the formal portrait of Johnson and Ida. A photograph of an Indian man and white woman is unheard of in this period, and yet Johnson and Ida struck a standard pose for husband and wife. Ida may well have had a relationship with the tall, handsome Johnson, and her family may have objected.

Despite their good work, the Fort Griffin scouts were still subject to a general order halting rations to Indians. The Interior Department authorized the purchase of cows and goats for the 119 Tonkawas and twenty-six Lipans, "whose condition is so deplorable that something should be done for them," Buell wrote. He asked that the President consider their case and sent some scouts out to hunt buffalo under the protection of troops. By October the Lipans were starving. A husband and wife left for the plains to "join the Apaches." Over the next year, the army contemplated moving the twenty-three Lipans to the Mescalero Reservation, "where most of the Lipans are," but had no funding for expenses.[32]

CHAPTER

Prairie Apaches

Doubtless, the Indians that have left the Reservation are on the war path and driven to it by a class of outlaws whose highest aspiration is to pilfer and plunder.

— *F. C. Crothers, 1875*[1]

The People returned to the Staked Plains. Comanches were settled on a reservation, and Apaches could roam freely. White men thought the Llano Estacado was dreary and monotonous, but Apaches knew where water stood in gleaming playas. Buffalo herds were thin, but the short buffalo grass still supported antelope. A thousand Apaches who had never lived on a reservation were in their former home, and their camps drew restless young men from the reservations. Troops were rarely seen, but scouting parties were beginning to thread their way across grassland and desert to etch new trails in the dust.

The No Water Lipans had been divided into small groups since the 1860s, when smallpox ravaged the tribes. Lipans suspected they got the disease from a shirt taken from a dead enemy along with his ammunition belt. They knew if they stayed together, more people would die. Chief Magoosh, who wore the scars of that epidemic the rest of his life, held a council and agreed to split up but rejoin when the sickness passed. Venego's group settled in the mountains near Zaragosa, where they lived on good terms with the Mexicans. Chief Josefa and his people went to the Kickapoos near McAllen and then to Mexico. Magoosh took his people to live among the Naishans.[2]

An agent in 1869 recorded three hundred unidentified Apaches joining three hundred Kiowa Apaches on their two-year-old reservation at Fort Sill.[3] In 1874 agents counted 602 Apaches: the resident Naishans and about 180 "Essaquetas" (Lipans), who were cultivating fields with their hosts. That year Lipans had just returned from Mexico when nearby Comanches and Kiowas fought with troops and tried to burn the Wichita Agency and the camps of peaceful Indians. The Lipans headed for the Pecos, but some stayed behind, including Magoosh's sister, whose husband was Naishan. For years, Magoosh roamed from the plains near present Roswell, New Mexico, to the Guadalupe Mountains, to Mexico, to the Kiowa Agency, and to his good friends, the Mescaleros.[4]

◄►

Through a window, Magoosh watched the Big Hat (the Lipans' term for Texans) read a "talking paper." The dog at Major Seth Mabre's place set up a commotion, as Magoosh's men rounded up horses that August evening in 1875. Magoosh took flight but fell into the well, fracturing his skull. He spent the rest of the night climbing out. From then on he wore a dent on the top of his bald head. Captain Dan Roberts and eight rangers picked up their trail where it crossed the Fort McKavett and Concho road. Rangers figured the Lipans would rest in the Lipan Mountains on the head of the South Concho, so they rounded the mountains and went on to Lipan Springs. Skirting the head brakes of the Concho, they reached the Staked Plains. Roberts wouldn't let his men smoke that night for fear the light would betray their presence.

The next day, the Lipans left their camp at a playa unknown to most white men (Big Lake, in the canyon country of Castle Gap). One warrior bragged that white men would never come there, and if they did, he could whip ten of them. As the sun rose high, Roberts ordered his men to form a line directly behind him so that only one man was visible from a distance. "They did and tracked as plumb as a new wagon," he wrote. When the rangers were nearly in shooting range, the Lipans saw them. Two warriors, moving slowly behind the main group, warned the

Magoosh, 1913. *Wanamaker Collection, Mathers Museum of World Cultures, University of Indiana*

others. "When Indians are driving a herd of stolen horses, they leave drag ropes to the best horses as an 'emergency clause.' In this case, they barely had time to jump down, grab ropes and change horses, which some of them did," Roberts wrote. They formed a line. The rangers got close enough to fire, stopped and dismounted. "They stood one good round and began to smell blood and left there like a covey of quail."

One warrior riding ahead was still unaware of danger. When they reached him, "he rallied them and they made another stand and fought like demons for a few minutes. We were wounding some of their horses, as well as warriors, and to lose a horse right then was 'goodbye John' to the rider." The rangers shot one warrior's horse from under him, the same bullet passing through the man's ankle. He jumped up behind a white warrior, who rode a big stallion. "Magoosh broke to the left with six men, and I put in after him with three men." The others broke into parties, and the rangers went after them. "We pursued Magoosh and his party at full speed for three or four miles, when we saw one of their horses weakening and gradually falling back and we had fired several times at the rider."

That man abruptly turned around and rode toward the rangers, yelling in broken Spanish that he was a friend. He was a Mexican captive. A second captive with the group was Rudolph Fischer, taken in 1865 near Fredericksburg when he was thirteen. Both had lived with their tribes so long they were Indian in everything but blood. After a few more miles the rangers' horses were tiring. They found a horse tied to a mesquite bush, left behind when one warrior joined a wounded comrade riding a big mule, probably to hold him on as they made their escape. The fleeing Lipans figured correctly that the tethered horse would buy them some time as the rangers stopped to examine it. The rangers never caught them.

Two men followed Fischer and the Lipan riding behind him for several miles. One ranger killed their horse, which pinned Fischer beneath. After a pursuit they killed the Lipan. Fischer worked himself from under the horse and escaped into the tall grass. Two years later, Fischer was discovered at Fort Sill and taken to his family, but he returned and spent his life with the Comanches. He later visited Lipans at the Mescalero Reservation. Magoosh said this was his last raid.[5] Was it? "Probably," said his great granddaughter, Meredith Magoosh Begay. "He had been living here [Mescalero] and asked the Mescalero Tribe if he could join them and the Mescaleros accepted him."[6]

◀▶

The treeless table-land of the Staked Plains was "a country almost entirely unknown except to Indians," Lieutenant Colonel William R. Shafter observed, and he wanted to explore it. Enabled by grass from recent rains, troops traveled thousands of miles in the latter half of 1875, keeping Apaches on the move and destroying their camps. Of greater military importance were the trails and water holes they discovered and mapped. In August Shafter's Tenth Cavalry troops, plus Seminole and Tonkawa scouts, trailed a large party across the southern plains. In the sand hills they found fresh signs of a small hunting party and a trail, five or six days old, leading north to some water holes where about three hundred people and hundreds of horses and mules had stayed. They were apparently in no hurry to leave and didn't try to hide their trail, "which could have been followed at a gallop by moonlight," Shafter wrote.

Soldiers found the body of a woman with her days-old, dead infant lying on her breast. The deaths most likely precipitated their departure. They followed the trail for three days to Dog Springs in New Mexico. At 1 a.m. a party of twenty or thirty warriors crossing back on the trail ran into soldiers, and they exchanged fire. The next morning, Shafter took the trail with forty-five of the best-mounted men. After twenty miles, he found a camp at a spring with enough water for thousands of horses. Soldiers spent the next day burning lodges. "From this point [Howard's Well] west to the Rio Grande the country is least known of any in this Department and is the most difficult to scout in," Shafter wrote. Deep, rocky ravines were impassable for wagons. Cactus, especially the aptly named Spanish dagger, made travel painful for horses. "There is undoubtedly plenty of water and this country has always been a favorite resort for the Apaches and Lipans."

A favorite Apache destination was what Shafter called the White Sand Hills (present Monahans Sandhills), twenty miles from the Pecos. Shaped by the wind into mounds, bowls and slopes as ribbed as a washboard, the sands were forbidding to man and horse. They were five miles wide and twenty-five miles long,[7] from northwest to southeast. From a distance, the dune fields could have been snow-covered hills. Shafter found quantities of water by digging a few feet in small depressions at the base of the dunes. Large willows and cottonwoods also signaled water below. This was probably the beloved home of Picax-andé. "The various scouts have shown how easily the plains can be traversed, in almost any direction, and to all the large watering places there are plain wagon roads that will show for years," Shafter wrote.

By December 25, 335 emaciated people had dragged themselves into the Mescalero Reservation, followed in January 1876 by another fifty-three. Shafter reported that the Indians had been "driven from the plains to Mexico, where they now are." He was satisfied there wasn't "an Indian east of the Pecos and south of Red River."[8]

◄►

After breaking from the Mescalero reservation in 1873, Chief Plata and his Llaneros joined Comanches living near the headwaters of the Brazos and Colorado rivers. By 1876, they were starving. Plata sent word that his five hundred people wanted to return to the agency, but they were afraid to come in without protection. Colonel Edward Hatch asked for authority to provide rations and send troops to accompany them, but General Philip Sheridan refused. If Plata and his people came in, Sheridan said, they should be dismounted; if they didn't come in, they should be attacked. The Eastern press picked up the story: "A BLOODTHIRSTY ORDER: General Sheridan Directs the Murder of a Peaceful Indian Tribe." Sheridan's December 6 dispatch to Fort Sill reached the president himself. "The tribe were in want, had been guilty of no depredation and were desirous of getting at the same time Government protection and support in return for their submission," the story said. Sheridan's response, the newspaper reported: "Issue no rations. Attack the tribe." President Grant condemned the order.

At Mescalero, Agent F. C. Godfroy believed Plata was key to "bringing back to the reservation all of the 'Prairie Apaches' of which there are a great number." Any attempt to take their horses would spur them to leave again, he said. Sheridan's orders might cause a "general stampede, thus destroying in one instant the work of many months."[9] Plata and his people stayed where they were, but in 1877 Natzili and Pinole returned from the plains with their people,[10] a concession to the growing scarcity of buffalo. When Sheridan made his famous statement in 1870 that buffalo hunters had done more to settle the "vexed Indian question than the entire regular army," buffalo hunting was a trade. Nearly three million would be killed between 1872 and 1874. Small, scattered herds foraged on the Southern Plains, but those too disappeared.[11] In that period, said Percy Big Mouth, his father and uncles went to the Pecos to hunt buffalo and met Tonkawa army scouts who warned them away. "Soldiers kill all the game and they kill you if you go. They think you are raiding and they sure get you. A Lipan scout, Dahnosti, was with the Tonkawas, so they never went there any more."[12]

◄►

Chief Natzili, whose name means "buffalo," led a large band that claimed territory from present Lubbock, Rabbit's Peak, Amarillo, the Texas Panhandle and the Pecos Valley to Tucumcari, New Mexico (traditional Llanero country), said Solon Sombrero, his grandson. "[They] were originally plains Apaches." Oral history tells that his older brother would have become a war leader, like their father, but a bear killed him during a hunt. After he and other men killed two bears, the people held a big council and decided young Natzili should be second chief. They placed a war bonnet on his head. He was a great leader after that.[13] Like Plata, Natzili was a member of the band called Gulgahende by Mescaleros, Cuelcahende by Lipans, and Llaneros by the Spanish. (Mescaleros always named this group when asked to list their bands, and Lipans did the same. The Llaneros were so closely tied to both groups, they were seen as relatives.) At the reservation, Natzili's people had the same rights as Mescaleros, said Solon Sombrero. Godfroy settled Natzili and his people at Twin Springs in the Sacramento Mountains because of a smallpox epidemic at the agency. There, without help from the agency farmer, they planted, cultivated and irrigated a garden.[14]

◄►

The Guadalupe Mountains jut from the desert floor in a V-shape pointing southward from New Mexico into West Texas, with the

Natzili. *Frank Randall photographer. Denver Public Library, Western History Collection, X-32927*

Guadalupe Mountains *(Sherry Robinson photo)*

point at El Capitan, which Apaches called Rock Nose. Its wings stretch into New Mexico; the forty-mile-long eastern escarpment grades into the Sacramento Mountains. From without, its limestone face seemed as impregnable as a walled castle; from within, its vertical canyons, pocked with caves, plunge thousands of feet to water sources.[15]

In March 1876 troops chased a large party of Apaches driving about three hundred head of stock toward the Guadalupes. Just as soldiers reached the mountains, Indians on a high lookout sent up a smoke signal to alert those in front. Army scouts picked their way through narrow, rocky canyons and over high mountains only to see the trail divide and the Apaches scatter. Scouts followed a few tracks over broken country until tracks disappeared in the stony soil.[16] That summer seventy rangers scoured the Pecos looking for Lipans and Kickapoos. At the mouth of Independence Creek they found abandoned camps with frames used to dry meat and evidence the Apaches had dressed a large number of deer hides and manufactured bows and arrows. At another abandoned camp in the waterless sixty miles between the Pecos and the headwaters of the South Concho, the Apaches had dressed so many antelope hides that the hair was a foot deep and thirty or forty skulls lay scattered.[17]

In the late 1870s many Apaches were still living in the Guadalupes. Citizen James Marr reported "a perfect reign of terror" for hundreds of miles. In the previous two years, fifty people had died and nearly a thousand head of stock were stolen within a hundred miles of Fort Davis. "It is well known that the Guadalupe Mountains, though 100 miles from their reservation, is the home of many of them, and that they only leave them on the one side to go and draw their government rations, and on the other to plunder and steal."[18]

General E. O. C. Ord charged that "nearly all the raiding is done by the Stanton Indians or those living in the Guadalupe Mountains." Godfroy retorted that the Apaches living in the Guadalupes were the general's responsibility.[19] Natzili and the other chiefs denied being away from the reservation long enough to raid in Texas. They told the Fort Stanton commander about forty or fifty "cutoffs" who had never been on the reservation. "They no doubt will take shelter in the Guadalupe Mountains if an attempt is made to follow them up, and it would be a difficult matter to catch them," Godfroy said. He hoped to lure these groups to the reservation with promises of rations.[20]

The People had always moved from place to place, but now soldiers and rangers were always behind them as they migrated among the Mescalero reservation, the mountains of Mexico, the Pecos, and the Guadalupes. Sometimes they were making raids; sometimes they were just trying to reach safety, stealing a few horses here and there for their own use and butchering a cow for food. They formed smaller groups, maybe just two or three. They cut telegraph lines and took the wire with them. They doubled back over their own tracks to confuse their pursuers, passed through the roughest escarpments, and watched as troops lost their trail in the rocks. They stole undetected around army camps. If they could remain in a place long enough, they made jerky, tanned skins and baked mescal.[21]

Ord exhorted his officers to spare "neither men nor animals" to punish or destroy them, but near constant patrols found little to report, and more often than not, they chased rumors and spurious reports

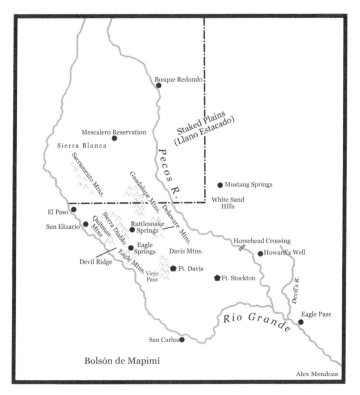

Map 9 Apache Haunts in West Texas

by freighters wanting protection or farmers hoping to sell supplies to the army. From September 1878 to September 1879, 128 patrols from thirteen Texas posts scouted 40,100 miles and fought just two engagements.[22] They did, however, become better acquainted with Apache geography, and their reports provide the first clear picture of Apache routes, water holes and landmarks.

In a typical patrol early in 1879, Lt. John Bullis, with fifteen soldiers, twelve packers, thirty-nine Black Seminole scouts, and three Lipan scouts, trailed a group traveling with women and children. They traced a wide loop from Independence Creek northeast to Castle Gap and on to the White Sand Hills, Horsehead Crossing on the Pecos, Antelope Wells in present Presidio County, and the Guadalupes. There they filled a spring with brush and stones, which delayed thirsty troops who invested hours cleaning it out. Their journey's end was the Mescalero reservation.[23]

Rangers led by Captain G. W. Arrington followed raiders coming from the west to strike cattle ranches along the headwaters of the Brazos, the Colorado and Concho. They picked up a trail on December 29, 1879, past the mouth of Yellow House Canyon, a broad gap in the caprock near present Lubbock, and followed it over rim rock, bending west toward spring-fed Tahoka Lake in present Lynn County, a favorite destination of raiders. A ranch cow, cut open with its paunch removed and emptied of contents, signaled a long desert ride. From Tahoka, they rode seven miles northwest to Double Lakes, the last known water before entering the Staked Plains.

Farther west, they plunged into white sand hills, which ranger J. B. Gibson called "the most complete picture of perfect desolation I had ever beheld." Taunted by mirages, they finally reached a real lake where they found ashes of four or five campfires and horses' bones. At other lakes along the trail were indications of a sizable camp. They were about 135 miles from their last known point and well inside New Mexico. Knowing they couldn't afford to mount an attack, the rangers retraced their steps to one of the lakes and waited for Indians to appear. While they waited, a few men went out to hunt antelope and found, instead, Apaches, who, guns lying across their saddles, formed a line of battle. Each side studied the other through field glasses.

"We had often heard of the desperate fighting qualities of the Apache Indians and we fully expected them, on account of their superior number, to attack us, and we prepared to give them one warm reception, and thus we stood and glared at each other for at least half an hour, but instead of them charging us as we expected they turned about and deliberately rode away."[24] The Apaches were undoubtedly having the same conversation and decided it was not a good day to die.

CHAPTER

Between Two Forces

The Lipans are very bold and desperate, and these people [the Mexicans] are afraid of them.

— *General E. O. C. Ord, 1878*

Historians like a tidy date to mark a rise or fall, and it would be easy to say the Lipan decline began July 1870, when the first Black Seminole scouts began arriving at American forts. Or we could say Mackenzie's Raid on May 18, 1873, was the beginning. We could name any single major conflict and conclude, as American or Mexican officers often did, that the Lipans would rise no more. Despite loss of life, horses and provisions, the Lipans were not only unwilling to give up, they continued stubbornly independent. They would re-establish themselves in new strongholds, rekindle old friendships, and reappear in different locations. If they couldn't trade for guns, their traditional weapons would do. They could draw on the superior numbers of the Llaneros and other Apaches of the plains, who were largely unknown until they came in to the Mescalero reservation.

Apaches had holed up in hidden corners of northern Mexico, described on maps at the time as *desconocido*, or unexplored. It was a vast expanse of desert, mountains and plains with water holes fifty miles apart—so unsettled and untraveled that nobody could say how many Apaches were living there. They might roam in the *desconocido* for fifty years without being discovered, said Ord. From these retreats the

Apaches could make their way to the canyons of Devils River, bide their time until the moon was full and then creep into Texas settlements.[1]

In 1876 Porfirio Díaz forced out President Sebastian Lerdo de Tejada. This single development would set off a cascade of grim consequences for the Lipans and their allies. Initially, Díaz made a treaty with the Indians remaining in Mexico, promising subsistence if they would live on permanent reservations and cease crossing the Rio Grande.[2] As Americans increased military and diplomatic pressure, the Apaches' role on the larger stage of border politics slipped from ally and trading partner to intruder.

On July 29, 1876, Shafter set out with twenty Black Seminole scouts and twenty Buffalo Soldiers and rode fifty-five miles in twelve hours. At 3 a.m. they located a camp of twenty-three lodges along the San Antonio River, about five miles from Zaragosa, and attacked at dawn. After the first volley, soldiers used the butts of their guns as clubs against the Lipans' lances. Fourteen Lipans died and four women were captured, along with a hundred horses and mules.[3] Scout Charlie Daniels called it a big fight. "Those Injuns was just the Lipans; they was mean fighters, yes sir, they was. [T]hey was two hundred and sixty warriors right there. [With just 23 lodges, the Lipans probably had no more than thirty men.] Well, we got 'em anyhow. We whipped 'em out, but the killin' were large, the killin' were large."[4]

Washington and Mexico City locked horns over American troop movements. Ord's superiors wanted permission to enter Mexico "in hot pursuit," but Díaz was adamantly opposed. John W. Foster, U.S. minister to Mexico, demanded that Mexico deliver the wild tribes living in Mexico—Lipans, Kickapoos, Mescaleros, Seminoles, Apaches and others—so they could be interned on reservations, and he made it clear that the president would withhold recognition until border raids and depredations ceased.[5]

Ord wholeheartedly supported Shafter and Lieutenant Bullis, but he also questioned how realistic it was to expect frontier Mexicans, who had suffered two centuries of Apache raids, "to make vigorous war upon their own neighbors, the Lipans and Mescaleros, for our protection" as long as Coahuileños were safe and the Apache plunder enriched their traders. The Mescalero reservation was part of the problem, he said. Mescaleros "and other Apache Indians formerly occupying the country between the Sierra Carmen in Mexico and the reservation" could leave the reservation to raid the country around forts Davis and Stockton and cooperate with tribes living south of the Rio Grande. The solution, he said, was to break up the reservation and move the Apaches west.[6]

Secretary of War George W. McCrary told Ord to use his discretion when pursuing raiders. "Discretion" must have been liberally interpreted. Bullis kept up his hunts for hostile Indians on Mexican soil, sustained by reports of mixed groups of Lipans, Mescaleros, Gileños and Comanches in the Sierra Pachona, Remolino, and the Burro Mountains in Coahuila, and in the villages of Metaje and San Carlos in Chihuahua. At times they had mules to trade for carbines. When pressed, they disappeared into the desconocido.[7]

◀▶

The hot-cold relationship of Lipans and Kickapoos cooled again in 1877, and they fought at least four times that summer; sometimes citizens of Santa Rosa helped the Kickapoos. At the end of July Kickapoos drove off the Lipans' horses, attacked a camp, and killed seventeen men, returning to Santa Rosa with scalps and one hundred twenty-five horses. The Lipans were then four leagues west of Zaragosa at Barrancas Coloradas and said to be "in a miserable situation, very poor," said Shafter. "If as many are killed as reported, it nearly wipes out the Lipans."[8]

Because it was riskier to raid in Texas, Lipans swept Mexican ranches, antagonizing their Mexican sponsors. Díaz sent the capable General Gerónimo Trevino to the northern frontier in search of Lipans. Ord told Trevino that it was necessary to pursue Lipans and other hostiles into the mountains of Coahuila and Chihuahua but assured him that he would also disband any armed revolutionaries organizing on

American soil to invade Mexico. Trevino asked that only regular forces be allowed to cross—in other words, no rangers.[9]

With ninety-one cavalry troops and scouts, Bullis crossed the Rio Grande on September 26, 1877, and four days later reached a Lipan village of twenty-seven tipis on Perdido Creek, about five miles west of Zaragosa. The Lipans were already racing toward Zaragosa. After a hard chase, troops captured three women, a boy and girl (the children of Ramón Castro) along with fifteen horses and two mules, most bearing brands from the Brackettville area. Soldiers destroying the camp found government-issue blankets.[10]

A month later Bullis and thirty-four Black Seminole scouts, guided by José Tafoya and Teresita, the daughter of Chief Costilietos, set out on a routine expedition up the Rio Grande. Learning of raiders returning to Mexico through the Sierra del Carmen, they crossed the Rio Grande on October 28 and followed the trail for four days to a camp on the Texas side. They could see Apaches driving a large herd of horses. Warriors took up positions among the rocks on the American side and opened fire; a nearly inaccessible network of bluffs sheltered their village of forty tipis. Eying this impregnable mass, Bullis withdrew.

He returned with 162 troops. In the Big Bend, they could see evidence of moving stock and different bands coming and going. The Apaches were moving camp and driving stock into the mountains on a trail up the opposite wall. They occupied a horseshoe-shaped ravine. A company deployed on one crest, Bullis's Black Seminole scouts deployed to cover the canyon's exit, and a second company was scrambling into position on the other side, concealed by a rocky crest, when Apaches leading their horses appeared suddenly about two hundred yards away and opened fire with Winchesters. Troops fired back as the Apaches dashed into the rocks. Shots thundered for several minutes, after which a charge by troops forced the warriors from their shelters; Lieutenant Andrew Geddes and his Twenty-fifth Infantry troops ran after them.

The Apaches fled up a narrow canyon to their ranchería at the top of a cliff. Troops continued firing but couldn't force the Apaches from their position without great loss of life, so they withdrew. The Apaches melted into the canyon but had to abandon seventeen horses, five mules and one burro. Troops found deer skins, buffalo robes, jerky, and equipment, some with markings from the Mescalero reservation. They burned anything they couldn't use.[11]

Washington was growing uneasy with the cross-border pursuits. General Grant questioned the military's motives, and Sherman wondered if Shafter was about to seize Coahuila. On December 5, 1877, the Committee on Military Affairs in Washington, which convened to examine border problems, asked Bullis if it was possible to annihilate these border Apaches.

"No, sir; they are too cunning," Bullis testified. "They can hide their families in the rocks and fastnesses of the mountains, and it is almost impossible to get at them. They have no regular villages whatever. They are broken up into small bands and the country is so very rough and broken that it is very difficult indeed to strike them." Asked the number of raiding Indians across the border, Bullis estimated no more than 225 men. The chairman observed that the army had more than four thousand troops on the frontier. Wasn't that a sufficient number? Bullis thought it was.[12]

◄►

Horizons were shrinking for the Lipans. Their bases in Mexico were eroding. The American army sent men, weaponry and provisions over Apache trails and drank from their water holes. Reservations provided little respite. As war claimed more of their people, Lipans and Mescaleros combined their dwindling forces with any likely ally for raids as desperate as they were brutal.

On April 14, 1878, when grass and water were abundant and new foliage would screen their passage, a group of forty-three Kickapoos, Lipans, Seminoles, Mexicans, and one white man forded the Rio

Grande from Coahuila at the foot of Big Apache Hill, in Webb County north of Laredo. They killed two vaqueros and took the main road toward Laredo. About dusk, they shot and lanced rancher Jorge Garcia and took his *chivarras* (goat-skin leggings), horse and saddle, along with a herd of saddle horses. His wife and friends heard him cry out, "No mi maten!" (Don't kill me.)

About fourteen miles from Laredo, they veered sharply northeast toward the Nueces, where they stole enough additional horses to mount the party and then divided up. Raiders appeared simultaneously at nearly every ranch in the area, chose the best horses, and raked a wide area for guns, money, clothing, camping equipment and blankets, before reuniting in Webb County. Now well armed with both Spencer and Remington rifles and bows and arrows, they wounded Tomás Solís with two pistol balls and an arrow. Driving a large herd of horses, they followed the Nueces east and converged at a place they had often used before. They killed John Steele, who didn't believe in carrying weapons, along with his two stepsons, Richard and George Taylor, plus Martín Martínez and Florentine Leo. Venturo Rodríguez, wounded with a rifle ball and eight arrows, survived. Mrs. Steele saved her other three children by placing them on a tree branch, wading into deep water, and pushing the branch ahead of her until she reached the other side, where she hid in tall grass for hours.

Twelve miles from the Nueces, one party killed Vicente Robledo, a shepherd, and left Tomás Zúñiga for dead. Another party encountered two Hispanic shepherds, took their clothing and forced them to run footraces for their amusement. The raiders said they would only kill "Americanos." In Duval County they killed Guadalupe Bazán and gathered up all the horses in the area. They killed a shepherd and his wife, tied their bodies on a horse and turned it loose. They killed two boys, John Jordan and Antonio Valdez, and mortally wounded Margarito Rodríguez in Encinal County. After killing José María Canales, a shepherd, they threw his body on the live coals of his campfire, which consumed half his body.

On the eighteenth Frank Gravis took up the trail and pursued the attackers for a hundred miles to their rendezvous point in Webb County. Gravis fired, sparking a brief gun battle before flying lead forced him into the trees. He watched them depart with about two hundred of the region's best horses, along with a quantity of clothing, saddles, blankets and other equipment. On at least two occasions they went out of their way to take socks. They floated their plunder across the river on rafts of dry wood and still left provisions, clothing and moccasins on the river bank. All the way home, Gravis heard about losses. In six days, this mixed group had traveled about 360 miles, killed at least eighteen people and stole horses—all within sixty miles of a fort. They moved in three divisions: An advance force killed and cleared the way, the next took the horses, and a well-armed third party guarded the rear.[13]

Mackenzie wanted to destroy the Lipans who lived near Santa Rosa and traded in Zaragosa, where the leading men supplied ammunition, blankets and sometimes money for their raids into Texas. Failing to interest Mexican General Anacleto R. Falcón in a joint campaign, he sent an expedition to destroy the Lipan village at El Mancherío, near Santa Rosa. Cavalry troops and scouts also searched the country between the Rio Grande and the Serranías del Burro and along the San Diego and San Rodrigo. They found no Lipans but met Mexican troops ordered to expel the Americans. Instead of turning around, they advanced; the Mexican soldiers retreated, and the Americans recrossed.[14]

Lipans and Kickapoos were a daily presence that summer in Santa Rosa (present Músquiz), a picturesque, tree-shaded town at the base of the Santa Rosa Mountains. Its deep canyons sheltered Lipan camps with thirty-four warriors, according to an American who lived there. Several miles away were the Kickapoo farms. Both groups sold American horses, brands intact, to prominent merchants in Santa Rosa for five or ten dollars or a few bottles of mescal.

Texans believed Mexican authorities condoned the April raid or even planned it. "They have pretended to not countenance raids, but now their mask is stripped," said the *Weekly State Gazette*, which accused Diaz of feigning cooperation in order to secure recognition. Confrontations with Mexican troops only meant they were shielding the robbers, said the newspaper. The accusations contained a seed of truth. Mexico had sent troops north from the interior because "local troops were bitterly hostile to Americans."[15] Santa Rosa officials, led by Jesús Galán, responded by rounding up the Americans and asking them, in the presence of armed Kickapoos, to sign a statement saying the article was a lie. A hundred yards away were Lipans sheltered by Galán, who reportedly profited from the raid. The Americans refused to sign.[16]

Kickapoo leaders maintained that only a few of their men joined the Lipans and said they were unjustly blamed for the Lipans' forays into Texas. A chief told the alcalde, if you don't attack the Lipans within twenty-four hours, we will leave. President Díaz himself ordered you to do this. The alcalde reluctantly agreed. Together, Mexicans and Kickapoos coordinated an attack. Kickapoos watched the road to the Lipan camp and intercepted a half dozen runners sent to warn the Lipans. The Mexicans killed five or six Lipans and captured eight or nine.[17]

Washington demanded action after the April raid, but the two nations were still debating whose Indians were responsible. Reservation Indians from the United States were depredating in Mexico, claimed Mexico's Minister of Foreign Affairs; Indians living in Coahuila and Chihuahua were depredating in Texas and New Mexico, claimed the United States Legation in Mexico.[18] Ord was confident that Trevino, his son-in-law, would be successful, which would relieve Americans of the responsibility "of hunting savages who do not belong to us, but to Mexico." Trevino in October marched into Piedras Negras with 1,200 soldiers. With Mexico's latest insurrection snuffed out, Trevino could focus on "the destruction of the Lipan and Mescalero Indians, who, by their frequent raids, are giving pretexts to the neighboring nation" to invade Mexico, said a newspaper in Nuevo León. "These Indians are the common enemies of both nations, and ought to be followed up until exterminated."[19]

◄ ►

San Carlos had long been a thorn in the side of both Americans and Mexicans. The village took root a century earlier near the San Carlos presidio south of the Rio Grande, in convenient proximity to Big Bend and the Bolsón de Mapimí, and soon cultivated such good relations with hostile Comanches that it was practically an arms depot.[20] Natividad Luján, a San Carlos native, said tribes made treaties with the village and "promised to be good to our people of the town and not to rob or kill any of them, no matter what they might do to other peoples; and we would on our part let them live among us." In the 1870s it sheltered at least four bands of Lipans and Mescaleros. With each strike by American or Mexican troops, more Lipans streamed in.[21]

When the army created the District of the Pecos in early 1878, Colonel Benjamin H. Grierson, the commanding officer, wanted a new post near San Carlos. His scouting parties in the Eagle, Chisos, and Guadalupe Mountains and along San Francisco Creek that summer sent small parties of Apaches toward the Mescalero reservation, but Apaches held out at San Carlos, moving frequently and keeping an eye on the soldiers. "Many of these Indians are miserably poor in appearance but some are well armed and correspondingly independent and surly," Grierson wrote.[22]

In October 1878 Trevino launched his campaign against Lipans, Mescaleros and Kickapoos with 5,000 troops from Coahuila, finally accommodating the Americans' goal of trapping the Lipans between their two forces. Mexican troops marched to the headwaters of the San Diego to drive Apaches from strongholds in the Sierra del Carmen between Santa Rosa and San Carlos.[23] Black Seminoles from Coahuila joined them to surround San Carlos, seizing the mayor and posting sentries to prevent locals from warning the Indians. John Horse knew they couldn't surprise the Indian camp, so he forced the

Johnson. Henry S. Shuster, photographer. *DeGrolyer Library, Southern Methodist University, Dallas, Texas. Ag2008.0005*

mayor, by threatening his family, to ride in with plenty of liquor. When the camp was vulnerable, the mayor released a nursing horse, which returned to its foal—a signal to the waiting combatants. They attacked, slaughtered all the men and took the women and children captive.[24]

◄►

Fort Griffin's troops hadn't seen a conflict since 1876; by 1879 it was running out of work for its scouts and again reduced their rations. Lipans and Tonkawas were "in a destitute, starving condition," wrote Captain J. B. Irvine, post commander and acting Indian agent. A local farmer, "Uncle Joe" Mathews, allowed the Tonkawas and Lipans to plant and even took them hunting. They earned a little money picking pecans and selling them to the local mercantile.[25]

Irvine suggested buying or leasing a permanent location along the river bottom opposite where they were then camped. "There are incorporated with the Tonkawas seventeen Lipan Indians," Irvine wrote. "These are particularly industrious and provident and have repeatedly asked for land to cultivate and own as a permanent home. The Tonkawas have made similar requests . . ." The government wanted to move both groups to Indian Territory, but the head men were opposed. They were born in Texas, they said, and had lived there in peace.[26]

The Lipan scouts in 1880 would be needed. Johnson, the Lipan scout sergeant at Fort Griffin, earned his commanding officer's praise for his work as acting guide at Fort McIntosh. That summer John Guerrero, Dahnosti, and Manti were at Fort Concho with a surveying expedition. In the fall all the remaining Lipan scouts transferred to Fort Clark. Juan Guerrero, known as Apache John, was Mexican. He and his sister Teresita (Apache name, Shonhata) were captured as children and grew up with the Lipans; Costilietos was their Lipan father. Guerrero heard his sister was living with the Black Seminole scouts at Fort Clark and wanted to bring her to Fort Griffin.[27] He would have learned at Fort Clark that his sister married a Seminole scout.

CHAPTER

Victorio!

[T]here were fully 150 bucks against us, being recruited from renegade
Navajos, Mescaleros, Comanches and Lapans.

— *Lieutenant Charles Gatewood, 1879*[1]

Apaches still weren't safe at Mescalero. "[T]he organized band of
desperados who infest this vicinity" continued their attacks, and
soldiers couldn't apprehend them, agent Godfroy wrote. The reservation, "situated in the most lawless county of the Territory" was "per-
fectly defenseless." Magoosh's grandson Richard said some white men
"would come to the reservation and help themselves . . . to the
horses. They would wait 'til the Indians had tamed the wild horses and
then steal them."[2]

Despite signs of an approaching hard winter, the government withheld blankets and clothing. On September 30, 1877, Natzili, and fifty
or sixty armed warriors rode in and demanded more beef and passes
for hunting on the Staked Plains and in the Burro and Eagle Mountains. They needed buffalo robes to keep warm. If the agent could provide blankets and clothing, they would stay, Natzili said. If not, they
had no choice but to provide for themselves. Godfroy stalled. While
he waited for instructions from Washington, seven people froze to
death, and twenty-seven young men left to hunt on the Staked Plains.
To keep more Apaches from leaving, he bought blankets and muslin
without permission.[3]

Throughout 1878 Apaches were often off the reservation. Authorities wrote it down to intransigence, but the challenges of their daily life were staggering. The Lincoln County War erupted in gunplay and bloodshed that spilled over to the agency. Delivery of supplies grew erratic because freighters were afraid to enter the county, and food from local sources was foul. Many reservation Apaches were afraid to leave the mountains because of armed white men roaming the area. Only 373 camped near the agency; in the Guadalupe Mountains were the groups of Natzili, Blanco (a Lipan), Patos Chiquito (Natzili's brother) and three Mescalero chiefs. Captain George Purington estimated the number of absent Apaches at 1,259, about half of them Mescaleros.[4]

Alexander McSween, a pivotal player in the Lincoln County War, informed the Interior Secretary in June 1878 that for the previous two years, Godfroy had purchased sick cattle and flour made of half rotten wheat from Lawrence Murphy's successors, James Dolan and John Riley. They inflated the number of people they claimed to feed and often received wagonloads of "surplus" Indian supplies. "The Indians are continually depredating on citizens," McSween said, "owing to the fact that the agent fails to give them what the Government has allotted them."[5]

On August 2, the president suspended Godfroy after an investigation found that he had appropriated goods for exaggerated numbers of Indians and sold "vast quantities of government property" for his own gain. Three days later Godfroy's clerk was murdered by partisans of the Lincoln County War, and more Apaches fled to the mountains.[6]

◄ ►

Chief Victorio took the war path on August 21, 1879. He and his Warm Springs (Gileño) Apaches had earlier slipped from their reservation in Arizona and reappeared at Mescalero, where they had many friends and relatives. Agent Samuel A. Russell allowed them to stay, but the chance appearance of law enforcement officers caused the edgy chief to flee. For the next year, he led two armies on a bloody chase through southern New Mexico, West Texas and northern Chihuahua. Apaches from the Mescalero reservation, Mexico and the Davis Mountains joined.[7] Lipans rode with Victorio. They also scouted against him for both the Americans and the Mexicans, an indication of how fragmented the tribe had become.

Victorio was still at the Mescalero reservation in late May 1879, when Lipans began trickling in. Ten weeks later, when the Lipans' presence became pronounced, Russell ordered them arrested. On July 24, an issue day, soldiers surrounded three men, a boy, four women, and two infants and removed them to Fort Stanton; another twenty Lipans were camped nearby. Agitated Mescaleros ran for the hills, but Victorio remained. Russell was sure the arrests would "have a good effect upon my Indians," and expected any excitement to be temporary. "I have improved the opportunity to lecture them on the importance of staying on the reservation and to warn them that by leaving it they may be liable to like treatment." The Commissioner of Indian Affairs scolded Russell for not arresting all the Lipans.

The army didn't know what to do with these prisoners. One man insisted that he was a Mescalero and that the other man, a Lipan, was his relative who was visiting. Officers were still asking in September, when they moved the Lipans from a tent to a room "to prevent further suffering and sickness." Some of the prisoners were related to the Mescalero Chief San Juan. They had lived in the Sierra del Fumo (Smoke Mountains) since the cowboys' attacks on the reservation in 1875 and came back because San Juan sent for them, with Godfroy's blessing. It took an unprecedented protest by the Mescalero chiefs, who sought help from attorney Alfred Fountain, to sway the officious Russell.

"The Mescaleros are very sad and very angry because these Indians have been imprisoned . . . They talk bad and some of them have gone away," said the medicine man Gregorio. "I feel sad for these poor people. All the Indians feel bad. They shed tears because these poor people are kept in the calaboose. Let them go back with us to their homes and their friends."[8]

The question of the Lipans' disposition rose through the chain of command to the Commissioner of Indian Affairs, the Secretary of State and the Secretary of War. Their solution: Turn them over to Mexican authorities as they would any captured "Mexican Indians." Before receiving that order, however, officers freed the Lipans.[9] The confusion was understandable. White officials were often unsure if Lipans were Mexican or American, and none could have known that the Upper (No Water) Lipans and Mescaleros had lived together so long that even to Apaches, the Tú é dine ndé were a blended group.[10]

Following the arrest, all the Lipans evaporated from the agency, as did thirty Comanches. It's not hard to imagine that they found a warm welcome with Victorio a month later. His recruiters frequented reservation camps, and the Lipans and Warm Springs people had previously spent time together. In the following months, two Mescalero chiefs and dozens of warriors joined Victorio as he swept back and forth across the border. Russell made Natzili principal chief. "I am fully satisfied that Natzili is the man for the plan," he wrote.[11]

General Edward Hatch suspected reservation Apaches of supplying Victorio with horses and weapons and wanted to disarm and dismount them. Over Russell's objections, he ordered them to move closer to the agency with their stock. On April 14, 1880, more than seven hundred soldiers abruptly assembled, including Grierson and his Tenth Cavalry troops from Texas and more than a hundred Chiricahua Apache scouts from Arizona. More Apaches moved deeper into the mountains. Two days later, Chiricahua scouts killed Natzili's father and a second man rounding up stock on Russell's orders. More people fled. That afternoon, Russell told the remaining Apaches they would have to give up their guns and horses, but he would return them when it was peaceful again.

The disarming started at 2 p.m., but before long Grierson spotted Apaches escaping up the mountain with their horses, as Natzili tried to turn them back. Troops began "attacking small parties of Indians here and there, and for a time the firing was quite lively," Grierson wrote.

They killed ten people, wounded others and forced many back to camp, but thirty to fifty escaped, including Magoosh and other chiefs. Chiricahua scouts pursued the fleeing Apaches, "not merely to find where they are but to kill [them] wherever found," Russell said.[12]

Soldiers placed about 250 men, women and children under guard and confiscated 199 horses and mules. Despite promises that their horses would be in the agent's care, Hatch gave fifteen to Gatewood and his scouts and sent the rest to Fort Stanton. Soldiers and scouts searched the captives and confiscated guns while helping themselves to anything of value. The following day, soldiers ordered the Apaches into a corral, where manure was nearly five inches deep. There they languished for five days until people began to sicken, and the agency doctor demanded their removal. Russell, frothing with indignation, protested the "total and complete violation of each and every pledge" Hatch made to the Apaches.[13] Hatch ignored him.

For three days, Natzili tried to turn back the fugitives. He couldn't make smoke signals in gale winds, so he sent runners. Another thirty surrendered, but most stayed out despite "the exceedingly humane treatment received by the Indians at the agency," reported Captain Charles Steelhammer, presumably with a straight face. The reservation Apaches were prisoners of war until March 1881. They never got their horses back. In May 1881 Natzili insisted that the Commissioner of Indian Affairs provide him a horse. "He says that he knows [the military] won't give him one, that you are his Great Father, that he is a large, heavy man and cannot get about on foot, which is true," Russell wrote.[14]

Lipans and Mescaleros never forgot this incident. Magoosh's grandson, Richard Magoosh, said: "When the army [came] to the [agency] they started to round all of them [up] there and they had done nothing. Some of them got away. They went on Jacinto Peak. My daddy [Willie Magoosh] was a small boy then. They were going up the side of the hill and trying to get over that into Nogal Canyon. They opened fire on them just like wild game. They were not fighting, just trying to get away. They killed some of them—I don't know how many... They didn't camp 'til they got to the east side of the Capitans. And they hid and went from there to Roswell, the Guadalupes and then to Mexico."

Percy Big Mouth said, "Our chiefs told us not to join them: 'We must remain on our own reservation.' A few slip away from here and go with them. Some of the men and women follow Victorio." For weeks, small groups traveled toward the Rio Grande, either to join Victorio or to escape the misery Hatch had visited upon the reservation. Others fled to West Texas and the Pecos. Magoosh went to his friends in Mexico.[15]

In mid-June, the army assessed Victorio's strength at 236 men, including a hundred renegade "Indians from Mexico." When Mexican troops hounded Victorio into west Texas, it was unfamiliar territory to the Warm Springs people but well known to Mescaleros and Lipans— and to Grierson's troops. On August 1 Grierson "vigorously repulsed" Victorio's stubborn approach to a waterhole near Eagle Springs and later outran Victorio to Rattlesnake Springs. A detachment of the Tenth on August 3 scrambled to the top of the Sierra Diablo, once an impenetrable Mescalero and Lipan fortress, and captured Victorio's supply camp.[16]

◄►

Reliable guides were scarce in west Texas, and Indian scouts were also in short supply because of harsh working conditions and minimal pay. Fort Quitman hired the experienced guide Charles Berger in late June 1880. The Tigua Pueblo scouts and their horses were "near dead," said the post telegraph operator, and yet they were still carrying important dispatches for both American and Mexican commanders.[17] When the army added Fort Griffin to the Pecos District on July 22, Grierson enlisted Lipan scouts in the hunt for Victorio.

In early August the Lipan scouts trailed the hostiles from Rattlesnake Canyon to the Sierra Diablos and accompanied Grierson and his troops in scaling a sheer face, scouting the heights on foot, and trailing

Victorio's forces as they limped south to the Rio Grande.[18] Berger, with two Lipans, two Pueblos and a Black Seminole, picked up the trail at the river crossing and followed it to a camp where Victorio's party had stayed a day or two. Then they struggled through mountains so rugged that the horses had to be led at times. In a valley of the Borracho Mountains, the Apaches scattered to confuse the trail. Evidence at another deserted camp revealed that a great many of Victorio's people were wounded, and their horses were played out. The Apaches emptied the water source to foil pursuers and headed for Lake Guzmán, although some remained in the Candelaria Mountains.[19]

On September 18 Berger returned to Mexico and learned that Colonel Joaquín Terrazas planned to strike Victorio with four hundred men. The exhausted and disgruntled Pueblo scouts mustered out, and no others were willing to enlist.[20] Berger and the Lipans scouts monitored the movements of the Apaches and the Mexican army almost to the end. On October 14, 1880, Terrazas ambushed Victorio and his beleaguered band in the Tres Castillos.[21] James Kaywaykla, who escaped with his mother, recalled: "There were two Lipan Indians who spoke Apache who were guides for the soldiers. That's what my grandmother said. She saw them. They told her and other Indians that were captured, 'Why didn't you get away? You had a chance.' The soldiers had been on the march a long time and their horses were given out. 'You made a bad mistake. You should have got away.'"[22]

CHAPTER

Renegades and Refugees

A long time till everything peaceful.

—Percy Big Mouth

On April 24, 1881, Lipans carried out the last Indian raid in Texas. From the cover of a rocky bluff overlooking the Frio, the small party could see for miles. They had come here every moon for twenty years, mostly to steal horses. For days, they monitored John McLauren's place, seven miles above Leakey. Finally, McLauren left, and they saw his wife, children and a teenaged hired hand, Allen Lease, leave the house and walk down a hill to work in the garden. The Lipans dropped down from their lookout, crept onto the property and proceeded to plunder the house. Had Kate McLauren not heard some commotion, that's probably all that might have happened that day, but she thought the pigs got loose and sent Lease to pen them up. When he spotted the Lipans, he turned to run but was shot in the head and died instantly.

Mrs. McLauren, who was sitting to nurse her infant, jumped to her feet. The Lipans shot her several times as she hurried toward the fence at the river, still holding her baby and shouting at the other two children to run. Six-year-old Maude instead ran back to the house, walked past the Lipans, who were still looting, and retrieved a pillow for her mother. After seeing to her mother's comfort, the plucky girl placed her three-year-old brother Alonzo and baby Frank next to the bleeding woman,

Costilietos and Teresita, photographed in 1873 in front of their jacal. *H. A. Doerr, photographer. DeGrolyer Library, Southern Methodist University, Dallas, Texas. Ag2008.0005*

climbed the fence and started down the river, where she found a neighbor fishing. He quickly summoned help. John McLauren found his two sons still at the side of his wife, who died minutes after his return. The Lipans had taken every bit of clothing from the house and emptied the mattresses of feathers.

Soon Bullis was on the trail with thirty-four Black Seminole scouts and Teresita. Although the raiders had wrapped their horses' hooves with rawhide to avoid leaving tracks, the scouts managed to follow their trail over rough terrain near Devils River. They killed thirty of the horses they were unable to drive before them, crossed the Rio Grande below the mouth of the Pecos and continued high into the Burro Mountains. Teresita, the leading guide, realized from signs on the trail that they were following her people and tried to divert the detachment to an older trail, but another scout caught on and returned troops to the fresh trail. She became so violent the scouts tied her to her horse. On May 2 they found the Lipans.

They hid until midnight and then crept toward the sleeping camp, leaving seven men behind with the still struggling Teresita and the horses. At daybreak on May 3 they attacked, killing four men and taking a boy and wounded woman captive. They recaptured twenty-one stolen horses. The woman said fifty or sixty families were still living in the Sierra Carmen and from there to the mouth of the Pecos and in

San Carlos. Bullis sent her to the Fort Sill reservation. The leader of the group was San-Da-Ve, (Santavi), the same man who fought Kickapoos with Chivato. Reportedly, he was mortally wounded, but he would later turn up at the Mescalero Reservation. This was the Black Seminole scouts' final campaign.[1]

◄►

The infamous Mescalero Alsate and his Lipan counterpart, Colorado, who had been a menace on both sides of the border for at least ten years, lost the last of many battles in 1881.[2] In late 1877, American troops, under cover of a snow storm, attacked the group in the Sierra Carmen and destroyed their well-stocked camp. A year later Mexican forces descended, killing six and capturing eighty-six, including the two chiefs. Soldiers took the prisoners to Santa Rosa, where some resident Apaches obtained the release of several children. Because the soldiers didn't receive their pay, they went on to Mexico City with their captives, and during the six-month journey some Apaches died of smallpox. In Mexico City, there was still no money for them, and they either freed their prisoners or let them escape.

The Apaches remained for a time in Mexico City and then returned to their old haunts, the Lipans first and the Mescaleros later. "Because of their bad treatment by the Mexicans, they resolved not to spare the lives of even those who had been their friends," reported a Texas newspaper. In early 1880, the Apaches "came down upon the ranches with a sweeping vengeance," killing entire families of Mexican ranchers, stealing hundreds of horses and retreating to the Sierra del Carmen.[3] In late 1881 Mexican officers, promising food and supplies, tricked the marauders into coming in. Soldiers surrounded and captured 63 warriors and about 150 women and children. They shot the three chiefs—Alsate, Colorado and Zorrillo—and gave the captives to families.[4]

◄►

In 1882 Texas patrols logged 3,662 miles and found no signs of hostile Indians. The Indian wars had ended in Texas. "A settled feeling of security heretofore unknown prevails throughout western Texas, causing a rapid and permanent increase of the population and wealth of the state, which is gratifying to citizens, and the military who have been instrumental and bringing about this very satisfactory condition of affairs," Grierson wrote in 1881. "The value of all this work to the great state of Texas . . . can hardly be overestimated."[5]

It's a revealing statement and confirms anthropologist Morris Opler's view that the military saw its mission as clearing the way for American occupation and prosperity. Mackenzie, Bullis and Shafter became heroes for their roles in subduing the last of the wild tribes, but without the remarkable skills, knowledge and fortitude of the Black Seminole scouts, their campaigns against a clever and intrepid enemy could have dragged on indefinitely. Despite the scouts' faithful service, they never received the land they were promised. They settled in Bracketville. In a similar vein, the American military was reluctant to share credit with Mexico's forces. In truth, the Lipans and Mescaleros could have hidden away in the Mexican mountains indefinitely. Only the combined effort of Mexican and American troops deprived them of every hideaway, and it was the Mexican army that struck the final blow.

In the region's conflicts, Lipans cast a longer shadow than much larger tribes. By the numbers, Comanches accounted for two-thirds of skirmishes in Texas before the Civil War, Apaches for one-fourth, according to historian F. Todd Smith. After the war, Comanches and Kiowas fought in half the engagements, Lipans and other Apaches, one third. Of depredations reported to the Commissioner of Indian Affairs between 1812 and 1889, 1,031 were blamed on Comanches and 759 on Apaches.[6]

While the Lipans and their allies waged a guerilla war of tactics and strategy, the army waged a war of brute force and resources. It must have seemed to the Apaches that white men were everywhere, and they were. Soldiers not on patrol were building roads and telegraph lines, digging out springs and seeps, and protecting railroad crews.

Grierson's men alone built and repaired more than a thousand miles of wagon roads and three hundred miles of telegraph lines and marched 1,335,710 miles by February 1881, when he could report a "vast region thoroughly scouted over, minutely explored, its resources made known and wonderfully developed."

Tactics and strategy played second fiddle to attrition; the two armies had only to inflict a few losses, destroy some camps, and wear the Apaches down. Each warrior's loss weighed heavily. Disease was the army's most efficient ally, cutting down an estimated three-fourths of Lipans and half of Mescaleros,[7] although it's all but impossible to estimate their numbers because the bands were scattered and Lipans were often with allies. It's reasonably safe to say their numbers plummeted from 4,365 in 1792 to about 750 in 1873. Despite such withering losses, the Lipans and their confederates waged a guerilla war that was monumental in its persistence despite overwhelming odds.

James Anson Farrer wrote in 1885 that wars between peoples with different standards of civilization do "more to barbarize the civilized than to civilise the barbarous," and soldiers who burned an Indian village were capable of burning Paris.[8]

◄►

As troops converged on both sides of the border to contain Victorio, Mexican military forces were driving Lipans from their strongholds in Coahuila and Chihuahua. In the heat of the campaigns and thereafter, Apaches—in groups, families, twos and threes—crept through mountains and trekked across deserts, trying to elude soldiers and make their way to refuge—the Guadalupes, various Mexican ranges, the Mescalero Reservation, or the village of San Carlos.

Troops following a tangle of tracks didn't always know whose trail they were on. A fresh recruit, who believed he pursued Victorio's Apaches, drew a bead on two people and was mortified to discover he shot a young woman carrying a baby; her tracks revealed she was not one of Victorio's Apaches. A lieutenant trailing Indians who raided near Zaragosa, obviously Lipans, wrote that they were believed to be Mescaleros belonging to Victorio's band "though I could discover no reason for this supposition."[9] Louis Scott, the United States Consul at Chihuahua, said it appeared that some small groups were not in the fight and "will now probably try and make their way back to the reservations, but this should not be allowed under any circumstances or conditions." Whether or not they were with Victorio, "they should be hunted to death every one of them." Grierson couldn't agree more.[10]

While the army's right hand in Texas was trying to kill all the Apaches, its left hand at Fort Stanton was sending runners to bring in renegades and stragglers. Captain C. H. Conrad instructed his troops to treat returning Apaches as they would reservation Indians, and he told Natzili, the subchiefs, and head men that the government wanted Indians then off the reservation to return and live in peace. Troops would protect them from "Texans" (cowboys), he said, and each family would receive two mares, plus other stock. They could select a white man to go with five Apaches to bring in renegades. At the chiefs' request, only Apaches were sent.[11]

A group arriving in January 1881 from the Smoke Mountains knew nothing of Victorio. Many had been away since Hatch's roundup. Ragged and miserable, with only a few guns and horses, they were hardly a threat. Because of Russell's arrests of Lipans in 1879, every newcomer for years claimed to be Mescalero. One of the returnees was Ayne, a married woman abducted by Victorio's people. After reuniting with her people, she married Natzili. Russell refused to provide for them because he wanted to care only for the "good Indians" who stayed, but he yielded to Purington's argument that for the army to feed them, troops would have to take them prisoner, which would only discourage others from coming in.[12]

To further complicate matters, Victorio's lieutenant, Nana, was still out and trying again to recruit from the Mescalero reservation. In summer 1881 the newly appointed agent William H. H. Llewellyn was traveling to the reservation with his wife and two small boys, when they came upon a horrifying sight—dead men inside an overturned wagon and, nearby, a woman's mutilated body. The agent left the road and traveled hard all night, reaching Tularosa the next morning.

"From all the information I can gather, it is my opinion that depredating hostiles are Indians on their way from Old Mexico to this Agency," he wrote. If not for an encounter with Chiricahua scouts still patrolling the reservation, the seventy people would have come in. Three weeks earlier they "attempted to come in but were chased and driven into the mountains thirty miles from the Agency to the south... Since that time they have made three ineffectual efforts to get into the agency, being prevented each time by the scouts and soldiers. Finding they could not return to the Agency as they had been led to believe they could, they concluded to go on the war path."[13]

Nonsense, growled Hatch. Troops fired on Nana and his warriors, who were raiding in the area.[14] Llewellyn wasn't mistaken. Refugees and renegades were both orbiting the reservation, and the military couldn't tell the difference. Apache remnants would drift in for several more years.

◄►

Most returning Apaches were relieved to be back to Mescalero, but for a few the war hadn't ended. Muchacho Negro, son of a Llanero chief, returned from Victorio's ranks with a small party on November 22, 1880, and clashed with Captain Conrad, who tried to have them arrested. They broke for the hills and strafed Conrad's camp for hours. Muchacho Negro was badly wounded, another man was killed, and four were captured.[15] The post trader lured Muchacho Negro and Give Me a Horse to his house with whiskey, and the two were arrested and sent to Fort Union.

Unfortunately, Natzili's son was also caught in the net. His only offense was associating with the wrong crowd, the eternal dilemma of parents. The chief pleaded tearfully with Llewellyn to get his son back, and the agent asked for the boy's release. "Nautzilli's boy was not a bad boy, and he had never been off the reservation," Llewellyn wrote, adding assurances about Natzili's sacrifice and friendship.[16] The inquiry passed through channels all the way to the Cabinet, and in February 1882, after nearly a year of confinement, One Eye was released, and Llewellyn brought him home.[17]

Muchacho Negro and Give Me a Horse escaped from the guardhouse at Fort Union in 1882, returned with stolen horses, and, with Muchacho Negro's brother Ishpiye, took over Natzili's camp. In a gun battle with the chiefs and Llewellyn's newly formed Indian police, three renegades were killed and Llewellyn was shot twice in the arm. Muchacho Negro and others and hid in the camp of Mescalero Chief Román Chiquito.[18]

On September 12, troops surrounded the camps of Natzili and Román Chiquito and disarmed them, and the agent demoted Natzili and made San Juan principal chief. Muchacho Negro and Ishpiye periodically haunted the reservation until their capture in 1883. The

Mescalero Police, ca. 1894. *Courtesy of Fort Stanton Inc. and Hubbard Museum of the American West.* **Sitting on ground:** Boneski (police captain) and Chino. **Middle row:** Patricio, Three Finger Charlie, Magoosh (in brimless hat) and Domingo. **Back row:** José Carrillo (interpreter), Sans Puer, and Natzili (hand raised, medallion visible).

military washed its hands of them (the War Department and the Interior Department were squabbling over which should pay to hold Indian prisoners), and so Llewellyn took responsibility. Without horses or arms, they posed no threat, the agent said.[19]

The second disarming and the demotion of Natzili didn't endear Llewellyn to the Apaches. He often seemed too eager to please the military, but then Hatch and others saw the Mescalero reservation as "an asylum for renegade Indians, who are beyond the control of the Indians now there and the agent." They wanted to abolish the reservation or take it over. Llewellyn was under pressure to earn their trust and cooperation.[20]

Natzili, caught between his obligations to relatives (Muchacho Negro was probably a nephew) and his responsibilities as principal chief, forfeited his position, but he still had a great deal of influence and was among a delegation taken to Washington, D.C., in the winter of 1884. Told he would meet President Arthur, Natzili dressed in his best beaded buckskin clothing and moccasins. He carried his bow and arrows and had a shield on his arm. When Natzili attempted, Indian fashion, to embrace his host, the president called for help. Natzili was so embarrassed that he never permitted anyone to mention the incident in his presence.[21]

"They went in and introduced themselves. The president came out to meet them," said Solon Sombrero. "My grandfather... hugged him. The president got scared. That's the way the Indians shake hands—no harm about it." Apache way, friends always embraced. Shaking hands was a white practice. Some Apaches used to say the white people shake with one hand so they can take something away from you with the other.[22]

CHAPTER

Lipan Exodus

I am now utterly opposed to their being coaxed back.

— *General Ranald S. Mackenzie, 1882*[1]

L ipans described their journey from Mexico during interviews with Morris Opler in the 1930s. This is their account: Most of the Lipans still in Mexico were living peacefully near the towns and trying to get along. Antonio Apache's grandfather was a mail carrier. The government couldn't keep mail carriers on the route between Zaragosa and Presidio del Norte because they would be waylaid and killed, but for three years, the wily Lipan mail carrier completed his rounds on horseback every six days, one way.

Some Lipans were then in the hills making trouble. (This could have been Alsate and Colorado.) One day they attacked a wealthy Mexican family traveling to their ranch and killed the entire party. Next they killed the employee of a Zaragosa man who was a friend to the Lipans. They took the hired man's clothes and killed the two steers he was driving, according to Antonio Apache. (In February 1880 unidentified Indians killed some people near Zaragosa, murdered an entire family at Guerrero [Presidio del Norte], and attacked a ranch. A party of Mexican citizens pursued them inland.) The wealthy Mexican called a meeting to organize and fight the Lipans, but the friendly Mexican, despite his losses, defended them. The wealthy man prevailed.

The Lipans' friend rode alone to the Indians, who were on the move. He called out to them, asking for a Lipan he knew. They told him the man had gone to the Mescaleros. He told the others they should speak to him because he had important news. They were afraid to approach, so he talked from a distance: "They are going to follow you right into the mountains and keep after you till they find you all. You Indians may think these are big mountains and this is rough country, but when they start to search for you, it will not be big enough, for there will be many men looking for you," he said. He suggested they go north to Fort Stanton in New Mexico.

He also informed the Lipan mail carrier and urged him to go to Fort Stanton. Each time the mail carrier made his rounds, he saw more soldiers. Finally the friendly Mexican warned him trouble was about to start. He gave the carrier a beef to butcher and make jerky and said they should leave for their own safety.

These Lipans departed in the early morning, leaving fires burning in all their camps so the Mexicans who wanted to kill them would think they were still there on the outskirts of town. They went to the mountains and traveled until they reached some distant Lipan camps. The mail carrier warned his people, but some didn't believe the Mexicans could find them. "These mountains are rough, and they don't know the country as we do," they said. The soldiers found them east of Zaragosa and attacked at dawn. They captured two women—a Lipan and a Mescalero—and some children. The Lipan woman, Liha, was wounded in the back; the Mescalero woman was Dule. (Both women came to Mescalero in 1904.) Others, including the sisters Conejo (Percy Big Mouth's mother) and Yeyu, escaped.[2]

The mail carrier continued on to warn relatives near Norte. They too ignored the warning and remained. They went to town to buy shells to hunt antelope, but shopkeepers had all been warned against selling ammunition to them. One said he would try to find them some shells. While they waited, they saw smoke signals[3] from the hills, which meant trouble.

Lipans in camps at the edge of town, led by Pancho Venego and his father, started for the mountains. Mexican friends told them that soldiers had trouble with Indians to the west (Victorio) and intended to fight them. "We Mexicans who live here don't bother you Indians, but these soldiers are from another place," they said. Another Mexican gave a butcher knife to a Lipan who was his friend and told him to stay in the hills and not return.

The Lipans, in two groups, gathered at a big mountain they called Pine. Some decided to return to a big camp near Norte. Pancho Venego said, "I came out here with my mind made up to go where you people are going. Now I see that my relatives are in the big camp. It doesn't look right to leave them. I ought to go back. If any trouble comes up I should share it and be with them no matter what happens." He and his people went back. Two families went to Flat Rock, where they found Chivato's group in a pretty place on a mountain top. They found more camps.

One big group stayed together on a ridge north of Norte. Three men who went into town to get liquor were seized and told to lead the soldiers to their people. Shosh led them to a ridge but claimed he forgot which ridge they were on. The other two Lipans were placed in a corral. After a while, the guards got drunk deliberately, and told the Lipans to escape when they fell asleep. The two scrambled over the wall and walked all night and day to reach the big Lipan camp, where they warned the people. The Lipans broke camp, packed their horses, and headed for the Rio Grande.

Shosh continued to lead the soldiers around, and a friendly soldier said they planned to kill him. He took them up a steep, winding trail. His feet were tied together under the horse. The friendly soldier gave him a stick, and he loosened the rope on one foot. Rounding a turn, Shosh jumped from the horse and ran. The guard waited and then shouted, "There he goes!" He fired some shots in that direction without taking good aim, as Shosh got the rope off and escaped into thickets on the other side of an arroyo. He found the tracks of about thirty Lipans from the big camp, who had traveled two days and nights toward the Rio Grande but hadn't yet crossed. Shosh ran all day and night without food. He tried to sleep, but it was too cold. It was then November. After two days without food or water, he found his people. Someone saw him coming.

The chief (Magoosh) said to the women: "Don't get excited. If a fight starts, just go to one side. We men will fight them here in the open. If they kill us, all right. But if you women run away to the hills when the fight starts, you will starve. No one will support you out there. They won't kill you; that's the promise they gave us long ago."

The men had slept with their guns close by and had their cartridges ready. Shosh stopped and said, "I am alone. Don't be afraid." One man said a ceremony over him, necessary before a captive could rejoin the group. The group moved to a place they called Wide Rocks, and when they saw fresh tracks of the Mexican soldiers' shod horses, they made for the summit of a mountain.

Four Mescaleros, including Big Mouth, approached. When they met, a Lipan told them, "We have had a great deal of trouble. This is all that is left of us in this district. The rest are captured. Just a few, Chivato's family, are elsewhere."

The Mescaleros said, "We have come from our reservation. We heard that some Lipans were left, and we want to bring you back to our reservation." Another Mescalero said, "The agency up our way told us to hunt other Apaches to the south and to bring them in."

When they headed out, they heard blasting from the railroad[4] being built at Eagle Pass. The Lipans stole mules from the construction crew, and others brought horses so they could ride to Mescalero. They crossed the river into Texas and stopped at Madzil, a mountain where they had once fought Comanches. "Then west of us we saw something like a star. It got bigger. Just as we got to the railroad it came around the hill. We could hear the thundering as it came. Some of us were on one side, some on the other. The leader told us to go far from the railroad track. Soon it passed right through us. We could see the red faces of the Americans in the cars."

The Mescaleros' leader had a pass. "In the paper it said that all those on the American side were our friends and would not harm us. But the Lipans were afraid and went cautiously around the hills, afraid to come out in the open." About thirty people crossed the track near Fort Davis and didn't stop until they were in New Mexico. They reached the Guadalupe Mountains and camped at a place they called Cedar Standing, which had a water hole. That night an old woman wandered off. They tried for two days to find her before going on. The woman rode alone toward Sierra Blanca. When her horse gave out, she continued on foot and arrived a few days later. The group went on to a place they called Turkey Roost, one of the first peaks of the Sacramentos. They stopped at Blue Water, fourteen miles from the present town of Weed. Another day's travel brought them to a place called Fir Tree Standing, southeast of present Cloudcroft, and then to Tularosa Canyon.

"From there we came on down. It was a Saturday. There were many Indians around. They were getting rations, all these Mescaleros. You could see red blankets all around that they were wearing. I asked about a relative I had here, San Juan. They told me, 'He's down below.' All of us went there. That was the end of my long journey from Old Mexico to this place. Since then I have lived here."[5]

"The Lipans came here when they got away from Old Mexico— twenty-five or thirty of them. Three times the Lipans brought a small band here," said Percy Big Mouth.[6]

◄►

As 1882 opened, Llewellyn was still trying to bring in distant Apaches, over the objections of Mackenzie, who was now commanding the Department of New Mexico. On January 4, the agent sent three Mescaleros to search the Guadalupes and bring back "Indians who belong here." They knew of one band of 135, and a small party was reported near Fort McRae. The larger group was probably Magoosh's band. Llewellyn was willing to discuss conditions and recognized that they might want some assurance they wouldn't be arrested.[7]

Mackenzie was adamant that Indians who were off the reservation should not be allowed back without first reporting to Fort Stanton for disarming, dismounting and confinement. Otherwise, "control over all the Mescaleros must be weakened," he said. He recognized the agent's authority, so long as the Indians were peaceful, but the moment they left without permission, the responsibility rested with troops, he said. The aging Indian fighter suggested to his subordinates that spies quietly collect information about renegade camps believed to be in the Guadalupes. The Commissioner of Indian Affairs supported Llewellyn's efforts to return renegades and said bluntly that arms and horses should be surrendered to the agent and not the military because of the Apaches' experience with Hatch.[8]

In late March, two Mescaleros sent south to find others returned, saying a large band would arrive in four or five weeks. They were vague about the band's location. Days later, a runner came in with twenty-one tattered, tired and hungry people on a few poor ponies. The eight men were armed with bows and arrows and one or two muzzle-loading rifles. They had been out since Hatch's roundup, scattered in small bands in the Guadalupe, Hueco and Davis Mountains but mostly in the Smoke Mountains and in communication with each other. Most had relatives at the agency. They said they had not been with Victorio and knew nothing of Nana and his group.

Llewellyn was unwilling to confine the men because the whole tribe would see it as treachery. Many more Apaches were still hiding, probably waiting to see how this group was treated, and they were expected within a month. If they didn't come in, Mackenzie intended to send troops after them. In early April Llewellyn rode out to meet the new arrivals. One Apache visited the agent's camp but hurried off without seeing Llewellyn after reservation Apaches told him the terms of surrender—Mackenzie's terms. The large group, probably Magoosh's people, stopped or turned back but remained in the area.[9]

◄ ►

In 1882 Magoosh returned to Mescalero from Mexico by way of Big Bend. The Lipans cut down a telegraph pole and used the wire to make bridle bits. They had only horsemeat to eat. "Magoosh one time came with . . . Magoosh Boy, who was a young boy. They came from Mexico. Magoosh had two wives and children with him. He left them at the south end of the Sacramentos toward El Paso. When they started walking close to Mescalero, Peso was living off toward the cemetery at the foot of the hill . . . They walked clear to the place where the Mormon Church is and asked for my father," said May Peso Second. "They told them where they came from. They wanted to come back to Mescalero. Peso let them return. Took them to the superintendent and told him. And he sent some of the scouts over there to get them . . ."[10]

When they reached Mescalero, said Willie Magoosh, Magoosh's son, they received rations—bacon, flour, coffee and sugar. Magoosh stayed for a time and then returned to Mexico, remaining several years. They returned on the same route and after that they stayed, he said.[11] There is no official record of Magoosh's return, but in 1883, Mackenzie was reassigned and Llewellyn was busily combining seven hundred unhappy Jicarilla Apaches[12] with the Mescaleros after Congress consolidated their two reservations. Nobody would notice the new faces.

Magoosh and his two wives, Cosa and Ekidda, were present for the first census in 1885. He is listed as "Mogul" because the agents were Americanizing Indian names, Before that, he was known to live across the Rio Grande from Eagle Pass, in Big Bend, and in the Chisos and Guadalupe Mountains. "[T]hey went south like a bird . . . When they were free they would go south for the winter and up here for the summer," said grandson Richard Magoosh. "What the government did was to pen them up here and keep them here."[13]

Lipans would quietly join the reservation through 1894, sometimes alone, sometimes in families. That year Caje, the last member of the Telkondaha band, appears on the census with his family, along with Antonio Apache, his wife and family, plus Antonio's sister and child, and Stella Lester and two sons.[14]

CHAPTER

Reservation Life

Most of the young men volunteered for scout duty. There were scouts in every Indian village or band.

— Solon Sombrero[1]

T roops from Fort Stanton had little to do except keep the Apaches and the settlers where they belonged, but even this duty could be lively. In April 1885, three horses strayed off the reservation into a wheat field in the Tularosa Valley owned by Andreas Wilson. Shosh, a Lipan, tracked his horses to Wilson's place and arrived just in time to see Wilson chase the animals from his field and shoot them. "There is great excitement and serious trouble may ensue. The Indians have quit planting and say they will retaliate," said Llewellyn. The shooting was malicious, "especially when he well knew that they would willingly have paid for any damages done by the animals, as they had always done on previous occasions."

Fifteen to twenty armed warriors headed for Wilson's ranch. Llewellyn ordered them back and intercepted a second group near the ranch, but that night they surrounded Wilson's house, built a fire in front, drove horses into his fields "and evidently did all they could to entice Wilson out." Troops arrived the next day. Llewellyn had his Indian police arrest Wilson and bring him to the agency. During a meeting with authorities and Apaches, Wilson denied shooting the horses but agreed to pay for them "to keep the peace."[2]

◄ ►

Apaches were settling into reservation life in 1885, when Geronimo broke out for his final adventure. This time, his recruiters stirred no interest at Mescalero. In fact, Mescaleros and Lipans scouted against him. It wasn't a hard decision for Lipans—Geronimo hadn't trusted Lipans, and Lipans believed that Chiricahuas led Mexican soldiers to Lipan camps.[3] The army first asked for scouts in 1883, and Chivato was the first Lipan to sign up. He was then thirty-three and tall, at five feet, ten inches. The agent also employed men as scouts; in 1884 he sent Lipans Shosh, Chivato and Dinero to search for Charley McComas, a white boy taken by the Warm Springs Apaches the year before.[4]

In summer 1885 troops seeking Geronimo crisscrossed the region, investigating every shadow and track reported by nervous residents, and caught only rumors and fabrications. Major John A. Wilcox set up four camps of Eighth Cavalry troops in the southwestern New Mexico mountains. By late June each camp had five scouts recruited by Llewellyn.[5]

In one squad were the Lipans Shosh and Blanco, along with Mescaleros Big Mouth (whose wife was Lipan), Caja, and Pinto. They served under Captain O. B. Boyd at a squalid, crowded outpost near the mining camp of Grafton. Because the only water, two miles away, was rank, all the officers and most of the enlisted men were sick. Apaches customarily moved camp at the first sign of illness. Even within the confines of the reservation, they moved often, for sanitary reasons. The scouts must have wondered why their captain would stay in such a dreadful place. By the end of July, Boyd was dead of dysentery, and the scouts wanted to return home because "they had their families and crops to look after," Wilcox reported. Congress failed to make appropriations, and Llewellyn was nearly out of rations.[6]

Appropriations or not, it was apparently government policy to maintain the Apaches at the brink of starvation. Llewellyn's orders were to divide supplies into fifty-two parts and issue one part each week. The quantities were often so minuscule, they couldn't be weighed, so he usually gave them a month's allowance, which they consumed in a day or two. The five hundred head of cattle he provided for twelve hundred Mescaleros and Jicarillas to begin a herd were mostly killed and eaten secretly or lost to rustlers.[7]

In 1886, the military requisitioned scouts repeatedly. At any given time, twenty-six to forty-eight men were on duty. Lipans serving in 1885 and in 1886 included Chivato, Shosh, Magoosh, Dinero and José Torres.[8] The scouts' pensions would support entire extended families during the Depression. The restless Jicarillas served in 1885 but not after. They wanted to return to their country and weren't interested in scouting or farming. In August 1886, the first group of Jicarillas left without permission, others soon followed, and the rest were allowed to go the following April.[9]

While Geronimo kept the army occupied to the west, more refugees slipped into the reservation. New families filled out the camps, and adult relatives joined existing Lipan households. The population of known Lipans jumped from twenty-eight to forty-three, and was probably much higher.[10]

Lipans were making the best of their new life but found, as the Jicarillas did, that it's one thing to be allies and quite another to be cooped up together on a reservation.

Occasional friction flared between Lipans and Mescaleros. As Chief San Juan lay dying in April 1886, a Mescalero medicine man blamed his death on witchcraft[11] by two Lipans who had a long-standing feud with the chief. Enraged Mescaleros wanted to kill the men. The Lipans hid their women and children in the mountains and prepared to fight. Agent Fletcher Cowart rushed in to find both groups saddled and armed. He calmed the Mescaleros by promising a thorough investigation; if the Lipans had done anything wrong they would be punished. He called in the medicine man, and, in the presence of his people, called him a fraud and troublemaker and threatened to put him in irons if he made any further accusations of witchcraft.[12]

Animosity still simmered a year later, when Chief Quannah Parker and three other Comanches visited the agency. Fifty people, mostly

Lipans, said they wanted to go to the Comanche reservation, and Parker told the agent he would be glad to have them. "Because of the trouble with San Juan's people, it might be best to let them go," Cowart said.[13] When Parker departed in August, Chivato, Dinero, and seven family members were with him. The Jicarillas had left without permission, and Chivato assumed they could too. He had a ninety-day pass, but Natzili informed the agent they had taken their families and intended to stay. They also cut the telephone line between the agency and Fort Stanton. After a two-hundred-mile chase, Lieutenant J. S. Scott found them and brought them back, and authorities in Washington ended visitation between reservations.[14]

Chivato began a letter-writing campaign and asked Parker's help. "I am much sorry here—here the Mescalero care for tiswin [fermented corn liquor] and are often crazy. I want to be with friends. I do not want my boy to grow to be a man here where there is much tiswin and no money," he wrote on October 25, 1888. A few months later, he wrote, "We are poor but we want to come to you soon. We want to work, to raise corn. Here we do not have land. I have a wagon and horses and a few cows. The Mescaleros are not good friends to us and are one people while we are not many [and] are another people." Hunting was good away from the agency, but the agent wouldn't let them go, "and he does not give us enough meat." To that letter he attached a list of thirty-five Lipans[15] who also wanted to move to Comanche country. Conspicuously absent from the list was Magoosh and his family, although one of his two wives, Cosa, wanted to go.[16]

Chivato's complaints about tiswin were probably exaggerated. Agents and Indian police destroyed the fermented corn liquor when they found it and tried to eradicate its use, but illicit drinking was a blight on all reservations. There was, however, a tiswin brawl in March 1887 at which several people died, including a Lipan woman's son. On July 3, 1888, the distraught mother killed a Mescalero woman in revenge. "Bad blood was engendered between the Mescalero and Lipans, and the Mescaleros were making threats," the agent reported.[17]

Chivato also knew the Comanches were farming successfully, while the Mescalero reservation had little arable land, limited water and a short growing season. In short, the Comanches weren't as poor. Other Lipans soon changed their minds about leaving. After San Juan's death, Cowart reinstated Natzili as principal chief. As he had in the past, Natzili probably took steps to restore unity. He and Chief Plata had come in from Comanche country just ten years earlier. It's logical that they and Magoosh, the only remaining Lipan chief, disabused the Lipans about life with the Comanches.

Cowart began including Shosh and José Torres, a Lipan head man, in councils and created the Court of Indian Offenses, "composed of three of the most sensible and influential Indians on the reservation." They were Boneski, captain of police and a non-drinker; Natzili; and Charlie, a Mescalero head man. Dressed in uniforms and dignified in bearing, they sentenced the guilty to a few days in the guardhouse and arbitrated differences, usually settling disputes to everyone's satisfaction.[18]

Boneski (White Teeth) was a Lipan head man in his mid-fifties who wore a goatee. "My whiskers stand for the Mexicans I have killed," he said. He once walked from Whitetail to Elk Springs in the January snow wearing only a G-string because others bet ten cartridges and two horses that he couldn't do it, and he needed those things. He tied his clothes in a bundle on his back and set out through deep snow and piercing wind. When he reached shelter, his head was covered with ice, but he sat nonchalantly before the fire and put his clothes on. "The cold is my friend," he said, and the snow bunting covered him with clothing. Boneski said he had spiritual power from the snow bunting, which gave him an edge in the hoop and pole game. Like all Lipan men, Boneski loved the game and cleaned up on many good hoop players.[19]

◄►

Within a few years, José Torres, Boneski's cousin, was also a judge. José Torres had power over horses. He carried an old wooden quirt

Boneski, 1913. *Wanamaker Collection, Mathers Museum of World Cultures, University of Indiana*

decorated with a white horse tail. When Plata's son Seth was badly injured during a horse race, he performed his horse ceremony and cured the boy.[20]

◄ ►

Personal trials probably magnified Chivato's discontent. In 1889 his son died, and his Mescalero wife, Zanagolecha, was abducted by Massai, a renegade Chiricahua.[21] The same year, he and Dinero recovered their sister from a family in Three Rivers, thanks to an order from the agent and the reservation police. Then Dinero, a sergeant in the tribal police, took up with a married woman and, confronted by the wronged husband, killed the man and was sentenced to death. He escaped from jail and vanished, reappearing on the Comanche reservation by 1891.[22]

In 1892, two Lipans—one was Magoosh's sister, the other a relative of Boneski—died in a drunken a brawl involving Natzili's brother Patos Chiquito, and Mariano, a Mescalero with a Lipan wife. When the agency police entered Natzili's camp, the chief asked in perfect Spanish, "What do you gentlemen want?" An agency employee observed that drinking unmasked some bitterness between Lipans and Mescaleros.[23]

At long last, Quanah Parker in 1893 prevailed on the commissioner, and Comanche John, Chivato and Sanavoy were allowed to leave. Sanavoy (Santavi, San Da Ve), who had fought Kickapoos with Chivato and led the last Indian raid in Texas, showed up on the Mescalero reservation with his wife in 1892. The three men departed in 1894, and their families joined them later.[24]

◄►

Elk Springs, in a high mountain valley of the Sacramento Mountains flanked by dense stands of Ponderosa pines, was called Nazitsai, "he comes back," after a captive of the Comanches who returned. It was here that Natzili established himself, as agent Cowart set about transforming nomadic hunters and raiders into farmers. Leveraging the Apaches' fear of losing their reservation to acquisitive settlers who were trying to pry open Mescalero lands, Cowart in 1888 gave them good advice: If you want to keep your land, build houses and start farms at all the best springs. Big camps broke up, and family clusters occupied nearly all the available water sources.

Most Lipans congregated with José Torres at White Oak Springs, but Magoosh was with his old friend Peso, a Mescalero chief, in Tularosa Canyon, where the best agricultural land unfolded from the creek bottom. A few Lipans remained with Natzili at Elk Springs. They

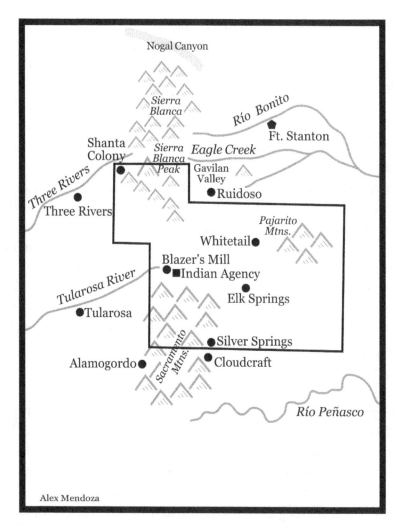

Map 10 Mescalero Apache Reservation

cultivated plots of a small, hardy corn, along with oats, potatoes and beans, and Cowart divided the remaining cattle, so each family owned a few head. "I believe in God and that labor is principal cause of men's welfare," said Natzili. "We are thankful to the Great Father for all gifts received in money and goods . . . And you will find that my people will work and raise crops if they can get the tools to work with."[25]

Non-Indians grazed thousands of head of livestock on reservation land without paying for the privilege, which cut into the Apaches' stock raising. After two years of drought, many of the Apaches' cattle died, and the hungry reservation dwellers solved two problems by filling their stomachs with trespassing cattle and sheep.[26]

After 1895, agent V. E. Stottler opened up Elk and Silver Springs and ditched the land to allow drainage, reasoning that the Apaches could take advantage of ample summer rainfall to grow crops. He settled more people there, and they fenced their lands and began planting wheat, barley and oats. Within a few years, Elk Canyon boasted thirty-five Apache ranches. By 1899 a visitor described "an endless succession of Indian farms" along the Elk Springs canyon road, all fenced and well cultivated. The nearby sawmill, operated by Apaches, was busy. This is probably when Magoosh moved to Elk, and it became the Lipans' community.[27]

"Magoosh got this land here. After the Lipans came here, he brought them all here and saw to their needs," said Meredith Magoosh Begay. "I'm hanging on to this land by living here. The younger generation goes out, and they want land here and there without thought. This land has history. That's why I don't let it go. The Lipans made their homesteads along this canyon and then infiltrated the Chiricahuas at White Tail. Most Lipans stayed within this canyon."[28] (Chiricahua Apaches moved from Fort Sill to the Mescalero reservation in 1913 and settled at Whitetail.)

Magoosh became the salaried assistant to the agency farmer in 1889 and was also a member of the police force. Stottler considered him "a man of strong personality." He was "efficient, doing what he could by example as well as precept to inspire his people to tend the land."[29]

CHAPTER

End of an Era

A hungry stomach was found to be an excellent mode of discipline.

— Agent Walter Luttrell, 1900[1]

Agents could be both advocates and tyrants. They pressured chiefs and head men to send their own children to the agency boarding school and to produce other pupils. When enrollment fell short, agents withheld rations and sent the Indian police to snatch shrieking children from the arms of their weeping mothers. Parents resorted to hiding their children or marrying off their young girls; some children faked insanity or sickness. At school, the children's dark tresses were shorn, and they were "stripped of their Indian garb, thoroughly washed, and clad in civilized clothing," wrote an agent. Once enrolled, they weren't allowed to go home, although parents could visit. There was one positive aspect to school: Apache children suddenly had enough to eat.

Students got new non-Indian names: José Torres's son became Horace Greeley and his daughter, Mollie Ohio; one of Magoosh's sons became William Stott[2]; Natzili's younger son became Len Smith and his daughter, Lucy Smith; Chivato's daughter became Carrie Heath and his son, Harry Heath. Agents also attempted to rename the parents; not surprisingly, Natzili refused to go by John Smith, and Magoosh never warmed to Mogul. Over time, children kept their first names, and many used their fathers' names as surnames.[3]

Portrait of Young Schoolgirl, 1900. A note identifies the girl as Lipan.
Ales Hrdlicka, National Anthropological Archives, Smithsonian Institution, NAA INV 02031302

From 1882 on, agents also sent children to schools in New Mexico, Colorado, Kansas and Pennsylvania. Willie Magoosh attended school in Fort Lewis, Colorado. Those who returned, even after years away from their camps, resumed wearing Apache attire and refused to speak English. Periodically, children escaped. In February 1891, Natzili's children, Len and Lucy Smith, fled a boarding school in Kansas, where they were mistreated. The chief still hadn't found them when he told the agent: "People have been displeased because instead of being taught to read and write, the children had to work too hard and do all sorts of menial labor. We are in favor of sending our children to school, all who are of school age, but the little ones should be left with their mothers . . . I am in favor of having our children attend our home school. I think it would be better than a distant school."[4]

Len Smith was found dying of tuberculosis and buried on the reservation. This dismal event further inflamed the Apaches' resistance to boarding schools, for good reason: The schools were disease incubators, and cases of appalling abuse would later surface. The first Apache student died of tuberculosis in 1888, and losses rose steadily, particularly at Fort Lewis and the reservation's own crowded, unventilated girls' dormitory. Stottler overcame their resistance through "firmness and a judicious use of the guardhouse and starvation of the parents . . . If then they can not be taught to be industrious and have all the warpath spanked out of them, it were high time to give up the effort."[5]

◄►

Clothing and dwellings were slower to change. Natzili offered in 1882 to discard his blanket and wear an overcoat if a large enough one could be found. After that more men added a shirt, vest, hat, boots, shoes and coat to their accustomed leggings, breech clout, blanket and moccasins. The women still wore a calico or gingham blouse, short skirt, and blankets. Llewellyn arranged in 1882 to have houses built for Natzili and his brother Patos Chiquitos, and Natzili paid a horse for the shingles. Most Apaches were unwilling to give up their tipis, made of ducking furnished by the government. "They declare that they will die if they attempt to live in houses," wrote Cowart. "He would not exchange his canvas lodge for Windsor palace as a residence."[6]

Stottler, beginning in 1895, addressed housing as he had schooling—with a heavy hand. He cut off the supply of canvas, and within

View of Lipan Tipis, 1900. *Ales Hrdlicka, National Anthropological Archives, Smithsonian Institution, NAA INV 02029802*

two years, Apaches were living in forty-five log cabins with cook stoves. (Tipis reappeared by 1911.) He reduced their rations because "[t]he indiscriminate issue of rations and other supplies to the worthy and unworthy alike simply beggars them and makes them feel the lack of any necessity for working for a self-support." He abolished the Court of Indian Offenses and dispensed his own justice.[7]

When he turned his attention to their appearance, he began with the police. Told they had to cut their hair, the police chief and one private refused. He fired them and threatened to fire the rest and cut off their rations.

"God meant it to be long," said Boneski.

"I'll give you a dollar," said the agent.

"I'll do it for five."

Boneski got his hair cut. Natzili also submitted to a haircut. For Magoosh, it wasn't an issue—he was bald. Stottler then sent the police to bring in every male Apache who had ever been to school and forced them to cut their hair and wear a hat, coat, vest, shirt, pants and shoes. In three weeks, with force and the guardhouse, he had the rest.[8]

Stottler could also be a benevolent dictator. He arranged for seventy-five impoverished single women and their children to garden on twenty acres, hired Apaches to do freighting (Magoosh was hauling freight before this), and ended the pass system around the time Fort Stanton closed in 1896. Apaches were now free to come and go. Finally, he bought and distributed five thousand sheep, believing they would provide a steady income, but only a few became successful sheepmen, including the Lipan descendents Frank Lester and Horace Torres and Natzili's grandson Solon Sombrero.[9]

"The best agent we had was Lieutenant Stottler," said Solon Sombrero. "He got the Indians to build log cabins and gave us wagons, horses, harnesses. We come to have our hair cut and get civilized clothing . . . We say Lieutenant Stottler was good because he was honest. He was a single man and was on the job. He got people to make gardens and taught them much . . . First I live in a tipi, then a shack, and then I built a good house. I set trees in 1912 and again in 1937. It is a little more than 7,000 feet in altitude here [Elk Springs] where I live."[10]

◄ ►

The latter 1890s were a time of loss for Natzili. Stottler acknowledged no chiefs or head men, nor did he recognize any tribal title to the land. His successor cut off rations, and the Apaches struggled to find enough to eat. In 1897 Natzili's son, One Eye, died after a horse fell with him. He had become known as Sombrero, for the time he killed a rich Mexican during a raid and returned home with the man's fancy saddle and bridle and a hat, festooned with four pounds of silver. He was buried with the hat and saddle, but before he died he gave Solon, then about twelve, the spurs and belt.[11]

Natzili's death in 1898 is something of a mystery. Agency records reveal no cause, but one of Opler's oral history accounts describes Natzili getting sick on mesquite gravy. Percy Big Mouth told historian Eve Ball that he choked to death, and she noted on the transcript, "It is said also that he froze." The census listed the chief's age as sixty-four, but he was probably older.[12]

Natzili, who brought his Gulgahende in from the plains and became chief of all the Apaches on the reservation, guided his people into a new life as he attempted to balance tradition with change. He led by example, becoming the first to live in a house and send his children to school, but he was also instrumental in maintaining culture and tradition, with an important role in the four-day girls' puberty ceremonies, as a peyote chief, and as a teacher. "[H]e practiced his peyote power. He used it toward the white man to make friends instead of trouble and used it for rain and to bring good summer weather, for he loved to see many fruits growing. He was the one to go after the peyote or told others where it grew," said Charlie Smith.

"Natzili was really a good leader in all things. He showed us how to hunt, to ride horses, to make saddles, bows and arrows, ropes, quirts, head bonnets, shields, and many other things; and in the making he showed us what to use, the stoutest things that would last a long time, buckskin and sinews. He also told stories . . . and we sat there days and nights listening, and sometimes we'd get sleepy. A head would begin to go forward. A boy would be asleep. Rap, he'd get it on the head and that head would come up again. He tapped me on the head many times . . .

"'My children and my relatives, there are many things I'd like to say to you. But we never come together as in the old days, so to the few who come to me I like to tell all I have learned and can still remember. I'm always glad to let you know.'"[13]

◄ ►

Venego was a head man. His father was a No Water Lipan and his mother, a Big Water Lipan. After he turned back from the Lipan exodus

Lucy Smith. *Photo by Daniel Castro Romero, Jr.*

to Mescalero in the early 1880s to return to his people, the Mexican army chased them from place to place and finally captured and enslaved them.

"There's a story about Philemon[14] Venego [Venego's son]. They put him to work in a field chopping weeds. He was chopping weeds in one direction and met his brother chopping weeds in another direction. They didn't see each other again," said Meredith Magoosh Begay.[15]

"They were at peace, moving around, but the government of Mexico, the Mexican soldiers were hunting down the Apaches," said Lucy Smith. "Somewhere in Mexico they were all captured. What they had, they burned all their stuff up. They took away their feathers and shell [used for the girls' puberty ceremonies] and burned them. They didn't carry anything with them."

Her father, Pedro Méndez, and his older brother Julio were boys when they were captured. After that they were placed with wealthy Mexicans to do cooking, washing, and field work. "They were loaned out to big, big rancheros, but they took off from them. The Lipans in Mexico escaped from the soldiers. The soldiers chased them all over. They were chased on both sides of the border. The Texas militia chased them. They were really in a predicament. They had no safe haven."[16]

Chivato and Sanavoy told Comanche Chief Quannah Parker they had relatives who were still in Mexico, and in 1902 Parker informed agent James Carroll that there were 107 Apaches living in the mountains in Mexico. Carroll assumed they were Mescalero remnants of Victorio's band and sent three Apaches to Mexico, who found thirty-seven people—Venego's Lipans—living in a narrow canyon in the Santa Rosa Mountains about twenty miles east of Zaragosa.

"The Indians referred to are . . . full-blooded Mescalero and Lippans, and the sons, daughters, brothers and sisters of those at this agency, and all are anxious to join their tribe. Reports are that there are about 40 of them, 14 being of school age. They have no land and no school," wrote Carroll. "They were in wretched circumstances, having to depend almost entirely on game and herbs and the sale of curios. They were anxious to remove to this reservation and requested their friends to convey such a message to this office."[17]

Carroll recommended their return, not only for the sake of unity and aid but because disease was decimating the reservation Apaches. "Tuberculosis, the dread enemy of the human race, has found its way to the mountain home of this little tribe and is rapidly depleting its ranks," he wrote. In 1903, the Office of Indian Affairs approved their removal and detailed Charles H. Dickson as a special representative to negotiate their release.[18]

Father Migeon and one Apache (probably Magoosh) went to Governor Terrazas, who received them courteously, and asked that the Lipans be allowed to come to Mescalero. Terrazas said they could leave if they wished. Father Migeon found Venego and his people held in an unsheltered corral at the outskirts of Ciudad Chihuahua. The Mexicans had burned their belongings and threw them ears of corn, as if they were cattle. With money from Carroll the priest chartered a car from Southern Pacific and bought food and clothing. On June 1, 1904 they arrived in Tularosa.

Philemon Venego, who was nine or ten years old, recalls getting off the train to find Apaches with wagons meeting them at the station. "We did not recognize our relatives, but they made themselves known to us. How glad our people were to see each other! Men embraced with tears streaming down their faces."[19] They had been separated for more than twenty-five years.

"Their arrival at the agency, the reuniting of families, the realization that many loved ones had gone to their last reward, the cries of joy commingled with wails of anguish, the tears, the shrieks, the groans—what tongue can tell, what pen describe, what brush portray the pathos of that scene!" wrote Carroll.

"When we got to Mescalero, the Nantan, Mr. Carroll, through his interpreter, José Carillo, made a talk to us," said Philemon Venego. "He told us that if we would keep the peace and be good Indians, that we were to have the privileges of the other Apaches already there . . . If we had grievances we were to report them first to Chief Magoosh and then to him. As Magoosh had promised, Mr. Carroll kept his word to the Lipans." Carroll and the resident Lipans soon noticed that the new arrivals were almost more Mexican than Indian, having acquired Mexican names, habits, language, dress and lifestyle. And they were industrious. Carroll believed they would be a good influence.[20]

Venego's people improved their lot, but not by much. School attendance was one hundred percent, Carroll wrote, not due to "a thirst for knowledge, but rather to a longing for something to eat and wear. The Indians have been on a starvation basis for years." The school's ramshackle facilities, subsequently condemned and torn down, were blamed for the deaths of twelve boys. White doctors and medicine men were powerless to check the spread of tuberculosis, and the agent feared that "historians may begin to record the final chapter of this division of the Apache nation." This is probably how Magoosh lost both of his wives within a week of one another in 1907.[21]

Pedro Méndez was about twenty when he came to Mescalero, and his mother, Juana Méndez, was about fifty. With them were Pedro's brother Julio, his Mescalero wife Delia, and their two little boys. They had visited Mescalero in the past and got along well with the people. Pedro, a relative of Chivato's, took his family to live in Oklahoma for a time. "When he came back, he lost his wife, and her family asked him to marry my mother [Jeanette, the daughter of Cariso Gallerito] to take her place," said Lucy Smith. "That's how the Apaches do. Gave her back to replace his wife, Apache way. Those times, they were strict about their Indian ways."[22]

Two of the Lipan newcomers married Geronimo's son and daughter. Around 1906, Juan Villa (whose name the agent misspelled as "Via") married Lenna, daughter of Geronimo and his Mescalero wife Ihtedda. Robert Geronimo, born after her return, married Ester Rodríguez in 1917. They had five children; when she succumbed to tuberculosis, her husband married her younger sister, Juanita.[23]

Conditions on the reservation deteriorated. Disastrous droughts in 1904 and 1910 dried up springs and painted grazing lands brown, and the courts restricted tribal use of the Tularosa River. As stubborn blue skies withheld their rains, the oat crop failed, and thousands of trees died. On March 2, 1909, outgoing President Theodore Roosevelt ordered 350,000 acres of timber on the reservation included in the new Alamo National Forest, to be supervised by the United States Forest Service.[24] Forest Service employees who came to the reservation were so arrogant the Apaches asked Carroll for help. He took the chiefs—Peso, Sans Peur and Magoosh—to Washington, D.C., a trip that included a stop in Chicago to buy clothing at Marshall Field. None had been in an elevator before, and when it began to move, Carroll noticed a fleeting look of fear on Magoosh's face before the chief regained his composure.

"Magoosh got a long-tailed coat and a derby hat, and the Indians called him Grasshopper, he looked so funny," recalled May Peso Second. During a boat trip Magoosh became seasick. "The Apaches thought he was sick from eating fish. [Lipans ate fish, but Mescaleros didn't.] He didn't want to get back on the boat, but he did." The three chiefs met with President William Howard Taft. On February 17, 1912, he revoked Roosevelt's executive order.[25]

Magoosh, who had raided Texas ranches for decades and wounded General Hugh L. Scott in battle, was a good neighbor to nearby white homesteaders. "Magoosh was my friend and neighbor for seven years. He was an intelligent man with a well-shaped head, piercing black eyes, good features, and with a wonderful memory and a gift for narrative and description in a mixture of Spanish, English and sign language," wrote Fred M. Griffin, Jr.

Griffin's father, a freighter and surveyor, lived in Elk Canyon on the edge of the reservation, where he got to know Magoosh. In December 1914, the senior Griffin set out to pick up a load of Christmas merchandise in Cloudcroft for the store at Elk, but was caught in a big storm. Apaches advised him to turn back and take refuge in an abandoned sawmill, which still had a stove and dry wood. Griffin turned around and headed back, but before he reached the sawmill he dozed off in the wagon, probably from hypothermia.

"Two Apache women found him and got him into the tipi, fed him coffee and jerked beef, rolled out his bedroll and told him to crawl in," Griffin Jr. recalled. The freighter spent the night in Sam Chino's camp and then went to Elk Springs and stayed in Magoosh's camp. By that time, Magoosh was married to Jakadecho, the widow of La Paz. The next day Griffin made it to Cloudcroft and returned safely. "With the help of the Indians, Santa Claus made his rounds on schedule."[26]

In 1915 pneumonia took Chief Magoosh in his cabin at the age of ninety-four. (The agent estimated his age at seventy-three.) Magoosh had witnessed the fall of the Alamo, harried three governments, outmaneuvered the Texas Rangers, led his people hundreds of miles through hostile country to safety on the reservation, and scouted against Geronimo. He never relinquished his traditional beliefs, and, to the end, he regarded San Antonio, his birthplace, as home. "Magoosh was a great chief," said Venego.[27]

CHAPTER

Lipan Diaspora

The Lipans, they were all scattered up. People were chasing them round and round. They were in different groups.

— Lucy Smith[1]

The Lipans at White Houses (San Antonio) liked it, but then they went to Many Houses (Zaragosa)[2] and made that their country. For a long time Many Houses was their country. Very long ago, before Many Houses, when no one was there, it was their country. Then the people moved this way to the mountains, and they went back and forth between Mescalero and Lipan country. And then they moved to Black Rock (Piedras Negras) and made that their country, along with Many Houses and other places in Mexico.

An old Lipan woman told her story to a younger woman, Augustina Zuazua, who wrote it down. The original lyrical account of Lipan migration, paraphrased here, describes the Lipans' wanderings and how the Mexicans helped them when they were poor. Lipans wove baskets[3] and used them to gather fruit and ripened yucca with its leaves. "Many Houses was our country, and we liked it there, but we came to Mescalero. Some here are our relatives, they told us . . . Thirty-one years have passed here since we arrived. We are Lipans. We are few. There remain nowhere any Lipan."[4]

The elder would have been cheered to learn that remnants of the tribe survived in Oklahoma, Louisiana, Mexico, and Texas.

FORT GRIFFIN

The government told Irvine to prepare his 115 wards for removal. In February 1880 Lieutenant R. N. Getty took three Tonkawas and two Lipans[5] to look over the Nez Percé and Ponca reservations in Indian Territory. After riding through a freezing storm, they learned that many of the Nez Percés who previously lived there had died of pneumonia, which extinguished any inclination to move. The Indian Commission pressed them to leave, but the tribes "still adhere to their determination to remain in Texas," reported the *Fort Griffin Echo.*[6]

Most frontier towns loathed their Indian neighbors, but the town of Fort Griffin instead took up their cause. In early 1881, with the fort scheduled to close, citizens circulated a strongly worded memorial to the Legislature. The scouts' "sacrifice in fighting for whites" had earned them the hatred of other tribes, and they were now further reduced by exposure and war. They asked the state government to buy at least three thousand acres, appoint an agent, build comfortable quarters, buy farm implements, and provide food and clothing for two years. "This is a step that should have been taken long ago," the petition stated. The newspaper demanded to know what would become of them. "These Indians are orderly and peaceable, always have been friendly toward the whites, always ready and willing to join and assist the military authorities in expeditions against hostile Indians, thereby incurring the deadly enmity of hostile tribes."[7]

After their final enlistments, the Tonkawa and Lipan scouts returned to Fort Griffin in 1881 and 1882. They helped a sheriff's posse now and then but had no other work, and drought destroyed their crops. Still, they hung on.[8] In 1884 anthropologist Albert Gatschet found seventy-eight Tonkawas living just south of the fort and nineteen Lipans just north, in brush wickiups, oilcloth tents or some combination of the two. The oblong shelters held beds, coffee mills, chickens, dogs, turkeys, barrels, bags, water casks, metates, trunks, women nursing babies, guns, pans, saucers, cups, and blankets. They ate twice a day, early in the morning and late in the evening.[9]

On October 22, 1884, the Tonkawas and Lipans left Texas. In covered wagons or on horseback, they followed agent Isaac Taylor to Cisco City, Texas, where a Lipan baby was born and named Railroad Cisco. After selling many of their horses, they traveled by rail to the Sac and Fox Agency near Stroud, Oklahoma. The destitute group wintered there, losing most of their remaining horses because there was no pasture.

The following spring, another jarring wagon ride brought them one hundred miles to the Iowa Reserve. Neither the Iowas nor the Tonkawas and Lipans accepted this arrangement, and the agent moved them to the just-vacated Nez Percé reservation. Traveling in the rain, they forded swollen rivers and sometimes sank axle deep in the mud. Ninety-two exhausted people reached the Oakland Agency on June 30, 1885. For the Tonkawas, this miserable journey was their "Trail of Tears." They commemorate it every year with a pow-wow.[10]

Deer and antelope were plentiful in their new home. Rather than live in the Nez Percés' houses, the Tonkawas and Lipans crouched near the agency in their dilapidated tents and wickiups—to receive rations, an agent assumed, but the Lipans would have feared spirits of the dead lurking in the abandoned houses. In 1886 the able-bodied people, with four old horses, several plows and some hoes, farmed thirty-five acres. G. C. Brewer, who became agent in early 1890, found them impoverished and starving and helped them plant 160 acres of wheat.

Elsie Buffalo, a Lipan, stood out in the memory of the agent's daughter Bertha. Captured in a battle between the Cheyennes and Tonkawas, Elsie was dragged for days by her thumbs, which were tied with a rope; her thumbs were bent and twisted the rest of her life. Elsie Buffalo buried her daughter the traditional way by strangling a horse at the grave site so it would go to the next life unblemished. After that, Brewer forbade the practice. Around 1892, disease did to the valiant Lipan scout sergeant Johnson what bullets couldn't during some of the army's most brutal campaigns.

Under the Dawes Act and an agreement made in October 1891, the Tonkawas (from the beginning, Lipans were counted as Tonkawas) ceded their 90,760-acre reservation to the government for $30,600. The surviving seventy-three people received allotments totaling 11,273 acres, and the rest was opened to white settlement in 1893. The Tonkawas had money for a while but soon spent it all. Tuberculosis and other diseases claimed many lives. By 1908 only forty-eight people survived. The Tonkawa Indian Agency at Oakland closed around 1910. Today the tribal government is headquartered at Tonkawa, Oklahoma. Lipan descendents among the Tonkawas still visit relatives at the Mescalero Reservation.[11]

NAISHAN

Lipans lived with the Naishans (Kiowa Apaches) off and on for decades before the reservation period. In 1869 Magoosh came with three hundred people, and in 1874 Lipans numbered one hundred-eighty.[12] The Naishans settled between forts Cobb and Sill and became farmers. Their population plummeted from 325 in 1891 to 150 in 1901. That year the government dissolved their reservation, gave the survivors 160-acre allotments, and opened the remaining lands to white settlement. The town of Apache became the tribe's community center. Despite additional allotments granted to tribal members, few could support themselves by farming alone. Some leased their unused lands to non-Indians, and many sold their allotments. In 1972 they adopted a constitution and became the Apache Tribe of Oklahoma.[13] They too have relatives at Mescalero.[14]

KESETTA/CASITA

In September 1877, Bullis's troops attacked a Lipan camp west of Zaragosa and captured Ramon Castro's daughter and son. Their mother died that day after trying to kill the girl with a stone "to keep the white men from getting me in the fight." She wore scars on her forehead and shoulder all her life. The girl was about ten, her brother a few years younger. A Fourth Cavalry soldier, Charles Smith, and his wife Mollie took them in, and for three years they traveled with the Fourth, becoming known as Kesetta and Jack; they called Mollie Smith "Mama."

On Mackenzie's orders, the children were sent to Carlisle Indian School to join Captain Richard Pratt's experiment in assimilation, an industrial boarding school in Carlisle, Pennsylvania. The object was to "civilize" Indian children by removing them from their families and tribal influence and teaching them to be productive citizens. More than 12,000 Indian children from all over the United States—but only three Lipans—would be enrolled between 1879 and 1918.

Arriving in March 1880, they were first called Kesetta and Jack Lipan. Because they were sent from Fort Hays, the school listed Kansas as their birthplace. Later on, Kesetta was called Kesetta Roosevelt. (Theodore Roosevelt was making a name for himself in neighboring New York.) They would have been forbidden to speak Apache, although after four years with the army, they may have forgotten their native tongue.[15]

After two years, Kesetta was sent to live with families in the region as part of the school's "outing" system, but she returned periodically. "Kesetta Roosevelt is with us again," reported the school newspaper. "She staid at her place nearly three years, and SOME of the time she did well." Following a series of jobs in Pennsylvania, New Jersey, Delaware and Maryland, she returned to Carlisle in October 1902 three months pregnant.

As a chief's daughter, Kesetta would have commanded respect, and many young men would have asked to marry her. Instead, her life was a series of stints as a domestic, interspersed with returns to the school, her only anchor. She became Carlisle's longest tenured student—twenty-three years. Kesetta had her baby May 22, 1903, in the Quakers' Rosine Home in Philadelphia. The white man who fathered her child never acknowledged him, and he was never known to Carlisle authorities. She found work in Lahaska, north of Philadelphia, and moved there with her son, Richard. In winter 1906, Kesetta died of tuberculosis. She was about forty.[16]

Kesetta and Jack, 1879–1880. *John N. Choate, photographer. Cumberland Historical Society, Carlisle, Pennsylvania*

Her brother's short life was somewhat better. Curiously, Mackenzie took an interest in the boy and wrote him letters until 1883, when the broken down Indian fighter entered an insane asylum, which "deprives Jack of his friend and guardian," said a school publication. At some point, Jack seriously injured his right index finger while making and using bows and arrows with his friends, and the school doctor had to amputate.

In 1884 Pratt reported to the Commissioner of Indian Affairs that Kesetta and Jack were "fairly well grown. They are entirely alienated

Richard Kesetta (Kaseeta), age 4, 1907. *Cumberland County Historical Society, Carlisle, Pennsylvania*

from their people, and it would be next to impossible to discover their friends or relatives, as they live in old Mexico. I am able to provide permanent homes for both of them." Pratt's statement was half true. Sarah Mather, a teacher who helped Pratt establish Carlisle, adopted Jack. He became Jack Mather and joined her in St. Augustine, Florida. Jack adjusted reasonably well, working in a hotel and then becoming a carpenter's apprentice. In 1888, diagnosed with tuberculosis, Jack returned to Carlisle and spent two weeks in the school's hospital. On February 5 he died at age nineteen and was buried in the school cemetery as "Jack Martha."[17]

Baby Richard's life was a far cry from his mother's. After Kesetta's death, the toddler was returned to the Rosine Home and then to Carlisle. On August 13, 1907, he was enrolled as Richard Roosevelt, a Lipan, but later called Richard Kasetta or various other misspelled versions of his mother's name. The little boy was popular with the school's older girls.

Five months later, he went to live with Martha Sharp and her daughter and son-in-law, Mary and Jack Culbertson, a prominent family in town. Richard had his own room and attended public school but was Carlisle's mascot. He knew the great athlete Jim Thorpe well enough to call him Uncle Jim; Thorpe carried Richard around on his shoulders. Carlisle residents remembered Richard skating on the pond on Saturdays.

When he was fourteen, Richard worked for a Philadelphia family as his outing experience and returned after a year with a recommendation that he receive strict military discipline. After the school closed in 1918, Richard returned to Martha Sharp's custody and lived out his life in the Culbertsons' home. When they died, he inherited a large tract of land on the boundaries of the school and married a local woman, Helen Rice. He died in 1970. His widow said he refused to talk about the school. Late in his life, Richard changed the spelling of his name to Kaseeta.[18] It's probably the way he heard his mother pronounce her name, which indicates her Spanish name was Casita (Little House).

CHOCTAW-APACHE TRIBE OF LOUISIANA

In 1716, the Spanish established a mission for the Adaes Indians fifteen miles from Natchitoches and added a military post in 1721. Spanish colonists moved to the area, and the Adaes were joined by Lipan captives. When Spanish authorities ordered settlers to leave Los Adaes in 1773 and move to Bexar, Antonio Gil Ybarbo kept his large ranch there, and some family members remained.

Ybarbo became justicia mayor of Bucareli, which was two leagues from the main village of the Bidais people, the Lipans' close allies and trading partners. Ybarbo apparently traded with the French and was accused of trading with Indians (probably Lipans) for mules and horses stolen from San Sabá, Béxar and Bahía. At Los Adaes, the Adaes and Lipans intermarried with the Ybarbos, and around 1789 they were joined by Apaches from the San Antonio missions. Dozens of Ybarbos continued to live near Los Adaes. An 1805 census counted 28 households totaling 178 people, including descendents of the two tribes. The same year, United States Indian agent John Sibley reported numerous "Cancee" (Lipans) in Louisiana.[19]

Choctaws, who originally lived on the Mississippi, began moving in at the turn of the nineteenth century, and many joined the Adaes and Lipans. Sibley moved more Choctaws to the area in the early 1820s. By 1850 the families were living on the eastern bank of the Sabine River, where they remain. Today the Choctaw-Apache Tribe of Ebarb, Louisiana, is second largest of the eight, state-recognized Native groups in Louisiana. In 2009 about 3,000 people were eligible for membership in the tribe—2,300 in the Ebarb area and another 700 elsewhere in Louisiana. Past census records have been inaccurate. "They told [census takers] whatever they wanted to so that they could stay on their homeland and not go to a reservation," said tribal member Jason Rivers in 2008. "It's time to tell people who we are."[20]

MEXICO

Many Lipans stayed in Mexico. The woman captured in the last raid in Texas said in April 1881 that several hundred Lipans were still living in the Sierra Carmen, San Carlos and other Lipan haunts, and two Lipan scouts at Fort Griffin said two hundred of their people remained in the Santa Rosa Mountains.[21] Lipans who came in 1904 mentioned relatives left behind, and Lipan descendants have encountered Apaches in places the Lipans once lived.

"I understand there's a band of Lipans at Zaragosa," said Meredith Magoosh Begay. "There's a village on the Rio Grande where they still live. My great-grandfather, some of his relatives are still on the other side. They used to say there were relatives in Eagle Pass. The people in Mexico are very evasive about being an Indian. They don't want to identify themselves. The government retaliates against them. They're leery of strangers."[22]

CHAPTER 38

We, the Apache Tribe

The whole state of Texas is the Lipan Nation. We had a lot of people then. The army kept killing them. Disease kept killing them.

— Meredith Magoosh Begay[1]

A s schools improved and education became a useful tool in the Apaches' entry to modern life, students wanted to attend school, and the community at Elk Canyon got its own day school. An educated younger generation, impatient for modern governance, organized a Business Committee in 1918 with representation by Mescaleros, Lipans and Chiricahuas; its president became the tribe's leader.[2] "[W]e finally got rid of the chiefs, who were getting old and feeble . . . We needed leaders, and the young educated people thought we should have a business committee," said Solon Sombrero. The surviving chiefs approved.[3]

The Business Committee wasn't immediately effective because the agent's power was undiminished. After logging began on Elk and Silver creeks in 1923, bringing new revenues to the reservation, the committee struggled to gain control of reservation resources, but income from timber sales and grazing still funneled through the government.

In 1934 the Wheeler-Howard (Indian Reorganization) Act gave tribes the right to organize and adopt a constitution and bylaws. Mescalero's residents voted that year to accept the act and two years later adopted a constitution and federal charter that made the ten-person

Business Committee the official governing body. The new tribal constitution began: "We, the Apache Tribe of the Mescalero Reservation," but the inclusive wording masked divisions.

"[N]ot one but three distinct tribes of Apache [are] represented on the Mescalero reservation, and . . . there was, too often, no love lost between the members of these ethnic groups," wrote Morris Opler in 1936. "The truth is that there is just enough similarity between Apache tribes so that the differences stand out like sore thumbs in the native mind." They didn't expect white people to understand their customs, but differences in beliefs with fellow Apaches weighed heavily.[4]

Time and intermarriage would melt those barriers. "My grandfather [Willie Magoosh] talked to me in Lipan, my grandmother [Hallie Magoosh] talked to me in Mescalero, and my other grandparents spoke Chiricahua. I had to be Apache trilingual," said Meredith Magoosh Begay with a chuckle.[5]

◄►

The new tribal administration, led by Victor Dolan (his maternal grandfather was Blanco, a Lipan, and his paternal grandfather was Chief Plata, a Llanero), borrowed from a new federal revolving loan fund to build homes, barns and poultry houses and buy implements and livestock. A Cattle Growers' Association managed reservation stock for new owners. Mescalero cattlemen terminated range leases to outsiders and began to graze their own cattle. The agency cut timber, sawed it and built four-room houses. By 1942 every family had a house.[6]

During World War II, many young Apaches served in the military; others found wartime employment off the reservation and lived for the first time in towns and cities. Richard Magoosh, grandson of the chief, learned welding at Holloman Air Force Base in nearby Alamogordo and later worked at Kelly Air Force Base in San Antonio. When the war boom ended, these young people returned to the reservation with new attitudes. Solon Sombrero, president of the Business Committee in 1943 and 1944, and Richard Magoosh, president in 1952, helped the people enter a new era.[7]

◄►

With the Indian Claims Commission Act of 1946, tribes could sue for any wrong or the taking of their land by the United States. On February 3, 1948, the Apache Nation (Lipans, represented by Pedro Méndez and Philemon Venego, and Mescaleros, represented by Solon Sombrero, Fred Pellman, Eric Tortilla and Victor Dolan) filed a claim saying they had aboriginal title to a vast area in Texas, New Mexico, Arizona and portions of adjoining states. Their attorney was Abe Weissbrodt, whose firm was one of the best Indian claims firms in Washington, D.C.[8]

Cloaked in noble sentiment, the claims commission was actually one facet of a larger scheme to terminate tribes: The government intended to compensate Indian people for lands taken and then close their reservations. The melting pot would complete the process, as liberated Indian people took their places in American society. The government gained clear title at bargain prices. In its thirty-year existence, the commission settled 484 claims for five cents to three dollars an acre. And it took decades to achieve "justice," as cases piled up in a bottleneck created by the commission's cumbersome procedures and understaffing and turnover in the Justice Department.[9]

During an early hearing, various Apache spokesmen tried to explain the different groups and their territories to commissioners, who preferred to pigeonhole bands into one convenient category. Asked if they were Mescaleros, Solon Sombrero deftly parried: "They are Apaches and talked the same language." San Juan led a group that lived near El Paso and around the Organ Mountains in southern New Mexico, he said; Natzili's group lived in the Guadalupe Mountains but traveled to the Texas panhandle and Amarillo for buffalo hunts and lived from there to Lipan country around San Antonio. "One band is up there [near the Jicarillas] sort of hold that country." He didn't know the band's name (possibly the Lipiyans), but they got their tent poles from the Canadian River. Asked if those people were Mescaleros, he said "Mescalero" was a name given to them by the Spanish, "only these people are Apaches, are in different bands, still one group." Apaches were living all over this country, he said.

Percy Big Mouth and Antonio Apache both said their mothers were Lipans who lived around San Antonio before moving to Mexico. "Mescaleros lived beyond the Pecos River clear up to the place they call San Angelo where they mixed with the Lipans," said Percy Big Mouth.[10]

◄►

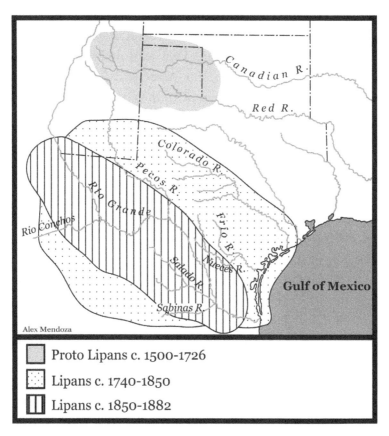

Map 11 Lipan Territories

While the claims process wore on, Truman's Indian Affairs Commissioner inaugurated a program to relocate reservation residents in major cities where they could find jobs. With unemployment approaching 80 percent on the Mescalero reservation, a number of families signed on and were sent to Los Angeles and San Francisco. They all came back.[11]

"My folks went on a BIA relocation program" in 1954, said Meredith Magoosh Begay. "Dad [Richard Magoosh] worked in a steel mill. We stayed three years and then returned . . . There were ten Mescalero families there, on the East Bay and San José. We gave a lot of things away when we moved home because we couldn't take them on the bus.

"The BIA promised a job to each family to get everyone to move to the big city. These people would report to the BIA. The first batch, they were successful. The second group and after got only temporary jobs. There were strikes and layoffs. They were no better off in the big city than they were on the reservation. Some of the younger ones were able to melt in. Others came home when they had the money to come back. I met Sioux people who were disappointed. They were trying to fix their cars to get back to South Dakota."[12]

◄►

In Texas during the early 1950s, many Lipans and Kickapoos got work building International Falcon Reservoir in former Lipan country on the Rio Grande, but during the summer of 1956, jobs were scarce. As the BIA was relocating reservation families to California, Modesto Castro decided to relocate his family to California in search of work. It meant dividing the family for the first time in decades, a heart-wrenching decision.[13]

Some of Chief John Castro's Lipans had quietly joined Mexican villages and lived as Mexicans. Gradually, many returned to Texas and settled in places they once called home—San Angelo, San Antonio, and Corpus Christi, among others. Valentina Castro Sambrano remembers her people talking about Cerralvo and Valle Hermosa in Mexico, "but many moved to Beeville, McAllen and Raymondville, Texas to live in the old places, I am told." In the Beeville area, prominent cattleman Ed Lasater befriended Lipans and gave them work on his Falfurrias Ranch.[14]

John Castro and his surviving family members settled nearby at a place where the family had lived and planted corn during the tribe's better days. His son Calixtro homesteaded land in McAllen, south of Falfurrias, and hunted in the oak belt near Falfurrias; he served as a scout in 1895 for the Texas Rangers and was also a sheriff. John Castro died on the family ranch in 1887, as did Calixtro in 1925. Calixtro's son Modesto Gonzalez Castro was born there in 1909. Calixtro once told Modesto in the presence of his young cousin Santiago Castro Castro, "'Remember the Ndé ways and show your children the Ndé ways and never forget. Never forget.'" Said Santiago, "I was scared when he said this to Modesto because he said it with much meaning and heart."[15]

"Before the peyote ceremony began, Modesto asked the family members to help him move, and instantly there was the cry of broken hearts I wish never to hear again from anyone," said his cousin Frank Vásquez Castro. "It was like one of our family members had died. It was very serious . . . I remember that the rest of the evening many prayers went to [Modesto] to change his mind about moving."[16]

◄►

In the late 1950s, President Eisenhower reshuffled the Indian Claims Commission, and the pace improved. On May 25, 1959, the Apache Tribe of the Mescalero Reservation, on behalf of Lipans and Mescaleros, filed an amended petition alleging loss of aboriginal lands in south and west Texas and claimed more than 60 million acres—all the land south and west of the Colorado River to the Rio Grande and the Texas-New Mexico border.

In August 1965, the commission dismissed the claims, saying the Republic of Texas never recognized any aboriginal rights to land. The Lipans appealed, and in 1967 the Court of Claims reversed the commission's decision, sending the case back to the commission with instructions to reconsider; the Apaches only had to prove their ancestors occupied the lands and were chased off by American troops around 1859.[17]

It was apparent to Weissbrodt that oral histories told by old men carried little weight with the commission; he decided the tribes needed expert witnesses and engaged anthropologist Morris Opler, who had written a great deal about Apaches during a long, distinguished career. The government chose Kenneth F. Neighbours, college professor and nephew of agent Robert Neighbors.[18] Opler considered Neighbours well informed about Indian affairs in Texas during the statehood period. "We shall have to know our stuff to cope with this fellow," he told Weissbrodt.

Opler argued that the Lipans and Mescaleros owned sixty million acres of Texas land until February 1, 1881, when the United States Army drove them from their land and extinguished their titles. Neighbours continued to argue that Texas granted them no such ownership. Both were taking liberties with the historical record. Opler well knew that many Lipans were in Mexico by the 1850s while others hugged the frontier borders to the west and that Texans, Texas rangers, and the army pushed them out. Neighbours well knew that Texas had acknowledged the Lipans' right to live there through treaties, policy and employment, and it benefited from their presence. Neighbours also knew that his revered uncle failed to establish reservations for the Lipans and Mescaleros and that the army declared all Indians not living on reservations to be hostile, which meant they had no place to live.

As the case dragged on, Weissbrodt grew pessimistic. "There are many new judges on the court of claims," he wrote Opler in 1973. "The old court was generally pro-Indian. It is not hard to detect an anti-Indian bias among some of the new judges. The outlook is most disturbing."

The commission rendered a new decision on March 14, 1975. Commissioner Brantley Blue, a member of the Lumbee Tribe who was consistently pro-Indian, wrote the opinion. The Apaches had a claim, he wrote, "but not to the extent as contended." The commission concluded that by 1854 the Lipans were fragmented; Blue cited as evidence an erroneous agent's report based on a visit to one camp even though contemporary reports demonstrated a far larger, cohesive group.

"Reports of Lipan activity in the Lipan claimed area following their exodus in 1854 to Mexico point to sporadic and inconsequential raiding activity along the Rio Grande River, mostly in the company of other renegade Indians from Mexico. Contrary to the plaintiff's contentions, we do not find these Lipan raids to reflect a serious effort to defend or regain lost tribal lands in Texas." This conclusion ignored persistent raids on former Lipan country that prompted petitions from settlers, diplomatic efforts, and counterattacks by the army. The Apaches certainly believed they were at war.

Equally in error is this conclusion: "For all intents and purposes, the Lipans had ceased to exist as a tribe sometime after 1854, having been compelled by circumstances beyond their control to remove themselves south of the border. Their subsequent history is simply one of further fragmentation and diminishing numbers."

The commission did grasp one key point: Under the 1846 peace treaty, the United States assumed the duty to protect Texas Indians and "did not fulfill its role . . . [T]he aboriginal rights of these Texas Indians to Texas lands were effectively extinguished by the United States. The fact that the Lipans fled to Mexico in 1854 and 1855 does not change their circumstances or alter their situation. The Lipan movement to Mexico could hardly be called a voluntary one . . ."

The commission settled on November 1, 1856, as the date Lipans lost their lands—the mid point between initial Lipan settlement in Mexico in January 1854 and the United States' removal from Texas of all the Texas tribes in August 1859. "It was a disappointing decision: about 10 million acres for Lipans and 6 million for Mescalero . . ." wrote Weissbrodt. He began talking to government lawyers about a settlement. In 1976 the commission awarded five million dollars to the Lipans—about fifty cents an acre—and an equal amount to the Mescaleros for lands lost in Texas. On December 6, 1975, sixty-one Lipan descendents unanimously approved the settlement; Mescalero descendents did the same.

Opler was philosophical: "The Lipan-Mescalero verdict is not too bad considering all circumstances. The heavy involvement of the State of Texas in the Apache removal probably makes U.S. responsibility seem less direct. The fact that American expansion pushed the Comanche westward and southwestward into Apache territory in the historic period probably raised doubts about exclusive Apache occupation of some areas. The state of U.S. government finances and the small size of the tribes involved may be psychological factors operating against any very large awards."[19]

◄ ►

As reservation Lipans assimilated under the agent's thumb, the Texas Lipans self-imposed their assimilation. Reservation Apaches feared losing their reservation, while the Texas Lipans feared being sent to one—or killed—if they revealed their identities, and so they passed as Mexican-Americans. When soldiers came around, Modesto's mother would say, "Speak English!" "They would beat us for speaking Indian," he said.

Modesto performed the Deer Dance in secret. He started a fire in a drum that would burn all night. "Once started, my grandfather would put his hands on each side of his head and, using four fingers pointing up to look like the antlers of a deer, would use the shadow of the fire to transform his likeness into a deer," recalled Daniel Castro Romero Jr. "Once grandfather had made his fingers look like antlers, he would start to dance around the barrel of fire in a clockwise direction and would turn in all four of the directions while singing. I remember asking my grandfather, 'Why do you cry when singing?' He would say, 'These are the old songs, and I cry for my people.' He always said, 'Soy Indio. Soy Apache.'" Modesto sometimes took the family to visit the Mescalero reservation or to see relatives among the Kickapoos. He died in 1968. To the end of his days, he regretted growing up Mexican-American and not Lipan.[20]

◄ ►

Traditionally, Lipans came together from all points of the compass for yearly buffalo hunts. It was an occasion of feasting, singing and socializing and also a time when the leaders made decisions together. In 1912 the Castro family revived the yearly gathering with a family reunion in Pettus. Descendents and relatives arrived in carriages, set up tents with the openings facing east, and spent the weekend eating, visiting, and singing. John Castro's son Manuel recited the family history. Attendance grew through the years as the family expanded: Calixtro had thirteen children, and so did Modesto. Two events anchored the gatherings—the blessing of the Grandfather Plate, a food offering in memory of those who passed on, and a retelling of the family history.

In 1980 the Castro elders decided to organize formally and try to reunify the Lipans. That year Daniel Castro Romero, Jr. attended the reunion in Fresno, California, with his mother (Modesto's daughter), Santos Peralez Castro. His uncle, Armando Castro Cavazos, blessed the Grandfather Plate. Daniel noticed his mother speaking with the elders, who were looking in his direction. At the end of the day, Armando approached Daniel from behind and tapped him on the shoulder.

"What can I do for you, uncle?"

"Listen."

His mother put her hands on his shoulders and said, "Mijo, you have been chosen to lead this family, and it is time for you to learn our traditional history." Others also came over to tap him on the shoulder. He had seen others similarly designated for duties in the past and knew that to refuse would shame his family.[21] That night, Armando recited the family history, as Daniel took notes on brown paper bags from the lunches—the first time Castro family history had been written. Daniel, the first member of the family with graduate degrees, listened and took notes for hours, finally asking, "Why me?"

"Because we just know—among our people, we just know," said Armando. "My time is short on this world, but I have faith that you will accomplish much for our people. Always remember the people." Three months later, Armando died.

"Their charge was, make us a tribe again. My uncle said, 'We know who we are, but make sure the government knows who we are.'"[22]

Daniel began the long process of gathering and contacting descendents scattered all over the country. He also posted his bibliography on a Lipan website—the modern equivalent of lining up stones for a historian to follow. The Lipan Apache Band of Texas incorporated in 1998 with Daniel as its General Council Chairman. On September 17, 2000, the Choctaw-Apache Community of Ebarb, Inc., proclaimed a shared heritage, culture and kinship with the Lipan Apache Band of Texas.

In 2007 the band members parted ways. The lawsuit involved is an artifact of modern times; historically bands divided simply by riding in different directions. The second group, the Lipan Apache Tribe of Texas, Inc., didn't respond to my requests for interviews. I wish them all well. Both groups are seeking federal recognition and both offer instruction and cultural events intended to help members reclaim their identities as Lipans. After years of hiding, physically and culturally, they're determined to understand what it means to be Lipan. Daniel's goal in seeking recognition is simple: "We want our name back."

Meredith Magoosh Begay, 1937–2006

Meredith Magoosh Begay.
Photo by Daniel Castro Romero, Jr.

When the great-granddaughter of Chief Magoosh died on April 28, 2006, her funeral drew hundreds of people and multiple groups of singers for a traditional Lipan ceremony. "We live by these songs. We live *for* these songs," said Ted Rodriguez, a fellow Lipan descendent.

They both grew up in Elk Canyon, where the families worked together to harvest wheat and barley. A few years earlier, Rodriguez wanted to introduce a new dance on the reservation as a way to honor war veterans. He went to Mrs. Begay, and she encouraged him to introduce the dance. Many people told stories of an encouraging word or a helping hand. "She was a grand lady," Rodriguez said. "She was a grand, grand lady."

Mrs. Begay touched many lives at Mescalero and beyond. She made cradleboards and placed the babies in them, gave many small children

their first hair cuts, and sponsored thirty-two girls in the puberty ceremony, a defining experience for Apache women. When the tribe
decided to add a culture and language program at the schools, it was
Mrs. Begay who helped develop the curriculum.

Meredith Magoosh Begay attended Elk Canyon Day School through
the eighth grade. After an unhappy experience at Tucson Indian Tribal
School, she transferred to South San Francisco High School when her
family was living in California. In San Francisco, she met a Navajo relo-
catee, Keith Begay, who returned with her to Mescalero after they married, and they had three children: Zachary, Zelda and Sharon.

"I was in that era when there were no scholarships," she said. "I
wanted to be an RN. I sent an application to Good Samaritan in Phoenix. They said I needed three hundred dollars. I used to wait tables at
the Summit [a tribal enterprise] for fifty cents an hour. I took courses—
chemistry, biology. I didn't get to be a nurse."

She became a secretary for the federal Bureau of Indian Affairs and
later attended New Mexico State University. During twenty-three years
with the BIA, she became a social services representative. She never
turned anyone away who needed her help.

For years, nobody owned a car in isolated Elk Canyon, and resi-
dents were glad to see visitors. Members of the Bahá'í faith got to know
Lipans there and brought some children their first birthday cakes. Mrs.
Begay, a traditional Apache, was also a Bahá'í for twenty years.

Mrs. Begay was a leader and bearer of Lipan culture, even as the
outside world assumed Lipans were extinct. Long after linguist Harry
Hoijer declared that "today there are no Lipan speakers," Mrs. Begay
and other elders were speaking—and singing—in Lipan. She also
chaired the 2004 centennial celebration of the arrival of the last Lipans.
The written program of her funeral testified to the great importance of
respect in the Lipan culture. She rests forever in beautiful Elk Canyon,
where her great-grandfather ended his wandering.

❧ Appendices ❧

Eastern Apache bands identified by Hugo Oconór in 1777

Mescaleros—Zetozendé

Faraones—Selcotisanendé

Ranchería of Pasqual—Culcahende

Ranchería of El Ligero—Cachuguindé

Ranchería of Alonso—Yncagendé

Ranchería of Capitan Bigotes—Sigilandé

Natagés—Zetozendé

Source: Cutter, 70–71.

Eastern Apache bands identified by Antonio Cordero in 1796

Faraones—Yntajen-ne

Mescaleros—Sejen-ne

Llaneros—Cuelcajen-ne (also included Lipiyans and Natagés)

Lipans—Lipajen-ne.

Source: Matson and Schroeder, 336.

Lipan Bands* named by Lipan Scouts in 1884:

Tséral tuétaha, "red hair"—below the Nueces River (extinct)

Tchecä, lived on Rio Grande—"Tchá is 'otter' in Lipan"

Kúne tsa, Big Water—lived on the Rio Grande

Kól kahä, "prairie"—west of Fort Griffin (Cúel ca hén ndé)

Tcó kanä, "pulverizing, rubbing"—west of Fort Griffin, west of Rio Grande, probably extinct.

Tséc kecénde, "painted wood"—in Lavon, Mexico.

Tazhä, uplanders—often with Mescaleros. (Upper Lipans)

Tcá cka ozhäye, "little breech clout"—on Pecos River

Tsél tátlidshä, "green mountain"—east of Rio Grande

Ndáwe góhä—west-southwest from Fort Griffin

Sha-á, "north"—on the other side of Dapeshte (Arkansas) River, then at Washita Agency about 300 Lipans

Tsés tsémbai—northwest of Griffin

Tel kóndahä—west, fight all the time

Source: Albert Gatschet, "Lipan, a dialect of the Apache-Tinné Family," 55–56 and "Lipan, of Tinné family, Apache subdivision," 183.

*Gatschet used the word "clans," but Lipans didn't have clans.

Lipan bands identified by Stella La Paz, 1935

Kunitsa or Chishene, "timber people"—lived northeast of the Rio Grande near the Gulf

Tuetenene—a Mescalero-Lipan group

Tuensane, Big Water People—lived southwest of the Rio Grande

Source: Edward Gifford, *Culture Element Distributions: Apache-Pueblo. University of California Anthropological Records*, Vol. 4, 188; Opler Papers, Box 44, Folder 54, Lipan History.

Lipan bands identified by Meredith Magoosh Begay, 2002

Tú é dine ndé—Tough People of the Desert, or No Water People, who lived from present El Paso to Del Rio;

Tú sís ndé—Big Water People, who lived from present Del Rio to Matamoros;

Cúel ca hén ndé—People of the High Grass, a prairie region;

Tas steé be glui ndé—Rock Tied to Head People, who lived between the Big Water and No Water people near present Del Rio and Piedras Negras;

Buií gl un ndé—Many Necklaces People, who once lived near the San Xavier mission; *Zuá Zuá ndé*—People of the Lava Beds, who lived in present southeastern New Mexico.

Source: Meredith Magoosh Begay, 2002 interview with Daniel Castro Romero Jr., in Daniel Castro Romero, Jr. *Cuélcahen Ndé: The Castros of the Lipan Apache Band of Texas.* ed. and trans. Santiago Castro Castro and Valentina Smbrano Rodriguez (San Antonio: Lipan Apache Band of Texas, 2004), 22.

LIPAN CHIEFS	DATES RECORDED
Cabellos Colorados	1734
Boca Comida	1749
Captain Coquin	1749
Pastellan	1750–1758
Chiquito (Tacu, Chico)	1754–1758
Pintas	1754
El Gordo	1754
El de Godo	1754
Bigotes	1754–1775
Casa Blanca	1757
Gran Cabezon	1761–1768
Teja	1762
Panocha	1762–1775
El Turnio	1762–1766
Boruca	1762–1768
Bordado	1762–1768
El Lumen	1762
El Cojo	1762
Casaca Colorado	1768–1773
Canos	1768
Juan Tuerto	1772–1773
Zapato Bordado	1772–1773
Malla	1773
Rivera	1773–1791
Cabello Largo	1774–1775
Poca Ropa	1774–1777
Boca Tuerta	1775–1792
El Cielo	1775

Continued

LIPAN CHIEFS	DATES RECORDED
El Flaco	1775
Xaviercillo	1775–1779
Pajarito	1775
Manteca Mucha	1775–1779
Josecillo, son of Xaviercillo	1777
Joyoso	1779
Josef Grande	1779
Josef (José) Chiquito	1779–1788
El Manco Roque	1779
Chiquito	1780–1801
Aga	1783–1791
Zapato Sas	1783–1791
Casaca, son of Chiquito	1784–1787
Cuernitos	1786
Panocha, son of Cuernitos	1786
Soxais	1787
Pobea	1787
Canoso	1787–1793
Cibolo	1787
Roque Torres	1790
Tomey	1790
Casachiquita	1790
José Antonio	1791–1792
Malave	1791
El Velazo	1791
José Lombrana	1791
Pinto	1791
Moreno	1792–1798

Continued

LIPAN CHIEFS	DATES RECORDED
Bidatja	1792
Tunayilten	1792
Pino Blanco	1792
Cabello Colorado	1792
El Cojo	1814–1822
Castro	1822–1842
Poca Ropa	1822
Juan Novale	1825
Flacco	1835
Juan Sais	1838–1841
Datil	1838
John (Juan) Castro	1842–1873
Chiquito	1844–1854
Roan	1844
Lemas (Lamos) Castro	1844–1851
Ramon Castro	1844–1873
Costilietos	1844–1873
Flacco Chico	1844
Simon Castro	1845
Magoosh	1846–1915
Palomo Blanco	1846
Chipota	1847–1853
Yekehtasna	1850
Kehrauch	1850
Capote	1850
Quaco	1851
Shanaca	1851
Coyote	1851

Continued

LIPAN CHIEFS	DATES RECORDED
Manuel	1851
John Flacco	1851
Castillo	1854
Venego	1861
Josefa	1861
Woodercarnervesta	1865
Gicare	1868
Soli	1868
Sabier	1868
Lagardo	1874
Washa Lobo	1875
Juan Galan	1877
Blanco	1878
Colorado	1878

Lipan Scouts who served at Fort Griffin and Fort Clark, 1878–1881

NAME	BIRTHPLACE	HEIGHT	SERVICE	AGE
Lipan Apache*	Mexico	5′7″	1878–1879	25
Juan Guerrera	Mexico	5′8″	1880–1881	35
Grant	Texas	5′7″	1881–1882	22
Jack**	Texas	5′10″	1881–1882	Unknown
Johnson	Texas	5′11″	1881–1882	Unknown
Hamilton Tardasta	Mexico	5′7″	1880–1881	35
Bill Turner***	Texas	5′10″	1881–1882	Unknown

*Deserted December 6, 1879.

**May be a Tonkawa.

***Died of internal hemorrhage at Fort Clark.

Source: Swanson, Enlistment Record of Indian Scouts

Known Lipans with Tonkawas, 1886

NAME	NAME, 1890	AGE	RELATIONSHIP
Elsie	Elsie Buffalo	45	
Emma		7	Daughter
Nellie		2	Granddaughter
Cisco		2	Grandson
Grant	Grant Richards	36	
Richard	Green Richards	6	Son
Johnson	Sargent Johnson	48	
Mariah	Mariah Johnson	93	Mother(?)
Louis	Louis Apache	30	
Osborne		6	Son
McMillin	William Apache	4	Son
Sophie	Kate Apache	2	Daughter
Teneste	Tarnasta	65	
Ocoyo		60	Sister

Source: Tonkawa Census 1886, 1890

Lipans at Mescalero in 1885–1888

NAME	SPANISH NAME	ENGLISH NAME	ESTIMATED AGE
Belin, widow			35–50
Big Chops			45–50
Henca, wife	Carmen		40–45
Baby			
Ge-getch-i-ka (Mescalero)	Guadalupe	Big Mouth	22–23
Zotsaha	Conejo	Eliza	17–23
Son		Percy	

Continued

NAME	SPANISH NAME	ENGLISH NAME	ESTIMATED AGE
Panosnincha	Blanco		40
Shahintahha, wife		Dinah	30–35
Wahgleigh, daughter			13–15
Daughter			
Boneski			50
Kawitses, wife		Mary	45–50
Dahbe, son			18–19
Daughter			
Husband	Caro Colorado		50–60
Yanconi, wife		Eva	50
Ichkotu, son		William Fargo	15–17
Naki, wife			
Daughter			
Daughter, widow			30–35
Louisa, niece			
Clo-it-so-e	Chino Gordo		50–60
(Mescalero wife)	Juanita		40–50
Son		Elmer Wilson	12
Daughter		Hallie	8
Daughter			4
Daughter			3 months
Chivato		William Heath	30–38
Zanagolecha (Mescalero wife)			24–28
Mineha, daughter		Carrie Heath	7–8
Alguno, son		Harry Heath	4–5
Dinero			24–25
Chalito (Mescalero wife)		Jane	18

Continued

NAME	SPANISH NAME	ENGLISH NAME	ESTIMATED AGE
Widow		Sarah Mooney	46–57
Grandson		Penn Scott	14
Magill			35–45
Wife		Jennie	30–40
Quenitz, daughter		Claudie	6
Magoosh		Mogul	50–56
Cosas, wife		Mamie	35
Ekidda (Mescalero wife)	Medicina	Susie	18–22
Son		William Stott	6–8
Zaki, infant son			
Mocha (ex-wife)		Louisa	50
Dotsina		Magoosh Boy	28
Yincan, wife		Helena	23
Daughter		Lola	3
Son	Cuchillo		1
Daughter		Daisy	3 months
Dech-e-la, widow			73
Chepah	Manuel		40–45
Dahchascha, wife	Mucho	Ellen	38–40
(Mescalero husband)	Mariano	Charles Wyeth	19–20
Gunarda, wife		Agatha	14
Nahilda Lipan, Widow			65
Grandson		Anthony Joseph	9
Husband		Peter	18
(Mescalero wife)			22
Shosh	Simon Santos		32–40
Gostuyah, wife	Bolita	Ann	25–30

Continued

NAME	SPANISH NAME	ENGLISH NAME	ESTIMATED AGE
Son			12
Doshkahla	Jose Torres		50–60
Benta (Mescalero wife)	Estella		45
Nashtodie, son		Horace Greeley	8
Eteddy, daughter		Mollie Ohio	13–15
Daughter		Pearl	2–3
Son		Benjamin	4 months
LATER ARRIVALS AT MESCALERO			
Kiokallah*		Antonio Apache	24
Wife			20
Daughter			1
Lawrence Belin***			32
Bujah		Eden	30
Dushque**		David Belin	24
Asthta		Sally	18
Caje*			36
Tadintoah, wife		Tillie	23
Mrs. Caje, mother			80
Son		James Caje	8
Son		Earl Caje	6 months
Sanavoy**			50
Wife			40
Yaoh,* widow		Stella	31
Son		Frank Lester	11
Son			2

*1894
**1891
***1889
Source: Mescalero Census, 1885–1894

Lipans from Mexico, 1904–1905

Juan Villa (Ska-en-to-en), 35

Pancho Venego, 40
   Wife Teodora Venego, 35
   Son Nicolas Venego, 14
   Son Felipe Venego, 11
   Son Philemon Venego, 9
   Son Julian Venego, 4
   Daughter Isabel Venego, 1
   Daughter Pascuala, 1 month
Daughter Genavera Venego, 17

Miguel Zuazua, 60
   Wife Josefa Zuazua, 40
   Daughter Rosa Zuazua, 16

Augustina Zuazua, 25

Jesus Zuazua, 20

Cardinal Rodriguez, 50
   Wife Cuera , 40
   Son Caterino Rodriguez, 15
   Daughter Maria Rodriguez, 12
   Daughter Encarnacion
   Rodriguez, 9

Daughter Ester Rodriguez, 4
Daughter Juanita Rodriguez, 2

Teresa Rodriguez, 21
Ricardo Rodriguez, 18
Juana, 50
Pedro Mendez, 20

Julio Mendez, 28
   Wife Otila Mendez, 20
   Son Lisandro Mendez, 2
   Son Eduardo Mendez, 3 months

Andrea, 70
Coyota, 80
Tanille, 70
Jahe, 40
Nicolasa, 70
Concha, 70

Luis Hernandez,* 35
   Wife Rosa, 25
   Son Ismall Carillo Hernandez, 5

*Arrived in 1905.
Source: Mescalero Census 1904 and 1905

Places Named for Lipans

Lipan Plains—Spanish name for flats between present Las Vegas and Bernal, New Mexico.

Lipan Creek—Texas has three such creeks. One rises with Lipan Spring in southeastern Tom Green County and runs northeast for thirty-three miles to its mouth on the Concho River, west of Vancourt; it is joined southwest of Mereta by Dry Lipan Creek. The second rises in eastern Bell County and runs southeast for eleven miles to its mouth on Big Elm Creek, three miles northeast of Buckholts. The third rises in extreme eastern Atascosa County and runs southwest for twenty miles to its mouth on the Atascosa River, three miles south of Campbellton.

Lipan Hills—A small range along Lipan Creek in Atascosa County.

Lipan Flat—a plain of high grass in the hilly country of east central Tom Green County that runs east and west for twenty miles just south of San Angelo.

Lipan, Texas, in the northwestern corner of Hood County, was established in 1873. Founder T. A. Burns named the community after Lipans because the area was their hunting ground earlier in the century.

Lipantitlán, which meant "Lipan land," was a presidio established in 1831 at Lipan camping grounds on the west bank of the Nueces River, near San Patricio.

Capote Draw, a shallow valley west of the Cuesta del Burro range, was most likely named for Chief Capote, who met the Whiting expedition in 1850.

Apache Canyon in eastern New Mexico, **Apache Peak** in northern New Mexico, and **Mesa Apache** and **Apache Valley** in northeastern New Mexico were most likely named for the Eastern Apaches who once lived there.

Lipan Crossing, 85 miles above the mouth of the Pecos.

Lipan Point, a popular lookout at the Grand Canyon, is far from Lipan country. It was called Lincoln Point until 1902 when cartographer Francois Mathes requested the change, for unknown reasons.

Ocate Creek in eastern New Mexico was named for Chief Ucate, who in 1706 was either an early Lipan chief or an early leader of the Eastern Apache Confederation.

Source: *Handbook of Texas Online*, Simmons, "Governor Anza, The Lipan Apaches and Pecos Pueblo," *El Palacio*, 36; Julyan, *The Place Names of New Mexico*, 19–20; McNamee, Grand Canyon Place Names, 77; USGS Topographical Maps, various.

⊰ Abreviations Used in Notes ⊱

AAAG   Acting Assistant Adjutant General

AAG   Assistant Adjutant General

AG   Adjutant General

AGN   Archivo General de la Nación

BA   Béxar Archives

CAH   Dolph Briscoe Center for American History, University of Texas at Austin

CIAAR   Commissioner of Indian Affairs, Annual Report

DT   Department of Texas, the District of Texas and the 5th Military District

H. Ex. Doc. House Executive Document

HRDNM   Headquarters Records of the District of New Mexico, RG 393, M 1088

HRDP   Headquarters Records of the District of the Pecos, RG 393, M 1381

HRFS   Headquarters Records of Fort Stockton, Texas, RG 393, M 1189

IC   Indian Census Rolls, U.S. Census Bureau, RG 75, M 595

OAG   Office of the Adjutant General, RG 393

OIA   Office of Indian Affairs, Letters Received, RG 75, M 234

OIANM   Office of Indian Affairs, New Mexico Superintendency, RG 75, M 234

OIAT   Office of Indian Affairs, Texas Agency, RG 75

NARA   National Archives and Records Administration

NMSA   New Mexico State Archives

S. Ex. Doc. Senate Executive Document

SANM   Spanish Archives of New Mexico

SWAR   Secretary of War, Annual Report

❈ Notes ❧

Introduction Endnotes

1. Enrique Gilbert-Michael Maestas, *Cúelcaén Ndé—Lipan Apache of Texas History* (Lipan Apache Band of Texas, 2004), 283.

2. Gary Clayton Anderson, *The Indian Southwest, 1580–1830: Ethnogenesis and Reinvention* (Norman: University of Oklahoma Press, 1999), 106.

3. Gary Clayton Anderson, *The Conquest of Texas: Ethnic Cleansing in the Promised Land, 1820–1875* (Norman: University of Oklahoma Press, 2005), 7.

4. Robert Wooster, *Frontier Crossroads: Fort Davis and the West* (College Station: Texas A&M University Press, 2006) 151, 152, 165.

5. Harry Hoijer, *The History and Custom of the Lipan as told by Augustina Zuazua* (New York: Moulton Publishers, 1975),

6. Thomas Schilz, *The Lipan Apache in Texas* (El Paso: Texas Western Press, 1987), 6–7, 38.

7. Schilz, 43, 52.

8. Thomas Britten, *The Lipan Apaches: People of Wind and Lightning* (Albuquerque: University of New Mexico Press, 2009), 11, 24.

9. Britten, 15, 76–77, 155.

10. Britten, 232.

11. Hampton Sides, "Writing Popular Nonfiction," June 16, 2012, Western Writers of America annual meeting, Albuquerque, New Mexico.

12. Bill Moyers, "The Big Story: A Journalist Looks at Texas History," *Southwestern Historical Quarterly* 101 (July 1997): 1–15.

13. Curtis D. Tunnell and W. W. Newcomb, *A Lipan Apache Mission: San Lorenzo de la Santa Cruz, 1762–1771* (Austin: Texas Memorial Museum, 1969), preface.

14. John H. Monnett, "Oh No, Not Another Battle Book!" *Western Writers of America Roundup Magazine* 17 (August 2010): 9–11.

Chapter 1

1. José Cortés, *Views from the Apache Frontier: Report on the Northern Provinces of New Spain*, ed. Elizabeth A. H. John (Norman: University of Oklahoma Press, 1989), 59.

2. Jean Louis Berlandier, *The Indians of Texas in 1830*, ed. John C. Ewers (Washington, D.C.: Smithsonian Institution Press, 1969), 56.

3. Morris E. Opler, *Myths and Legends of the Lipan Apache Indians,* Memoirs of the American Folk Lore Society 36 (New York: J. J. Augustin Publisher, 1940), 3,169, 277–278.

4. Morris E. Opler, *The Lipan and Mescalero Apaches in Texas* (New York: Garland Publishing, 1974), 15, 277–278.

5. Morris Edward Opler Papers, 14-25-3238, Subseries D: Lipan, "Warpath and raid," Box 44, Folder 25, Division of Rare and Manuscript Collections, Cornell University Library.

6. Opler, *Myths,* 110.

7. Opler, *Myths,* 5, 98. The Jicarillas are the only other Apache group with the same beliefs.

8. Percy's version differs in certain details with the creation story anthropologist Morris Opler recorded from Antonio Apache, with Percy translating. In parentheses are additional details from Antonio Apache's story and from a story Percy wrote for Carolyn Sue Edwards.

9. Opler, *Myths,* 13.

10. Sue Edwards Black Collection, Provo Special Collections & Manuscripts, Harold B. Lee Library, Brigham Young University, Provo, Utah.

11. Opler, *Myths,* 14–15.

12. Opler (*Myths,* 16 and 16 fn 3) wrote that the Sun is Killer-of-Enemies and then explained that Killer-of-Enemies is associated with the sun.

13. Opler, *Myths,* 15–18.

14. Black Collection.

15. Opler, *Myths,* 18–22, 29–32.

16. Opler, *Myths,* 3–5; Morris E. Opler, "The Apachean Culture Pattern and Its Origins," in *Handbook of North American Indians* 10, ed. Alfonso Ortiz (Washington, DC: Smithsonian Institution Press, 1983), 368–369.

17. Opler, *Myths,* 11, 15 fn 3.

18. Percy Big Mouth, interview with Eve Ball, Mescalero Reservation, November 10, 1954, Eve Ball Papers and Letters, MSS3096, Perry Special Collections & Manuscripts, Harold B. Lee Library, Brigham Young University, Provo, Utah.

19. Carolyn Sue Black, "Token of a Redman," manuscript, Black Collection; Percy Big Mouth to Sue Black, January 13, 1951, Black Collection.

20. Eve Ball to Henry Schnautz, January 14, 1959, Ball Collection.

21. Eve Ball, manuscript, undated, Ball Collection.

Chapter 2

1. Narrative Given by Captain Juan Jaramillo, in Richard and Shirley Cushing Flint, *Documents of the Coronado Expedition: "They Were Not Familiar with His Majesty Nor Did They Wish to Become His Subjects"* (Dallas: Southern Methodist University Press, 2005), 514.

2. Maestas, 7.

.3 Pedro de Castañeda, "Expedition to Cibola, 1540," in Flint and Flint, *Documents,* 408.

4. Coronado to the King, Province of Tiguex, October 20, 1541, in George P. Hammond and Agapito Rey, *Narratives of the Coronado Expedition, 1540–1542* (Albuquerque, University of New Mexico Press, 1940), 186. The Flints' interpretation was, "The people are the best disposed I have seen . . ."

5. Frederick W. Hodge, "The Narrative of the Expedition of Coronado, by Pedro de Castañeda," in *Spanish Explorers in the Southern United States, 1528–1543* (New York: Barnes & Noble Inc., 1965), 362. The Flints' translation is essentially the same.

6. Hammond and Rey, 186, 235–236; Albert H. Schroeder, *A Study of the Apache Indians*, vol. 1, *The Apaches and Their Neighbours, 1540–1700* (Santa Fe, 1959–60), 27. Susan Vehik, Albert Schroeder and other anthropologists accept a location northeast of the Canadian River. Vehik, "Cultural Continuity and Discontinuity in the Southern Prairies and Cross Timbers," in *Plains Indians, A.D. 500–1500: The Archaeological Past of Historic Groups*, ed. Karl H. Schlesier (Norman: University of Oklahoma Press, 1994), 251; Schroeder, vol. 1, 27. Judith Habicht-Mauche and others believe they could have been south of the same river near the present New Mexico-Texas state line. Archeological evidence supports either location, but Coronado encountered people on the move during buffalo season, not permanent villages. Scholars have long debated Coronado's route, but the chroniclers' descriptions indicate they crossed the Pecos River in eastern New Mexico and then passed over the broad grasslands of the Llano Estacado before entering the Plains. Habicht-Mauche, "Coronado's Querechos and Teyas in the Archaeological Record of the Texas Panhandle," *Plains Anthropologist* 37, no. 140 (1992): 248–249.

7. George Parker Winship, *The Coronado Expedition* (Chicago: Rio Grande Press, 1964), 111.

8. Hodge, 362–363.

9. Hammond and Rey, 235–236.

10. *Lipan Apache Band of Texas, Inc.* http://members.aol.com/_ht_a/ceolipan//lipan.html (accessed August 7, 2002). Some scholars agree: William W. Newcomb, *The Indians of Texas: Prehistory to Present* (Austin: University of Texas Press, 1961), 106; Karl H. Schlesier, "Commentary: A History of Ethnic Groups," in *Plains Indians, A.D. 500–1500: The Archaeological Past of Historic Groups*, ed. Karl H. Schlesier (Norman: University of Oklahoma Press, 1994), 358; Paul H. Carlson, *Deep Time and the Texas High Plains* (Lubbock: Texas Tech University Press, 2005), 77.

11. Morris Opler didn't care for the term "Plains Apaches" and pointed out that the Lipans showed more of a plains orientation than did the Jicarillas. Opler, "The Apachean Culture Pattern and Its Origins," in *Handbook of North American Indians Volume 10: The Southwest* (Washington, DC: Smithsonian Institution Press, 1983), 380. Archeologist Deni Seymour's archeological evidence suggests that early Mescaleros were mountain people (Deni Seymour, email, June 8, 2011). "Plains Apaches" is now a term used by Naishan (Kiowa Apache) people.

12. Habicht-Mauche, 256; Winship, 367. Historians and anthropologists have debated the identity of the Teyas. Castañeda muddied the discussion by lumping them together in an account written 25 years after his journey. A few have argued the Teyas were Apachean (Hammond, 292–293). Schroeder, vol. 1, 34–36, said "Querecho" was a term the Pecos people used for the plains group nearest them, while "Teya" indicated those farther east; he concluded that the Teyas were Caddoan. Another group sometimes mistaken for Apaches were the Escanxaques, who probably were a Kansa or Wichita people. They bore no resemblance to the Vaqueros, spoke a different language, and the Spanish found several Apaches in the Escanxaques' camp, indicating the Spanish could tell them apart.

13. Douglas Boyd, "Querechos and Teyas: Protohistoric Hunters and Gatherers in the Texas Panhandle-Plains, A.D. 1540–1700," *Bulletin of the Texas Archeological Society* 72 (2001): 5–7, 10; Habicht-Mauche, 247, 253. Boyd makes a strong case for Apaches at Tierra Blanca, but

others, like David Hughes, maintain the evidence is too sparse to know definitely. Hughes calls it a "reasonable hypothesis" (Hughes, "Tierra Blanca: A complex Issue," ms. in *From the Land of Ever Winter to the American Southwest: Athapaskan Migrations, Mobility, and Ethnogenesis*, ed. Deni Seymour [Salt Lake City: University of Utah Press, 2012]).

14. Dolores A. Gunnerson, "The Southern Athabascans: Their Arrival in the Southwest," *El Palacio* 63 (November–December 1956): 348, 352, 363; Schroeder, vol. 1, 6.

15. Richard J. Perry, "The Apachean Transition from the Subarctic to the Southwest," *Plains Anthropologist* (1980): 281; David Wilcox, "The Entry of Athapaskans Into the American Southwest: The Problem Today," in *The Protohistoric Period in the North American Southwest, AD 1450–1700*, ed. David Wilcox and Bruce Masse (Tempe: Arizona State University, 1981), 222; Deni Seymour, *Conquest and Concealment: After the El Paso phase on Fort Bliss, an archaeological study of the Manso, Suma, and early Apache* (El Paso: Lone Mountain Archaeological Services, 2002), 320. This is also the position of Enrique Maestas, anthropologist of the Lipan Apache Band of Texas (Maestas, 23–24).

16. Kevin P. Gilmore and Sean Larmore, "Looking for Lovitt in all the Wrong Places: Migration Models and the Athapaskan Diaspora as Viewed from Eastern Colorado," ms. to be published in *From the Land of Ever Winter*.

17. Jack T. Hughes, "Prehistoric Cultural Developments on the Texas High Plains," *Bulletin of the Texas Archeological Society* 60 (1989): 8–9, 34–35; Wilcox, 226; Seymour, *Conquest and Concealment*, 35.

18. Seymour, *Protohistoric and Early Historic Temporal Resolution in the Southern Southwest*, 2003, 1; Seymour, *Conquest and Concealment*, 360; Seymour, "A Ranchería in the Gran Apachería," *Plains Anthropologist* 49, no. 190 (2004): 186; Seymour, "Despoblado or Athapaskan Heartland: A Methodological Perspective on Ancestral Apache Landscape Use in the Safford Area," in *Crossroads of the Southwest: Culture, Ethnicity, and Migration in Arizona's Safford Basin*, ed. David E. Purcell (New York: Cambridge Scholars), 121–162.

19. Judith Habicht-Mauche, "Southwestern-style Culinary Ceramics on the Southern Plains: A Case Study of Technological Innovation and Cross-Cultural Interaction," *Plains Anthropologist* 32 (1987): 175–176, 252–253; Hughes, "Prehistoric Cultural Developments," 43.

20. Katherine A. Spielman, "Late Prehistoric Exchange Between the Southwest and Southern Plains," *Plains Anthropologist* 28 (November 1983): 258–261, 264–267.

21. James H. Gunnerson, *An Introduction to Plains Apache Archeology: The Dismal River Aspect* (Washington DC: Smithsonian Institution Bureau of American Ethnology Bulletin 173, 1960), 243; Timothy G. Baugh, "Ecology and Exchange: The Dynamics of Plains-Pueblo Interaction," in *Farmers, Hunters, and Colonists: Interaction Between the Southwest and the Southern Plains*, ed. Katherine A. Spielmann (Tucson: University of Arizona Press, 1991), 121.

22. Marc Simmons, "Call of the Canadian," *New Mexico Magazine* 68 (June 1990): 35, 39, 41, 43. For an excellent exploration of how the Staked Plains were named, see John M. Morris, *El Llano Estacado: Exploration and Imagination on the High Plains of Texas and New Mexico, 1536–1860* (Austin: Texas State Historical Association, 1997), 162–166.

23. Gallegos, Hernán, "The Rodriguez Expedition," *New Mexico Historical Review* 2 (July 1927): 252–253.

24. George P. Hammond and Agapito Rey, *The Rediscovery of New Mexico, 1580–1594; The Explorations of Chamuscado, Espejo, Castaño de Sosa, Morlete, and Leyva de Bonilla and Humaña* (Albuquerque: University of New Mexico Press, 1966), 87.

25. Opler said the term "vaqueros" probably included both non-Apachean groups and the groups later called Cuartelejos and Palomas. Schroeder believed most Vaqueros became Lipan. Opler, *Handbook*, 388. Given their location, they were Apaches.

26. Hernan Gallegos, *The Gallegos Relation of the Rodriguez Expedition to New Mexico*, trans. and ed. George P. Hammond and Agapito Rey (Santa Fe: El Palacio Press, 1927), 31–32, 90–92; Baltasar de Obregón, *Obregon's History of 16th Century Explorations in Western America*, translated and edited by George P. Hammond and Agapito Rey (Los Angeles: Wetzel Publishing Company, 1928), 303–305.

27. Morris,138; Hammond and Rey, *Don Juan de Oñate, Colonizer of New Mexico, 1595–1628* (Albuquerque: University of New Mexico Press, 1953), 852.

28. Jerry R. Craddock, *Zaldívar and the Cattle of Cibola: Vicente de Zaldívar's Report of His Expedition to the Buffalo Plains in 1598* (Dallas: Southern Methodist University, 1999), 32–34; Andrée Sjoberg, "Lipan Apache Culture in Historical Perspective," *Southwestern Journal of Anthropology* 9 (1953): 88.

29. Schroeder, vol. 1, 166. A Spanish priest (Benavidez, 302 fn 111), said the name Apache came from the Zuni word "Apachu," or "enemy." Schroeder doubted the Zuni source. Oñate hadn't yet encountered Zuni people, but he could have met Utes. "Thus, there is abundant evidence that the name 'Apache' seems not to have been derived from the Zunis," he wrote. Schroeder to Ives Goddard, Handbook of North American Indians, November 14, 1981, Albert Schroeder Papers, New Mexico State Archives.

30. Herbert Eugene Bolton, *Spanish Exploration in the Southwest*, 1542–1706 (New York: Barnes & Noble Inc., 1916), 251–255.

31. Schroeder, vol. 1, 48–49; Hammond and Rey, *Oñate*, 752 fn 11, 841, 854; Vehik, 251. George P. Hammond and Agapito Rey, *Narratives*, 235–236.

32. Hodge, 330, 362, 363.

Chapter 3

1. Alonso de Benavides, *The Memorial of Fray Alonso de Benavides, 1630*, trans. and ed. Mrs. Edward E. Ayer (Chicago: Privately Printed, 1916), 41.

2. Who were the Acho Apaches? Bernice S. Eiselt ("The Emergence of Jicarilla Apache Enclave Economy During the 19th Century in Northern New Mexico," Ph.D. diss., University of Michigan, 2006, 79) wrote that the Achos, Rio Colorados and Jicarillas may have been the Apaches led by Chief Quinia, who in the early 1600s lived on both sides of the upper Rio Grande near Taos. Dolores Gunnerson, in *The Jicarilla Apaches: A Study in Survival* (Dekalb, Ill.: Northern Illinois University Press, 1974), 91, and Albert Schroeder ("Castañeda's 'Acha'—Picuris, Hopi or Apache?" *El Palacio* 65 [February 1958]: 6) held the same opinion. Eiselt also mentions a group she calls the Manansas, but there were no such people; Manansas was the name of one of Quinia's captains. However, Schroeder reported that the Quinias moved farther west by 1628 and became a western branch of the Navajos; Gunnerson also links Quinia to the Navajo clan Kin-ya ni. Eiselt asserts that the Achos and Rio Colorados were proto-Jicarillas, and yet all three groups are listed separately in a 1702 Spanish document. Schroeder apparently changed his mind (*The Jicarilla Apaches*, vol. 2 [Santa Fe: 1959–60], 2, 5, 6), noting that the Achos were consistently described as living near Picuris or Taos. Between 1706 and 1719, the Jicarillas were in the Cimarron-Ponil Creek area, said Schroeder, and "could not have developed out of the Achos." He

said no identity was established for the Achos but later agreed with Karl Schlesier ("Rethinking the Dismal River Aspect and the Plains Athapaskans, A.D. 1692–1768," *Plains Anthropologist* 15 [1972]: 111), who concluded the Achos were an early Lipan group who lived from the Sangre de Cristos to present Eagle Nest.

3. La Cañada was a village near present Cochiti Lake.

4. Fray Juan Sanz de Lezaun, 1760, in Charles Wilson Hackett, *Historical Documents Relating to New Mexico, Nueva Vizcaya, and Approaches Thereto, to 1773*, vol. 3 (Washington, D.C.: Carnegie Institution of Washington, 1937), 468; Alonso Garcia, September 4, 1680, in Charles W. Hackett, *Revolt of the Pueblo Indians of New Mexico and Otermín's Attempted Reconquest, 1680–1682*, vol. 1 (Albuquerque: University of New Mexico Press, 1942), 57; Hackett, *Revolt*, lxv; Fray Antonio de Sierra, September 4, 1680, in Hackett, *Revolt*, 60; Governor Antonio de Otermín, in Hackett, *Revolt*, 99–100; Juan de la Cruz, December 24, 1681, in Hackett, *Revolt*, vol. 2, 330; Opler, *Handbook*, 390.

5. Ramón Gutiérrez, *When Jesus Came, the Corn Mothers Went Away: Marriage, Sexuality, and Power in New Mexico, 1500–1846* (Stanford: Stanford University Press, 1991), xxvii.

6. Jack D. Forbes, *Apache, Navajo, and Spaniard* (Norman: University of Oklahoma Press, 1960), 98–99; Hammond and Rey, *Oñate*, 1072.

7. John L. Kessell, *Kiva, Cross and Crown: The Pecos Indians and New Mexico, 1540–1840* (Albuquerque: University of New Mexico Press, 1987), 123; Elinore M. Barrett, *Conquest and Catastrophe: Changing Rio Grande Pueblo Settlement Patterns in the Sixteenth and Seventeenth Centuries* (Albuquerque: University of New Mexico Press, 2002), 69, 71.

8. Francis Haines, "The Northward Spread of Horses among the Plains Indians," *American Anthropologist* 40 (1938): 431–434; Lipan Apache Band of Texas, 1; Schroeder, vol.1, 168; Hammond & Rey, *Oñate*, 1059.

9. Schroeder, vol. 1, 168; "Notes and Reflection on the War with the Apache Indians in the Provinces of New Spain," in Elizabeth John, "A Cautionary Exercise in Apache Historiography," *Journal of Arizona History* 25 (Autumn 1984), 306–307; Antonio Cordero, "Cordero's Description of the Apache—1796," Daniel S. Matson and Albert H. Schroeder, eds. *New Mexico Historical Review* 32 (October 1957), 345–346.

10. George P. Hammond and Agapito Rey, *Apostolic Chronicle of Juan Domingo Arricivita: The Franciscan Mission Frontier in the Eighteenth Century in Arizona, Texas, and the Californias* (Berkeley: Academy of American Franciscan History, 1996), 25.

11. Ayer, 39–41. Father Gerónimo de Zárate Salamerón in 1626 made similar comments. Charles Wilson Hackett, *Pichardo's Treatise on the Limits of Louisiana and Texas*, vol. 2 (Austin: University of Texas Press, 1934), 324–325.

12. S. Lyman Tyler and Darrell H. Taylor, "The Report of Fray Alonso de Posada in Relation to Quivira and Teguayo," *New Mexico Historical Review* 3 (October 1958): 303.

13. Hammond and Rey, *Oñate*, 1089, 1094. Frank Reeve argued that Navajos were the more likely refuge "because of growing corn," but Plains Apaches also grew corn. Reeve, "Seventeenth Century Navajo-Spanish Relations," *New Mexico Historical Review* 32 (July, 1957): 39.

14. Gunnerson, *Jicarilla*, 87-88, 90, 96–97; Karl H. Schlesier, "Rethinking the Dismal River Aspect," 104; Myra Ellen Jenkins, "Taos Pueblo and Its Neighbors, 1540–1847," *New Mexico Historical Review* 41 (April 1966): 88; Jack D. Forbes to Albert Schroeder, August 1, 1959, Schroeder Papers. Around 1662 Governor Diego de Peñalosa allegedly sent soldiers to

capture thirty-three Pueblo people remaining at El Cuartelejo and destroy the village. Schroeder said this document from Peñalosa was a fraud prepared to obtain money and there was no such expedition. "Forbes mixed up the dates of the father and son of the same name. The Taos took off in 1641 or 2 and Archuleta went out in 1664," he wrote to Karl Schlesier on January 16, 1973, Schroeder Papers.

15. Declarations of Juan Dominguez de Mendoza, December 20, 1681, and Diego Lopez Sambrano, December 22, 1681, in Hackett, *Revolt*, 266, 299.

16. Barrett, 76–77; Forbes, 158-159; Fray Juan Bernal to Tribunal, April 1, 1669, in Hackett, *Historical Documents*, vol. 3, 191–192, 271–272.

17. France Scholes, "Troublous Times in New Mexico," *New Mexico Historical Review* 12, no. 4 (October 1937): 397–398; Scholes, "Civil Government in New Mexico," *New Mexico Historical Review* 10, no. 2 (April 1935): 84–85; Gutiérrez, 154. Of the 3,294 Indians in Spanish homes between 1700 and 1849, Navajos were 37.5 percent and Apaches, 24 percent.

18. Gunnerson, *Jicarilla*, 85; Ayer, 56–57; France Scholes, "The Supply Service of the New Mexican Missions in the Seventeenth Century," *New Mexico Historical Review* 5 (April 1930): 188.

19. Scholes, "Church and State in New Mexico," *New Mexico Historical Review* 11 (October 1936): 300–301; Kessell,158–159; Gunnerson, *Jicarilla*, 88; Jack D. Forbes, "Unknown Athapaskans: The Identification of the Jano, Jocome, Jumano, Manso, Suma, and other Indian Tribes of the Southwest," *Ethnohistory* 6 (Spring 1959): 118.

20. Declaration of Captain Andrés Hurtado, September, 1661, in Hackett, *Historical Documents*, vol. 3, 186-187; Donald E. Worcester, "The Beginnings of the Apache Menace of the Southwest," *New Mexico Historical Review* 16 (January 1941): 10.

21. Scholes, "Troublous Times," 147; John L. Kessell, *Spain in the Southwest: A Narrative History of Colonial New Mexico, Arizona, Texas, and California* (Norman: University of Oklahoma Press, 2002), 114; Kessell, "Diego Romero, the Plains Apaches, and the Inquisition," *The American West* 15 (May–June 1978): 13–15.

22. Jane Sanchez, "Spanish-Indian Relations During the Otermín Administration, 1677–1683," *New Mexico Historical Review* 58 (April 1983): 142–143; Gunnerson, *Jicarilla*, 94–95.

23. Juan de la Cruz, December 24, 1681, in Hackett, *Revolt*, vol. 2, 330; Opler, *Handbook*, 390; Junta de Guerra, October 2, 1680, in Hackett, *Revolt*, vol. 1, 169; Cabildo of Santa Fe, October 3, 1680, in Hackett, 180; Juan Dominguez de Mendoza to Otermín, December 10, 1681, in Hackett, vol. 2, 227; Fray Francisco de Ayeta, December 23, 1681, in Hackett, 308; Sanchez, 145.

24. Schroeder, undated, draft review of *The Mescalero Apaches* by C. L. Sonnichsen, Schroeder Collection; Otermín, March of the army, November 5 to December 8, 1681, in Hackett, *Revolt*, vol. 2, 210.

25. Account of Fray Juan Sanz de Lezaún, 1760, in *Historical Documents*, vol. 3, 470–472.

Chapter 4

1. Alfred B. Thomas, *After Coronado: Spanish Exploration Northeast of New Mexico* (Norman: University of Oklahoma Press, 1935), 64.

2. Haines, 431.

3. S. Lyman Tyler and H. Darrell Taylor, "The Report of Fray Alonso de Posada in Relation to Quivira and Teguayo," *New Mexico Historical Review* (October 1958): 300–301; Maria de Fatima

Wade, *The Native Americans of the Texas Edwards Plateau, 1582–1799* (Austin: University of Texas Press, 2003), 71.

4. Bolton, 320–322, 331–332, 334–335. Another diary of the expedition indicates that Juan Sebeata was not sent away (Wade, 71).

5. Bolton, 336–338; Frederick W. Hodge, George P. Hammond, and Agapito Rey, *Fray Alonso de Benavides' Revised Memorial of 1634* (Albuquerque: University of New Mexico Press, 1945), 313; Maestas, 126; Del Weniger, *The Explorers' Texas: The Lands and Waters* (Austin: Eakin Publications, 1984), 76–77.

6. George C. Martin, *The Indian Tribes of the Mission Nuestra Señora del Refugio* (Corpus Christi: Bootstraps Press, 1972), 33–34, 50 fn 15, 77 fn 19. Archeological evidence indicates the Lipans occupied the area from Baffin Bay to the Nueces for a long time before.

7. Tyler and Taylor, 300–302; Hodge, *Benavidez*, 313; Forbes, 169.

8. Hodge, Hammond and Rey, 313.

9. The Ervipiame people were Coahuiltecans, who lived in northern Coahuila and central Texas. They were unable to hold out and entered missions in the 1690s, eventually becoming absorbed by the Tonkawas. (Walter Prescott Webb, et al., "Ervipiame Indians," in *The Handbook of Texas* [Austin: Texas State Historical Association, 1952]).

10. The people called Jumanos living on the central plains were Taovayas, who would be absorbed by the Wichitas. They were not related to the Jumanos living to the south, who were displaced by the Apaches (Newcomb, 225–226, 249.)

11. Maestas, 128, 337; Declaration of Cuis Benive, April 11, 1689, in Hackett, *Historical Documents*, vol. 2, 275; William Foster, *Spanish Expeditions into Texas, 1689–1768* (Austin: University of Texas Press, 1928), 113; William Edward Dunn, "Apache Relations in Texas, 1718–1750," *Texas State Historical Association Quarterly* 14 (January 1911): 203–204.

12. Pekka Hämäläinen (*The Comanche Empire* [New Haven: Yale University Press], 30) also notes that these tribes "were in the midst of an expansionist burst of their own" at the time they began fighting Comanches.

13. Gunnerson, *Jicarilla*, 112.

14. Manuel J. Espinosa, *Crusaders of the Rio Grande: The Story of Don Diego de Vargas and the Reconquest and Refounding of New Mexico* (Chicago: Institute of Jesuit History, 1942), 138; Albert B. Thomas, *The Plains Indians and New Mexico, 1751–1778* (Albuquerque: University of New Mexico Press, 1940), 7; Opler, *Handbook*, 390; Forbes, 254.

15. Tyler and Taylor, 303.

16. Schroeder, vol. 1, 213–214; Espinosa, 177, 183–184, 192; Gunnerson, *Jicarilla*, 120; Kessell, *Kiva*, 263–264. Vargas called the chief a Faraon, but this chief lived far to the east of the Faraons.

17. Thomas (*After Coronado*, 13) said the Chipaines were Faraons, which is incorrect. For a discussion of the Achos, see note 2 in Chapter 3.

18. Schlesier, "Rethinking," 111; Schroeder, vol. 1, 214; Schroeder, vol. 2, 6–7.

19. Espinosa, 236, 251–253.

20. Espinosa, 286–288; Gunnerson, *Jicarilla*, 124; Schlesier, 104; Schroeder, vol. 2, 10, 12. Schroeder disagrees with the route suggested by Thomas.

21. Diary of Juan de Ulibarri to El Cuartelejo, 1706, in Thomas, *After Coronado*, 61.

22. Schroeder, vol. 1, 48–49 and vol. 2, 7.

23. Diary, 63; Schlesier, "Rethinking," 111; Schroeder, vol. 2, 8–9; Schroeder, *A Study of the Apache Indians*, vol. 2, 8–9 and vol. 3, *The Mescalero Apaches* (Santa Fe, 1959–60), 16; Opler, *Handbook*, 390.

24. Diary, 64 and Thomas, *After Coronado*, 263 fn 13; Opler, *Handbook*, 391; Schroeder, vol. 3, 16; Declarations of Pecos Indians, March 1702, Albert Schroeder collection, New Mexico Archives, Santa Fe. Schlesier ("Rethinking," 112, and "Commentary," 335) thinks they were the Colorado division of the Dismal River aspect.

25. Diary, 63–64. Ulibarri wrote the chief's name as "Ucase," but the original Spanish text indicates it's Ucate, which also explains the present name of the area, "Ocate." (James Gunnerson, "Apache Archaeology in Northeastern New Mexico," *American Antiquity* 34 [1969]: 36.) Opler says the word is Nahuatl, Ocóte. (Opler, "Review of Gunnerson's '*The Jicarilla Apaches*," *Plains Anthropologist* 20 [1975]:155.)

26. Some historians have speculated that the Apaches feared punishment for their role in the Pueblo Revolt, but it's unlikely the Spanish carried a grudge for 26 years.

27. Diary, 64; Schroeder, vol. 2, 23. The two describe slightly different routes.

28. James Gunnerson, 143.

29. Diary, 66–69; James H. Gunnerson and Dolores A. Gunnerson, "Apachean Culture: A Study in Unity and Diversity" in *Apachean Culture, History and Ethnology*, ed. Keith H. Basso and Morris E. Opler (Tucson: The University of Arizona Press, 1971), 11; Schroeder, vol. 2, 26–27.

30. Diary, 69–75; Schlesier, "Rethinking," 101–102, 106, 109–110.

31. Opler (*Handbook*, 388) says the Sierra Blanca, who lived north of the Raton River in southeastern Colorado were the same as Carlanas. Schlesier ("Rethinking," 110) says the Sierra Blancas were the same as Flechas de Palo.

32. James Gunnerson to Albert Schroeder, April 1, 1970, Schroeder Papers; Hammond and Rey, *Oñate*, vol. 1, 484–485.

33. James Gunnerson, 178–179, 248–249, 252. Gunnerson described Cuartelejo as a pan–Apache home ("Plains Apache Archeology: A Review," *Plains Anthropologist* 13 [August 1968]: 167–169), while Schroeder (vol. 1, 10–11) thought it was Lipan. Opler, citing the unusual dwellings, presence of a coyote bone necklace, and lack of horse remains, said that Dismal River wasn't Apache at all (Opler, *Handbook*, 383–384), but historical records describing Apaches here along with the absence of fish bones clinch the argument that the site was, in fact, Apache. Opler claimed the Lipans were afraid of coyotes, but Daniel Castro Romero, Jr., Lipan Band chief, says the coyote was not only the bearer of cultural stories and lessons but had the power to foretell the future. Lipans were not afraid of the coyote but were cautious, he said (Daniel Castro Romero, email, July 2, 2006).

34. Gunnerson and Gunnerson, 21; Kevin P. Gilmore and Sean Larmore, "Migration Models and the Athapaskan Diaspora as Viewed from the Colorado High Country," presented March 27, 2008 at the Symposium "The Earliest Athapaskans in the Southern Southwest," at the Society for American Archaeology, Vancouver, British Columbia, 3.

35. Gunnerson, James, "An Introduction to Plains Apache Archeology—The Dismal River Aspect," (Washington, D.C.: Smithsonian Institution Bureau of American Ethnology Bulletin 58, 1960), 141, 143, 145–146, 175–176, 240, 245, 250–251.

36. Schlesier, "Rethinking," 101–102; Anna Lewis, *Along the Arkansas* (Dallas: The Southwest Press, 1932), 48; Gunnerson and Gunnerson, 12, 14–15, 21–22.

37. Schlesier ("Rethinking," 110) said the Sierra Blancas were the Flechas de Palo; Opler (*Handbook*, 388) said they were Carlanas. However, they are listed separately from the other groups so many times in Spanish records that they were clearly a separate group.

38. Schlesier, "Rethinking," 101–102, 109–110, 118. Schlesier says the Panhandle group also included Limitas and Trementinas, but these were Faraon bands. Schroeder also thought these groups were related to the Chipaines.

39. Schlesier, 112.

40. Schroeder to Schlesier, January 16, 1973, Schroeder Papers. Schroeder also wrote to William C. Sturtevant, of the *Handbook of North American Indians*, that archeologist Jim Gunnerson "should refer to Karl H. Schlesier's article . . . This is the most thorough coverage to date on clues of early historic period Athapaskan locations that might relate to late prehistoric locales. While it does contain a few errors and perhaps a few questionable interpretations, the article is a good one." He didn't identify what he believed was in error. (Schroeder to William Sturtevant, April 13, 1973.)

41. Opler, *Handbook*, 388; Maestas, 71; Hodge, *Benavidez*, 302–304, fn 111; Hodge, *Handbook*, 453. Hodge said the Carlanas were a division of the Jicarillas and Orozco y Berra said the Carlanas were a division of the Faraons, but neither is correct.

42. Juan Ygnacio Florez Mogollon, Santa Fe, December 16, 1712, State Archives of New Mexico II.

43. Testimony of Don Gerónimo, July 20, 1715, in Thomas, *After Coronado*, 80–81.

44. After 1726 the name "Faraon" was replaced by Natagé and then Mescalero in 1814, but Faraons appeared on maps up to 1858 (Opler, *Handbook*, 390).

45. Kessell, *Kiva*, 361–363; Juan Tindé declaration, Santa Fe, August 20, 1714, Albert Schroeder Papers.

46. Testimony of Don Gerónimo, Testimony of Don Lorenzo, July 22, 1715, Council of Wark, July 23, 1715, Order to Hurtado, August 26, 1715, in Thomas, *After Coronado*, 80–87.

47. Diary of the Campaign of Juan Páez Hurtado, 1715, in Thomas, *After Coronado*, 94–98.

Chapter 5

1. Declaration of Felipe de Tamariz, November 15, 1720, in Thomas, *After Coronado*, 175, 177. By Sierra Blanca, he meant the mountains near present Raton, home of the Carlanas.

2. Opler (Gunnerson review, 154) insists that only tipis and wickiups were Apachean and that other kinds of houses were "attributed to them." Their mobility, their death practices and their in-law avoidance would have made life in a multi-room pueblo difficult. He thinks the houses were built by Pueblo refugees. However, Opler himself reported (*Myths*, 7) that Lipans didn't practice in-law avoidance, and chances are their confederates didn't either. Also, the refugees didn't live here—they were farther east on the plains with the Cuartelejos.

3. Diary of the Campaign of Governor Antonio de Valverde, 1719, in Thomas, *After Coronado*, 111, 114; Thomas, *Plains Indians*, 12; Schlesier, "Rethinking," 116. University of California graduate student Michael Glassow identified the locations during field work in 1966. (Glassow to Schroeder, December 14, 1966, Schroeder Papers.)

4. Valverde, 112–133; Antonio de Valverde Cosio to Viceroy, November 30, 1719, in Thomas, 144; Sjoberg, 89–90; Schroeder, vol. 2, 35–36, 40; Frank Norall, *Bourgmont, Explorer of the Missouri, 1698–1725* (Lincoln: University of Nebraska Press, 1988), 158–160.

5. Thomas, *After Coronado*, 34, 36, 38; A. B. Thomas, "The Massacre of the Villasur Expedition at the Forks of the Platte River August 12, 1720," *Nebraska History* 7 (1924): 71–80; Declaration of Phelipe Tamaris to General Juan Domingo de Bustamante, April 19 to May 4, 1724, Schroeder Papers; Diary of the Reconnaissance Expedition of Colonel Don Pedro de Villasur, 1720, in Thomas, *After Coronado*, 134.

6. Thomas, *Plains*, 11, 165–166; Charles L. Kenner, *A History of New Mexican-Plains Indian Relations* (Norman: University of Oklahoma Press, 1969), 31.

7. Diary of Governor Bustamante, November 17–27, 1724, in Thomas, *After Coronado*, 197–201.

8. Schroeder, vol. 1, 107; Vehik, 254; Opler, *Handbook*, 390. Other terms were *Canecy, Canze, Canchy,* and *Cannecy*. Schroeder (vol. 1, 48–49) thought the French also referred to Acho and Conejero Apaches (Lipan ancestors) as Cancy; Opler thought they could be Lipan or Jicarilla.

9. Anna Lewis, "La Harpe's First Expedition in Oklahoma, 1718–1719," *Chronicles of Oklahoma* 2 (December 1924): 333–335; Ralph A. Smith, "Account of the Journey of Bénard de la Harpe: discovery Made by Him of Several Nations Situated in the West," *Southwest Historical Quarterly* 62 (1959): 377, 384; Subseries D: Lipan, "Alien People," Box 44, Folder 10, Opler Papers.

10. Robert S. Weddle, *The French Thorn: Rival Explorers in the Spanish Sea, 1682–1762* (College Station: Texas A&M University Press, 1991), 192–193; Juan Agustin Morfi, *History of Texas, 1673–1779* (Albuquerque: Quivira Society, 1935), 170; "Bonilla's Brief Compendium of the History of Texas, 1772," *Texas State Historical Association Quarterly* 8 (July, 1904): 24. Dunn (204, fn 5) doubted these people were Apaches, but the Tejas with St. Denis would have known the difference. Dunn described the river as the San Marcos.

11. Katherine Bridges and Winston De Ville, eds., "Natchitoches and the Trail to the Rio Grande," *Louisiana History* 8 (Summer 1967): 247–248; Weddle, 200–203. Bridges and DeVille said the river was the Brazos; Weddle said it was the Colorado.

12. Lewis, "La Harpe's First," 344–345, 347; Lewis, *Along the Arkansas*, 48; Schroeder, vol. 3, 17–18. Scholars have also questioned the Padoucas' identity, but the written and archeological records make it clear they were Apaches. (Donald J. Blakeslee, *Along Ancient Trails: The Mallet Expedition of 1839* [Niwot, Colorado: University Press of Colorado, 1995], 35).

13. A camp of this size would normally house 700 people; obviously, most of these people were visiting.

14. Frank Norall, 36, 58–78, 153–160; Henri Folmer, "De Bourgmont's Expedition to the Padoucas in 1724, the First French Approach to Colorado," *The Colorado Magazine* 14 (July 1937): 121–127; Schlesier, "Rethinking," 114.

15. Declaration of Captain Alonsso Rael de Aguilar to General Juan Domingo de Bustamante, April 19 to May 4, 1724, Schroeder Papers.

16. Hackett, *Pichardo's Treatise*, 244–246; Tiller, Veronica E. Velarde, *The Jicarilla Apache Tribe: A History* (Albuquerque: BowArrow Publishing Co., 2000), 8; Schlesier, "Rethinking," 116; Stanley Noyes, *Los Comanches: The Horse People, 1751–1845* (Albuquerque: University of New Mexico Press, 1993), 22. A faction of the Jicarillas returned to the Cimarron-Ponil area and stayed.

17. Opler (*Handbook*, 389) said Cuartelejos by 1719 had begun to merge with other Plains Apaches and were last recorded in 1727.

Chapter 6

1. Bridges and De Ville, 248–249; Dunn, "Apache Relations," 201; T. N. and T. J. Campbell, *Indian Groups Associated With Spanish Missions of the San Antonio Missions National Historical Park* (San Antonio: Center for Archeological Research, University of Texas at San Antonio, 1996), 6, 22, 27–28.

2. Dunn, 204–205; Morfi, *History of Texas,* 199.

3. Governor Cabello, Informe, September 30, 1784, Béxar Archives, Dolph Briscoe Center for American History, University of Texas at Austin.

4. Spaniards in New Mexico meant the Canadian River when they referred to the Rio Colorado. In Texas, they meant the Colorado River of their province.

5. Hackett, *Pichardo's Treatise,* 463; Dunn, 206–208; Hammond and Rey, *Arricivita,* vol. 2, 25.

6. Dunn, 222; Jeff Hengesbaugh, "Massacre on the Platte," *Wild West* (October 1995): 37.

7. Hammond and Rey, *Arricivita,* 27–28.

8. Dunn, 208; Elizabeth John, *Storms Brewed in Other Men's Worlds: The Confrontation of Indians, Spanish, and French in the Southwest, 1540–1795* (College Station: Texas A&M University Press, 1975), 260; Hackett, *Pichardo's Treatise,* 463.

9. *Arricivita,* 27–9; Dunn, 209–212; Maestas, 163–166.

10. Fray Francisco Hidalgo, statement, January 14, 1724, Archivo General de la Nación, Mexico City, Provincias Internas; Dunn, 215–219; Almazán auto, March 12,1724, AGN; Maestas, 166.

11. Cabello, Informe, BA.

12. Maestas, 215; Morris E. Opler, "Problems in Apachean Cultural History, with Special Reference to the Lipan Apache," *Anthropological Quarterly* 48 (1975): 187.

13. Dunn, 222–224; Morfi, 246; Schroeder, vol. 3, 32.

14. Max Moorhead, *The Apache Frontier: Jacobo Ugarte and Spanish-Indian Relations in Northern New Spain, 1769–1791* (Norman: University of Oklahoma Press, 1968), 15–16.

15. Herbert Eugene Bolton, *Texas in the Middle Eighteenth Century; Studies in Spanish Colonial History and Administration* (New York: Russell & Russell, 1962), 5–6.

16. Dunn, 225–228; *Arricivita,* 32; Paul D. Nathan, trans., and Lesley Byrd Simpson, ed., *The San Saba Papers: A Documentary Account of the Founding and Destruction of San Sabá Mission* (Dallas: Southern Methodist University Press, 2000), xv.

17. Carlos E. Castañeda, *Our Catholic Heritage in Texas, 1519–1936,* vol. 3 (Austin: Von Boeckmann-Jones Co., 1938), 37; Opler, *Handbook,* 375; Dunn, 227–228; Robert E. Bolton, "The Jumano Indians in Texas 1650–1771," *Southwestern Historical Quarterly* 15 (July 1912): 80–81.

18. Maestas, 176; Forbes, "Unknown Athapaskans," 135.

19. Morris, *El Llano Estacado,* 146; Tyler and Taylor, 301; Bolton, "Jumano Indians," 82.

20. Anderson, *Indian Southwest,* 117.

21. Opler, *Handbook,* 390. Opler argued that the two terms were interchangeable, but later Spanish records listed Faraons and Natagés, indicating separate groups.

22. Tunnell and Newcomb, 147–148; Enrique R. Madrid, ed., *Expedition to La Junta de los Rios, 1747–1748: Captain Commander Joseph de Ydoiaga's Report to the Viceroy of New Spain,* (Austin: Office of the State Archeologist, 1992), 37, 52–53, 86; Opler, *Handbook,* 391.

23. Castañeda, 38–39.

24. Dunn, "Apache Relations," 231–3, 269; Castañeda, 39; Schlesier, 117; Schroeder, vol. 3, 28b–28c, 32; Nathan and Simpson, xvi.

25. Wade, 173–174, 251 fn 4.

26. In one implausible interpretation, Juliana Barr writes that soldiers, "perhaps in mute recognition of the Apache men's grief," wanted to move their families. (Juliana Barr, *Peace Came in the Form of a Woman: Indians and Spaniards in the Texas Borderlands* [Chapel Hill: University of North Carolina Press, 2007], 173.)

27. Dunn, 234–241, Nathan and Simpson, xvii; John, 272–273; Anderson, *Indian Southwest,* 119 and 304 fn 58.

28. Dunn, 241, 241 fn 4, 243.

Chapter 7

1. Nathan and Simpson, xvi.

2. Testimony of Mateo Perez, Ignacio Lorenzo, Prudencio de Orobio Basterra, and Juan Corbinal, December 1739, AGN; Maestas, 184 and 184 fn 99; Dunn, 240–241, 241 fn 4, 243–25l.

3. Juan de Balbuena, October 21, November 4, and December 7, 1739, AGN; Pedro Malo de Villavicencio to Viceroy, October 27 and November 23, 1739, AGN; Max L. Moorhead, "Spanish Deportation of Hostile Apaches: The Policy and the Practice," *Arizona and the West* 17 (Autumn 1975): 206, 210–211, 215, 217; Santiago Martinez Ros to Francisco Xavier Ramos Martín Gonzalez, May 1739, AGN.

4. In her revisionist history, Juliana Barr (168–170) warps the known facts to conjure up an innocent chief victimized by Spanish military policy, but the Lipans were at war. She wrote that the *capitan grande* was a "nonexistent entity," which is incorrect, and relies on Moorhead's flawed translation to conclude, as he did, that a guardian "absconded" with the dying Maria, which simply makes no sense.

5. Moorhead, 205–206.

6. Dunn, 249, 251; Morfi, 290.

7. Father Santa Ana attributed this gesture to fear, but sparing one person to intimidate the enemy was not uncommon among Apaches.

8. Castañeda, vol. 3, 343–344.

9. Blakeslee, 171; Torribio Urrutia to Viceroy, December 17, 1740, in *The San José Papers: The Primary Sources for the History of Mission San José y San Miguel de Aguayo from its Founding in 1720 to the Present* (San Antonio: Old Spanish Missions Historical Research Library at San José Mission, 1978), 77–78.

10. *Arricivita,* 36.

11. Tomás Felipe de Winthuysen, "Texas as Seen by Governor Winthuysen," *Southwestern Historical Quarterly* 88 (October 1984):176–177. Father Santa Ana believed the Natagés included the Mescaleros and Salineros, but those groups were Natagé allies with their own territories.

12. Dunn, "Apache Relations," 250–259, 266–268; *Arricivita,* 35–38.

13. John, 277, 280–283; Robert H. Thonhoff, *El Fuerte del Cibolo: Sentinel of the Bexar-La Bahia Ranches* (Austin: Eakin Press, 1992), 16; Dunn, 254–255, 259; Handbook of Texas Online, "Brushy Creek" and "San Gabriel River" *www.tsha.utexas.edu/handbook* (accessed August 30, 2007).

14. *Arricivita,* 40.

15. Herbert Eugene Bolton, "The Mission as a Frontier Institution in the Spanish-American Colonies," *The American Historical Review* 23 (1918): 19–21; Diana Hadley, Thomas H. Naylor and Mardith K. Schuetz-Miller, eds., *Presidio and Militia on the Northern Frontier of New Spain: A Documentary History*, vol. 2, part 2 (Tucson: University of Arizona Press, 1997), 483–485; Mardith K. Schuetz, "The Indians of the San Antonio Missions, 1718–1821," Ph.D. diss. (University of Texas at Austin, 1980), 346.

16. Cabello may have confused his tribes. In 1786, when DeAnza made peace with the Comanches, they dug a hole and "symbolically buried the war" (Noyes, 81).

17. Hadley, 486 and fn 17; Dunn, 261–262 and fn 1; William E. Dunn, "Missionary Activities among the Eastern Apaches Previous to the Founding of the San Saba Mission," *Southwestern Historical Quarterly* 15 (1912): 189 and fn 1; Thoribio de Urrutia, testimony, November 29, 1749, Marc Simmons Papers, courtesy of Marc Simmons. Domingo Cabello reported incorrectly that the prisoners were released August 18.

18. *Arricivita*, 42–46; Father Mariano Francisco de Los Dolores, Report on the Reduction of Indians at the San Xavier mission in Texas, undated, The Dolph Briscoe Center for American History, University of Texas, Austin, Texas; Morfi, 308–309; Maestas, 206; Dunn, "Missionary Activities," 192.

19. Hadley, 483, 486–491; Dunn, "Missionary Activities," 194–195; William E. Dunn, "The Apache Mission on the San Sabá River: Its Founding and Failure," *Southwestern Historical Quarterly* 17 (1914): 382.

20. John, 286–287.

Chapter 8

1. Hadley, Naylor and Schuetz-Miller, 191.

2. Tobosos were a small but aggressive tribe of unknown affiliation.

3. Thomas Naylor and Charles Polzer, eds., *The Presidio and Militia on the Northern Frontier of New Spain*, vol. 1 (Tucson: University of Arizona Press, 1986), 304 and footnotes 5 and 6; Schroeder, vol. 3, 32.

4. The Tobosos were still enough of a threat that in 1746 an argument for moving the presidio of Sacramento in northern Coahuila to the San Xavier River in Texas was the need to defend Coahuila and Nueva Leon against the Tobosos and the "Apaches Jumanes" from the Rio Grande (Bolton, "Jumano Indians," 83).

5. Hadley, Naylor and Schuetz-Miller, 170–171, 177–178, 191; Maestas, 193.

6. Berroterán was placed under arrest at about that time, after long conflict with his superiors (Hadley, 174).

7. Madrid, "Expedition to La Junta," 37, 52–53, 86; Maestas, 193–197; Anderson, *Indian Southwest*, 115–116; Opler, *Handbook*, 388.

8. Handbook of Texas Online, "La Junta de los Rios" and "Pedro de Rábago y Rábago," *http://wwwtsha.utexas.edu/handbook/online/articles/PP/uqp4.html* (accessed December 14, 2006); J. Charles Kelley, "The Historic Indian Pueblos of La Junta de Los Rios," *New Mexico Historical Review* 27 (October 1952): 276–278, and 28 (January 1953), 48, 50; Howard G. Applegate and C. Wayne Hanselka, "La Junta de los Rios del Norte y Conchos," *Southwestern Studies Monograph* 41 (El Paso: University of Texas, 1974): 9–10; Anderson, *Indian Southwest*, 118.

9. Anderson, *Indian Southwest*, 116. Schroeder (vol. 3, 31) argued that Lipans "could not have been the Apaches . . . near the Rio Grande-Concho junction," but they were clearly a presence there.

10. "The Founding of Missions at La Junta de Los Rios," *Supplementary Studies of the Texas Catholic Historical Society* 1 (April 1938): 17–18, 24.

11. Maestas, 378; Forbes, "Unknown Athapaskans," 140; Newcomb, *Indians of Texas*, 31; Opler, "Use of Peyote by the Carrizo and Lipan Apache Tribes," *American Anthropologist* 40 (1938): 271–2; Hadley, 188; *Handbook of Texas Online*, "San Agustín Church, Laredo, Texas," *http://www.tshaonline.org/handbook/online/articles/LL/hdl2.html* (accessed September 15, 2009) and "Laredo" *http://www.tshaonline.org/handbook/online/articles/LL/hdl2.html* (accessed September 15, 2009).

12. Omer Stewart, "Origin of the Peyote Religion in the United States," *Plains Anthropologist* 19 (1974): 214–215; Maestas, 384; Opler, "Use of Peyote," 271–274.

13. Pedro de Rábago y Terán, Diary of Campaign, Walter Webb Papers, Dolph Briscoe Center for American History, University of Texas at Austin.

14. Rábago, Diary; Cordero, 345–346.

15. Schroeder, vol. 1, xii. Thirty years later, Father Juan Agustin Morfi would write that Lipans might throw adult captives into the fire, stab them, apply coals to body parts, cut off a piece of flesh and eat it. Juan Agustin Morfi, *Excerpts from the Memorias for the history of the province of Texas* (San Antonio: Privately published, 1932), 18.

16. Rábago, Diary; Handbook of Texas Online, s.v. "Presidio Del Norte," *http://wwwtsha.utexas.edu/handbook/online/articles/PP/uqp4.html* (accessed December 14, 2006.)

17. "Instruction of Don Thomas Vélez Cachupín, 1754," in Thomas, *Plains Indians*, 132.

18. Gunnerson, *Jicarilla Apaches*, 228; Thomas, *Plains Indians*, 2, 31–32, 124, 135–137; Kessell, *Kiva*, 385, 510; Schlesier, 126. Thomas identifies the Chilpaines as Faraons, but this is incorrect. Vélez doesn't mention Jicarillas, but apparently a few eastern Jicarillas were there. According to Eiselt (107), some time around 1770 the confederated El Cuartelejos and the Pecos Jicarillas became known collectively as the Lipiyanes or Llaneros, but the Jicarillas returned to their own country in 1768 (Schlesier). "The Jicarilla alone did not participate" in the southern migration. Later records make it clear that the plains Jicarillas were separate from the Lipiyans and Llaneros.

Chapter 9

1. Verne F. Ray, *Ethnohistorical Analysis of Documents Relating to the Apache Indians of Texas* (New York: Garland Publishing Inc., 1974), 28.

2. Castañeda, vol. 3, 369–374.

3. Morfi, *History*, 328–329.

4. Tunnell and Newcomb, 157–158; Dunn, "Apache Mission," 383; *Arricivita*, 48.

5. Castañeda, 369–375; *Arricivita*, 54.

6. Castañeda, 379–380.

7. John, *Storms Brewed*, 290.

8. Robert S. Weddle, *San Juan Bautista: Gateway to Spanish Texas* (Austin: University of Texas Press, 1968), 246–248; Dunn, "Missionary Activities," 197–200; *Arricivita*, 51.

9. Dunn, "Apache Mission," 386, 388–389; John, 291–292, 294; Castañeda, 378–379, 386, 388–390.

10. John, 293–294; Dunn, "Apache Mission," 387.

11. Tlaxcaltecans from Mexico were often used as teachers and colonists in the northern missions. Vanquished by Cortés, they became trusted allies of the Spaniards and helped extend Spanish rule (Robert E. Bolton, "The Mission as a Frontier Institution," 54–55).

12. Tunnell and Newcomb, 158–159; John, 295; Dunn, "Apache Mission," 391–397; Schlesier, 125.

13. *Arricivita*, 59–62; Fr. Benito Varela to Parrilla, San Marcos, May 9, 1757, Simmons Papers; Parrilla statements, May 22 and 29, 1757, Simmons Papers; Tunnell and Newcomb, 159; Dunn, "Apache Mission," 398.

14. *Arricivita*, 63–66; Tunnell and Newcomb, 159; Dunn, "Apache Mission," 399–402, 381 fn 3; John, 296; Colonel Parrilla to Marqués de las Amarillas, April 8, 1758, in Nathan and Simpson, 132.

15. Statement by Fray Francisco Aparicio to Colonel Parrilla, April 5, 1758, in Nathan and Simpson, 128.

16. Dunn, "Apache Mission," 403–404; Tunnell and Newcomb, 160.

17. Depositions of Andrés de Villareal and Juan Leal, March 22, 1758, and Father Miguel de Molina, Joseph Gutiérrez, and Joseph Antonio Flores, March 21, 1758, in Nathan and Simpson, 44, 46–48, 68–71, 73–76, 85.

18. *Arricivita*, 70. Schilz (15) claims that Parilla "appealed to friendly Lipan chiefs for warriors to defend the Spanish settlement. The unenthusiastic Lipans, however, left the presidio dangerously exposed to attack."

19. Dunn, "Apache Mission," 413–414.

20. Parrilla to Viceroy, April 8, 1758, 149–150, and Molina Deposition, in Nathan and Simpson, 91.

21. W. W. Newcomb Jr., *The Rock Art of Texas Indians* (Austin: University of Texas Press, 1967), 153–155; Maestas, 221.

22. *Arricivita*, 72–73; Henry Easton Allen, "The Parrilla Expedition to the Red River, *Southwestern Historical Quarterly* 43 (July 1939): 57.

23. Parrilla to Viceroy, April 8, 1758, in Nathan and Simpson, 148–149; John, 301.

24. Father Mariano Francisco de los Dolores to Parrilla, March 30, 1758, in Nathan and Simpson, 123–124.

25. Nathan and Simpson: Navarrete to Toribio de Guevara, March 23, 1758, and Navarrete to Rodríguez, March 23, 1758, 17–23; Nieto and Castilla y Therán to Governor, March 24, 1758, 14; Jack Jackson, *Imaginary Kingdom: Texas as Seen by the Rivera and Rubí Military Expeditions, 1727 and 1767* (Austin: Texas State Historical Association, 1995), 179–180; Casteñeda, vol. 4, 193; Dunn, "Missionary Activities, 196 fn 2.

26. Casteñeda, 114–117; *Arricivita*, 71.

27. John, 302; Nathan and Simpson, 154–155; Allen, 65.

28. Diary of Juan Angel de Oyarzún, in Robert S. Weddle, *After the Massacre: The Violent Legacy of San Sabá Mission* (Lubbock: Texas Tech University Press, 2007), 107–108, 110–117, 120–123.

29. Tunnell and Newcomb, 161–162; Allen, 67–70; Lathel F. Duffield, "The Taovayas Village of 1759: In Texas or Oklahoma?" *Great Plains Journal* 4 (April 2, 1965): 44; Robert S. Weddle, "The San Sabá Mission: Approach to the Great Plains," *Great Plains Journal* 4 (April 2, 1965): 33.

Chapter 10

1. Tunnell and Newcomb, 162.

2. Maestas, 249.

3. L. B. Bloom, "Bourke on the Southwest," *New Mexico Historical Review* 11 (July 1936): 277. The name may have evolved over time from various designations used by the Spanish: Ipande, Ypande, Hipandis, Hipanes, and Lypanes (Tunnell and Newcomb, 149; Gunnerson, *Jicarilla Apaches*, 154–155, 166; Schroeder Papers, Box 10715, card catalogue 445, New Mexico Archives).

4. Morfi, *History*, 399–400; Castañeda, vol. 4, 154, 158, 160–161, 163; Tunnell and Newcomb, 163–165.

5. Castañeda, Vol. 4, 162–166; *Handbook of Texas Online*, s.v. "Camp Wood," http://www.tsha.utexas.edu/handbook/online/articles/CC/hrc17.html (accessed October 11, 2007); Tunnell and Newcomb, 166.

6. John, *Storms Brewed*, 362; Opler, *Lipan and Mescalero*, 4; Cordero, 338–339.

7. John, 362–365; Castañeda, vol. 4, 168–172, 175, 178–182; *Arricivita*, 80–82, 84; Morfi, 402–403; Weddle, *San Juan Bautista*, 275–276; Tunnell and Newcomb, 168–171.

8. Anderson, *Indian Southwest*,125–126.

9. Castañeda, 183; Tunnell and Newcomb, 172–173; *Arricivita*, 86–87.

10. Castañeda, 196.

11. Bolton, "Mission," 4.

12. Daniel Castro Romero Jr., "Castro Family History in Bee County," 8. WPA workers in 1936 reconstructed the presidio's chapel, walls and one tower. A guest book at the site, adjacent to Menard's country club, shows regular visitation.

13. Subseries D: Lipan, "Alien People," Box 44, Folder 10, Opler Papers.

14. Bidais were Atakapans who lived in eastern Texas along the upper Brazos.

15. Nicolas de Lafora, *The Frontiers of New Spain: Nicholas de Lafora's Description, 1766–1768*, trans. Lawrence Kinnaird (Berkeley: Quivira Society, 1958), 1–3, 77; Rubí Dictamen, in Jackson, 179–180; Newcomb, *Indians of Texas*, 319; Castañeda, 247–248; Thomas, *Plains Indians*, 37; Moorhead, *Apache Frontier*, 26; Bonilla, 60.

16. Foster, 181, 276. Lafora mentions a canoe, and Kinnaird says "dugout" canoe, but the original text doesn't specify a dugout canoe. Lipans told Opler they never made or used canoes, but they were known to use rafts and bullboats (Morris Opler, "Lipan Apache Navigation," *The Masterkey* 49 [April–June 1975], 70–72). The bullboat was a circular rawhide with rope threaded through holes around the edge; pulling the rope drew the edges up, and it could hold goods or children. They also used a raft of two parallel logs with cross pieces topped by hides, which could carry baggage, children and old people. Men swam ahead and pulled it by ropes, with women and some men behind. They could also float across by placing a large gourd under an armpit. Subseries D: Lipan, "Artifacts," Box 44, File 5, Opler Papers.

17. Lafora, 147–148; Castañeda, Vol. 4, 190, 197, 199.

18. Lafora, 7–8, 214–217.

19. Rubí Dictamen, in Jackson, 179, 181; Lafora, 149–150; Viceroy Francisco, Marques de Croix to Hugo Oconor, Mexico City, September 3, 1768, Simmons Papers; Foster, 182.

20. Thomas, *Plains Indians*, 37–38; Rubí Dictamen, 181–182;

Chapter 11

1. David M. Vigness, "Don Hugo O'Conor and New Spain's Northeastern Frontier, 1764–1776," *Journal of the West* 6 (1967): 39.

2. Moorhead, *Apache Frontier*, 27–28.

3. Maestas, 256; *Handbook of Texas Online*, s.v. "Gálvez Crossings on the Pecos River," *http://www.tsha.utexas.edu/handbook* , accessed September 16, 2006.

4. Bernard E. Bobb, *The Viceregency of Antonio Maria Bucareli in New Spain, 1771–1779* (Austin: University of Texas Press, 1962), 134; Moorhead, *Apache Frontier*, 35–36.

5. Ugarte to Bucareli, July 11, 1772 and Bucareli to Arriaga, Mexico, August 27, 1772, AGN.

6. Ripperda to Viceroy, July 6 and August 25, 1772, in Herbert Eugene Bolton, *Athanase de Mezieres and the Louisiana-Texas Frontier, 1768–1780*, vol. 1 (Cleveland: Arthur H. Clark Co., 1914; New York: Kraus Reprint Co., 1970), 328–329, 342.

7. Ripperda to Viceroy, July 4, 1772, in Bolton, 317–319.

8. Robert S. Weddle, *San Juan Bautista*, 304–305; Moorhead, *Apache Frontier*, 16–18; Mark Santiago, *The Red Captain: The Life of Hugo O'Conor, Commandant Inspector of the Interior Provinces of New Spain* (Tucson: Arizona Historical Society, 1994), 40, 43–48, 97 note 125; Vigness, 35–36. Flying companies were units of soldiers experienced in Indian fighting.

9. Opler, "Apachean Culture Pattern," 388; John, *Storms Brewed*, 363; Tunnell and Newcomb, 169. In September 1762, the Tejas attacked a Lipan camp on the Frio near San Antonio and captured his sister; she escaped the following spring and made her way to the San Sabá presidio. Bigotes' band, whose Apache band name was Sigilande, was then camped at Paint Rock.

10. Santiago, 48.

11. Ugarte to Bucareli, May 11, 1773, AGN.

12. Weddle, 327; Santiago, 55, 58–59.

13. Roque de Medina, November 29, 1773, AGN.

14. Santiago, 57–59; Moorhead, *Apache Frontier*, 38.

15. Moorhead, *Apache Frontier*, 37–38; Alfred B. Thomas, *Forgotten Frontiers: A Study of the Spanish Indian Policy of Don Juan Bautista de Anza, Governor of New Mexico, 1777–1787* (Norman: University of Oklahoma Press, 1932), 10–11.

16. Ugarte, diary, January 14, 1776, and Vicente Rodriguez, diary, January 1776, AGN.

17. Opler, "Apachean Culture Pattern," 388; Maestas, 71; Santiago, 67–68.

18. Alejo de Garza Falcon, diary, January 1776, AGN; Opler, "Apachean Culture Pattern," 388; Maestas, 71; Santiago, 67–68; Moorhead, *Apache Frontier*, 40–41.

19. Ugarte to Bucareli, September 11, 1776, AGN; Minutes of the Council of Chihuahua, June 11, 1778, Béxar Archives, Briscoe Center for American History, University of Texas at Austin.

20. Moorhead, 41; Santiago, 72–73; Thomas, 64.

Chapter 12

1. Croix to Lord Baron de Ripperdá, Chihuahua, September 15, 1778, BA.

2. Report of the Council at Monclova, December 11, 1777, in Bolton, *Mezieres*, vol. 2, 153–154; Ugarte to Bucareli, September 11, 1776, and Minutes of the Council of Chihuahua, June 11, 1778, BA.

3. Cabello to Viceroy, June 17, 1776, BA.

4. Minutes of the Council of Chihuahua, June 11, 1778, BA.

5. Testimony of Juan Domingo Ochoa to Ugarte, November 1, 1776, AGN.

6. Albert B. Thomas, *Teodoro de Croix and the Northern Frontier of New Spain, 1776–1783*, vol. 1 (Norman: University of Oklahoma Press, 1941), 7; Report of the Council at Monclova, 152–154; Croix's Report of 1781, in Thomas, 115, 120.

7. Bernardo de Gálvez, *Instructions for Governing the Interior Provinces of New Spain, 1786*, ed. Donald E. Worcester (Berkeley: Quivira Society, 1951), 18; Ripperdá to Croix, April 27, 1777, Simmons Papers.

8. Thomas, *Forgotten Frontiers*, 16; Antonio Bonilla, January 5, 1778, in Bolton, vol. 2, 165–167; Report of the Council at Monclova, 153, 156–157, 161–162.

9. Opler, "Apachean Culture Pattern," 388.

10. Sjoberg (78) dates the division around 1780, but use of the Apache name for Big Water Lipans in 1771 indicates an earlier division. The fact that Oconór found Bigotes with Natagés and Mescaleros in New Mexico indicates they were No Water Lipans.

11. Castañeda, vol. 4, 176; Thomas, *Croix*, 6; Schroeder, vol. 3, 35, 45–47; Cordero, 353–356; Concha to Nava, December 13, 1792, AGN. Gunnerson (*Jicarilla Apaches*, 277) argues that Lipiyans and Llaneros were the same group.

12. Donald C. Cutter, trans. and ed., *Northern New Spain: Hugo O'Conor's Report to Teodoro de Croix, July 22, 1777* (Dallas: DeGolyer Library, 1994), 73.

13. Weddle, *San Juan Bautista*, 340–342; Report of the Council at Monclova, 155; Croix's Report of 1781, 89–90.

14. Morfi, *Excerpts*, 17–19.

15. Bolton, *Mezieres*, vol. 1, 111; Minutes of the Council of Chihuahua, June 11, 1778, BA; Report of the Council at Monclova, 157, 161–162.

16. Croix's Report, 90.

17. Thomas, *Forgotten Frontiers*, 16.

18. Croix to Jose de Galvez, September 23, 1778, 221 and Méziéres to Croix, April 7, 1778, in Bolton, vol. 2, 197; Morfi, *History*, 430–432.

19. John, *Storms Brewed*, 529–530; Croix's Report, 82.

20. Donald E. Chipman and Harriett Denise Joseph, *Notable Men and Women of Spanish Texas* (Austin: University of Texas Press, 1999), 202–204, 207–208.

21. Croix to Cabello, January 13, 1779, BA; Cabello to Croix, March 18, 1779, BA; Thonhoff, *El Fuerte*, 113.

22. Cabello to Croix, March 18, 1779, BA.

23. Croix's Report of 1781, in Thomas, *Teodoro de Croix*, 73–74, 90–93.

24. Croix to Cabello, September 16, 1779, BA.

25. Croix to Cabello, August 16, 1779, BA

26. Cabello to Croix, August 19, 1779, BA.

27. Cabello to Croix, September 3, 1779, BA.

28. Croix's Report of 1781, 92–93, 96, 125–127.

29. Cabello to Croix, Oct. 19, 1779, BA.

30. Cabello to Croix, November 2, 1779, BA.

31. Cabello to Croix, February 12, 1780, BA; John, 613; Croix's Report, 77, 98–99, 129; Morfi, *History*, 440; Chipman and Joseph, 211–212.

32. Cabello to Croix, October 20, 1780, BA; Croix to Ripperdá, September 15, 1778, BA.

33. Revilla to Josef Antonio de la Garza Falcon et al., March 30, 1783, in Robert D. Wood, *Archivos de Laredo: Documents on the Indians* (Laredo Archives Series No. 2, 1998), 8.

34. Cabello to Croix, January 31, 1781, BA.

35. Marc Simmons, "New Mexico's Smallpox Epidemic of 1780–1781," *New Mexico Historical Review*, 41 (October 1966): 321–324; John, 541–542; Morfi, 434–435; Joaquín Rivaya-Martinez, "Captivity and Adoption Among the Comanche Indians, 1700–1875," Ph.D. diss., University of California at Los Angeles, 2006, 391.

36. Morfi, *Excerpts*, 19; Jean Louis Berlandier, *The Indians of Texas in 1830*, ed. John C. Ewers (Washington, D.C.: Smithsonian Institution Press, 1969), 84–85; Cabello to Croix, October 20 and November 20, 1780 and January 31, 1781, BA; Simmons, 321–324.

Chapter 13

1. Revilla Gigedo to Falcon, March 30, 1783 in Wood, 8.

2. David La Vere, *Life Among the Texas Indians: The WPA Narratives* (College Station: Texas A&M University Press, 1998), 8; Morfi, *History*, 437–438; Cabello to Croix, November 30, 1780, BA.

3. John, *Storms Brewed*, 541–542, 634–636; Cabello to Rengel, June 4, 1785, BA; Raphael Martínez Pacheco to Ugalde, December 9, 1787, BA; Verne Huser, *Rivers of Texas* (College Station: Texas A&M University Press, 2004), 201, 203, 205.

4. Cabello to Croix, March 14, 1780, BA; Morfi, *Excerpts*, 4. The Cocos were a Karankawan group and the Mayeyes, a Tonkawan group. The Bidais were related to the Atakapas, who lived along the coast and in the bayous of southwestern Louisiana and southeastern Texas, and to the Akokisas, an Atakapan group living south of the Bidais on the lower Trinity and San Jacinto rivers and along the eastern shores of Galveston Bay. Handbook of Texas Online, "Atakapa Indians," *http://www.tshaonline.org/handbook/online/articles/AA/bma48.html* (accessed February 5, 2008); Newcomb, *Indians of Texas*, 316.

5. Wood, 8; Luis Cazorla, Response to Charges, December 18, 1780, BA; Handbook of Texas Online, "Karankawa Indians," *http://www.tshaonline.org/handbook/online/articles/KKbmk5.html* (accessed February 5, 2008).

6. John, *Storms Brewed*, 634–636; Phelipe de Neve to Cabello, December 26, 1783, BA.

7. Schilz (29–30) wrote that the Lipan Chief Josef Chiquito "was especially active as a diplomat and helped spread El Mocho's ideas of a grand Indian confederacy among other Apaches," and that Cabello had Spanish soldiers assassinate him, all of which is incorrect.

8. Cabello to de Neve, September 30, 1783, BA; de Neve to Cabello, December 26, 1783, BA.

9. John, 641–642, 644, 646; Cabello to viceroy, September 30, 1782, April 30, May 31 and October 31, 1783, BA.

10. Cabello to de Neve, March 31, June 20 and September 20, 1784, BA; John, 647–648.

11. Cabello to Rengel, June 4 and 7, 1785 and January 25, 1786, BA.

12. Cabello to Rengel, September 19, 1785, and January 25, March 18, and November 20, 1786, BA; John, 698–699.

13. Cabello to Rengel, November 25, 1785, BA; Cabello to Ugarte, July 30, 1786, BA.

14. Cabello, diary, June 8, 1786; Cabello to Ugarte, July 3, 1786, BA.

15. Opler, *Handbook*, 377.

16. Cabello to Ugarte, July 2 and 3 and September 25, 1786, BA.

17. John, *Storms Brewed*, 717–718.

18. Cabello to Ugarte, September 25, 1786, BA; Pacheco to Ugalde, December 24, 1787, and February 3, 1788, BA.

19. Ugalde to Pacheco, August 23, 1787, BA; Pacheco to Ugalde, September 29, 1787, BA; Pacheco to Ugarte, March 10, 1787, BA.

20. Pacheco, report, February 1787, BA; Ugarte Pacheco, February 1, 1787, BA.

21. Fray José Raphael Oliva to Pacheco, February 11, 1787, BA; Pacheco to Oliva, February 14, 1787, BA.

22. Curvelo to Pacheco, September 25, 1787, BA; Manuel de Urrutia to Pacheco, September 28, 1787, BA.

23. José Antonio Rapahel Curvelo to Pacheco, September 25, 1787, BA; Cabello to Croix, August 17, 1780, BA; Urrutia to Pacheco, September 28, 1787. Chiquito had been a chief since August 1780.

24. Ugarte to Pacheco, February 1, 1787.

25. Curvelo to Pacheco, September 25, 1787.

26. Al B. Nelson, "Campaigning in the Big Bend of the Rio Grande in 1787," *Southwestern Historical Quarterly* 39 (January 1936): 202, 205, 207–208, 211, 213, 223, 225.

27. Reports of expenditures, December 27, 1786 to June 30, 1787, BA; Pacheco to Ugalde, March 17, 1788, BA; Curvelo to Pacheco, September 25, 1787, BA.

28. Ugarte to Pacheco, February 1, 1787, BA; Ugalde to Pacheco, August 23, 1787, BA; Pacheco to Ugarte, March 10, 1787, BA; Pacheco to Ugalde, September 29, 1787, BA.

29. Gálvez, *Instructions*, 21, 38, 40–47, 75, 80.

Chapter 14

1. Al B. Nelson, "Juan de Ugalde and Picax-ande InsTinsle," *Southwestern Historical Quarterly* 63 (April 1940): 438–439, 441–444; Blas Maria Ecay Musquis testimony, April 3, 1792, AGN.

2. Nava to Concha, June 28, 1792, AGN; Diaz to Nava, April 30, 1792, SANM II; Nava to Concha, June 28, 1792, AGN. Sandhills are common in the region, but the two largest fields are just east of Monahans and south of present Muleshoe stretching into eastern New Mexico. While other historians have chosen the latter as Picax-andé's sandhills, Monahans logistically makes the most sense. It was in the middle of their territory; the northern sands were outside Apache territory and squarely in the thick of Comanchería, although it's possible that Apaches also used those sandhills on occasion.

3. Interpretive exhibit, Dunagan Visitor Center, Monahans Sandhills State Park, Monahans, Texas; Morris, 322.

4. Nelson, 441–442.

5. Cordero, 345.

6. Opler, "Apachean Culture Pattern," 370, 373.

7. Castro to Captain Jose Maria de Echeagaray, March 24, 1792, AGN; Echeagaray, informes, March 25, 1792, AGN.

8. Nelson, 453.

9. The Lipiyans' ties to the Jicarillas is another indication they were Carlanas.

10. Kenner, 59; Marc Simmons, "Governor Anza, The Lipan Apaches and Pecos Pueblo," *El Palacio* 77 (December 1970): 36–40.

11. Nelson, 452–457. The Spanish saw Picax-andé's exchange with the first Lipan chiefs he met on the Rodrigo as gruff, but his exchanges were customarily curt; he was probably issuing orders to prepare for the ceremony held in their camps.

12. Ugalde to Flores, March 10, 1788, AGN.

13. Nelson, 456-462; Ugalde to Flores, March 22, 1788, AGN.

14. Nelson, 461, 463–464.

15. Nelson, 459.

16. This may be a Hispanicized word; the Spanish had a similar term, *tlatolero*, from Nahuatl. (Joaquin Rivaya-Martinez, manuscript note, January 23, 2012.)

17. Simmons, "Governor Anza", 36–40; Cordero, 343; Jacobo Ugarte, journal, 1788, AGN; Pacheco to Ugalde, September 29, 1788, BA; Ugarte to Flores, September 24, 1788, AGN.

18. Ugalde to Pacheco, November 12, 1787, BA.

19. Ugalde to Flores, May 2, 1788, AGN; Pacheco to Ugalde, September 15, 1788, BA; Luis Cazorla to Pacheco, June 22, 1788, BA.

Chapter 15

1. Ugalde to Pacheco, December 19, 1789, BA.

2. Nelson, "Juan de Ugalde," 453; Ugalde to Flores, April 28, 1788, AGN; Diaz to Ugarte, June 15, 1790, AGN; Ugalde to Picax-andé, April 28, 1788, AGN; Ugarte to Flores, September 24, 1788, AGN.

3. Ugalde to Flores, April 20, 1789, AGN; Ugarte, July 30, 1790, AGN.

4. Ugalde to Picax-andé, April 28, 1788, AGN; Casimiro Valdés to Ugalde, January 21, 1789, AGN; Valdés to Ugalde, January 11, 1789, AGN.

5. Valdés to Ugalde, January 21, 1789, AGN.

6. Moorhead, *Apache Frontier*, 253–255; Ugalde to Flores, April 20 and May 13, 1789, AGN; Ugalde to Pacheco, December 19, 1789, BA.

7. Pacheco to Ugalde, August 1789, BA; Report of expenditures, September 15, 1789, BA.

8. Pacheco to Ugalde, September 6 and 30, 1789, BA; Pacheco report, March 1, 1790, Nacogdoches Archive, Marc Simmons Papers.

9. Ugalde to Pacheco, December 19 and 24 1789, BA; Pacheco to Ugalde, December 23, 1789, BA; Pacheco diary, December 1789, Nacogdoches Archives, Simmons Papers.

10. Pacheco to Manuel de Espadas, December 29, 1789, BA; Pacheco report, March 1, 1790, Nacogdoches Archive, Simmons Papers; Pacheco diary, December 1789, Nacogdoches Archive, Simmons papers; Moorhead, 255.

11. Muñoz to Sierragorda, August 3, 1790, AGN; Muñoz to Revilla Gigedo, September 10, 1790, AGN.

12. Benedict Leutenegger, "New Documents on Father José Mariano Reyes," *Southwestern Historical Quarterly* 71 (April 1968): 596.

13. Seb Wilcox, "The Spanish Archives of Laredo," *Southwestern Historical Quarterly* 49 (January 1946): 350–351.

14. Governor of Nuevo Santander, December 1790, AGN; Ugarte to Revilla Gigedo, September 10, 1790, AGN.

15. Moorhead, *Apache Frontier*, 255, 257–258.

16. Ugarte to Diaz, June 29, 1790, AGN; Muñoz to Revilla Gigedo, undated, AGN; Diaz to Ugarte, June 15, 1790, AGN.

17. Nava to Chacon, April 9, 1798, SANM.

18. Moorhead, 263–264; Ugarte, August 13, 1790, AGN.

19. Moorhead, 264–268.

Chapter 16

1. Muñoz to Nava, February 26, 1791, AGN.

2. Nava to viceroy, February 8, 1791, AGN; Francisco Xavier Uranga to Concho, February 20, 1791, SANM.

3. Muñoz to Nava, February 26, March 1, 7, and 16, 1791 and April 22, 1792, AGN.

4. Castro to Muñoz, March 29 and April 2, 1791, AGN; Muñoz to Castro, April 17 and 18, 1791, AGN; Muñoz to Juan Gutierrez de la Cueva, undated, AGN.

5. De la Cueva to Muñoz, May 2, 1791, AGN; Revilla Gigedo to Castro, October 10, 1792, AGN.

6. Medina to Nava, July 18, 1791, AGN; Nava to Grimarest, September 5, 1791, AGN.

7. Galindo Navarro, testimony, August 31, 1791, AGN.

8. Bernardo Fernandez to Muñoz, May 9, 1791, AGN; Muñoz to Revilla Gigedo, May 7, 1792, AGN; Muñoz to Castro, May 9, 1791, AGN; Antonio Gil Ybarbo to Muñoz, June 13, 1791, AGN.

9. Muñoz to Castro, May 9 and 22, 1791, AGN; Concha to viceroy, July 20, 1792, AGN; Revilla Gigedo? to Ramon de Castro, June 8, 1791, AGN; Nava to Concha, July 22, 1791, SANM II, Simmons Papers; Nava, November 21, 1791, SANM II; Nava to Concha, August 6, 1792, SANM, Simmons Papers.

10. J. Richard Salazar, *Spanish-Indian Relations in New Mexico during the Term of Commandant General Pedro de Nava, 1790–1802* (Guadalupita, New Mexico: Center for Land Grant Studies, 1994), 9.

11. Muñoz to Castro, September 12, 1791, AGN.

12. Gunnerson, *Jicarilla Apaches*, 271–272. Although Gunnerson believed the Lipiyanes and Llaneros were the same group, (Gunnerson, 265), references like this make it clear they were separate groups. They were mentioned repeatedly as distinct groups with different leaders.

13. Concha to Nava, November 1, 1791, SANM II; Nava, November 21, 1791, SANM II; Muñoz to Revilla Gigedo, undated, AGN.

14. Revilla Gigedo to Nava, February 25, 1792, AGN.

15. Population estimates were derived by multiplying tents or warriors by five or more. Vehik, 255.

16. Nava to Castro, March 7, 1792, AGN; Nava to Revilla Gigedo. September 14, 1792, AGN.

17. Juan Bautista de Elquezabel to Juan Gutierrez de la Cueva, February 12, 1792, AGN.

18. Castro to Revilla Gigedo, April 3, 1792, AGN.

19. Castro to Revilla Gigedo, April 3 and May 29, 1792, AGN; Castro to Sierra Gorda, June 16, 1792, AGN; Revilla Gigedo to Castro, October 10, 1792, AGN.

20. Nava to Concha, June 28, 1792, AGN; Díaz to Nava, April 30, 1792, SANM II; Nava to Castro, September 14, 1792, AGN ; Muñoz to Díaz, May 10, 1792, AGN.

2.1 Gunnerson, *Jicarilla Apaches*, 273; Díaz to Nava, July 31, 1792, AGN.

22. Concha to Revilla Gigedo, July 20, 1792, SANM; Concha to Nava, November 1792, SANM II.

23. Nava to Díaz, June 7, 1792, AGN; Nava to Revilla Gigedo, July 26, 1792, AGN; Juan Cortes to Sierra Gorda, July 9, 1792, AGN.

24. Díaz to Nava, July 31, 1792, AGN; Castro to Sierra Gorda, July 16, 1792, AGN.

25. Revilla Gigedo to Castro, October 10, 1792, AGN.

26. Diego de Borica to Diaz, October 23, 1792, AGN; Nava to Castro, September 14, 1792, AGN; Diaz to Nava, July 31, 1792, AGN; Nava to Concha, December 1792, Simmons Papers; Nava to Revilla Gigedo, October 1792, AGN.

27. Concha to Nava, December 13, 1792, Simmons Papers; Nava to Concha, December 1792, Simmons papers; Salazar, 14–15.

28. Ramon Diaz de Bustamante to Castro, December 27, 1792, AGN.

Chapter 17

1. Cordero, 341.

2. Juan Gutierrez de la Cueva to viceroy, February 10 and March 27, 1793, AGN; Nava to Castro, September 14, 1792, AGN; Manuel Martinez, "Lipan Peace," September 14, 1792, AGN; Nava to Concha, February 2, 1793, AGN.

3. Max L. Moorhead, *The Presidio* (Norman: University of Oklahoma Press, 1975), 109, 258–259, 261; Gunnerson, *Jicarilla Apaches*, 274–275.

4. F. Todd Smith, *From Dominance to Disappearance: The Indians of Texas and the Near Southwest, 1786–1859* (Lincoln: University of Nebraska Press, 2006), 46.

5. Nava to Muñoz, June 6 and 20, 1793 and August 20, 1793, Simmons papers; Bustamante to Cordero, September 3, 1803, Simmons Papers; Muñoz to Viceroy, October 5, 1805, Simmons Papers; Nava to Chacon, April 9, 1798, SANM; Cordero, 353–356.

6. Cordero, 338–339, 341.

7. Smith, 46; Moral to Muñoz, January 18, 1799, Simmons Papers; Weddle, *San Sabá*, 190. Lipans would be recorded at missions until 1817.

8. Elizabeth A. H. John, ed., "Views from a Desk in Chihuahua: Manuel Merino's Reports on Apaches and Neighboring Nations, ca. 1804," *Southwestern Historical Quarterly* 95 (July 1991): 164.

9. Elizabeth A. H. John, "Nurturing the Peace: Spanish and Comanche Cooperation in the Early Nineteenth Century," *New Mexico Historical Review* 59 (October 1984): 353–357, 360; John Sibley, *A Report from Natchitoches in 1807* (New York: Museum of the American Indian, 1922),

93–94. Sibley estimated the Lipans at 1,200 to 1,300, with about 200 to 250 warriors, which is probably the number of Lower Lipans; he probably didn't know about the Upper Lipans.

10. Nava made repeated references to "Lipiyans *or* Llaneros," which has led to confusion about whether they were the same people. During this period the two groups joined periodically, especially as the Lipiyans' numbers diminished. In early 1792 the fact that Llaneros separated from the Lipiyans to live in peace at El Norte is one instance of many demonstrating their autonomy.

11. Nava to Chacón, October 19, 1797 and January 3, 1798, SANM; Chacón to Nava, November 19, 1797, SANM.

12. Nava to Chacón, June 13, 1798, SANM.

13. Chacón to Nava, November 18, 1798, SANM. The Jicarillas later divided into two groups— Olleros and Llaneros, or mountain and plains people. The Jicarilla Llaneros knew Picax-andé's Llaneros, but they were not the same group.

14. Joseph Manuel de Ochoa to Chacón, December 27, 1800, SANM.

15. Ochoa to Chacón, August 29, 1801, SANM; Cortés, 28–30.

16. Gunnerson, *Jicarillas*, 289–292; Hämäläinen, 162.

17. Nava to Chacón, Santa Fe, August 5, 1801, SANM; Ochoa to Chacón, August 29, 1801, SANM; Ochoa to Nava, August 29, 1801, Marc Simmons Papers.

18. Gunnerson, 290; Elizabeth A. H. John, ed., "View from a Desk," 155, 157, 162–164.

19. H. Bailey Carroll and J. Villasana Haggard, *Three New Mexico Chronicles: The Exposición of Don Pedro Bautista Pino 1812; the Ojeada of Lic. Antonio Barreiro 1832; and the additions by Don José Agustín de Escudero, 1849* (Albuquerque: The Quivira Society, 1942), 128.

20. Zebulon Montgomery Pike, *The Journals of Zebulon Montgomery Pike, with Letters and Related Documents*, ed. Donald Jackson (Norman: University of Oklahoma Press, 1966), 74. Pike estimated 750 warriors, which was probably somewhat low.

21. Félix D. Almaráz, *Tragic Cavalier: Governor Manuel Salcedo of Texas, 1808–1813* (College Station: Texas A&M University Press, 1991), 111; Julia Kathryn Garrett, *Green Flag Over Texas: A Story of the Last Years of Spain in Texas* (New York: The Cordova Press, 1939), 62; Berlandier, *Indians of Texas*, 131; "Elizondo, Ignacio," *Handbook of Texas Online, http://www.tsha.utexas.edu/ handbook/online/articles/view/EE/fel8.html*, accessed December 30, 2003; Hobart Huson, *Refugio: A Comprehensive History of Refugio County from Aboriginal Times to 1953,* vol. 1 (Woodsboro, TX: Rooke Foundation, 1953–55), 49.

22. Garrett, 84; Jarrett Rie, *Gutiérrez de Lara, Mexican-Texan: The Story of a Creole Hero* (Austin: Creole Texana, 1949), 8; Handbook of Texas Online, "José Menchaca," http://www.tshaonline. org/handbook/online/articles/MM/fme11.html (accessed May 10, 2010); Carlos Beltran, "San Antonio's First Great Tragedy," *Frontier Times* 3 (October 1925): 43.

23. Harry M. Henderson, "The Magee-Gutierrez Expedition," *Southwestern Historical Quarterly* 55 (July 1951): 43–44; Henry Walker, "William McLane's Narrative of the Magee-Gutierrez Expedition, 1812–1813," *Southwestern Historical Quarterly* 66 (April 1963): 577.

24. Henderson, 50; H. Yoakum, *History of Texas from Its First Settlement in 1685 to Its Annexation to the United States in 1846*, vol. 1 (New York: Redfield, 1855), 166; Opler, *Lipan and Mescalero Apache*, 56.

25. James M Day, *The Texas Almanac 1857–1873: A Compendium of Texas History* (Waco: Texian Press, 1967), 461; Henderson, 51; John Henry Brown, *History of Texas* (St. Louis: L. E. Daniell,

c.1892–93), 57. Yoakum (167) said the Americans placed Indian auxiliaries in front to receive the charge of the Spanish cavalry while the Americans outflanked them, and the Indians fled except for the Coushattas and a few others, who withstood two more charges, losing two killed and several wounded. A veteran of this fight, Colonel W. D. C. Hall, took issue with the accuracy of this account (Day, 458).

26. Carlos Beltran, "The Battle of the Alazan," *Frontier Times* 3 (November 1925): 43–48; Beltran, "The Battle of the Medina," *Frontier Times* 3 (December 1925): 9.

27. Henderson, 56-60; Handbook of Texas Online, "Miguel Menchaca," *http://www.tshaonline. org/handbook/online/articles/MM/fme15.html* (accessed May 10, 2010); Beltran, "Battle of the Medina," 10, 12.

28. Joaquin de Arredondo, "Joaquin de Arredondo's Report of the Battle of the Medina, August 18, 1813" *Texas Historical Association Quarterly* 11 (January 1908): 224–225.

29. Berlandier, *Indians of Texas*, 131; Jean Louis Berlandier, *Journey to Mexico During the Years 1826 to 1834*, vol. 1 (Austin: The Texas State Historical Association, 1980), 284; Huson, vol. 2, 44; Ted Schwarz, ed., *Forgotten Battlefield of the First Texas Revolution: The Battle of Medina, August 18, 1813* (Austin: Eakin Press, 1985), 64; Arredondo, 226. Arredondo said the Tonkawas, Taovayas, Tawakonis and Lipans fled early in the action, the Lipans first. Huson wrote, "In the Battle of the Medina the Lipans' ranks broke although they were brave and loyal."

30. Cordero, 34; Berlandier, *Journey to Mexico*, 284; Vicente Filisola, *Memoirs for the History of the War in Texas*, vol. 2, trans. Wallace Woolsey (Austin: Eakin Press, 1987), 31.

31. Harris Gaylord Warren, *The Sword Was Their Passport: A History of American Filibustering in the Mexican Revolution* (Baton Rouge: Louisiana State University Press, 1943), 69; Joseph C. McElhannon, "Imperial Mexico and Texas," *Southwestern Historical Quarterly* 53 (October 1949): 125–127; Austin to Bustamonte, May 10, 1822, in Moses Austin, *The Austin Papers*, vol. 1, part 1 (Austin: University of Texas, 1924), 507–510; Hubert Howe Bancroft, *History of the North Mexican States and Texas*, vol. 2 (San Francisco: The History Company, Publishers, 1889), 31–32.

32. *Reports of the Committee of Investigation Sent in 1873 by the Mexican Government to the Frontier of Texas* (New York: Baker & Godwin, 1875), 417; McElhannon, 125.

33. Berlandier, *Indians of Texas*, 132–133, 132 fn 189; Berlandier, *Journey to Mexico*, 352–353, 425, 430; Anderson, *Indian Southwest*, 195. DeLay writes that the Lipans became "consummate survivors" after being "driven from the plains, abandoned and preyed upon by the Spanish . . . and impoverished and nearly annihilated by Comanches . . ." Obviously, the Lipans were neither poor nor vanquished. (Brian DeLay, *War of a Thousand Deserts: Indian Raids and the U.S. Mexican War* [New Haven: Yale University Press, 2008], 54).

34. J. Cameron to Lamar, in Charles A. Gulick, et al., eds., *The Papers of Mirabeau B. Lamar*, vol. 1 (Austin: The Pemberton Press, 1968), 476. Chariticas are often thought to be Arapahoes, but the name could also apply to Apaches. (Melburn D. Thurman, "On the Identity of the Chariticas," *Plains Anthropologist* 33 [May 1988], 159.) In this case, since only the Naishans spoke Apache, these Chariticas were Arapahoes.

35. In 1828, the Mexican emissary José Francisco Ruiz described a group he called "Lipans of the Plains," numbering 80 to 100 families, who lived with the Chariticas. "The Lipans of the Plains are ferocious Indians. Their customs differ somewhat from those of the southern Lipans." (José Francisco Ruiz, *Report on the Indians of Texas in 1828*, ed. John C. Ewers [New Haven: Yale University Press, 1972], 8.)

36. "Letters of Antonio Martínez, The Last Spanish Governor of Texas, 1817–1822," *Southwestern Historical Quarterly* 39 (April 1936): 330–331; "Calendar of the Letters of Antonio Martínez, Last Spanish Governor of Texas, 1817–1822," *Southwestern Historical Quarterly* 59 (January 1956): 373–374 and (July 1956): 482; McElhannon, 121.

37. F. Todd Smith, *Dominance*, 107, 109–110.

38. Antonio Muzquiz to Juan Jose Elguezabal, September 5, 1819, AGN; Juan Jose Elguezabal to Manuel Pardo, September 5, 1819, AGN; Joaquin de Arredondo to viceroy, September 14, 1819, AGN; Miguel Sanches Navarro to Manuel Pardo, Santa Rosa, September 5, 1819, AGN.

39. Joaquin de Arredondo to viceroy, September to October, 1819, AGN; Huson, Vol. 2, 45.

40. Douglas C. McMurtrie, "The First Texas Newspaper," *Southwestern Historical Quarterly* 36 (July 1932): 45; "Calendar of the Letters," 142–14; Padilla, 56.

Chapter 18

1. Berlandier, *Indians of Texas*, 134.

2. Berlandier, *Indians of Texas*, 66; McElhannon, 128.

3. McElhannon, 128; Ruiz, 6–8.

4. McElhannon, 123; Nettie Lee Benson, "Texas as Viewed from Mexico, 1820–1834," *Southwestern Historical Quarterly* 90 (January 1987): 228.

5. Romero, 24–25; Maestas, 212, 272–274; Lipan Apache Tribe of Texas web site (accessed March 23, 2009); Berlandier, *Indians of Texas*, 129, 132 and 132 note 189, 134; Berlandier, *Journey to New Mexico*, 352–353.

6. Berlandier, *Indians of Texas*, 42 and 42 fn 16; Smith, 107, 110; Bethel Coopwood, "Route of Cabeza de Vaca," *Southwestern Historical Quarterly* 3 (April 1900): 234, 237; McElhannon, 130.

7. Treaty of 1822, Eberstadt Collection, Dolph Briscoe Center for American History, University of Texas at Austin; Herrera to Alcaldes, August 17, 1822, in Wood, 18; José María Sánchez, "A Trip to Texas in 1828," *Southwestern Historical Quarterly* 29 (April 1926): 251.

8. Berlandier, *Indians of Texas*, 131, 133–134; DeLay, 55–56; Gulick, 191–192.

9. Huson, vol. 1, 47–48; Smithwick, Noah, "Reminiscences of an Old Texan," *Santa Ana Standard*, January 22, 1898; Ray, 32.

10. Berlandier, *Indians of Texas*, 6, 85–86; Berlandier, *Journey to Mexico*, 262, 268–269; Sánchez, 252.

11. Berlandier, *Indians of Texas*, 129. "They are of gallant appearance, and much cleaner than their compatriots," wrote Cordero (355).

12. Berlandier, *Indians of Texas*, 128–130, 134, 129 note 179; Berlandier, *Journey to Mexico*, 269; Pike, 53–55; Francis S. Latham, *Travels in the Republic of Texas, 1842* (Austin: Encino Press, 1971), 30.

13. Berlandier, *Indians of Texas*, 32, 65–66, 66 fn 63, 130; *Journey to Mexico*, 269–270.

14. James Kerr to Austin, February 26, 1827 in *The Austin Papers*, vol. 1, part 2, 1607; Huson, vol. 2, 48.

15. Berlandier, *Indians of Texas*, 13; Berlandier, *Journey*, 258, 269.

16. Ohland Morton, *Terán and Texas: A Chapter in Texas-Mexican Relations* (Austin: The Texas State Historical Association, 1948), 134; Le Roy Graf, "Colonizing Projects in Texas South of the Nueces, 1820–1845," *Southwestern Historical Quarterly* 50 (April 1947): 436; Coopwood, 237.

17. Berlandier, *Indians of Texas*, 47 and 47 fn 27; Berlandier, *Journey to Mexico*, 357.

18. Juan Gutierrez de la Cueva to viceroy, February 10 and March 27, 1793, AGN; Nava to Castro, September 14, 1792, AGN; Manuel Martinez, "Lipan Peace," September 14, 1792, AGN.

19. Anderson, 130; Sánchez, 252.

20. Dan Flores, "Bringing Home All the Pretty Horses," *Montana* (Summer 2008): 4, 12–13; Virginia H. Taylor, ed., "Calendar of the Letters of Antonio Martínez, Last Spanish Governor of Texas, 1817–1822." *Southwestern Historical Quarterly* 59 (July 1956): 478; Berlandier, *Indians*, 129–130.

21. Subseries D: Lipans, "Artifacts," Folder 5, and "Horses and Pets," Folder 13, Box 44, Opler Papers.

22. Stephen L. Hardin, *Texian Iliad: A Military History of the Texas Revolution, 1835–1836* (Austin: University of Texas Press, 1994), 97; Smith, 122.

23. Opler, *Lipan and Mescalero*, 56; Passport from S. F. Austin to Captain Huan Novale, 1825, in Winfrey and Day, vol. 1, 1.

24. Mary Austin Holley, *Texas Observations: Historical, Geographical and Descriptive* (Arno Press, New York, 1973), 103–104; Huson, vol. 1, 125.

25. "Indian difficulties From Col. Pettus," in Gulick, vol. 4, 247–248; Huson, vol. 1, 47–48.

26. Benavides to José Andrés de Sobrevilla, February 1832, in Wood, 33; José Francisco de la Garza et al, to the government of Laredo, March 11, 1824, in Wood, 20–22; Fernando Garcia Davila to viceroy, August 8, 1825, in Wood, 24; Manuel Lafuente to Government of Tamaulipas, February 20, 1833, in Wood, 39–40; J. Marvin Hunter, "Bowie's Battle Ground on the San Saba," *Frontier Times* 16 (February 1939): 214–219; Smith, 124.

27. José Antonio Leal, August 10, 1829, in Wood, 31; Francisco V. Fernandes to Governor of Tamaulipas, January 7, 1835, in Wood, 44.

28. J. M. Guerra to Commander of Tamaulipas, November 16, 1835, in Wood, 47.

Chapter 19

1. Lamar to Castro, March 6, 1838, in Gulick, vol. 2, 43.

2. William C. Binkley, ed., *Official Correspondence of the Texan Revolution, 1835–1836*, vol. 1 (New York: D. Appleton-Century Co., 1936), 25; J. M. Guerra, November 16, 1835, in Wood, 47; Daniel Castro Romero Jr., interview with Sherry Robinson, August 14, 2005.

3. Griffin, 18; Gilberto Miguel Hinojosa, *A Borderlands Town in Transition: Laredo, 1755–1870* (College Station: Texas A&M University Press, 1983), 50; James Presley, "Santa Anna in Texas: A Mexican Viewpoint," *Southwestern Historical Quarterly* 62 (April 1959): 499; Hardin, 104.

4. Stephen L. Moore, *Savage Frontier: Rangers, Riflemen, and Indian Wars in Texas*, vol. 1 (Denton: University of North Texas Press, 2002), 74; D. C. Barrett, et al., to Acting Governor J. W. Robinson, January 27 and February 14, 1836, in Binkley, 347, 426.

5. Maestas, 290; Romero, 40.

6. Richard Magoosh, interview with Eve Ball, Mescalero, New Mexico, September 29, 1963, Ball Papers.

7. Meredith Magoosh Begay, interview with Sherry Robinson, Mescalero, New Mexico, August 14, 2005.

8. Rusk to Houston, August 9, 1836, in John Jenkins, *The Papers of the Texas Revolution, 1825–1836*, vol. 8 (Austin: Presidial Press, 1973), 183.

9. Carlos Castañeda, ed., *The Mexican Side of the Texan Revolution (1836) by the Chief Mexican Participants* (Dallas: P. L. Turner Company, 1956), 326–327.

10. Tate, "Indian-White Relations in Texas," in Winfrey and Day, Vol. 1, ix; A. K. Christian, "Mirabeau Buonaparte Lamar," *Southwestern Historical Quarterly* 24 (July 1920): 44.

11. Anna Muckleroy, "The Indian Policy of the Republic of Texas," *Southwestern Historical Quarterly* 25 (April 1922): 242; Morfit to Forsyth, August 27, 1836, in Jenkins, vol. 8, 335–336; I. W. Burton, "Report of Standing Committee on Indian Affairs," October 12, 1837, in Winfrey and Day, vol. 1, 23–24.

12. Manuel Lafuente, June 11, 1838, in Wood, 55–56; J. B. Wilkinson, *Laredo and the Rio Grande Frontier* (Austin: Jenkins Publishing Co., 1975), 156; Juan N. Seguín, *A Revolution Remembered: The Memoirs and Selected Correspondence of Juan N. Seguín* (Austin: Texas State Historical Association, 2002), 158.

13. David Vigness, "Indian Raids on the Lower Rio Grande, 1836–1837," *Southwestern Historical Quarterly* 59 (July 1955): 14, 17, 22.

14. Ray, 40–41.

15. Treaty Between Texas and Lipan Indians, January 8, 1838, in Winfrey and Day, vol. 1, 30–32; Maestas, 292–293; Drafts on the Government during March, 1838 in Winfrey and Day, vol. 1, 33.

16. *Telegraph and Texas Register*, March 10, 1838; R. A. Irion to Houston, March 14, 1838, in Winfrey and Day, vol. 1, 44–45; John Hunter Herndon, "Diary of A Young Man in Houston, 1838," *Southwestern Historical Quarterly* 53 (January 1950): 290–291; Thomas W. Cutrer, "Smith, Erastus [Deaf] Smith," *Handbook of Texas Online* (*http://www.tshaonline.org/handbook/online/articles/fsm10*), Texas State Historical Association, accessed April 22, 2012.

17. T. C. Allan, "Reminiscences of Mrs. Annie Fagan Teal," *Southwestern Historical Quarterly* 34 (April 1931): 323.

18. John J. Linn, *Reminiscences of Fifty Years in Texas* (Austin: The Steck Company, 1935), 292–293. Linn claimed the woman cut off the hand of a dead Comanche and proposed they eat it. This is a tall tale. Lipans didn't eat human flesh, and their beliefs about the dead would have prevented them from carrying around a body part.

19. Latham, 28–33; William Bollaert, "Observations of the Indian Tribes in Texas," *Journal of the Ethnological Society of London* 2 (1850): 277.

20. Fred M. Griffin, "Under Five Flags." *New Mexico Magazine* 21 (July 1943): 18–19.

21. Opler, 231–232.

22. Christian, 50–51; Tate, x–xi; W. J. Jones to Lamar, June 23, 1838, in Gulick, vol. 2, 170; Lamar to Castro, March 6, 1838, in Gulick, vol. 2, 44.

23. Christian, 53; Jones, 34.

24. Privates were: Chipeta (probably Chipota, who also served under Captain Bell in Corpus Christi), Casa, Charcia, Conpah, Cooshatee, Deisaslishta (Eishashlishta), Ellorttes, Fernando, Flacco (who served with Mounted Volunteers and Rangers), Ganto, Gosly, Hawneeky, Helliama, Hoesky, Hosey (José), Jack, Joshua, Moccasin, Muess, Mondoisi, Musconttish, Neckinina, Nehelki, Neuhantis, Nuchl, Pecar, Pehenial, Saeonkell, Satella, Sechi, Sentika, Shilkoe, Shindial, Slarshal, Sockersiss, Sockins, Tazazanto, and Tohotoliny. Manuel and Plata also held the rank of captain. Quansise (Juan Sais) was a lieutenant. (Frances T. Ingmire, *Texas Ranger Service Records, 1830–1846*, 25, 47 and Moore, *Savage Frontier*, vol. 2, 163.) Most served in 1839 and 1841.

25. Joseph Baker to Lamar, January 2, 1839, in Gulick, vol. 2, 398; Frederick Wilkins, *The Legend Begins: The Texas Rangers, 1823–1845* (Austin: State House Press, 1996), 46; Frances T. Ingmire, *Texas Ranger Service Records, 1830–1846* (St. Louis: Privately published, 1982), 25, 47. The only other Indian units were Choctaw, Cherokee, Delaware and Shawnee.

26. Huson, vol. 1, 46.

Chapter 20

1. Noah Smithwick, *The Evolution of a State, or, Recollections of Old Texas Days* (Austin: Steck-Vaughn Company, 1968), 221.

2. J. C. Neill to the Governor and Council, undated, in Binkley, 25; Dudley Wooten, *A Comprehensive History of Texas, 1685 to 1897*, vol. 1 (Dallas: William G. Scarff, 1898), 737.

3. J. B. R. Austin, *Texas Sentinel* (Austin, October 28, 1841).

4. James K. Greer, *Colonel Jack Hays: Texas Frontier Leader and California Builder* (New York: E. P. Dutton & Company, 1952), 29–30.

5. Smithwick, 215–220; Manuel Lafuente, June 11, 1838, in Wood, 55–56; Report of Capt. J. H. Moore to Albert Sidney Johnston, March 10, 1839, in Winfrey and Day, vol. 1, 57–58; Moore, vol. 2, 158–159, 161, 163–165; Wilkins, *Legend Begins*, 48–49. Wooten (vol. 1, 737) wrote that Juan Castro tried to run off two thousand Comanche horses but didn't succeed.

6. Moore, vol. 2, 342–343, 347–349.

7. *Telegraph and Texas Register*, June 1, 1840.

8. Walter Prescott Webb, *The Texas Rangers: A Century of Frontier Defense* (Austin: University of Texas Press, 1965), 45; John Henry Brown, *Indian Wars and Pioneers of Texas* (Austin: Statehouse Press, 1988), 83; Moore, vol. 2, 148–151; Kevin Ladd, *Gone to Texas: Genealogical Abstracts from The Telegraph and Texas Register, 1835–1841* (Bowie, MD: Heritage Books, 1994), 210; Donaly Brice, *The Great Comanche Raid* (Austin: Eakin Press, 1987), 50.

9. Wilkins, 87; Ladd, 212.

10. *Brazos Courier*, November 24, 1840; Burnet to Schoolcraft, August 20, 1847, in Winfrey and Day, vol. 3, 96. "Charitica" could refer to Arapahoes or Apaches, but because Castro could speak to them, they were Apaches. They weren't Naishans, who never numbered more than 300 (Thurman, 159–160).

11. *Telegraph and Texas Register*, December 23, 1840.

12. Robert M Utley, *Fort Davis National Historic Site, Texas* (Washington, D.C.: National Park Service, 1965), 5–7.

13. Greer, *Hays*, 67–68.

14. Greer, *Hays*, 29, 60.

15. Lipan rangers were Plasedonce, Colquie, Tom, Juan, Wash and Antonio.

16. James K. Greer, *Texas Ranger: Jack Hays in the Frontier Southwest* (College Station: Texas A&M University Press, 1993), 49–51; Gulick, vol. 4, 235; Moore, vol. 3, 321–325.

17. J. B. R. Austin, *Texas Sentinel* (Austin, October 28, 1841); Latham, 28–33.

Chapter 21

1. Smithwick, 222.

2. J. B. R. Austin, *Texas Sentinel*; Latham, 28–33.

3. Ladd, 166–167, 188.

4. J. Frank Dobie, *A Vaquero of the Brush Country* (New York: Grosset & Dunlap, 1929), 76.

5. See Chapter 27.

6. *Telegraph and Texas Register* (December 16, 1840), Robert Simpson Neighbors Papers, Dolph Briscoe Center for American History, University of Texas at Austin.

7. Manuel Lafuente to military commander of Laredo, June 18, 1841, in Wood, 58; Mayor C. H. Guilbeau to Lamar, July 27, 1841, in Gulick, vol. 4, 559.

8. Adele B. Looscan, "Capt. Joseph Daniels," *Texas Historical Association Quarterly* 5 (July 1901): 26; Huson, vol. 1, 54; Moore, vol. 3, 353.

9. Noah Smithwick, "Webber's Prairie," *The Galveston Semi-Weekly* (July 13, 1897), Smithwick Papers, Dolph Briscoe Center for American History, University of Texas at Austin.

10. Muckleroy, 184–185; Houston to G. W. Adams, Houston, April 14, 1842, in Williams and Barker, vol. 3, 32–34.

11. Tate, in Winfrey and Day, vol. 1, xi; Houston to Major Thomas J. Smith, March 25, 1842, in Williams and Barker, vol. 2, 535.

12. Kenneth F. Neighbors, *Robert Simpson Neighbors and the Texas Frontier, 1836–1859* (Waco: Texian Press, 1975), 25; Houston to Colonel L. B. Franks, February 1, 1842, in Williams and Barker, vol. 2, 461–462, May 9 and 21, 1842, in vol. 3, 46, 55–56; Proclamation, August 15, 1842 in Williams and Barker, vol. 3, 146.

13. General Miguel A. Sánchez Lamego, *The Second Mexican-Texas War, 1841–1843* (Hillsboro, TX: Hill Junior College, 1972), 19; Report of General Mariano Arista to the Secretary of War and Navy, March 27, 1842, in Lamego, 87; Joseph M. Nance, *Attack and Counter-Attack: The Texas-Mexican Frontier, 1842* (Austin: University of Texas Press, 1964), 41, 44; Frederick C. Chabot, *Texas Expeditions of 1842* (San Antonio: Artes Graficas, 1942), 23.

14. *Telegraph and Texas Register* (June 1, 1840); Nance, 66–68, 86, 116, 229, 446–447; Smithwick, 221.

15. Nance, 116; Report of the Secretary of War and Marine, June 23, 1842, in *Telegraph and Texas Register*, July 6, 1842; "Diary of Adolphus Sterne," *Southwestern Historical Quarterly* 13 (October 1929): 167 and 9 (October 1928): 174; "A Request in Behalf of Castro, the Lipan Chief," June 21, 1842, in Williams and Barker, vol. 3, 73. Flacco had previously received $355 on March 18, 1841, for the services of himself and fifteen men under General Morehouse. Castro received $1,140 for himself and his men for services rendered against the Cherokees under Burleson in 1839 and against the Comanches in 1840 under Moore (Texas State Library and Archives Commission, *http://www.tsl.state.tx.us/index.html* [accessed July 3, 2010]).

16. Huson, vol. 1, 54; Nance, 193, 226; Lamego, 24–27; *Telegraph and Texas Register*, July 6 and 20, 1842.

17. Romero, 44. Bollaert ("Observations of the Indian Tribes," 277) said Castro drank so much in Houston that "he bursted his boiler with rotgut." Bollaert wasn't always accurate, but Castro was known to be fond of liquor.

18. Romero, 41–42; *Telegraph and Texas Register*, January 11, 1843. A newspaper reported that the second group, faithful to Texas, was led by Flacco, but Flacco was already in Mexico (*Telegraph and Texas Register*, November 23, 1842).

19. Houston, testimonial, March 28, 1843, in Williams and Barker, vol. 3, 343–344.

20. *Telegraph and Texas Register,* January 11, 1843 and March 29, 1843; Greer, 82–89; Smithwick, 221–222; Brown, *Indian Wars,* 65; Nance, 575–576; Gulick, vol. 6, 297.

21. Flacco to Houston, Little River, March 24, 1843 in Williams and Barker, vol. 3, 343.

22. Sam Houston to Flacco, March 28, 1843, in Williams and Barker, vol. 3, 341–343.

23. Houston to Benjamin Bryant, March 28, 1843, in Williams and Barker, vol. 3, 344–345. Britten (193) wrote that law enforcement apprehended Flacco's murderers in Seguin, still in possession of his horses and blankets.

24. Houston, testimonial, March 28, 1843, in Williams and Barker, vol. 3, 343–344; Romero, 42; *Telegraph and Texas Register,* November 1, 1843; Smith, *Dominance* (2006), 189; Kelly F. Himmel, *The Conquest of the Karankawas and the Tonkawas, 1821–1859* (College Station: Texas A&M University Press, 1999), 87–88; Weniger, 135.

25. Wooten, vol. 1, 738; J. W. Wilbarger, *Indian Depredations in Texas* (Austin: Hotchings Printing House, 1889), 282–283.

26. Smithwick, 222–223; Handwritten note, Smithwick Collection; Wooten, vol. 1, 737. A lifelong scoundrel named James Reavis later served time in New Mexico for forgery ("Prince of Bunco Steerers," *Alamogordo News,* July 20, 1899).

Chapter 22

1. David G. Burnet to Henry R. Schoolcraft, August 20, 1847, in Winfrey and Day, vol. 3, 96.

2. Opler, *Lipans and Mescaleros,* 18.

3. Muckleroy, "Indian Affairs," 191; Romero, 41; C. Green to Major T. G. Western, Dec. 14, 1844 and Neighbors to Western, Jan. 14, 1845, in Winfrey and Day, 150–151, 166–167; *Telegraph and Texas Register,* April 24, 1844.

4. Minutes of Council at the Falls of the Brazos, October 7, 1844, in Winfrey and Day, vol. 2, 105.

5. Western to Benjamin Sloat, September 22, 1844, and Neighbors to Western, January 15, 1845, in Winfrey and Day, vol. 2, 97, 168–169.

6. A Treaty Signed in Council at Tehuacana Creek, October 9, 1844, in Winfrey and Day, 114–119; Muckleroy, 196. Captain Chico was probably Flacco Chico, then referred to simply as Chico because the Apaches would have avoided using his father's name.

7. Opinion of the Secretary of State on the Financial and War Policy of the Country, December 22, 1841, in Anson Jones, *Memoranda and Official Correspondence Relating to the Republic of Texas, Its History and Annexation* (Chicago, Rio Grande Press Inc., 1966), 124; Muckleroy, 204–205; *Texas National Register* (November 15, 1845).

8. Minutes of Council Held at Tehuacana Creek, September 19, 1845, in Winfrey and Day, vol. 2, 334–338.

9. Muckleroy, 198; L. H. Williams to Western, August 20, 1845, in Winfrey and Day, vol. 2, 326–327.

10. Neighbours, 25–26, 28; "Neighbors, Robert Simpson," The Handbook of Texas Online. <http://www.tsha.utexas.edu/handbook/online/articles/view/NN/fne8.html> (Accessed Wed Jan. 28 13:00:37 US/Central 2004); Smith, 189.

11. Julia Nott Waugh, *Castro-Ville and Henry Castro, Empresario* (San Antonio: Standard Printing Company, 1934), 92; Romero, 42; Western to Neighbors, July 8 and 18, 1845, in Winfrey and Day, vol. 2, 273, 292–293; DeLay, 195.

12. Neighbors to Western, September 15, 1845, in Winfrey and Day, vol. 2, 361–362; Alice Neighbors, "Life and Works of Robert S. Neighbors," Master's Thesis, University of Texas, 1936, 46–47.

13. Report of Council with the Comanche Indians, November 23, 1845, and William G. Cooke to Anson Jones, December 12, 1845, in Winfrey and Day, vol. 2, 411–412, 422–423.

14. Neighbors, *Life and Works*, 48–50; *Telegraph and Texas Register*, November 19 and 26, 1845.

15. Grant Foreman, "The Texas Comanche Treaty of 1846," *Southwestern Historical Quarterly* 51 (April 1948): 313–315; A Report of Messrs Butler and Lewis Relative to the Indians of Texas and the Southwestern Prairies, February 3, 1847, 29th Congress, second session, 1846–1847, House Executive Doc. 76, Serial Set 500, 4; Grant Foreman, "The Journal of Elijah Hicks," *Chronicles of Oklahoma* 13 (March 1935): 89, 96.

16. A Report of Messrs Butler and Lewis, 4.

17. Stan Hoig, *White Man's Paper Trail: Grand Councils and Treaty-Making on the Central Plains* (Boulder: University Press of Colorado, 2006), 74–77; Neighbours, 29–30; Treaty with the Comanche and Other Tribes, May 15, 1846, in Winfrey and Day, vol. 3, 43–49; Ray, 64; Foreman, "Journal," 98; Howard Lackman, "The Howard-Neighbors Controversy: A Cross-Section in West Texas Indian Affairs," *Panhandle-Plains Historical Review* 25 (1952): 32; Lena Clara Koch, "The Federal Indian Policy in Texas, 1845–1846," *Southwestern Historical Quarterly* 28 (April 1925): 263; Smith, 189.

18. Foreman, "Journal," 90, 95–96; *Texas Democrat*, January 20, 1847.

19. Rafael H. Garcia to Prefect, January 31, 1845, in Wood, 75; Calisto Bravo to Commander, July 4 and 17, 1845, in Wood, 81–82; Bravo, September 30, 1845, in Wood, 84.

20. James Buckner Barry Papers, Dolph Briscoe Center for American History, University of Texas at Austin.

21. James Pinckney Henderson to Neighbors, January 15, 1847, in Williams and Barker, vol. 5, 24–25; R. L. Biesele, "The Relations between the German Settlers and the Indians in Texas, 1844–1860," *Southwestern Historical Quarterly* 31 (October 1927): 117; Gerald S. Pierce, *Texas Under Arms: The Camps, Posts, Forts and Military Towns of the Republic of Texas, 1836–1846* (Austin: Encino Press, 1969), 114.

22. Domenech, 122–124.

23. Lipan boys sometimes shot fish with a bow and arrow but usually caught them in the shallows with their bare hands (Gifford, 90).

24. Theodore Gentilz, *Gentilz: Artist of the Old Southwest: Drawings and Paintings by Theodore Gentilz* (Austin: University of Texas Press, 1974), 14–15; Sam DeShong Ratcliffe, *Painting Texas History to 1900* (Austin: University of Texas Press, 1992), 65–67, 69; William W. Newcomb, "German Artist on the Pedernales," *Southwest Historical Quarterly* 82 (October 1978): 149, 153; Pauline A. Pinckney, *Painting in Texas: The Nineteenth Century* (Austin: University of Texas Press, 1967), 79, 83.

25. *The Texas Democrat* (January 13, 1847), Neighbors Papers; Darwin Payne, "Camp Life in the Army of Occupation: Corpus Christi, July 1845 to March 1846," *Southwestern Historical Quarterly* 73 (January 1970): 336; Neighbors, *Life and Works*, 48–50; *Texas Democrat*, May 6, 1846; *Telegraph and Texas Register*, November 5, 1845.

26. Neighbors, *Life and Works*, 49; Opler, *Lipan and Mescalero*, 68; *Democratic Telegraph and Texas Register*, May 13, 1846.

27. The term Esikwita could also refer to Mescaleros and other Apaches (Rivaya-Martinez, 150 fn 34), but in this context it meant Lipans.

28. A Report of Messrs Butler and Lewis, 6–7; Hoig, 74; Albert Gatschet, "Lipan, a dialect of the apache-Tinné family," September 1884, Archives of the Bureau of American Ethnology, 81-a, Smithsonian Institution, 30.

29. James Pinckney Henderson to Neighbors, January 15, 1847, in Williams and Barker, vol. 5, 24–25; *Texas Presbyterian* (January 1, 1848).

30. Opler, *Lipan and Mescalero*, 22–23, 39–40.

31. Burnet to Schoolcraft, in Williams and Barker, 96–99.

32. Himmel, 91; Mildred P. Mayhall, *Indian Wars of Texas* (Waco: Texian Press, 1965), 84.

Chapter 23

1. Ray, 96.

2. John Wright and William Wright, *Recollections of Western Texas, 1852–55, by Two of the U.S. Mounted Rifles,* ed. Robert Wooster (Austin: Book Club of Texas, 2003), 52.

3. A. Wislizenus, Memoir of a Tour to Northern Mexico, January 13, 1848, Senate Miscellaneous Document 26, 30th Congress, first session, Serial Set 511, 72; Tate, in Winfrey and Day, vol. 1, xii; Delay, xiii.

4. Robert S. Neighbors to Commissioner, Annual Report of the Commissioner of Indian Affairs, House Executive Document 1, 30th Congress, second session, Serial Set 503 (June 22, 1847), 896–898 and (September 14, 1847), 896–898, 903.

5. Romero, 43; Neighbors, House Executive Document 1, 30th Congress, second session (September 14, 1847), 903.

6. Domenech, 176.

7. Neighbors, House Executive Document 1, 30th Congress, second session (January 20, 1848), 574-575.

8. The teller of this tale said her name was Chipeta, but that was also a name the rangers used for Chipota.

9. A. J. Sowell, *The Life of Bigfoot Wallace* (Austin: The Steck Company, 1957), 80–85; Weniger, 142.

10. John Duval, "The Adventures of Bigfoot Wallace," *Frontier Times* 8 (December 1930): 116.

11. Neighbors to Commissioner, March 2, 1848, Annual Report of the Commissioner of Indian Affairs, House Executive Document 1, 30th Congress, second session, Serial Set 537, 581–587.

12. Ray, 95–96.

13. Thomas M. Likens, *The Texas Democrat*, August 16, 1848, Neighbors Papers.

14. Neighbors to Commissioner, November 7, 1848, Annual Report of the Commissioner of Indian Affairs, Senate Executive Document 1, 30th Congress, second session, Serial Set 537, 599–600; Neighbours, 47; John Salmon Ford, *Rip Ford's Texas* (Austin: University of Texas Press, 1963), 449–450.

15. Neighbors, 49; Neighbors, "Texas Indians in 1849," in Winfrey and Day, vol. 3, 108–109; Neighbors to Commissioner, March 7, 1849, Commission of Indian Affairs, Annual Report, 1849, House Executive Document 1, 31st Congress, first session, Serial Set 550, 963, 966.

16. Richard H. Kern to James S. Calhoun, June 19, 1850, in James S. Calhoun, *The Official Correspondence of James S. Calhoun while Indian Agent at Santa Fé and Superintendent of Indian Affairs in New Mexico*, ed. Annie Abel (Washington, D.C.: Government Printing Office, 1915), 266.

17. J. M. Smith to Meriwether, September 5, 1853, Letters Received by the Office of Indian Affairs, New Mexico Superintendency, Record group 75, Roll 547, NARA; Emmanuel Henri Domenech, *Seven Years' Residence in the Great Deserts of North America*, vol. 2 (London: Longman, Green, Longman, and Roberts, 1860), 6; Neighbors to Commissioner, September 16, 1853, Annual Report of the Commissioner of Indian Affairs, Senate executive document 1, 33rd Congress, first session, Serial Set 690, 428.

18. Claim of H. L. Kinney against the United States, January 1, 1861, in Winfrey and Day, vol. 4, 51–52.

19. Lackman, 30, 36.

20. Opler, *Lipan and Mescalero*, 226; Thomas T. Smith, *Fort Inge: Sharps, Spurs, and Sabers on the Texas Frontier, 1849–1869* (Austin: Eakin Press, 1993), 22–23, 34–36; Joseph I. Lambert, *One Hundred Years with the Second Cavalry* (Fort Riley, Kansas: Capper Printing Company Inc., 1939), 47–48.

Chapter 24

1. Rollins to Lea, March 4, 1851, Verne Ray's digest, Box 85, Folders 10–12, Opler Papers.

2. Rollins to G. M. Brooke, September 25, 1850, in Winfrey and Day, vol. 3, 124–125; Negotiations Between the United States and the Comanche, Lipan and Mescalero Tribes of Indians, October 26, 1851, in Winfrey and Day, vol. 3, 142–147; *Texas State Gazette*, February 26, 1853.

3. Rollins to C. S. Todd, March 25, 1951, Senate Executive Document 1, 32nd Congress, first session, Serial Set 636, 518–520.

4. Rollins to Commissioner, May 8, 1850, Letters Received by the Office of Indian Affairs, Texas Agency, Record Group 75, Roll 858, NARA; Rollins to Orlando T. Brown, June 8, 1850, Box 85, Folders 10–12, Opler Papers; Lt. Col. W. J. Hardee, report, August 29, 1851, Secretary of War Annual Report, 1851, 32nd Congress, 1st session, Senate executive document 1, Serial Set 611, 123; *Texas State Gazette*, December 28, 1850.

5. Rollins to G. M. Brooke, September 25, 1850, in Winfrey and Day, vol. 3, 124–125.

6. *Texas State Gazette*, September 28, 1850.

7. Treaty between United States and the Comanche, Caddo, Lipan, Quapaw, Tawakoni, and Waco Tribes of Indians, December 10, 1850, in Winfrey and Day, vol. 3, 130–137; Webb, 139.

8. Rollins to Lea, March 4, 1851; Bvt. Lt. Col. William J. Hardee to Deas, May 28, 1851; Rogers to Lea, August 28, 1851; Hardee to Deas, August 29, 1851; J. P. Mullin and John Conner to Rogers, September 12, 1851. All in Opler Papers.

9. Negotiations Between the United States and the Comanche, Lipan and Mescalero Tribes of Indians, October 26, 1851, in Winfrey and Day, vol. 3, 142–147; *The Western Texan* (November 20, 1851).

10. Proceedings Prior to a Treaty Between the United States and the Southern Comanche, Lipan and Mescalero Tribes of Indians, San Sabá, October 27, 1851, in Winfrey and Day, vol. 3, 148–152.

11. Rollins to Howard, February 26, 1852, OIAT, RG 75, Roll 858, NARA.

12. Lackman, 31-32; Howard to Lea, March 23, 1852, OIAT, RG 75, Roll 858, NARA; Ray, 137.

13. Howard to Lea, July 10, 1852, and Petition from Citizens of Gillespie County to Gov. H. P. Bell, July 12, 1852, Opler Papers; Robert Penniger, *A Brief Account of the German Colonies in Texas Established by the Mainzer Noblemen's Society and Chronicles of the City of Fredericksburg* (Fredericksburg, TX: Privately published, 1896), 34.

14. Capron to Howard, August 12, 1852, CIAAR, 1852, 32nd Congress, Second session, S. ex. doc. 1, Serial Set 658, 431–432; Howard to Peter H. Bell, September 11, 1852, in Winfrey and Day, vol. 5, 127–128; Kenneth F. Neighbours, An Ethnohistorical Report, Together with Supporting Exhibits Relating to the Cause of Action in the Lipan Apache Tribe, the Mescalero Apache Tribe, et al, v. United States, Docket No. 22-C, Before the Indian Claims Commission, 42.

15. Opler, *Lipan and Mescalero Apache*, 7; Howard to Lea, August 15, 1852, S. ex. doc. 1, 32nd Congress, Second session, Serial Set 673, 430-431; *Texas State Gazette*, February 26, 1853; Capron to Howard, September 30, 1852, OIAT, RG 75, Roll 858.

16. Opler, *Apache Culture*, 127; Capron to Howard, September 30, 1852, Opler papers.

17. William Henry Chase Whiting, *Exploring Southwestern Trails, 1846-1854* (Philadelphia: Porcupine Press, 1974), 260–261, 263–264.

18. Zenas Randall Bliss, *The Reminiscences of Major General Zenas R. Bliss, 1854–1876: From the Texas Frontier to the Civil War and Back Again* (Austin: Texas State Historical Association, 2007), 65–66, fn 38, 40; Whiting, 271–278, 336; Albert Schroeder, notes, Albert Schroeder Papers. Many place names originated with that expedition. The 6,320-foot peak forming the northeastern buttress of the Davis Mountains became Gómez Peak. Howard's Well, named for the party's guide, Richard Austin Howard, became a primary watering stop on the San Antonio–El Paso Road and a focal point for Indian attacks.

19. Hays to Ewing, January 3, 1950; Whiting, 336; Bvt. Major E. B. Babbitt to War Dept., October 15, 1849, Box 85, Folders 10–12, Opler Papers.

20. Captain Henry B. Judd to Lt. L. M. Laws, March 30, 1850, OIANM, RG 75, Roll 546, NARA.

21. These Jicarillas, also called Llaneros, were then living in northeastern New Mexico on the plains and along the Sangre de Cristo Mountains (Tiller, 13–14). They were a different group than the Llaneros proper, although they certainly associated with one another.

22. Abel, 212; Albert Schroeder, notes, Schroeder Papers; Tiller, 13–14; Schroeder, *Mescalero Apaches*, 56, 58.

23. Opler, *Myths*, 246–252.

24. John Russell Bartlett, *Personal Narrative of Explorations and Incidents in Texas, New Mexico, California, Sonora and Chihuahua Connected with the United States and Mexican Boundary Commission During the Years 1851, '52, and '53*, vol. 1 (New York: D. Appleton & Company, 1854), 76–82.

Chapter 25

1. Williams and Barker, vol. 7, 62–63; *Texan Mercury*, November 26, 1853.

2. Koch, "Federal Indian Policy," 28 (April 1925): 281, and 29 (July 1925): 19–23; Opler, *Lipan and Mescalero*, 22; Ray, 91–92.

3. Frank D. Reeve, "The Apache Indians in Texas," *Southwestern Historical Quarterly* 50 (October 1946): 206 fn 68.

4. Capron to Lea, January 23 and February 18, 1853, OIAT, RG 75, Roll 859, NARA; Opler, *Lipan and Mescalero Apache*, 77–78; Ray, 131–132.

5. Artist Richard Petri captured the scene in an unfinished painting. Pinckney, 86; Ratcliffe, 76; Newcomb, "German Artist," 170–172.

6. Neighbours, *Robert Simpson Neighbors*, 110, 112; Lackman, 38; Opler, *Apache Culture*, 130; Meriwether to Manypenny, November 28, 1853, OIANM, RG 75, Roll 547, NARA; Ray, 130; Neighbors to Commissioner, CIAAR 1853, 428.

7. Romero, 32–35, 38, 46.

8. *Tri-Weekly State Times* (Austin), March 21, 1854; Major General Persifor Smith, June 2, 1854, SWAR, 34th Congress, first session, S. ex. doc. 1, vol. 2, 52–54, Serial Set 811; Edmund J. Davis to Pease, March 13, 1854, in Winfrey and Day, vol. 5, 161–162; H. P. Bee to Pease, March 13, 1854, in Winfrey and Day, vol. 5, 164–165.

9. Wright, 51–52, 83–87; General Persifor Smith, May 10 and 15, 1854, SWAR, S. ex. doc. 1, 34th Congress, first session, Serial Set 747, 29.

10. Neighbors to commissioner, May 3, 1854, and Petition to Pease, undated, OIAT, RG 75, Roll 859, NARA; Smith, *Dominance*, 215; Neighbours, *Robert Simpson Neighbors*, 113–114.

11. Frederick Law Olmsted, *A Journey through Texas: Or a Saddle Trip on the Southwestern Frontier* (Austin: University of Texas Press, 1978), 288–290; Reading W. Black, *The Life and Diary of Reading W. Black* (Uvalde, TX: Privately printed, 1997), 21, 39–40.

12. Neighbors to Commissioner, May 3, 1854 and Howard to commissioner, May 4, 1854, OIAT, RG 75, roll 859, NARA; Olmsted, 290–295. Schilz (56) wrote that Lipans, believing the Tonkawas were guilty, deserted rather than fight their allies, and Howard arrested Chiquito and Ramon Castro, which is incorrect.

13. Ray, 134; Himmel, 112–113; CIAAR, November 25, 1854, S. ex. doc. 1, 33rd Congress, second session, Serial Set 746, 222; Caleb Pirtle III and Michael F. Cusack, *The Lonely Sentinel: Fort Clark on Texas's Western Frontier* (Austin: Eakin Press, 1985), 13; James G. Bell, "A Log of the Texas-California Cattle Trail, 1854." *Southwestern Historical Quarterly* 35 (January 1932): 208–209, 213; *Gonzales Inquirer*, May 13, 1854.

14. Kenneth Porter, "The Seminole in Mexico, 1850–1861," *The Hispanic American Historical Review* 31 (February 1951): 1–3; Kevin Mulroy, *Freedom on the Border: The Seminole Maroons in Florida, the Indian Territory, Coahuila, and Texas* (Lubbock: Texas Tech University Press, 1993), 46–47.

15. Kenneth W. Porter, "The Seminole Negro-Indian Scouts, 1870–1881," *Southwestern Historical Quarterly* 55 (January 1952): 359–361; Porter, "Seminole in Mexico," 4–6, 13–14.

16. Howard to Commissioner, May 4, 1854, OIAT, RG 75, roll 859; Neighbours, *Robert Simpson Neighbors*, 114; *Reports of the Committee of Investigation*, 418; Neighbors to Pease, April 10, 1854, in Winfrey and Day, vol. 5, 170–171; Neighbors to Charles Mix, September 10, 1855, CIAAR, 1855, 34th Congress, first session, H. ex. doc. 1, Serial Set 840, 499; Porter, "Seminole in Mexico," 15–16; Wooten, 738; Reeve, 205.

17. Report of R. B. Marcy and R. S. Neighbors to P. H. Bell, September 30, 1854, in Winfrey and Day, vol. 3, 186, 189–190; Koch, "Federal Indian Policy," 29 (October 1925): 99–100.

18. Koch, 109; Ray, 124–125; Neighbors, 97–98, 101–104; CIAAR, 1855, 330, 497, 499; Neighbors to Commissioner, September 18, 1856, CIAAR, H. ex. doc. 1, 34th Congress, third session,

Serial Set 893, 725, 727. Teacher Zachariah Ellis Coombes, who arrived in 1858, recalled Lipan students among the Tonkawas, Caddos, Wacos, and others (Barbara Neal Ledbetter, *The Fort Belknap of Yesterday and Today, 1851–1963*, 55).

19. Walker to Smith, October 6, 1854, and Smith to AG, October 9, 1854, OAG, RG 94, Roll 506; Robert Wooster, *Frontier Crossroads: Fort Davis and the West* (College Station: Texas A&M University Press, 2006), 43.

20. John Pope, Report of Exploration of a Route for the Pacific Railroad near the Thirty–second Parallel of Latitude, from the Red River to the Rio Grande, 33rd Congress, 1855, H. ex. doc. 129; Major General Persifor Smith, March 14, 1855, SWAR 1854, 52–54.

21. Newspaper Item Concerning Indian Depredations, August 6, 1855, in Winfrey and Day, vol. 3, 230–231; Petition to E. M. Pease for Rangers in Goliad County, September 13, 1855, 238; Bexar County Committee to Pease, September 22, 1855, 232–234; Jones to Pease, September 22, 1855, 245–246; R. H. Hord and E. Basse to Pease, Brownsville, December 10, 1855, 261–262; *Depredations on the Frontiers of Texas*, 1873, H. ex. doc. 257, 43rd Congress, first session, 23.

22. Ernest C. Shearer, "The Callahan Expedition, 1855," *Southwestern Historical Quarterly* 54 (April 1951): 433, 435–436; Pease to Smith, September 5, 1855, in Winfrey and Day, Vol. 3, 235.

23. Frederick Wilkins, *Defending the Borders: The Texas Rangers, 1848–1861* (Austin: State House Press, 2001), 46–47; Shearer, 431; Ronnie Tyler, "The Callahan Expedition of 1855: Indians or Negroes?" *Southwestern Historical Quarterly* 70 (April 1967): 574–576.

24. Tyler, 579–580; Wilkins, 50–59, 62; Shearer, 436, 438; *Texas State Gazette* (Austin), October 13, 1855; Jesse Sumpter, *Paso del Águila: A Chronicle of Frontier Days on the Texas Border as Recorded in the Memoirs of Jesse Sumpter*, ed. Ben E. Pingenot (Austin: Encino Press, 1969), 74, fn 10 and 11.

25. Cora Montgomery, *Eagle Pass or Life on the Border* (Austin: The Pemberton Press, 1966), 119–120.

Chapter 26

1. Johnston to Thomas, November 17, 1856, RG 393, M 1165, Letters Sent by the Department of Texas, the District of Texas and the 5th Military District, Roll 1.

2. *Kinney County: 125 Years of Growth, 1852–1977* (Kinney County Historical Society, 1977), 19; "Cavalry Post, Haven of Lee, Sheridan, Will Celebrate," *San Antonio Evening News*, April 22, 1952; Pirtle and Cusack, 18–19; H. I. Richards to J. W. Throckmorton, March 19, 1867, in Winfrey and Day, vol. 4, 179.

3. Bliss, 43–44.

4. *Galveston Weekly News*, February 26, 1856.

5. Kenneth F. Neighbours, *Robert Simpson Neighbors*, 167.

6. CIAAR, 1855, 330–331; Neighbors to Manypenny, February 4, 1856, Neighbors Papers, Neighbors to Commissioner, September 18, 1856, 725, 727.

7. *San Antonio Texan*, April 3, 1856; Shearer, 443; *Reports of the Committee*, 419–420.

8. J. K. F. Mansfield, "Colonel J. K. F. Mansfield's Report of the Inspection of the Department of Texas in 1856," *Southwestern Historical Quarterly* 42 (January 1939): 237; Reeve, 206; Porter, "Seminole in Mexico," 22; *Report of the Committee*, 333–334, 421; Johnston to Thomas, November 17, 1856.

9. Philip Sheridan, *Personal Memoirs of P. H. Sheridan, General, United States Army* (New York, C. L. Webster & Company, 1888), 20, 25, 29–30.

10. Buell to Lt. Col. John B. Magruder, May 18, 1856, RG 393, M 1165, DT, Roll 1, NARA; Buell to Captain Robert Granger, September 29, 1856; Buell to Captain Albert Brackett, July 14, 1856; Opler, *Lipan and Mescalero*, 81–82; Thomas T. Smith, *The Old Army in Texas: A Research Guide to the U.S. Army in Nineteenth-Century Texas* (Austin: Texas State Historical Association, 2000), 140, 142.

11. Col. Albert S. Johnston to Cooper, December 5, 1856, and Johnston to Col. L. Thomas, November 8, 1856; Irwin McDowell, November 13, 1857, SWAR, S. ex. doc. 11, first session, 35th Congress, Serial Set 920, 54; Olmsted, 451–452.

12. John Bell Hood, *Advance and Retreat: Personal Experiences in the United States and Confederate States Armies* (New York: Kraus Reprint Company, 1969), 8–10; Bliss, 65–66.

13. "Devils River," The Handbook of Texas Online, *http://www.tshaonline.org/handbook/online/articles/DD/rnd3.html* [accessed Wed Jan 28 13:0037 US/Central 2004]; Romero, 47.

14. Hood, 10–15; Charles M. Robinson, *Frontier Forts of Texas* (Houston: Lone Star Books, 1986), 83; Reeve, 206; Price, 59–61.

15. Porter, "Seminole Negro-Indian Scouts," 26; Price, 62; Robert S. Neighbors, "The Indians and Their Outrages," *Texas State Gazette*, February 13, 1858; Neighbors to Charles Mix, September 10, 1858, and Guy M. Bryan to J. Thompson, September 27, 1848, Neighbors Papers; Neighbors, Annual Report, September 16, 1858, H. ex. doc. 2, 35th Congress, second session, Serial Set 997, 526.

16. John S. Ford to H. R. Runnels, June 2, 1858, 241–243; John S. Hodges to Runnels, June 6, 1858, 244; Richards to Governor, January 3, 1859, 302–303, all in Winfrey and Day, vol. 5.

17. Cooper to Twiggs, January 19, 1859, and SWAR, April 5, 1859, S. ex. doc. 2, first session, 36th Congress, Serial Set 1023, 357–358; Smith, *Fort Inge*, 117–118; Pirtle and Cusack, 39–40; Smith, 118.

18. Koch, "Federal Indian Policy" (October 1925): 116, 123; Webb, 172; Raymond Estep, "Lieutenant William E. Burnet Letters," *Chronicles of Oklahoma* 38, no. 4 (1960): 386; Murial H. Wright, *A Guide to the Indian Tribes of Oklahoma* (Norman: University of Oklahoma Press, 1986), 181.

19. Paul Adams, "Amelia Barr in Texas, 1856–1868," *Southwestern Historical Quarterly* 49 (January 1946): 368.

20. SWAR, October 8, 1860, S. ex. doc., 36th congress, second session, Serial Set 1079, 3, 32.

21. Tate in Winfrey and Day, vol. 1, xiv–xvi; Opler, *Lipan and Mescalero*, 85–86.

22. Smith, *Frontier Defense*, 156, 158–161.

23. Smith, *Fort Inge*, 140–141; Sergeant W. Barrett to Lt. John Bradley, October 16, 1861, in *War of the Rebellion*, Series I, vol. 4, 34.

24. Smith, *Frontier Defense*, 23, 30, 38; Tate in Winfrey and Day, vol. 1, xiv–xvi; Depredations on the Frontiers of Texas, 12; Clayton E. Jewett, *Texas in the Confederacy: An Experience in Nation Building* (Columbia: University of Missouri Press, 2002), 79.

25. Report of the Committee of Investigation, 334. Baylor and Hamner, editor and publisher of the anti-Indian newspaper *The White Man*, were probably two of the "designing men" Neighbors referred to.

26. CIAAR, 1866, H. ex. doc. 1, 39th congress, second session, Serial Set 1284, 55; Compact made between the Confederate Indian tribes and the Prairie tribes at Camp Napoleon on the Washita River, May 26, 1865, in *War of the Rebellion*, Series 1, vol. 48, part 2, 1102–1103.

27. John M. Elkins, *Indian Fighting on the Texas Frontier* (Amarillo: Russell & Cockrell, 1929), 37–39; CIAAR, 1862, H. ex. doc. 1, 37th Congress, third session, Serial Set 1157, 382–384, 391–392; Utley, *Fort Davis*, 18; James Collins to William P. Dade, October 10, 1862 and April 12, 1863, OIANM, RG 75, Roll 551; Collins to Dade, February 8, 1863, CIAAR, 1863, H. ex. doc. 1, 38th Congress, first session, Serial Set 1182, 136; Collins to Dade, April 12, 1863.

28. Griffin, 33–34; Meredith Magoosh Begay, interview with Sherry Robinson, Mescalero, September 24, 2005.

29. Steck to Dade, December 10, 1863; Labadi to Dade, May 1, 1864, and Labadi to Steck, May 18, 1864, J. G. Thrapp to Dale, February 4, 1865, all in OIANM, RG 75, Roll 552; Percy Big Mouth, interview with Eve Ball, Mescalero, November 16, 1951, Ball Papers.

30. Clayton Williams, *Texas' Last Frontier: Fort Stockton and the Trans-Pecos 1861–1895* (College Station: Texas A&M University Press, 1982), 61–62.

31. Depredations on the Frontiers, 21, 24; Report of Indian Depredations in Medina County, 1865–1866, and Record of Indian Depredations in Bandera County, June 25, 1867, in Winfrey and Day, vol. 4, 134–137, 225–230; Bliss, 427.

32. Robinson, *Frontier Forts*, 59; Ray, 151–152.

33. Captain William Frohock to post adjutant, Fort Stockton, December 27, 1867, and Hatch to AAG, January 3, 1868, HRFS, Roll 1; Robinson, *Frontier Forts*, 50; William and Shirley Leckie, *The Buffalo Soldiers: A Narrative of the Black Cavalry in the West* (Norman: University of Oklahoma Press, 2003), 87; Williams, 102–103.

Chapter 27

1. F. M. Buckelew, *Life of an Indian Captive* (Philadelphia: Dorrance, 1865), 30.

2. *Uvalde Leader-News*, April 16, 1937; Kinney County, 24–26.

3. N. M. C. Patterson and W. B. Knox to Throckmorton, April 29, 1867, and Record of Indian Depredations in Bandera County, June 25, 1867, in Winfrey and Day, vol. 4, 202, 226.

4. Buckelew, 12–91; Record of Indian Depredations in Bandera County, June 25, 1867, 229; Deposition of F. M. Buckelew, March 21, 1868, in Winfrey and Day, vol. 4, 258–259; Waugh, 90.

5. Jeff's claim that Geronimo bought him may seem unlikely, but Chiricahuas did have contact with Comanches, and the boy's observation about Geronimo's fear of being captured is consistent with his known patterns of behavior.

6. Clinton L. Smith, *The Boy Captives: Being the True Story of the Experiences and Hardships of Clinton L. Smith and Jeff D. Smith* (Bandera, TX: Frontier Times, 1927), 28–34, 36–46, 64, 126–127, 165, 198, 208–209; Subseries D: Lipan, "Warpath and Raid," Box 44, Folder 25, Opler Papers.

7. Scott Zesch, *The Captured: A True Story of Abduction by Indians on the Texas Frontier* (New York: St. Martin's Press, 2005), 194–195.

Chapter 28

1. H. I. Richards to Pease, May 18, 1868, and Report from H. I. Richards to Throckmorton, February 25, 1867, in Winfrey and Day, vol. 4, 263, 167; N. M. Davis, September 15, 1868, CIAAR, H. ex.doc.1, 40th Congress, third session, SS 1366, 620.

2. S. S. Brown to Reynolds, September 1, 1868, in Winfrey and Day, vol. 4, 271–276.

3. Extracts from Official Mexican Papers, September 1, 1868, in Winfrey and Day, vol. 4, 276–288; Opler, *Myths*, 222–229; Subseries D: Lipan, "Alien People," Box 44, Folder 10, Opler Papers.

4. CIAAR, 1868, 547; "Depredations on the Frontiers of Texas," 23.

5. William Chebahtah and Nancy McGown Minor, *Chevato: The Story of the Apache Warrior Who Captured Herman Lehmann* (Lincoln: University of Nebraska Press, 2007), 3, 19–22.

6. Chebatah and Minor, 4–5, 32, 45–47; Opler, *Myths*, 230–235.

7. Wilson to Commanding Officer, Fort Union, November 3, 1867, HRFS, RG 393, Roll 1, NARA; *Handbook of Texas Online*, "Sierra Diablo," *http://www.tshaonline.org/handbook/online/articles/SS/rjs33.html* (accessed July 6, 2010).

8. Stanwood to AAG, August 26, 1869, and Hennisee to Superintendent Gallegos, July 31, 1869, HRFS, Roll 2; CIAAR, 41st Congress, 3rd session, H. ex. doc. 1, SS 1449, 469.

9. Hennisee to Clinton, May 31, 1870, CIAAR, 1870.

10. CIAAR, 1871, 42nd Congress, second session, H. ex. doc. 1, SS 1505, 441, 787.

11. J. Evetts Haley, *Fort Concho and the Texas Frontier* (San Angelo: San Angelo Standard-Times, 1952), 165–167; Paul Carlson, "William Rufus Shafter with the Frontier Army in the Big Bend," *Journal of Big Bend Studies* 1 (January 1989): 72–73; Mackenzie to Commander, Fort Griffin, August 11, 1871, HRFS, Roll 1.

12. James Trainor, July 30, 1873, HRFS, Roll 1, NARA; Captain J. P. Dodge to Post Adjutant, Fort Stockton, August 1872, HRFS, Roll 8, NARA.

13. Curtis to Grant, August 8, 1872, OIANM, RG 75, Roll 561; Curtis to Commissioner, August 31, 1872, CIAAR, 1872, H. Ex. Doc. 1, 42nd Congress, third session, SS 1560, 689.

14. Randlett to AG, Washington, July 22, 1873, HRFS, Roll 1, NARA.

15. Maurice G. Fulton, *History of the Lincoln County War* (Tucson: University of Arizona Press, 1997), 45–46; Robert M. Utley, *High Noon in Lincoln: Violence on the Western Frontier* (Albuquerque: University of New Mexico Press, 1987), 14.

16. Dudley to Commissioner, September 3, 1873, CIAAR, 1873, H. Ex.Doc. 1, 43rd Congress, 1st session, SS 1601, 632; Fulton, 49–50.

17. Lawrence G. Murphy to Crothers, January 14, 1877, OIANM, Roll 570, NARA.

18. Randlett to Price, September 18, 1873, OIANM, Roll 563, NARA; William A. Keleher, *The Fabulous Frontier* (Albuquerque: University of New Mexico Press, 1962), 60–61; *Las Vegas Gazette*, November 25, 1875; CIAAR, 1874, 43rd Congress, second session, H. ex. doc. 1, SS 1639, 382, 529, 542; SWAR, 1874, 43rd Congress, second session, H. ex. doc. 2, SS 1635; CIAAR, 1876, 44th Congress, second session, H. ex. doc. 1, SS 1749, 545, 766, 774.

19. Dudley to Commissioner, March 11, 1874, OIANM, Roll 562, NARA; Crothers to Dudley, May 2 and May 13, 1874, OIANM, Roll 563; CIAAR, 1874, 373, 613–614.

20. Major D. R. Clendenin to AAAG, New Mexico, January 5, 8 and 29, 1875, OAG, Roll 187, NARA; J. W. Daniels, to Smith, February 26, 1875, Reports of Field Inspections, Bureau of Indian Affairs, RG 75, Roll 25, NARA; Captain E. G. Fechit, to Clendenin, January 27, 1875, OIANM, Roll 564; Crothers to Smith, January 20 and March 30, 1875, OIANM, Roll 564; Fulton, 25–26.

21. A protracted search failed to locate the Smoke Mountains on any map of Texas. The agent and various army officers described these locations: near Fort Davis, adjacent to the Carrizo

Mountains, south of Fort Quitman, and between forts Davis and Quitman. Captain D. A. Carpenter, of the Tenth Cavalry at Fort Davis, provided the most detailed descriptions, along with the source of the name. During a scout, he found an Apache trail on the east side of Smoke Mountain that led east to the Guadalupes. Just as they arrived, Indians on a high lookout on Smoke Mountain sent up a smoke signal to alert those in front (Carpenter to AG, March 22, 1876). The most likely candidates are the Eagle Mountains and the Sierra Vieja to the south. Agent Godfroy, who knew their habits best, asked that scouting parties be sent to the Eagle Mountains (Godfroy to Smith, September 29, 1877).

22. Carpenter to Adjutant, October 8, 1878.

23. Andrew W. Sharpe to Smith, June 2, 1875 and Crothers to Smith, October 15, 1875, OIANM, NARA.

24. Captain George A. Purrington to AAAG, New Mexico, June 19, 1876, OIANM, Roll 566, NARA; Crothers to Smith, November 10, 1876 and Godfroy to Smith, August 10, 1876, OIANM,R rolls 569–570, NARA.

Chapter 29

1. Bliss, 431.

2. Utley, *Fort Davis*, 20, 25; Leckie, 88

3. Wooster, 31, 34; SWAR, 1868, H. ex. doc. 3, 40th congress, third session, SS 1367, xvi–xvii, 716; SWAR, 1869, H. ex. doc. 2, 41st congress, second session, SS 1412, 17–18, 144.

4. Major J. Wade to AAAG, May 31, 1869, HRFS, Roll 1, NARA; *Depredations on the Frontiers of Texas*, 22; Kenneth W. Porter, "Negroes and Indians on the Texas Frontier, 1834–1874," *Southwestern Historical Quarterly* 53 (October 1949), 101.

5. *Depredations on the Frontiers of Texas*, 3, 13, 17, 23.

6. Porter, "Seminole Negro-Indian Scouts," 360; Kenneth W. Porter, *The Black Seminoles: History of a Freedom-Seeking People* (Gainesville: University Press of Florida, 1996), 162–166, 182.

7. Bliss to Brevet Colonel H. Clay Wood, July 14, 1870, HRFS, Roll 1, NARA; Montgomery, 145; Porter, *Black Seminoles*, 219; Porter, "Seminole Negro-Indian Scouts," 360–364, 369; Mulroy, 114.

8. Mulroy, 117–118.

9. Edward S. Wallace, "General Ranald Slidell Mackenzie Indian Fighting Cavalryman," *Southwestern Historical Quarterly* 56 (January 1953), 378, 386–387, 392; Robert G. Carter, *On the Border with Mackenzie, or Winning West Texas from the Comanches* (Washington, D. C.: Eynon, 1935), 18; Wooster, "The Army and Politics," 154.

10. Schilz (61) wrote that most of the Kickapoo warriors were absent, and so "Mackenzie aimed the heaviest blows at the Lipan village" and struck while many of the inhabitants were taking a siesta. He concluded the Lipans' power was broken by Mackenzie's soldiers.

11. Porter, *Black Seminoles*, 182–183; Carter, 438–442, 447; Mulroy, *Freedom*, 118; Frost Woodhull, "The Seminole Indian Scouts on the Border," *Frontier Times* 15 (December 1937): 121; Robert Wooster, "The Army and the Politics of Expansion: Texas and the Southwestern Borderlands, 1870–1886," *Southwestern Historical Quarterly* 93 (October 1989): 154–155.

12. Oral account of Calixtro Gonzalez Castro, born in 1858 in Beeville, in Romero, 8.

13. Maestas, 295–297; Romero, 48–50, 53.

14. Woodhull, 121; Mulroy, 118–119; Robinson, *Frontier Forts*, 47–48; Edward S. Wallace, "General John Lapham Bullis: Thunderbolt of the Texas Frontier, II," *Southwestern Historical Quarterly* 55 (July 1951): 79; Carter, 436–437, 444–445, 447–448.

15. "The Lipan Indians," *Texas State Gazette* (Austin), October 25, 1873; Clarence C. Clendenen, *Blood on the Border: The United States Army and the Mexican Irregulars* (London: The Macmillan Company, 1969), 69–70.

16. Augur, Annual Report, September 30, 1873; Mackenzie to Augur, June 6, 1873; and Shafter to Augur, June 27, 1873; all in "Ranald S. Mackenzie's Official Correspondence Relating to Texas, 1873–1879," *Museum Journal* 10 (1966): 23, 35, 62. Mackenzie to AAG Texas, May 23, 1873, 173, and Schuhard to Mackenzie, May 19, 1873, 175, all in "Ranald S. Mackenzie's Official Correspondence Relating to Texas, 1871–1873," *Museum Journal* 9 (1965); *Houston Daily Mercury*, July 11, 1873.

17. Shafter to Augur, June 27, 1873, in Mackenzie, 36; Porter, "Seminole Negro-Indian Scouts," 365; Mulroy, 119. Porter wrote that Teresita and James Perryman had two children, and their son Warren (Juan) Perryman was a community leader and a deacon in the church at Brackettville. When the army disbanded the Seminole Negro Indian Scouts in 1914, James and Warren Perryman were among a handful of people allowed to remain on the Fort Clark Military Reservation until the senior Perryman died (Order of Col. Sibley, May 7, 1914, Fort Clark Museum).

18. Shafter to Mackenzie, July 1, 1873, "Official Correspondence," 37–38.

19. Reports of the Committee of Investigation, 336.

20. Wooster, "Army and the Politics of Expansion," 157.

21. Augur, Annual Report, 1873, 61–62; Mackenzie to Augur, June 28, 1873, 33; Sherman to Sheridan, July 17, 1873, 35; Sheridan, endorsement, July 15, 1873, 34; Augur to AAG, July 5, 1873, 34; all in "Official Correspondence, 1873–1879"; *Houston Daily Mercury*, July 13, 1873.

22. Atkinson to Augur, July 12, 1873, 40–41; Williams to Augur, July 28, 1873, 43; Atkinson and Williams to Cepeda, July 22, 1873, 43–44; Mackenzie to Augur, July 18, 1873, 46; all in "Official Correspondence, 1873–1879."

23. Atkinson and Williams to Secretary of Interior, October 21, 1873, 43rd Congress, first session, H. ex. doc. 2, 2; Atkinson to Mackenzie, July 25, 1973, "Official Correspondence, 1873–1879," 48.

24. A small group of Kickapoos joined the group in Indian Territory in 1875, but the rest stayed in Mexico and still live on a reservation near Musquiz.

25. George R. Nielsen, *The Kickapoo People* (Phoenix: Indian Tribal Series, 1975), 56–59; Mackenzie, 49 fn 5 and Augur's Annual Report, 61–3, in "Official Correspondence, 1873–1879"; Robinson, *Frontier Forts*, 47.

26. Mackenzie to AAG Texas, May 23, 1873, in "Ranald S. Mackenzie's Official Correspondence Relating to Texas, 1871–1873," 173; Lester W. Galbreath, *Fort Griffin and the Clear Fork Country* (Albany, Texas, Self-published, 1997), 87–89.

27. Michael Tate, "Indian Scouting Detachments in the Red River War, 1874–1875," *Red River Valley Historical Review* 3 (Spring 1978): 214–217, 222; Tate in Winfrey and Day, vol. 1, xix; Mulroy, 122.

28. Mackenzie thought Johnson was half Tonkawa.

29. Tonkawa Indians at Fort Griffin, Texas, 44th Congress, first session, H. ex. doc.102, SS 1689, 1–5; Ernest Wallace, *Ranald S. Mackenzie on the Texas Frontier* (Lubbock: West Texas Museum

Association, 1964), 125; Donald A. Swanson, *Enlistment Record of Indian Scouts* (Bronte, TX: Ames-American Printing Co., 1990), 2, 18, 20, 22, 43, 45; Deborah Lamont Newlin, "The Tonkawa People: A Tribal History from Earliest Times to 1893," *The Museum Journal* 21 (1982): 82; Ty Cashion, *A Texas Frontier: The Clear Fork Country and Fort Griffin, 1849–1887* (Norman: University of Oklahoma Press, 1996), 144.

30. Edna Greer Hatfield Collection, Box 1, Folder 1, Western History Collections, University of Oklahoma Libraries, Norman, Oklahoma; Subseries D: Lipan, "Childhood and Child Training," Box 44, Folder 6, Opler Papers.

31. Troy Milton Morris, "Tale of Old Fort Griffin," *Dallas Morning News*, August 26, 1928.

32. Tonkawa Indians at Fort Griffin; Mulroy, 129; Leckie, 143.

Chapter 30

1. Crothers to Smith, January 8, 1875.

2. Eve Ball, "The Last of the Lipan Apaches," undated manuscript, Ball Papers; John C. Ewers, "The Influence of Epidemics on the Indian Populations and Cultures of Texas," *Plains Anthropologist* 18 (May 1973): 107; Romero, 44; Griffin, 34.

3. CIAAR, 1870, 728.

4. CIAAR, 1874, 382, 529, 542, 545; Augur's Report, September 28, 1874, SWAR, 1874, 42; CIAAR, 1875, H. ex. doc. 1. 44th Congress, first session. SS 1680, 540, 543; CIAAR, 1876, 545, 766, 774; *Record of Engagements with Hostile Indians within the Military Division of the Missouri, from 1868 to 1882* (Washington: Government Printing Office, 1882), 41; Albert Gatschet, "Lipan, a dialect of the Apache-Tinné family," September 1884. *Archives of the Bureau of American Ethnology*, 81-a (Washington, D.C.: Archives of the Bureau of American Ethnology, Smithsonian Institution), 30; Meredith Magoosh Begay, interview with Sherry Robinson, Mescalero, September 24–25, 2005.

5. Griffin, 34; Dan W. Roberts, *Rangers and Sovereignty* (San Antonio: Wood Printing & Engraving Co., 1914), 67–75; Zesch, 39–40, 204–205, 208, 282–283, 301; R. Radcliff to AAG, November 22, 1869, HRFS, Roll 2. Ranger James B. Gillett told the same story about a white boy with long red hair. Gillett and Ed Sieker killed the warrior but lost the white boy. A Mexican boy said they were Lipans from Mexico. Gillett believed the white boy was Herman Lehmann, who was then a captive (Williams, 183), but Roberts spoke to Fischer about the episode.

6. Meredith Magoosh Begay, interview.

7. A. B. Gray, chief engineer of the Pacific and Texas Western Railways, in 1854 estimated their extent at fifty to sixty miles and ten miles wide. "These singular-looking hills seem to be an accumulation of fine white sand heaped together near the lower part of the plain . . . and innumerable hillocks and ridges forty to eighty feet high that at night resemble waves of the sea" (Weniger, 56).

8. Major William R. Price to Willard, October 8, 1873, OIANM, Roll 561, NARA; Shafter to AAG, January 4, 1876, in William Shafter, "Shafter's Explorations in Western Texas, 1875," *West Texas Historical Association Year Book* 9 (October 1933): 82–95; Captain S. T. Norvell to AAG, November 1, 1875, HRFS, Roll 3, NARA; Shafter to AG, Texas, September 29, 1875, HRFS, Roll 3; Crothers to Commissioner, January 31, 1876, OIANM, roll 566, NARA.

9. Secretary of War to Secretary of the Interior, December 15, 1876; Godfroy to Major Lawrence G. Murphy, January 6, 1877; Godfroy to Smith, Janury 25 and February 1, 1877; all on OIANM, Roll 570, NARA.

10. Godfroy to Smith, November 7, 1877, OIANM, Roll 572, NARA; Llewellyn to Van Horn, August 4, 1884, HRDNM, Roll 55, NARA; Mescalero Census, 1885, IC, Roll 254, NARA.

11. Tate, in Winfrey and Day, vol. 1, xix; Smith, *Fort Inge*, 173; CIAAR, 1871, 419, 918-919; Colonel Ranald Mackenzie to Commander, August 11, 1871, HRFS, Roll 2; Weniger, 18-29.

12. Percy Big Mouth, interview with Eve Ball, Mescalero, October 27, 1954, Ball Papers.

13. Eve Ball, *Indeh: An Apache Odyssey* (Provo, UT: Brigham Young University Press, 1980), 211–212, 273; Opler, *Apache Odyssey*, 58.

14. Solon Sombrero, interview with Eve Ball, Elk Canyon, October 20, 1954 and June 22, 1962, Ball Papers; Russell to Commissioner, March 27, 1880, OIANM,Rroll 580, NARA; Godfroy, annual report, September 1, 1877, CIAAR, 1877, H. ex. doc. 1, 45th Congress, second session, SS 1800, 551-553; Charlie Smith, interview with Eve Ball, Ruidoso, January 3, 1968, Ball Papers. Charlie Smith, a Mescalero, referred to Natzili's band as Mescaleros (Odyssey, 59), but in an interview with Eve Ball, he referred to a time before the "Buffalo Indians and Lipans came."

15. *Guadalupe Mountains National Park* (Washington, D.C.: National Park Service, undated); Subseries D: Lipan, "Bands and Place Names," Box 38, Folder 19, Opler Papers.

16. Captain D. A. Carpenter to Post Adjutant, Fort Davis, March 22, 1876, HRFS, Roll 3, NARA.

17. James B. Gillett, *Six Years with the Texas Rangers, 1875–1881* (New Haven: Yale University Press, 1925), 58–60.

18. James Marr to Carl Schurz, Interior Secretary, February 14, 1878, HRFS, Roll 1, NARA.

19. Ord to AG, Texas, February 8, 1878 and Godfroy to Dudley, April 22, 1878, OIANM, Roll 573, NARA.

20. Dudley to AAAG, New Mexico, May 24, 1878, OAG, RG 393, Roll 406, NARA; Godfroy to Hoyt, May 14, 1878, OIANM, Roll 573, NARA.

21. Viele to AAAG, Pecos, October 11, 1879; Carpenter to AAAG Pecos, July 19, 1879; Nordstrom to AAAG, Pecos, August 2, 1879; Eggleston, to CO, Camp Charlotte, August 2, 1879; all in HRDP, Roll 2, NARA.

22. Smither to Grierson, March 28 1879, HRDP, Roll 2, NARA; Smith, "U.S. Army Combat Operations," 506.

23. Bullis to Ord, May 9, 1879, in SWAR, 1880, H. ex. doc. 1, 46th Congress, third session, SS 1952, 115; M. L. Crimmins, "The Mescalero Apaches," *Frontier Times* 8 (September 1931): 553–554; Tabular statement of expeditions and scouts against Indians, etc. made in the Department of Texas in the year ending September 1, 1879, in SWAR, 1879.

24. J. B. Gibson, "Texas Rangers Scouting After Apache Indians," *Frontier Times* 11 (February 1934): 220–231.

Chapter 31

1. Ord, Testimony Taken by the Committee on Military Affairs in Relation to the Texas Border Troubles, 1878, H. Misc. Doc. 64, 45th Congress, second session, SS 1820, 14, 79, 83; Shafter testimony, 159.

2. Wooster, "Army and the Politics of Expansion," 159; CIAAR, 1876, 537–538.

3. Bullis testimony, *Texas Border Troubles*, 190; Porter, *Black Seminoles*, 198.

4. Woodhull, 122.

5. Ord testimony, *Mexican Border Troubles*, H. ex. Doc. 13, 45th Congress, first session, 1877, SS 1773, 9, 73–74; Schuchardt to Shafter, March 29, 1877, Special Collections, Eagle Pass Public Library; Wooster, "Army and the Politics of Expansion," 145, 158–159; Daniel Cosio Villegas, *The United States Versus Porfirio Díaz* (Lincoln: University of Nebraska Press, 1963), 110–111; *Weekly State Gazette*, February 2, 1878.

6. Ord testimony, *Texas Border Troubles*, 13–14; Ord to AG, July 12, 1877, *Mexican Border Troubles*.

7. Wooster, "Politics of Expansion," 159; Bullis testimony, 195, and Ord testimony, *Mexican Border Troubles*, 178, 195; Mulroy, 127; Porter, *Black Seminoles*, 200–201.

8. William Schuchardt, September 7, 1877, and Shafter to Ord, August 10, 1877, *Mexican Border Troubles*, 208–209.

9. Bruce Dinges, "The Victorio Campaign of 1880: Cooperation and Conflict on the United States-Mexico Border," *New Mexico Historical Review* 62 (January 1987): 83–84; Ord Testimony, *Texas Border Troubles*, 13–14; Villegas, 102–103.

10. Expeditions and Scouts against Indians, &c., made in the Department of Texas During the Year ending September 30, 1878, HRDNM, Roll 36, NARA.

11. Mulroy, 128; Expeditions and Scouts; M. L. Crimmins, "The Mescalero Apaches," 552–553.

12. Ord to Shafter, November 22, 1877, Special Collections, Eagle Pass Public Library; Bullis testimony, *Texas Border Troubles*, 203.

13. Peter Steffian, et al., "The Duval and Nueces County Raid," submitted with citizens' petition to Secretary of State, September 30, 1878, in SWAR, 1878, H. ex. doc. 2, 45th Congress, third session, SS1843; "The Mexican and Indian Raid of '78," *Texas Historical Association Quarterly* 5 (January 1902): 214–215.

14. Mackenzie, Report of Expedition into Mexico, in "Official Correspondence," 204 and 204 fn 3–4; Mackenzie to Shafter, February 25, 1878, "Official Correspondence," 202; J. M. Kelly to AAG, April 6, 1878, "Official Correspondence," 212; Schofield to AG, November 8, 1877, Special Collections, Eagle Pass Public Library; Expeditions and Scouts against Indians, &c., made in the Department of Texas During the Year ending September 30, 1878, OAG, M 666, Roll 406, NARA.

15. *Weekly State Gazette*, June 29 and July 13, 1878; *Lampasas Dispatch*, September 13, 1877.

16. Anonymous, Santa Rosa, to Mackenzie, August 28, 1878 and Mackenzie to AAG, Texas, undated, OAG, M 666, Roll 406, NARA. Mackenzie said two men who profited from the April raid were Jesús Galán and Tirso Castellón.

17. Judge Thomas Paschal to Ord, August 26, 1878, in SWAR, 1878, 83–84; S. D. Myres, ed., "O. W. Williams' Stories from the Big Bend," *Southwestern Studies* 3 (1965): 39 fn 34.

18. John W. Foster, Legation of United States in Mexico, to William M. Evarts, Secretary of State, July 23, 1879; Foster to Miguel Buelas, Mexican Minister of Foreign Affairs, July 18 and 22, 1879, HRDNM, Roll 38, NARA.

19. Ord, annual report, October 2, 1878, in SWAR, 1878, 85; *Weekly State Gazette*, October 19, 1878; "Editorial," *Periodico Official* (Monterey, Nuevo Leon, September 7, 1878).

20. Britten (229) confuses the village with the San Carlos Apache Reservation in Arizona.

21. Myres, 9–10; Beck to AAAG, Pecos, December 21, 1878, HRDP, Roll 2, NARA; Moses Kelley to Bullis, September 16, 1877, in *Mexican Border Troubles*, 241; Bullis testimony, *Texas Border Troubles*, 203; E. Bush to AAG, August 31, 1874, HRFS, Roll 1, NARA; James F. Brooks,

Captives and Cousins: Slavery, Kinship, and Community in the Southwest Borderlands (Chapel Hill: University of North Carolina Press, 2002), 324; Ord, October 2, 1878.

22. Grierson to AAG, Texas, March 8 and June 27, 1878, HRDP, Roll 1, NARA; Maxon to AAAG, Pecos, August 5, 1878, HRDP, Roll 2.

23. Ord, annual report, 1878, 85; Maxon to Grierson, November 6, 1878, HRDP, Roll 2, NARA; AAG to Grierson, December 11, 1879, HRDP, Roll 2; AAG to CO, Fort Stockton, November 8, 1878, HRDFS, Roll 3; Wooster, "Politics of Expansion," 161–162.

24. Porter, *Black Seminoles*, 200, 220.

25. *Fort Griffin Echo*, November 15, 1879, and November 6, 1880.

26. Irvine to Secretary of Interior, May 12 1879; Irvine to Commissioner of Indian Affairs, July 4, 1879, October 7, 1879, and January 7, 1880; all in Pawnee Agency Census and Enrollment, Indian Archives Division, Oklahoma Historical Society, Roll PA 1.

27. Irvine to Commanding Officer, January 23, 1880; Swanson, 18; *Handbook of Texas Online,* "Fort Griffin," *http://www.tshaonline.org/handbook/online/articles/FF/hnf35.html* (accessed March 2, 2010; Phelps to Adjutant, Fort McIntosh, February 28, 1880, HRDP, Roll 2, NARA; *Fort Griffin Echo* (May 29, 1880).

Chapter 32

1. Dan L. Thrapp, *Victorio and the Mimbres Apaches* (Norman: University of Oklahoma Press, 1974), 250.

2. Godfroy to Smith, September 27, 1877, OIANM, Roll 571, NARA; Richard Magoosh, interview with Eve Ball, Ruidoso, August 1954, Ball Papers.

3. Godfroy to Smith, October 1, 1877, OIANM, Roll 571, NARA; Godfroy to E. A. Hoyt, November 7 and December 8, 1877, OIANM, Roll 572, NARA.

4. Captain George Purington to E. C. Watkins, U.S. Indian Inspector, July 2, 1878, OIANM, Roll 574, NARA; Godfroy to Commissioner, July 5, 1878, OIANM, Roll 573, NARA; J. Staab to Hoyt, June 18, 1878.

5. Alexander McSween to Carl Schurz, February 11, 1878, OIANM, Roll 574, NARA.

6. Rutherford B. Hayes, Executive Order, August 2, 1878; Report to C. Schurz, Secretary of the Interior, October 2, 1878; Godfroy to Hoyt, August 5 and 15, 1878; all in OIANM, roll 574, NARA.

7. Godfroy to Smith, September 29, 1877, OIANM, Roll 571, NARA; Thrapp, 216–217; Russell to Commissioner, August 21, 1879, OIANM, Roll 577, NARA.

8. Russell to Colonel G. A. Purington, July 19, 1879, OIANM, Roll 577, NARA; Goodwin to Post Adjutant, Fort Stanton, July 24, 1879, HRDNM, Roll 38, NARA; Rucker to AAAG, New Mexico, July 25, 1879, HRDNM, Roll 38, NARA; Russell to Commissioner, July 22, September 3, October 3 and 13, 1879, OIANM, Roll 577-578, NARA; Swaine to AAAG, September 21, 1879, HRDNM, Roll 38, NARA; A. J. Fountain to Russell, October 11, 1879, OIANM, Roll 580, NARA; Statements taken before Lt. Col. P. T. Swain, October 11, 1879, HRDNM, Roll 39, NARA.

9. William M. Evarts, Department of State, to George W. McCray, Secretary of War, October 10, 1879, and McCray to Evarts, November 10, 1879, OIANM, Roll 580, NARA.

10. Opler, "Use of Peyote," 282; Edward Gifford, *Culture Element Distributions: Apache-Pueblo,* vol. 4, University of California Anthropological Records (Berkeley: University of California

Press, 1940), 188; Gatschet, "Lipan, a dialect," 55. The Tú é dine ndé have been described as a Mescalero band; Meredith Magoosh Begay described them as a Lipan band. Lipan scouts at Fort Griffin called the Lipans in this group Tazhä. When Opler interviewed Lipans in 1935, he was surprised to learn that the Lower Lipans, or Big Water People, considered themselves the more true representatives of Lipan culture because they had less contact with the Mescaleros (Opler, *Myths*, 2).

11. Russell to Commissioner, September 3, 1879 and March 16 and 27, 1880, OIANM, Roll 580, NARA; Pope to Sheridan, November 5, 1879, HRDP, Roll 2, NARA.

12. Grierson to AAG, May 21, 1880, HRDP, Roll 1, NARA; Russell to Commissioner, April 17, 1880, OIANM, Roll 580, NARA.

13. Kelley to AG, Pecos, April 22, 1880, HRDP, Roll 2, NARA; Russell to Commissioner, April 17, 1880; Russell to Hatch, April 17, 1880, OIANM, Roll 580, NARA; Carter to Russell, April 21, 1880, OIANM, Roll 580, NARA.

14. *Thirty-Four* (Las Cruces) April 14, 1880; Captain Charles Steelhammer to AAAG NM, May 14, 1880, HRDNM, Roll 40, NARA; Pope, annual report, Department of Missouri, September 22, 1881, SWAR, 1881, H. Ex. Doc.1, 47th Congress, first session. SS 2010; Russell to Commissioner, May 2, 1881, OIA, RG 75, Box 19, File 7879.

15. Percy Big Mouth, interview with Eve Ball, Ruidoso, October 27, 1954, Ball Papers; Richard Magoosh, interview with Eve Ball, Ruidoso, August, 1954 and September 29, 1963, Ball Papers. Ball (*In the Days of Victorio*, 75) wrote that Magoosh joined Victorio, but that's unlikely.

16. Thrapp, 283-284; Colonel A. F. Valle, Mexican Army, to Grierson, July 26, 1880, HRDP, Roll 2, NARA; Thrapp, 286; Grierson to AAG, July 31, 1880, HRFS, Roll 1, NARA; Grierson to AAG, September 20, 1880, HRDP, Roll 1, NARA; Theophilus Rodenbough and William Haskins, eds, *The Army of the United States: Historical Sketches of Staff and Line with Portraits of Generals-in-Chief* (Ann Arbor: Argonaut Press, 1966), 295–296.

17. E. D.Townsend, AAG, general order, April 19, 1867, HRDP, Roll 1; Andrews to AAG, Pecos, March 13, 1878, HRDP, Roll 1; Carpenter to A, Davis, October 8, 1878, HRDP, Roll 2; Charles S. Palmer to Grierson, June 25 and July 26, 1880, HRDP, roll 2, NARA.

18. Nolan to AAAG, Pecos, August 14 and undated (probably September 9), 1880, HRDP, Roll 4, NARA; Thrapp, 289; Grierson to AAG, August 14 and September 20, 1880, HRDP, roll 1, NARA; Grierson, Report of the Campaign in Western Texas, July–August 1880, September 22, September 1880, RG 393, Part 1, Entry 2546, 639-644, courtesy of Robert Watt.

19. Vincent to Grierson, July 22, 1880, HRDP, Roll 2, NARA; Lt. William H. Beck, to CO, Eagle Springs, August 12, 1880 and Beck to CO, Fort Quitman, August 18, 1880, HRDP, Roll 1; Berger to Beck, August 23, 1880; Grierson to AAG, September 20, 1880; all in HRDP, roll 2.

20. Nolan to AAAG, Pecos; undated (probably September 9, 1880) and September 16, 1880; Grierson to AAG, September 20, 1880; Nolan to Beck, September 21, 1880 and October 6, 1880, HRDP, Roll 2; Nolan to Beck, September 21, 1880 and October 6, 1880, HRDP, Roll 2.

21. Berger to Nolan, September 28, 1880; Nolan to Carpenter, October 4, 1880; Brinkerhoff to Nolan, October 22, 1880, HRDP, Roll 2, NARA.

22. Sherry Robinson, *Apache Voices: Their Stories of Survival as Told to Eve Ball* (Albuquerque: University of New Mexico Press, 2000), 19.

Chapter 33

1. "Last Indian Raid in Southwest Texas," *Frontier Times* 4 (August 1927): 58–59; A. J. Sowell, *Early Settlers and Indian Fighters of Southwest Texas* (New York: Argosy-Antiquarian Ltd., 1986), 513–518; Mulroy, 119, 130–131; Augur, annual report, September 27, 1881 in ARSW, 1881. Teresita died in 1881 and was reportedly buried in the Seminole Negro Scouts' cemetery near Fort Clark. In a visit to the cemetery, the author found no grave site with her name, and she's not in B. Max Burleson's listing of the Seminole Indian Scouts Cemetery.

2. Wooster, *Fort Davis*, 94; Smith, "Old Army," 149; Williams, 89.

3. Ord report, 1878, 85; Carpenter to AAAG, December 22 and 28, 1878, HRDP, Roll 2; AAG to Commanding Officer, Fort Stockton, November 8, 1878, HRDFS, Roll 3; Wooster, "Politics of Expansion," 161–162; "The Indians of Mexico," *San Antonio Express* (undated but early 1880); Tabular statement of expeditions and scouts against Indians, etc. made in the Department of Texas during the year ending September 30, 1880, in SWAR, 1880; *Herald and Planter*, December 26, 1877.

4. *El Progresista* (Paso del Norte), December 30, 1881; Myres, 15–19.

5. Augur to AG, February 6, 1882; Porter, *Black Seminoles*, 207; Grierson, General Order, February 7, 1881, HRDP, Roll 5, NARA.

6. Porter, "Seminole Negro-Indian Scouts," 376–377; Smith, "U.S. Army Combat Operations," 512, 514.

7. Ewers, 104–113; David La Vere, *Life Among the Texas Indians*, 18. La Vere estimates Lipan losses to disease at 88 percent.

8. Sven Linkquist, "A History of Bombing," *Harper's Magazine* 303 (September 2001).

9. Kennedy to AAAG, Pecos, August 9, 1880, HRDP, Roll 2, NARA; Pope to Vincent, September 21, 1880, HRDP, Roll 1, NARA; AAG to McLaughlin, October 7, 1880, HRDP, Roll 1, NARA; Phelps to Post Adjutant, Fort McIntosh, February 28, 1880, HRFS, Roll 4, NARA; Captain J. J. Spencer to AAG Pecos, November 4, 1880, HRDP, Roll 2, NARA; Baldwin to Nolan, November 12, 1880, HRDP, Roll 2, NARA.

10. Louis Scott, U.S. Consul at Chihuahua, to John Hay, Department of State, October 22, 1880, HRDP, Roll 2, NARA; Grierson to AAG, December 31, 1880, HRDP, Roll 1.

11. Conrad to AAAG NM, September 23, 1880, October 27, 1880, November 13, 1880, HRDNM, Roll 41, NARA; Russell to Commissioner, October 29, 1880, OIANM, Roll 582, NARA.

12. Lt. Walter Finley to Post Adjutant, Fort Stanton, January 9, 1881, HRDNM, Roll 42; Morris E. Opler, *Apache Odyssey: A Journey between Two Worlds* (New York: Holt, Rinehart and Winston, 1969), 48; Llewellyn to Major Guy V. Henry, September 26 and October 12, 1881, HRDNM, Roll 43, NARA; Russell to Commissioner, November 23, 1880.

13. Llewellyn to CO, July 22, 1881 and Llewellyn to Commissioner, July 28, 1881, HRDNM, Roll 43.

14. Hatch to AAG, Department of Missouri, September 12, 1881, HRDNM, Roll 43.

15. Conrad to Post Adjutant, Stanton, December 1 and 2, 1880, HRDNM, Roll 41, NARA; Conrad to CO, Fort Stanton, November 13, 1880, HRDNM. Roll 41, NARA; Russell to Commissioner, November 23 and December 3, 1880, OIANM, Roll 582, and March 4, 1881, HRDNM, Roll 42; E.M. Marble, Acting Commissioner to Interior Secretary, December 21, 1880, OIANM, Roll 582, NARA.

16. Llewellyn to Commissioner, December 3, 1881, OIA, Letters Received, Box 53, #21760, NARA.

17. Mackenzie endorsement of reports and letters from Interior Department, February 8, 1882, OIA, LR, Box 61, #2108, NARA; G. W. Maxwell to CO, Stanton, January 23, 1882, OIA LR, Box 65, #4182, NARA; Llewellyn to Mackenzie, January 15, 1882.

18. Llewellyn to Henry, September 26, 1881, HRDNM, Roll 43, NARA; Wood to Post Adjutant, Stanton, June 23, 1882 and Llewellyn to Crofton, June 23, 1882, in HRDNM, Roll 47; Llewellyn to Commissioner, annual report, September 1, 1882, CIAAR, 1882, H. ex. doc. 1, 47th Congress, second session, SS 2100; Llewellyn to Commissioner, September 12, 1882, OIA LR, Box 97, #17309, NARA; Llewellyn to Crofton, August 16, 1882, HRDNM, Roll 47; Llewellyn to Mackenzie, September 18, 1882, HRDNM, Roll 47; Charlie Smith, interview with Eve Ball, Ruidoso, January 3, 1968, Ball Papers.

19. Llewellyn to Commissioner, September 12, 1882, OIA LR, Box 97, #17309, NARA; Van Horn to AAAG, September 21, 1882, HRDNM, Roll 47; Gale to Post Adjutant, Stanton, November 18, 1882, HRDNM, Roll 48; Wood to Post Adjutant, Stanton, February 6, 1883, HRDNM, Roll 49; Llewellyn to Mackenzie, March 21, 1883, HRDNM, Roll 49, and June 5 and 18, 1883, HRDNM, Roll 50; Gale to Post Adjutant , Fort Stanton, May 6, 1883, HRDNM, roll 50; Llewellyn to Fletcher, September 12, 1883, HRDNM, Roll 51; Robert T. Lincoln, Secretary of War, to President of Senate, February 28, 1882, HRDNM, Roll 45; Van Horn to AAAG NM, November 2, 1884, HRDNM, Roll 55.

20. Llewellyn to Mackenzie, August 19, 1882, HRDNM, Roll 47; Guilfoyle to Hatch, July 30, 1881; Hatch to AAG Department of Missouri, August 10 and 16 and September 12, 1881; Inspector General J. J. Coppinger to Pope, August 15, 1881; Whipple to Adjutant General, Washington, D.C., August 24, 1881; Hatch, annual report, October 3, 1881, all in OAG RG 94, M 689, Roll 44.

21. Llewellyn, annual report, August 15, 1884, CIAAR, 1884, H. ex. doc. 1, 48th Congress, second session, SS 2287, 176; Eve Ball wrote (*Indeh*, 215) that agent Carroll took Natzili to Washington, but Carroll didn't become Mescalero agent until 1901; Natzili died in 1898.

22. Solon Sombrero interview with Eve Ball, Ruidoso, December 15, 1954, Ball Papers; Subseries D: Lipan, "Alien People," Box 44, Folder 10, Opler Papers.

Chapter 34

1. Mackenzie to AAG, Department of Missouri, January 10, 1882, HRDNM, Roll 45, NARA.

2. Yeyu (Stella La Paz) and Conejo were Big Water Lipans, born in southern Texas.

3. Lipans used green leaves to make a signal with thick smoke to warn camps far away.

4. In 1882 the Galveston, Harrisburg and San Antonio Railway reached Eagle Pass.

5. Opler, *Myths*, 260–273; Phelps to Post Adjutant, Fort McIntosh, February 28, 1880, HRFS, Roll 4; General Augur, Annual Report, September 27, 1881, SWAR, 1881, 128; Solon Sombrero, interview with Eve Ball, Elk Canyon, October 20, 1954, Ball Papers; Subseries D: Lipan, "Warpath and raid" and "Lipan history," Box 44, Folders 25 and 54, Opler Papers. Antonio Apache dated the journey at around 1869, but there was no railroad or reservation at that time.

6. Percy Big Mouth, interview with Eve Ball, Mescalero, November 10, 1954, Ball Papers.

7. Llewellyn to CO, Stanton, January 4, 1882 and Crofton to Wood, January 8, 1882, HRDNM, Roll 45, NARA.

8. Mackenzie to Llewellyn, January 9, 1882; Mackenzie to Crofton, January 9, 1882; Mackenzie to AAG, Department of Missouri, January 10, 1882, all in HRDNM, Roll 45, NARA; Commissioner to Llewellyn, March 3, 1882 and Llewellyn to Mackenzie, March 14, 1882, HRDNM, Roll 46, NARA.

9. Llewellyn to Crofton, March 25 and April 5, 1882; Crofton to Mackenzie, March 31, 1882; Mackenzie to AAG, Department of Missouri, March 31 and April 2, 1882; all in HRDNM, Roll 46, NARA.

10. Eve Ball ms, undated, Ball Papers; Willie Magoosh, interview with C. L. Sonnichsen, Mescalero, February 5, 1955, Box 73, Folder 171, C. L. Sonnichsen Papers, MS 141, C. L. Sonnichsen Special Collections Department, University of Texas at El Paso; May Peso Second, interview with Eve Ball, Ruidoso, December 17, 1964, Ball Papers. The agent described Magoosh Boy as Magoosh's son, but Solon Sombrero said he wasn't a son but a relative (Sombrero, October 20, 1954).

11. Willie Magoosh, interview with C. L. Sonnichsen, Sonnichsen Papers.

12. Lipans probably noticed that their spoken language was more like the Jicarillas' than it was the Mescaleros' and that the Jicarillas, like themselves, had an emergence story, while the Mescaleros didn't. They also had the same concept of the afterlife and many stories in common (Opler, *Myths and Legends*, 3–6.)

13. Mescalero Census, 1885, IC, NARA, Roll 254; Meredith Magoosh Begay, interview with Sherry Robinson, Mescalero, September 24 and 25, 2005; Richard Magoosh, interview with Eve Ball, Ruidoso, August 1954, Ball Papers.

14. John Gallarito to Eve Ball, July 1970, Ball Papers; Gatshet, 183; Mescalero Census, 1894. Gallarito said Caje was the last member of a group that was all dead; it was named for the woodpecker. Gatshet (183) listed only one band, the Telkondaha, named for a bird.

Chapter 35

1. Solon Sombrero, interview with Eve Ball, Ruidoso, June 22, 1962, Ball Papers.

2. Llewellyn to Van Horn, April 29 and May 1, 1885; Clerk to Lt. J. J. Neinberg, April 29, 1885; Van Horn to AAAG NM, May 3, 1885, all in HRDNM, Roll 56, NARA.

3. Bradley, District of New Mexico, annual report, September 10, 1885, HRDNM, Roll 58, NARA; Opler, *Myths*, 274.

4. Chebahtah and Minor, 132–133; Llewellyn to Van Horn, August 4, 1884, HRDNM, Roll 55, NARA.

5. Van Horn to AG, New Mexico, June 1, 1885; Wallace to Van Horn, June 10, 1885; Cruse to Van Horn, June 20, 1885; Van Horn to AAAG, New Mexico, June 21, 1885; Cruse to CO, Stanton, June 28, 1885; all in HRDNM, Roll 56, NARA; Wilcox to AAG, New Mexico, July 7, 1885, and Llewellyn to Captain H.J. Farnsworth, August 10, 1885, HRDNM, Roll 57, NARA.

6. Wilcox to AAG, New Mexico, July 7 and 23, 1885, Fechét to AG, Washington, July 23, 1885; Gaston to AAG, New Mexico, July 25, 1885; Muster-Roll of a Detachment of Indian Scouts serving at camp near Fairview under the command of Lt. William A. Shunk, August 17, 1885; Norbert Strong, assistant surgeon, to Wilcox, July 26, 1885; all in HRDNM, Roll 57, NARA; Llewellyn to Commissioner, August 20, 1885, CIAAR, H. ex. doc. 1, 49th Congress, first session, SS 2379.

7. Llewellyn to CO, Fort Stanton, July 10, 1885, HRDNM, Roll 57, NARA; Cowart, August 1, 1887, CIAAR, 1887, H. ex. doc. 1, 50th Congress, first session, SS 2542, 250; V. E. Stottler, June 30, 1895, CIAAR, 1895, H. ex. doc. 5, 54th Congress, first session, SS 3382, 215.

8. Chebahtah and Minor, Appendix 2; Returns from U.S. Military Posts, 1800-1916, Fort Stanton, New Mexico, RG 94, M 617, Roll 1218, NARA; Robert S. Gardner, October 13, 1886, Reports of Field Inspections, Bureau of Indian Affairs, RG 75, M 1070, Roll 25, NARA; Cowart, August 12, 1886, CIAAR, 1886, H. ex. doc., 49th Congress, second session, SS 2467, 419. The army estimated Magoosh and Jose Torres to be in their mid-thirties, but both were in their fifties. Shosh and Dinero's estimated age was thirty.

9. Superintendents' Annual Narrative and Statistical Reports from Field Jurisdictions of the BIA, 1936, RG 75, M 1011, Roll 82, NARA; Gardner report; Vance to AAAG, New Mexico, August 25, 1886, and Crittenden to AAAG, New Mexico, April 10, 1887, OAG, Roll 489, NARA.

10. Mescalero Census 1887, IC, NARA.

11. Opler (*Handbook*, 373) wrote that all Apaches had a fear of witches and often blamed prolonged sickness on witchcraft, but this belief may have been more common among Mescaleros. "Witches were unknown in old Lipan country," said Stella La Paz. "They have been heard of just since coming in contact with the No Water People" (Subseries D: Lipan, "Alien People," Box 44, Folder 10, Opler Papers).

12. Cowart to Commissioner, August 12 and 13, 1886, CIAAR, 1886, 420.

13. Cowart to Commissioner, May 5, 1887, OAG, RG 94, M 689, Roll 548, NARA.

14. Howard to AG, Washington, D.C., August 12, 1887 and Adjutant General's Office Brief, November 19, 1887, OAG, RG 94, M 689, Roll 548, NARA; Cowart to Commissioner, August 11, 1887, Office of Indian Affairs, Letters Received, Box 414, #21783; Chebahtah and Minor, 150.

15. The list included, besides Chivato and his family, Mariano, Blanco, José Torres, Manuel, Shosh, and Stella Lester and their families (Chebahtah and Minor, *Chevato*, Appendix 1).

16. Mescalero Census, 1886, 1887 and 1888, IC, NARA; Chebahtah and Minor, 151–152 and Appendix 1.

17. Cowart to Smith, November 1, 1887, CIAAR, 1887; Cowart, July 31, 1888, CIAAR, 1888.

18. Cowart to Commissioner, January 29 and October 15, 1887, HRDNM, Roll 62-63, NARA; Cowart to Commissioner, July 28, 1888, HRDNM, Roll 65, NARA; Joseph F. Bennett, August 15, 1890, CIAAR, 1890, H. ex. doc. 1, 51st Congress, second session, SS 2841, 156.

19. Opler, *Apache Odyssey*, 168–169; Subseries D: Lipan, "Names," Box 44, Folder 35, Opler Papers.

20. Bennett, August 15, 1890; Subseries D: Lipan, "Horse, burro, mule," Box 38, Folder 10 and "Childhood and child training," Box 44, Folder 6, Opler Papers; Percy Big Mouth, undated, Sue Edwards Black Papers.

21. Sherry Robinson, *Apache Voices*, 92; Mrs. Jake Cojo, interview with Eve Ball, Mescalero, June 19, 1956. Apache oral history fixes this abduction in 1887, about six months after Massai escaped from the train, but the Mescalero Census shows Zanagolecha with Chivato until 1889. In 1890 Chivato married Chenoco, then about eighteen, and they had a baby, Joco (Mescalero Census, 1890).

22. Chebahtah and Minor, 156–158; Inspector Arthur Tinker to Secretary of Interior, April 19, 1890, Reports of Field Inspections, Bureau of Indian Affairs, RG 75, M 1070, NARA; Bennett to Commissioner, undated but probably August 1889, Blazer Family Papers, MS 110, Box 6, Folder 3, NMSU Special Collections.

23. John Meadows, "Tribal Fight Between Mescalero and La Pan Indians," *Alamogordo News*, February 20, 1936.

24. Walter Luttrell, Report of School Superintendent in Charge of Mescalero Agency, June 30, 1900, CIAAR, 1900, H. ex. doc. 5, 56th Congress, second session, SS 4101, 290; Mescalero Census 1887, 1888 and 1895, CI, NARA; Browning to Baldwin, June 8, 1896, Letters Sent and Received, Kiowa Agency, Oklahoma Historical Society, Microfilm Publications, Roll KA 1. Sanavoy returned in December 1895 to get his wife, and a year later Chivato's daughter, Carrie Heath, enrolled in the Comanche Tribe. Chivato's son, Harry Heath, enrolled on May 22, 1901. The young Lipan Penn Scott, a relative of Dinero, asked to go live at Fort Sill, repeating the complaint about tiswin. He remained, got married and raised a family.

25. Cowart to Commissioner, August 15, 1888, CIAAR, 1888, H. ex. doc. 1, 50th Congress, second session, SS 2637, 186; Mescalero Census, 1888; Subseries B: Mescalero, "Bands and Place Names," Box 38, Folder 19, Opler Papers; Hinman Rhodes to Commissioner, February 1891, Ball Papers. Also in Tularosa Canyon were Boneski, and Dinero. Magoosh Boy was at Elk Springs.

26. Joséph F. Bennett to Commissioner, August 22, 1889, CIAAR, 1889, H. ex. doc. 1, 51st Congress, first session, SS 2725, 254; Richard Hudson, July 20, 1893, CIAAR, 1893, H. ex. doc. 1, 53rd Congress, second session, SS 3210, 215; James Carroll, August 15, 1903, CIAAR, 1903, H. ex. doc. 5, 58th Congress, second session, SS 4645, 216.

27. Luttrell, June 30, 1900, 286, 290; "Salado Coal Fields," *Alamogordo News*, June 8, 1899.

28. Meredith Magoosh Begay, interview, August 14 and September 24 and 25, 2005.

29. Reports of Field Inspections, May 17, 1889 and December 12, 1992, Bureau of Indian Affairs, RG 75, Roll 25, NARA; Luttrell, June 30, 1900, 290.

Chapter 36

1. Walter M. Luttrell to Commissioner, June 30, 1900, CIAAR, 1900, 291.

2. "One time, when I was working in the BIA office, a tall white man came in—William Stott from Dallas. He said he knew my grandfather well. How, he didn't explain" (Meredith Magoosh Begay, September 24–25, 2005).

3. Andrew Atchison to Rhodes, July 20, 1893, CIAAR, 1893; Cowart, August 12, 1886; Cowart, August 1, 1887; Mescalero Census, 1886.

4. Atchison to Rhodes, July 30, 1892, CIAAR, 331; Meredith Magoosh Begay, September 24–25, 2005; Hudson, July 20, 1893; Levi F. Burnett to Commissioner, July 14, 1894, CIAAR, 206; Atchison to Rhodes, July 20, 1893; Rhodes to Commissioner, February 6, 1891, Ball Papers; Mescalero Census, 1892.

5. Rhodes, February 6, 1891; Henry Banta, agency physician, to Commissioner, May 3, 1891, Office of Indian Affairs, Letters Received, RG 75, Box 732, #17326; Burnett, July 14, 1894; A. E. Marden, agency physician, to Rhodes, July 15, 1892, CIAAR; V. E. Stottler to Commissioner, July 1, 1897, CIAAR, 193; Mescalero Census, 1888; Cowart, August 15, 1888; Stottler to Commissioner, June 30, 1896, CIAAR, 213.

6. Howard Thompson, agency physician, to Cowart, August 11, 1886, CIAAR, 1886, 418; Cowart, August 12, 1886, 416; Cowart, August 15, 1888; Llewellyn to Commissioner, January 26, 1882, Office of Indian Affairs, RG 75, Box 60, #1785, and June 10, 1882, Box 83, #11192, NARA.

7. Stottler to Commissioner, June 30, 1895, CIAAR, 215-216; Stottler, July 1, 1897.

8. Stottler, June 30, 1896, 211; Series B: Mescalero, "Biography," Box 38, Folder 20, Opler Papers; Opler, *Odyssey*, 59.

9. Stottler, June 30, 1896, 210; Stottler, July 1, 1897, 198; Luttrell, June 30, 1901, 282; Series B: Mescalero, "Birds," Box 40, Folder 26, Opler Papers.

10. Solon Sombrero, interview with Eve Ball, Elk Springs, October 20, 1954, Ball Papers.

11. Stottler, June 30, 1895, 218; Luttrell to Commissioner, July 18, 1899, CIAAR, 244; Mary V. Barclay to Luttrell, October 16, 1901, CIAAR, 1901, 288; Ball, *Indeh*, 213; Mescalero Census 1897 and 1898; Solon Sombrero, October 20, 1954.

12. Percy Big Mouth to Eve Ball, October 15, 1950, Ball Papers; Opler, *Odyssey*, 129–130.

13. Opler, *Odyssey*, 59; Series B: Mescalero, "Childhood and child training," Box 38, Folder 33, Opler Papers.

14. Eve Ball interviewed Philemon Venego over a 20-year period at White Tail.

15. Subseries D: Lipan, "Myths and tales," Box 44, Folder 37, Opler Papers; Meredith Magoosh Begay, September 24–25, 2005.

16. Lucy Smith, interview with Sherry Robinson, August 13, 2005, Mescalero.

17. Eve Ball (*Indeh*, 270) told the story of how Antonio Apache, an unmarried man, determined to find Magoosh and his people and take those in Mexico to join them on the Mescalero reservation. He made his way to the reservation, found Magoosh and told the chief that his people were barely surviving and wanted to come to Mescalero. Magoosh believed the agent would help. However, Antonio Apache had been living on the reservation with his wife and daughter since 1893 or 1894 (Mescalero Census 1894). It was probably then that he crept into the reservation and looked for Magoosh.

18. James A. Carroll to Commissioner, August 15, 1902, CIAAR, 253; Carroll to Commissioner, August 15, 1903, CIAAR 1903, 214; Carroll to Commissioner, May 25, 1903, Ball Papers. Carroll said they were living in the Guadalupe Mountains in Mexico, which is incorrect.

19. Eve Ball, "The Last of the Lipan Apaches," draft manuscript, Ball Papers; *Indeh*, 267–272; Mrs. Carroll, July 10, 1951, Blazer Family Papers, MS 110, Box 6, Folder 3, NMSU Special Collections.

20. Carroll to Commissioner, August 17, 1904, CIAAR, 251; Ball, "Last of the Lipan," Ball Papers. A year later Luis Hernandez appeared; he was a Mexican captive, married to the Lipan Rosa Hernandez. He had the same privileges as an Apache but returned to Mexico (Subseries B: Mescalero, "War," Box 40, Folder 23, Opler Papers; Mescalero Census, 1904 and 1905).

21. Carroll, August 15, 1902 and August 15, 1903; Carroll, May 25, 1904, Ball Papers; Willie Magoosh, interview with Eve Ball, Mescalero, October 23, 1953, Ball Papers.

22. Mescalero Census, 1904; Lucy Smith, interview.

23. Mescalero Census, 1906; Angie Debo, *Geronimo: The Man, His Time, His Place* (Norman: University of Oklahoma Press, 1976), 342; Dorothy Emerson, *Among the Mescalero Apaches: The Story of Father Albert Braun, O.F.M* (Tucson: University of Arizona Press, 1973), 39–41.

24. Carroll to Commissioner, August 9, 1905, CIAAR, 266; Carroll to Commissioner, August 9, 1910, Superintendents' Annual Narrative and Statistical Reports from Field Jurisdictions of the BIA, M 1011, Roll 82, NARA; Henry F. Dobyns, *The Mescalero Apache People* (Phoenix: Indian Tribal Series, 1973), 76.

25. May Peso Second, interviews with Eve Ball, Ruidoso, December 17, 1964 and January 30, 1967, Ball Papers; Ball, *Indeh*, 229; Dobyns, 76–77; Carroll to Commissioner, July 12, 1912, Superintendents' Annual Narrative and Statistical Reports from Field Jurisdictions of the BIA, M 1011, Roll 82, NARA.

26. Griffin, 34; Fred M. Griffin Jr., "Fred M. Griffin Family," oral account (Cloudcroft, NM: Sacramento Mountains Museum); Series B: Mescalero, "Photographs and documentation," Box 39, Folder 22, Opler Papers.

27. Solon Sombrero, October 20, 1954; Willie Magoosh, October 23, 1953; Eve Ball, unpublished draft, Ball Papers.

Chapter 37

1. Lucy Smith, August 13, 2005.

2. Hoijer says Many Houses was San Antonio, but Opler says Many Houses was Zaragosa and White Houses was San Antonio. The context indicates Opler was correct. Subseries D: Lipans, "Alien people," Box 44, Folder 10, Opler Papers.

3. Stella La Paz said Lipans used rawhide containers and made pottery of sticky, reddish clay but didn't make baskets until they lived in Mexico (Subseries D: Lipans, "Artifacts," Box 44, Folder 5, Opler Papers). Meredith Magoosh Begay said (August 14, 2005): "Apache baskets are all made the same way. Two to four strands are crossed, then they start weaving. They used suma berry, cottonwood, devil's claw, yucca. They'd soak and make the strips. Then they were very pliable. They'd make them into plates."

4. Hoijer, *Augustina Zuazua*, 25–37.

5. They were George Miles, Standing Buffalo, Johnson, John Williams, and John Kaise.

6. Irvine to Secretary of Interior, May 12 1879; Irvine to Commissioner of Indian Affairs, July 4, 1879, October 7, 1879, and January 7, 1880; all in Pawnee Agency Census and Enrollment; *Fort Griffin Echo*, February 7, March 5 and December 4, 1880; Grant Foreman, *The Last Trek of the Indians* (Chicago: The University of Chicago Press, 1946), 286–287; Tonkawa Public Schools Collection, Western History Collections, University of Oklahoma Libraries, Norman, Oklahoma; Tonkawa Indians, Indian Census Rolls, 1886, RG 75, M 595, Roll 386, NARA.

7. *Fort Griffin Echo*, February 5 and April 16, 1881.

8. Swanson, 18; *Handbook of Texas Online*, "Fort Griffin," *http://www.tshaonline.org/handbook/online/articles/FF/hnf35.html* (accessed March 2, 2010); Collinson, 85-88; Cashion, 274.

9. Albert Gatschet, "Lipan, a dialect," 55–56, and "Lipan, of the Tinné family," 183. Gatschet spoke to Juan Guerrero and Louis, both captives. Born in 1863 between the Pecos and the Rio Grande, Louis was captured by Comanches when he was about three. Big Water Lipans bought him around 1872 for four horses and two mules. He went with them to Fort Sill, where there were more than one hundred Lipans.

10. Hatfield Collection, Box H45, Folder 13, and Box H46, Folder 101, Western History Collections, University of Oklahoma Libraries, Norman, Oklahoma; The Tonkawa Tribe of Oklahoma, http://www.tonkawatribe.com/history.htm (accessed April 1, 2009); Foreman, 288–289.

11. Hatfield Collection; Tonkawa Public Schools Collection; Tonkawa Census, 1886–1893, IC, rolls 386-387, NARA; Wright, 251-252; Foreman, 290. Elsie Buffalo raised Railroad Cisco and Bertha Jesse, her grandchildren, and in 1893 married the Tonkawa head man Standing Buffalo; Meredith Magoosh Begay, September 24, 2005.

12. Wright, 181, states that Lipans once led by Woodercarnervesta joined their friends in 1895, but the Lipans had dispersed and resettled many years earlier. Foreman (*Last Trek*, 292) misinterpreted Hodge's numbers to state incorrectly that thirty-five Lipans joined the Kiowa Apaches. Hodge (Handbook 1, 769) calculated that only thirty-five Apaches total had survived, which was also incorrect.

13. Julia A. Jordan, *Plains Apache Ethnobotany* (Norman: University of Oklahoma Press, 2008), 25, 34–35, 37, 129; *Handbook of Texas Online*, "Kiowa Apaches," *http://www.tshaonline.org/handbook* (accessed October 9, 2008).

14. Meredith Magoosh Begay (August 14, 2005) said her oldest living relative there was Carrie Redbone. Percy Big Mouth's mother, Conejo, was born in Oklahoma when her people were visiting relatives there. Kiowa-Apache Chief Black Bear's mother Edidjo was related to Conejo and her sister Stella (Subseries D: Lipan, "Biography," Box 44, Folder 34; Kiowa Apache Census, 1879–1880, Oklahoma Historical Society, roll KA 1).

15. Jacqueline Fear-Segal, *White Man's Club: Schools, Race, and the Struggle of Indian Acculturation* (Lincoln: University of Nebraska Press, 2007), 259–260, 353 fn 14; Marc Simmons, "Indian Schools' Checkered History," *Santa Fe New Mexican*, August 22, 2009; Jerry Reynolds, "Boarding school dismantled families and cultures" and "'In The White Man's Image' a sad but vivid story of Indian history," *Navajo Times*, February 4 and 13, 1992.

16. Fear-Segal, 265–266, 268–269; *The Indian Helper* 1 (Carlisle Indian School: November 20, 1885); *The Red Man and Helper* 16 (August 3, 1900) and 18 (October 10, 1902).

17. Pratt to Commissioner, November 22, Commission of Indian Affairs, LR, 1884, #22556, Box 216, NARA; Fear-Segal, 261, 264-265; Paul Adams Yates, James Ramsay Humer, Russell D. Smith and William Bentz Carroll, *The Carlisle Indian School Cemetary: A List of Those Buried There* (Carlisle, Pennsylvania: Cumberland County Historical Society, undated).

18. Fear-Segal, 270, 275–277.

19. *Handbook of Texas Online*, "Adaes Indians," *http://www.tsha.utexas.edu/handbook/online/articles/AA/bma5.html* (accessed March 15, 2006); Joan Roche, "Sociocultural aspects of diabetes in an Apache-Choctaw community in Louisiana," Ph.D. diss., Catholic University of America, 1982, 60–62; Herbert E. Bolton, "The Spanish Abandonment and Re-Occupation of East Texas, 1773–1779," *Texas Historical Association Quarterly* 9 (October 1905): 84–85, 88–93, 99–100, 105 fn 2, 106–107; Choctaw-Apache Tribe of Louisiana, *http://www.choctaw-apache.org/* (accessed December 11, 2009); *Handbook of Texas Online*, "Antonio Gil Ibarvo," *http://www.tsha.utexas.edu/handbook* (accessed September 13, 2006).

20. Roche, 65, 68; Patrick Brendel, "Restoring ancient remains," *Victoria Advocate*, April 2, 2006; Choctaw-Apache website; "Choctaw-Apache Tribe grows under new leadership," *Shreveport Times*, December 11, 2008.

21. Albert Gatschet, "Lipan, a dialect," 55–56, and "Lipan, of the Tinné family," 183.

22. Meredith Magoosh Begay, August 13, 2005.

Chapter 38

1. Meredith Magoosh Begay, August 13, 2005.

2. Superintendent's Annual Narrative and Statistical Reports, Mescalero Agency, 1924, 1925, 1927, and 1930, RG 75, M 1011, Roll 83, NARA; Dobyns, 79–80. Maggie Lester Sampson, a Lipan woman who was assistant girls' matron, taught beadwork to girls.

3. Subseries B: Mescalero, "Biography," Box 38, Folder 20, Opler Papers.

4. Morris Opler, "Report on Observations at Mescalero Reservation" (Whiteriver, Arizona: Office of Indian Affairs, 1936), 5–6, 9; Michael Lieder and Jake Page, *Wild Justice: The People of Geronimo vs. the United States* (New York: Random House, 1997), 73–74, Dobyns, 82; Superintendent's Annual Narrative and Statistical Reports, Mescalero Agency, 1935, RG 75, M 1011, Roll 83, NARA.

5. Meredith Magoosh Begay, August 14, 2005.

6. Dobyns 82–83, Subseries D: Lipans, Miscellaneous, Box 44, Folder 32; Mescalero Census, 1887 and 1904.

7. Dobyns, 84; Meredith Magoosh Begay, September 24–25, 2005. Richard Magoosh also ran cattle with an Apache brand and was on the Cattle Growers' Association board.

8. Lieder and Page, 64, 66, 157; *Indian Claims Commission Decisions* 36 (Boulder: Native American Rights Fund, 1978), 7.

9. Sherry Robinson, "ICC: Clear title at bargain prices," *Americans Before Columbus* 2 (Fall 1983): 4; Lieder and Page, 158.

10. Testimony of Solon Sombrero, Percy Big Mouth and Antonio Apache, Subseries B: Mescalero, Hearing, Mescalero, May 13, 1950, Box 41, Folder 6, Opler Papers.

11. Lieder and Page, 154; Dobyns, 85.

12. Meredith Magoosh Begay, September 24–25, 2005.

13. Romero, August 14, 2005; Romero, *Castro Family History*, 5.

14. "Lipan Apache Nation," *El Mesteño* 4 (December 2000); *Handbook of Texas Online*, "Falfurrias, Texas," *http://www.tshaonline.org/handbook/online/articles/FF/hff1.html* (accessed December 8, 2009); *Handbook of Texas Online*, "Lasater, Edward Cunningham," *http://www.tshaonline. org/handbook/online/articles/LL/fla42.html* (accessed December 8, 2009). He said *falfurrias* was a Lipan word meaning "land of heart's delight," but the word was the Spanish name for a desert flower known as the heart's delight.

15. Romero, *Cuélcahen Ndé*, 3, 52–53; Daniel Castro Romero Jr., interview with Sherry Robinson, Mescalero, August 14, 2005; Romero, telephone interview, April 4, 2006; Romero, *Castro Family History in Bee County* (San Antonio: Lipan Apache Band of Texas, 2004), 10.

16. Romero, August 14, 2005; Romero, *Castro Family History*, 5.

17. Lieder and Page, 158–159; *Indian Claims Commission Decisions* 36, 8, 11; "Court Claims Indians Own Florida: Ancestry Snags New Mexico Case," *Navajo Times*, June 22, 1967.

18. Robert Neighbors Americanized the spelling of the family name.

19. Morris Opler to Abe Weissbrodt, October 1, 1968, and Weissbrodt to Opler, June 20, 1973, December 31, 1975, and January 9, 1976, Series III: Miscellaneous Native American Material, Box 85, Folder 2, Opler Papers; Lieder and Page, 161–162, 205; *Indian Claims Commission Decisions* 36, 8,10–11, 17–20 and Vol. 37, 229, 232, 234.

20. Daniel Castro Romero, interview with Sherry Robinson, Albuquerque, April 4, 2006, and Mescalero, August 14, 2005; Romero, *Cuélcahen Ndé*, 52–53; Maestas, 286, 3305.

21. The relatives who chose him were, in addition to his mother and uncle: Frank Vasquez Castro, an uncle, whose father was Albino Castro, son of Calixto Gonzalez Castro; Paula Castro Cavazos, an aunt, whose mother was Juanita Gonzalez Castro and daughter of Chief John Castro; and Porfiria Castro Cavazos, whose mother was Juanita Gonzalez Castro, daughter of John Castro (Maestas, 282).

22. Maestas, 282; Romero, April 4, 2006.

❈ Bibliography ❈

Archives and Collections

Archivo General de la Nación, Mexico City, Provincias Internas.

Ball, Eve, Papers and Letters. Perry Special Collections and Manuscripts, MSS 3096, Harold B. Lee Library, Brigham Young University, Provo, Utah.

Barry, James Buckner, Papers. The Dolph Briscoe Center for American History, University of Texas, Austin, Texas.

Béxar Archives. The Dolph Briscoe Center for American History, University of Texas, Austin, Texas.

Black, Sue Edwards, Papers. Perry Special Collections and Manuscripts, Harold B. Lee Library, Brigham Young University, Provo, Utah.

Blazer Family Papers. Special Collections. Branson Library. New Mexico State University, Las Cruces.

Carlisle Indian School Collection. Cumberland Historical Society. Carlisle, Pennsylvania.

Eberstadt Collection. The Dolph Briscoe Center for American History, University of Texas, Austin, Texas.

Harris, Gene Neyland, Papers. Courtesy of Gene and Jackson Harris, Memphis, Tenn.

Neighbors, Robert Simpson, Papers. The Dolph Briscoe Center for American History, University of Texas at Austin.

Opler, Morris Edward, Papers. 14-25-3238. Division of Rare and Manuscript Collections, Cornell University Library.

Porter, Edna Greer, Hatfield Collection. Western History Collections, University of Oklahoma Libraries, Norman, Oklahoma.

Schroeder, Albert, Papers. New Mexico State Archives. Santa Fe, New Mexico.

Simmons, Marc, Papers. Courtesy of Marc Simmons. Cerrillos, New Mexico.

Smithwick, Noah, Papers. The Dolph Briscoe Center for American History. University of Texas, Austin, Texas.

Sonnichsen, C. L., Papers, MS 141, C. L. Sonnichsen Special Collections Department, University of Texas at El Paso.

Spanish Archives of New Mexico, I and II, New Mexico State Archives. Santa Fe, New Mexico.

Special Collections, Eagle Pass Public Library. Eagle Pass, Texas.

Tonkawa Public Schools Collection. Western History Collections, University of Oklahoma Libraries, Norman, Oklahoma.

Webb, Walter Prescott, Papers. The Dolph Briscoe Center for American History, University of Texas, Austin, Texas.

U.S. Government Documents

Annual Report of the Commissioner of Indian Affairs, 1847. House Executive Document 1. 30th Congress, second session. Serial Set 503.

———. 1848, House Executive Document 1. 30th Congress, second session. Serial Set 537.

———. 1849. Senate Executive Document 1. 31st Congress, first session. Serial Set 550.

———. 1852. Senate Executive Document 1. 32nd Congress, second session. Serial Set 658.

———. 1853. Senate Executive Document 1. 33rd Congress, first session. Serial Set 690.

———. 1854, Senate Executive Document 1. 33rd Congress, second session. Serial Set 746.

———. 1855. Senate Executive Document 1. 34th Congress, first session. Serial Set 840.

———. 1856. House Executive Document 1. 34th Congress, third session. Serial Set 893.

———. 1858. House Executive Document 2. 35th Congress, second session. Serial Set 997.

———. 1862. House Executive Document 1. 37th Congress, third session. Serial Set 1157.

———. 1863. House Executive Document 1. 38th Congress, first session. Serial Set 1182.

———. 1866. House Executive Document 1. 39th Congress, second session. Serial Set 1284.

———. 1868. House Executive Document 1. 40th Congress, third session. Serial Set 1366.

———. 1870. House Executive Document 1. 41st Congress, third session. Serial Set 1449.

———. 1871. House Executive Document 1. 42nd Congress, second session. Serial Set 1505.

———. 1872. House Executive Document 1. 42nd Congress, third session. Serial Set 1560.

———. 1873. House Executive Document 1. 43rd Congress, 1st session. Serial Set 1601.

———. 1874. House Executive Document 1. 43rd Congress, second session. Serial Set 1639.

———. 1875. House Executive Document 1. 44th Congress, first session. Serial Set 1680.

———. 1876. House Executive Document 1. 44th Congress, second session. Serial Set 1749.

———. 1877. House Executive Document 1. 45th Congress, second session. Serial Set 1800

———. 1882. House Executive Document 1. 47th Congress, second session. Serial Set 2100.

———. 1883. House Executive Document 1. 48th Congress, first session. Serial Set 2191.

———. 1884. House Executive Document 1. 48th Congress, second session. Serial Set 2287.

———. 1885. House Executive Document 1. 49th Congress, first session. Serial Set 2379.

———. 1886. House Executive Document 1. 49th Congress, second session. Serial Set 2467.

———. 1887. House Executive Document 1. 50th Congress, first session. Serial Set 2542.

———. 1888. House Executive Document 1. 50th Congress, second session. Serial Set 2637.

———. 1889. House Executive Document 1. 51st Congress, first session. Serial Set 2725.

———. 1890. House Executive Document 1. 51st Congress, second session. Serial Set 2841.

———. 1892. House Executive Document 1. 52nd Congress, 2nd session. Serial Set 3088.

———. 1893. House Executive Document 1. 53rd Congress, second session. Serial Set 3210.

———. 1894. House Executive Document 1. 53rd Congress, third session. Serial Set 3306.

———. 1895. House Executive Document 5. 54th Congress, first session. Serial Set 3382.

———. 1896. House Executive Document 5. 54th Congress, second session. Serial Set 3489.

———. 1897. House Executive Document 5. 55th Congress, second session. Serial Set 1077.

———. 1899. House Executive Document 5. 56th Congress, first session. Serial Set 3915.

———. 1900. House Executive Document 5. 56th Congress, second session. Serial Set 4101.

———. 1902. House Executive Document 5. 57th Congress, second session. Serial Set 4458.

———. 1903. House Executive Document 5. 58th Congress, second session. Serial Set 4645.

———. 1904. House Executive Document 5. 58th Congress, third session. Serial Set 4798.

———. 1905. House Executive Document 5. 59th Congress, first session. Serial Set 4960.

Annual Report of the Secretary of Interior, 1861. Senate Executive Document 1. 37th Congress, second session. Serial Set 1117.

Annual Report of the Secretary of War, 1851. Senate Executive Document 1. 32nd Congress, first session. Serial Set 611.

———. 1854. Senate Executive Document 1, 34th Congress, first session. Serial Set 747.

———. 1854. Senate Executive Document 1, Vol. 2, 34th Congress, first session , Serial Set 811.

———. 1857. Senate Executive Document 11, 34th Congress, first session. Serial Set 920.

———. 1859. Senate Executive Document 1, 36th Congress, first session. Serial Set 1023.

———. 1860. Senate Executive Document 1. 36th Congress, second session. Serial Set 1079.

———. 1868. House Executive Document 3. 40th Congress, third session. Serial Set 1367.

———. 1869. House Executive Document 2. 41st Congress, second session. Serial Set 1412.

———. 1874. House Executive Document 2. 43rd Congress, second session. Serial Set 1635.

———. 1878. House Executive Document 2. 45th Congress, third session. Serial Set 1843.

———. 1880. House Executive Document 1. 46th Congress, third session. Serial Set 1952.

———. 1881. House Executive Document 1. 47th Congress, first session. Serial Set 2010.

Atkinson and Williams, Report to Secretary of Interior, October 21, 1873. House Executive Document 90. 43rd Congress, first session. Serial Set 1607.

Depredations on the Frontiers of Texas, 1873. House Executive Document 257. 43rd Congress, first session. Serial Set 1615.

Committee on Military Affairs. *The Texas Border Troubles*. House Misc. Document 64. 45th Congress, second session. Serial Set 1820.

Guadalupe Mountains National Park. Washington, D.C.: National Park Service, no date.

Headquarters Records of the District of New Mexico. Record group 393, M 1088. National Archives and Records Administration.

Headquarters Records of the District of the Pecos, 1878–1881. Record Group 393, M 1381. National Archives and Records Administration.

Headquarters Records of Fort Stockton, Texas, 1867–1886. Record Group 393, M 1189. National Archives and Records Administration.

Indian Claims Commission Decisions, Vols. 36–37. Boulder: Native American Rights Fund, 1978.

Indian Census Rolls. U.S. Census Office, Record Group 75, M 595. National Archives and Records Administration.

Letters Received by the Office of the Adjutant General. Main series (1822–1860). Record group 94, M 567. National Archives and Records Administration.

———. (1861–1870). Record group 94, M 619.

———. (1871–1880). Record group 94, M 666.

———. (1881–1889). Record group 94, M 689.

Letters Received by the Office of Indian Affairs, 1824–1881. Record group 75, M 234. National Archives and Records Administration.

Letters Sent and Received, Kiowa Agency, Microfilm Publications, Oklahoma Historical Society.

Mexican Border Troubles, 1877. House Executive Document 13, 45th Congress, first session. Serial Set 1773.

Pawnee Agency Census and Enrollment. Indian Archives Division, Oklahoma Historical Society.

Pope, John, Report of Exploration of a Route for the Pacific Railroad near the Thirty-second Parallel of Latitude, from the Red River to the Rio Grande, 33rd Congress, 1855, H. ex. doc. 129.

Record of Engagements with Hostile Indians within the Military Division of the Missouri, from 1868 to 1882. Washington: Government Printing Office, 1882.

Report of Messrs. Butler and Lewis Relative to the Indians of Texas and the Southwestern Prairies, 1846–1847, February 3, 1847. House Executive Document 76. 29th Congress, second session. Serial Set 500.

Reports of Field Inspections, Bureau of Indian Affairs. Record Group 75, M 1070. National Archives and Records Administration.

Resolution of the Legislature of Texas, May 24, 1870. Senate Miscellaneous Document 150. 41st Congress, second session.

Returns from U.S. Military Posts, 1800–1916, Fort Stanton, New Mexico, RG 94, M 617.

Superintendent's Annual Narrative and Statistical Reports from Field Jurisdictions of the Bureau of Indian Affairs, 1907–1938. RG 75, M 1011. National Archives and Records Administration.

Tonkawa Indians at Fort Griffin, Texas, January 31, 1876. House Executive Document 102. 44th Congress, first session. Serial Set 1689.

War of the Rebellion: A Compilation of the Official Records of the Union and Confederate Armies. Series 1, vol. 4. Washington, D.C.: Government Printing Office, 1882.

———. Series 1, vol. 48. Washington, D.C.: Government Printing Office, 1896.

Wislizenus, A. *Memoir of a Tour to Northern Mexico*, January 13, 1848. Senate Miscellaneous Document 26. 30th Congress, first session. Serial Set 511.

Books

Almaráz, Félix D. *Tragic Cavalier: Governor Manuel Salcedo of Texas, 1808–1813*. College Station: Texas A&M University Press, 1991.

Austin, Moses. *The Austin Papers*. Edited by Eugene C. Barker. Vols. 1–3. Austin: University of Texas, 1924, 1926.

Anderson, Gary Clayton. *The Conquest of Texas: Ethnic Cleansing in the Promised Land, 1820–1875*. Norman: University of Oklahoma Press, 2005.

———. *The Indian Southwest, 1580–1830: Ethnogenesis and Reinvention*. Norman: University of Oklahoma Press, 1999.

Applegate, Howard G. and Hanselka, C. Wayne. *La Junta de los Rios Del Norte y Conchos*. El Paso: Texas Western Press, 1974.

Ball, Eve. *Indeh: An Apache Odyssey*. Provo: Brigham Young University Press, 1980.

———. *In the Days of Victorio*. Tucson: University of Arizona Press, 1970.

Bancroft, Hubert Howe. *History of the North Mexican States and Texas*. Vol. 2. San Francisco: The History Company, Publishers, 1889.

Barr, Juliana. *Peace Came in the Form of a Woman: Indians and Spaniards in the Texas Borderlands*. Chapel Hill: University of North Carolina Press, 2007.

Barrett, Elinore, M. *Conquest and Catastrophe: Changing Rio Grande Pueblo Settlement Patterns in the Sixteenth and Seventeenth Centuries*. Albuquerque: University of New Mexico Press, 2002.

Bartlett, John Russell. *Personal Narrative of Explorations and Incidents in Texas, New Mexico, California, Sonora and Chihuahua connected with the United States and Mexican Boundary Commission during the Years 1851, '52, and '53*. Vol. 1. New York: D. Appleton & Company, 1854.

Benavides, Alonso de. *The Memorial of Fray Alonso de Benavides, 1630*. Translated and edited by Mrs. Edward E. Ayer. Chicago: Privately Printed, 1916.

Berlandier, Jean Louis. *The Indians of Texas in 1830*. Edited by John C. Ewers. Washington, D.C.: Smithsonian Institution Press, 1969.

———. *Journey to Mexico During the Years 1826 to 1834.* Vol. 1. Austin: The Texas State Historical Association, 1980.

Binkley, William C., ed. *Official Correspondence of the Texan Revolution, 1835–1836.* Vol. 1. New York: D. Appleton-Century Co., 1936.

Black, Reading W. *The Life and Diary of Reading W. Black.* Uvalde, TX: Privately printed, 1997.

Blakeslee, Donald J. *Along Ancient Trails: The Mallet Expedition of 1839.* Niwot, CO: University Press of Colorado, 1995.

Bliss, Zenas Randall. *The Reminiscences of Major General Zenas R. Bliss, 1854–1876: From the Texas Frontier to the Civil War and Back Again.* Austin: Texas State Historical Association, 2007.

Bolton, Herbert Eugene. *Athanase de Mezieres and the Louisiana-Texas Frontier, 1768–1780.* Vols. 1–2. Cleveland: Arthur H. Clark Co., 1914. Reprint, New York: Kraus Reprint Co., 1970.

———. *Spanish Exploration in the Southwest, 1542–1706.* New York: Barnes & Noble Inc., 1916.

———. *Texas in the Middle Eighteenth Century: Studies in Spanish Colonial History and Administration.* New York: Russell & Russell, 1962.

Bobb, Bernard E. *The Viceregency of Antonio Maria Bucareli in New Spain, 1771–1779.* Austin: University of Texas Press, 1962.

Brice, Donaly. *The Great Comanche Raid.* Austin: Eakin Press, 1987.

Britten, Thomas. *The Lipan Apaches: People of Wind and Lightning.* Albuquerque, University of New Mexico Press, 2009.

Brooks, James F. *Captives and Cousins: Slavery, Kinship, and Community in the Southwest Borderlands.* Chapel Hill: University of North Carolina Press, 2002.

Brown, John Henry. *History of Texas.* St. Louis: L. E. Daniell, 1892–93.

———. *Indian Wars and Pioneers of Texas.* Austin: Statehouse Press, 1988.

Buckelew, F. M. *Life of an Indian Captive.* Philadelphia: Dorrance, 1865.

Calhoun, James S. *The Official Correspondence of James S. Calhoun while Indian Agent at Santa Fé and Superintendent of Indian Affairs in New Mexico.* Edited by Annie Abel. Washington, D.C.: Government Printing Office, 1915.

Campbell, T. N. and T. J. Campbell. *Indian Groups Associated With Spanish Missions of the San Antonio Missions National Historical Park.* San Antonio: Center for Archeological Research, University of Texas at San Antonio, 1996.

Carlson, Paul H. *Deep Time and the Texas High Plains.* Lubbock: Texas Tech University Press, 2005.

Carroll, H. Bailey, and J. Villasana Haggard, trans. *Three New Mexico Chronicles: The Exposición of Don Pedro Bautista Pino 1812; the Ojeada of Lic. Antonio Barreiro 1832; and the Additions by Don José Agustín de Escudero, 1849.* Albuquerque: The Quivira Society, 1942.

Carter, Robert G. *On the Border with Mackenzie, or Winning West Texas from the Comanches.* Washington, D. C.: Eynon, 1935.

Cashion, Ty. *A Texas Frontier: The Clear Fork Country and Fort Griffin, 1849–1887.* Norman: University of Oklahoma Press, 1996.

Casteñeda, Carlos E. *Our Catholic Heritage in Texas, 1519–1936.* Vols. 3–4. Austin: Von Boeckmann-Jones Co., 1938, 1939.

———. ed. *The Mexican Side of the Texan Revolution (1836) by the Chief Mexican Participants.* Dallas: P. L. Turner Company, 1956.

Chabot, Frederick C. *Texas Expeditions of 1842: Corpus Christi.* San Antonio: Artes Graficas, 1942.

Chebahtah, William and Nancy McGown Minor. *Chevato: The Story of the Apache Warrior Who Captured Herman Lehmann*. Lincoln: University of Nebraska Press, 2007.

Chipman, Donald E. and Harriett Denise Joseph. *Notable Men and Women of Spanish Texas*. Austin: University of Texas Press, 1999.

Clendenen, Clarence C. *Blood on the Border: The United States Army and the Mexican Irregulars*. London: The Macmillan Company, 1969.

Collinson, Frank. *Life in the Saddle*. Norman: University of Oklahoma Press, 1964.

Cortés, José. *Views from the Apache Frontier: Report on the Northern Provinces of New Spain*. Edited by Elizabeth A. H. John. Norman: University of Oklahoma Press, 1989.

Craddock, Jerry R. *Zaldívar and the Cattle of Cibola: Vicente de Zaldívar's Report of His Expedition to the Buffalo Plains in 1598*. Dallas: Southern Methodist University, 1999.

Cutter, Donald C., ed. *Northern New Spain: Hugo O'Conor's Report to Teodoro de Croix, July 22, 1777*. Dallas: DeGolyer Library, 1994.

Day, James M. *The Texas Almanac 1857–1873: A Compendium of Texas History*. Waco: Texian Press, 1967.

Debo, Angie. *Geronimo: The Man, His Time, His Place*. Norman: University of Oklahoma Press, 1976.

DeLay, Brian. *War of a Thousand Deserts: Indian Raids and the U.S. Mexican War*. New Haven: Yale University Press, 2008.

Dobie, J. Frank. *A Vaquero of the Brush Country*. New York: Grosset & Dunlap, 1929.

Dobyns, Henry F. *The Mescalero Apache People*. Phoenix: Indian Tribal Series, 1973.

Domenech, Emmanuel Henri. *Seven Years' Residence in the Great Deserts of North America*. Vol. 2. London: Longman, Green, Longman, and Roberts, 1860.

Elkins, John M. *Indian Fighting on the Texas Frontier*. Amarillo: Russell & Cockrell, 1929.

Emerson, Dorothy. *Among the Mescalero Apaches: The Story of Father Albert Braun, O.F.M.* Tucson: University of Arizona Press, 1973.

Espinosa, J. Manuel. *Crusaders of the Rio Grande: The Story of Don Diego de Vargas and the Reconquest and Refounding of New Mexico*. Chicago: Institute of Jesuit History, 1942.

Fear-Segal, Jacqueline. *White Man's Club: Schools, Race, and the Struggle of Indian Acculturation*. Lincoln: University of Nebraska Press, 2007.

Filisola, Vicente, *Memoirs for the History of the War in Texas*. Vol. 2. Translated by Wallace Woolsey. Austin: Eakin Press, 1987.

Flint, Richard, and Shirley Cushing Flint, eds. and trans. *Documents of the Coronado Expedition: "They Were Not Familiar with His Majesty Nor Did They Wish to Become His Subjects."* Dallas: Southern Methodist University Press, 2005.

Forbes, Jack D. *Apache, Navajo, and Spaniard*. Norman: University of Oklahoma Press, 1960.

Ford, John Salmon. *Rip Ford's Texas*. Edited by Stephen B. Oates. Austin: University of Texas Press, 1963.

Foreman, Grant. *The Last Trek of the Indians*. Chicago: The University of Chicago Press, 1946.

Foster, William. *Spanish Expeditions into Texas, 1689–1768*. Austin: University of Texas Press, 1928.

Fulton, Maurice G. *History of the Lincoln County War*. Tucson: University of Arizona Press, 1997.

Galbreath, Lester. *Campfire Tales: True Stories from the Western Frontier*. Albany, TX: Bright Sky Press, 2005.

———. *Fort Griffin and The Clear Fork Country*. Albany, TX: self-published, 1997.

Gálvez, Bernardo de. *Instructions for Governing the Interior Provinces of New Spain, 1786*. Edited by Donald E. Worcester. Berkeley: Quivira Society, 1951.

Garrett, Julia Kathryn. *Green Flag Over Texas: A Story of the Last Years of Spain in Texas*. New York: The Cordova Press Inc., 1939.

Gentilz, Theodore. *Gentilz: Artist of the Old Southwest: Drawings and Paintings by Theodore Gentilz*. Austin: University of Texas Press, 1974.

Gifford, Edward. *Culture Element Distributions: Apache-Pueblo*. Vol. 4, in University of California Anthropological Records. Edited by A. L. Kroeber, R. H. Lowie, and R. L. Olson. Berkeley: University of California Press, 1940.

Gillett, James B. *Six Years with the Texas Rangers, 1875–1881*. New Haven: Yale University Press, 1925.

Greer, James K., *Colonel Jack Hays: Texas Frontier Leader and California Builder*. New York: E. P. Dutton & Company Inc., 1952.

———. *Texas Ranger: Jack Hays in the Frontier Southwest*. College Station: Texas A&M University Press, 1993.

Gulick, Charles A., et al., eds. *The Papers of Mirabeau B. Lamar*. Vols. 1, 2 and 4. Austin: The Pemberton Press, 1968.

Gunnerson, Dolores A. *The Jicarilla Apaches: A Study in Survival*. Dekalb, IL: Northern Illinois University Press, 1974.

Gunnerson, James H. *An Introduction to Plains Apache Archeology—The Dismal River Aspect*. Washington, D.C.: Smithsonian Institution Bureau of American Ethnology Bulletin 173, Anthropological Papers, No. 58, 1960.

Gunnerson, James H., and Dolores A. Gunnerson. "Apachean Culture: A Study in Unity and Diversity." In *Apachean Culture, History and Ethnology*. Edited by Keith H. Basso and Morris E. Opler. Tucson: The University of Arizona Press, 1971.

Gutiérrez, Ramón. *When Jesus Came, the Corn Mothers Went Away: Marriage, Sexuality, and Power in New Mexico, 1500–1846*. Stanford: Stanford University Press, 1991.

Hackett, Charles Wilson. *Historical Documents Relating to New Mexico, Nueva Vizcaya, and Approaches Thereto, to 1773*. Washington, D.C.: Carnegie Institution of Washington, 1937.

———. *Pichardo's Treatise on the Limits of Louisiana and Texas*. Vol. 2. Austin: University of Texas Press, 1934.

———. *Revolt of the Pueblo Indians of New Mexico and Otermín's Attempted Reconquest, 1680–1682*. Vols. 1–3. Albuquerque: University of New Mexico Press, 1942.

Hadley, Diana, Thomas H. Naylor and Mardith K. Schuetz-Miller, eds. *Presidio and Militia on the Northern Frontier of New Spain: A Documentary History*. Vol. 2, part 2. Tucson: The University of Arizona Press, 1997.

Haley, J. Evetts. *Fort Concho and the Texas Frontier*. San Angelo: San Angelo Standard-Times, 1952.

Hämäläinen, Pekka. *The Comanche Empire*. New Haven: Yale University Press, 2008.

Hammond, George P., and Agapito Rey. *Apostolic Chronicle of Juan Domingo Arricivita: The Franciscan Mission Frontier in the Eighteenth Century in Arizona, Texas, and the Californias*. Berkeley: Academy of American Franciscan History, 1996.

———. *Don Juan de Oñate, Colonizer of New Mexico, 1595–1628*. Albuquerque: University of New Mexico Press, 1953.

———. *Narratives of the Coronado Expedition, 1540–1542*. Albuquerque: University of New Mexico Press, 1940.

———. eds. *The Gallegos Relation of the Rodriguez Expedition to New Mexico*. Santa Fe: El Palacio Press, 1927.

———. *The Rediscovery of New Mexico, 1580–1594; The Explorations of Chamuscado, Espejo, Castaño de Sosa, Morlete, and Leyva de Bonilla and Humaña*. Albuquerque: University of New Mexico Press, 1966.

Hardin, Stephen L. *Texian Iliad: A Military History of the Texas Revolution, 1835–1836*. Austin: University of Texas Press, 1994.

Himmel, Kelly F. *The Conquest of the Karankawas and the Tonkawas, 1821–1859*. College Station: Texas A&M University Press, 1999.

Hinojosa, Gilberto Miguel. *A Borderlands Town in Transition: Laredo, 1755–1870*. College Station: Texas A&M University Press, 1983.

Hodge, Frederick W., ed. *Spanish Explorers in the Southern United States, 1528–1543*. New York: Barnes & Noble Inc., 1965.

Hodge, Frederick W., George P. Hammond, and Agapito Rey, trans. *Fray Alonso de Benavides' Revised Memorial of 1634*. Albuquerque: University of New Mexico Press, 1945.

Hoig, Stan. *White Man's Paper Trail: Grand Councils and Treaty-Making on the Central Plains*. Boulder: University Press of Colorado, 2006.

Hoijer, Harry. *The History and Custom of the Lipan as told by Augustina Zuazua*. New York: Moulton Publishers, 1975.

Holley, Mary Austin. *Texas Observations: Historical, Geographical and Descriptive*. Arno Press, New York, 1973

Hollon, W. Eugene, and Ruth Lapham Butler. *William Bollaert's Texas*. Norman: University of Oklahoma Press, 1956.

Hood, J. B. *Advance and Retreat: Personal Experiences in the United States and Confederate States Armies*. New York: Kraus Reprint Company, 1969.

Huser, Verne. *Rivers of Texas*. College Station: Texas A&M University Press, 2004.

Huson, Hobart. *Refugio: A Comprehensive History of Refugio County from Aboriginal Times to 1943*. Woodsboro, TX: Rooke Foundation, 1953–55.

Ingmire, Frances T. *Texas Ranger Service Records, 1830–1846*. St. Louis: Privately published, 1982.

Jackson, Jack. *Imaginary Kingdom: Texas as Seen by the Rivera and Rubí Military Expeditions, 1727 and 1767*. Austin: Texas State Historical Association, 1995.

Jenkins, John, ed. *The Papers of the Texas Revolution, 1825–1836*. Vol. 8. Austin: Presidial Press, 1973.

Jewett, Clayton E. *Texas in the Confederacy: An Experience in Nation Building*. Columbia: University of Missouri Press, 2002.

John, Elizabeth. *Storms Brewed in Other Men's Worlds: The Confrontation of Indians, Spanish, and French in the Southwest, 1540–1795*. College Station: Texas A&M University Press, 1975.

Jones, Anson. *Memoranda and Official Correspondence Relating to the Republic of Texas, Its History and Annexation*. Chicago: Rio Grande Press Inc., 1966.

Jordan, Julia A. *Plains Apache Ethnobotany*. Norman: University of Oklahoma Press, 2008.

Keleher, William A. *The Fabulous Frontier*. Albuquerque: University of New Mexico Press, 1962.

Kenner, Charles L. *A History of New Mexican-Plains Indian Relations*. Norman: University of Oklahoma Press, 1969.

Kessell, John L. *Kiva, Cross and Crown: The Pecos Indians and New Mexico, 1540–1840.* Albuquerque: University of New Mexico Press, 1987.

———. *Spain in the Southwest: A Narrative History of Colonial New Mexico, Arizona, Texas, and California.* Norman: University of Oklahoma Press, 2002.

Kinney County: 125 Years of Growth, 1852–1977. Kinney County Historical Society, 1977.

Ladd, Kevin. *Gone to Texas: Genealogical Abstracts from The Telegraph & Texas Register, 1835–1841.* Bowie, MD: Heritage Books, 1994.

Lafora, Nicolas de. *The Frontiers of New Spain: Nicholas de Lafora's Description, 1766–1768.* Translated by Lawrence Kinnaird. Berkeley: Quivira Society, 1958.

Lamar, Mirabeau Buonaparte. *The Papers of Mirabeau Buonaparte Lamar, Edited from the Original Papers in the Texas State Library.* Vol. 4. New York: AMS Press, 1973.

Lambert, Joseph I. *One Hundred Years with the Second Cavalry.* Fort Riley, KS: Capper Printing Company Inc., 1939.

Lamego, General Miguel A. *The Second Mexican-Texas War, 1841–1843.* Hillsboro, Texas: Hill Junior College, 1972.

Latham, Francis S. *Travels in the Republic of Texas, 1842.* Austin: Encino Press, 1971.

LaVere, David. *Life Among the Texas Indians: The WPA Narratives.* College Station: Texas A&M University Press, 1998.

Leckie, William, with Shirley Leckie. *The Buffalo Soldiers: A Narrative of the Black Cavalry in the West.* Norman: University of Oklahoma Press, 2003.

Ledbetter, Barbara Neal. *The Fort Belknap of Yesterday and Today, 1851–1963.* Newcastle, TX: Privately published, 1963.

Lewis, Anna. *Along the Arkansas.* Dallas: The Southwest Press, 1932.

Lieder, Michael, and Jake Page. *Wild Justice: The People of Geronimo vs. the United States.* New York: Random House, 1997.

Linn, John J. *Reminiscences of Fifty Years in Texas.* Austin: The Steck Company, 1935.

Mackenzie, Ranald Slidell. *Ranald S. Mackenzie's Official Correspondence Relating to Texas, 1873–1879.* Edited by Ernest Wallace. Lubbock: West Texas Museum Association, 1968.

Madrid, Enrique R., ed. *Expedition to La Junta de los Rios, 1747–1748: Captain Commander Joseph de Ydoiaga's Report to the Viceroy of New Spain.* Special Report 33. Austin: Office of the State Archeologist, 1992.

Mayhall, Mildred P. *Indian Wars of Texas.* Waco: Texian Press, 1965.

Martin, George C. *The Indian Tribes of the Mission Nuestra Señora del Refugio.* Corpus Christi: Bootstraps Press, 1972.

Mier y Terán, Manuel de. *Texas by Terán: The Diary Kept by General Manuel de Mier y Terán on His 1828 Inspection of Texas.* Edited by Jack Jackson. Austin: University of Texas Press, 2000.

Montgomery, Cora. *Eagle Pass or Life on the Border.* Austin: The Pemberton Press, 1966.

Moore, Stephen L. *Savage Frontier: Rangers, Riflemen, and Indian Wars in Texas.* Vols. 1–3. Denton: University of North Texas Press, 2002, 2006, 2007.

Moorhead, Max. *The Apache Frontier: Jacobo Ugarte and Spanish-Indian Relations in Northern New Spain, 1769–1791.* Norman: University of Oklahoma Press, 1968.

———. *The Presidio: Bastion of the Spanish Borderlands.* Norman: University of Oklahoma Press, 1975.

Morfi, Juan Agustin. *Excerpts from the Memorias for the history of the province of Texas, being a translation of those parts of the Memorias which particularly concern the various Indians of the province of Texas; their tribal divisions, characteristics, customs, traditions, superstitions, and all else of interest concerning them*. Translated by Frederick C. Chabot. San Antonio: Privately published, 1932.

————. *History of Texas, 1673–1779*. Albuquerque: Quivira Society, 1935.

Morris, John Miller. *El Llano Estacado: Exploration and Imagination on the High Plains of Texas and New Mexico, 1536–1860*. Austin: Texas State Historical Association, 1997.

Morton, Ohland. *Terán and Texas: A Chapter in Texas-Mexican Relations*. Austin: The Texas State Historical Association, 1948.

Mulroy, Kevin. *Freedom on the Border: The Seminole Maroons in Florida, the Indian Territory, Coahuila, and Texas*. Lubbock: Texas Tech University Press, 1993.

Nance, Joseph M. *Attack and Counter-Attack: The Texas-Mexican Frontier, 1842*. Austin: University of Texas Press, 1964.

Nathan, Paul D., trans., and Lesley Byrd Simpson, ed. *The San Saba Papers: A Documentary Account of the Founding and Destruction of San Sabá Mission*. Dallas: Southern Methodist University Press, 2000.

Naylor, Thomas, and Charles Polzer. *The Presidio and Militia on the Northern Frontier of New Spain*. Vol. 1. Tucson: University of Arizona Press, 1986.

Neighbours, Kenneth F. *Robert Simpson Neighbors and the Texas Frontier, 1836–1859*. Waco: Texian Press, 1975.

Newcomb, William W. Jr. *The Indians of Texas: Prehistory to Present*. Austin: University of Texas Press, 1961.

————.*The Rock Art of Texas Indians*. Austin: University of Texas Press, 1967.

Nielsen, George R. *The Kickapoo People*. Phoenix: Indian Tribal Series, 1975.

Norall, Frank. *Bourgmont, Explorer of the Missouri, 1698–1725*. Lincoln: University of Nebraska Press, 1988.

Noyes, Stanley. *Los Comanches: The Horse People, 1751–1845*. Albuquerque: University of New Mexico Press, 1993.

Obregón, Baltasar de. *Obregon's History of 16th Century Explorations in Western America, entitled Chronicle, Commentary, or Relation of the Ancient and Modern Discoveries in New Spain and New Mexico, Mexico, 1584*. Translated, edited, and annotated by George P. Hammond and Agapito Rey. Los Angeles: Wetzel Publishing Company, 1928.

Olmsted, Frederick Law. *A Journey through Texas: Or a Saddle Trip on the Southwestern Frontier*. New York: Dix, Edwards, 1857.

Opler, Morris E. *Apache Odyssey: A Journey between Two Worlds*. New York: Holt, Rinehart and Winston, 1969.

————. "The Apachean Culture Pattern and Its Origins." In *Handbook of North American Indians*, Vol. 10, *The Southwest*. Edited by Alfonso Ortiz. Washington, D.C.: Smithsonian Institution Press, 1983.

————. *The Lipan and Mescalero Apaches in Texas*. New York: Garland Publishing, 1974.

————. *Myths and Legends of the Lipan Apache Indians*. Memoirs of the American Folk Lore Society 36. New York: J. J. Augustin Publisher, 1940.

Penniger, Robert. *A Brief Account of the German Colonies in Texas Established by the Mainzer Noblemen's Society and Chronicles of the City of Fredericksburg*. Fredericksburg, TX: Privately published, 1896.

Pierce, Gerald S. *Texas Under Arms: The Camps, Posts, Forts and Military Towns of the Republic of Texas, 1836–1846*. Austin: Encino Press, 1969.

Pike, Zebulon Montgomery. *The Journals of Zebulon Montgomery Pike, with Letters and Related Documents.* Edited by Donald Jackson. Norman: University of Oklahoma Press, 1966.

Pinckney, Pauline A. *Painting in Texas: The Nineteenth Century.* Austin: University of Texas Press, 1967.

Pirtle, Caleb III, and Michael F. Cusack. *The Lonely Sentinel: Fort Clark on Texas's Western Frontier.* Austin: Eakin Press, 1985.

Porter, Kenneth W. *The Black Seminoles: History of a Freedom-Seeking People.* Gainesville: University Press of Florida, 1996.

Ray, Verne F. *Ethnohistorical Analysis of Documents Relating to the Apache Indians of Texas.* New York: Garland Publishing Inc., 1974.

Ratcliffe, Sam DeShong. *Painting Texas History to 1900.* Austin: University of Texas Press, 1992.

Reports of the Committee of Investigation Sent in 1873 by the Mexican Government to the Frontier of Texas. New York: Baker & Godwin, 1875.

Rie, Jarratt. *Gutiérrez de Lara, Mexican-Texan: The Story of a Creole Hero.* Austin: Creole Texana, 1949.

Robinson, Charles M. *Frontier Forts of Texas.* Houston: Lone Star Books, 1986.

Robinson, Sherry. *Apache Voices: Their Stories of Survival as Told to Eve Ball.* Albuquerque: University of New Mexico Press, 2000.

Rodenbough, Theophilus, and William Haskins, eds. *The Army of the United States: Historical Sketches of Staff and Line with Portraits of Generals-in-Chief.* Ann Arbor: Argonaut Press, 1966.

Roberts, Dan W. *Rangers and Sovereignty.* San Antonio: Wood Printing & Engraving Co., 1914.

Ruiz, José Francisco. *Report on the Indians of Texas in 1828.* Edited by John C. Ewers. New Haven: Yale University Press, 1972.

The San José Papers: The Primary Sources for the History of Mission San José y San Miguel de Aguayo from its Founding in 1720 to the Present. San Antonio: Old Spanish Missions Historical Research Library at San José Mission, 1978.

Santiago, Mark. *The Red Captain: The Life of Hugo O'Conor, Commandant Inspector of the Interior Provinces of New Spain.* Tucson: Arizona Historical Society, 1994.

Schilz, Thomas. *The Lipan Apache in Texas.* El Paso: Texas Western Press, 1987.

Schlesier, Karl H. "Commentary: A History of Ethnic Groups," in *Plains Indians, A.D. 500–1500: The Archaeological Past of Historic Groups.* Edited by Karl H. Schlesier. Norman: University of Oklahoma Press, 1994.

Schroeder, Albert H. *A Study of the Apache Indians.* Vol. 1: *The Apaches and Their Neighbours, 1540–1700.* Vol. 2: *The Jicarilla Apaches.* Vol. 3: *The Mescalero Apaches.* Santa Fe: Np, 1959–60.

Schwarz, Ted, ed. *Forgotten Battlefield of the First Texas Revolution: The Battle of Medina, August 18, 1813.* Austin: Eakin Press, 1985.

Seguín, Juan N. *A Revolution Remembered: The Memoirs and Selected Correspondence of Juan N. Seguín.* Austin: Texas State Historical Association, 2002.

Seymour, Deni. *Conquest and Concealment: After the El Paso Phase on Fort Bliss, an archaeological study of the Manso, Suma, and Early Apache.* El Paso: Lone Mountain Archaeological Services, 2002.

———. *Protohistoric and Early Historic Temporal Resolution in the Southern Southwest.* El Paso: Lone Mountain Archaeological Services, 2003.

———. ed. *From the Land of Ever Winter to the American Southwest: Athapaskan Migrations, Mobility, and Ethnogenesis.* Salt Lake City: University of Utah Press, 2012.

Sheridan, Philip H. *Personal Memoirs of P. H. Sheridan, General, United States Army.* New York, C. L. Webster & Company, 1888.

Sibley, John. *Indian Notes and Monographs: A Report from Natchitoches in 1807.* New York: Museum of the American Indian, 1922.

Smith, Clinton L. *The Boy Captives: Being the True Story of the Experiences and Hardships of Clinton L. Smith and Jeff D. Smith.* Bandera, TX: Frontier Times, 1927.

Smith, F. Todd. *From Dominance to Disappearance: The Indians of Texas and the Near Southwest, 1786–1859.* Lincoln: University of Nebraska Press, 2006.

Smith, Thomas T. *Fort Inge : Sharps, Spurs, and Sabers on the Texas Frontier, 1849–1869.* Austin: Eakin Press, 1993.

———. *The Old Army in Texas: A Research Guide to the U.S. Army in Nineteenth-Century Texas.* Austin: Texas State Historical Association, 2000.

Smithwick, Noah. *The Evolution of a State, or, Recollections of Old Texas Days.* Austin: Steck-Vaughn Company, 1968.

Sowell, A. J. *Early Settlers and Indian Fighters of Southwest Texas.* New York: Argosy-Antiquarian Ltd., 1986.

———. *Life of "Big Foot" Wallace.* Austin: The Steck Company, 1957.

Spielmann, Katherine A., ed. *Farmers, Hunters, and Colonists: Interaction Between the Southwest and the Southern Plains.* Tucson: University of Arizona Press, 1991.

Thomas, Alfred B. *After Coronado: Spanish Exploration Northeast of New Mexico.* Norman: University of Oklahoma Press, 1935.

———. *Forgotten Frontiers: A Study of the Spanish Indian Policy of Don Juan Bautista de Anza, Governor of New Mexico, 1777–1787.* Norman: University of Oklahoma Press, 1932.

———. *The Plains Indians and New Mexico, 1751–1778.* Albuquerque: University of New Mexico Press, 1940.

———. *Teodoro de Croix and the Northern Frontier of New Spain, 1776–1783.* Norman: University of Oklahoma Press, 1941.

Thonhoff, Robert H. *El Fuerte del Cibolo: Sentinel of the Bexar-La Bahia Ranches.* Austin: Eaken Press, 1992.

Thrapp, Dan L. *Victorio and the Mimbres Apaches.* Norman: University of Oklahoma Press, 1974.

Tiller, Veronica E. Velarde. *The Jicarilla Apache Tribe: A History.* Albuquerque: BowArrow Publishing Co., 2000.

Tunnell, Curtis D., and W. W. Newcomb. *A Lipan Apache Mission: San Lorenzo de la Santa Cruz, 1762–1771.* Austin: Texas Memorial Museum, 1969.

Utley, Robert M. *Fort Davis National Historic Site, Texas.* Washington, D.C.: National Park Service, 1965.

———. *High Noon in Lincoln: Violence on the Western Frontier.* Albuquerque: University of New Mexico Press, 1987.

Vehik, Susan. "Cultural Continuity and Discontinuity in the Southern Prairies and Cross Timbers," in *Plains Indians, A.D. 500–1500: The Archaeological Past of Historic Groups.* Edited by Karl H. Schlesier. Norman: University of Oklahoma Press, 1994.

Villegas, Daniel Cosio. *The United States Versus Porfirio Díaz.* Lincoln: University of Nebraska Press, 1963.

Wade, Maria F. *The Native Americans of the Texas Edwards Plateau, 1583–1799.* Austin: University of Texas Press, 2003.

Wallace, Ernest. *Ranald S. Mackenzie on the Texas Frontier.* Lubbock: West Texas Museum Association, 1964.

Warren, Harris Gaylord. *The Sword Was Their Passport: A History of American Filibustering in the Mexican Revolution*. Baton Rouge: Louisiana State University Press, 1943.

Waugh, Julia Nott. *Castro-Ville and Henry Castro, Empresario*. San Antonio: Standard Printing Company, 1934.

Webb, Walter Prescott. *The Texas Rangers: A Century of Frontier Defense*. Austin: University of Texas Press, 1965.

Webb, Walter Prescott, et al. *The Handbook of Texas*. Austin: Texas State Historical Association, 1952.

Weddle, Robert S. *After the Massacre: The Violent Legacy of the San Sabá Mission*. Lubbock: Texas Tech University Press, 2007.

———. *The French Thorn: Rival Explorers in the Spanish Sea, 1682–1762*. College Station: Texas A&M University Press, 1991.

———. *San Juan Bautista: Gateway to Spanish Texas*. Austin: University of Texas Press, 1968.

Weniger, Del. *The Explorers' Texas: The Lands and Waters*. Austin: Eakin Publications, 1984.

Whiting, William Henry Chase. *Exploring Southwestern Trails, 1846–1854*. Philadelphia: Porcupine Press, 1974.

Wilbarger, J. W. *Indian Depredations in Texas*. Austin: Hotchings Printing House, 1889.

Wilcox, David R. "Entry of Athapaskans into the American Southwest: The Problem Today," in *The Protohistoric Period in the North American Southwest, AD 1450–1700*. Edited by David Wilcox and Bruce Masse. Tempe: Arizona State University, 1981.

Wilkins, Frederick. *Defending the Borders: The Texas Rangers, 1848–1861*. Austin: State House Press, 2001.

———. *The Legend Begins: The Texas Rangers, 1823–1845*. Austin: State House Press, 1996.

Wilkinson, J. B. *Laredo and the Rio Grande Frontier*. Austin: Jenkins Publishing Co., 1975.

Williams, Amelia W., and Eugene C. Barker, eds. *The Writings of Sam Houston*. Vols. 2–5 and 7. Austin: University of Texas Press, 1939, 1940, 1941, 1942.

Williams, Clayton. *Texas' Last Frontier: Fort Stockton and the Trans-Pecos 1861–1895*. College Station: Texas A&M University Press, 1982.

Winfrey, Dorman, and James M. Day. *The Indian Papers of Texas and the Southwest, 1825–1916*. Vols. 1–4. Austin: Texas State Historical Association, 1966.

Winship, George Parker. *The Coronado Expedition*. Chicago: Rio Grande Press, 1964.

Wood, Robert D. *Archivos de Laredo: Documents on the Indians*. Laredo Archives Series No. 2, 1998.

Wooster, Robert. *Frontier Crossroads: Fort Davis and the West*. College Station: Texas A&M University Press, 2006.

Wooten, Dudley G. *A Comprehensive History of Texas, 1685 to 1897*. Vol. 1. Dallas: William G. Scarff, 1898.

Wright, John, and William Wright. *Recollections of Western Texas, 1852–55, by Two of the U.S. Mounted Rifles*. Edited by Robert Wooster. Austin: Book Club of Texas, 2003.

Wright, Murial H. *A Guide to the Indian Tribes of Oklahoma*. Norman: University of Oklahoma Press, 1986.

Yoakum, H. *History of Texas from Its First Settlement in 1685 to Its Annexation to the United States in 1846*. Vol. 1. New York: Redfield, 1855.

Zesch, Scott. *The Captured: A True Story of Abduction by Indians on the Texas Frontier*. New York: St. Martin's Press, 2005.

Articles

Adams, Paul. "Amelia Barr in Texas, 1856–1868." *Southwestern Historical Quarterly* 49 (January 1946): 362–373.

Allan, T. C. "Reminiscences of Mrs. Annie Fagan Teal." *Southwestern Historical Quarterly* 34 (April 1931): 317–328.

Allen, Henry Easton. "The Parrilla Expedition to the Red River in 1759." *Southwestern Historical Quarterly* 43 (July 1939): 53–71.

Arredondo, Joaquin de. "Joaquin de Arredondo's Report of the Battle of the Medina, August 18, 1813." Mattie Austin Hatcher, transl. *Texas Historical Association Quarterly* 11 (January 1908): 220–232.

Bell, James G. "A Log of the Texas-California Cattle Trail, 1854." *Southwestern Historical Quarterly* 35 (January 1932): 208–237.

Beltran, Carlos. "The Battle of the Alazan." Translated by John Warren Hunter. *Frontier Times* 3 (November 1925): 41–48.

———. "The Battle of the Medina." Translated by John Warren Hunter. *Frontier Times* 3 (December 1925): 9–16.

———. "San Antonio's First Great Tragedy." Translated by John Warren Hunter. *Frontier Times* 3 (October 1925): 41–48.

Benson, Nettie Lee. "Texas as Viewed from Mexico, 1820–1834." *Southwestern Historical Quarterly* 90 (January 1987): 219–291.

Biesele, R. L. "The Relations between the German Settlers and the Indians in Texas, 1844–1860." *Southwestern Historical Quarterly* 31 (October 1927), 116–129.

Bloom, L. B. "Bourke on the Southwest." *New Mexico Historical Review* 11 (July 1936): 217–282.

Bollaert, Willliam. "Observations of the Indian Tribes in Texas." *Journal of the Ethnological Society of London* 2 (1850): 262–283.

Bolton, Robert E., "The Jumano Indians in Texas 1650–1771," *Southwestern Historical Quarterly* 15 (July 1912): 66–86.

———. "The Mission as a Frontier Institution in the Spanish-American Colonies." *The American Historical Review* 23 (1918): 42–61.

———. "The Spanish Abandonment and Reoccupation of East Texas 1773–1779," *Texas Historical Association Quarterly* 9 (October 1905): 67–137.

Bonilla, Lt. Don Antonio. "A Brief Compendium of the Events Which Have Occurred in the Province of Texas from its Conquest, or Reduction, to the Present Date." *Texas State Historical Association Quarterly* 8 (July 1904): 9–78.

Boyd, Douglas. "Querechos and Teyas: Protohistoric Hunters and Gatherers in the Texas Panhandle-Plains, A.D. 1540–1700." *Bulletin of the Texas Archeological Society* 72 (2001): 5–16.

Bridges, Katherine and Winston De Ville, eds. and trans. "Natchitoches and the Trail to the Rio Grande." *Louisiana History* 8 (Summer 1967): 239–259.

"Calendar of the Letters of Antonio Martínez, Last Spanish Governor of Texas, 1817–1822." Edited by Virginia H. Taylor. *Southwestern Historical Quarterly* 59 (January 1956): 372–381; (July 1956): 473–486; 60 (January 1957): 80–99; (April 1957): 292–305; 61 (July 1957): 125–146; (October 1957): 289–304.

Carlson, Paul. "William Rufus Shafter with the Frontier Army in the Big Bend." *Journal of Big Bend Studies* 1 (January 1989): 72–82.

Christian, A. K. "Mirabeau Buonaparte Lamar," *Southwestern Historical Quarterly* 24 (July 1920): 39–80.

Coopwood, Bethel. "Route of Cabeza de Vaca," *Southwestern Historical Quarterly* 3 (April 1900): 229–264.

Cordero, Don Antonio. "Cordero's Description of the Apache—1796." Edited by Daniel S. Matson and Albert H. Schroeder. *New Mexico Historical Review* 32 (October 1957): 335–56.

Crimmins, M. L. "Colonel J. K. F. Mansfield's Report of the Inspection of the Department of Texas in 1856." *Southwestern Historical Quarterly* 42 (January 1939): 215–257.

———. "The Mescalero Apaches." *Frontier Times* 8 (September 1931): 551–560.

Dinges, Bruce. "The Victorio Campaign of 1880: Cooperation and Conflict on the United States-Mexico Border." *New Mexico Historical Review* 62 (January 1987): 81–94.

Duffield, Lathel F. "The Taovayas Village of 1759: In Texas or Oklahoma?" *Great Plains Journal* 4 (1965): 39–48.

Dunn, William E. "The Apache Mission on the San Saba River: Its Founding and Failure." *Southwestern Historical Quarterly* 17 (April 1914): 379–414.

———. "Apache Relations in Texas, 1718–1750." *Texas State Historical Association Quarterly* 14 (January 1911): 198–274.

———. "Missionary Activities among the Eastern Apaches Previous to the Founding of the San Saba Mission." *Southwestern Historical Quarterly* 15 (January 1912): 186–200.

Duval, John C. "The Adventures of Big-Foot Wallace." *Frontier Times* 8 (December 1930): 113–119.

Estep, Raymond. "Lieutenant William E. Burnet Letters." *Chronicles of Oklahoma* 38, no. 4 (1960), 369–396.

Ewers, John C. "The Influence of Epidemics on the Indian Populations and Cultures of Texas." *Plains Anthropologist* 18 (May 1973): 104–115.

Flores, Dan. "Bringing Home All the Pretty Horses." *Montana* 58 (Summer 2008): 3–21.

Folmer, Henri. "De Bourgmont's Expedition to the Padoucas in 1724, the First French Approach to Colorado." *The Colorado Magazine* 14 (July 1937): 121–128.

Forbes, Jack D. "Unknown Athapaskans: The Identification of the Jano, Jocome, Jumano, Manso, Suma, and other Indian Tribes of the Southwest." *Ethnohistory* 6 (Spring 1959): 97–159.

Foreman, Grant. "The Journal of Elijah Hicks." *Chronicles of Oklahoma* 13 (March 1935): 68–99.

———. "The Texas Comanche Treaty of 1846." *Southwestern Historical Quarterly* 51 (April 1948): 313–332.

"The Founding of Missions at La Junta de Los Rios." *Supplementary Studies of the Texas Catholic Historical Society* 1 (April 1938).

Gallegos, Hernán. "The Rodriguez Expedition." *New Mexico Historical Review* 2 (July 1927): 17–268.

Gibson, J. B. "Texas Rangers Scouting After Apache Indians." *Frontier Times* 11 (February 1934): 220–231.

Graf, Le Roy P. "Colonizing Projects in Texas South of the Nueces, 1820–1845." *Southwestern Historical Quarterly* 50 (April 1947): 431–448.

Griffin, Fred M. "Under Five Flags." *New Mexico Magazine* 21 (July 1943): 18, 33–34.

Gunnerson, Dolores A. "The Southern Athabascans: Their Arrival in the Southwest." *El Palacio* 63 (November–December 1956): 346–365.

Gunnerson, James H. "Apache Archaeology in Northeastern New Mexico." *American Antiquity* 34 (1969): 23–39.

————. "Plains Apache Archeology: A Review," *Plains Anthropologist* 13 (August 1968), 167–199.)

Habicht-Mauche, Judith. "Coronado's Querechos and Teyas in the Archaeological Record of the Texas Panhandle." *Plains Anthropologist* 37 (1992): 247–259.

————. "Southwestern-style Culinary Ceramics on the Southern Plains: A Case Study of Technological Innovation and Cross-Cultural Interaction." *Plains Anthropologist* 32 (1987): 175–186.

Haines, Francis. "The Northward Spread of Horses among the Plains Indians." *American Anthropologist* 40 (1938): 429–437.

Hatcher, Mattie Austin. "Letters of Antonio Martinez: Last Spanish Governor of Texas, 1817–1822." *Southwestern Historical Quarterly* 39 (October 1935): 139–147 and (April 1936): 327–332.

Henderson, Harry McCorry. "The Magee-Gutierrez Expedition." *Southwestern Historical Quarterly* 55 (July 51): 43–61.

Hengesbaugh, Jeff. "Massacre on the Platte," *Wild West* (October 1995): 37–42, 87–90.

Herndon, John Hunter. "Diary of A Young Man in Houston, 1838." *Southwestern Historical Quarterly* 53 (January 1950): 290–291.

Hughes, Jack T. "Prehistoric Cultural Developments on the Texas High Plains." *Bulletin of the Texas Archeological Society* 60 (1989): 1–43.

Hunter, J. Marvin. "Bowie's Battle Ground on the San Saba." *Frontier Times* 16 (February 1939), 213–220.

Jenkins, Myra Ellen. "Taos Pueblo and Its Neighbors, 1540–1847." *New Mexico Historical Review* 41 (April 1966): 85–111.

John, Elizabeth A. H. "A Cautionary Exercise in Apache Historiography." *Journal of Arizona History* 25 (Autumn 1984): 301–315.

————. "Nurturing the Peace: Spanish and Comanche Cooperation in the Early Nineteenth Century." *New Mexico Historical Review* 59 (October 1984): 345–369.

————. "Views from a Desk in Chihuahua: Manuel Merino's Reports on Apaches and Neighboring Nations, ca. 1804." *Southwestern Historical Quarterly* 95 (July 1991): 139–175.

Kelley, J. Charles. "The Historic Indian Pueblos of La Junta de Los Rios." *New Mexico Historical Review* 27 (October 1952): 257–295 and 28 (January 1953): 21–51.

Kessell, John L. "Diego Romero, the Plains Apaches, and the Inquisition." *The American West* 15 (May–June 1978): 12–16.

Koch, Lena Clara. "The Federal Indian Policy in Texas, 1845–1846." *Southwestern Historical Quarterly* 28 (April 1925): 259–286

————. "The Federal Indian Policy in Texas, 1845–1860." *Southwestern Historical Quarterly* 29 (July 1925): 19–35.

————. "The Federal Indian Policy in Texas, 1845–1860." *Southwestern Historical Quarterly* 29 (October 1925): 98–127.

Lackman, Howard. "The Howard-Neighbors Controversy: A Cross-Section in West Texas Indian Affairs." *Panhandle-Plains Historical Review* 25 (1952): 29–44.

"Last Indian Raid in Southwest Texas." *Frontier Times* 4 (August 1927): 58–59.

Leutenegger, Benedict, ed. "New Documents on Father José Mariano Reyes," *Southwestern Historical Quarterly* 71 (April 1968): 597–602.

Lewis, Anna. "La Harpe's First Expedition in Oklahoma, 1718–1719." *Chronicles of Oklahoma* 2 (December 1924): 331–349.

Linkquist, Sven. "A History of Bombing." *Harper's Magazine* 303 (September 2001).

Looscan, Adele B. "Capt. Joseph Daniels." *Texas State Historical Association Quarterly* 5 (July 1901): 19–27.

McElhannon, Joseph Carl. "Imperial Mexico and Texas." *Southwestern Historical Quarterly* 53 (October 1949): 119–133.

McMurtrie, Douglas. "The First Texas Newspaper." *Southwestern Historical Quarterly* 36 (July 1932): 41–46.

"The Mexican and Indian Raid of '78." *Texas State Historical Association Quarterly* 5 (January 1902): 212–251.

Monnett, John H. "Oh No, Not Another Battle Book!" *Western Writers of America Roundup Magazine* 17 (August 2010): 7–12.

Moorhead, Max L. "Spanish Deportation of Hostile Apaches: The Policy and the Practice." *Arizona and the West* 17 (Autumn 1975): 205–220.

Moyers, Bill. "The Big Story: A Journalist Looks at Texas History," *Southwestern Historical Quarterly* 101 (July 1997), 1–15.

Muckleroy, Anna. "The Indian Policy of the Republic of Texas." *Southwestern Historical Quarterly* 25 (April 1922): 229–260 and 26 (January 1923): 184–206.

Myres, S. D., ed. "O. W. Williams' Stories from the Big Bend." *Southwestern Studies* 3 (1965): 3–44.

Nelson, Al B. "Campaigning in the Big Bend of the Rio Grande in 1787." *Southwestern Historical Quarterly* 39 (January 1936): 200–227.

———. "Juan de Ugalde and Picax-ande InsTinsle." *Southwestern Historical Quarterly* 43 (April 1940): 438–464.

Newcomb, William W. "German Artist on the Pedernales," *Southwestern Historical Quarterly* 82 (October 1978): 149–172.

Newlin, Deborah Lamont. "The Tonkawa People: A Tribal History from Earliest Times to 1893." *The Museum Journal* 21 (1982): 7–119.

Opler, Morris E. "The Lipan Apache Death Complex and Its Extensions." *Southwestern Journal of Anthropology* 1 (1945): 122–141.

———. "Lipan Apache Navigation." *The Masterkey* 49 (April–June 1975): 70–72.

———. "Problems in Apachean Cultural History, with Special Reference to the Lipan Apache." *Anthropological Quarterly* 48 (1975): 182–192.

———. "Review of Gunnerson's *The Jicarilla Apaches.*" *Plains Anthropologist* 20 (1975): 150–157.

———. "Use of Peyote by the Carrizo and Lipan Apache Tribes," *American Anthropologist* 40 (1938): 271–285.

Padilla, Juan Antonio. "Texas in 1820," *Southwestern Historical Quarterly* 23 (April 1919): 47–60.

Payne, Darwin. "Camp Life in the Army of Occupation: Corpus Christi, July 1845 to March 1846." *Southwestern Historical Quarterly* 73 (January 1970): 326–342.

Perry, Richard J. "The Apachean Transition from the Subarctic to the Southwest." *Plains Anthropologist* (1980): 279–296.

Porter, Kenneth W. "Negroes and Indians on the Texas Frontier, 1834–1874." *Southwestern Historical Quarterly* 53 (October 1949): 151–163.

——. "The Seminole in Mexico, 1850–1861." *The Hispanic American Historical Review* 21 (February 1951): 1–36.

——. "The Seminole Negro-Indian Scouts, 1870–1881." *Southwestern Historical Quarterly* 55 (January 1952): 358–377.

Presley, James. "Santa Anna in Texas: A Mexican Viewpoint." *Southwestern Historical Quarterly* 62 (April 1959): 489–512.

"Ranald S. Mackenzie's Official Correspondence, 1873–1879." *Museum Journal* 10 (1966): 3–227.

"Ranald S. Mackenzie's Official Correspondence Relating to Texas, 1871–1873." *Museum Journal* 9 (1965): 3–190.

Reeve, Frank. "The Apache Indians in Texas." *Southwestern Historical Quarterly* 50 (October 1946): 189–213.

———. "Seventeenth Century Navajo-Spanish Relations." *New Mexico Historical Review* 32 (July 1957): 36–52.

Sanchez, Jane. "Spanish-Indian Relations During the Otermín Administration, 1677–1683," *New Mexico Historical Review* 58 (April 1983): 133–151.

Sánchez, José María. "A Trip to Texas in 1828," *Southwestern Historical Quarterly* 29 (April 1926): 249–288.

Schlesier, Karl H. "Rethinking the Dismal River Aspect and the Plains Athapaskans, A.D. 1692–1768." *Plains Anthropologist* 15 (1972): 101–133.

Scholes, France. "Civil Government in New Mexico." *New Mexico Historical Review* 10 (April 1935): 71–111.

———. "Church and State in New Mexico." *New Mexico Historical Review* 11 (October 1936): 297–333.

——. "The Supply Service of the New Mexican Missions in the Seventeenth Century." *New Mexico Historical Review* 5 (April 1930): 186–209.

——. "Troublous Times in New Mexico." *New Mexico Historical Review* 12 (October 1937): 380–452.

Schroeder, Albert. "Castañeda's 'Acha'—Picuris, Hope or Apache?" *El Palacio* 65 (February 1958): 1–7.

Seymour, Deni J. "A Ranchería in the Gran Apachería." *Plains Anthropologist* 49 (2004): 153–192.

Shafter, William. "Shafter's Explorations in Western Texas, 1875." *West Texas Historical Association Year Book* 9 (October 1933): 82–95.

Simmons, Marc. "Call of the Canadian," *New Mexico Magazine* 68 (June 1990): 35–43.

——. "Governor Anza, The Lipan Apaches and Pecos Pueblo," *El Palacio* 77 (December 1970): 35–40.

——. "New Mexico's Smallpox Epidemic of 1780–1781." *New Mexico Historical Review* 41 (October 1966): 319–326.

Shearer, Ernest C. "The Callahan Expedition, 1855." *Southwestern Historical Quarterly* 54 (April 1951): 430–451.

Sjoberg, Andrée. "Lipan Apache Culture in Historical Perspective." *Southwestern Journal of Anthropology* 9 (1953): 76–98.

Smith, Ralph A. "Account of the Journey of Bénard de la Harpe: Discovery Made by Him of Several Nations Situated in the West." *Southwest Historical Quarterly* 62 (1959): 246–259, 371–385, 525–541.

Smith, Thomas T. "U.S. Army Combat Operations in the Indian Wars of Texas, 1849–1881." *Southwestern Historical Quarterly* 99 (April 1996): 501–532.

Spielmann, Katherine A. "Late Prehistoric Exchange between the Southwest and Southern Plains." *Plains Anthropologist* 28 (November 1983): 257–272.

Sterne, Adolphus. "Diary of Adolphus Sterne." *Southwestern Historical Quarterly* 32 (October 1928): 165–179 and 23 (October 1929) 160–168.

Stewart, Omer. "Origin of the Peyote Religion in the United States." *Plains Anthropologist* 19 (1974): 211–223.

Tate, Michael L. "Indian Scouting Detachments in the Red River War, 1874–1875." *Red River Valley Historical Review* 3 (Spring 1978): 202–225.

Thomas, A. B. "The Massacre of the Villasur Expedition at the Forks of the Platte River August 12, 1720." *Nebraska History* 7 (1924): 68–81.

Thurman, Melburn D. "On the Identity of the Chariticas." *Plains Anthropologist* 33 (May 1988): 159–170.

Tyler, Ronnie C. "The Callahan Expedition of 1855: Indians or Negroes?" *Southwestern Historical Quarterly* 70 (April 1967): 574–585.

Tyler, S. Lyman, and Darrell H. Taylor. "The Report of Fray Alonso de Posada in Relation to Quivira and Teguayo." *New Mexico Historical Review* 3 (October 1958): 285–314.

Vigness, David M. "Don Hugo O'Conor and New Spain's Northeastern Frontier, 1764–1776." *Journal of the West* 6 (1967): 27–40.

——. "Indian Raids on the Lower Rio Grande, 1836–1837." *Southwestern Historical Quarterly* 59 (July 1955), 14–23.

Walker, Henry P., ed. "William McLane's Narrative of the Magee-Gutierrez Expedition, 1812–1813." *Southwestern Historical Quarterly* 66 (April 1963): 569–588.

Wallace, Edward S. "General John Lapham Bullis: Thunderbolt of the Texas Frontier, II." *Southwestern Historical Quarterly* 55 (July 1951): 77–85.

——. "General Ranald Slidell Mackenzie: Indian Fighting Cavalryman." *Southwestern Historical Quarterly* 56 (January 1953): 378–393.

Weddle, Robert S. "The San Sabá Mission: Approach to the Great Plains," *Great Plains Journal* 4 (1965): 29–38.

West, Elizabeth Howard. "Bonilla's Brief Compendium of the History of Texas, 1772." *Texas State Historical Association Quarterly* 8 (July 1904): 3–8.

Wilcox, Seb S. "The Spanish Archives of Laredo, *Southwestern Historical Quarterly* 49 (January 1946): 341–360.

Winthuysen, Tomás Felipe de. "Texas as Seen by Governor Winthuysen," *Southwestern Historical Quarterly* 88 (October 1984): 167–180.

Woodhull, Frost. "The Seminole Indian Scouts on the Border." *Frontier Times* 15 (December 1937): 118–127.

Wooster, Robert. "The Army and the Politics of Expansion: Texas and the Southwestern Borderlands, 1870–1886." *Southwestern Historical Quarterly* 93 (October 1989): 151–167.

Worcester, Donald E. "The Beginnings of the Apache Menace of the Southwest." *New Mexico Historical Review* 16 (January 1941): 1–14.

Newspapers

Alamogordo News	*San Antonio Evening News*
Americans Before Columbus	*San Antonio Texan*
Brazos Courier	*Santa Fe New Mexican*
Dallas Morning News	*Shreveport Times*
El Mesteño	*Telegraph and Texas Register*
Fort Griffin Echo	*Texan Mercury*
The Galveston Semi-Weekly	*Texas Democrat*
Galveston Weekly News	*Texas National Register*
Gonzales Inquirer	*Texas Presbyterian*
Herald & Planter	*Texas Sentinel*
Houston Daily Mercury	*Texas State Gazette*
The Indian Helper	*Thirty-Four*
Lampasas Dispatch	*The Western Texan*
Las Vegas Gazette	*Tri-Weekly State Times*
Navajo Times	*Uvalde Leader-News*
The Northern Standard	*Victoria Advocate*
Periodico Official	*Weekly State Gazette*
The Red Man and Helper	

Web Sites

Choctaw-Apache Tribe of Louisiana. *http://www.choctaw-apache.org/*, accessed December 11, 2009.

Lipan Apache Band of Texas, Inc. http://members.aol.com/_ht_a/ceolipan//lipan.html (accessed August 7, 2002).

Handbook of Texas Online. *http://www.tshaonline.org/handbook/online/*

"Fred M. Griffin Family." Sacramento Mountains Museum. *www.mountaintimes.net.*

The Tonkawa Tribe of Oklahoma, *http://www.tonkawatribe.com/history.htm*

Unpublished Papers and Interviews

Begay, Meredith Magoosh, interview with Sherry Robinson, Mescalero, August 14 and September 24–25, 2005.

Black, Carolyn Sue, "Token of a Redman," ms. Provo Special Collections & Manuscripts, Harold B. Lee Library, Brigham Young University, Provo, Utah.

Eiselt, Bernice Sunday. The Emergence of Jicarilla Apache Enclave Economy During the 19th Century in Northern New Mexico." Ph.D. diss., University of Michigan, 2006.

Gatschet, Albert. "Lipan, a dialect of the Apache-Tinné family," September 1884. Archives of the Bureau of American Ethnology, 81-a, and "Lipan, of the Tinné family, Apache subdivision. Fort Griffin, Shackleford County, Texas." October 1884, 81-b. Washington, D.C.: Archives of the Bureau of American Ethnology, Smithsonian Institution.

Gilmore, Kevin P. and Sean Larmore. "Migration Models and the Athapaskan Diaspora as Viewed from the Colorado High Country." Presented March 27, 2008, at the Symposium "The Earliest Athapaskans in the Southern Southwest," at the Society for American Archaeology, Vancouver, British Columbia.

Fred M. Griffin Jr. "Fred M. Griffin Family," oral account. Cloudcroft, New Mexico: Sacramento Mountains Museum.

Maestas, Enrique Gilbert-Michael. *Cúelcaén Ndé—Lipan Apache of Texas History*. Lipan Apache Band of Texas, 2004.

Neighbors, Alice. "Life and Works of Robert S. Neighbors." Master's Thesis, University of Texas, 1936.

Neighbours, Kenneth F. An Ethnohistorical Report, Together with Supporting Exhibits Relating to the Cause of Action in the Liipan Apache Tribe, the Mescalero Apache Tribe, et al, v. United States, Docket No. 22-C, Before the Indian Claims Commission, 1974.

Opler, Morris Edward. "Report on Observations at Mescalero Reservation." Whiteriver, Arizona: Office of Indian Affairs, 1936.

Rivaya-Martinez, Joaquín. "Captivity and Adoption Among the Comanche Indians, 1700–1875." Ph.D. diss., University of California at Los Angeles, 2006.

Roche, Joan. "Sociocultural Aspects of Diabetes in an Apache-Choctaw Community in Louisiana." Ph.D. diss., The Catholic University of America, 1982.

Romero, Daniel Castro. "Cuélcahen Ndé: The Castros of the Lipan Apache Band of Texas." Edited and translated by Santiago Castro Castro and Valentina Sambrano Rodriguez. San Antonio: Lipan Apache Band of Texas, 2004.

———. *Castro Family History in Bee County*. San Antonio: Lipan Apache Band of Texas, 2004.

Romero, Daniel Castro, interview with Sherry Robinson, Mescalero, August 14, 2005; Albuquerque, November 28, 2005; and telephone interview April 4, 2006.

Salazar, J. Richard. "Spanish-Indian Relations in New Mexico during the Term of Commandant General Pedro de Nava, 1790–1802." Guadalupita, NM: Center for Land Grant Studies, 1994.

Schuetz, Mardith K. "The Indians of the San Antonio Missions, 1718–1821." Ph.D. diss., University of Texas at Austin, 1980.

Smith, Lucy. Interview with Sherry Robinson, Mescalero, August 13, 2005.

Swanson, Donald A. "Enlistment Record of Indian Scouts Who Served in One of the Scout Detachments at Fort Clark, Texas." Bronte, TX: Ames-American Printing Company, 1990.

Yates, Paul Adams, James Ramsay Humer, Russell D. Smith and William Bentz Carroll. "The Carlisle Indian School Cemetary: A List of Those Buried There." Carlisle, PA: Cumberland County Historical Society, undated.

❧ Index ❧